Kitchen Sense

Kitchen Sense

More Than 600 Recipes to Make You a Great Home Cook

MITCHELL DAVIS

CLARKSON POTTER / PUBLISHERS
NEW YORK

All rights reserved.
Published in the United States by Clarkson Potter/Publishers,
an imprint of the Crown Publishing Group,
a division of Random House, Inc., New York.
www.crownpublishing.com
www.clarksonpotter.com

Clarkson N. Potter is a trademark and Potter and colophon
are registered trademarks of Random House, Inc.

Library of Congress Cataloging-in-Publication Data

Davis, Mitchell.
Kitchen sense : more than 600 recipes to make you a
great home cook / Mitchell Davis.—1st ed.
Includes index.
1. Cookery. I. Title.
TX714.D396   2006
641.5—dc22   2005037241
ISBN-13: 978-1-4000-4906-6
ISBN-10: 1-4000-4906-7

Printed in the United States of America

Design by Maggie Hinders

10 9 8 7 6 5 4 3 2 1

First Edition

For my mother and father,
no doubt at a dining-room table in the sky,
happily reunited and laughing over a flank steak,
broiled to medium-well, thinly sliced on the bias, and smothered with
mushrooms and onions sautéed in plenty of butter.

■ ■ ■

Contents

Introduction   ix

Hors d'Oeuvres, Spreads, Dips, and Other Finger Foods   2

Soups   32

Salads   54

Sandwiches and Pizza   83

Breakfast, Brunch, and Eggs   103

Vegetables, Beans, and Potatoes   141

Grains   214

Pasta, Noodles, and Dumplings   238

Fish and Shellfish   274

Poultry   307

Meat   338

Sauces and Condiments   389

Desserts   411

Understanding the Recipes in This Book   475

Kitchen Words   480

Further Reading   485

Acknowledgments   489

Index   491

Introduction

YOU HAVE JUST OPENED a cookbook written by someone who loves to cook. If you like to cook already, you've found a new friend. If you are the sort of person who loves food but would rather make reservations than make dinner, keep reading. By the time you finish flipping through these pages, I bet you will want to roll up your sleeves and cook something. If nothing else, I'm going to make you hungry.

I love to cook for several reasons, not the least of which is that I love to eat. I have rarely met a food I didn't like, provided it was prepared with quality ingredients and care. I enjoy eating at expensive French restaurants as much as at cheap roadside stands—from tuna tartare to tuna casserole, and everything in between. You could say I am an equal opportunity eater. Moreover, I like to eat well, by which I mean that I prefer to eat food that is both good *and* good for me. Cooking for yourself, your family, and your friends is the only way to be certain you know what everyone is really consuming. Save for the occasional exotic ethnic dish or crusty loaf of bread or intricate pastry, there just aren't that many things you cannot make at home better than anything you can buy.

The joy I get in feeding people is another reason I like to cook. Knowing that I'm serving my sister Leslie her favorite chocolate cake (page 443) or my friend Izabela her favorite macaroni and cheese (page 259) gives *me* as much pleasure as it gives them. Eating is a social act, and many of the best times I've had with family and friends have happened around the table.

Perhaps most important, I simply enjoy being in the kitchen. Cleaning vegetables, making a stew, baking a cake, making jam—these are all simple, satisfying activities that slow down my world for a minute and help me relax. It's not that I have a lot of time—I lead a busy life and I'm always on the go—but for me, cooking is restorative, and the direct link between what I'm doing and how it is going to taste makes for a very tangible, satisfying, and rewarding payoff.

As vice president and director of communications at the James Beard Foundation and an adjunct professor of Food Studies at New York University, I spend a large part of my day wondering what it will take to make people understand the importance of food, not just in their personal health and well-being (we are all made up of what we have consumed) but in the health and well-being of our society at large. (Food is our country's biggest private-sector industry.) I've come to think learning to cook is part of the solution.

Often I hear that noncooks are frustrated with their attempts in the kitchen because recipes don't work and the time spent in the kitchen and the money spent on ingredients is wasted. Some people I know don't cook because they associate it with the resentment they felt from their mothers' having to put three square meals on the table every day. I know people who stopped cooking because their children won't eat anything. And I know people whose friends are all on special diets so it's become too complicated to figure out what to make. More than explain why people aren't cooking, these reasons underscore our complicated relationship with food here in America.

Food has become something to fear. It makes us overweight. It tempts us to overindulge. It can adversely affect our blood pressure, our cholesterol level. But the way to develop a healthy relationship to food is not to pretend it doesn't exist. It's to embrace it, live with it, learn about it, and enjoy it. Let Italy and France be our examples. The easiest, most effective way to accomplish all of that is to cook.

Further complicating our relationship with food has been the drastic change in the food scene. New interest in and enthusiasm for cooking shows and other food media, chefs, and restaurants have resulted in more people who may know a lot about food and how it is made—people who can have a heady conversation about the effects of Spanish cooking on restaurants in France and the benefits of organic agriculture over conventional growing methods—but fewer people who actually know how to turn a bagful of groceries into dinner.

This is a paradox I wrestle with as I walk past stands at my local greenmarket overflowing with beautiful produce or lose myself in the aisles of cookbook shelves at my neighborhood bookstore. Interest in food has never been higher, yet all you hear is that fewer people are cooking. Houses are built with custom dream kitchens and expansive dining areas, while the take-out food business is booming and Americans supposedly now eat more meals outside their homes than they do in them. I was intrigued by the thesis of Laura Shapiro's book on the history of women in the kitchen in twentieth-century America, called *Something from the Oven* (Viking, 2004). Shapiro explains how early food industry marketers set out to turn cooking, which many 1950s housewives found the most satisfying of their daily tasks, into a dreary chore. Enter cake mixes and instant rice, frozen dinners and dehydrated potato flakes. Evidence would suggest that the marketers succeeded in that transformation. Luckily, over the last few decades, there has been a strong, growing group of prolific advocates for cooking—I consider myself one of them—who are trying to force the pendulum back and get people into the kitchen again. Won't you join us?

This book is my way of helping to get people into the kitchen by encouraging them to enjoy cooking. I've titled the book *Kitchen Sense* because a little common sense in the kitchen goes a long way and is all you really need to get started. This book contains hundreds of well-tested, good recipes and plenty of sound advice. If you are an experienced cook who already loves being in the kitchen, I'm confident you will find fresh ideas and new techniques to take away from the following pages. If you've never made more than a piece of toast before, I think you will be surprised how easy and effortless some of the recipes are. Cooking well is, part and parcel, an attitude about life—make the most of it.

Kitchen Sense

Hors d'Oeuvres, Spreads, Dips, and Other Finger Foods

A T THE JAMES BEARD FOUNDATION, where I work, we organize almost 300 guest-chef dinners a year. Each dinner begins with an hour-long cocktail reception, during which five or six hors d'oeuvres are served. It is often my favorite part of the meal. Some chefs let their imaginations run wild, serving explosive flavors in intricate little bites. Other chefs go the traditional route, sticking to dips and puffs that have a retro feel. Long before there were tapas and tasting menus at every restaurant in New York, there were cocktail parties where you could sample a variety of flavorful nibbly things. James Beard himself had so much respect for and skill in making hors d'oeuvres that his first foray into the professional food world was to open a catering company in 1937 on Manhattan's Upper East Side, which he called Hors d'Oeuvre, Inc.

Concocting hors d'oeuvres requires care. But that doesn't mean that preparing hors d'oeuvres or finger foods at home has to be complicated or expensive. It just means that it requires a little forethought.

Because you put just a little bite in your mouth, an hors d'oeuvre should be intensely flavorful. That also helps fulfill its main function, which is to stimulate the appetite. Like a good cocktail, a good hors d'oeuvre or a selection of finger foods should provide a balance of flavors—sweet, salty, sour, bitter, spicy—to jump-start your guests' taste buds. When planning a menu, you should keep the hors d'oeuvres in the theme of the overall meal. Just as it would be odd to serve a gelatin salad with a classic Italian pasta, it would be weird to serve Middle Eastern meze before a macaroni-and-cheese dinner. Tasty, but weird, nevertheless.

Hors d'oeuvres are also designed to keep your guests from getting hungry while they wait for everyone else to arrive. And from getting too tipsy while they sip cocktails or wine. That's a lot of responsibility for a small bite of food, so treat them with respect. If you keep a few cans or bottles of imported ingredients in your cupboard, some tasty meats and cheeses in your fridge, and pastry dough in your freezer, you are never far away from some impressive little creations.

Party Nuts

Of course, a dish of salted peanuts, or those tasty Spanish Marcona almonds that have started popping up in gourmet shops all over the place, is a fine thing to serve with cocktails. But when I want to get a little fancy, I make these spicy nuts. They have a delicate flavor that lingers long after you eat them. For the best taste and presentation, be sure the nuts are fresh and whole (i.e., not broken or chopped). You can use either raw or roasted nuts, but raw nuts will require a little more time in the oven, so keep them separate when you are measuring.

Makes 2 cups

> 2 tablespoons unsalted butter
> 1 teaspoon Worcestershire sauce
> 2 cups mixed unsalted nuts, such as walnuts,
>   pecans, almonds, macadamia nuts, or peanuts
> 1 tablespoon sugar
> 1 teaspoon kosher salt
> 1/2 teaspoon cayenne pepper
> 1/2 teaspoon ground cumin
> 1/2 teaspoon dry mustard

Preheat the oven to 325°F.

Place the butter in a 9 by 13-inch baking dish or sheet pan and add the Worcestershire sauce. Place the pan in the preheating oven until the butter is melted. Remove the pan and swirl it around to evenly distribute the Worcestershire sauce. Add the nuts and sugar to the pan and toss to coat. Place in the oven to toast for 10 to 12 minutes, until the nuts begin to brown, stirring them once or twice to ensure even cooking.

Meanwhile, combine the salt, cayenne pepper, cumin, and mustard. Remove the pan from the oven and sprinkle the spice mixture over the nuts. Toss to coat with the spices. Return to the oven and toast for another 10 to 12 minutes, or until you smell the aroma of the spices. Remove from the oven and cool slightly. Serve warm or at room temperature.

PREP TIME: 5 minutes
COOKING TIME: 20 to 24 minutes
TOTAL TIME: 25 to 30 minutes

ADVANCE PREP *The nuts can be prepared a day or two in advance, though they are best just after they are made.*
LEFTOVERS *Party Nuts will keep for about three days in an airtight container. They can also be frozen for up to two weeks. If you like them warm, reheat the nuts for 5 or 6 minutes in a 350°F oven before serving. These nuts make an excellent addition to a tossed salad.*

Edamame

Better than bar nuts, a traditional Japanese snack, edamame—that's Japanese for "soybeans"—are one of my favorite things to nibble on with cocktails. And nothing is easier to prepare. You can serve edamame hot, room temperature, or cold. Because one of the principal flavors is salt, I use a fancy salt for the final sprinkling, but you can use ordinary salt, too. Be sure to serve them with some sort of receptacle for the pod, which, by the way, you don't eat.

Makes 3 cups

> 1 tablespoon kosher salt
> 1 pound frozen or fresh (cleaned) edamame
>   (soybeans in the pod)
> 1/2 to 1 teaspoon fancy salt, such as
>   fleur de sel, Maldon, or any Asian
>   flaked salt, or an additional teaspoon
>   kosher salt

PARTY PLANNING: WHAT AND HOW MANY HORS D'OEUVRES TO PREPARE

Knowing how many hors d'oeuvres to make for a party requires some simple calculations. There are several variables to consider, each of which has an impact on the final number of hors d'oeuvres you should prepare. For instance, what time of day is it? What else are you serving? Will there be more men than women? Any vegetarians coming? How long will drinks be served? These are the sorts of questions you should be asking yourself when you set out to determine what and how many hors d'oeuvres to make. I'm lucky enough to have a sixth sense when it comes to yields and portion size, but it's easy enough to figure out if you follow a few simple guidelines:

Dinner Party

When I host a dinner party, I figure three to four hors d'oeuvres per person. I don't want my guests to fill up before the main meal. The idea is to give them something to hold them over while they drink and wait for everyone to arrive.

As a rule, for variety, I like to offer at least three different things, choosing from different genres (i.e., spreads, puffs, tarts) and ingredients (i.e., vegetables, meats, cheeses). I might serve a dip for vegetables, a crostini, and a bowl of olives. Or maybe a pâté, a pizza, and some spiced nuts. Try not to repeat any of the principal ingredients you are using in the main part of the meal.

Cocktail Party

Figure six to eight hors d'oeuvres per person per hour for an early-evening cocktail party: fewer if you suspect guests will be heading off to dinner after they leave your place, more if you think most people will be making a meal of your finger foods. If you plan on serving dessert, count it separately (it goes into a different stomach). Again,

it's important to have a variety of offerings. I like to have a dip or spread, maybe a bowl of pickled shrimp, a savory tart, perhaps some beautiful cherry tomatoes with coarse sea salt; in other words, use your imagination.

If your party is going to take place over a couple of hours, don't put everything out at once. Start with two or three items at the beginning, then spread the flow of new items from the kitchen over the duration of the party. That way people get excited about trying something new throughout the evening.

From the host's perspective, the preparations should still allow you to enjoy your own party. For example, you don't want to choose five hot finger foods that have you tied to the oven all night. It's okay to have to finish one or two things as the party progresses—that way your guests know you actually did the cooking—but be sure to have some stuff that can be made ahead and can sit out while guests serve themselves. Replenish and neaten the table as necessary as the evening proceeds.

FACTORS THAT AFFECT THE QUANTITY OF HORS D'OEUVRES NEEDED

	More d'Oeuvres	Fewer d'Oeuvres
More men	X	
More women		X
Cold weather	X	
Hot weather		X
Large dinner following		X
Early evening		X
Later evening (i.e., dinnertime)	X	

In a medium pot, bring about 6 cups of cold water to a boil. Add the tablespoon of kosher salt. Add the fresh or frozen (straight from the freezer) soybeans. When the water comes back to a boil, turn down the heat and simmer the beans for 7 to 10 minutes, until the pods are easy to pop open and the beans inside are tender. Drain. Transfer about half of the pods to a serving bowl and sprinkle with $1/4$ to $1/2$ teaspoon of the fancy salt. Add the remaining pods and sprinkle with the remaining $1/4$ to $1/2$ teaspoon salt, or to taste.

PREP TIME: 10 minutes
COOKING TIME: 15 minutes
TOTAL TIME: 25 minutes

LEFTOVERS *I like having edamame in the fridge, where they will last about a week in an airtight container before they develop a slightly sour flavor and become a little slimy. Cooked soybeans are great in any dish that calls for beans, such as succotash or chili. They are also good stirred into scrambled eggs. Simply pop them out of their pods and use them as you would any cooked bean.*

Spicy Moroccan Olive Salad

When you want to offer guests something more than just a plain dish of olives, consider this spicy combination of olives, herbs, hot pepper, and preserved lemon. For the best visual impact, choose olives of different colors, sizes, and shapes. Use the best brine- or oil-cured olives you can find, with or without pits. Avoid canned California black olives like the plague. If you use only pitted olives and you stir in some other vegetables, like blanched carrots and cauliflower, this salad makes a great condiment for Italian cold-cut sandwiches, like the classic Muffuletta (page 91) that is a tradition of New Orleans. Makes 3½ cups

> 3 cups (about 1½ pounds) assorted green and black olives, such as Kalamata, Lucques, Niçoise, Spanish, Cerignola, Picholine, or Sicilian, with or without pits
> 4 wedges Preserved Lemon (page 409), cut in half lengthwise, or 5 or 6 strips lemon zest removed with a vegetable peeler
> 1 medium shallot, minced
> 1 garlic clove, minced
> ½ cup extra-virgin olive oil
> ½ teaspoon cumin seeds, toasted (see page 10)
> ¼ teaspoon crushed red pepper flakes, or to taste
> Juice of ½ lemon (about 2 tablespoons)
> Freshly ground black pepper

Combine the olives in a medium bowl. Add the lemon, shallot, garlic, olive oil, cumin seeds, red pepper flakes, lemon juice, and black pepper to taste. Toss to coat.

TOTAL TIME: 5 minutes

ADVANCE PREP *The salad is best if it sits, covered, in the refrigerator for a day before serving. Stir it occasionally as it sits to infuse the flavors evenly. Bring to room temperature before serving.*
LEFTOVERS *The olive salad will keep in the refrigerator for at least a week, depending on the freshness of the olives when the salad was made. It's best to bring the salad back to room temperature before serving so the olive oil in the dressing returns to its liquid state. Leftover olive salad can be used as a seasoning or condiment for baked fish or*

chicken or just about any Mediterranean-flavored dish. With the lemon or lemon zest removed, it can be stirred into pasta sauces, stews, and the like.

VARIATION

Herbed Olive Salad with Orange

Follow the recipe as indicated, substituting strips of orange zest for the preserved lemon, orange juice for the lemon juice, and 2 or 3 tablespoons chopped fresh herbs (such as thyme, marjoram, oregano, parsley, or a combination) for the toasted cumin seeds. You can use the red pepper flakes or omit them, as you wish.

Marinated Artichoke Hearts

I'm a big fan of marinated artichoke hearts and other types of preserved vegetables. I serve them as part of an assortment of hors d'oeuvres or as a side dish; I use them to garnish sandwiches and pizzas; and I cook with them, adding them as an ingredient in other recipes, such as pasta. The artichoke hearts you buy in jars in the grocery store are fine, but the flavor and texture of freshly prepared artichoke hearts are far superior to those that are available commercially.

Makes 3 pints

1 cup extra-virgin olive oil, plus more to cover
½ cup fresh lemon juice (about 3 lemons); reserve 1 squeezed lemon half
2 garlic cloves, thinly sliced
1 tablespoon chopped fresh mint, thyme, marjoram, flat-leaf parsley, or a combination
3 small bay leaves
2 teaspoons kosher salt
2½ to 3 pounds baby artichokes (about 2 dozen)

When handling artichokes, it's important to work quickly to prevent them from prolonged exposure to air or they will darken. In a large bowl, combine the olive oil with the lemon juice, garlic, herbs, bay leaves, and salt. Cut the reserved lemon half into wedges and add the wedges to the olive oil mixture. Trim and pare the artichokes to reveal the hearts as described in detail on page 174. As finished, drop each artichoke heart in the olive oil mixture, swishing it around to coat.

Transfer the artichokes and marinade to a large frying pan and set over medium heat. Cook, stirring often, for 7 or 8 minutes, until the artichokes are tender but not mushy when pricked with the point of a knife. Transfer to a large jar and let cool completely to room temperature.

TOTAL TIME: 45 minutes

***ADVANCE PREP** Marinated artichoke hearts are actually better if allowed to sit for a day or two in the refrigerator before serving.*
***LEFTOVERS** The marinated artichokes will keep in the refrigerator for two to three weeks. Bring the artichokes back to room temperature before serving. Use marinated artichoke hearts everywhere: in pasta sauces, in baked chicken dishes, with fish, as a garnish for sandwiches, or in salads. Don't discard the marinade; it makes a delicious salad dressing.*

Roasted Red Pepper and Garlic Dip

This creamy, beautifully colored dip blends the sweet taste of roasted red peppers and the mild taste of roasted garlic. Vegetables, chips, and crostini are all improved by a dunk in this dip. Omit the sour or heavy cream, and you'll have a rich spread or schmear for bagels or thick slices of crusty peasant bread. If you roast the peppers yourself, pop the garlic into the oven after 30 minutes and roast everything together for 30 minutes more.

Makes about 2½ cups

3 large red bell peppers (1½ pounds), roasted (see page 146), or 1 12-ounce jar roasted red peppers, drained very well
1 large head of garlic, roasted (see page 152)
Kosher salt and freshly ground black pepper
1 pound cream cheese, at room temperature
2 to 3 tablespoons sour or heavy cream
2 tablespoons extra-virgin olive oil
Juice of ½ lemon (about 2 tablespoons)

Place the roasted peppers in the bowl of a food processor fitted with a metal chopping blade or in a blender. Separate the garlic into cloves. Holding the pointy end, squeeze each clove into the food processor or blender to extract the pulp. Be careful not to get any of the papery peel in the bowl. Using on/off pulses, purée the peppers and garlic, and then let the machine run continuously until the mixture is very smooth, about 2 minutes. Season with ½ teaspoon salt and pepper to taste. You should have about 1 cup of purée.

Place the cream cheese and sour cream in the bowl of an electric mixer fitted with the paddle attachment; beat on medium speed until smooth, about 2 minutes. Scrape down the sides. Add the olive oil and lemon juice and beat until smooth. Slowly beat in the red pepper purée. Keep beating until well blended, scraping down the sides occasionally. If the mixture is too thick for dipping, adjust the con-

sistency with additional cream and/or olive oil. Adjust the seasoning with salt and pepper.

TOTAL TIME: 45 minutes

ADVANCE PREP *The roasted red pepper and garlic purée can be made up to a week in advance. It can also be frozen for up to two months. Defrost before finishing the dip. The dip can be eaten as soon as it is made, but the flavor is best if the dip sits, chilled, for a day or two before serving. The dip will thicken when chilled but will come back to the proper consistency at room temperature.*
LEFTOVERS *The dip will keep for about two weeks in the fridge. It is delicious stirred into a cream sauce for pasta or drizzled over warm focaccia.*

Artichoke Spread

The tang of lemon and the fresh taste of artichokes give this spread a light, summery taste. It's delicious if you use commercially prepared marinated artichoke hearts, whether in jars or bottles, but if you happen to have homemade Marinated Artichoke Hearts (page 7) lying around, they make the spread divine. Serve with fresh bread or focaccia as a substitute for butter, or as a condiment on sandwiches.

Makes 2 cups

2 (12-ounce) cans or jars marinated artichoke hearts, well drained, or homemade Marinated Artichoke Hearts (page 7), drained
¼ cup extra-virgin olive oil
Juice of 1½ lemons (about 6 tablespoons)
1 tablespoon drained capers, minced
Salt and freshly ground black pepper

In the bowl of a food processor fitted with a metal chopping blade or in a blender, finely chop the artichoke hearts with on/off pulses. Scrape down the sides. Add the olive oil, lemon juice, and capers and run the machine for 2 to 3 minutes to purée until smooth. Adjust the seasoning to taste with salt and pepper. Transfer to a container and chill until ready to serve.

TOTAL TIME: 7 minutes

LEFTOVERS *The spread will keep in the refrigerator for about two weeks. It is delicious on sandwiches, but you can also stir it into pasta sauces, Mediterranean vegetable soups, or other dishes with flavors that will complement the artichoke and lemon.*

Garlicky Walnut and Potato Spread

This garlicky Mediterranean spread makes a delicious hors d'oeuvre served with warm pita. Although I've seen recipes for similar spreads that have you make the whole thing in the food processor, I find the result has an unappetizingly pasty texture because of the potato, which never fares well when it comes in contact with a food processor's chopping blade. Although it's a bit of a hassle, using a food mill or ricer for the potato produces a more delicate texture.

Makes 2½ cups

2 large baking potatoes (1 to 1¼ pounds), such
   as Russet or Yukon Gold
Kosher salt
1 cup walnut halves, toasted (see page 10)
5 large garlic cloves
Juice of 1 lemon (about ¼ cup)
¼ cup white wine vinegar

KITCHEN SENSE

SPREADS VS. DIPS
Besides consistency, there isn't much difference between a dip and a spread. Any of the spreads in this book could be turned into dips by adding olive oil, sour or heavy cream, lemon juice, brandy, or other complementary liquids to thin the consistency. Conversely, by omitting liquid or adding solids—such as cream cheese or butter—most dips can be turned into spreads. One thing to keep in mind is that because you are likely to consume dips in smaller amounts— how much dip can you actually get onto a potato chip?—the flavor of a dip needs to be more intense to make an impact. Also be aware that if you add liquids or solids to your dips or spreads you will have to adjust the seasoning to compensate. Most dips and spreads thicken when chilled, especially if they contain cream cheese, butter, and/or extra-virgin olive oil, but as they come back to room temperature they will return to their original consistency.

½ cup extra-virgin olive oil
Freshly ground black pepper

Place the potatoes in a small pot and cover with cold water. Add 1 tablespoon of salt. Set over high heat and bring to a boil, uncovered, until the potatoes are soft, about 40 minutes. Add more water if necessary to be sure the potatoes remain submerged while cooking. When cooked, drain the potatoes and set aside to cool slightly.

Meanwhile, place the walnuts in the bowl of a food processor fitted with a metal chopping blade. Add the garlic and process with on/off pulses, scraping down the sides once or twice, until the nuts are finely ground and the garlic is

TOASTING NUTS, SEEDS, AND SPICES

In almost every recipe that calls for nuts, seeds, and most spices, it is best to toast them first. Toasting nuts improves their flavor and texture—even if they've already been roasted or blanched. Toasting seeds and spices intensifies and freshens their flavor. This is one of the secrets that separates good cooks from great cooks, but for some reason it is left out of many cookbooks, despite the fact that it takes a mere 5 to 10 minutes to do. You will see that I almost always call for nuts, seeds, and spices to be toasted. The only exceptions are recipes in which they will toast as part of the cooking procedure—such as in Party Nuts (page 4) or Dukkah (page 408).

Just about any nut benefits from toasting—walnuts, pecans, pine nuts, almonds, peanuts, what have you. And you can toast them in just about any form—whole, halves, broken pieces, chopped, or ground. I prefer to work with nuts in their whole form, which is usually when they are the freshest. After the nuts are toasted and cooled, I chop, or slice, or grind them as the recipe requires. Seeds and spices should also be ground after they are toasted.

There are two basic techniques for toasting: in the oven and on top of the stove. I prefer the oven technique because I find it toasts more uniformly and because I often have to preheat the oven anyway for a recipe, so it's easy to just pop in a pan while the oven heats up. But on hot days when I don't want to turn on the oven, or when I'm in a hurry, I toast in a frying pan. Both techniques are described below.

Oven-Toasting

You can toast nuts and seeds in any oven set between 300° and 350°F. Place the nuts on a sheet pan or in a baking dish with enough room to spread them out in an even layer without touching too much. Place the pan in the oven and set a timer for 5 minutes. (If you don't set a timer, you will forget about the nuts or seeds and burn them. Trust me, it happens to me all the time.) Toss the nuts or seeds around and return them to the oven. Set the timer for 4 more minutes. When you begin to smell the distinct aroma of toasted nuts or seeds and they have browned somewhat, they are done. They should have a slightly shiny look to them because the heat brings the oils to the surface. Some seeds may pop. Remove the toasted nuts or seeds from the oven, transfer to a clean plate (if you keep them on the baking pan they continue cooking and may burn), and cool before proceeding with your recipe.

Pan-Toasting

To toast nuts or seeds on top of the stove, place them in a dry, heavy frying pan and set over medium heat. Swirl the pan as it begins to heat, keeping the nuts or seeds in motion. You can let them sit still periodically, but as the pan gets hotter, they are more likely to burn. Don't walk away from the pan or you'll be sorry. Keep heating and swirling until the nuts or seeds begin to brown and become shiny, 3 to 4 minutes for seeds and 5 to 6 minutes for nuts. Again, don't worry about popping. Remove from the pan to a plate to cool.

minced. Add the lemon juice, and pulse a few times to almost purée the mixture. Transfer to a large bowl.

Peel the potatoes while they are still somewhat warm. Using a food mill or a potato ricer, mash the potatoes. Alternatively, you can force the potatoes through a fine sieve using a large metal or wooden spoon. You should have about 1¾ cups mashed potato. Add the mashed potato to the nut-and-garlic mixture along with the vinegar and 1 teaspoon of salt; blend this mixture into a paste with a wooden spoon. Slowly add the olive oil, a tablespoon or two at a time, stirring to combine completely before adding more oil. When all of the oil is incorporated, season to taste with pepper and additional salt, if necessary. Serve at room temperature.

PREP TIME: 25 minutes
COOKING TIME: 45 minutes
TOTAL TIME: 1 hour 10 minutes

ADVANCE PREP The spread can be made several hours in advance and refrigerated, but for the best texture, bring it to room temperature before serving.
LEFTOVERS The spread will keep in the refrigerator for four or five days. Bring it back to room temperature before serving. If any of the oil separates out of it as it warms up, beat the mixture until light and fluffy again. The spread is delicious on sandwiches.

The Best Hummus You've Ever Tasted

I used to think I made a pretty good hummus. But I was never happy with the texture. I wanted mine to be ethereally creamy and smooth, but it always had a slight graininess to it. Then my friend Bonnie went to Israel. And when she came back she told me the secret was in peeling the chickpeas. "You've got to be kidding me," I said. It seemed crazy. But then I tasted Bonnie's hummus, and indeed the texture was incredible.

So here's my version of a pain-in-the-neck hummus that is, I believe, worth the extra effort if you have the time. Of course you can make a perfectly acceptable hummus without peeling your chickpeas. Heck, you can just open a couple of cans of chickpeas and make a decent hummus in 10 minutes (see Variation, below). But when you want something special, I suggest you cook dried chickpeas and peel them. While you're at it, why not toast and grind your own cumin, too? Trust me, if you do, you will understand why the name of this recipe isn't an exaggeration.

Makes 2½ to 3 cups

1 cup dried chickpeas
3 large garlic cloves, 1 left whole, the other 2 chopped
1 bay leaf
¼ cup tahini or sesame butter
1 teaspoon cumin seeds, toasted and ground (see page 10)
Pinch of cayenne pepper
Kosher salt
Freshly ground black pepper
Juice of 1½ lemons (about 6 tablespoons)
5 tablespoons extra-virgin olive oil

Place the chickpeas in a large bowl and add enough cold water to cover by 3 inches. Let sit at room temperature for 8 to 12 hours or overnight.

Drain and rinse the chickpeas. Place them in a pot and add enough water to cover by 2 inches or so. Add the whole garlic clove and the bay leaf. Bring to a boil over high heat, turn down the heat so that the water simmers, loosely cover the pot, and cook the chickpeas for 50 minutes to 1 hour, or until they are soft. Remove from the heat and let the chickpeas cool in their cooking water. Remove the garlic and bay leaf.

When the chickpeas are cool enough to handle, drain them, reserving about half of their cooking liquid. To peel the chickpeas, I find it fastest to pinch them gently one at a time between my forefinger and thumb. The outer skin stays between my fingers while the inner bean pops out without mashing. It should take 45 minutes to 1 hour to peel all of the chickpeas. (This is a good task to do while watching television or talking on the phone.)

You should have about 2½ cups of peeled chickpeas. Place them in the work bowl of a food processor fitted with a metal chopping blade or in a blender. Add the chopped garlic, tahini, cumin, cayenne, 1½ teaspoons salt, black pepper to taste, ¼ cup of the reserved chickpea cooking liquid, and about 4 tablespoons of the lemon juice. Pulse about 10 times to grind the beans to a paste (you cannot overprocess the hummus). With the machine running continuously, pour the olive oil in a steady stream down the feed tube and process until the hummus becomes a smooth, creamy paste. Adjust the consistency by adding more chickpea cooking water, if necessary. Taste and adjust the seasoning with more salt, pepper, or lemon juice. Transfer to a container and chill, adjusting the seasoning again before serving.

PREP TIME: 1 hour
COOKING TIME: 1 hour
TOTAL TIME: 10 hours (includes overnight soaking)

ADVANCE PREP *The chickpeas can be cooked and stored in their cooking liquid for up to a week in the refrigerator until you are ready to make the hummus. Once the chickpeas have been peeled, you should prepare the hummus within a day or the beans will dry out.*

LEFTOVERS *The hummus will keep in the refrigerator for over two weeks. As it sits, the flavors become more intense.*

VARIATION
Hummus in a Hurry
For a less smooth hummus with the same flavor, forget peeling the chickpeas and proceed with the recipe as directed. Be sure the chickpeas are well cooked and very soft; otherwise the finished texture will be grainy. For an even faster hummus that doesn't have as good a flavor or texture but is perfectly acceptable, substitute 2 (15-ounce) cans of chickpeas, drained, for the home-cooked chickpeas, and 1 teaspoon ground cumin for the cumin seed. Use water or vegetable stock instead of the cooking liquid called for in the recipe.

Fava Bean Hummus
This is a delicious, light, creamy, quick spread, a nice change from the more familiar hummus made with chickpeas (see page 11). Fava beans are broad, green beans that resemble lima beans in shape. For this recipe, use dried peeled fava beans, which are sometimes also referred to as "split." Without the peel they are very soft so there is no need to soak them before cooking.
Makes 1½ cups

 1 cup dried split fava beans
 1 shallot or ¼ medium white or yellow onion, chopped

1 medium garlic clove, chopped

Kosher salt

Juice of $\frac{1}{2}$ lemon (2 tablespoons)

About $\frac{1}{2}$ teaspoon ground cumin

About $\frac{1}{8}$ teaspoon cayenne pepper or other
   hot pepper

Freshly ground black pepper

3 tablespoons extra-virgin olive oil

2 tablespoons chopped fresh mint or flat-leaf
   parsley or a combination (optional)

Place the fava beans in a small saucepan and cover with about 4 cups of cold water. Add the shallot, garlic, and 1 teaspoon salt. Bring to a boil, turn down the heat, and simmer for about 40 minutes, or until the fava beans are cooked through and look like they are falling apart. Turn off the heat and let cool to room temperature. Drain the fava beans and reserve the cooking liquid (you should have about $\frac{1}{2}$ cup). Refrigerate the cooking liquid.

Transfer the beans, along with the shallot and garlic, to the bowl of a food processor fitted with a metal chopping blade or to a blender. Add the lemon juice, cumin, cayenne, and black pepper to taste and purée until very smooth. With the machine running, add the olive oil in a slow, steady drizzle. Don't worry that the texture is soupy; the purée will stiffen as it chills.

Transfer the hummus to a container and chill for a couple of hours or overnight before serving. Once chilled, stir in the chopped mint, if using, and adjust the seasoning with more salt, pepper, cumin, hot pepper, or lemon juice, to taste (the chilling will soften the flavors). If the hummus is too stiff after chilling, beat in some of the reserved cooking liquid from the beans.

PREP TIME: 20 minutes

COOKING TIME: 45 minutes

TOTAL TIME: 1 hour 10 minutes (plus chilling time)

ADVANCE PREP *The beans can be cooked a day or two in advance and chilled before puréeing with the other ingredients. Drain just before puréeing.*

LEFTOVERS *The spread will keep for about a week in the refrigerator. Use as a dip with pita chips or as a spread in sandwiches.*

Baba Ghanoush

For me, the sign of a great baba ghanoush, which is sometimes called *moutabal* or eggplant spread, is the subtle, haunting smoky flavor that comes from charring the skin of the eggplant while it roasts. I find that two techniques work best for achieving the taste I'm looking for: If you have a gas stove, roasting the eggplant directly over the flame of a burner works well. Otherwise, if you have access to a charcoal or gas grill, you can roast it that way. Finally, you can make a perfectly good baba ghanoush by roasting the eggplant in a 500°F oven. It won't have much of that smoky flavor, but it will still be delicious.

Makes about 1$\frac{1}{2}$ cups

One 1$\frac{1}{2}$- to 2-pound firm eggplant

5 tablespoons tahini (sesame paste)

Juice of 1 lemon ($\frac{1}{4}$ cup)

1 small garlic clove, minced

6 tablespoons cold water

Kosher salt and freshly ground black pepper

3 tablespoons extra-virgin olive oil

If using a gas burner or charcoal or gas grill, wrap the eggplant well in two or three sheets of aluminum foil. Set the eggplant directly over the highest flame or in the hottest coals and roast, turning often with tongs, until the eggplant softens and deflates, about 40 minutes, depending on the heat of your flame. The foil will blacken a little bit and you'll smell something burning—which is the point. Be careful not to puncture the foil or the eggplant skin, or you'll have a bit of a mess on your hands. Alternatively, place the eggplant on a foil-lined sheet pan (for easy clean up) and roast in a preheated 500°F oven for about 45 minutes, or until the skin has blackened and the eggplant is soft and deflated. When cool enough to handle, remove any foil and transfer the eggplant to a colander. Make two or three slashes in the eggplant to allow it to drain while it cools to room temperature.

When cool, cut the eggplant in half lengthwise. Remove the long veins of seeds and discard. Scrape out all of the pulp leaving behind the burnt, papery skin. You should have $1\frac{1}{4}$ to $1\frac{1}{2}$ cups of pulp.

In a food processor or blender, combine the tahini, lemon juice, and garlic with the cold water. Purée this mixture until smooth and creamy. (Alternatively, you can use an immersion blender.) Add $\frac{3}{4}$ teaspoon salt and pepper to taste. Remove 2 tablespoons of this tahini mixture and set aside. Add the roasted eggplant pulp and 2 tablespoons of the olive oil to the food processor and purée until smooth. Adjust the seasoning with more salt and pepper, if necessary.

To serve, spoon the baba ghanoush out onto a plate and swirl it into a circular pattern with the back of the spoon. Add a tablespoon or two of water and/or lemon juice to the reserved tahini mixture, just enough to make it pourable, and drizzle it over the baba ghanoush along with the remaining tablespoon olive oil.

PREP TIME: 30 minutes
COOKING TIME: 45 minutes
TOTAL TIME: 1 hour 30 minutes (includes cooling time)

LEFTOVERS *The baba ghanoush will last for about a week in the fridge. After it has been served the first time, simply stir the garnish of oil and tahini into the spread. Use leftovers in sandwiches or as a condiment for falafel or other fried legume or meat dishes.*

Guacamole

There can be no guacamole without ripe avocados. And since most avocados are sold hard as rocks, guacamole, though simple, requires a little advance planning. Unlike peaches and plums, which are purposely picked and shipped unripe so they don't bruise (even if it means they will never have much flavor), avocados are the rare fruit that actually doesn't ripen until after it is picked. To store avocados, growers actually keep them on the trees. Select the avocados with dark green, mottled skin, called Hass avocados. They have the most flavor. The avocados should be firm but give a tiny bit when you press them. Keep them at room temperature until the flesh feels soft and dense when squeezed, usually two to three days or up to a week.

There's no way around it: you have to make guacamole just before you serve it. Though you will see a lot of tricks about how to keep it from turning brown, including keeping an avocado pit in the bowl or covering the top of the guacamole with a layer of oil, in my humble opinion none of these tricks works. But since guacamole takes just 10 minutes to make, this isn't such a big deal. **Makes 2½ to 3 cups**

3 ripe Hass avocados
Juice of 3 limes (about ¾ cup)
1 ripe medium tomato, chopped
1 handful fresh cilantro, finely chopped
½ small red onion or large shallot, finely chopped
½ fresh jalapeño chile, seeded and minced
1 tablespoon extra-virgin olive oil
Kosher salt
Freshly ground black pepper

With a sharp knife, cut each avocado in half lengthwise around the pit. Separate the halves, remove the pit, and scoop out the flesh into a bowl. Using a fork, roughly mash the avocados. I like to keep my guacamole somewhat lumpy so that it has more body and texture. Add two thirds of the lime juice, the tomato, cilantro, red onion, japaleño, and olive oil, and about ¾ teaspoon salt and freshly ground black pepper. Taste and adjust the seasoning with more lime juice, salt, and pepper, as necessary. Serve immediately.

TOTAL TIME: 15 minutes

LEFTOVERS Guacamole really doesn't keep well at all. If it makes you feel better, you can keep one of the avocado pits in the bowl when you mix and serve the guacamole, but I don't find it makes much difference. If you have leftovers, press plastic wrap right on the surface of the guacamole and keep it in the fridge for a day or two. It will darken unappetizingly, but it is fine to eat. If you want to serve it again, scrape off the discolored top layer of guacamole to salvage what's underneath. Leftover

guacamole makes a nice garnish for chilled Tomato Gazpacho (page 34).

Fresh Red and Yellow Tomato Salsa

Although I remember the day it was announced that salsa outsold ketchup as America's favorite condiment, the truth is there's very little difference between most jars of commercially made salsa and ketchup. *Fresh salsas are a different thing altogether.* This one, made with red and yellow tomatoes and peppers, is a clean, fresh-tasting alternative to bottled salsa. It is delicious on its own, but it also makes a nice garnish to things like Guacamole (page 14), Hummus (page 11), or Baba Ghanoush (page 13). Salsa is also a good accompaniment to grilled fish or chicken.

Makes 3 cups

2 ripe medium red tomatoes, finely diced
1 ripe large yellow tomato, finely diced
½ red bell pepper, cored, seeded, and finely chopped
½ yellow bell pepper, cored, seeded, and finely chopped
½ medium red onion or 4 scallions, white and green parts, finely chopped
1 large garlic clove, minced
1 small jalapeño or habanero chile, seeded and minced
1 bunch fresh cilantro, leaves and some of the stems, finely chopped
¼ cup extra-virgin olive oil
Juice of 2 limes (about ⅓ cup) or ¼ cup white wine vinegar
1 teaspoon sugar (optional)
1 teaspoon kosher salt
Coarsely ground black pepper

In a large bowl, combine the red and yellow tomatoes, red and yellow bell peppers, onion, garlic, jalapeño, cilantro, olive oil, lime juice, sugar if using, salt, and black pepper. Taste and adjust seasoning. Let sit at room temperature for about thirty minutes before serving.

TOTAL TIME: 15 minutes

LEFTOVERS *Fresh salsa keeps for only about two days in the refrigerator because the salt and sugar cause the tomatoes to shrivel and wilt; though it is perfectly okay to eat, it will get more liquidy as it sits. Use leftover salsa as a condiment for scrambled eggs, tacos, fish, or other dishes. You can drain off some of the liquid and stir the vegetables into sour cream to make a tasty dip for chips.*

Grilled Tomato and Corn Salsa with Chipotle

The combination of grilled vegetables and chipotle chile (smoked jalapeño) in this salsa gives it a deep, smoky flavor. It is delicious with sour cream and fresh tortilla chips or on grilled fish. If you don't have a grill, you can broil the tomatoes, corn, and red onion very close to the flame to char them. Because most of the ingredients in this salsa are cooked, it keeps longer than the fresh salsa on page 16.

Makes 2 cups

    3 ripe medium tomatoes (1 1/4 pounds), cut in half
        but not cored
    2 ears fresh corn, shucked
    1 small red onion, cut into 1/2-inch-thick slices
    1 handful fresh cilantro, finely chopped
    1 chipotle chile in adobo (from a can), minced
    1 large garlic clove, minced

    2 tablespoons extra-virgin olive oil
    Juice of 2 limes (about 1/3 cup)
    Kosher salt and coarsely ground black pepper

Heat a gas or charcoal grill, grill pan, or broiler. Grill or broil the tomatoes cut side toward the heat until charred, about 5 minutes. Turn and grill or broil the second side until the skin blisters, another 3 or 4 minutes or so. Remove to a plate to cool. Grill or broil the ears of corn and the slices of onion until they are marked, but not quite charred, 3 or 4 minutes per side. Remove and discard the tomato skin and finely chop the pulp. Using a sharp knife, cut the corn kernels off the cob and add them to the tomatoes. Finely chop the grilled onion, and add it to the tomato mixture. Add the cilantro, chipotle, garlic, olive oil, and lime juice and stir to combine. Add about 1/2 teaspoon salt and some freshly ground black pepper to taste. Adjust the seasoning with more lime juice, salt, and pepper, as necessary.

PREP TIME: 10 minutes
COOKING TIME: 15 minutes
TOTAL TIME: 25 minutes

LEFTOVERS *This salsa will keep for four or five days in the refrigerator. It makes a delicious condiment to scrambled eggs, grilled fish, cold roast pork, nachos, and other dishes.*

VARIATION
Grilled Pineapple Salsa
A delicious salsa can be made using the same recipe but substituting grilled pineapple for the grilled tomatoes and corn. Use four or five 3/4-inch-thick circular slices of fresh, ripe, peeled pineapple for the tomatoes and corn. Grill until

nicely marked, 4 or 5 minutes per side. Finely dice the pineapple, discarding the core, and combine with the remaining ingredients, including the grilled red onion, as directed.

Cheese Spread

This is a simple but delicious spread for bread that's a great way to use up old bits of cheese you have in your fridge. Serve it as an hors d'oeuvre with slices of baguette or as a condiment for sandwiches.

Makes 2 cups

 4 ounces cream cheese or fresh goat cheese,
    at room temperature
 ¼ cup sour cream
 4 ounces sharp white Cheddar or other strong
    aged cheese, shredded (1 cup)
 3 ounces strong blue cheese, such as Roquefort
    or Cabrales, crumbled (½ cup)
 2 tablespoons freshly grated Parmigiano
    Reggiano or Pecorino Romano cheese
 ¾ teaspoon Worcestershire sauce
 1 teaspoon Dijon mustard
 1 tablespoon minced shallot (optional)
 1 tablespoon Cognac or brandy
 Freshly ground white pepper

In the bowl of a food processor fitted with a metal blade, combine the cream or goat cheese, sour cream, Cheddar, blue cheese, Parmigiano, Worcestershire sauce, mustard, shallot if using, Cognac, and pepper. Pulse on/off until the mixture forms a ball around the blade. Alternatively, you can beat the ingredients together in a large bowl with a wooden spoon. Transfer to a container, cover, and chill to firm up. Remove from the refrigerator about 15 minutes before serving.

TOTAL TIME: 5 minutes

LEFTOVERS The spread will last for up to two weeks in the refrigerator. It also freezes well for up to a month. If any moisture forms when the spread defrosts, simply beat it back into the spread before serving. Use this spread wherever you want a little kick of cheese flavor. You can even stir it into the sauce for The Ultimate Macaroni and Cheese (page 259).

Liptauer

This is a traditional, cheesy Hungarian spread with lots of flavor. Be sure you have fresh sweet Hungarian paprika on hand. Old, stale paprika will ruin this dish. (I made liptauer once accidentally with hot paprika, which I liked very much, but some of my friends found the kick overwhelming.)

Makes 2 cups

 ½ cup (1 stick) unsalted butter, at room
    temperature
 4 ounces strong, imported feta cheese, such as
    Bulgarian feta
 8 ounces cream cheese, at room temperature
 ¼ medium red onion or 1 large shallot, minced
 1 large garlic clove, minced
 2 anchovies or 1 tablespoon anchovy paste
    (optional, but desirable)
 1 tablespoon capers, rinsed, drained, and minced
 1 teaspoon caraway seeds, toasted (see
    page 10)
 5 tablespoons very fresh sweet Hungarian paprika
 Kosher salt and freshly ground black pepper

In the bowl of an electric mixer fitted with a paddle attachment, combine the butter and feta. Beat until blended, about 1 minute. (Alternatively, you can beat it by hand using a wooden spoon.) Add the cream cheese and beat, scraping down the sides, until smooth, another minute or two. Add the onion, garlic, anchovies, if using, capers, and caraway seeds, and beat to combine, about 1 minute or so. Add the paprika and beat, scraping down the sides, until it is incorporated. The spread should have a nice red color, which will darken as the liptauer sits. Adjust the seasoning with salt and pepper. Transfer to a container and chill until ready to serve.

TOTAL TIME: 15 minutes

LEFTOVERS *Liptauer will keep for about three weeks in the refrigerator. Use leftovers in cheese sauces or as an accent on cheese sandwiches.*

Chicken Liver Mousse with Green Apple and Toasted Walnuts

With enough butter and cream beaten into them, chicken livers end up tasting remarkably like the French delicacy foie gras. This mousse (or pâté) is a simple, make-ahead hors d'oeuvre that you can serve on toast or crackers. The apple adds a tangy sweetness and the nuts provide a gentle bitterness that softens the taste of the liver. A garnish of tiny pickled onions or chopped herbs complements the flavors.

Makes 2½ cups

1 pound chicken livers (2 cups)
10 tablespoons (1¼ sticks) unsalted butter, at room temperature
½ medium red onion, finely chopped (about ½ cup)

1 small Granny Smith apple, peeled and shredded (about 1 cup)
1 tablespoon balsamic vinegar
¼ cup dry sherry, Madeira, white Port, Cognac, or brandy
2 tablespoons heavy cream
Pinch of grated nutmeg or mace
Kosher salt
Freshly ground black pepper
⅓ cup walnut halves, toasted (see page 10) and finely chopped

Clean the chicken livers by trimming any fat, nerves, or membranes with a sharp paring knife. Cut away any green patches. Rinse under cold water and place in a sieve or colander to drain. Pat dry with paper towel.

In a large frying pan, melt 2 tablespoons of the butter over medium-high heat. Add the onion and sauté until soft, about 5 minutes. Add the apple and continue cooking for 5 to 6 minutes, until the apple has softened, given off its water, and that water has evaporated. Add the balsamic vinegar, cook until it evaporates, and then transfer this mixture to the bowl of a food processor fitted with a metal chopping blade.

In the same pan, melt 2 more tablespoons of the butter over medium-high heat. Add the chicken livers and cook until they curl up, shrink, give off their liquid, and start to brown, about 8 minutes. There should be enough room in the pan so the livers are not touching. I use tongs to turn the livers while they cook, so that they brown evenly. If there's too much liquid to evaporate, pour it off so the livers don't boil. When done, the livers should still be slightly pink inside. Place them in the food processor, too. Add the sherry to the pan and return to the heat to evaporate for a minute or so, scraping up all the bits on the bottom of the pan. Pour this into the food processor. Add the cream, nutmeg, ¾ teaspoon salt, and ¼ teaspoon pepper to the processor and purée with on/off pulses, until the mixture becomes a smooth paste. Let the machine whirl for a minute or so to be absolutely sure there are no lumps. (If using a blender, process in two batches.)

Transfer the liver mixture to a medium bowl and let cool completely to room temperature; stirring helps the mixture cool faster. When the liver is cool, beat in the remaining 6 tablespoons of butter with a wooden spoon or rubber spatula to make a smooth, light paste. Stir in the walnuts. Adjust the seasoning with salt and pepper, keeping in mind that when chilled, the flavors will be less intense—very slightly oversalting and overpeppering the mousse will produce the right taste when chilled. Transfer to an attractive crock or other serving dish and smooth the top. (The mousse will firm up when chilled, so it's best to make it look good now, while it is still soft.) Press plastic wrap or waxed paper right down on the surface of the mousse to prevent it from darkening as it sits and chill for at least 2 hours before serving. Remove from the fridge 10 to 15 minutes before serving to make the mousse more spreadable.

PREP TIME: 20 minutes
COOKING TIME: 20 minutes
TOTAL TIME: 40 minutes

ADVANCE PREP *The mousse is actually best after a day, once the flavors have had time to come together.*
LEFTOVERS *The chicken liver mousse will keep covered, with plastic wrap or waxed paper pressed directly onto the surface, for about two weeks.*

Cheese Lace

Italy's answer to raclette, this thin, crisp, fried cheese "pancake," known as *frico*, makes a delicious hors d'oeuvre as is or as an accompaniment to a tangy vegetable dip or garlicky potato spread. I like to make my frico small—individual size.
Makes 6 fricos

> **6 ounces imported Italian hard cheese, such as aged Montasio, aged Asiago, Parmigiano Reggiano, Grana Padano, or a combination, preferably shredded (as opposed to grated; about 1½ cups)**

Heat a small, well-seasoned cast-iron or nonstick frying pan over medium-high heat. Have a clean rolling pin or wine bottle nearby. Take a handful of the shredded cheese, a scant ¼ cup, and scatter it on the bottom of the pan in the shape of a pancake about 4 inches in diameter. Be sure the center is uniformly covered with cheese; the edges can be left wispy. Watch carefully as the cheese begins to melt and bubble. It should fill in any holes as it melts. When the edges begin to turn golden brown, after about 2 minutes, carefully work a thin spatula under the cheese to loosen it from the pan. Flip and let the second side brown for a minute or two.

Remove from the pan and drape onto the rolling pin or wine bottle to give the cheese a slightly curved shape as it cools and firms up for a couple of minutes. Carefully remove the cooled frico to a serving plate and continue until the rest of the cheese is used up. You should get about 6 fricos. Pay attention to the temperature of the pan, which may get too hot as you work. If so, remove it from the heat for a minute or so to cool before you add more cheese.

PREP TIME: 5 minutes
COOKING TIME: 25 minutes
TOTAL TIME: 30 minutes

VARIATION
Cheese Lace for a Crowd

When I want to make a lot of fricos, I do them in the oven. Preheat the oven to 375°F. Line a baking sheet with a silicone mat. Arrange the cheese in 3-inch circles on the mat, about 6 per tray. Bake for 10 to 12 minutes, until the cheese has melted and browned. Cool 2 to 3 minutes, lift off the pan, and finish cooling draped over a rolling pin or bottle.

Cheese and Nut Biscuits

These delicate, savory shortbread-like biscuits have a rich, cheesy flavor and a sandy texture that melts in your mouth. They are perfect with cocktails, as an accompaniment to soups, or as part of an after-dinner cheese course. What's more, because you can keep the dough in the freezer for a very long time, you are always only minutes away from a terrific tidbit.

1 cup pecan halves, toasted (see page 10)
¾ cup (1½ sticks) unsalted butter, at room
    temperature
6 ounces extra-sharp Cheddar cheese, grated
    (1½ cups)
1 ounce Parmigiano Reggiano cheese, grated
    (¼ cup)
¾ cup unbleached all-purpose flour
¾ cup cake flour
1 teaspoon salt
Pinch of ground cayenne pepper

Place the pecans in the bowl of a food processor fitted with a metal blade. Using on/off pulses, finely chop the nuts. Transfer the nuts to a medium bowl and reserve. Reassemble the food processor, but there is no need to clean it. Combine the butter, Cheddar, and Parmigiano in the food processor, and process until blended. The mixture will start to form a ball around the blade. Sift the all-purpose and cake flours, salt, and cayenne directly into the food processor and then pulse to combine; stop just before the mixture forms a ball. Transfer the cheese mixture to the bowl with the chopped nuts and blend with a rubber spatula until the nuts are evenly mixed in.

Divide the mixture into thirds among three sheets of waxed or parchment paper. Roll each third into a log about 1 inch in diameter in the paper. The dough will be soft. Wrap the logs (still in the paper) in aluminum foil so they hold their shape. Refrigerate until firm, at least an hour or two.

Preheat the oven to 350°F.

Unwrap and slice the logs into ¼-inch-thick rounds. Place on an ungreased or parchment-lined cookie sheet. The biscuits will not spread, but leave a little room between them so they color nicely. Bake for 13 to 15 minutes, until the tops and the edges have become golden brown and the biscuits have set. Remove from the oven and carefully transfer to a wire rack to cool.

PREP TIME: 15 minutes
COOKING TIME: 15 minutes
TOTAL TIME: 1 hour 30 minutes (includes chilling time)

ADVANCE PREP *The dough can be made in advance and refrigerated for up four or five days or* *frozen for up to six months. Defrost the logs in the refrigerator for 3 or 4 hours or overnight before slicing and baking.*

LEFTOVERS *The biscuits can be stored in an airtight container at room temperature for up to two days or in the freezer for up to two months.*

VARIATIONS

Appenzeller and Peanut Biscuits

Although pecans and Cheddar cheese are a classic duo in the South, this combination is equally delicious.

Follow the same directions as for Cheese and Nut Biscuits, above, substituting skinned, unsalted, dry-roasted peanuts for the pecans, 6 ounces extra-aged imported Appenzeller cheese for the Cheddar, and 1 ounce Pecorino Romano for the Parmigiano Reggiano.

Mini Cheese and Nut Biscuits

For bite-size hors d'oeuvres, make the logs only ½ inch in diameter and bake the biscuits for only 10 minutes.

Goat Cheese Tots

These crispy goat cheese croquettes make an excellent hors d'oeuvre, and the simple technique by which they are made lends itself to experimentation. Try using herbed goat cheese (delicious served with Quick Tomato Sauce, for dipping, page 250) or stuffing a piece of sun-dried tomato or roasted red pepper in the center of each one (these are tasty with a dab of Pesto, page 398). The croquettes should be served warm, but not so warm that your guests burn their mouths. The recipe can be multiplied as necessary.

Makes 16 tots

8 ounces fresh goat cheese
16 tiny cubes of sun-dried tomato (oil-packed) or
   roasted red pepper (optional)
¼ cup all-purpose flour
1 large egg
½ cup panko (Japanese bread crumbs),
   or unseasoned dry bread crumbs
About ¾ cup peanut or vegetable oil, for frying

Divide the goat cheese into 16 equal portions. Use your hands to roll each portion into a ball, about ¾ inch in diameter. If stuffing the tots, flatten the balls into disks in the palm of your hand. Place a tomato cube in the center of each disk and carefully reform the ball to envelop the tomato. Put the flour in a small bowl. Beat the egg with 2 teaspoons cold water in a second bowl. Put the panko in a third bowl. Using a fork, toss one ball in the flour, lift it out, tapping off any excess flour, and dip into the egg. Lift out of the egg and roll in panko until evenly coated. Set aside on a clean plate. Repeat with the remaining cheese. Chill for about 30 minutes.

Heat about ½ inch of peanut or vegetable oil in a medium cast-iron or other heavy skillet over medium-high heat. Gently drop in the chilled cheese balls. Fry until golden brown on all sides, about 1 minute per side. Transfer to paper towels to drain. Serve warm.

PREP TIME: 15 minutes
COOKING TIME: 5 minutes
TOTAL TIME: 45 minutes (includes chilling time)

ADVANCE PREP *The tots can be shaped and breaded up to a day in advance; cover and refrigerate overnight. Fry them just before serving.*

Quesadilla

I keep flour tortillas and grated cheese in my freezer so I can whip up a quesadilla when guests come over unexpectedly. There's no need to defrost the tortillas or cheese before making the quesadilla, though it can be a challenge to separate the tortillas while frozen without breaking them. I insert a flexible spatula between the tortillas to peel them off carefully.

You can use just about any cheese for the filling. I've even made quesadillas with crumbled Roquefort. Serve with pickled jalapeños, salsa, and sour cream.

Makes 1 large quesadilla

2 large (11-inch) flour tortillas
2 ounces strong cheese, such as Manchego,
    extra-sharp Cheddar, or aged Gouda, grated
    ($\frac{1}{2}$ cup)
2 tablespoons freshly grated Pecorino Romano or
    other hard grating cheese
1 scallion, white and green parts,
    thinly sliced
3 or 4 sprigs fresh cilantro, leaves only
Hot sauce

Preheat the oven to 425°F.

Lay one of the tortillas on a cookie sheet or other baking pan. Sprinkle evenly with the grated cheeses. Scatter the scallion and cilantro leaves evenly over the cheese. Drizzle a small amount of hot sauce over the top. Cover with the second tortilla and press down lightly to compact. Place the quesadilla in the oven and bake for 12 to 15 minutes, until the tortilla has browned around the edges and crisped. (The edges have a tendency to curl up.) Remove from the oven. Using a pizza cutter or sharp knife, cut into 8 or 12 wedges and serve immediately.

PREP TIME: 5 minutes
COOKING TIME: 15 minutes
TOTAL TIME: 20 minutes

LEFTOVERS The quesadilla will last for about a week in the fridge. Recrisp in a preheated 350°F oven for a few minutes before eating.

Crostini

Crostini is Italian for "little crunchy things." These are toasts or rusks you can serve with pâtés or spreads. (For a grilled version, see Bruschetta, page 23.) Although some people suggest that to make crostini all you have to do is slice bread and let it go stale, what you get if you do that is "stale bread." In fact, stale bread is the starting point, not the finishing point, of crostini. A quick brush with olive oil and a sprinkling of salt and pepper add a boost of flavor.

Makes 2 to 3 dozen

1 day-old baguette
$\frac{1}{2}$ cup extra-virgin olive oil
1 teaspoon kosher salt
Freshly ground black pepper

Preheat the oven to 325°F.

With a serrated knife, slice the baguette on the diagonal between $\frac{1}{4}$ and $\frac{1}{2}$ inch thick. Arrange the slices in a single layer on a cookie sheet or two. Lightly brush each slice with olive oil. Don't worry if you don't evenly coat the entire surface of the bread with the oil. Sprinkle to taste with salt and pepper. Turn over the slices and repeat. Place in the oven and bake until the bread begins to brown, about 15 minutes. Turn over each slice and continue baking until the crostini are a nice, even golden brown, another 10 minutes or so. Remove from the oven and leave on the pans to cool completely.

PREP TIME: 10 minutes
COOKING TIME: 25 minutes
TOTAL TIME: 35 minutes

ADVANCE PREP *The crostini can be made up to a week in advance and stored in an airtight container.*
LEFTOVERS *If you have more crostini than you need, pulverize them in a food processor and use them as seasoned bread crumbs.*

VARIATION
Bruschetta
When I have a crusty peasant-style bread, I prefer to make Bruschetta (pronounced broo-SKAY-ta). Slice the bread about $1/2$ inch thick. Toast the bread on a preheated charcoal, wood-fired, gas, or electric grill for a minute or two until lightly marked. Flip and toast the second side. Rub the bread on both sides with the cut side of a halved garlic clove and drizzle the bread generously with extra-virgin olive oil. Season with salt and pepper.

Wild Mushroom and Hazelnut Crostini
I find the deep, woodsy flavors of wild mushrooms and hazelnuts complementary. By cutting the wild mushrooms with cultivated mushrooms, such as portobellos, you can stretch their strong flavor and economize.

Makes 16 hors d'oeuvres

$1\frac{1}{2}$ ounces dried porcini
$3/4$ cup boiling water
6 tablespoons extra-virgin olive oil
1 small yellow or white onion or 2 shallots, minced
2 garlic cloves, minced
2 pounds assorted mushrooms, such as chanterelles, bluefoots, black trumpets, portobellos, oyster mushrooms, button mushrooms, or whatever else looks good and fresh, finely chopped
1 teaspoon kosher salt, or to taste
Freshly ground black pepper
$3/4$ cup blanched hazelnuts, toasted (see page 10) and coarsely chopped
$1/4$ cup chopped flat-leaf parsley
Juice of $1/2$ lemon (about 2 tablespoons)
16 or so Crostini (page 22)

Preheat the oven to 325°F.

Place the dried porcini in a small bowl, cover with the boiling water, and let sit for about 20 minutes to soften. (Alternatively, you can cover them with cold water and place them in the microwave for 2 minutes on high.) Let cool to room temperature. Lift the swollen porcini out of the water with a fork (don't disturb the sandy sediment in the bottom of the bowl). Remove any tough pieces and discard. Finely chop the procini. Set aside and reserve the soaking liquid.

Heat the olive oil in a medium sauté pan set over medium-high heat. Add the onion and cook until soft, about 5 minutes. Add the garlic and cook 2 or 3 minutes more. Add the chopped mushrooms and cook until they wilt and give off their water, about 10 minutes.

Add the porcini along with some of their soaking liquid—pour it carefully off the top of the bowl without disturbing the sediment on the bottom. Keep cooking until the mushroom cooking liquid evaporates, about 10 minutes more. Season with salt and pepper. Add the hazelnuts and heat through. Toss in the parsley and add the lemon juice. Remove from the heat and spoon over the crostini. Serve hot, lukewarm, or at room temperature.

PREP TIME: 10 minutes
COOKING TIME: 30 minutes
TOTAL TIME: 1 hour 10 minutes (includes soaking time)

ADVANCE PREP *You can prepare the mushroom mixture three or four days in advance, but don't stir in the hazelnuts until you are ready to serve or they will get soggy. Reheat the mushrooms in a frying pan, add the nuts, and spoon onto the crostini just before serving.*
LEFTOVERS *Stir leftover mushroom mixture into a stuffing, into the mixture for a meatloaf, or into scrambled eggs.*

Grilled Pita Triangles with Za'atar

It's easy enough to heat plain pitas on a grill or in the oven to warm them. Only slightly more complicated, and a whole lot more impressive, is this recipe for grilled pita sprinkled with Za'atar (a combination of dried thyme, marjoram, toasted sesame seeds, and sumac), which you can make (see page 407) or buy. Serve the grilled pita with Hummus (page 11) or Baba Ghanoush (page 13).
Makes 3 to 4 dozen

4 pitas with pockets
1/3 cup extra-virgin olive oil
2 to 3 tablespoons Za'atar (page 407)

Preheat a charcoal, gas, or electric grill or grill pan. Separate the pitas into two circles, cutting around the edge. Brush both sides with olive oil and sprinkle with the za'atar.

Place the pita circles, inner side down, on the grill just for a minute or two, depending on the temperature of your grill, until the bread is warmed and grill marks are visible. Turn for another minute to brown and then remove. Cut into triangles and serve warm.

PREP TIME: 5 minutes
COOKING TIME: 5 minutes
TOTAL TIME: 10 minutes

ADVANCE PREP *The pita shouldn't be grilled more than a few minutes before serving. If you are making a lot, keep them warm by wrapping them in a dish towel or in foil. You can reheat the grilled pita in foil in a 300°F oven for a few minutes if necessary.*

Savory Pear and Gorgonzola Tart

This savory, free-form tart makes a beautiful hors d'oeuvre when presented whole on a cutting board for your guests to help themselves. The sweetness of the pears offsets the bite of the Gorgonzola. You can use either store-bought frozen puff pastry or Cream Cheese Pastry (page 431) for the base. If you are buying puff pastry, try to find one that's made with real butter.
Makes one 8 by 12-inch tart

3 tablespoons unsalted butter
2 large white or yellow onions, finely chopped (about 1 1/2 cups)
2 large, ripe pears, such as Anjou, Bartlett, or Bosc, peeled and finely diced (about 2 1/2 cups)

2 tablespoons sherry or cider vinegar

1 tablespoon fresh thyme leaves

Kosher salt and freshly ground black pepper

12 ounces frozen puff pastry, defrosted,
  or ½ recipe Cream Cheese Pastry
  (page 431), chilled

4 ounces imported Italian Gorgonzola or other
  blue cheese, such as Roquefort, Maytag, or
  Danish Blue, crumbled

1 ounce mild cheese, such as white Cheddar,
  Gouda, or Parmigiano Reggiano, grated

Preheat the oven to 425°F.

In a large skillet, melt the butter over medium-high heat. Add the onions and cook for 7 or 8 minutes, until they soften and begin to brown. Add the pears and continue cooking for another 8 minutes or so, until the pears soften and the whole mixture begins to caramelize. Add the vinegar and cook until it is evaporated. Stir in the thyme, ½ teaspoon kosher salt, and some pepper to taste. Remove from the heat and set aside.

On a lightly floured work surface, roll out the pastry to a rectangle, approximately 8 by 12 inches. Transfer to an ungreased baking sheet. If using puff pastry, prick the entire surface of the pastry with a fork. (There is no need to prick the cream cheese pastry.) Set the pan in the oven and bake the pastry for 12 to 15 minutes, or until it begins to puff and brown. Remove from the oven.

Turn down the oven temperature to 375°F. Arrange the cooked onion and pear mixture on top of the pastry, leaving a 1-inch border free around the edges. Scatter the Gorgonzola and mild cheese evenly over the top. Return to the oven and bake for 15 minutes, or until the cheese has melted, the pastry has risen and browned, and the pear and onion mixture is heated through.

Remove from the oven and cool for 5 to 10 minutes before transferring to a serving dish and cutting into pieces. Serve warm or at room temperature.

PREP TIME: 20 minutes
COOKING TIME: 45 minutes
TOTAL TIME: 1 hour 5 minutes

ADVANCE PREP *You can prepare the onion and pear filling up to four days in advance. Cover and refrigerate until ready to assemble and bake the tart.*
LEFTOVERS *The tart will last for about one week wrapped well in the refrigerator. You can recrisp the crust and warm the tart in a 325°F oven 10 minutes or so before serving.*

VARIATION
Savory Apple and Cheddar Tart
The classic combination of apple and Cheddar cheese makes a lovely savory tart, too. Substitute 2 large Golden Delicious, Northern Spy, or Granny Smith apples for the pears. Use 1 teaspoon minced fresh rosemary instead of the thyme, and replace the Gorgonzola and mild cheese with 5 ounces shredded Cheddar. Follow the recipe as directed.

Chorizo and Pepper Puffs
Hors d'oeuvres are supposed to intrigue your mind and stimulate your appetite for the meal ahead. These little sausage-stuffed puffs have just the right amount of sweet and spice to do both perfectly. I use a dab of red or jalapeño pepper jelly to offset the piquant sausage.
Makes 24 hors d'oeuvres

½ recipe Cream Cheese Pastry (page 431), chilled

¼ cup red or jalapeño pepper jelly

5 ounces spicy dried chorizo, sliced into ¼-inch-thick rounds

Preheat the oven to 425°F.

On a generously floured work surface, roll out the pastry to a ¼-inch thickness. Cut the pastry into 2-inch squares. Place a dab of pepper jelly in the center of each square and lay a slice of chorizo on top. Fold the corners of the squares up and over the chorizo to meet in the middle. Press the corners together to seal, forming a little packet. Place on an ungreased baking sheet and chill while you finish forming the rest of the puffs.

Bake the puffs for 12 to 13 minutes, until the pastry has risen and browned. Remove from the oven, transfer to a wire rack, and cool for 5 to 10 minutes before serving.

PREP TIME: 20 minutes
COOKING TIME: 15 minutes
TOTAL TIME: 35 minutes

ADVANCE PREP *The puffs can be formed and chilled up to a day before baking. They can also be frozen for up to one month. To freeze, lay the puffs on a baking sheet and set in the freezer until hard. Transfer to a resealable freezer bag to store. To bake, arrange the frozen puffs on an ungreased sheet pan and bake as directed. The frozen puffs will take 4 to 5 minutes longer to cook.*

LEFTOVERS *Although the puffs are best freshly baked, they can be stored in an airtight container at room temperature for up to three days.*

VARIATION
Cheese and Pepper Puffs

You can substitute cheese for the chorizo in this recipe to make an equally delicious, vegetarian hors d'oeuvre. I like to use a strong blue cheese, such as Cabrales, Gorgonzola, or Roquefort, or else a sharp white cheese, such as Manchego. Cut about 5 ounces of cheese into ½-inch cubes. Proceed with the recipe as directed, replacing the slice of chorizo with a cube of cheese in each puff. Some of the cheese will melt out of the puffs as they bake, but don't worry about it. Break off any unwieldy crispy bits before serving.

Homemade Potato Chips

While everyone was trying to figure out how to make the perfect french fry, I wanted to know how to make the perfect potato chip. Potato chips are one of those things you regret ever making at home because they are so delicious, they spoil you from ever being able to truly enjoy store-bought potato chips again. (Well, almost.) The key is slicing the potatoes as thin as possible; I use a mandoline to get paper-thin slices. Soaking the slices in ice water serves to bring the starch to the surface, which makes for a crispier chip. If you have a deep-fryer, use it as directed; I usually just use a small pot and work in small batches, frying fresh chips while my friends enjoy cocktails before dinner. They are excellent topped with Salmon Tartare (page 293).
Makes 3½ cups

1 pound Russet potatoes, either peeled or not

2 to 3 cups peanut or vegetable oil, for frying

Fine sea salt

Fill a large bowl with ice and cold water. Using a mandoline, a food processor fitted with a thin slicing blade, or a very sharp knife, thinly slice the potatoes, about $\frac{1}{16}$ inch thick, and place the slices in the ice water. Let them sit for 45 minutes to 1 hour in the refrigerator, until they curl up.

Heat about 2 inches of peanut oil in a deep-fryer or heavy saucepan to 375°F. Remove a handful of potato slices from the ice water and drain them on paper towels. Pat dry. Drop the potatoes into the hot oil and fry until golden brown and crisp, about 4 minutes. Lift out of the oil with a slotted spoon and drain on paper towels. Sprinkle with salt while still warm. Repeat with the remaining potato slices.

PREP TIME: 10 minutes

COOKING TIME: 15 minutes

TOTAL TIME: 1 hour 25 minutes (includes soaking time)

ADVANCE PREP The potatoes can be sliced and soaked up to a day in advance. Store them in water in the refrigerator.

LEFTOVERS The potato chips will theoretically keep for a couple of days, but there won't be any left. Store them on a paper towel in an airtight container. Chop up any leftovers and stir them into mashed potatoes, or sprinkle them onto a vegetable gratin.

Baked Parsnip Chips

A tasty alternative to potato chips, these crisp parsnip chips are baked, not fried. They are good for cocktail snacks or piled beside a sandwich. Look for fresh white parsnips that are not shriveled or discolored, and slice them as thin as possible to make crisp chips.

Makes about 3 cups

> 2 medium parsnips (about 1 pound), peeled
> 3 to 4 tablespoons extra-virgin olive oil
> $\frac{1}{4}$ to $\frac{1}{2}$ teaspoon fine sea salt

Preheat the oven to 425°F. Line one or two baking sheets with parchment paper.

Using a mandoline, a food processor fitted with a thin slicing blade, or a very sharp knife, thinly slice the parsnips on the diagonal less than $\frac{1}{8}$ inch thick. The thinner they are, the crispier your chips will be. Lay the slices out on the parchment-lined baking sheets. They can be close, but not touching.

Using a pastry brush, brush each side of each slice very lightly with olive oil. Sprinkle with salt. Bake for 10 to 12 minutes, until the edges have browned and curled and the center of each slice is cooked. Remove from the oven and cool for a minute or two before transferring to a bowl or other container to cool completely.

PREP TIME: 15 minutes

COOKING TIME: 10 to 12 minutes

TOTAL TIME: 30 minutes

ADVANCE PREP The chips can be made several hours in advance and stored unwrapped at room temperature until ready to eat.

LEFTOVERS The parsnip chips will keep in a airtight container for a day at room temperature, but they lose their crispness. If you don't want to dip them, you can use leftover chips as a garnish for just about anything, such as a soup or a salad.

Devilish Eggs

Deviled eggs have been making a comeback on restaurant menus of late, but they've never gone out of style at my home. You can pretty much add anything you want to the mixture—minced parsley, shallot, or pickle, for example. Whatever you add, be sure to mince it as fine as possible so you don't detract from the yolks' creamy texture. To keep it vegetarian, substitute finely minced capers for the anchovies.

Makes 16 deviled eggs

> 8 hard-cooked eggs (see page 29), peeled
> 1/4 cup mayonnaise
> 1 teaspoon anchovy paste, or 1 mashed anchovy
>   fillet, or 1 1/2 teaspoons finely minced capers
> 1 teaspoon Dijon mustard
> Pinch of sweet or hot Hungarian paprika or
>   cayenne pepper, plus extra for garnish
> Freshly ground white pepper
> 5 or 6 drops hot sauce, or to taste
> 1 tablespoon finely chopped chives (optional)

Slice the eggs lengthwise in half. With a small teaspoon, remove the yolks and place them in a medium bowl, being careful not to damage the whites. Add the mayonnaise to the yolks and mash with a fork or rubber spatula to make a smooth, creamy paste. Mash in the anchovy, mustard, paprika, white pepper to taste, and hot sauce. Taste and adjust the seasoning.

Transfer the yolk mixture to a small pastry bag fitted with a wide star nib, and pipe rosettes of yolk into the cavity of each egg white. Alternatively, you can use two teaspoons to shape the yolk mixture and deposit it into the cavity. Garnish with chives or an additional sprinkling of paprika or cayenne.

TOTAL TIME: 10 minutes

ADVANCE PREP *The deviled eggs can be made a couple of hours in advance, but you have to wrap them carefully because the yolk mixture will darken and discolor. Before wrapping, I invert a glass or two on the plate or tray they are on to prevent the plastic wrap from touching them. Don't garnish the deviled eggs until you are ready to serve them.*
LEFTOVERS *Deviled eggs will keep three or four days in the refrigerator, but they will not be suitable for guests. Eat them yourself or chop them up to make egg salad.*

Shrimp Cocktail

It may be old-fashioned, but that doesn't mean shrimp cocktail isn't delicious. When I was a kid, shrimp cocktail was a treat reserved for special occasions, like birthdays. Now, with places like Red Lobster offering all-you-can-eat-shrimp dinners, it hardly seems special. But if you take a little care in the preparation of your shrimp and your cocktail sauce, there's nothing mundane about it. Cocktail sauce made with fresh horseradish has an unexpected delicacy, but if you can't find it, prepared white horseradish provides a familiar thwack of flavor.

Makes 4 servings

> 1/2 cup ketchup
> 1/2 cup chili sauce
> Juice of 1/2 lemon (2 tablespoons)
> 1/4 cup finely grated fresh horseradish or
>   3 tablespoons prepared white horseradish
> 1/2 teaspoon dry mustard
> Freshly ground black pepper
> Hot sauce
> 1 pound jumbo shrimp, 16 to 20 count, cooked,
>   peeled, and chilled (see page 279)

Hard-Cooked Eggs

Seems simple enough, right? But how often do you see hard-boiled eggs ruined by overcooking, which produces that unappealing dark gray-green sulphurous ring around the yolk? Here's a simple and foolproof way to hard-boil (or hard-cook) eggs perfectly every time. The recipe can be increased as needed. For easy peeling, use eggs that are at least a week old.

Makes 6 hard-boiled eggs

6 large, extra-large, or jumbo eggs
Pinch of salt

Fill a small to medium saucepan with cold water and carefully place the eggs in the pot in a single layer with some space between them. It doesn't really matter if your eggs are taken directly from the refrigerator or if they are at room temperature. The water should come to about 1 inch over the top of the eggs; add more or pour some off if necessary. Add a pinch of salt to the water to help coagulate the white more firmly, making peeling easier. Set the pot over high heat and bring to a boil. As soon as the water starts to boil, cover the pot and turn off the heat. Set a timer for 12 minutes for large eggs, 13 minutes for extra-large eggs, and 15 minutes for jumbo eggs.

As soon as the time is up, dump out the hot water and fill the pot with cold water to stop the eggs from cooking further. Keep the pot under cold running water until the eggs are cool to the touch. Remove from the water and dry with paper towels. You can leave the eggs intact or peel them before storing, wrapped in plastic or in a plastic bag, in the refrigerator.

TOTAL TIME: 20 to 25 minutes

LEFTOVERS Hard-boiled eggs will keep for about a week in the fridge. I prefer to keep them unpeeled in a resealable plastic bag, and then I remove the shell when I go to use them. I put hard-boiled eggs in and on everything. For instance, I slice them and put them in sandwiches; I dice them and sprinkle them on asparagus or steamed green beans; and I cut them into wedges and put them on my salads.

In a small bowl, combine the ketchup, chili sauce, lemon juice, horseradish, and mustard, and mix well. Season with black pepper and hot sauce to taste. You will have about 1 cup of sauce. Chill for 30 minutes, or until needed.

Serve the chilled shrimp in shrimp cocktail dishes or small bowls with the cocktail sauce on the side.

TOTAL TIME: 5 minutes (plus chilling time)

LEFTOVERS Cocktail sauce will keep in a covered container in the refrigerator for up to 1 month. The cooked shrimp will keep for only 2 or 3 days in the fridge.

Evelynne's Pickled Shrimp

This is a delicious hors d'oeuvre or appetizer from my friend Evelynne that's welcome at any large dinner party. You can easily double or triple the recipe for a crowd.

Makes 8 to 10 servings

2½ pounds shrimp in the shell, cooked, peeled, and deveined (see page 279), but with the tails left intact

1 large red or white onion, very thinly sliced

8 bay leaves

⅔ cup extra-virgin olive oil

⅔ cup vegetable oil, such as soybean, safflower, or grapeseed

⅔ cup distilled white vinegar or white wine vinegar

2 teaspoons celery seeds

1½ teaspoons salt

Freshly ground black pepper

Hot sauce

In a resealable plastic bag or lidded nonreactive container, layer the shrimp, sliced onion, and bay leaves. In a small bowl, combine the olive oil, vegetable oil, vinegar, celery seeds, salt, and pepper to taste, and mix well. Pour this dressing over the shrimp. Seal the bag or cover the container and let the shrimp marinate, refrigerated, for at least 24 hours and up to 3 days before serving.

Serve the shrimp in a glass container, with the bay leaves mixed in for decoration and a bottle of hot sauce on the side. Put out only half the shrimp at a time and keep the rest chilled so you can replenish the dish.

PREP TIME: 5 minutes

TOTAL TIME: 1 to 3 days (includes marinating time; plus chilling time)

ADVANCE PREP *The shrimp can be made up to three days in advance and refrigerated.*

LEFTOVERS *Depending on how long they were marinated, the shrimp will keep for another two or three days in the refrigerator before the vinegar*

---

starts to affect the texture of the flesh, turning it mealy.

White Anchovies with Garlic and Parsley

Served with plenty of fresh country bread or Bruschetta (page 23), to sop up the dressing, these marinated white anchovies make a quick, delicious hors d'oeuvre. White anchovies have very little to do with the dark, salty anchovies most people pick off of their pizzas. Be sure to find soft, white anchovies that are marinated in vinegar, not dried or salted or preserved in olive oil. They are available at Italian gourmet shops, and recently I even saw them at Costco.

Makes 4 to 6 servings

---

8 ounces white anchovies in vinegar
½ cup finely chopped flat-leaf parsley
⅓ cup extra-virgin olive oil
2 large garlic cloves, minced
Grated zest of 1 lemon
Freshly ground black pepper

Drain the anchovies and arrange in a compact, contiguous layer on a small, rimmed serving dish. In a small bowl, mix the parsley, olive oil, garlic, and lemon zest. Spread this mixture out over the anchovies and grind some black pepper evenly over the top.

TOTAL TIME: 5 minutes

ADVANCE PREP *The anchovies can be made up to a day in advance. Cover with plastic wrap and refrigerate until ready to serve.*
LEFTOVERS *The marinated anchovies will keep three or four days.*

■ ■ ■

Soups

CAMPBELL'S WAS RIGHT. Soup *is* good food (though whether Campbell's soup qualifies is another story). The recipes in this chapter are indeed good food, if by good you mean simple, flavorful, healthful, and—to use a word that seems appropriate for something as homey as soup—downright yummy. There are soups that are thick and rich enough to warm you on the coldest winter's night, and soups that are light and refreshing enough to cool you down on a hot summer's day. There are soups that are hearty enough to serve as an entire meal, and others that are delicate enough to stimulate your appetite for what lies ahead.

Soup isn't only good, it is practical. You can use up odds and ends of vegetables, meats, grains, starches, wine—you name it. (Though always keep in mind what my great-grandmother used to say when she cooked: "You put in good, you get out good.")

A large pot of soup will feed a lot of people. Most soups keep well, too, and are better the second day; if you have time to let them sit, I'd encourage you to do so. I freeze leftovers in individual portions and take them out of the freezer to bring to work for lunch.

You will note in the recipes that follow that my technique for making soup is similar from one to the next. I usually begin by sautéing some aromatic vegetables (onions, carrots, celery) in fat (olive oil, butter, or bacon fat). Then I add liquid in the form of wine or milk or stock or water. Next I add the principal ingredients, whether beans or vegetables or meats or a combination, and simmer them until the ingredients are tender and the flavors have come together. Recipes for all but the most traditional soups are really guidelines. Don't let yourself get hung up if you are missing an ingredient or you want to throw something else into the pot.

■ ■ ■

Tomato Gazpacho

There is nothing more refreshing on a hot summer day than a glass or bowl of chilled gazpacho, Spain's most famous soup. Only make gazpacho with fresh tomatoes if you are in high tomato season and you have access to super-ripe, locally grown tomatoes. Even then, I give them a little boost with some tomato juice. The rest of the year, top-quality canned tomatoes work perfectly well. For a more substantial soup, add a garnish of cooked, chilled shrimp.

Makes 4 cups, enough for 4 servings

5 tablespoons extra-virgin olive oil

Four $1/2$-inch-thick slices baguette

$1/4$ green bell pepper, cored, seeded, and chopped

1 medium cucumber, peeled, seeded, and chopped

$1/2$ medium red onion, diced

1 jalapeño or other hot chile, seeded and chopped

1 garlic clove, chopped

About $1/4$ cup sherry vinegar, white wine vinegar, or cider vinegar

3 large ripe tomatoes ($1 1/2$ pounds), chopped, plus 1 cup tomato juice, or 1 (28-ounce) can top-quality plum tomatoes

Kosher salt and freshly ground black pepper

1 scallion, white and green parts, chopped

2 tablespoons chopped fresh cilantro or parsley

In a small frying pan, heat 2 tablespoons of the olive oil over medium heat. Add the bread slices and toast until nicely browned, about 2 minutes. Flip and toast the second side for 2 minutes. Transfer the bread to the work bowl of a food processor fitted with a metal chopping blade or a blender. Set aside a few pieces of the bell pepper and cucumber for garnish. Add the rest of the bell pepper and cucumber to the food processor, along with the onion, jalapeño, garlic, vinegar, and the remaining 3 tablespoons olive oil. Using on/off pulses, finely chop the vegetables. Scrape down the sides. Add the fresh tomatoes and tomato juice or the canned tomatoes. If using canned, rinse the can out with $1/2$ cup cold water and add the water, too. Add 1 teaspoon salt and some black pepper and pulse to purée the tomatoes. Let the machine run continuously for a minute or two to liquefy the soup.

Strain the soup through a vegetable mill or mesh sieve into a bowl. Be sure to scrape off and incorporate any pulp from the underside of the strainer. Adjust the seasoning with vinegar, salt, and pepper. Chill for at least 1 hour. Serve in chilled bowls or glasses, garnished with the reserved chopped cucumber and green pepper, the scallion, and cilantro.

PREP TIME: 15 minutes
COOKING TIME: 5 minutes
TOTAL TIME: 20 minutes (plus chilling time)

ADVANCE PREP *The soup can be made two or three days in advance and chilled until ready to serve.*

LEFTOVERS *Gazpacho makes a delicious Bloody Mary-like cocktail. Thin it if necessary with a little more tomato juice and add vodka and your favorite seasonings. I also use leftover gazpacho as a base for salad dressing, adding more olive oil, vinegar, and seasonings to taste. Made with canned tomatoes, the soup will keep for ten days in the refrigerator. Made with fresh tomatoes, it will last for only three days.*

Yellow Tomato Gazpacho

When ripe, local yellow tomatoes are available, use them to make a pretty yellow gazpacho. You can even serve red and yellow gazpacho swirled together in a bowl to make an attractive pattern. Substitute 1 1/2 pounds yellow tomatoes for the red tomatoes and use 3/4 cup vegetable stock instead of tomato juice. Increase the vinegar to 5 tablespoons to account for the lower acidity of the yellow tomatoes.

Watermelon Gazpacho

Lighter than tomato gazpacho, watermelon gazpacho may be even more refreshing and delicious. It is certainly unexpected, though the melding of flavors is seamless, perhaps because cucumbers and watermelon are close relatives. I prefer to use seedless watermelon so I don't have to remove the seeds, but if watermelon with seeds is all you can find, it doesn't take that long to deal with them. Depending on the size of your food processor or blender, you may want to work in two batches: even though this recipe makes a small amount, the soup has a thin consistency, and as a result, it has a tendency to overflow while you whiz it. A garnish of crumbled feta cheese, chopped black olives, and chopped scallion holds the sweet-and-sour taste of the soup in balance.

Makes 4 1/2 cups, enough for 4 servings

4 1/2 pounds watermelon

1 medium cucumber, peeled, seeded, and chopped

1 small red chile, seeded and chopped

1/4 red bell pepper, cored, seeded, and chopped

1/2 small red onion or 1 large shallot, chopped

1/2 cup tomato juice

3 tablespoons extra-virgin olive oil

Juice of about 1 lime (3 tablespoons) or about 3 tablespoons sherry vinegar, white wine vinegar, or cider vinegar

Kosher salt and freshly ground black pepper

1 1/2 ounces feta cheese, crumbled

2 tablespoons finely chopped black olives, such as Kalamata

1 scallion, white and green parts, chopped

Remove the rind from the watermelon, seed the melon, and cut it into chunks. (You'll have about 6 cups of melon.)

Place the watermelon, cucumber, chile, bell pepper, onion, tomato juice, olive oil, lime juice, 1/2 teaspoon salt, and some black pepper in the bowl of a food processor fitted with a metal chopping blade or in a blender. Using on/off pulses, purée the ingredients until they begin to liquefy. Keep the machine running continuously for a minute or two to be sure the mixture is as smooth as possible. Pass the purée through a vegetable mill or mesh sieve into a bowl. Adjust the seasoning with additional lime juice, salt, or pepper. Chill for at least 1 hour. Serve garnished with the feta, olives, and scallion.

PREP TIME: 15 minutes

TOTAL TIME: 15 minutes (plus chilling time)

ADVANCE PREP *The soup can be made a day or two in advance and refrigerated until served.*

LEFTOVERS *Like Tomato Gazpacho (page 34), this soup can be used as the base of a delicious cocktail mixed with vodka and served over ice. The watermelon gazpacho will keep for up to four days in the refrigerator.*

Roasted Tomato Soup with Chickpeas, Spinach, and Cumin

Slow-roasting tomatoes concentrates their flavor, almost as though they've been artificially ripened. What that means is that even in the dead of winter, when all you can find at the grocery store is pale, hard, plum tomatoes, you can actually transform them into a lovely tomato soup. The deep tomato and cumin flavor of this soup is equally enjoyable in winter and summer.

Makes about 8 cups, enough for 6 to 8 servings

    4 pounds fresh plum tomatoes, cored and cut in
        half lengthwise
    1 head of garlic (8 to 10 cloves), separated into
        cloves and smashed but not peeled
    2/3 cup extra-virgin olive oil
    Kosher salt and freshly ground black pepper
    2 large yellow or white onions, chopped
    1 small carrot, chopped
    2 bay leaves
    About 6 cups vegetable or chicken stock
    1 teaspoon cumin seeds, toasted (see page 10)
    Juice of 1 lemon (1/4 cup)
    2 cups cooked chickpeas (see page 201)
    1 pound fresh spinach, cleaned

Preheat the oven to 325°F.

Place the tomatoes on a large rimmed baking sheet. Scatter the garlic cloves on the pan and drizzle the whole thing with 1/3 cup of the olive oil. Season generously with salt and pepper. Toss the tomatoes to coat with the oil and seasoning. Place the tomatoes in the oven and roast for 2 hours, or until the tomatoes have shriveled and browned around the edges. (To save time, you can preheat the oven to 375°F and roast for 1 hour, but the tomato flavor of the finished soup will be less intense.) Cool. Remove and discard the peel of the garlic.

In a large saucepan over medium-high heat, heat the remaining 1/3 cup olive oil. Add the onions and cook until translucent, about 7 minutes. Add the carrot, bay leaves, and stock and bring to a boil. Loosely cover the pot and turn down the heat so that the liquid is simmering. Let cook for 20 minutes or until the carrots are tender. Add the roasted tomatoes and garlic along with any pan juices. The tomatoes should be covered by the stock; if not, add more stock or water. Return to a boil, reduce the heat, cover, and simmer for 20 minutes more, or until the flesh of the tomatoes has disintegrated. Remove the bay leaves.

Pass the soup through a food mill or purée with a blender, immersion blender, or food processor and pass through a fine sieve. Return the puréed soup to a pot and bring back up to a simmer. Adjust the seasoning with salt and pepper. Add the cumin and lemon juice, along with the chickpeas and spinach. Cook for 3 or 4 minutes, or until the spinach has wilted and the chickpeas are heated through.

PREP TIME: 30 minutes
COOKING TIME: 1 1/2 to 2 1/2 hours
TOTAL TIME: 2 to 3 hours

ADVANCE PREP *The soup can be made up to two days in advance and refrigerated. Don't add the toasted cumin, spinach, or chickpeas until you reheat the soup to serve.*
LEFTOVERS *The soup will keep for about ten days in the refrigerator. It can also be frozen for up to two months.*

Cream of Broccoli Soup

The principal flavor in this classic American soup is broccoli, so if, like George Bush, Sr., you don't like broccoli, scroll down. The same technique can be used with just about any other vegetable—asparagus, carrot, cauliflower, celery—to make a creamed soup. Although some people use flour to thicken their cream soups, I prefer the lighter taste and texture of an unthickened soup. For a thicker soup, add half a small potato to the mixture with the stock or water.

Makes 8 cups, enough for 8 servings

    3 tablespoons unsalted butter
    1 large white or yellow onion, chopped
    3 large broccoli stalks (about 1 1/2 pounds),
        trimmed and roughly chopped
    6 cups chicken or vegetable stock or water
    1 bay leaf
    Kosher salt
    1/2 to 1 cup heavy cream
    Freshly ground black pepper

In a large saucepan, heat the butter over medium-high heat. Add the onion and sauté until soft, about 5 minutes. Add the broccoli and sauté until wilted, 5 minutes more. Add the stock, bay leaf, and 2 teaspoons salt. Bring to a boil, reduce the heat, and simmer, with the cover ajar, until the broccoli is very tender, about 30 minutes. Remove the bay leaf.

Using an immersion or regular blender or food processor, purée the soup until smooth, working in batches if necessary. (For a smoother texture, pass this purée through a mesh sieve back into the pot.) Stir in the cream—1/2 cup at first, more if desired—and adjust the seasoning with salt and pepper. Bring the soup back to a simmer, turn down the heat,

and cook for just a couple of minutes to bring the flavors together before serving.

PREP TIME: 20 minutes
COOKING TIME: 45 minutes
TOTAL TIME: 1 hour 5 minutes

ADVANCE PREP The soup can be made a day or two in advance, cooled, covered, and refrigerated. Reheat gently to serve. Stir any skin that forms on top of the soup back into the pot as the soup warms.
LEFTOVERS The soup will keep for about a week in the fridge. You can also freeze it for up to a month.

VARIATIONS
Cream of Asparagus Soup
Substitute 1 large bunch of asparagus (about 1 1/2 pounds) for the broccoli. Remove and reserve the tips for garnish (you'll have to blanch them in salted water for 2 minutes; see page 163) or for another purpose. Use only the asparagus stalks, cut into chunks, for the soup. Strain the soup before adding the cream.

Cream of Carrot Soup
Substitute about 2 pounds of carrots, peeled and cut into chunks, for the broccoli. The carrots will take longer to soften, about 40 minutes. A pinch of nutmeg adds a nice flavor.

Cream of Cauliflower Soup
Substitute 1 1/2 pounds of cauliflower for the broccoli and proceed as directed.

Cream of Three Celery Soup
Substitute the top half of a bunch of celery, with leaves, or 6 or 7 whole celery stalks with leaves (about 1 pound), cut into chunks, for the

broccoli. Also add an 8-ounce piece of celery root, peeled and diced, and add $\frac{1}{4}$ teaspoon celery seeds to the pot before simmering. Strain before adding the cream.

Butternut Squash Soup with Apple and Nutmeg

This is a delicious and beautiful soup, ideal for the fall and winter holidays. I've made the cream optional because without it, the soup has a homey, comforting quality; with it, the soup is a little more refined. For even more sophistication, make a garnish of sautéed apple cubes, toasted pumpkin seeds, crumbled bacon, and/or buttered croutons.

Makes 3 quarts, enough for 12 servings

> 4 tablespoons ($\frac{1}{2}$ stick) unsalted butter
> 1 large white or yellow onion, chopped
> One 3-pound butternut squash, peeled, seeded, and cut into cubes (about 6 cups)
> 2 medium carrots, peeled and chopped
> 2 medium cooking apples, such as Northern Spy or Golden Delicious, peeled, cored, and chopped
> 1 small Yukon Gold or other all-purpose potato, peeled and chopped
> 1 bay leaf
> Scant $\frac{1}{4}$ teaspoon ground nutmeg
> Kosher salt and freshly ground black pepper
> 1 cup heavy cream (optional)

In a large pot, melt the butter over medium-high heat. Add the onion and sauté until soft, about 7 minutes. Add the squash, carrots, apples, potato, bay leaf, nutmeg, 4 teaspoons salt, and a scant $\frac{1}{4}$ teaspoon pepper, as well as 6 cups of water—the water should be at least 1 inch or so above the vegetables; if not, add more. Bring to a boil. Turn down the heat, cover the pot, and simmer for 45 minutes, or until the carrots are fall-apart tender.

Remove the bay leaf. Using an immersion blender, a food processor fitted with a metal chopping blade, or a regular blender, purée the soup until smooth, working in batches if necessary. If you cooked the soup long enough, there will be no need to strain it. If not using the cream, adjust the seasoning and serve. If using cream, stir in the cream and bring the soup back up to a simmer. Cook for a couple of minutes. Adjust the seasoning (you'll need another teaspoon or so of salt and more pepper) and serve.

PREP TIME: 20 minutes
COOKING TIME: 1 hour
TOTAL TIME: 1 hour 20 minutes

ADVANCE PREP The soup can be made a day or two in advance, cooled, covered, and refrigerated. If made with cream, a skin may form on top as it reheats. Simply stir it back into the pot.
LEFTOVERS Made without cream, the soup will keep for up to two weeks in the refrigerator; made with cream, it will last for one week. The soup can also be frozen for up to four months.

Roasted Cauliflower and Pear Soup

The addition of pears to a simple cauliflower soup underscores the flavor of the cauliflower. I find roasting the cauliflower first intensifies its flavor, but if you are short on time, you can skip that step entirely.

Makes 10 cups, enough for 10 servings

1 large (2- to 2½-pound) head of cauliflower,
   including the stems and stalk, roughly chopped
2 tablespoons extra-virgin olive oil or vegetable oil
2 bacon strips, finely chopped, or 2 tablespoons
   unsalted butter
1 large yellow or white onion, chopped
1 garlic clove, minced
1 celery stalk, chopped
1 large carrot, chopped
1 large ripe pear, such as Anjou or Bartlett,
   peeled, cored, and diced
4 cups chicken or vegetable stock or water
Kosher salt and freshly ground black pepper
Pinch of freshly grated nutmeg
1 tablespoon chopped flat-leaf parsley

Preheat the oven to 400°F.

Spread out the cauliflower on a baking sheet lined with parchment or aluminum foil and roast until browned, 35 to 40 minutes.

Meanwhile, in a large pot, heat the oil with the bacon. Add the onion and cook for about 5 minutes, until soft. Add the garlic and celery and cook for another 5 minutes or so. Add the carrot and pear, and continue cooking for about 5 more minutes. It's okay if the vegetables begin to color slightly. Add the roasted cauliflower, along with the stock and an additional 4 cups cold water. Add 1 tablespoon salt, ¼ teaspoon black pepper, the nutmeg, and parsley. Bring to a boil. Reduce the heat so that the soup simmers, set on a cover slightly ajar, and cook slowly for 30 to 40 minutes, until the cauliflower is very soft.

Using a food mill, purée the soup into a clean pot. Alternatively, you can use a blender, immersion blender, or food processor and then pass the puréed soup through a fine-mesh strainer. Bring the puréed soup back to a simmer and adjust the

seasoning. The soup can be served right away, but like most soups it's best after it has sat for a day or two in the refrigerator.

PREP TIME: 20 minutes
COOKING TIME: 1 hour 20 minutes
TOTAL TIME: 1¾ hours

ADVANCE PREP *The soup can be made several days in advance, cooled, covered, and refrigerated. Reheat gently before serving.*
LEFTOVERS *The soup will keep in the refrigerator for a week or in the freezer for several months.*

VARIATION
Curried Cauliflower Soup
Add 2 tablespoons curry powder (see page 409) when you add the carrot, cabbage, and pear. Continue with the recipe as directed.

Izabela's Polish Pickle Soup
The idea for this soup sounds weird, but it is based on a delicious, traditional Polish soup of pickles and potatoes, and it has a light, refreshing flavor. Better still, it's a very quick soup, perfect for when you think you have nothing in the house . . . except pickles.
Makes 6 cups, enough for 6 servings

4 cups chicken stock
2 medium Yukon Gold potatoes, peeled and diced
4 large kosher or Polish sour dill pickles, shredded
¼ cup pickle juice
¼ cup heavy cream
Freshly ground black pepper
1 hard-cooked egg (see page 29), chopped
Chopped flat-leaf parsley, for garnish

In a medium pot, bring the chicken stock to a boil. Add the potatoes, turn down the heat, and simmer until tender, about 20 minutes. Add the pickles and pickle juice and bring back to a boil. Stir in the heavy cream and a generous amount of black pepper. Bring to a simmer and adjust the seasoning.

Divide the hard-cooked egg and parsley among the serving bowls and ladle in the hot soup.

TOTAL TIME: 40 minutes

ADVANCE PREP *You can shred the pickles and keep them in their juice in advance. You can also dice the potatoes, but they must be kept submerged in cold water.*

LEFTOVERS *The soup will keep for about one week in the fridge. Don't worry about a thin film that forms on top. Just stir it back into the soup.*

Split Pea Soup

A soup traditionalist, I like to use the classic smoked ham hock or a ham bone to infuse my split pea soup with a rich, smoked-pork flavor. But if you'd rather not use pork, I find a smoked turkey wing is a perfectly acceptable substitute. Sometimes I also add shredded kale or cabbage to the soup. Small croutons fried in butter or bacon fat make the perfect garnish.

Makes 6 cups, enough for 6 servings

2 tablespoons unsalted butter or bacon fat

1 large white or yellow onion, chopped

1 large garlic clove, minced

1 large carrot, chopped

1 celery stalk, chopped

1 bunch green kale, leaves only, or 1/4 head of green cabbage, shredded (about 2 cups; optional)

2 cups yellow or green split peas (1 pound), rinsed

1 smoked ham hock, ham bone, or smoked turkey wing

1 small bay leaf

Kosher salt and freshly ground black pepper

1 tablespoon chopped fresh thyme or marjoram

1 tablespoon chopped fresh flat-leaf parsley

In a large saucepan, heat the butter over medium-high heat. Add the onion and sauté until soft, about 5 minutes. Add the garlic and sauté for another minute more. Add the carrot and celery and cook until wilted, about 5 minutes. Add the kale, if using, split peas, ham hock, bay leaf, 2 teaspoons salt, and a generous amount of pepper, along with 8 cups cold water. Bring to a boil, reduce the heat, cover, and simmer for 1 hour, skimming off any white froth or scum that accumulates on the surface. Add the thyme and parsley, and continue simmering for about 15 minutes, until the herbs have infused the soup. Remove the ham hock, discard the skin and bone, chop up any meat, and return it to the soup. Discard the bay leaf. For a thicker soup, continue simmering until it reaches your desired consistency. Adjust the seasoning with salt and pepper.

PREP TIME: 20 minutes
COOKING TIME: 1 hour 40 minutes
TOTAL TIME: 2 hours

ADVANCE PREP *The soup is actually better if it is made a day or two in advance, refrigerated, and reheated before serving. The soup will solidify when it chills, but it will return to its liquid state as it reheats.*

MAKING CROUTONS

Little cubes of toasted bread add flavor and a delicious textural component to soups, salads, and other dishes. There are two basic techniques for making them: in a frying pan on top of the stove or in the oven. Stove-top croutons are often heavier because they absorb the fat they are fried in; I prefer them in soups. Oven-toasted croutons are lighter, so I prefer them in salads, where they gain flavor by soaking up the dressing. Each of these recipes makes 1 to 1½ cups croutons. Once cool, they will keep in an airtight container for three days.

Stove-Top Croutons

Remove and discard the crusts from two or three ½-inch-thick slices of slightly stale, dense country white bread. Cut the bread into ½-inch cubes (or smaller). In a medium skillet, heat 2 to 3 tablespoons unsalted butter, extra-virgin olive oil, or bacon fat over medium-high heat. Add the bread cubes and toast, tossing continuously, until golden brown, 4 or 5 minutes. You should not need to add more fat to the pan because even if the croutons have absorbed it all, they will still brown evenly. Season the croutons with salt and pepper and use them to garnish soups.

Oven-Toasted Croutons

Preheat the oven to 350°F. Remove and discard the crusts from two or three ½-inch-thick slices of slightly stale, dense country white bread. Cut the bread into ½-inch cubes (or smaller). If you have one of those newfangled olive oil atomizers, lightly spray the bread cubes with extra-virgin olive oil. Otherwise, drizzle them with a small amount of olive oil and toss to evenly distribute. Place the croutons in the oven and toast, tossing frequently, for about 8 minutes, or until golden brown.

LEFTOVERS Split pea soup will keep for about ten days in the refrigerator. It can also be frozen for several months.

Mushroom Barley Soup

This hearty soup has a rich beef flavor from a generous amount of beef short ribs. Any cut of short ribs will work fine, whether English-style square cut or Jewish-style flanken strips. I use lentils in the soup to add body and a depth of flavor that just using barley alone doesn't give. And of course, the more varieties of cultivated and wild mushrooms you use, the more complex a mushroom flavor your soup will have.

Makes 10 cups, enough for 8 to 10 servings

> 2½ pounds beef short ribs, rinsed
> 1 (14-ounce) can plum tomatoes, with juice, cut into chunks
> ¾ cup brown lentils, picked over and rinsed
> ½ cup pearl barley
> 1 large yellow or white onion, diced
> 2 large carrots, peeled, 1 cut into 2 chunks, 1 diced
> 3 celery stalks, 2 cut into 2 chunks each, with leaves; 1 diced, without leaves
> 5 sprigs flat-leaf parsley
> 1 bay leaf
> Kosher salt and freshly ground black pepper
> 12 ounces assorted mushrooms, such as button, portobello, cremini, or porcini, sliced
> ½ cup frozen peas (optional)

In a large pot, combine the short ribs, tomatoes, lentils, barley, onion, chunked carrot and celery, parsley, and bay leaf. Add 2½ teaspoons salt, about ½ teaspoon pepper, and 6 cups cold water. Set over medium-high heat and bring to a boil.

Skim off any scum that rises to the surface, turn down the heat, cover, and simmer for 2 hours.

With a slotted spoon or tongs, remove the carrot, celery, parsley, and bay leaf and discard. Add the remaining diced carrot and celery, the mushrooms, and peas; cover and continue simmering for about 1 hour, or until the meat falls from the bones and the vegetables are very tender. Remove the bones and gristle from the short ribs, and discard. Dice the meat and return it to the pot. Adjust the seasoning with additional salt and pepper.

PREP TIME: 20 minutes
COOKING TIME: 3 hours 30 minutes
TOTAL TIME: 3 hours 50 minutes

ADVANCE PREP *The soup is best made a day or two in advance. It will thicken as it sits. Cool and refrigerate it. Remove and discard any fat that coagulates on the surface. To reheat, add some more water if necessary to thin it down.*
LEFTOVERS *The soup will keep refrigerated for about two weeks. It can be frozen for several months.*

Bean Soup with Stinging Nettles

I know, this sounds like some sort of witch's brew. But I promise there's no eye of newt in this delicious, Tuscan-inspired soup. Stinging nettles have a fresh, green taste that gives this soup a complex flavor. I find them occasionally in my local greenmarket. Wear rubber gloves while handling the nettles because they really do sting, but don't worry about harming your family or friends—the nettles' sting disappears when they are cooked. If you can't find nettles, use pungent mustard greens or deep, dark leafy kale.

Makes 12 cups, about 10 servings

¼ cup extra-virgin olive oil
2 tablespoons minced pancetta, bacon, or prosciutto (optional)
½ large yellow onion, chopped
1 large red onion, chopped
2 garlic cloves, minced
2 large celery stalks, chopped
6 medium carrots, peeled and chopped
1 medium fennel bulb, cored and chopped
2 small dried mild red chiles, stemmed, halved, and seeded
4 ounces stinging nettles or 8 ounces mustard greens or kale, leaves removed from the stems and coarsely chopped
5 cups cooked beans, such as cannellini, borlotti, navy, or baby limas (see page 201), drained, cooking water reserved
2 cups reserved bean cooking water
Kosher salt and freshly ground black pepper
A 2- by 3-inch rind of Parmigiano Reggiano cheese (see page 43, optional)
Handful of chopped parsley
Best-quality extra-virgin olive oil

In a large, heavy-bottomed soup pot, heat the olive oil. Add the pancetta, if using, and the onions and garlic. Sauté until the onions are translucent, about 8 minutes. Add the celery, carrots, fennel, and chiles, and continue sautéing until the vegetables have wilted and start to brown, about 10 minutes. Add the nettles and cook for another 3 or 4 minutes, until wilted. Add the cooked beans, the bean cooking water, 6 cups cold water, 1½ tablespoons salt, some black pepper, and the Parmigiano Reggiano rind, if using, and bring to a boil. Turn down the heat and simmer for about 30 minutes, until the vegetables are tender but not mushy and the flavors have blended. Remove the cheese rind.

CHEESE RINDS

Another way my frugality in the kitchen rears its cheapskate head is that I almost never throw out the hard rind of natural-rind cheeses, especially Parmigiano Reggiano or Grana Padano. (If you are not sure whether a cheese has a natural rind, ask your cheese monger.) Once I've consumed all the desirable insides of the cheese, I throw the rind into a bag in my freezer. Then when I go to make something like an Italian vegetable soup, for which the rind of a Parmigiano adds richness and flavor to the broth, or a cheese sauce that could use the boost of flavor a few rinds of different cheese could give, I throw them in. Before serving, be sure to remove the rind.

Adjust the seasoning with more salt and pepper, as needed, and stir in the parsley. Ladle the soup into bowls and drizzle some of the best extra-virgin olive oil you can find on top.

PREP TIME: 15 minutes
COOKING TIME: 1 hour
TOTAL TIME: 1 hour 15 minutes

ADVANCE PREP This soup, like most soups, is best after it has sat for a day or two in the fridge. If making it in advance, don't add the parsley until you reheat it.

LEFTOVERS The soup will keep for up to two weeks in the refrigerator or it can be frozen for up to three months.

VARIATION

Ribollita

Ribollita, literally "reboiled," is another classic of Tuscany. Once the soup has sat for a day or two, bring it back to a boil. Toast several thick pieces of stale country bread and rub each side with a split garlic clove to make a basic bruschetta. In a large soup tureen or pot, arrange a layer of bread. Drizzle the bread with a generous amount of best-quality extra-virgin olive oil. Ladle the soup over the bread to cover. Make another layer of bread and repeat until the tureen is full or the soup is gone. Keep warm but let the soup sit for 20 minutes or so before serving.

Cuban Black Bean Soup

This simple, traditional Cuban soup has a complex flavor from the combination of herbs and spices. It's lick-the-bowl good. To save time, you can use canned beans as explained in the variation below, but the flavor and texture of the finished soup is best when you cook dry beans from scratch.

Makes 6 cups, enough for 4 to 6 servings

> 1 cup dried black or turtle beans
> 2 ounces salt pork, pancetta, country ham, or other cured pork
> 2 tablespoons extra-virgin olive oil
> 1 medium white onion, chopped
> 1 large garlic clove, minced
> ½ small green bell pepper, cored, seeded, and chopped
> ½ small jalapeño chile, seeded and minced, or ¼ teaspoon cayenne pepper
> ½ teaspoon ground cumin
> ½ teaspoon dried oregano
> ½ teaspoon dry mustard
> Juice of 1 lime (about 3 tablespoons)
> Kosher salt
> ¼ teaspoon cayenne pepper, or to taste (optional)

1 hard-cooked egg (see page 29), chopped
Handful of fresh cilantro leaves
Wedges of lime

Place the beans in a large bowl, add enough water to cover by 3 inches, and let soak for 8 to 12 hours or overnight at room temperature.

Drain and rinse the beans. Place the beans in a large saucepan. Add 5 cups cold water and the salt pork. Bring to a boil over high heat, reduce the heat, cover loosely, and let simmer for 50 minutes to 1 hour, until the beans are tender but have not turned to mush.

Meanwhile, in a sauté pan, heat the olive oil. Add the onion, garlic, bell pepper, and jalapeño, if using, and sauté until soft, about 7 minutes. Stir in the cumin, oregano, and mustard and continue cooking for a minute or so to toast the spices. Add about ½ cup of the cooking liquid from the beans and the lime juice. Turn down the heat to a simmer, cover, and let cook for about 15 minutes, until the vegetables are very tender. Stir this mixture into the beans along with 1 tablespoon salt and the cayenne pepper, if using, and continue simmering the beans for another 30 minutes or so. Remove the salt pork and discard.

In a blender or food processor, purée about 1 cup of the cooked beans until smooth and stir the purée back into the pot to thicken the mixture. Alternatively, you can use an immersion blender to purée some of the soup in the pot, but be sure to leave most of the beans whole. To serve, ladle the soup into hot bowls and garnish with chopped egg, fresh cilantro, and lime wedges.

PREP TIME: 20 minutes

COOKING TIME: 2 hours

TOTAL TIME: 10 hours 20 minutes (includes soaking time)

ADVANCE PREP The beans can be cooked and stored in their cooking liquid in the refrigerator for up to a week before finishing the soup.

LEFTOVERS The soup will keep for two weeks in the refrigerator or in the freezer for two months. Don't add the garnish of chopped egg and cilantro until ready to serve.

VARIATION

Black Bean Soup in a Hurry

Substitute 2 (15-ounce) cans black beans for the dried beans. Drained, the cans should yield about 2¼ cups of beans. Place the beans in a saucepan with 2½ cups chicken or vegetable stock and bring to a simmer while you proceed with the recipe as directed.

Cheddar Cheese Soup

When I was a child, Cheddar cheese soup was popular on menus in all sorts of restaurants. Today, it's all but disappeared. I'm not sure why—the low-fat craze, perhaps? But with low-carb unseating low-fat, I think it's time creamy, rich, delicious Cheddar cheese soup were the soup du jour again. I start by grinding my vegetables because I like the flavor and texture of the finished soup better. If you prefer, you can chop the vegetables by hand and then purée the soup base when it has finished cooking, before you add the cheese. I serve my Cheddar Cheese Soup with any or all of the following garnishes: Buttermilk Fried Onions (page 193), Roasted Cauliflower (page 147), or crumbled bacon.

Makes 10 cups, enough for 8 to 10 servings

2 celery stalks, cut into chunks
1 large yellow onion, peeled and cut into chunks

2 medium carrots, peeled and cut into chunks

5 sprigs flat-leaf parsley, leaves only

6 tablespoons ($\frac{3}{4}$ stick) unsalted butter, softened

2 cups chicken or vegetable stock

2 cups beer (lager or ale), dry white wine, or additional chicken or vegetable stock

4 cups whole milk

2-inch square rind of Parmigiano Reggiano (see page 43), or 2 tablespoons grated Parmigiano Reggiano cheese

$\frac{1}{4}$ cup all-purpose flour

$\frac{1}{2}$ teaspoon dry mustard or 1 tablespoon Dijon mustard

$\frac{1}{4}$ to $\frac{1}{2}$ teaspoon cayenne pepper

Kosher salt and freshly ground white pepper

1 pound extra-sharp Cheddar cheese, shredded (about $3\frac{1}{2}$ cups)

Using a food processor fitted with a metal chopping blade or a meat grinder, finely mince the celery, onion, carrots, and parsley (see headnote).

In a medium pot, melt 4 tablespoons of the butter over medium-high heat. Add the minced vegetables and cook for 5 or 6 minutes to soften. Add the stock, beer, milk, and cheese rind, if using. Bring to a boil, reduce the heat, and simmer, uncovered, for 10 minutes, stirring occasionally.

Meanwhile, in a small bowl, combine the remaining 2 tablespoons soft butter with the flour and work with a spoon to form a smooth paste. When the soup base has finished simmering, remove the cheese rind and discard. Using a whisk, mix in the butter and flour paste (see box, right). Whisk in the mustard, cayenne, 1 teaspoon salt, and white pepper to taste, and continue simmering the soup for 5

KITCHEN SENSE

THICKENING SOUPS

If your soup doesn't quite come together, or has a thinner, more watery consistency than you desire, here are a few remedies you can try:

1. Continue simmering—some soups will thicken by evaporation if you continue simmering them, uncovered, until they attain the desired consistency. Be careful about seasoning, though. As the liquid evaporates, salt and other spices will concentrate. And don't let the soup burn.

2. Purée some of the solids—you can take a cup or two of your soup and purée it with a blender, immersion blender, or food processor. Stir the purée back into the soup to thicken it.

3. Add something starchy—potato, rice, barley, toasted bread, or other starches will thicken a soup. Be sure to continue cooking the soup long enough to thoroughly cook whatever it is that you've added. If you add potato, mashing some of it on the side of the pot will thicken the soup even more. Don't forget to adjust the seasoning. (Adding a starch to soup is also a good fix if you've oversalted your soup. The extra starch will absorb excess salt.)

4. Whisk in a beurre manié—a paste made from equal parts butter and flour is called a *beurre manié*, and it is used to thicken cream soups and other rich soups. I like to make the beurre manié in a small bowl and dip a whisk into the bowl to pick up some of the paste. Whisk it into the simmering soup, making sure there are no lumps. Let the soup simmer for 5 or 6 minutes to thicken and properly cook the flour. If the soup is still not thick enough, add more beurre manié, simmering for at least 5 minutes after each addition.

to 8 minutes, until it has thickened and there is no perceptible raw flour taste.

Using the whisk, stir in the shredded Cheddar cheese and the grated Parmigiano, if using. Do not allow the soup to boil, or it may break and curdle. Serve in warmed bowls with your choice of garnish.

PREP TIME: 20 minutes
COOKING TIME: 30 minutes
TOTAL TIME: 50 minutes

ADVANCE PREP *You can prepare the soup up to the point that you add the shredded cheese three or four days in advance and refrigerate it. To finish the soup, bring it back up to a simmer over low heat, adding more liquid if necessary to thin it. Then add the cheese and stir to melt before serving. You can complete the soup a couple of hours in advance of serving, but keep it at room temperature before reheating it gently or it may break.*

LEFTOVERS *The soup will keep for a week or so in the refrigerator. When reheated, the soup has a slightly less silken texture, but otherwise it is delicious. Heat it over low heat, adding a small amount of liquid if necessary, to prevent scorching or breaking. If the soup breaks, you can beat in additional beurre manié to help bring it back together.*

Peanut Soup with Pickled Cherries and Crumbled Bacon

Peanut soup is a Virginia classic that sounds a little odd but is amazingly satisfying. When served with a garnish of pickled cherries, which add a tart sweetness like a grown-up jelly to cut through the soup's richness, and crumbled bacon, which makes everything better, the combination of flavors is simply delicious.

Makes 12 cups, enough for 10 servings

1/2 cup (1 stick) unsalted butter
1 small white or yellow onion, chopped
1 large carrot, chopped
2 large celery stalks, chopped
3 tablespoons all-purpose flour
3 quarts chicken or vegetable stock
2 cups smooth, unsweetened natural peanut
    butter
Juice of 1/2 lemon (about 2 tablespoons)
1/4 teaspoon celery salt
Kosher salt and freshly ground white or
    black pepper
1/4 cup dried cherries, chopped
1/4 cup balsamic vinegar
Crumbled bacon
1/2 cup dry-roasted, salted peanuts, toasted
    (see page 10) and finely chopped

In a large saucepan, melt the butter over medium heat. Add the onion, carrot, and celery, and cook until soft but not colored, about 6 minutes. Add the flour and continue cooking for a couple of minutes more until the flour blends with the butter and begins to give off a nutty aroma. Whisk in the chicken stock. Bring to a boil, turn down the heat, and simmer for about 30 minutes, or until the soup base has the consistency and flavor of a light gravy and the carrot is soft.

Remove from the heat. For a more refined soup (my preference), pass this soup base through the fine disk of a vegetable mill or purée in batches with a blender or food processor and pass through a sieve or strainer. Return the soup to the pot and bring it back to a simmer over medium heat. For a homier, chunky soup, you can omit this step. Whisk in the peanut butter and bring the soup back to a simmer again. It may be a little lumpy until the peanut butter melts. Stir in the lemon juice, celery salt, 1 teaspoon salt, and pepper to taste. Simmer gently for 4 or 5 minutes. The soup should have a pourable consistency, not too thick or too thin. Adjust the consistency with more stock or water if necessary, and adjust the seasoning with more salt and pepper.

Meanwhile, place the cherries in a small bowl. You can either heat the vinegar and pour it over the cherries or pour the cold vinegar over the cherries and heat the whole thing in a microwave for 2 minutes to soften. Let sit for about 15 minutes, then strain. (You can use the vinegar in salad dressing or for another purpose.)

To serve, divide the bacon and cherries among warmed soup bowls. Ladle in the hot soup and sprinkle each bowl with the peanuts.

PREP TIME: 25 minutes
COOKING TIME: 50 minutes
TOTAL TIME: 1 hour 15 minutes

ADVANCE PREP The soup base can be made to the point before you add the peanut butter one or two days in advance and refrigerated. Before serving, reheat the base and proceed with the recipe as directed. The garnishes can also be made up to a day in advance and kept at room temperature.
LEFTOVERS You can keep the soup in the refrigerator for up to a week. You can also freeze the soup for up to a month. Reheat leftovers gently over low heat, adding more chicken stock if necessary to thin down the soup.

Clam Chowder

The debate continues: New England (with cream) versus Manhattan (with tomatoes). If menus around the country are any indication, New England is winning, but I like them both, and so I have included recipes for each. Both are best if you start with big, plump chowder clams, or Quahogs. But you can also use smaller littleneck, cherrystone, or Manila clams, or any other clams you can find. You first have to steam them to open them and to produce a stock that you can later use for your soup. Chop the clams and you are ready to make your chowder. Of course, if you don't want to bother with fresh clams, you can buy already shucked and/or cooked and chopped clams and clam juice to make a fine soup.

NEW ENGLAND CLAM CHOWDER

This is the creamy one. I prefer my New England–style clam chowder on the thinner side rather than thicker, so I don't add flour. If you prefer a thicker soup, you could add up to 2 tablespoons of flour to this recipe. In fact, if you are using milk instead of cream, I would recommend you add at least 1 tablespoon of flour, not only for its thickening properties but also because it will help prevent the soup from curdling. If it curdles, strain out the solids and use a blender to whip the liquid back to smooth and frothy. If that doesn't work, stir in a slurry of 1 tablespoon cornstarch mixed with 3 tablespoons cold water or white wine, bring to a boil, and simmer a few minutes until thickened.

Makes 8 cups, about 8 servings

1 tablespoon unsalted butter

1 1/2 to 2 ounces salt pork or bacon, finely
    chopped (about 1/3 cup)

1 large white or yellow onion, chopped

1 to 2 tablespoons all-purpose flour (optional;
    see headnote)

1 1/2 cups half-and-half

1 1/2 cups milk or additional half-and-half

Steamed clams (see page 283), chopped,
    juice reserved; or 2 cups chopped clams and
    2 cups bottled clam juice

1 tablespoon chopped fresh thyme or 1/2 teaspoon
    dried

1/2 bay leaf

2 large Yukon Gold or other all-purpose potatoes,
    peeled and diced

Kosher salt and freshly ground black pepper

In a large saucepan over medium heat, melt the butter and add the salt pork. Cook until the fat from the pork renders, 3 or 4 minutes. Add the onion and cook for about 8 minutes, until soft but not browned. If using milk, stir in the optional flour. Add the half-and-half, milk, and 2 cups clam cooking liquid or juice, stirring, along with the thyme and bay leaf. Bring to a simmer. Add the potatoes. Set the cover ajar and simmer until the potatoes are tender, about 15 minutes. Add the clams and cook for another 5 minutes. Adjust the seasoning with salt and pepper and discard the bay leaf. For a slightly thicker soup, mash some of the cooked potato pieces against the side of the pan and stir into the soup.

PREP TIME: 10 minutes

COOKING TIME: 35 minutes

TOTAL TIME: 45 minutes

ADVANCE PREP *This chowder is best made a day in advance. Reheat over low heat just until simmering.*

LEFTOVERS *The soup will keep for four or five days in the fridge. Because of the potatoes, the soup does not freeze well.*

MANHATTAN CLAM CHOWDER

Here's a recipe for the tomato-based clam chowder that's named for the island I call home. I add toasted caraway or cumin seed and a touch of Tabasco to give the final flavor a little oomph.

Makes 2 quarts, enough for 8 servings

1 tablespoon unsalted butter

1 1/2 to 2 ounces salt pork or bacon, finely
    chopped (about 1/3 cup)

1 large white or yellow onion, chopped

1 garlic clove, minced

1 celery stalk, finely chopped

1 medium carrot, peeled and diced

1 teaspoon caraway or cumin seeds

1 (28-ounce) can tomatoes, chopped, with juice
    (without basil)

Steamed clams (see page 283), chopped,
    juice reserved; or 2 cups chopped clams and
    2 cups bottled clam juice

1 bay leaf

2 tablespoons chopped fresh thyme or 1 teaspoon
    dried thyme

1 large potato, peeled and diced

3 or 4 drops Tabasco sauce, or to taste (optional)

Kosher salt and freshly ground black pepper

In a large saucepan over medium heat, melt the butter. Add the salt pork and cook until the fat has rendered, 3 or 4 minutes. Add the onion and garlic and cook until soft, 4 or 5 minutes. Add the celery, carrot, and caraway, and cook until the vegetables are wilted, about 5 minutes. Add the tomatoes, clam cooking liquid or juice, and 1 cup of water, along with the bay leaf and thyme. Bring to a boil. Add the potato. Bring back to a boil, turn down the heat, set the cover ajar, and simmer for about 15 minutes, until the potato is tender. Add the clams and simmer for another 5 minutes. Add the Tabasco if using, discard the bay leaf, and adjust the seasoning with salt and pepper.

PREP TIME: 10 minutes
COOKING TIME: 35 minutes
TOTAL TIME: 45 minutes

ADVANCE PREP *Like New England Clam Chowder (page 47), this is best made a day in advance. Reheat over low heat just until simmering.*
LEFTOVERS *The soup will keep about a week in the fridge. Because of the potatoes, the soup does not freeze well.*

Fresh Corn Chowder

There's no point to making this soup if it isn't corn season. Sweet, local corn produces a wonderful corn chowder. I make mine so heavy with corn that it's more like a corn stew. For a thinner soup, add less corn and/or more milk, adjusting the seasoning as necessary.

Makes 8 cups, enough for 8 servings

2 tablespoons unsalted butter
2 double-smoked bacon strips, or an additional
    2 tablespoons unsalted butter
1 large white or yellow onion, chopped
1 large carrot, chopped
1 celery stalk, chopped
6 ears sweet corn, kernels removed from the cobs
    (about 5 cups; see page 50), cobs reserved
6 cups whole milk
1 bay leaf (optional)
2 medium Yukon Gold or other all-purpose
    potatoes, peeled and diced
¼ red bell pepper, finely chopped, or ½ small
    red chile, minced
Kosher salt and fresh ground black pepper
1 teaspoon fresh thyme leaves

In a large saucepan, melt the butter over medium-high heat. Add the bacon and fry until the bacon renders its fat but doesn't begin to brown, 3 or 4 minutes. Add the onion and sauté for 4 or 5 minutes, until soft. Add the carrot and celery and continue cooking for 4 or 5 minutes more. Add the corn cobs (break them in half if necessary) along with the milk and bay leaf, if using. Bring to a boil, reduce the heat so the milk simmers very gently, cover the pot, and cook for 30 minutes. Discard the cobs and the bay leaf. Add the potatoes, red pepper, 1 tablespoon salt, and a generous amount of pepper, and simmer for 15 minutes, or until the potatoes are almost fork-tender. Raise the heat. Add the corn kernels and the thyme; bring to a boil, reduce the heat, and simmer for 5 minutes.

TOTAL TIME: 1 hour 10 minutes

LEFTOVERS *The corn chowder will keep for about five days in the refrigerator. It does not freeze well.*

Chicken Soup

There are no secrets to chicken soup. You put a nice, old, flavorful hen or chicken and a lot of vegetables into a pot, cook it for a while, and you get a delicious cure for the common cold and whatever ails you. I strain my chicken soup and serve it with a garnish of cooked carrots and other vegetables, as well as noodles or rice. A lighter chicken soup is a chicken stock (see page 51). You can also add some of the cooled chicken meat back into the soup before serving.

Makes 4 quarts, enough for 10 servings

> 1 (4$\frac{1}{2}$-pound) stewing hen or chicken, cut into quarters and rinsed, or 5 pounds chicken bones (necks, backs, wings), rinsed
>
> 2 pounds yellow onions (about 4 large), roughly chopped
>
> Top half of a bunch of celery, with leaves
>
> 6 large carrots, peeled and cut into chunks
>
> 10 sprigs flat-leaf parsley
>
> 1 small turnip, peeled and cut into chunks
>
> 1 medium parsnip, peeled and cut into chunks
>
> 1 tablespoon black peppercorns
>
> 1 point of star anise
>
> 1 whole clove
>
> 2 tablespoons kosher salt
>
> 6 sprigs fresh dill, plus extra for garnish (optional)

In a 12-quart stockpot, place the hen or bones, onions, celery, carrots, parsley, turnip, parsnip, peppercorns, star anise, clove, and salt. Add 5 quarts cold water. Place over high heat, bring to a boil, and skim off any scum that floats to the top. Set the cover ajar, turn down the heat so that the water simmers, and cook about 2 hours, skimming as necessary. Add the dill, if using, and simmer for an additional 45 minutes or so. Turn off the heat and let cool.

Strain the soup into a clean pot or large container. Remove the cooked chicken meat and reserve (for this soup or for Chicken Salad, if you like; see page 78) and chill the soup overnight. Remove any fat that has congealed on top of the soup, and reheat to boiling before serving. Adjust the seasoning with additional salt and pepper, if necessary. Add a handful of chopped fresh dill, too, if you like.

PREP TIME: 15 minutes
COOKING TIME: 3 hours 15 minutes
TOTAL TIME: 3$\frac{1}{2}$ hours (plus chilling time)

ADVANCE PREP *The soup can be made several days in advance and refrigerated. Be sure to bring back to a boil before serving.*

LEFTOVERS *The soup will last for about ten days in the fridge and up to six months in the freezer. Freeze in small, 2- or 3-cup containers so you can defrost only what you need. Leftover chicken soup can be used like chicken stock (see below) as a base for other soups or in gravies, sauces, or other dishes.*

Poultry or Meat Stock

The ready availability of commercially prepared stocks made with all-natural ingredients and little or no sodium has revolutionized home cooking to some extent. At the Whole Foods store on the corner of my street I can choose from many varieties of stock produced by various brands. Although I have found my favorites through trial and error, none compares with homemade stock. What's more, making stock at home allows you to use up so many of the odds and ends you've got lying around the kitchen—bones, meat scraps, herb stems, vegetable tops; just about everything has a place in some stock or another.

There was a time when important distinctions were made between stocks, broths, and other technical culinary terms. In professional kitchens many of these still hold sway, but at home, I think a flavorful stock or broth, call it what you will, is the most versatile thing you can have. You can make as much or as little stock as you want. I periodically make large pots of different types of stock and keep them in my freezer in 1- or 2-cup portions so I don't have to defrost a large amount when I only need a little. As far as I'm concerned, once frozen, stock keeps nearly indefinitely.

COOK-INS FOR SOUPS

Chicken soup and other clear broth types of soup lend themselves to garnishes that cook quickly in the broth itself. Small pastas, delicate grains, and chopped vegetables and herbs are among the categories of garnishes to consider.

• **Pasta:** Pastina or stelle (little stars) are the most common choices for pastas that cook in the soup in which they are served. Very fine egg noodles can be cooked in broth, as can both Moroccan- and Israeli-style couscous.

• **Grains:** Quick-cooking grains, such as bulgur, can be added as a garnish to broths because they don't throw off much starch. I also like to add other grains such as rice and barley. To expedite cooking, rinse the grains thoroughly and soak them in water before cooking them in the soup.

• **Vegetables:** For soups, such as chicken soup, which require long, slow cooking, I rarely serve the vegetables that were cooked in the soup. Although I happen to like carrots, celery, and onions that have been cooked to death, I don't think they are appropriate to serve to guests. Instead I cut vegetables into small dice and pretty shapes and cook them in the strained soup before serving. Among my favorite vegetable garnishes are parsnip, turnip, celery root, and carrot. Although usually these all take a long time to cook, if you cut them small enough, they are ready in minutes.

You are not supposed to add any salt to stock because you are presumably going to use it in another dish that will then be seasoned, but I add a little because I think it's better that way and everything you cook is going to need some salt, anyway. Some people say you should be very restrained with the aromatic vegetables you use in a stock, but I say if you have another carrot, put it in. The principle behind using stocks in the kitchen is a simple one: Why add anything flavorless to a dish, such as water, when you could add something with flavor, such as stock? Take that sentiment to heart and your cooking will improve immediately.

Makes about 3 quarts

> 4 to 5 pounds bones, such as chicken, turkey, veal, pork, ham, lamb, or duck, raw or cooked
> 2 large yellow or white onions, cut into chunks
> 3 large carrots, peeled and cut into chunks
> 3 celery stalks, peeled and cut into chunks
> 1 leek, white and green parts, cleaned well and cut into chunks (optional)
> 1 bay leaf
> 1 teaspoon black peppercorns
> 1 whole clove
> Handful of flat-leaf parsley sprigs or stems
> 1 teaspoon kosher salt

Place the bones in a large, 10-quart stockpot. Add the onions, carrots, celery, leek if using, bay leaf, peppercorns, clove, parsley, and salt. Add enough cold water to cover the ingredients, about 4 quarts. Set the pot over high heat and bring to a boil. Skim off any froth and/or scum that rises to the surface. Reduce the heat, cover loosely, and simmer the stock for about 3 hours. Strain, discarding the solids. Cool, and if you have the time, chill. Any fat in the stock will coagulate on the top; skim it off and reserve for another purpose (such as roasting potatoes).

Portion the stock and refrigerate or freeze as desired.

PREP TIME: 15 minutes
COOKING TIME: 3 hours 15 minutes
TOTAL TIME: 3½ hours (plus chilling time)

ADVANCE PREP *Stock can be made far in advance. It keeps in the fridge for about two weeks and in the freezer for months—possibly even years.*

VARIATIONS

Darker, Richer Stock

By roasting the raw bones and vegetables before making a stock, you produce a broth with a deeper color and richer taste. (The carcasses from roasted chicken, turkey, and duck produce a stock somewhere between the two.) Preheat the oven to 500°F. Place the bones in a roasting pan and set in the oven for about 1 hour, or until very nicely browned. Add the vegetables and continue roasting for another 30 minutes or so, until they have browned, too. Place the roasted ingredients in a pot and add the remaining ingredients. Cover with cold water and proceed with the recipe as directed.

Chinese Stock

Use a combination of pork, chicken, and turkey bones. Add 1 head garlic split in half, 4 ounces of sliced fresh ginger, 1 bunch of scallions, chopped, and 1 whole star anise. This stock is an excellent base for Asian soups and other dishes.

Fish Stock

Use the heads and bones of fresh, white-fleshed fish such as snapper, sea bass, grouper—what have you. Avoid the bones of oily fish, such as salmon. Remove and discard the gills. Follow the recipe for stock, substituting 4 to 5 pounds fish heads and bones for the bones and omitting the clove. Add 1 cup dry white wine and enough water to cover the ingredients. Simmer the stock for only 1½ hours.

Lobster or Shrimp Stock

Lobster and shrimp shells produce a rich, flavorful stock, but because the flavor components of the shells are largely fat-soluble, you have to cook the shells in butter to extract their essence before you proceed with making the stock. Use the shells from 3 or 4 lobsters, 2 to 3 pounds of shrimp, or a combination. Melt 8 tablespoons (1 stick) unsalted butter over medium heat in the bottom of the stock pot. Add the shells and cook, mashing with a potato masher or metal spoon, for about 10 minutes, until the aroma of the seafood is strong. Add the remaining ingredients for the stock (omitting the bones) and proceed with the recipe as directed, simmering the stock for only 1½ hours.

Vegetable Stock

Vegetable stock is a little tricky because however hard you try, it just never has the richness of a meat stock. I do three things to help. First, I save the cooking water when I make vegetables like broccoli or Brussels sprouts for other purposes and I use that cooking water instead of some of the water for the liquid in my vegetable stock (watch the salt). Second, I use a ton of vegetables in the stock, including the stems of leafy greens, asparagus ends, broccoli stems, and plenty of carrots and celery. And third, I cut an unpeeled onion in half and cook it, cut side down, in a dry cast-iron pan over high heat until the onion is black. I add the burnt onion, peel and all, to my vegetable stockpot. I know it sounds weird, but the onion adds a browned taste and richness that I think gives the stock some body.

To make about 4½ quarts of vegetable stock, slice an unpeeled onion in half and place it cut side down in a dry skillet over medium-high heat. Let the onion sizzle and burn to black while you prepare the rest of the stock. Into a large stock pot place 2 medium onions, roughly chopped; 6 carrots, chopped; 4 stalks celery, with leaves, chopped; 1 leek, roughly chopped; 1 small parsnip or turnip, chopped; and 4 to 6 cups of other green vegetables, stems, or leaves, such as broccoli, kale, lettuce, asparagus, or spinach. Add the burnt, unpeeled onion. Cover the vegetables with 5 to 6 quarts cold water and bring to a boil. Add 1 teaspoon black peppercorns, 1 point of a star anise, and 1 whole clove. Bring to a boil, reduce the heat, and simmer for 1½ hours. Strain and chill.

■ ■ ■

Salads

ALTHOUGH AMERICANS AREN'T EXACTLY known for the creativity or healthfulness of their diet, when it comes to salad making I think we can hold our own. Large bowls of salad greens with various fixings and creative dressings are commonplace on the American table. I miss American-style salads when I travel. I have a big salad of leafy greens and other vegetables with just about every meal. I often even make a little tomato or avocado salad at breakfast to eat with my eggs. At dinner, I make myself a big salad in a giant serving bowl—probably large enough to serve six people—and I eat it right out of the bowl, sometimes with my fingers. I can't get enough, especially if there's a really good dressing on it.

Of course, the world of salads is vast and varied. Lettuce is the base for just one type of salad. Grains, potatoes, meat, and even bread can all be turned into delicious salads. Almost all salads contain vegetables, which are usually raw, and they are served chilled or at room temperature, for the most part—although wilted salads made with hot dressings are also a favorite of mine. Salads also always have a certain acidity, whether it be from vinegar, citrus juice, or other tart ingredients in their dressings, which can be thick or thin, creamy or not. But these salad similarities are only minor, and actually serve to illustrate just how vast the possibilities for different salads are.

At what part of the meal you eat a salad is ripe for cultural analysis. Americans, English, and Italians generally eat their salads—we're talking lettuce, here—before the main course, a case for which can be made because the acidity in the dressing helps to stimulate the appetite. The French eat their salads after their main course, when the same acidity helps cleanse the palate. (Of course they might just do that because the English don't.) Sommeliers and wine aficionados generally prefer to have people eat salad before the meal because the vinegar in any leftover salad at the end of the meal kills the taste of any wine leftover from the main course. Many Vietnamese and Thai main courses are really salads, combining raw and cooked elements with tangy dressings. In Greece, Turkey, and Middle Eastern countries a typical meal comprises a huge assortment of salads eaten with plenty of fresh bread;

this is one of my favorite ways to eat. Meanwhile, a lot of Americans prefer to eat their salads as a side dish to their main meal, perhaps a holdover from the TV-dinner era, when all of our food was supposed to come at the same time.

Regardless of when you eat it, I think salad should be part of every good, properly balanced meal. There are plenty of recipes in this chapter to choose from, but don't feel limited by my indications. If you have different ingredients or your own ideas, use these recipes as a starting point for creating your own salads.

■ ■ ■

Simple Green Salad

During college I spent a year in Paris. I lived with a French family not far from the Arc de Triomphe. Every night after our main course, Madame would mix a quick Dijon mustard vinaigrette in the bottom of a salad bowl. She'd toss delicate leaves of Bibb lettuce in the dressing and serve everyone a pile of what was for me at the time one of the simplest and most satisfying salads I had ever eaten. A few years later, when I was working in a restaurant in Italy, every "family meal" with the staff included a similarly simple salad of mixed greens and herbs dressed only with a drizzle of olive oil, a squirt of wine vinegar, and a handful of salt. This was another salad revelation. Although I love large, American-style salads piled high with cheese, bacon, grilled chicken, and thick dressings, the understated elegance of a simple green salad remains for me the pinnacle of the salad maker's art.

SALAD À LA FRANÇAISE

Here's a recipe for a simple green salad prepared in the French manner.
Makes 4 servings

1 tablespoon Dijon mustard
1 small shallot, minced
3 tablespoons white wine vinegar
½ cup extra-virgin olive oil
Kosher salt and freshly ground black pepper
2 small heads Boston or Bibb lettuce or 1 large
    head red or green leaf lettuce, dark outer
    leaves discarded, tender inner leaves separated

In the bottom of a large salad bowl, combine the mustard, shallot, and vinegar with 1 tablespoon cold water. Beat with a fork to blend. Continue beating while you dribble in the olive oil in droplets. Be sure to incorporate the olive oil from each addition before you add more; you are creating a temporary emulsion. As you continue to beat in the olive oil, the dressing will thicken. When all of the oil has been incorporated, add a pinch of salt and some freshly ground pepper. Add the lettuce and gently toss with salad servers or tongs to coat the leaves with the dressing without bruising them.

TOTAL TIME: 10 minutes

SALAD ALL'ITALIANA

This is an Italian version of a simple green salad.
Makes 4 servings

8 ounces mesclun or mixed greens, such as
    arugula, mizuna, tatsoi, frisée, radicchio,
    or other lettuces
¼ cup loosely packed assorted fresh herbs,
    leaves only, such as flat-leaf parsley, thyme,
    marjoram, chervil, chives, or tarragon
⅓ cup extra-virgin olive oil
3 tablespoons white or red wine vinegar
Kosher salt and freshly ground black pepper

In a large salad bowl, toss the mixed greens with the herbs to distribute. Drizzle with the olive oil and vinegar. Season generously with salt and pepper. Toss and serve.

TOTAL TIME: 5 minutes

ADVANCE PREP *You can prepare the lettuces several hours before serving. Cover with damp paper towels and refrigerate. The dressings can be mixed and kept at room temperature. Do not toss the lettuce in the dressing until just before serving—the salt and vinegar will wilt the leaves.*
LEFTOVERS *Dressed salad does not keep.*

VINAIGRETTE

Perhaps the easiest, most versatile salad dressing—besides a splash of oil and vinegar—is a simple French vinaigrette made from Dijon mustard, red or white wine vinegar, and olive oil. You can use it to dress green salads, vegetable salads, potato salads, even meat salads. It is the base of other, more complicated dressings, such as Gorgonzola dressing. By changing the ingredients slightly—using a tarragon-infused vinegar or lemon juice or a grainy mustard, or adding any number of other ingredients, such as shallots, herbs, anchovies, and capers, for example—you can create a totally different dressing.

When made properly, a vinaigrette should be creamy. That's because you've created a temporary emulsion by suspending tiny oil and vinegar droplets beside each other in the medium of the mustard. As the name implies, the creaminess won't last. (Mayonnaise, by contrast, is a permanent emulsion because egg yolk is a more effective emulsifier than mustard.) To achieve this texture, you must add the oil to the other ingredients very slowly and beat vigorously during and after each addition. For more about the emulsification process, see page 395.

Besides the texture, the most important detail is the ratio of oil to vinegar. I'm a sour person—it's not that I'm unhappy, it's just that I like to eat acidic things. To my taste, a good vinaigrette should be pretty tart. But vinegars can have a wide range of acidity, and you can adjust the proportions to suit your own tastes. See page 393 for some suggestions for vinaigrette variations.

Avocado Salad

There is no other fruit or vegetable quite like a ripe avocado. The texture is somewhere between melon and custard. The flavor is subtle but distinct. I love it. (Unripe avocadoes, however, are like raw potatoes. I hate them.) To make a good avocado salad, it is important that you have good, ripe avocados. I prefer Hass avocados, the small ones with dark green mottled skin from California, to the larger, paler-green avocados with smooth skin from Florida. Be sure to allow some time for your avocados to ripen. Depending on how hard they are when you buy them, they can take up to one week to become ready. A ripe avocado has a soft but dense texture when you squeeze it gently. Because avocados discolor quickly once they are cut, this salad must be made just before it is served. It does not keep.

This salad has a mayonnaise-like dressing emulsified with avocado and raw egg yolk (see page 125). Because the texture of the flesh of a ripe avocado is so delicate, I don't toss avocados with dressing—which would mash them. Instead, I simply slice them and drizzle the slices with the dressing. For a more substantial salad, add chilled lump crab meat or cooked shrimp (see page 279).

Makes 4 servings

2 ripe Hass avocados
1 large egg yolk
1 small garlic clove
2 tablespoons chopped fresh herbs, such as cilantro, tarragon, chervil, or flat-leaf parsley, or a combination
2 teaspoons drained capers, rinsed
Juice of 1 lime (3 tablespoons)
Kosher salt and freshly ground black pepper
1/2 cup extra-virgin olive oil
4 leaves green leaf or Bibb lettuce
1/2 cup cherry tomatoes, cut in half
2 scallions, white and green parts, chopped

6 ounces chilled lump crab meat or cooked
    shrimp (see page 279; optional)
½ lime, cut into 4 wedges

Split the avocados in half lengthwise around the pits. Remove and discard the pits, and carefully remove the skin, peeling it back off the flesh while keeping the halves intact. Place the avocado halves cut side down on a cutting board. Slice each half crosswise into ¼-inch-thick slices. In a blender or food processor, place the egg yolk, garlic, herbs, capers, lime juice, and one piece of each avocado half (taken from the top or bottom so it isn't obviously missing). Pulse this mixture, scraping down the sides, until puréed. Add a generous pinch of salt and some freshly ground black pepper. With the machine running, slowly drizzle in the olive oil to create a thick emulsion. Adjust the seasoning with additional salt and pepper.

On each of four chilled serving plates, place a leaf of lettuce. Using a spatula, carefully lift the avocados off the cutting board and place them on the lettuce, fanning out the slices in an attractive pattern. Arrange the cherry tomato halves, scallions, and crab if using around the avocado in an attractive way. Spoon the dressing over each avocado and around the plate. Serve with a wedge of lime.

TOTAL TIME: 20 minutes

Tomato Salad with Browned Butter and Caper Dressing

The flavors of browned butter and tomatoes go surprisingly well. The acidity of the tomato helps cut through the richness of the butter. Only make this salad in tomato season, when ripe beefsteak tomatoes are available. Slice them thick and serve them with plenty of salt—I prefer the large, crunchy flakes of Maldon salt on my tomatoes, but any good-quality salt is just fine.

Makes 4 servings

2 ripe beefsteak tomatoes (2 pounds), sliced
    crosswise ¾ inch thick, at room temperature
½ cup (1 stick) unsalted butter
1 tablespoon drained capers, rinsed
Maldon salt, fleur de sel, or other good-quality
    salt
Freshly ground black pepper
Chopped flat-leaf parsley

Arrange 2 or 3 thick slices of tomato on each of four serving plates. In a medium skillet, melt the butter over medium-high heat. As soon as the foaming subsides, about 4 minutes, add the capers. Swirl the pan and watch it closely for any indication that the milk solids are beginning to brown. You will know it when you can smell a nutty, toasted aroma. As soon as the butter starts to brown, remove it from the heat and pour it over the tomatoes, being sure the capers are evenly divided among the plates. Sprinkle the tomatoes with salt, pepper, and parsley and serve immediately.

PREP TIME: 3 minutes
COOKING TIME: 7 minutes
TOTAL TIME: 10 minutes

LEFTOVERS Because the tomatoes wilt when they come into contact with the hot butter and the salt, this salad doesn't keep. Leftovers can be chopped up and used in sauces and soups.

CLEANING AND STORING LEAFY GREENS
I'm an impulsive cook so I like to have ingredients on hand and ready to use. This means that when I buy lettuces and other leafy greens, I clean them before I put them away in the refrigerator. To clean them, separate the leaves, discarding any that seem dark and tough or bruised. Soak the leaves in a generous amount of cold water. (I keep a plastic basin under the sink expressly for this purpose.) Gently swish the leaves around in your best impersonation of a washing machine's agitator (on the gentle cycle, of course). Lift the leaves out of the water, leaving any sand and dirt behind. (If instead of lifting them out of the water you dump them into a colander with the water, you will deposit the dirt back onto the leaves.) If your greens are particularly dirty or sandy, repeat this procedure. The most difficult green to clean is spinach, which usually requires three soakings.

If you have a salad spinner, spin the leaves dry. Transfer them to resealable plastic bags. Take two sheets of paper towel and wet them with cold water. Wring out any excess water and unfurl the damp sheets. Place the paper towels in the bag with the greens. This will keep their environment cold and damp. Keep the greens in the refrigerator. They will keep for three to five days, depending on the type of greens and their state of freshness when you purchased them.

If you don't have a spinner, lay out several contiguous sheets of paper towel. Lay the leaves on the paper towel and gently roll them up in the towel like a sleeping bag. Place the roll of leaves in a resealable plastic bag and refrigerate.

Roasted Seckel Pear and Roquefort Salad with Walnuts

Pear and Roquefort is a classic French combination. For this autumnal salad, I roast small Seckel pears with shallot and walnuts, stuff them with the cheese, and serve them on a bed of frisée dressed with vinaigrette. It's a simple but impressive combination of flavors and ingredients.

Makes 4 servings

3 tablespoons unsalted butter

1 medium shallot, thinly sliced

4 ripe Seckel pears, split in half lengthwise and cored

Kosher salt and freshly ground black pepper

¼ cup walnut pieces

4 ounces Roquefort, Gorgonzola, or other blue cheese, at room temperature

1 tablespoon sour cream or heavy cream (optional)

⅓ cup vinaigrette (see page 391)

1 head frisée, dark outer leaves removed

Chopped flat-leaf parsley

Preheat the oven to 400°F. Place the butter and shallot in a small baking dish. Arrange the pear halves in the pan, cut side up. Season with salt and pepper. Place the pan in the oven and roast, basting frequently, for 20 minutes. Add the nuts to the pan, turn down the heat to 350°F, and continue roasting and basting for 10 minutes more, or until the pears are tender when pricked with the point of a knife and browned around the edges. Remove from the oven and cool to room temperature.

Place the Roquefort in a small bowl and with the back of a spoon, work it into a paste. If the cheese is too crumbly, add a drop of sour cream. Spoon a dollop of the Roquefort onto the center of each pear half and set aside. Place the vinaigrette in a large bowl and scrape the pan juices from the roasted pears, including the shallots and nuts, into the bowl. Mix the dressing. Add the frisée and toss to coat with the dressing. Divide the salad among four serving plates, being sure each plate gets an equal number of nuts. Arrange the pears on each plate and sprinkle with chopped parsley.

PREP TIME: 10 minutes
COOKING TIME: 30 minutes
TOTAL TIME: 1 hour (includes cooling time)

ADVANCE PREP *The pears can be roasted in the morning and kept at room temperature until dinner. Stuff them and dress the salad just before serving.*
LEFTOVERS *The roasted pears will keep refrigerated for two or three days, but once dressed, the salad will not last.*

Carrot and Caraway Salad

This salad was inspired by a dish I enjoy at a local Middle Eastern restaurant. It's simple, but the flavors add up to more than the sum of their parts: you add the dressing to the hot carrots so they absorb it while they cool.

Makes 6 servings

1 1/2 pounds carrots, peeled and sliced about
   1/4 inch thick
1 teaspoon caraway or cumin seeds
1/2 cup extra-virgin olive oil
Juice of 2 lemons (about 1/2 cup)
2 garlic cloves, crushed
Kosher salt and freshly ground pepper

Bring a medium pot of salted water to a boil. Add the carrots and cook for 4 to 5 minutes,

THE JOY AND PAIN OF MESCLUN
Only ten years ago, nobody had ever heard of mesclun, the French word for a colorful mixture of (traditionally wild) baby greens and lettuces. (For some reason the Italian equivalent, *misticanza*, never caught on.) Nowadays, practically every supermarket sells the stuff. Because mesclun is sold cleaned and ready to eat and because it provides a simple way to jazz up the salad bowl, I think the popularity of mesclun is a good thing. But the mesclun marketplace is not without its problems. For starters, some stores pass off ordinary lettuces torn into small bit as mesclun. Others stretch a perfectly fine selection of baby greens with ordinary lettuces. This is fraud. But an even bigger problem is that mesclun contains a variety of leaves that do not all age at the same rate. This means that sometimes a perfectly good mesclun will be ruined by brown, slimy bits of some rotten leaf or another.

I store mesclun like other greens in resealable plastic bags with a piece or two of damp paper towel in the bag. Unless you can be absolutely sure of its freshness, you should plan on keeping mesclun for only two or three days. One conscientious purveyor in my neighborhood sells all of the different components of mesclun separately, so you can assemble the mix yourself and be sure nothing is past its prime.

If your mesclun begins to brown or wilt, don't toss it out just yet. By sautéing limp mesclun in a little olive oil with some garlic, you can make a delicious side dish for meat or fish.

until tender but not soft. Drain but do not rinse. Place in a medium bowl. Meanwhile, heat a dry pan over medium heat and add the caraway seeds. Swirl the pan for about 3 minutes to evenly toast the seeds. Add the toasted seeds to the hot carrots along with the olive oil, lemon juice, garlic, and salt and pepper to taste. Toss and let cool to room temperature, about 1 hour. Adjust the seasoning and serve at room temperature or chilled.

PREP TIME: 7 minutes
COOKING TIME: 5 minutes
TOTAL TIME: 12 to 15 minutes (plus chilling time)

ADVANCE PREP *The salad can be made two or three days in advance and refrigerated.*
LEFTOVERS *The salad will keep for about a week in the fridge. You can use leftovers in other salads, or even as a garnish for soups.*

Celery Root Rémoulade

A sort of French coleslaw, this celery root salad is a favorite of mine on summer picnics and with light lunches. It's also nice in winter, when celery roots are available and you begin to get sick of other winter vegetables. I usually make my rémoulade with a light vinaigrette dressing, but sometimes I'm in the mood for a creamier salad, enriched with mayonnaise, for which I've given directions in the Variation, below.
Makes 8 servings

1 large (1-pound) celery root
1/4 cup Dijon mustard
1 small shallot, minced
2 tablespoons white wine vinegar
Juice of 1/2 lemon (about 2 tablespoons)

1/2 cup extra-virgin olive oil
Kosher salt and freshly ground black pepper
2 tablespoons assorted chopped herbs, such as
    marjoram, chives, tarragon, or flat-leaf parsley

With a sharp paring knife or vegetable peeler, peel the celery root, cutting off any deep crevices you can't peel. Remove any dark patches on the root, too. I prefer to julienne the celery root by slicing it into paper-thin slices and then cutting the slices into matchsticks. The julienne must be long and fine or the celery root will be tough. If you find julienne too much of a hassle, you can simply shred the celery root on a box grater or in a food processor.

Place the mustard in a large mixing bowl. Whisk in the shallot, 3 tablespoons water, the vinegar, and lemon juice. While mixing, slowly dribble in the olive oil to make a creamy emulsion. Beat in a pinch of salt and some freshly ground pepper. Add the celery root and toss to coat with the dressing. Before serving, stir in the fresh herbs.

TOTAL TIME: 15 minutes if you shred, 30 minutes if you julienne

ADVANCE PREP *The salad is best if it is made in advance and allowed to sit overnight in the refrigerator. Don't stir in the chopped herbs until just before you serve it.*
LEFTOVERS *The celery root will keep for about a week in the refrigerator.*

VARIATION
Creamy Celery Root Rémoulade
Stir 1/2 cup mayonnaise (page 405) into the vinaigrette before adding the celery root. Adjust the seasoning with salt and pepper.

Strained Yogurt

Strained yogurt, which is sometimes called yogurt "cheese," is another staple in my kitchen. I hold it in almost as high regard as cream cheese for its versatility. In some ways it's even better because it manages to be thick and rich and delicious without being high in fat.

For best results, choose a tangy, plain, low-fat organic yogurt without any gums, pectins, or other additives. Even better still, use your own homemade yogurt (see page 133). Of course, you can use full-fat yogurt if you like, but the rich texture of the strained yogurt makes low-fat yogurt cheese perfectly satisfying. It's delicious as is on a toasted bagel. If you like, season it with salt to taste. Someone actually gave me a yogurt strainer once—like a muslin jelly bag suspended on a wire ring—but cheesecloth works perfectly well.

Makes 1 1/2 cups

1 quart yogurt, low-fat, reduced-fat, or full-fat

1/2 teaspoon kosher salt, or to taste (optional)

Line a fine sieve with two layers of cheesecloth and set over a bowl or other container. Dump the yogurt into the sieve. Allow the yogurt to sit on the counter and drain for 2 to 6 hours, depending on how thick you want it to be. (For spreading, you want it really thick; for a sauce it can be thinner.) You can also place the strainer in the refrigerator overnight. Discard the liquid that gathers in the bowl. If you want to use the strained yogurt as a spread like cream cheese, blend in the salt. Otherwise, leave it plain. Store in an airtight container in the refrigerator for up to two weeks. Discard any liquid that forms while it sits.

PREP TIME: 5 minutes

TOTAL TIME: 2 to 6 hours (includes draining time)

Creamy Cucumber Salad

Mayonnaise makes this cucumber salad creamy. And using a wide variety of fresh herbs makes it delicious.

Makes 4 to 6 servings

2 pounds (3 or 4 large) meaty, firm cucumbers

1/2 cup Hellmann's or Best Foods mayonnaise

3 tablespoons distilled white vinegar

3/4 teaspoon kosher salt

1/4 teaspoon freshly ground black pepper

1/4 cup assorted minced herbs, such as basil, tarragon, sage, pineapple sage, oregano, marjoram, chervil, thyme, lemon thyme, lemon balm, dill, and/or flat-leaf parsley

Peel the cucumbers and cut them in half lengthwise. Using a small spoon, scoop out the soft center that has the seeds and discard. (I even scoop out seedless cucumbers for this salad; otherwise the dressing gets too runny.) Cut the scooped-out halves in half lengthwise again. Cut each of these long, curved quarters crosswise into slices about 1/4 inch thick. You should have 4 to 5 cups of cucumber slices. Place them in a medium bowl.

In a small bowl, combine the mayonnaise with the vinegar, salt, pepper, and herbs. Mix until smooth. Toss the cucumbers with the dressing and chill until ready to serve.

TOTAL TIME: 15 minutes (plus chilling time)

ADVANCE PREP *The salad is best if made in advance and allowed to sit overnight in the refrigerator. The salt in the dressing wilts the cucumbers slightly to give them a pleasant texture.*

LEFTOVERS *The salad will keep four or five days in the fridge, but the texture of the cucumbers is best during the first day or two.*

VARIATIONS

Herbed Coleslaw

Substitute 12 ounces finely sliced or shredded green cabbage (about 4 cups) for the cucumbers. Toss the cabbage with 1 tablespoon kosher salt and let sit for about 1 hour, covered, at room temperature to wilt. Rinse in cold water, drain well, and toss with the dressing as directed above.

Creamy Carrot Slaw

Substitute $1\frac{1}{2}$ pounds carrots, peeled and shredded (about $3\frac{1}{2}$ cups), for the cucumbers and proceed as directed.

Cucumber and Yogurt Salad

This cucumber salad has the flavors of Greek tzatziki, but because the cucumbers are sliced instead of shredded, it's more of a side dish than a spread. Salting the cucumbers in advance draws out extra moisture, which improves the texture and flavor of the finished salad.

Makes 4 to 6 servings

> 2 English cucumbers (about 2 pounds), peeled and thinly sliced
> Kosher salt

1 cup Greek-style or strained yogurt (see page 63)
1 shallot, minced
1 medium garlic clove, minced
2 heaping tablespoons chopped fresh dill
$\frac{1}{4}$ teaspoon freshly ground white pepper

Place the cucumbers in a large bowl. Toss with 1 tablespoon salt. Invert a small plate over the cucumbers to weight them down and let sit for about 1 hour at room temperature. Rinse the cucumbers quickly under cold water and drain well. Add the yogurt, shallot, garlic, dill, and pepper and stir to blend. Adjust the seasoning with more salt if necessary.

PREP TIME: 10 minutes
TOTAL TIME: 1 hour 10 minutes (includes salting time)

ADVANCE PREP *The salad can be mixed several days in advance and refrigerated until ready to serve. Stir any liquid that forms back into the salad before serving.*

LEFTOVERS *The salad will keep for about a week. Use leftovers as a garnish for pita-pocket sandwiches.*

Red Cabbage Slaw with Toasted Hazelnuts and Buttermilk Orange Dressing

I like the taste of orange in savory foods, and the dressing for this slaw, which uses buttermilk instead of mayonnaise, provides a delicate platform for the flavor of orange to come through. It's a good salad for brunches, picnics, or barbecues. You can substitute mayonnaise or plain yogurt for the buttermilk.

Makes 8 to 10 servings

SHREDDING CABBAGE

I like the cabbage in coleslaw, braised cabbage, and other cabbage dishes to have some texture to it, and I find most graters—such as box graters or food processor disks—shred it too fine. Instead, I prefer to slice the cabbage on a mandoline or by hand. To use the mandoline, cut the cabbage into quarters through the core, but do not remove the core. Instead, use the core to hold the cabbage while you work the leaves back and forth over the cutting blade. When you get close to the core, discard it. To cut the cabbage by hand, It also helps to keep the core intact because it holds the leaves together. With a sharp knife, thinly slice the cabbage crosswise on both sides of the core.

1 small head (1½ to 2 pounds) red cabbage, shredded (about 6 cups)

Kosher salt

1 cup buttermilk, plain yogurt, mayonnaise, or a combination

Grated zest and juice of 1 orange (about ½ cup) or 2 tablespoons orange juice concentrate, thawed

2 tablespoons peanut or vegetable oil

1 to 2 teaspoons honey or sugar

3 medium carrots, peeled and shredded (1¼ cups)

1 shallot, minced, or 2 scallions, chopped

1 tablespoon chopped fresh tarragon

1 tablespoon chopped fresh flat-leaf parsley

Freshly ground black pepper

2 tablespoons hazelnuts, toasted (see page 10)

Place the cabbage in a large bowl and toss with 2 tablespoons salt. Cover with a small inverted plate to weight it down and let sit at room temperature for at least 1 hour and up to 3 hours to wilt. Rinse quickly in cold water and drain well.

In a small bowl, beat together the buttermilk, orange zest and juice, oil, and honey. Pour this dressing over the cabbage. Add the carrots, shallot, tarragon, parsley, and some black pepper, and toss. Adjust the seasoning with additional salt and pepper. Stir in the toasted hazelnuts just before serving.

PREP TIME: 20 minutes
TOTAL TIME: 1½ to 3½ hours

ADVANCE PREP *The salad is best after it has sat overnight in the fridge. Don't add the toasted hazelnuts until just before you go to serve it, though, or they will become soggy.*

LEFTOVERS *The salad will keep for about one week in the refrigerator.*

Jícama Slaw with Yogurt and Lime

I think the flavor, sweetness, juiciness, and crunch of jícama fall somewhere between green apple and cucumber. It's also slightly astringent. All of these qualities are balanced in this salad by the tart creaminess of the dressing.

Makes 6 servings

⅔ cup plain yogurt

1 large lime, sectioned (see page 70)

1 small garlic clove, minced

1 small shallot or ¼ red onion, very thinly sliced

¼ cup loosely packed cilantro leaves

Kosher salt and freshly ground black pepper

1 medium jícama (about 1¼ pounds), peeled, sliced, and cut into matchsticks

In a medium bowl, combine the yogurt, lime sections and their juice, garlic, shallot, cilantro, ½ teaspoon salt, and freshly ground black pepper to taste. Add the jícama and toss to coat with the dressing.

TOTAL TIME: 15 minutes

ADVANCE PREP *The salad can be made several hours in advance and refrigerated until serving.*
LEFTOVERS *The salad will keep up to one week in the refrigerator.*

Asian Bean Sprout Salad

This quick salad flavored with soy sauce goes well with most Asian meals, whether Chinese, Korean, Vietnamese, or Thai. One of my favorite things about the salad is that it doesn't require a stove burner to prepare it, which can be a godsend if you are cooking with a large wok. The fresh taste and crisp texture of the raw bean sprouts are always a welcome foil to other heavier-bodied Asian dishes.

Makes 4 servings

2 tablespoons vinegar, such as rice, red, or white wine
2 tablespoons toasted Asian sesame oil
2 tablespoons soy sauce
1 garlic clove, minced
¼ teaspoon kosher salt
3 or 4 grinds of black pepper
2 to 3 scallions, white and green parts, chopped

2 to 3 cups mung bean sprouts, picked over to remove any wilted beans
1 tablespoon sesame seeds, toasted (page 10)

In a large bowl, combine the vinegar, sesame oil, soy sauce, garlic, salt, and pepper. Mix with a fork to blend. Add the scallions and bean sprouts and toss gently with the dressing to coat. Avoid breaking the sprouts as you toss. Sprinkle with sesame seeds.

TOTAL TIME: 20 minutes

ADVANCE PREP *The salad should be made no more than a half hour before you intend to serve it.*

Chopped Middle Eastern Salad

I'm calling this chopped cucumber and tomato salad generically Middle Eastern Salad because it's been served to me under as many names as there are countries in the Middle East. While it is best made in the height of tomato season, I make it year-round with plum tomatoes that I've let ripen for a few days in a brown paper bag.

Makes 4 to 6 servings

2 ripe beefsteak tomatoes or 4 ripe plum tomatoes (about 1 pound), seeded and cut into ¼-inch dice
1 medium cucumber (about ½ pound), peeled, seeded, and cut into ¼-inch dice
½ small white or red onion, chopped
2 small radishes, chopped (optional)
Juice of 1 lemon (¼ cup)
¼ cup extra-virgin olive oil
1 tablespoon chopped flat-leaf parsley
Kosher salt and freshly ground black pepper

WHAT YOU SHOULD KNOW ABOUT OLIVE OIL

Despite the popularity of olive oil in this country, I think the liquid gold of the Mediterranean is misunderstood. For starters, extra-virgin olive is the only oil you should cook with, whether you are frying eggplant or tossing a salad. Somewhere along the way toward Mediterranean fettishism Americans started to believe that they shouldn't cook with extra-virgin olive oil, and instead ought to use what is sold as pure olive oil or olive pomace oil for frying because of its higher "smoke point" (the temperature at which it burns). This is nonsense. Pure olive oil is mostly used for industrial purposes in Italy, and it is actually illegal to sell pomace oil (made from olive pits)—they ship it all to the United States.

That's not to say I don't make a distinction among olive oils in my kitchen. I have at least two different ones on the go at all times: I use a relatively inexpensive, commercial, imported extra-virgin olive oil for frying or for any dish in which the flavor and textural qualities of the oil are not important. Many chains such as Whole Foods and Trader Joe's now bottle their own oils, and these are fine for most purposes. For salad dressings, pasta sauces, to drizzle raw on soups or fish, or to garnish other dishes, I keep an expensive, imported extra-virgin olive oil on hand. In fact, I usually have several, with different flavor profiles, that I pair to different dishes. The rich, spicy oils of Tuscany, for instance, can stand up to strong flavors, while the soft, sweet, grassy oils of Sardegna (Sardinia) are perfect for more subtle flavors.

You will see extra-virgin olive oils marketed as "cold pressed." While true, the fact is that by (legal) definition, an extra-virgin designation *means* the oil was cold pressed, so there are in fact no other types of extra-virgin olive oil on the market. The "extra-virgin" designation also refers to the percentage of free oleic acid in the oil, the result of poor handling, which by law must be less than 1 and which is usually much less than that in better oils. Oleic acid is a fatty acid, a component of fat, not a taste. You will hear pretentious olive oil aficionados relate this percentage to an acidic taste in the oil, but in fact you cannot perceive the free oleic acid profile of an oil on your tongue. It can be determined only through chemical analysis. Off tastes in oils are usually the result of rancidity.

The best olive oils are quite perishable. In fact, their health-promoting qualities are due to volatile phytochemicals whose effectiveness diminishes over time. Olive oil should be stored in dark bottles in cool dark places and should be used within a year. Opened, it should be used in six months. Never buy an expensive oil (upwards of $15 or $20 for 500 ml) that does not have a vintage date on the label. At those prices it should be from the most recent harvest.

In a medium bowl, combine the tomatoes, cucumber, onion, and radishes. Drizzle with the lemon juice and olive oil, sprinkle with the parsley, and toss. Season to taste with salt and pepper.

TOTAL TIME: 5 minutes

LEFTOVERS The salad doesn't keep more than a day or two in the fridge. Pack leftovers into a falafel or other pita sandwich. The salad is also delicious served mixed into cottage cheese.

Chickpea and Spinach Salad

There's a wonderful Middle Eastern restaurant, Moustache, not far from my house that serves this lemony salad as part of its selection of meze. It's best, of course, if you prepare the chickpeas from scratch, but it's perfectly acceptable to use canned. The same goes for the spinach: fresh is best, but frozen is fine, too. The salad is better if it has a chance to sit, refrigerated, for a day.

Makes 6 servings

> 2 pounds fresh spinach, cleaned, or 2 (10-ounce) packages frozen spinach, defrosted
> 3 cups cooked chickpeas (see page 201) or 2 (15-ounce) cans chickpeas, drained
> 1 large shallot or $1/4$ medium red onion, finely chopped
> 2 large garlic cloves, minced
> $1/2$ cup extra-virgin olive oil
> Juice of 2 lemons ($1/2$ cup)
> Pinch of cayenne pepper (optional)
> Kosher salt and freshly ground black pepper

Bring a large pot of salted water to a boil, add the spinach, and blanch for 1 minute, until wilted. Rinse with cold water to stop the cooking. If using frozen spinach, skip the blanching. Drain, squeeze out any excess moisture, and chop. In a large bowl, combine the spinach with the chickpeas, shallot, and garlic. Add the olive oil, lemon juice, cayenne if using, $1/2$ teaspoon salt, and a generous amount of fresh pepper. Toss, adjust the seasoning, and chill.

TOTAL TIME: 15 minutes (plus chilling time)

ADVANCE PREP The salad is best if it chills for a day so the chickpeas and spinach absorb the dressing.
LEFTOVERS The salad will keep for one week in the refrigerator. You can use the salad as a topping for Crostini (page 22) or as a filling for pita sandwiches.

Bread Salad

This is my version of a Tuscan specialty known as *panzanella*. (For a variation of panzanella made with wheat berries, see page 72). It's a great way to use up a country-style or peasant loaf that's gone stale. It's best made several hours in advance. And since it doesn't require you to turn on the stove, it makes a perfect, light, summertime dish.

Makes 6 servings

> $1/2$ pound stale country or peasant loaf, white, sourdough, or partially whole wheat, torn into bite-size pieces (about 4 cups)
> $1/3$ cup red or white wine vinegar
> 1 large shallot or $1/4$ medium red onion, minced
> 1 garlic clove, minced

2 large tomatoes, diced, or 1 cup cherry
   tomatoes, cut into halves or quarters
   depending on their size

3/4 cup finely chopped fresh fennel, sweet turnip,
   carrot, celery, cucumber, or any other crunchy
   vegetable, or a combination

1/4 cup extra-virgin olive oil

10 to 12 large pitted black or green olives,
   chopped, or 2 tablespoons black or green olive
   paste or tapenade

2 tablespoons finely chopped flat-leaf parsley

1 tablespoon finely chopped fresh thyme or
   marjoram, or 4 or 5 leaves fresh basil, shredded

Kosher salt and freshly ground black pepper

Place the bread in a large bowl. In a small bowl, combine 1 3/4 cups cold water with the vinegar. Pour this mixture over the bread. Using your hands, push the bread around to make sure it is all soaked. Then, using a strainer or just your hands, drain the bread, squeezing out any excess liquid. Don't worry if you've broken the bread into little wet bits—that's desirable. Return the bread to the bowl.

Add the shallot, garlic, tomatoes, crunchy vegetable, olive oil, olives, parsley, other herbs, 1/2 teaspoon salt, and a generous amount of pepper, and mix well. Let the salad sit at room temperature or in the refrigerator for at least 2 hours before serving so the flavors have a chance to meld. Adjust the seasoning with additional salt and pepper and the tanginess with additional vinegar, if necessary. Stir gently before serving chilled or at room temperature.

TOTAL TIME: 15 minutes (plus chilling time)

ADVANCE PREP *This salad can be made as much as a day or two in advance without losing much of its*
freshness. *The only thing to watch out for is that the tomatoes don't start to wilt; you can tell because the tomato skin wrinkles. In fact, if you are going to make the salad more than 8 hours in advance, don't chop or add the tomatoes until closer to serving time.*

LEFTOVERS *The salad will keep up to a week in the refrigerator, but the tomatoes will start to look a little tired.*

Spiced Orange Couscous Salad with Currants and Carrots

This simple, beautiful couscous salad has a delicate flavor and buttery texture. It takes only a few minutes to prepare.

Makes 4 servings

1 cup couscous

1/4 cup dried currants

2 tablespoons frozen orange juice concentrate

2 tablespoons white wine, cider, or white vinegar

1/4 teaspoon ground cumin

1/4 teaspoon ground coriander

Kosher salt and freshly ground black pepper

3 tablespoons extra-virgin olive oil

1 medium carrot, peeled and shredded

2 scallions, green and white parts, finely chopped

2 to 3 tablespoons chopped fresh cilantro

Orange sections (see page 70), for garnish
   (optional)

In a medium bowl, combine the couscous and currants and mix to distribute the currants. In a small saucepan, combine the orange juice concentrate, vinegar, cumin, coriander, 1 teaspoon salt, 1/4 teaspoon black pepper, and 1 1/2 cups cold water. Bring to a boil and pour the hot liquid over the couscous and currant mixture.

SECTIONING CITRUS

When a recipe calls for any citrus to be sectioned—whether orange, grapefruit, lemon, or lime—the idea is to cut the juicy pulp from the tough membranes that encase the flesh and hold the fruit together. This gives you luscious, delicate sections that are called *filets* or *suprêmes* in French. At first this can seem like a chore, but with a little practice it becomes second nature.

To section any citrus fruit, take a sharp paring knife and slice off the top and bottom, cutting through the peel and pith, to reveal the ends of the sections beneath. Sit the fruit on a cutting board. Using the knife and following the curvature of the fruit, cut away the peel and pith from the sides of the citrus, making your cuts deep enough to reveal the glistening flesh beneath. Trim any white pith or membrane. Holding the peeled fruit over a bowl to catch the juice, insert the knife along one side of one of the membranes that divides the sections. Turn the blade to come back up the second side of the membrane around that particular section, releasing the fruit and letting it drop into the bowl below. Remove and discard any pits. When you have finished sectioning the fruit, squeeze the empty membrane in your fist to release any extra juice into the bowl. Cover and refrigerate for up to 1 day.

Cover the bowl with plastic wrap and let sit for 5 minutes.

Uncover and fluff the couscous with a fork. Add the olive oil, carrot, scallions, and cilantro and mix well. Adjust the seasoning with additional salt and/or pepper. Serve lukewarm, at room temperature, or chilled, garnished with orange sections, if desired.

PREP TIME: 15 minutes
COOKING TIME: 2 minutes
TOTAL TIME: 22 minutes

ADVANCE PREP *This salad can be made up to a day in advance and refrigerated until ready to use. I prefer the flavor at room temperature, and so I take it out of the fridge about 30 minutes before serving.* **LEFTOVERS** *It will keep in the fridge for about a week.*

Tabbouleh

Bulgur, a key ingredient in tabbouleh, is wheat that has been steamed, hulled, and cracked. Because it is precooked, all you need to do is soak it in hot water for a few minutes to make it edible—though, like couscous, it can also be cooked longer to make it lighter, fluffier, and more digestible. Bulgur is available in different sizes, of which I prefer medium. This tomato, herb, and bulgur salad is a staple in the Middle East, where the proportion of herbs to bulgur is much higher than we usually see here at home. This recipe falls somewhere in the middle. Serve it with dips and spreads and other salads at the start of meal.

Makes 4 servings

> 1/2 cup medium bulgur
> Kosher salt
> 1 cup boiling water
> 1/4 cup finely chopped flat-leaf parsley
>   (about 15 sprigs)
> 1/4 cup finely chopped fresh mint (about 10 sprigs)
> 4 scallions, white and green parts, chopped
> 1/8 teaspoon ground cumin
> Freshly ground black pepper
> 2 tablespoons fresh lemon juice (1/2 lemon)

2 tablespoons orange juice (¼ orange)

1 or 2 medium ripe tomatoes, diced

3 tablespoons extra-virgin olive oil

Place the bulgur in a medium bowl. Add ½ teaspoon salt to the boiling water, pour over the bulgur, and let sit for 15 to 20 minutes, until the grains have swollen. Fluff with a fork. If any liquid remains, drain the bulgur well and return it to the bowl. Add the parsley, mint, scallions, and cumin, and season generously with black pepper. Toss. Add the lemon and orange juices and toss again. Stir in the tomatoes. Cover the bulgur with plastic wrap and let sit at room temperature for about 1 hour so the grain absorbs the dressing and the flavors come together. Add the oil, then adjust the seasoning with additional salt and pepper.

PREP TIME: 10 minutes

TOTAL TIME: 1 hour 30 minutes (includes resting time)

ADVANCE PREP *The bulgur can be made a day or two in advance, refrigerated, and tossed with the other ingredients when you finish the recipe.*

LEFTOVERS *Tabbouleh will keep in the refrigerator for a day or two, but it deteriorates as it sits because the tomatoes become mealy. One way to salvage it is to serve it tossed with lettuce instead of as a stand-alone salad.*

Israeli Couscous with Favas, Feta, Olives, Preserved Lemon, and Mint

A relatively recent invention, Israeli couscous is neither a relative of couscous nor traditional in Israel. Nevertheless, it is a delicious toasted pasta product that has caught on because of its pleasing texture, flavor, and versatility. You can cook it just like pasta, in copious boiling salted water, or you can use the "pilaf" method described on page 216. Unlike pasta, though, Israeli couscous can develop a strong, off flavor if it is stale. Be sure yours is fresh. Israeli couscous takes to any flavoring, whether sweet or savory, mild or pungent. This summery salad is excellent with grilled meats.

Makes 6 to 8 servings

Kosher salt

1½ cups (8 ounces) Israeli couscous

2 pounds fresh fava beans in the pod, shelled, blanched, and peeled (see page 170; about 1 cup), or 1 cup frozen peas or edamame

1 roasted red pepper (see page 146), peeled, seeded, and chopped

½ small red onion, finely chopped

10 to 12 black olives, such as Kalamata, pitted and chopped

1 wedge Preserved Lemon (page 409), pulp removed, skin finely minced

4 ounces sharp feta cheese, crumbled (½ cup)

¼ cup finely chopped fresh mint or flat-leaf parsley

Juice of 1 lemon (¼ cup)

½ cup extra-virgin olive oil

Freshly ground black pepper

Bring a large pot of water to a boil. Add 1 tablespoon salt and stir in the Israeli couscous. Boil rapidly for 8 to 9 minutes, or until the couscous is tender but not mushy; it should retain a certain chewiness. Drain and cool to room temperature. Transfer to a large bowl. Add the fava beans, roasted pepper, onion, olives, preserved lemon, feta, and mint and toss to mix well. In a small bowl, beat together the lemon juice, olive oil, and a generous amount of black pepper. Pour this dressing over the couscous salad and toss to coat. Let sit for about 30 minutes at room temperature and adjust the seasoning with salt and pepper before serving.

PREP TIME: 20 minutes
COOKING TIME: 8 to 9 minutes
TOTAL TIME: 30 minutes (plus resting time)

ADVANCE PREP *The couscous can be cooked up to a day in advance and refrigerated.*
LEFTOVERS *The salad will keep in the refrigerator for up to a week, but the flavors tend to cloud each other out after three or four days.*

Wheat Berry Salad

Wheat berries are dried whole kernels of wheat before they are ground into flour. They are available peeled or unpeeled. No matter how long you cook them, unpeeled berries always remain chewy. You can use either for this salad. You can also use farro, an ancient variety of wheat known as emmer wheat (not spelt), which would make this salad similar to a type of panzanella served in Tuscany.

Makes 6 servings

   1 cup wheat berries or farro
   1 small bay leaf
   1 sprig rosemary
   1 large garlic clove
   1/4 cup extra-virgin olive oil
   3 tablespoons white or red wine vinegar
   Kosher salt and freshly ground black pepper

   1 large ripe tomato, diced
   1/2 medium red onion, chopped
   1/3 cup cubed sheep's milk cheese, such as
      Pecorino Toscano or feta (optional)
   1 tablespoon chopped flat-leaf parsley

Place the wheat berries in a medium bowl and cover with cold water. Let sit at room temperature for 8 hours or overnight. Drain the wheat berries and place in a medium saucepan. Cover with fresh water; add the bay leaf, rosemary, and garlic, and bring to a boil. Lower the heat and simmer the wheat berries for 50 to 60 minutes, or until tender but still slightly chewy. Drain well and remove the bay leaf, rosemary, and garlic.

While still warm, toss the berries with the olive oil, vinegar, 3/4 teaspoon salt, and a generous amount of pepper. Let cool to room temperature or chill. Mix in the tomato, red onion, cheese if using, and parsley. Adjust the seasoning and serve at room temperature or chilled.

PREP TIME: 15 minutes
COOKING TIME: 1 hour
TOTAL TIME: 12 hours (includes soaking time)

ADVANCE PREP *The wheat berries can be cooked a day or two before you assemble the salad and refrigerated, and the salad can be assembled and refrigerated up to a day before you intend to serve it.*
LEFTOVERS *The salad will keep for about one week in the refrigerator, though the tomatoes wilt and become slightly mealy after a day or two.*

VARIATION
Barley Salad
Pearl barley provides a delicious, quick alternative to wheat berries for this salad because

barley does not have to be soaked overnight before it is cooked. Bring a large pot of salted water to a boil. Add 1 cup of pearl barley and cook for 20 to 25 minutes, or until the barley is tender but retains a slight chewiness. Drain well and proceed with the recipe as directed above.

Warm Barley Salad with Corn and Green Beans

This warm salad makes a colorful and delicious side dish in the summer, when local corn and green beans area available. It is equally delicious served chilled. The key is not to overcook the barley or the vegetables so that they retain their bright color, chewy texture, and fresh flavor.

Makes 6 servings

Kosher salt

8 ounces green beans, ends trimmed

2 to 3 ears fresh corn

1 cup pearl barley

Juice of 1 to 2 lemons

$1/4$ cup extra-virgin olive oil

$1/2$ roasted red pepper (see page 146), finely chopped

3 scallions, white and green parts, or $1/4$ medium red onion, chopped

$1/4$ cup black olives, such as Kalamata (not canned), pitted and chopped

1 to 2 tablespoons chopped fresh lemon, opal, or regular basil

Freshly ground black pepper

Bring a large pot of water with about 1 tablespoon kosher salt to a boil. Add the green beans and blanch for 2 or 3 minutes, until they turn bright green and are tender with a delicate crunch. Lift the beans out of the pot with a strainer and rinse under cold running water to stop the cooking. Cut the green beans into $1/2$-inch pieces, place in a large bowl, and set aside.

Bring the water back to a boil. Add the ears of corn and cook for 3 or 4 minutes, just until the kernels are cooked. Remove the corn from the pot and rinse under cold water. Using a sharp paring knife, remove the kernels from the cob (see page 50) and add them to the green beans.

Bring the water to a boil one last time. Add the barley and cook until the barley is tender but not mushy, 30 to 35 minutes. Drain the barley, do not rinse, and add to the beans and corn. Toss with the lemon juice and olive oil. Add the red pepper, scallions, black olives, and basil, and mix well. Adjust the seasoning with salt and pepper. Serve warm, at room temperature, or chilled.

PREP TIME: 10 minutes
COOKING TIME: 35 minutes
TOTAL TIME: 45 minutes

ADVANCE PREP *The salad can be made up to a day or two in advance and refrigerated until served. If desired, reheat in a microwave on high for a couple of minutes before serving.*
LEFTOVERS *The salad will keep for about a week in the refrigerator.*

Potato Salad

If you looked in an American culinary dictionary, this is the recipe you would find next to the definition of potato salad. It's about as "summer picnic" and "apple pie" as you can get. The secret is to use plenty of chopped pickle and pickle juice.

Makes 6 to 8 servings

2 pounds Red Bliss or other boiling potato (about 3 large), unpeeled

2 large eggs

Kosher salt

2 celery stalks, finely chopped

1 small white or red onion or 3 scallions, white and green parts, finely chopped

5 sweet (midget) gherkins or 1 large dill pickle, finely chopped, with 2 tablespoons pickle juice

2 teaspoons Dijon mustard

¾ cup Hellmann's or Best Foods mayonnaise

1 to 2 tablespoons chopped flat-leaf parsley or other herbs

Freshly ground black pepper

Place the potatoes and the eggs in a large saucepan and cover with cold water. Add 2 teaspoons salt and bring to a boil. Turn down the heat so the water simmers and cook for 10 minutes. Lift out the eggs and cool under cold, running water. Continue simmering the potatoes until they are tender when pricked with a fork, but not so tender that they fall apart, an additional 20 minutes or so. It's important not to overcook the potatoes, or the salad with be mushy; better to err on the side of underdone.

Drain the potatoes and let cool to room temperature. If you have the time, chill them along with the eggs for 2 or 3 hours or overnight. Peel the potatoes and eggs. Cut the potatoes into ½-inch cubes and place in a large bowl. Chop the eggs and add them to the bowl along with the celery, onion, pickles, pickle juice, mustard,

mayonnaise, parsley, ½ teaspoon salt, and a generous amount of black pepper. Mix well. Taste and adjust the seasoning. Chill until ready to serve.

PREP TIME: 10 minutes
COOKING TIME: 30 minutes
TOTAL TIME: 40 minutes (plus chilling time)

ADVANCE PREP *The potatoes and eggs can be boiled up to two or three days in advance and refrigerated until ready to use.*
LEFTOVERS *The potato salad will keep for about one week in the refrigerator.*

Curried Rice and Fresh Corn Salad with Golden Raisins

This is a salad I sometimes make with leftover corn on the cob and/or leftover white rice. Cooked barley works well, too; substitute 2 cups for the rice. It's also a good way to use up leftover cooked vegetables, such as cauliflower or asparagus. Simply chop them up and mix them in.

Makes 6 to 8 servings

½ cup white wine or cider vinegar

⅓ cup golden raisins or currants

2 tablespoons curry powder (page 409)

2 tablespoons canola or vegetable oil

½ medium white onion, finely chopped

1 small garlic clove, minced

1 tablespoon minced fresh ginger

2 cups cooked corn kernels from fresh or frozen corn

3 cups cooked white rice

2 scallions, white and green parts, chopped

1 tablespoon chopped fresh cilantro

¼ cup extra-virgin olive oil
Kosher salt and freshly ground black
    pepper

In a small saucepan, bring the vinegar to a boil. Pour it over the raisins and let sit until the raisins are swollen. Alternatively, you can combine the vinegar and the raisins in a small bowl and heat them in the microwave on high for 1 minute 30 seconds before letting them sit.

In a small bowl, mix the curry powder with about 2 tablespoons cold water to form a paste. Set aside. In a small, nonstick frying pan, heat the canola oil over medium-high heat. Add the onion and cook until it begins to soften, about 5 minutes. Add the garlic and ginger and cook for a minute or two, until the perfume of garlic and ginger is strong. Stir in the curry paste and let cook for 1 or 2 minutes, until the water has evaporated and the aroma of toasted spices is perceptible. Turn off the heat. Pour in the raisins with their vinegar. Using a wooden spoon or rubber spatula, scrape the spice mixture off the bottom of the pan. Let cool completely to room temperature.

In a large bowl, combine the corn and rice. Add the curried onion and raisin mixture along with the scallions, cilantro, and olive oil. Season with salt and pepper and chill before serving.

PREP TIME: 10 minutes
COOKING TIME: 10 minutes
TOTAL TIME: 20 minutes (plus chilling time)

ADVANCE PREP *The salad can be made a day in advance and refrigerated until serving.*
LEFTOVERS *The salad will keep for about one week in the refrigerator.*

Macaroni Salad

My tips for making a better macaroni salad than you are used to are to use Italian durum wheat pasta, which has a better texture and better flavor than any American brand of elbow macaroni I've tried. Also, do not over- or undercook it; the pasta should retain some texture but not stick in your teeth. And do not use too much mayonnaise, which drowns the flavor of all the other ingredients.
Makes 6 to 8 servings

½ cup fresh peas, or frozen peas or shelled
    edamame, defrosted
8 ounces pasta corkscrews, fusilli, or elbow
    macaroni
4 ounces smoked ham or Polish kielbasa, finely
    diced
1 small red onion, finely chopped
1 celery stalk, finely chopped
1 small carrot, shredded
6 or 7 slices bread and butter pickles, chopped
⅔ cup Hellmann's or Best Foods mayonnaise
1 tablespoon white wine vinegar
2 tablespoons finely chopped flat-leaf parsley
Kosher salt and freshly ground black pepper

Bring 4 quarts of heavily salted water to a boil. If using fresh peas, add them to the water and blanch for 1 minute. Scoop them out with a strainer or slotted spoon and rinse under cold water. Drain well and set aside. Add the pasta to the boiling water. Cook, stirring, until the noodles are just slightly past al dente, about 9 minutes. Drain and rinse in cold water. Drain well. In a large bowl, combine the peas, ham, onion, celery, carrot, and pickles. Add the pasta and toss to distribute the ingredients. Mix in the mayonnaise, vinegar, parsley, 1 teaspoon salt, and some pepper. Chill for at least 1 hour and adjust the seasoning before serving.

PREP TIME: 20 minutes

COOKING TIME: 10 minutes

TOTAL TIME: 30 minutes (plus chilling time)

ADVANCE PREP *The salad can be made a day or two in advance and refrigerated.*

LEFTOVERS *The salad will keep for about one week in the refrigerator. As it sits, the noodles will absorb the mayonnaise. To make the salad creamy again, stir in a little more mayo before eating.*

Chilled Soba Salad

I love the buckwheat taste of soba. This chilled soba salad with soy-sauce dressing makes a refreshing lunch on a hot summer's day. You can use any number of vegetable garnishes, but I prefer either grated daikon radish or shredded napa cabbage.

Makes 4 to 6 servings

  8 ounces 100% buckwheat soba noodles, or as
      close to 100% as you can get
  2 teaspoons toasted Asian sesame oil
  ¾ cup vegetable or chicken stock
  2 tablespoons soy sauce
  1 tablespoon mirin
  1 tablespoon rice vinegar
  3 tablespoons fresh orange juice or 1 tablespoon
      frozen orange juice concentrate, defrosted
  One 4-inch piece daikon, peeled and grated
      (about 1 cup)
  1 carrot, cut into matchsticks
  2 scallions, white and green parts, finely
      chopped
  2 teaspoons sesame seeds, toasted (see page 10)

Bring about 5 quarts of salted water to a boil in a large pot. Add the soba and stir, using tongs or a large fork, to be sure the noodles don't stick together. Boil until the noodles are just al dente, 7 or 8 minutes. Remove ¼ cup of the cooking water and reserve. Drain the noodles and rinse in cold water to stop the cooking. Drain well. Toss the noodles with the sesame oil and chill.

To prepare the dressing, in a small bowl combine the vegetable stock, soy sauce, mirin, rice vinegar, orange juice, and the reserved ¼ cup of soba cooking water. Pour this mixture over the chilled soba, toss, and let sit for 10 minutes or so.

Divide the noodles evenly among the serving bowls and spoon any remaining dressing into the bowls. Divide the daikon among the bowls and mound it on top of the noodles. Arrange the carrot on top of the daikon. Sprinkle the scallions and the sesame seeds on top of that. Serve chilled.

PREP TIME: 10 minutes

COOKING TIME: 8 minutes

TOTAL TIME: 20 minutes (plus chilling time)

ADVANCE PREP *The noodles can be cooked a day or two in advance and kept in the refrigerator until needed. Dress and garnish them just before serving.*

LEFTOVERS *The soba will keep about a week in the fridge, but it will lose its nice al dente texture.*

Shrimp and Green Mango or Green Papaya Salad

This is a simple, fresh Thai-style salad that's loaded with flavor and easy to make. Green mango or green papaya are simply underripe fruits. Whichever you use, it should be firm and have a definite greenish hue to the skin. You can play around with the ingredients based on what you can find in the market.

Makes 4 to 6 appetizer servings

3 tablespoons boiling water

2 tablespoons sugar

1/4 cup fresh lime juice (about 1 large lime)

3 tablespoons Asian fish sauce, such as Thai *nam pla* or Vietnamese *nuoc nam*

1 or 2 red chiles, fresh or pickled, seeded and chopped

1 large firm green mango or green papaya, peeled

8 ounces medium shrimp, cooked and peeled (see page 279), sliced lengthwise in half

1 small sweet red or white onion, thinly sliced

3 scallions, white and green parts, thinly sliced

1/2 red bell pepper, cored, seeded, and sliced into matchsticks

1 handful (about 15) fresh mint or basil leaves, chopped

5 to 7 sprigs fresh cilantro, leaves only

1/3 cup salted peanuts, toasted (see page 10) and finely chopped (optional)

1 bunch watercress, large, tough stems removed

Place the boiling water in a small bowl. (Alternatively, you can heat the water in a bowl in the microwave until boiling.) Add the sugar and stir until dissolved. Cool to room temperature. Stir in the lime juice, fish sauce, and chile. Set aside.

Slice the mango or papaya very thin using a mandoline or a very sharp knife. Cut these slices into very thin, long strips or julienne. Place the mango or papaya in a medium bowl. Add the shrimp, onion, scallions, bell pepper, chopped mint leaves, whole cilantro leaves,

and peanuts if using. Add the dressing and toss with a fork, being careful not to break up the strips of mango. Arrange the watercress on serving plates and spoon the salad on top. Spoon some of the dressing from the bottom of the bowl onto the watercress around the salad and serve.

TOTAL TIME: 20 minutes

ADVANCE PREP *You can prepare the dressing and cut up the ingredients several hours in advance. Refrigerate the shrimp and store the other ingredients at room temperature. Toss the salad with the dressing just before you intend to serve it.*

Smoked Trout Salad with Pickled Beets and Beans

My sister Leslie has a summer cottage about 2 1/2 hours northeast of Toronto. It's pretty much in the middle of nowhere, especially as far as food provisioning is concerned. The one thing that we look forward to is smoked trout from a local trout farm run by a lovely German couple. This is a *composed* salad, meaning the different elements are arranged on a plate, not tossed together, and the eater mixes them together as he or she eats. It makes a delicious starter for a hearty meal or an entrée for brunch.

Makes 4 servings

1/3 cup sour cream

1 tablespoon finely grated fresh horseradish or 1 teaspoon prepared white horseradish, or to taste

1 tablespoon chopped fresh dill

Kosher salt and freshly ground black pepper

4 leaves Bibb or green or red leaf lettuce

10 ounces smoked trout, skin and bones removed

8 slices Pickled Beets with Caraway (page 210), cut in half

4 ounces thin French-style green beans, trimmed and blanched (see page 163)

½ cup cooked white beans, such as cranberry, cannelloni, or navy beans (see page 201)

2 or 3 very thin slices red onion, separated into rings

In a small bowl, combine the sour cream with the horseradish and dill. Season with a pinch of salt and some pepper. Set aside. On each of four chilled serving plates, place a leaf of lettuce. Arrange the trout, beets, green beans, white beans, and red onion attractively on the plates. Place a dollop of the dressing in the center of each plate and grind some additional pepper on top.

TOTAL TIME: 10 minutes

ADVANCE PREP *The sour cream dressing can be made and refrigerated up to a day in advance.*

Chicken Salad

Perhaps we have Jack Nicholson's character in *Five Easy Pieces* to thank for making a chicken salad sandwich on toast an iconic American lunch. Regardless, it's one of my favorites. Use the cooked chicken from a chicken soup or leftover roast chicken or turkey for the meat, and play around with any number of ingredients to make a tasty salad.

Makes 6 servings

3 cups cubed cooked chicken

1 large celery stalk, finely chopped

½ large red or white onion or 4 scallions, white and green parts, finely chopped

1 large dill pickle, finely chopped

1 hard-cooked egg, finely chopped (page 129)

1 tablespoon chopped flat-leaf parsley

½ cup Hellmann's or Best Foods mayonnaise

1 teaspoon grainy French mustard

Kosher salt and freshly ground black pepper

In a large mixing bowl, combine the chicken, celery, onion, pickle, egg, parsley, mayonnaise, mustard, ¼ teaspoon salt, and some pepper. Stir to blend. Chill and adjust the seasoning before serving.

TOTAL TIME: 15 minutes (plus chilling time)

ADVANCE PREP *The salad can be made several days in advance and refrigerated until serving.*
LEFTOVERS *The salad will keep for about a week in the fridge.*

VARIATIONS

Feel free to add all sorts of things, such as chopped toasted nuts; dried currants, cranberries, or raisins; shredded carrot or shredded green apple; and pickled onions, olives, or other tasty condiments.

Curried Turkey Salad with Dried Cranberries and Yogurt Dressing

Here's a quick, low-fat turkey salad that packs a flavor punch. Cooking the curry powder before mixing it with the dressing brings out the rich flavor of the spices—a modern take on the retro curried chicken salad my mother served in the 1970s. This is an excellent way to use up leftover cooked turkey or chicken.

Makes 4 servings

> 1/4 cup dried cranberries or cherries
>
> 1/4 cup white or red wine vinegar
>
> 1 tablespoon curry powder (page 409)
>
> 2 tablespoons peanut or vegetable oil
>
> 3/4 cup plain yogurt
>
> 3 cups cubed cooked white-meat turkey or chicken
>
> 1 medium carrot, shredded
>
> 1 medium cucumber, peeled, seeded, and shredded
>
> Kosher salt and freshly ground black pepper
>
> 1 to 2 tablespoons cashews, toasted (see page 10) and finely chopped

Place the dried cranberries in a small, microwavable bowl and pour over the vinegar. Microwave on high for 1 1/2 minutes. Alternatively, you can bring the vinegar to a boil on the stove and pour it over the cranberries. Set aside to cool.

Meanwhile, place the curry powder in a small dish and add 2 tablespoons of cold water to make a paste. Set a small nonstick frying pan over medium heat. Add the oil, and when it is hot, add the spice paste, stirring as it sizzles and the water evaporates. After a minute or two, the paste will thicken and coat the bottom of the pan, giving off a strong aroma. Remove from the heat. Add the soaked cranberries and the vinegar to the pan, and using a wooden spoon or rubber spatula, stir to loosen the spices from the bottom of the pan. Cool to room temperature.

Add the yogurt to the spice mixture and stir to blend. In a medium bowl, combine the turkey, carrot, and cucumber. Add the yogurt mixture to the turkey and vegetables, season to taste with salt and pepper, and toss to distribute the dressing. Chill for at least 30 minutes. Garnish with chopped cashews.

PREP TIME: 15 minutes

COOKING TIME: 4 minutes

TOTAL TIME: 20 minutes (plus chilling time)

ADVANCE PREP *The salad is best after having chilled a few hours or overnight before serving.*

LEFTOVERS *The salad will keep for about four days in the refrigerator. Some liquid will come off of the yogurt and the cucumber; simply stir it back in before serving.*

Wilted Arugula with Anchovy and Garlic Dressing

Gentle cooking removes the harsh edge of garlic and anchovies in the warm dressing on this arugula salad. It's a takeoff on traditional Piemontese bagna cauda. It is also good on bitter greens, such as escarole, frisée, or dandelions.

Makes 4 servings

> 1 pound arugula, tough stems removed
>
> 2/3 cup extra-virgin olive oil
>
> 2 large garlic cloves, minced
>
> 5 to 7 anchovy fillets in oil, drained
>
> 1/3 cup red or white wine vinegar
>
> Freshly ground black pepper
>
> Sliced or chopped hard-cooked egg (see page 29)
>
> Chopped flat-leaf parsley, for garnish

Place the arugula in a large bowl and set aside. In a small frying pan over low heat, heat the olive oil for a minute or two until warm. Add the garlic and cook slowly, stirring frequently, until the garlic gives off a strong aroma, 3 or 4 minutes. Add the anchovies, and using a wooden spoon or heat-proof rubber spatula, mash the anchovies on the bottom of the pan to make them into a paste. Cook slowly until the garlic begins to color slightly, about 3 more minutes. Pour in the vinegar, stir, add some black pepper, and pour the hot dressing over the arugula. Toss quickly and divide the salad among serving plates. Garnish with egg and chopped parsley.

PREP TIME: 7 minutes
COOKING TIME: 8 minutes
TOTAL TIME: 15 minutes

ADVANCE PREP *You can make the dressing several hours in advance and keep it at room temperature until ready to serve. Gently reheat it before tossing the salad.*
LEFTOVERS *The dressing will keep in the refrigerator for a couple of days, but the flavor begins to diminish. Once dressed, the salad will not keep.*

Wilted Spinach Salad with Red Onion and Bacon

While it may be messy and retro, spinach salad with warm bacon dressing is nevertheless delicious.
Makes 4 servings

1½ pounds fresh spinach, stems removed
¾ cup cherry tomatoes, cut in half
2 ounces white button mushrooms, very thinly sliced (optional)

½ cup croutons (see page 41)
1 tablespoon chopped flat-leaf parsley
1 tablespoon vegetable oil
3 thick-cut bacon strips, diced
½ small red onion, sliced
⅓ cup red wine vinegar
Kosher salt and freshly ground black pepper
1 hard-cooked egg (see page 29), sliced or cut into wedges

In a large bowl, toss together the spinach, cherry tomatoes, mushrooms if using, croutons, and parsley. In a large frying pan, heat the oil with the bacon over medium-high heat. Cook until the fat has rendered out of the bacon and the bacon begins to brown, about 6 minutes. Add the onion and cook until wilted, 4 or 5 minutes. Add the vinegar, a pinch of salt, and a generous amount of pepper. Cook for a minute or so, just until the vinegar begins to evaporate. Pour the hot dressing over the spinach mixture and toss. Divide among four serving plates and garnish with the hard-cooked egg. Serve immediately.

PREP TIME: 10 minutes
COOKING TIME: 10 minutes
TOTAL TIME: 20 minutes

ADVANCE PREP *You can get all of your ingredients ready several hours in advance, but do not assemble the salad or make the dressing until just before serving.*

Frisée aux Lardons

One of the great salads of all time, this combination of frisée (curly endive), bacon, and poached egg is simply delicious. A runny, poached egg offsets the tart dressing.

Makes 4 servings

2 thick-cut double-smoked bacon strips, cut crosswise into $1/4$-inch-wide pieces (lardons)

1 small shallot, thinly sliced

1 heaping teaspoon Dijon mustard

3 tablespoons white or red wine vinegar

5 tablespoons extra-virgin olive oil

Kosher salt and freshly ground black pepper

2 heads of frisée (about 1 pound), dark outer leaves removed

4 poached eggs, warmed (see page 122)

Handful of chopped flat-leaf parsley

Heat a large frying pan over medium-high heat and add the bacon. Cook, stirring, until the bacon is browned and crisp, about 4 minutes. Remove the bacon to a paper-towel–lined plate and pat off any excess fat. Fry the shallot in the bacon fat over medium-high heat until soft, 3 or 4 minutes. Remove the shallot to drain on the paper towel, too.

Place the mustard in the bottom of a large bowl. With a small whisk or fork, whisk in the vinegar until smooth. Whisk in the olive oil in a slow, steady stream to make a creamy emulsion. Season with salt and pepper. Add the frisée, bacon, and shallot, and toss. Arrange the salad on plates, top each with a poached egg, and sprinkle with parsley.

PREP TIME: 12 minutes
COOKING TIME: 8 minutes
TOTAL TIME: 20 minutes

ADVANCE PREP *The various components of the salad can be made in advance. The eggs can be poached a day or two before serving and kept refrigerated in water. Reheat the eggs as directed on page 122. The bacon and dressing can be made several hours in advance and kept at room temperature until ready to assemble the salad. Toss the salad right before serving.*

Vietnamese Beef Salad with Watercress

This is a simple, light salad with a pungent dressing that makes for a superb summer appetizer or light main course. Play with the selection of vegetables based on what's available and to suit your taste.

Makes 4 appetizer or 2 main-course servings

$1/4$ cup boiling water

$1/4$ cup sugar

$1/2$ cup fresh lime juice (about 2 limes)

$1/3$ cup Asian fish sauce, such as Thai *nam pla* or Vietnamese *nuoc nam*

2 or 3 red chiles, fresh or pickled, seeded and chopped

1 ($3/4$-pound) rib eye or top round steak

2 teaspoons minced fresh ginger

1 large garlic clove, minced

1 tablespoon peanut or vegetable oil

1 tablespoon soy sauce

$3/4$ teaspoon freshly ground or cracked black pepper

1 bunch watercress

$1/2$ medium cucumber, peeled, seeded, and sliced into long sticks

1 small sweet, white onion, sliced

1 medium ripe tomato, cut into wedges

3 or 4 sprigs fresh cilantro

$1/4$ cup salted peanuts, toasted (see page 10) and finely chopped

To prepare the dressing, pour the boiling water into a small bowl. Add the sugar and stir until dissolved. Cool to room temperature. Stir in the lime juice, fish sauce, and chiles. Keep at room temperature.

Place the steak in a small, shallow container. Add the ginger, garlic, peanut oil, soy sauce, and 2 tablespoons of the dressing. Move the steak around to coat it with the ingredients. Cover and refrigerate for 2 hours.

When you are ready to serve, heat a grill, broiler, or grill pan until very hot. Lift the steak out of the marinade, draining off any excess liquid, and lay the steak on the hot grill. After 4 or 5 minutes, flip the steak to cook the other side. The cooking time will depend on how thick the steak is. I like the meat to be quite rare for this salad, but cook it until it is done enough for you and your guests. Once you flip the steak, coat the cooked side with half of the black pepper. When the second side is done, flip the steak just for a minute or so and coat the other side with the remaining black pepper. (This gives the steak a strong peppery flavor without a burnt pepper taste.) When cooked, remove to a cutting board and let rest 10 to 15 minutes.

Meanwhile, arrange the salad attractively in serving bowls. Lay down a bed of watercress and scatter the cucumber, onion, and tomato around the cress. Pick the leaves off the stems of the fresh cilantro and scatter them around the bowls, too. Using a sharp knife, slice the steak on an angle across the grain into thin slices. Stir up the dressing and spoon some over the arranged salad (don't do this beforehand or the vegetables will wilt). Lay the strips of steak on top of the salad, spoon a little more dressing on the meat, and sprinkle with peanuts. Serve immediately.

PREP TIME: 20 minutes

COOKING TIME: 10 minutes

TOTAL TIME: 2$\frac{1}{2}$ hours (includes marinating time)

LEFTOVERS Once the salad is dressed, it does not keep well, but the meat can be kept in the refrigerator for a day or two.

■ ■ ■

Sandwiches and Pizza

W HAT EXACTLY THE EARL of Sandwich is supposed to have invented in the eighteenth century I am not quite sure, since just about every culture is proud of some form of sandwich, from France's Croque Monsieurs to Italy's pressed panini. Still, I think it is safe to say that, for the rest of the world, Americans are most closely identified with sandwich eating, perhaps because of our close ties to the hamburger. And in fact, even though many cultures enjoy sandwiches, I think that only in America is a sandwich considered an equally appropriate meal for breakfast, lunch, or dinner.

And with good reason. A properly made sandwich is a delight to behold. It should be constructed on some form of good bread or an appropriate alternative, such as a pita or tortilla. It should have a complex combination of flavors, including elements of spice, sweet, tart, and salt. It should have an equally intriguing combination of textures, including soft, crisp, and chewy. Condiments are key. They should add flavor and moistness, bringing all the flavors and textures of the sandwich together. Whether you toast or press or bake or grill depends on the sandwich you are making and your personal taste.

Most sandwiches are intended to be eaten with hands, and this fact should be taken into consideration when they are constructed. A pet peeve of mine is sandwiches that fall apart when you eat them, whether because you can't easily bite through the bread or the filling or the bread is so soft that it can't hold the whole thing together. Likewise, I am opposed to sandwiches stuffed so thick that you can't get your mouth around them. I recall a scene at a panini stand in Florence, where a student of mine tasted her first Italian sandwich. She was shocked by how little filling was inside the big, crusty bun. And then she was surprised at how satisfying the sandwich was because what little filling there was was so intensely flavorful, she didn't need more. There is a lesson in restraint to be learned in this story.

Sandwich-like choices such as tacos, wraps, panini, pita pockets, open-faced sandwiches, and even pizzas provide a wide variety of alternatives to the piece-of-meat-on-two-pieces-of-bread idiom. Add them to your repertoire and you'll never be hungry for sandwich ideas.

"Grilled" Cheese

Grilled cheese isn't usually grilled anyway (it's griddled), so I feel perfectly justified in calling this baked version "Grilled" Cheese. I find baking these sandwiches less of a hassle than frying them individually, and using this technique allows you to make a large number of sandwiches simultaneously if you need to feed a crowd.

Makes 4 sandwiches

8 thin slices fresh, dense white sandwich bread
6 ounces aged Emmentaler, Gruyère, or other
    Swiss cheese, or sharp Cheddar, thinly sliced
Freshly ground black pepper
4 tablespoons ($\frac{1}{2}$ stick) unsalted butter, at room
    temperature

Preheat the oven to 400°F. Line a baking sheet with parchment or aluminum foil.

Lay 4 slices of bread on a flat work surface. Arrange a thin layer of cheese on the bread. Sprinkle with one or two grinds of black pepper. Top with the remaining cheese and the remaining bread. Press down on the sandwiches to compact. If desired, cut off the crusts and any overhang of filling to make perfect squares. Butter the tops of the sandwiches with half of the butter and invert them, buttered side down, on the prepared sheet pan. Butter the other side of the sandwiches with the remaining butter.

Bake for about 10 minutes, until the bread begins to brown. With a spatula, push down gently on the sandwiches to further compact them, but don't push so hard that you force the cheese to ooze out. (A little of the cheese will melt out of the sandwich, naturally.) Flip the sandwiches, and bake for another 5 minutes or so, until the second side is evenly browned.

Remove from the oven and let sit at room temperature for 2 or 3 minutes so the melted cheese firms up—but don't let them sit long enough to harden, or you'll never get them off the pan. Lift off of the baking sheet and let cool for another minute or two before cutting diagonally into halves or quarters to serve.

PREP TIME: 15 minutes
COOKING TIME: 15 minutes
TOTAL TIME: 30 minutes

LEFTOVERS Reheat leftovers in a 300°F oven for 10 minutes or so, or just eat them cold, dipped in ketchup, out of the fridge.

VARIATIONS
Grilled Cheese with Bacon and Tomato
Place 2 strips of crisp bacon and 1 thin slice of ripe tomato between the layers of cheese in each sandwich. Increase the baking time by 2 or 3 minutes to be sure the sandwiches are heated through.

Grilled Cheese with Ham and Onions
Place 2 thin slices of Black Forest ham and a small handful of Buttermilk Fried Onions (page 193), or caramelized onions, or a couple of rings of grilled onions between the layers of cheese in each sandwich. Increase the baking time by 2 or 3 minutes to be sure the sandwiches are heated through.

Grilled Cheese with Smoked Salmon
(with a nod to chef Eric Ripert of Le Bernardin)
Place 1 or 2 thin slices of smoked salmon, 1/8 teaspoon finely minced Preserved Lemon (page 409) or lemon zest, and a pinch of

chopped chives between the layers of cheese in each sandwich. Bake as directed. If desired, garnish each sandwich quarter with a spoonful of fresh salmon or sturgeon caviar before serving.

Croque Monsieur

This version of the classic French ham-and-melted-cheese sandwich is based on one I enjoyed at Tartine in San Francisco.

Makes 4 sandwiches

1 1/2 teaspoons Dijon mustard
1 cup Cream Sauce (page 404), made with a
    pinch of nutmeg
Four 1/2-inch-thick slices crusty country bread
2 tablespoons unsalted butter, at room
    temperature
8 thin slices Jambon de Paris, Black Forest ham,
    or regular boiled ham
8 ounces imported Emmentaler, Gruyère,
    or other Swiss cheese, shredded (about
    1 cup)

Preheat the broiler, or set the oven to 450°F. Stir the mustard into the cream sauce.

Toast the bread in a toaster or toaster oven, or in the preheating oven, until light golden brown. Lay the toasted bread on a nonstick or parchment- or foil-lined baking sheet (to ease cleanup). Spread the toast with a light layer of the butter. Divide the cream sauce among the pieces of toast and spread to form an even layer. Depending on the size of your slices, you may have leftover sauce. Arrange the ham on top of the sauce, folding as necessary to prevent too much overhang. Cover the ham with the shredded cheese. Place under the broiler or in the

preheated oven and cook for 5 to 10 minutes, until the cheese has melted and browned. Remove from the oven and let cool for 2 or 3 minutes before lifting the sandwiches off the pan with a spatula—don't let them sit long enough for the cheese to harden, or you'll never get them off the pan. Serve warm or at room temperature.

PREP TIME: 10 minutes
COOKING TIME: 10 minutes
TOTAL TIME: 20 minutes

ADVANCE PREP *The sandwiches can be assembled up to 4 hours in advance, refrigerated, and then broiled or baked just before serving. Take them out of the refrigerator 15 minutes before baking. They can also be baked in advance and reheated or served at room temperature.*
LEFTOVERS *Cooked sandwiches will keep for three or four days in the refrigerator, but their texture will suffer considerably. Reheat in a 300°F oven for 10 minutes or until warm. Do not microwave.*

VARIATION
Croque Madame

You can switch your sandwich's gender by serving it with a fried, sunny-side-up egg on top. Prepare the Croque Monsieur as directed (sometimes for a Madame I substitute smoked salmon for the ham). Preheat the broiler. In a nonstick pan, heat a tablespoon or so of unsalted butter over medium-high heat. When the butter is sizzling, crack an egg into the pan—the fresher the egg, the less it will spread. Fry until the white has turned opaque and the egg is browned around the edges, about 4 minutes. Pop the pan under the broiler for a minute or so to firm up the white. Slide the egg out of the pan (butter and all) onto the hot sandwich. Repeat with more eggs for whoever wants them.

Grilled Portobello and Sun-Dried Tomato Sandwich with Garlic Herbed Mayonnaise

Here's a vegetarian sandwich that is as satisfying as one with meat. Kaiser rolls are the perfect shape for the portobello caps, and their thick crust catches the mushroom juices. Fresh hamburger buns are good, too.

Makes 4 sandwiches

> 4 kaiser rolls
> 1/3 cup Hellmann's or Best Foods mayonnaise
> 2 teaspoons white wine vinegar or lemon juice
> 1 teaspoon minced garlic
> 1 tablespoon finely chopped flat-leaf parsley
> 1 teaspoon minced fresh rosemary
> 4 large portobello mushroom caps
>   (about 1 1/4 pounds)
> 1/4 cup extra-virgin olive oil
> Kosher salt and freshly ground black pepper
> 4 to 8 sun-dried tomato halves packed in olive oil
> 2 large leaves romaine lettuce

Preheat the oven to 325°F.

Individually wrap the rolls in aluminum foil and set them in the oven while it heats. Combine the mayonnaise, vinegar, garlic, parsley, and rosemary. Set aside.

Preheat a grill, grill pan, or large, heavy frying pan to medium-high. Brush the portobello caps with olive oil and season liberally with salt and pepper on both sides. Place the mushrooms on the hot grill or in the hot pan, and cook until they begin to sear, soften, and shrink, 5 to 8 minutes. Flip and cook the second side for 4 or 5 minutes.

Meanwhile, remove a roll from the oven, unwrap it, and slice it in half. Spread both halves with the prepared mayonnaise. Place 1 or 2 sun-dried tomato halves on the bottom half of the roll and top with a mushroom cap. Finish with half a leaf of romaine lettuce and crown with the top of the roll. Repeat to prepare the other sandwiches and serve.

PREP TIME: 15 minutes
COOKING TIME: 10 minutes
TOTAL TIME: 25 minutes

ADVANCE PREP *You can grill the mushrooms in advance if you want to serve the sandwiches at room temperature, but I prefer them hot.*
LEFTOVERS *The grilled mushrooms will keep for about a week in the fridge. Slice leftovers and use them in pasta, salads, soups, or any dish that might taste good with some mushrooms in it. Use any leftover mayonnaise as a dressing for potato or chicken salad.*

Panini

Although in Italy the term *panini* refers to any kind of sandwiches on bread (the singular in Italian is *panino*), here in America the same word has recently come to refer only to a sandwich that has been pressed and toasted (what the French call "un toast"). The pressing and toasting compact and heat the filling, compress the bread, and create a pleasant crunch. Literally any sandwich can be pressed and toasted, though for best results I think the filling ought to include cheese, vegetables, and some sort of moistening condiment or dressing, or else a spread that oozes and melts when it is heated.

For best results, you should use a panini press or a double-sided electric grill that closes with enough room to fit a sandwich between the plates. Do not stuff the sandwiches so full that you cannot close the press. I have made very respectable panini in a frying pan, using a sturdy spatula or my heavy, smooth meat tenderizer to press the sandwiches on both sides while they heat.

Makes 4 sandwiches

1 ciabatta or other crusty Italian bread
2 tablespoons extra-virgin olive oil
6 ounces sweet or hot sopressatta or other Italian salami, thinly sliced
8 thin slices grilled zucchini or 4 thin slices grilled eggplant (see page 153)
1 roasted red or yellow bell pepper (see page 146), seeded and cut into 4 strips
4 thin slices ripe tomato
Kosher salt and freshly ground black pepper
6 ounces fresh mozzarella cheese, thinly sliced
¼ cup black olive paste or tapenade

Preheat a panini press or double-sided electric grill. Cut the ciabatta crosswise into 4 sections. Cut each section lengthwise in half. On each bottom half of bread spoon about ½ tablespoon of the olive oil. Divide the sopressatta on top of the oil. Arrange the zucchini, red pepper, and tomato on top of the sopressatta. Season with salt and pepper. Top with the mozzarella. Spread the black olive paste on the cut side of the top piece of bread and set on top of the sandwich. With your palm, firmly press the sandwich to compact.

Place the sandwiches, one or two at a time, into the press. Close and toast for about 8 minutes, or until the filling is warm, the cheese has melted, and the bread is toasted. Repeat with the remaining sandwiches. Alternatively, you can prepare the panini in a large skillet. Heat a dry skillet over medium-high heat. Add the

sandwiches to the pan without crowding. Using a sturdy spatula or a smooth, heavy meat tenderizer, press down on the sandwiches as they cook and toast. When the bread is browned and the filling is warm, in 4 or 5 minutes, flip and toast the other side.

PREP TIME: 10 minutes
COOKING TIME: 20 to 40 minutes
TOTAL TIME: 30 to 50 minutes

ADVANCE PREP *The panini can be assembled, wrapped, and stored in the refrigerator for up to a day before you toast them. Although the panini are best eaten immediately after toasting, to keep them warm while you finish making all of them, wrap them in foil and set them in a preheated 275° F oven until ready to serve.*

LEFTOVERS *Once toasted, panini will keep refrigerated for a couple of days, though they tend to get soggy.*

Cuban Sandwich

Before every deli in Manhattan served trendy Panini (page 87), you could find *cubanos*, traditional pressed sandwiches of roast pork, ham, pickles, and cheese, at Latin holes-in-the-wall around town. Though Cuban in origin, my favorite local version comes from a Dominican place that uses juicy pulled pork instead of roast pork. The secret is to press the sandwich while it cooks so it turns out flat and crisp. It helps to have a panini press or double-sided electric grill, but you can use a cast-iron pan and a sturdy spatula with fairly good results. This simple recipe can be enhanced with any number of fillings, such as grilled or pickled onions, flavored mayonnaise, or other meats or condiments.

Makes 4 sandwiches

1 slightly stale baguette, cut into 4 equal portions

1 to 2 tablespoons mustard

4 large, long slices dill pickle

4 slices boiled ham (about 4 ounces)

6 to 8 ounces Pulled Pork without barbecue sauce (page 376) or sliced Roast Pork (page 372)

4 thick slices mild white cheese, such as Swiss cheese, Monterey Jack, or Munster (about 4 ounces)

Preheat a panini press or double-sided electric grill, or set a dry cast-iron pan over medium heat. Slice each piece of baguette in half lengthwise without going all the way through so that you do not separate the top and bottom halves. Open them up and flatten both halves. Spread the bottom half of each piece of bread very lightly with mustard and place a slice of pickle on top. Lay a slice of ham on top of that and then a mound of pork. Top with a slice of cheese and fold the sandwich back in half. Press the sandwiches firmly to flatten.

If using a panini press or electric grill, place the sandwiches, one or two at a time depending on the size of the grill, in the center and close the grill. Cook for 5 to 8 minutes, until the sandwiches are hot and compacted, the bread is crisp, and the cheese has melted. Remove from the press and cut each sandwich in half. Repeat with remaining sandwiches and serve immediately.

If using a cast-iron pan, place one or two sandwiches in the pan and heat on a medium-high burner. Using a sturdy spatula or a smooth, heavy meat tenderizer, keep pressing down on the sandwich while it cooks. When the bottom of the baguette has toasted, 4 or 5 minutes, flip the sandwiches and press again to toast the top and melt the cheese, an-

other 3 or 4 minutes or so. Remove from the pan and slice in half. Repeat with remaining sandwiches and serve immediately.

PREP TIME: 10 minutes

COOKING TIME: 20 to 40 minutes

TOTAL TIME: 30 to 50 minutes

ADVANCE PREP *The sandwiches can be assembled, wrapped in plastic, and refrigerated for up to a day before toasting.*

LEFTOVERS *The pressed sandwiches will keep for two or three days in the refrigerator. Reheat in a 300°F oven for 15 minutes or so until the bread is crisp and the filling is warm.*

Lobster Roll

To the uninitiated, lobster rolls are a strange concept. A specialty of Maine, they are basically hot dog buns stuffed with lobster salad. (Some insist it should be a split-top potato-bread roll, but even so, it still looks and tastes a lot like a hot dog bun.) The lobster salad should be chilled and dripping with mayonnaise. When the lobster meat is sweet and in big chunks, and the roll is warm and dripping with butter, the combination of flavors and textures is downright addictive. Here's a simple recipe that will produce a very satisfying lobster roll for those who know them and an entrée into the world of the lobster roll for those who don't. You can substitute chilled cooked shrimp (page 279) or lump crab meat with perfectly delicious results.

Makes 4 rolls

12 ounces cooked lobster meat (see page 288), from 2 to 3 one-pound lobsters, cut into chunks (about 2 cups), chilled

½ cup Hellmann's or Best Foods mayonnaise

1 celery stalk, very finely diced

Juice of ½ lemon (2 tablespoons)

2 tablespoons minced flat-leaf parsley,
    tarragon, chervil, or chives, or a combination
    (optional)

Kosher salt and freshly ground black pepper

4 hot dog buns or potato rolls

3 to 4 tablespoons unsalted butter, at room
    temperature

Iceberg or other lettuce, for garnish
    (optional)

In a medium bowl, combine the lobster meat, mayonnaise, celery, lemon juice, parsley, a pinch of salt, and some pepper. Mix well to coat the lobster with the mayonnaise. Chill.

Flatten the hot dog buns without splitting them apart, if you can. Generously butter the cut side and sprinkle with some salt. Heat a cast-iron or nonstick frying pan or griddle over medium-high heat. Place the buns in the pan buttered side down and toast until golden brown, 4 or 5 minutes. (You'll smell the delicious, buttery aroma when the buns start to toast.) Remove the buns to serving plates, toasted side up. Place a lettuce leaf on top, if using, and spoon one fourth of the lobster salad on each sandwich. Pull up the sides, and serve.

PREP TIME: 10 minutes

COOKING TIME: 4 or 5 minutes

TOTAL TIME: 15 minutes

ADVANCE PREP *The salad can be made a day or two in advance, covered, and refrigerated. Toast the buns and assemble the sandwiches just before serving.*

VARIATIONS

Shrimp Roll

Substitute 2 cups chilled, cooked and peeled small shrimp (from about 12 ounces in the shell; see page 279; cut larger shrimp into chunks) for the lobster. Proceed as directed.

Crab Roll

Substitute 2 cups (1 pound) chilled lump crab meat for the lobster and proceed with the recipe as directed.

Italian Tuna and Shaved Fennel Sandwich with Black Olive Paste

The strong Mediterranean flavors in this satisfying sandwich were jointly inspired by a trip to Tunisia and my frequent visits to the original 'wichcraft sandwich shop in New York City.

Makes 4 sandwiches

1 baguette, split in half and cut into 4 sections

1 small fennel bulb

Juice of 1 lemon (about ¼ cup)

2 tablespoons extra-virgin olive oil

Kosher salt and freshly ground black pepper

¼ cup black or green olive paste or tapenade

Peel of ¼ Preserved Lemon (page 409), very
    thinly sliced (optional)

10 to 12 ounces finest imported Italian tuna
    packed in olive oil, drained

1 tablespoon harissa or other hot pepper sauce

Preheat the oven to 325°F.

Individually wrap the 4 sections of baguette in aluminum foil and set in the oven to warm, about 10 minutes. Trim the fennel bulb of any fronds or stalks and remove a slice or two from the root end. Using a mandoline, a sharp knife, or a food processor, shave the fennel as thin as possible—the shavings should be nearly transparent. Toss the fennel with the lemon juice, olive oil, a pinch of salt, and some pepper. Set aside.

Remove one of the baguette sections from the oven. Spread the bottom half with a tablespoon or so of the olive paste. Lay on top 2 to 4 slices of Preserved Lemon, if using. Arrange one fourth of the tuna on the sandwich. Dot with some of the harissa, and top with a scattering of the fennel salad. Close the sandwich and wrap up again with foil. Set aside. Repeat with the remaining bread to form 4 sandwiches. Cut each in half through the foil and serve.

PREP TIME: 20 minutes
COOKING TIME: 10 minutes
TOTAL TIME: 30 minutes

LEFTOVERS *Assembled sandwiches will keep for eight hours or so, but no more. As they sit, the bread gets a little soggy, but that isn't such a bad thing.*

Muffuletta

Here's a recipe to re-create the taste of an authentic muffuletta from the source, Central Grocery in New Orleans. Like an Italian hero only better, a true muffuletta has a generous amount of Central Grocery's famous olive salad. Although nobody has their secret recipe, you can make a perfectly respectable muffuletta if you make my olive salad (see page 6) with pitted olives. If you add a little shredded carrot, chopped celery, and cooked chopped cauliflower, you'll be even closer to the original. If you don't have olive salad handy, you can get the same taste by spreading the roll with a few tablespoons of both green and black olive pastes.

Makes 2 sandwiches

2 large, crusty Italian rolls
2 tablespoons extra-virgin olive oil
Kosher salt and freshly ground black pepper
4 ounces thinly sliced Genoa salami
4 ounces thinly sliced mortadella
4 ounces thinly sliced sharp provolone or Swiss cheese
1/2 cup Spicy Moroccan Olive Salad (page 6) or 2 tablespoons each green and black olive paste

Split the rolls in half. Spoon 1 tablespoon of olive oil on the bottom of one half of each roll. Season with salt and pepper. Arrange half of the salami, mortadella, and cheese on each roll. Divide the olive salad between the two sandwiches. Top with the top half of the roll and gently push down to compact the sandwich.

TOTAL TIME: 10 minutes

ADVANCE PREP *I happen to like these muffulettas best after they sit for 30 minutes or more before serving. This softens the bread and brings the flavors together.*

Smoked Turkey Sandwich with Green Apple, Curried Mayonnaise, and Pickled Red Onions

I like to sneak slices of green apple into sandwiches because their tart flavor and crunchy texture add pleasant, contrasting elements to many fillings. With this particular combination of flavors, smoked chicken or ham are excellent alternatives to turkey.

Makes 4 sandwiches

1/4 cup red wine vinegar
2 tablespoons sugar
1/2 medium red onion, thinly sliced

1 teaspoon curry powder

1/3 cup Hellmann's or Best Foods mayonnaise

1 medium Granny Smith apple

8 slices pumpernickel bread

6 ounces thinly sliced smoked turkey

In a small, nonstick pan over medium-high heat, heat the vinegar. Add the sugar and stir to dissolve. Put the onion in a small bowl. When the vinegar mixture boils, pour it over the onion and set aside to cool.

Mix the curry powder with 2 tablespoons water to make a thin paste. Return the small pan to medium-high heat. Pour in the curry powder mixture and cook until most of the water evaporates and you smell the strong aroma of toasted spices, about 1 minute. Be careful not to let the spices burn. Remove from the heat and cool. Stir the curry into the mayonnaise. Just before serving, peel the apple and, using a mandoline or a sharp knife, thinly slice it.

To assemble the sandwich, lay 4 slices of bread on a flat work surface. Spread with the curried mayonnaise. Arrange the turkey to cover the bread. Place a layer of sliced apple on top of the turkey and then scatter some of the pickled onion on top of that (use a fork to lift out the onion so it drains somewhat). Spread the top of the bread with more curried mayonnaise, and invert on top of the sandwich.

PREP TIME: 15 minutes

COOKING TIME: 5 minutes

TOTAL TIME: 20 minutes

ADVANCE PREP *You can prepare the onion and the mayonnaise several days in advance. Keep refrigerated.*

Soft Turkey Taco

If you have the time—it takes just an hour—brining makes the turkey in these light, spicy tacos juicier and more flavorful. You can substitute chicken if desired. Chipotles are smoked jalapeños, and chipotle sauce is available in small cans in the Latin foods section of most supermarkets. If you can find only cans of chipotles in adobo, which are more common, you can purée a few peppers with some of the adobo sauce in a food processor or blender and use this purée as a substitute.

Makes 4 servings

Kosher salt

1 pound turkey or chicken tenders

5 tablespoons chipotle sauce or puréed chipotles in adobo (see note above)

1/2 cup sour cream or plain yogurt

8 scallions, ends trimmed

8 (6-inch) corn tortillas

1 cup shredded lettuce

1/2 medium cucumber, peeled and diced

1/2 ripe Hass avocado, cubed

1 ripe medium tomato, diced

1/2 cup shredded Monterey Jack cheese (2 ounces)

1/4 cup loosely packed cilantro leaves

1 lime, quartered

If you have time to brine the turkey, place 2 tablespoons kosher salt in a small bowl or cup. Add 1/4 cup hot water to dissolve the salt. (Alternatively, you can heat the salt and water in a microwave to dissolve.) Pour this solution into a large, shallow bowl. Add 1 1/2 cups cold water and stir to combine. Place the turkey tenders in this bowl and refrigerate for 1 hour. Remove the meat, discard the brine, and rinse out the bowl.

Slice the turkey tenders on the diagonal into

strips about $1/2$ inch thick and place the strips back into the bowl. Add 4 tablespoons of the chipotle sauce or purée, and turn the meat to coat evenly with the sauce. Set aside. Stir the remaining tablespoon of chipotle sauce into the sour cream and set aside.

Preheat a charcoal, gas, or electric grill or grill pan to medium-high. Grill the scallions for 2 or 3 minutes, until tender. Set aside. Place the tortillas on the grill and cook for a minute or two, turning frequently, until they have browned and softened. Remove from the grill and wrap in a clean dish towel to keep warm. (Alternatively, you can cook them over an open-flame gas burner on high, turning them frequently to prevent burning.) Grill the marinated turkey strips for 2 or 3 minutes per side, until cooked through.

To assemble, lay out the tortillas on four plates. Divide the turkey, lettuce, cucumber, avocado, tomato, cheese, and cilantro leaves among them. Top each taco with a grilled scallion and a dollop of the sour cream mixture. Serve with a wedge of lime.

PREP TIME: 15 minutes

COOKING TIME: 10 minutes

TOTAL TIME: 1 hour 25 minutes (includes brining time)

ADVANCE PREP *You can brine the turkey up to a day in advance. You can marinate the meat in the chipotle sauce, refrigerated, for up to 12 hours.*

LEFTOVERS *Store cooked meat refrigerated in an airtight container for up to a week to use in sandwiches and salads.*

VARIATION
Soft Beef Taco
Because of its rich flavor and texture, I like to use hanger steak (aka butcher's tender) or skirt steak for tacos. Substitute 1 pound hanger steak for the turkey. Do not brine the steak, but marinate it in the chipotle sauce and proceed with the recipe as directed.

Fish Taco
A favorite of the folks In San Diego and other parts of southern California, fish tacos are easy to love. The fish—I prefer cod—is usually made in one of two ways: fried or grilled. This is a recipe for grilled fish tacos, which I think are more practical to make at home. They are great for a summer barbecue or picnic. If you don't want to bother with a grill, you can also cook the fish in a dry, hot cast-iron or nonstick pan; prepared this way, the fish is reminiscent of Cajun blackened fish.

Makes 4 servings

$1/4$ cup canola or vegetable oil

Juice of 1 lime (about 3 tablespoons)

1 tablespoon ancho chile powder

Kosher salt and freshly ground black pepper

1 pound mild, flaky white fish fillets, such as cod, halibut, or snapper

4 scallions, ends trimmed

4 ($1/4$-inch-thick) slices red onion

4 (10-inch) flour tortillas

1 cup shredded green cabbage

$1/4$ cup sour cream

Handful of cilantro leaves

Fresh Red and Yellow Tomato Salsa (page 15), Guacamole (page 14), and/or hot sauce, for serving

In a shallow container or bowl, mix the oil, lime juice, chile powder, a pinch of salt, and some freshly ground black pepper. Add the fish and turn the fillets over to coat. Cover and let marinate, refrigerated, for 30 minutes to 1 hour.

Preheat a charcoal, gas, or electric grill to medium-high.

Grill the scallions and onion slices until lightly charred, 3 or 4 minutes. Remove from the grill and set aside. Place the tortillas on the grill, and grill until soft and slightly charred, about 2 minutes per side. Remove from the grill and wrap in a clean dish towel to keep warm. Lift the fish out of the marinade, allowing some but not all of the oil to drain off. Lay the fish on the grill and grill until the flesh turns opaque white and grill marks are evident, 3 or 4 minutes per side, depending on how hot the grill is. As it is cooked, remove the fish from the grill and divide it among the 4 tortillas. Top with shredded cabbage, the grilled onion, a dollop of sour cream, a sprinkling of cilantro leaves, a grilled scallion, and a spoonful or two of salsa, guacamole, and/or hot sauce.

PREP TIME: 10 minutes

COOKING TIME: 15 to 20 minutes

TOTAL TIME: 1 to 1½ hours (includes marinating time)

ADVANCE PREP *The garnishes and the vegetables can be made several hours in advance and kept at room temperature. The fish should not marinate for much longer than 1 hour, or the marinade begins to affect the texture of the flesh.*
LEFTOVERS *The cooked fish will keep for two or three days in the refrigerator.*

Mushroom and Bean Burrito

Despite the Mexican-style ingredients, giant flour-tortilla burritos stuffed with rice, beans, cheese, guacamole, sour cream, and other fixin's are an American creation. This recipe includes a garnish of sautéed mushrooms, but you could also use the chipotle-marinated turkey, chicken, or beef from the taco recipe on page 93.

Makes 4 servings

4 (10-inch) flour tortillas
2 tablespoons canola or vegetable oil
1 small shallot or ¼ medium red onion, finely chopped
1 small garlic clove, minced
1 jalapeño, seeded and finely chopped
8 ounces button mushrooms, quartered
Juice of 1 lime (about 3 tablespoons)
¼ cup chopped fresh cilantro
Kosher salt and freshly ground black pepper
3 cups "Refried" Beans (page 204)
2 cups Rice Pilaf (page 220), or other cooked rice
8 ounces Monterey Jack cheese, shredded (1 cup)
¼ medium sweet white onion, minced
2 scallions, white and green parts, chopped
Sour cream, Guacamole (page 14), Fresh Red and Yellow Tomato Salsa (page 15), and/or hot sauce, for serving

Preheat the oven to 300° F. Wrap the tortillas well in aluminum foil and set in the oven to heat.

In a large skillet, heat the oil over medium-high heat. Add the shallot and cook until soft, about 4 minutes. Add the garlic and jalapeño and cook for another minute or until you can smell the garlic. Turn up the heat to high and add the mushrooms. Sauté until the mushrooms have browned, given off their water, and shrunk, about 7 minutes. The liquid should have evaporated from the pan. Add the lime juice and 2 tablespoons of the cilantro. Season with salt and pepper and set aside.

Remove the tortillas from the oven and lay them on a work surface. Turn up the oven to 350°F. Toward the bottom of each tortilla, about one third of the way up, spoon ³⁄₄ cup of refried beans in a line, leaving a 1¹⁄₂-inch margin at the edges. Top with ¹⁄₂ cup rice and one fourth of the sautéed mushroom mixture. Sprinkle with ¹⁄₄ cup cheese and 1 or 2 tablespoons minced onion. Fold up the bottom over the filling and fold in the sides. Roll up the tortilla to envelope the filling. Wrap each tortilla in aluminum foil and set on a baking sheet. Return to the oven for about 15 minutes, or until the filling has heated through and the cheese has melted (insert a metal skewer or the point of a knife into the center of the burrito and press it on the back of your hand to check the temperature of the filling). Slice each burrito in half through the foil and serve with scallions, sour cream, guacamole, salsa, and hot sauce.

PREP TIME: 10 minutes
COOKING TIME: 30 minutes
TOTAL TIME: 40 minutes

ADVANCE PREP *The individual components of the filling can be prepared three or four days in advance and refrigerated.*

Hamburger Heaven

My friend George Motz likes hamburgers so much that he traveled across America for two years to make a documentary about them. Appropriately, it's called *Hamburger America*, and watching the movie makes me very hungry. Everyone in it has been serving the same kind of hamburgers for more than forty years. And besides a few odd toppings—like peanut butter or a quarter pound of butter—none of the burgers he filmed is made from anything more than ground beef.

Like George, I have to say I am a bit of a purist when it comes to burgers. I don't need braised short ribs or sake-drinking cows to make me happy. All I need is a decent amount of freshly ground, naturally raised meat with plenty of fat and I'm happy. Salt, pepper, and the most basic seasonings are all that are called for if your meat is top quality. The only trick is making sure you have mixed your meat well to evenly distribute the seasonings.

Makes 4 to 5 hamburgers

1¹⁄₂ pounds ground beef (chuck, not lean),
    preferably from naturally raised cows (see
    page 347)
1 tablespoon Worcestershire sauce or Dijon
    mustard (optional)
Kosher salt and freshly ground black pepper
4 hamburger buns
Ketchup, pickles, onions, tomatoes, lettuce,
    mustard, mayonnaise, or whatever garnishes
    you like

In a large bowl with a wooden spoon, or in a wooden chopping bowl with a metal chopper, combine the meat with the Worcestershire or Dijon, if using. Add ¹⁄₂ teaspoon salt if you are using the Worcestershire or Dijon, and 1¹⁄₄ teaspoons if you are not. Add a generous amount of pepper. Mix the meat well to be sure there will be no unpleasant pockets of salt in your burgers. Divide the meat into four or five equal portions. Shape each portion into a ball, and then flatten each ball to form a patty about 1 inch thick.

Heat a dry cast-iron skillet, grill pan, broiler, or grill until quite hot. Place the burgers in the skillet, in a pan under the broiler, or on the grill and cook for about 4 minutes per side for rare, 5 to 6 for medium, and up to 10 for well done.

PREP TIME: 5 minutes
COOKING TIME: 8 to 20 minutes
TOTAL TIME: 15 to 25 minutes

ADVANCE PREP The hamburgers can be mixed and shaped in advance. Wrap them in plastic wrap and keep them in the refrigerator for up to one day or freeze for up to one month. Defrost in the refrigerator overnight before cooking.

LEFTOVERS Fully cooked, hamburgers will keep for about four days in the fridge. Crumble leftover burgers into spaghetti sauce or chili rather than serve them again as burgers, which are never as good as when they are hot off the grill.

VARIATIONS
Gussied Up Burgers
If you are not a minimalist, you might consider mixing any number of things into your hamburger meat, including finely chopped onion, minced garlic, chopped jalapeños, ketchup, raw egg, bread crumbs, minced capers, minced anchovies, and/or finely chopped flat-leaf parsley.

Cheeseburgers
Save your fine, farmstead cheeses for your cheese plate. Hamburgers call for slices of good ol' American cheese. Sure, Cheddar, Jack, Swiss, and blue are tasty, but they don't give you that quintessential cheeseburger flavor.

PIZZA AND FOCACCIA
I've grouped these two seemingly different dishes together because, when it comes down to it, they are both just flat breads baked with stuff on top. (I've put them together with sandwiches, because what is a pizza but a large open-faced sandwich?) The distinction between pizza and focaccia may reside in the sauce and cheese, which some say make a pizza unique. But I've had "pizza" with neither and "focaccia" with both! Shape is another variable—focaccia is usually rectangular; pizza is usually round. But again, that distinction doesn't hold firm. And where does the square Sicilian "slice" fit in?

I think the most important difference between pizza and focaccia is in the dough. But for simplicity's sake (and because I usually have one or the other on hand in the freezer), I use Quick Pizza Dough (page 98) and Neapolitan-style Pizza Dough (page 99) interchangeably to make pizza or focaccia. The quick dough has some olive oil in it so the baked crust is shorter (as in less chewy) and less breadlike. The Neapolitan dough has a good yeasty flavor and chewy texture. In the end it comes down to a question of time. Quick Pizza Dough can be made in a couple of hours. Neapolitan Pizza Dough needs almost a day of fermentation.

A lot of time and money have been spent figuring out how to bake a pizza in a home oven. Terra-cotta tiles, natural stones, perforated pans, and other technologies have been invented to recreate that coal- or wood-fired oven taste in a household range. What I'm about to say is blasphemous, but true: having tried plenty of different techniques, I manage to get the best results out of my oven without any newfangled pizza technology. I set a rack as high as it will go—heat rises, so the top of the oven is hotter than the bottom. I turn the dial as high as it will go—about 500° F. And I bake the pie in an ordinary, round, aluminum pizza pan, without any holes in the bottom. With this low-tech arrangement, I find the topping and the dough bake at the same rate and are done at the same time. The crust is gently risen and crisp, and thoroughly browned. Of course, every oven is different and if you have a technique that works well for you in yours, please feel free to use it.

On to the topping. As with most things in the kitchen, I am a believer in restraint when it comes to pizza and focaccia toppings. The sight of pies piled high with broccoli and chicken and cheese in New York pizzerias offends my pizza sensibility. I prefer the simple austerity of a schmear of tomato sauce and a sparse layer of cheese baked to bubbly golden brown. I think pizza is about the crust as much as it's about the topping, so if your crust is flavorful and crunchy, you shouldn't have to cover it up with loads of junk.

Pizza

Makes one 14-inch pie or two 10-inch pies

2 teaspoons coarse semolina or cornmeal
½ batch Quick Pizza Dough (page 98) or
    Neapolitan-Style Pizza Dough (page 99)
Your choice of topping from pages 100 to102

Place a rack in the top portion of the oven, as high as it will go, and preheat the oven to 500° F. Sprinkle the semolina or cornmeal evenly over the bottom of a round aluminum pizza pan, cookie sheet, or half-sheet pan, or two pans if baking smaller pies.

Remove the dough from the refrigerator. Flatten it into one or two disks and let the dough sit at room temperature for 15 to 20 minutes to take the chill off. Pick each disk up in your hands to stretch it into a sort of Frisbee. My technique is to hold it so the disk is perpendicular to the work surface and stretch it gently between my fingers and thumb as I turn it like a steering wheel. Gravity will help it to stretch. Tug gently on any part that seems thicker than the others. (Although it is disheartening to make any holes in the dough, they don't really affect the finished pizza.) When the dough is about 12 inches round for large pies or 8 inches round for small pies, lay it out on the prepared pan and finish stretching it on the pan, pulling at opposite sides until it is around 14 (or 10) inches in diameter. Use your fingertips to push the dough to the edges of the pan. Sometimes it helps to stick the dough to the side of the pan while you stretch the other side. (Note: I know some people who swear that a rolling pin is the best way to make a pizza crust. It works well enough, but it doesn't give you the same sense of pride or tactile sensation that making a hand-stretched dough does.) If making smaller pies, repeat with the second disk of dough.

Cover the pizza evenly with your topping of choice and bake for the time specified for each topping. I tend to prefer my pizza and focaccia cooked more rather than less, so that the crust is crisp and the topping is nicely browned. Serve hot.

PREP TIME: 10 minutes
COOKING TIME: 10 to 25 minutes, depending on the topping
TOTAL TIME: 20 to 35 minutes

Quick Pizza Dough

This is my sister Carrie's recipe for a simple, tasty dough that can be whipped up in a pinch to make a pizza, focaccia, or any number of baked (or even grilled) savory pies. According to the guidelines of the governing body of Italian pizzas, Verace Pizza Napoletana (I'm not kidding), there should be no olive oil in the crust. But without the benefit of a long fermentation, I think the dough needs a little olive oil, which adds flavor and texture when baked. There is also quite a bit of yeast in the dough, given the amount of flour—another way to cheat by adding flavor while cutting back on time.

Makes 2¼ pounds dough, enough for two 14-inch pizzas or four 10-inch individual pies

> 4 teaspoons (1½ packets) active dry yeast or 3 teaspoons instant yeast
> 1⅓ cups lukewarm water (about 110°F)
> 6 tablespoons extra-virgin olive oil, plus extra for greasing the bowl
> 4 cups all-purpose flour or a combination of 2 cups all-purpose flour and 2 cups bread flour
> 1½ teaspoons kosher salt

TO MAKE THE DOUGH BY HAND

Place the yeast in the bottom of a large bowl. Add the lukewarm water and stir with a heavy whisk or wooden spoon to dissolve. Add the 6 tablespoons of olive oil and 1 cup of the flour and whisk until smooth. Add another cup of flour and the salt and mix well. Add the remaining 2 cups of flour and stir with a wooden spoon to incorporate as much of the flour as you can. Turn the dough out onto a clean work surface and scrape out all the flour and flakes of dough from the bowl. Begin kneading the dough with both hands, folding the dough over, pressing it out, turning it a half turn and folding it again. Incorporate any flour and dough flakes on the counter as you work. After about 10 minutes of kneading, the dough should have a soft, smooth texture, and it won't be sticky. Shape the dough into a ball.

TO MAKE THE DOUGH WITH AN ELECTRIC MIXER

Place the yeast in the bowl of an electric mixer fitted with a paddle attachment. Add the lukewarm water and stir with the paddle attachment on low to dissolve. Add the 6 tablespoons of olive oil and 1 cup of the flour and beat on medium-low speed for a minute or so until smooth. Switch to the dough hook. Add another cup of flour and the salt and mix well. Add the remaining 2 cups of flour and put the machine on low until the dough forms a mass around the hook. Let the machine knead the dough for 2 minutes. Turn the dough out onto a clean work surface and scrape out the bowl. Knead for a minute or two, until the dough is smooth and elastic. Shape the dough into a ball.

Place a teaspoon of olive oil in the bottom of a large, clean bowl. Place the ball of dough in the bowl and move it around to coat with the oil. Cover the bowl with a clean dish towel and set in a warm place, such as near a preheating oven or in an oven that has a pilot light, to rise until the dough doubles in bulk, 45 minutes to 1 hour. Punch down the dough and divide in half (or into quarters, if making smaller pies).

PREP TIME: 15 minutes
TOTAL TIME: 1 hour 15 minutes

***ADVANCE PREP** The dough will keep in a plastic bag in the refrigerator for up to three days or it can be frozen for up to two months. Defrost overnight in the fridge before using.*

Neapolitan-Style Pizza Dough

Here's a recipe for pizza dough that adheres to the regulations of the Verace Pizza Napoletana association. It has a texture and flavor more like bread than Quick Pizza Dough (page 98), and it is my favorite for traditional pizzas, such as Pizza Margherita (page 101). Make it when you have enough time to let the dough rise for at least 8 hours.

Makes 2½ pounds dough, enough for two 14-inch pizzas or four 10-inch individual pies

- 4½ cups unbleached all-purpose flour, or a combination of 2½ cups all-purpose flour and 2 cups bread flour
- ¾ teaspoon instant yeast or 1 teaspoon dry active yeast dissolved in 2 tablespoons warm water
- 2 teaspoons kosher salt
- 1½ cups warm water (about 110°F)
- Extra-virgin olive oil, for greasing the bowl

TO MAKE THE DOUGH BY HAND

In a large bowl, combine the flour, yeast, and salt, and mix well with a wooden spoon. Pour in the water and continue stirring until a dough begins to form. Turn the dough out onto a clean work surface. Be sure to scrape out the bowl and scrape off the spoon. Keeping your hands floured with the excess flour on the dough, knead the dough for about 10 minutes, until it becomes smooth and elastic and is no longer sticky. Shape the dough into a ball.

TO MAKE THE DOUGH WITH AN ELECTRIC MIXER

Place the flour, yeast, and salt in the bowl of an electric mixer fitted with a dough hook. Turn the machine to low for a few seconds to combine. Pour in the water, and with the machine on low, work the mixture into a smooth dough. As the dough starts to form into a ball around the dough hook, you can increase the speed slightly to knead for a minute or two. The dough should be smooth and elastic. Turn it out onto a lightly floured work surface and knead for just a minute or two by hand to form a smooth ball.

Place a teaspoon of olive oil in a large, clean bowl. Put the dough in the bowl and move it around to coat with the oil. Cover the bowl with plastic wrap and lay a clean dish towel on top. Set in a warm, dark place to rise for about 8 hours, until the dough just more than doubles in bulk. Remove the towel and plastic wrap, punch down the dough to compact it to its original size, and divide in half (or in quarters).

PREP TIME: 15 minutes
TOTAL TIME: 8½ hours (includes rising times)

ADVANCE PREP The dough will keep in a plastic bag in the refrigerator for up to three days or it can be frozen for up to two months. Defrost overnight in the fridge before using.

Focaccia

Focaccia dough is traditionally formed into a rectangle. Omit the semolina. Flatten the dough into a square or rectangle and place it on a well-oiled half-sheet pan or cookie sheet. Using your fingertips, push, pull, and stretch the dough into as close to a rectangular shape as you can get it. If the dough becomes too elastic and retracts as soon as you push or stretch it, let it sit undisturbed for 20 minutes to relax the gluten, and then try to stretch it again. Sometimes for leverage I tack one corner of the dough over the edge of the sheet pan and then pull the rest of the dough from there. Top as desired and bake as described for pizza on page 97, increasing the baking time as indicated in the recipe.

TOPPINGS

Each of these topping recipes makes enough to top one 14-inch pizza or two 10-inch pies.

White Pizza

About as simple as it gets.

    4 ounces buffalo mozzarella or fresh mozzarella,
        thinly sliced (optional)
    2 tablespoons extra-virgin olive oil
    1 large garlic clove, minced
    1½ teaspoons minced fresh herbs, such as
        rosemary, oregano, or marjoram (optional)
    3 tablespoons freshly grated Parmigiano
        Reggiano cheese
    Kosher salt and freshly ground black pepper

KITCHEN SENSE

MAKING PIZZA ON A GRILL

Grilled pizza has become very trendy lately. One taste of a pizza hot off the grill with a crisp, slightly smoky crust and you know why. The technique is simple, though it requires a small leap of faith to believe that the dough will actually cook properly and not adhere to the grill. Use any pizza dough. Be sure that your grill is clean and has a cover. Have all of your toppings assembled near the grill and ready to go. And make sure the grill is well heated before beginning.

On a well-oiled sheet pan, pull and stretch the pizza dough into a thin, roundish shape and let it rest for 15 minutes before grilling. Move the pan over to the grill. Stretch the dough again to make it as thin as possible without tearing it and lay it over the hot grill. Don't worry if it is not perfectly round. Let the dough cook for a minute or two, until it begins to rise, bubble, and brown. When it is firm enough to lift, use tongs to turn it over. Immediately arrange the toppings on the cooked side of the dough. Cover the grill and cook for about 2 minutes more, or until the cheese has melted, the toppings have bubbled, and the dough has risen and browned. Lift off the grill and serve immediately.

If using mozzarella, arrange the slices on the dough.

Using the back of a spoon or a pastry brush, spread the oil over the pizza. Sprinkle the garlic, herbs if using, and grated cheese evenly on top. Season to taste with salt and pepper and bake until crisp, about 15 minutes.

Pizza Margherita

This is the classic pizza topping from Naples, arguably the home of the best pizza on earth.

> 5 or 6 small, very ripe plum tomatoes, cut into
> ½-inch chunks, or 5 or 6 canned plum
> tomatoes, preferably San Marzano, with juice
> 3 ounces fresh mozzarella, thinly sliced
> 1½ tablespoons freshly grated Parmigiano
> Reggiano or Pecorino Romano cheese
> 1½ tablespoons extra-virgin olive oil
> Pinch of kosher salt
> Freshly ground black pepper
> 3 or 4 basil leaves

Scatter the fresh tomatoes over the crust or squeeze the canned tomatoes between your fingers onto the crust. Arrange the slices of mozzarella evenly on top of the pizza and sprinkle with the Parmigiano. Drizzle the olive oil over the pizza and season to taste with salt and pepper. Bake for about 20 minutes, until the cheese is browned and bubbly and the crust is crisp. When you take the pizza out of the oven, scatter the basil on top and serve.

A New York Slice

New York–style pizza is made with sauce, not tomatoes. To be true to the sad, present-day pizza reality, you should use the rubbery, pre-shredded mozzarella sold in grocery stores, but for a more traditional pie with better flavor, I recommend only fresh mozzarella.

> ⅓ cup Quick Tomato Sauce (page 250)
> ⅔ cup shredded fresh mozzarella cheese
> 3 ounces pepperoni, thinly sliced (optional)
> 1½ tablespoons extra-virgin olive oil

> 1½ tablespoons freshly grated Parmigiano
> Reggiano or Pecorino Romano cheese
> Pinch of crushed red pepper flakes
> Pinch of dried oregano

With the back of a spoon, spread the sauce evenly over the crust. Sprinkle the mozzarella cheese on top and arrange the slices of pepperoni, if using, on top of the cheese. Drizzle with olive oil. Bake 20 to 25 minutes, until the cheese and the crust are nicely browned. Remove from the oven and sprinkle with the Parmigiano, red pepper flakes, and dried oregano.

Eggplant Focaccia

When I can find them, I use a variety of eggplants of different sizes and colors to make an attractive pattern and to give a more complex eggplant flavor.

> ½ small eggplant (6 ounces), sliced paper-thin
> lengthwise
> Kosher salt
> 3 tablespoons extra-virgin olive oil
> 1 garlic clove, minced
> 1½ teaspoons minced fresh herbs, such as
> rosemary, oregano, marjoram, or basil
> Freshly ground black pepper

Lay out the eggplant slices on a plate and sprinkle both sides with 3 teaspoons of salt. Let sit at room temperature for about 30 minutes, or until the salt draws out water from the eggplant. Rinse the slices under cold water and pat dry.

Arrange the eggplant in an attractive pattern on the pizza crust. Spoon or brush half of the oil evenly over the eggplant and on the edge of the dough. Sprinkle the garlic and herbs evenly over the top. Bake for 25 to 30 minutes, until the eggplant and the crust are nicely browned. Remove from the oven and brush with the remaining olive oil and sprinkle with additional salt and black pepper to taste.

Potato Focaccia

This is one of my favorite types of focaccia. I cut it into small rectangles and serve it as an hors d'oeuvre.

1 large Red Bliss or Yukon Gold potato
   (12 ounces)
3 tablespoons extra-virgin olive oil
1 1/2 teaspoons minced fresh rosemary
Kosher salt and freshly ground black pepper

Preheat the oven to 350°F.

Bake the potato for about 35 to 40 minutes. It should give ever so slightly when pressed, but still be firm. Remove from the oven and cool. Peel and slice very thin. (I use a mandoline to get paper-thin slices.) Arrange the potato slices in an attractive pattern on the crust. Spoon or brush half of the olive oil evenly over the potato. Sprinkle with the rosemary, salt, and pepper. Bake for about 25 minutes, until the potatoes and the crust are nicely brown and crisp. Remove from the oven, brush or drizzle with the remaining olive oil, and serve.

■ ■ ■

Breakfast, Brunch, and Eggs

I F I HAD TO CHOOSE, I would say breakfast is my favorite meal of the day, followed closely by brunch. Before I go to sleep at night I think about what I'm going to have for breakfast the next morning. I'm not like those people who eat the same thing every morning of their lives. I mix it up, making scrambled eggs with scallions and a tomato salad one morning, and cold cereal and toast with peanut butter the next. I'm one of the few westerners I know who, while traveling in Japan, enjoyed the traditional breakfast of steamed rice, pickled vegetables, seaweed salad, and broth.

In the mood for pancakes but craving a salad? At brunch you can have them both. Brunch is a thoroughly American invention, but it is quickly becoming popular around the world. One of my favorite bakery/cafés in Paris now serves "le Brunch" to young Parisians excited to have another excuse to share a meal. It's becoming popular in Italy, too. The advantage of brunch is that you simultaneously get both sides of the flavor spectrum, savory and sweet.

While people in New York meet regularly in restaurants for power breakfasts and ritual Sunday brunches, I am almost always disappointed by the food when I have either of those meals outside my home. It is so easy and inexpensive to make breakfast and brunch dishes better than almost anything you are ever served in a restaurant that it's almost never worth the price or the schlep to go out.

What's more, I think brunch is an excellent way to entertain. The food is easy to prepare. (If you have a few jars of jam, some eggs, a piece of good cheese, and some ripe fruit, you practically have brunch already made.) The timing means you can clean up and still have the afternoon to yourself; and people are almost always more chipper on Sunday morning than they are after a long day of work during the week. Inviting guests for brunch requires a little planning since you don't want to get up at four in the morning to start cooking. Choose a menu with a good mix of dishes, some of which can be prepared in advance, some served hot, some served cold. Do as much as you can the day before, including setting the table before you go to bed, and ask a guest to pick up bagels on her way over so you don't have to leave the house in the morning.

Breakfast Strudel

I served this "strudel" as an entrée at my sister Carrie's wedding brunch. It's ideal for a large crowd because it's one of those rare breakfast egg dishes you can make and assemble in advance. But it's also simple enough to whip up for a romantic breakfast for two. You can scale the recipe up or down as needed. For a refresher on working with phyllo, see page 106.

Makes 4 to 6 servings

6 tablespoons (¾ stick) unsalted butter

1 small white or yellow onion, chopped

2 tablespoons heavy cream

5 large eggs

Kosher salt and freshly ground black pepper

2 ounces smoked sturgeon or smoked salmon, diced

1 tablespoon finely chopped flat-leaf parsley

4 sheets phyllo dough

2 ounces crumbled feta cheese (about ¼ cup)

Melt 3 tablespoons of the butter and set aside to cool. Place the remaining 3 tablespoons of butter in a large skillet and set over medium-high heat. Add the onion and cook until translucent, about 5 minutes. While the onion is cooking, beat the heavy cream and the eggs together in a medium bowl until light and fluffy. Season with salt and pepper. When the onion is soft, add the smoked fish and cook for a minute. Pour in the egg mixture and continue cooking, stirring, just until the eggs set and are no longer runny; they should still be quite moist. Remove from the heat, transfer to a clean medium bowl, stir in the parsley, and let cool.

Preheat the oven to 450° F.

To form the strudel, lay out one sheet of phyllo and brush liberally with the melted butter. Fold the sheet in half crosswise and brush again with butter. Repeat with another sheet of phyllo, and place the second on top of the first, creating four layers of dough. Arrange half the cooled egg mixture in a log along the long end of the rectangle of phyllo, leaving a 1-inch border free on each of the three sides. Sprinkle with half of the feta. Fold the short edges of the phyllo rectangle over the egg mixture, then roll up to form a longish tube, like a strudel. Brush the dough with melted butter as you roll it up. Transfer to a parchment-lined baking sheet. Repeat with the remaining phyllo and egg mixture.

Brush the strudels with any remaining butter and bake for about 15 minutes, or until golden brown and crisp. Remove from the oven, cool slightly, and slice on the diagonal with a serrated knife before serving.

PREP TIME: 25 minutes

COOKING TIME: 20 minutes

TOTAL TIME: 45 minutes

ADVANCE PREP *The strudels can be assembled up to a day in advance. Wrap in plastic and refrigerate until ready to bake.*

LEFTOVERS *The strudels will keep for three or four days in the refrigerator. They can be crisped in a 325° F oven.*

French Toast

Despite its name, French toast is about as American as Sunday brunch. You can use any stale bread to make it, but my favorite is stale challah (Jewish egg bread) sliced about 1 inch thick. The Italian Christmas bread

WORKING WITH PHYLLO

Every good home cook should know how to work with phyllo because there isn't much to learn, and with a package of phyllo in the freezer, you are never very far from an impressive hors d' oeuvre, appetizer, entrée, or dessert. Phyllo are the paper-thin sheets of dough (the word is Greek for "leaf") that are used to make delicate sweet and savory pastries, such as baklava or spaniko-pita. Phyllo is similar to strudel dough (and in fact it's what I use for strudel).

To use frozen phyllo it has to be defrosted first, preferably overnight in the refrigerator. Slow defrosting alleviates condensation on the package, which can sometimes create sticky patches on the dough. In a hurry, you can defrost the dough at room temperature and forgo the loss. The secret to attaining crisp, buttery phyllo in pastries is using a lot of butter and stacking the layers at least three or four sheets high. Because phyllo dries out very easily, have your butter (I use unsalted so I can control the seasoning) melted and cooled before you unwrap the dough.

Once defrosted, open the box and the internal packaging and unwrap the phyllo. The sheets of dough are usually folded in half, with a sheet of waxed paper in between the two halves, and then rolled up to fit in the box. Unroll and unfold the phyllo but don't remove the paper. Lay the sheets of dough on a clean, flat work surface with the paper on top. Cover with a clean, damp kitchen towel that has been thoroughly wrung out. This will keep the dough from drying out. Be sure to keep whatever dough you are not using covered while you work. Place one sheet of dough in front of you, and using a pastry brush, brush it with a generous amount of melted butter all the way to the edges. You can fold the phyllo in half and brush with more butter to create the first layers, or place another sheet on top and brush that, depending on how large a piece of pastry you need.

For added texture and flavor, you can sprinkle ingredients between the layers of phyllo as you stack them. When I'm making a dessert strudel, I use a very light sprinkling of a mixture of ground nuts, sugar, cinnamon, and bread, cake, or cookie crumbs between the layers. For savory dishes, I sometimes use bread crumbs that I season myself. In addition to their flavor and texture contribution, bread crumbs between the layers help keep the pastry dry and crisp as it bakes. For the same reason, I like to bake phyllo pastries at a high temperature, at or above 400°F, which causes the pastry to turn golden brown and to crisp nicely.

---

panettone also makes delicious French toast when stale. Be sure to let the bread soak up the egg-and-milk mixture; in my opinion, there's nothing more disappointing than a golden-brown piece of French toast that's bready in the middle instead of custardy. In my family, we like a crunchy granulated sugar coating, but feel free to pour on the maple syrup.

Makes 4 servings

2 large eggs
2/3 cup whole milk
1/3 cup half-and-half, or additional whole milk
2 teaspoons pure vanilla extract
1/4 teaspoon ground cinnamon

About 4 tablespoons (½ stick) unsalted butter
Eight ¾- to 1-inch-thick slices day-old bread,
    preferably challah or panettone
2 tablespoons sugar

Preheat the oven to 350°F.

In a wide, shallow bowl, beat the eggs with the milk and half-and-half until well blended and frothy. Beat in the vanilla and cinnamon (don't worry that the cinnamon will sort of float on top). In a large, heavy pan, such as a cast-iron one, heat a tablespoon or so of the butter over medium-high heat. As the butter is melting, dip a piece or two of bread (depending on the size of your bowl) into the egg mixture. Push the bread down for a few seconds, then flip it over and let it sit. When the butter begins to sizzle audibly, lift the bread out of the bowl with a spatula or large fork, drain it for a few seconds, and transfer it to the hot pan. Repeat with another piece or two of bread so that the pan is full, but the bread is not touching.

Fry the bread until crisp around the edges and dark golden brown, 6 to 8 minutes. Peek underneath to make sure it is cooking evenly. If the center is browning faster than the edges, rotate the slices in the pan. When the bottom is evenly browned, flip the French toast and cook for 3 or 4 minutes to brown the second side. Transfer the French toast to a cookie sheet in a single layer while you finish cooking the rest in batches, using the remaining butter, bread, and batter. Let the pan cool for a minute off the heat between batches so the butter doesn't burn.

Once the last pieces of French toast are on the cookie sheet, sprinkle the toast with the sugar. Set the sheet in the oven for 8 to 10 minutes to melt the sugar and heat and crisp up the French toast.

PREP TIME: 10 minutes
COOKING TIME: 40 minutes
TOTAL TIME: 50 minutes

ADVANCE PREP You can keep French toast warm in a 250°F oven for a maximum of 15 minutes before it begins to dry out.
LEFTOVERS Leftovers can be kept for a day or two in the refrigerator. Reheat them in the microwave or in a 300°F oven.

VARIATION
Lemon- or Orange-Infused French Toast
Omit the cinnamon and reduce the vanilla to 1 teaspoon. Add 1 tablespoon lemon or orange liqueur and 1 teaspoon grated lemon or orange zest to the egg mixture.

Buttermilk Pancakes
This pancake recipe is my old standby. It never disappoints. Many is the time I have served these simple buttermilk pancakes to guests who have declared them the best they have ever eaten. They are thin, feathery light, and delicate, with what could only be described as an intense pancake flavor. You can increase the recipe or cut it in half as necessary. While the pancakes are cooking, add whatever flavorings you like, such as chocolate chips, blueberries, banana slices, or nuts.
Makes 3 or 4 servings

About 4 tablespoons (½ stick) unsalted butter

1 cup unbleached all-purpose flour

2 teaspoons sugar

½ teaspoon baking powder

¼ teaspoon baking soda

½ teaspoon kosher salt

1 large egg

¾ cup buttermilk

¼ cup milk

In a small saucepan or the microwave, melt 2 tablespoons of the butter. Set aside to cool. In a medium bowl, combine the flour, sugar, baking powder, baking soda, and salt. Mix with a fork to blend. In a small bowl, beat together the egg, buttermilk, and milk. Be sure the egg is thoroughly blended. Pour the egg mixture into the dry ingredients and stir with a fork to make a smooth batter. Just before all of the flour is incorporated, stir in the melted butter.

Meanwhile, in a large, heavy frying pan, preferably a cast-iron one, heat about 1 table-spoon of the remaining butter over medium heat. When the butter is sizzling, fill the pan with pancakes, using about 3 tablespoons batter for each one. Avoid crowding; the pancakes shouldn't touch. Once the pancakes have set, turn down the heat to low. Cook until the pancakes are bubbly and the edges have browned, about 4 minutes. If the pancakes aren't cooking evenly, carefully rotate them in the pan. Flip the pancakes and cook the second side for 2 minutes or so until browned. Serve immediately. Remove the pan from the heat for a minute or so to cool slightly between batches. Repeat, adding more butter to the pan before cooking the next batch.

PREP TIME: 10 minutes

COOKING TIME: 25 minutes

TOTAL TIME: 35 minutes

ADVANCE PREP The batter can be mixed up to 1 hour before making the pancakes. Keep it at room temperature.

LEFTOVERS Once cooked, the pancakes can be refrigerated for three or four days, though the texture doesn't hold up well. To reheat, microwave them on high for about 25 seconds apiece.

Multigrain Pancakes

Despite the combination of whole grains, these healthful pancakes have a light, delicate texture and flavor. You can substitute other grain flours for the rye and whole wheat, such as oat or buckwheat. The pancakes are delicious plain, or you can add any of your favorite pancake fillings, such as blueberries, chocolate chips, pecans, or sliced bananas.

Makes 4 servings

About 4 tablespoons (½ stick) unsalted butter

¼ cup rye flour

¼ cup whole wheat flour

½ cup unbleached all-purpose flour

2 tablespoons cornmeal

1 tablespoon ground flax seed

2 tablespoons sugar

1½ teaspoons baking powder

Scant ¼ teaspoon baking soda

¾ teaspoon kosher salt

2 large eggs

1¾ cups buttermilk or sour milk, or plain yogurt or sour cream thinned with milk

1 teaspoon pure vanilla extract

In a small pan or the microwave, melt 2 tablespoons of the butter. Set aside to cool. In a medium bowl, combine the rye flour, whole wheat flour, all-purpose flour, cornmeal, flax seed, sugar, baking powder, baking soda, and salt, and mix well to blend. In a small bowl, beat together the eggs, buttermilk, melted butter, and vanilla. Pour the egg mixture into the dry ingredients and mix with a fork or whisk just until blended. Do not overmix.

Meanwhile, in a large, heavy frying pan, preferably a cast-iron one, heat about 1 tablespoon of the remaining unsalted butter over medium heat. When the butter is sizzling, fill the pan with pancakes, using about 3 tablespoons batter for each one. Avoid crowding; the pancakes shouldn't touch. Once the pancakes have set, turn down the heat to low. Cook until the pancakes are bubbly and the edges have browned, about 4 minutes. If the pancakes aren't cooking evenly, carefully rotate them in the pan. Flip the pancakes and cook the second side for 2 minutes or so until browned. Serve immediately. Remove the pan from the heat for a minute or so to cool slightly between batches. Repeat, adding more butter to the pan before cooking the next batch.

PREP TIME: 10 minutes
COOKING TIME: 25 minutes
TOTAL TIME: 35 minutes

ADVANCE PREP *The batter can be mixed up to 1 hour before making the pancakes. Keep it at room temperature.*
LEFTOVERS *Once cooked, these pancakes can be refrigerated for three or four days. Because of the various grains, which provide texture, they actually reheat very well. Microwave them on high for about 25 seconds apiece.*

Cranberry Johnnycakes

This recipe produces hefty cornmeal pancakes studded with dried cranberries that are thoroughly satisfying. Though they are substantial they aren't dense because the yogurt that holds them together makes them light and because I use less cornmeal than for a traditional johnnycake. For a different effect you can substitute semolina for the cornmeal and use any dried fruit in place of the cranberries. Serve with warm pure maple syrup.

Makes 4 servings

About 6 tablespoons (3/4 stick) unsalted butter
1 cup unbleached all-purpose flour
1/2 cup cornmeal or semolina
3 tablespoons sugar
2 teaspoons baking powder
1 teaspoon baking soda
Pinch of kosher salt
1/4 cup dried cranberries or other dried fruit, chopped
2 large eggs
1 1/4 cups plain yogurt or a combination of sour cream and buttermilk or milk

In a small saucepan or in the microwave, melt 4 tablespoons of the butter and set aside to cool. Meanwhile, in a medium bowl, combine the flour, cornmeal, sugar, baking powder, baking soda, and salt. Mix in the cranberries. In a small bowl, beat the eggs. Add the yogurt and mix well. Add this mixture to the flour mixture along with the melted butter and stir just until blended. The batter will be quite thick, almost the texture of pudding.

Heat a large cast-iron or nonstick skillet over medium-high heat. Add some of the remaining butter. When the foaming subsides, spoon about ¼ cup of the batter into the pan to make each pancake. Don't crowd the pan. The batter will seem gloppy, but it will spread out as it heats. When the surfaces of the pancakes begin to bubble and the undersides are brown, 3 or 4 minutes, flip and cook for another 3 minutes or so until the second sides have browned. Remove from the pan and serve immediately. Allow the pan to cool slightly off the heat for a minute or so before adding more butter and cooking the second batch of pancakes.

PREP TIME: 10 minutes

COOKING TIME: 25 minutes

TOTAL TIME: 35 minutes

ADVANCE PREP *You can mix the dry and liquid ingredients in advance, but do not combine them until just before you intend to cook the pancakes.* **LEFTOVERS** *The texture of these pancakes lends itself to reheating better than most. Store leftovers wrapped in the fridge for up to four days. Reheat in the microwave on high for 25 seconds per pancake.*

Yeast-Raised Waffles

I gave up on my quest for the perfect waffle recipe when I stumbled on a yeast-raised waffle recipe by Marion Cunningham, the woman responsible for reviving and revising *The Fannie Farmer Cookbook*. Actually I saw the recipe in someone else's book and thought I had stumbled on something relatively undiscovered. Since then I have seen references to Cunningham's famous yeast-raised waffles in cookbooks and magazine articles all over the place. I have adapted her recipe for instant yeast, my preference for home use. These waffles have a delicate texture, a superb flavor, and a nice crunch. I really do think they are perfect. The only difficulty is remembering to mix up the batter the night before so the yeast can work its magic overnight.

Makes 4 servings

2½ cups milk

2 cups unbleached all-purpose flour

2½ teaspoons (1 packet) active dry yeast or 2 teaspoons instant yeast

½ cup (1 stick) unsalted butter, melted and cooled

1 teaspoon sugar

1 teaspoon kosher salt

2 large eggs, beaten

¼ teaspoon baking soda

½ teaspoon pure vanilla extract

Nonstick vegetable oil cooking spray

The night before you intend to make the waffles, place the milk in a saucepan and heat gently over medium heat (about 110°F) for 2 or 3 minutes until it feels just slightly warm to the touch. Transfer the warm milk to a large bowl. Stir in the flour, yeast, butter, sugar, and salt to form a batter. If the batter is lumpy, beat with a whisk until smooth. Cover the bowl with plastic wrap and let sit at room temperature for 8 to 12 hours. The batter should rise an inch or two and bubble on the surface.

Preheat a waffle iron, preferably nonstick. Stir the eggs into the batter along with the baking soda and vanilla, and mix well. The batter will be somewhat thinner than most waffle batters. Spray the waffle iron with nonstick cooking spray and ladle the batter into the iron, using $\frac{1}{2}$ to $\frac{3}{4}$ cup batter per waffle. The batter should be thin enough to fill out the iron without help. Close the iron and cook until the waffles have risen, turned golden brown, and crisped, 7 to 8 minutes or so, depending on your waffle iron. Repeat with the remaining batter.

PREP TIME: 5 minutes
COOKING TIME: 20 minutes
TOTAL TIME: 8½ to 12 hours (includes rising time)

ADVANCE PREP *The waffle batter will keep for three or four days in the refrigerator.*
LEFTOVERS *Refrigerate or freeze leftover waffles and reheat them in the toaster.*

Sour Cream Waffles

When I forget to make up my yeast-raised waffle batter in advance (page 110), and I want waffles for breakfast anyway, these are the ones I make. The recipe was given to me by my friend Jennifer, who also gave me my waffle iron. She was surprised to learn I didn't have one and acted quickly, stuffing this recipe in the box. The eggs are separated and the whites are beaten and folded back into the batter, giving the waffles a lovely light, airy texture.

Makes 4 servings

1½ cups unbleached all-purpose flour
2 tablespoons sugar
1½ teaspoons baking powder
¾ teaspoon baking soda
Kosher salt
1½ cups sour cream or plain yogurt
3 large eggs, separated
3 tablespoons unsalted butter, melted and cooled
2 teaspoons pure vanilla extract
Nonstick vegetable cooking spray

Preheat the waffle iron, preferably nonstick.

In a large bowl, blend the flour, sugar, baking powder, baking soda, and a pinch of salt. In a small bowl, beat together the sour cream, egg yolks, butter, and vanilla. Beat the egg whites with an electric mixer or by hand with a whisk until they form stiff peaks. Stir the sour cream mixture into the flour mixture just until blended. Using a large rubber spatula, fold one fourth of the egg whites into the batter to lighten it and then fold the rest of the egg whites into the batter until the whites are fully incorporated, being careful to deflate the whites as little as possible.

Spray the waffle iron with cooking spray. Ladle about ¾ cup batter per waffle into the waffle iron and spread it out with a spatula to fill the iron evenly. Close and let cook for about 8 minutes, or until the waffle has risen, browned, and crisped. Repeat with the remaining batter.

PREP TIME: 10 minutes
COOKING TIME: 35 minutes
TOTAL TIME: 45 minutes

ADVANCE PREP *The batter can be mixed just to the point that you fold in the egg whites up to several hours in advance and refrigerated. Whip and fold in the whites just before cooking the waffles.*
LEFTOVERS *Store leftover waffles in the refrigerator or freezer and reheat them in the toaster.*

Clafoutis

A clafoutis (pronounced klah-foo-TEE) is like a French pancake that's baked in the oven. Although it is traditionally served as a dessert, I find myself making clafoutis more often as part of a brunch. Sour cherries are the classic filling, but you can use just about any fruit or nuts or even chocolate chips. Because it requires only a few ingredients and takes only a couple of minutes to get in the oven, clafoutis is a good thing to remember when you find yourself needing a quick brunch dish or dessert. The end product, best served right out of the oven, is a cross between a sweet, crustless quiche, a baked custard, and a giant pancake. Yum.

Makes 4 to 6 servings

2 tablespoons unsalted butter

4 large eggs

3/4 cup granulated sugar

1/2 teaspoon kosher salt

1 teaspoon pure vanilla extract

2 tablespoons brandy or Cognac

Grated zest of 1/2 lemon (optional)

3 tablespoons all-purpose flour

1 cup heavy cream

1 to 1 1/2 cups pitted sour or Bing cherries, diced mango, fresh raspberries, fresh blueberries, diced fresh or poached pear, diced ripe mango, diced fresh pineapple, toasted and chopped hazelnuts, or dark chocolate bits

Confectioners' sugar, for serving

Preheat the oven to 425°F. Place the butter in a 9-inch cast-iron pan or straight-sided pie plate and set in the oven to melt. When the butter is melted, remove the pan from the oven and set aside to cool slightly. Swirl the butter around to evenly coat the bottom and the sides of the pan.

Meanwhile, in a large bowl, whisk the eggs until frothy. Add the sugar and beat vigorously for 4 or 5 minutes, until the eggs have become thick and pale. Alternatively you can use an electric mixer. Stir in the salt, vanilla, brandy, and lemon zest, if using. Whisk in the all-purpose flour. Add the heavy cream and continue whisking to make a smooth, rich batter.

Arrange the fruit or other filling in an even layer on the bottom of the pan. Whisk the egg and cream mixture again and pour slowly into the pan, directing the batter to different positions in the pan so that it doesn't disperse the filling. Set into the oven and bake for 20 to 25 minutes, until the clafoutis has begun to rise and brown. Turn down the oven temperature to 375°F and continue baking until it has risen evenly, set firm to the touch in the center, and turned a deep brown, an additional 20 minutes or so. Remove from the oven. Dust with confectioners' sugar and serve immediately, before the clafoutis sinks.

PREP TIME: 15 minutes
COOKING TIME: 45 to 55 minutes
TOTAL TIME: 1 hour

ADVANCE PREP The clafoutis batter can be made up to one day in advance and stored in the refrigerator. Bring back to room temperature before baking.
LEFTOVERS The leftovers will keep for three or four days in the fridge, although as the pancake cools it will sink in the center.

Fruity Oatmeal Porridge

I came to eat oatmeal late in life—about a year ago. I quickly developed a preference for Irish steel-cut oats or old-fashioned rolled oats, both of which have a chewier texture and nuttier flavor than instant or quick-cooking oats. My friend Peggy turned me onto cooking oatmeal with fruit juice and dried fruit, both of which add a little acidity, a little sweetness, and a lot of taste. Whether you make sweet or savory oatmeal, be sure to add enough salt to bring out the flavor of the oats.

Makes 2 to 4 servings

1 cup fresh orange juice or apple cider
Pinch of salt
1 cup steel-cut Irish or Scottish oats, also known as pinhead oats
1/4 cup chopped pitted dates, prunes, raisins, or other dried fruit
1 tablespoon unsalted butter
1/2 teaspoon pure vanilla extract
Pinch of ground cinnamon
Heavy cream, for serving (optional)
Brown sugar, for serving (optional)

In a medium saucepan, combine the fruit juice with the salt and 3 cups water and bring to a boil. Stir in the oats and bring back to a boil. Reduce the heat so that the mixture simmers and cook, stirring occasionally, for about 20 minutes. Add the dried fruit and continue cooking for another 10 to 15 minutes or until the oatmeal reaches the desired consistency. Stir in the butter, vanilla, and cinnamon and serve with cream and brown sugar, if you like.

TOTAL TIME: 30 to 40 minutes

ADVANCE PREP *Oatmeal should be made just before it is served. You can hold it in a double boiler or over a very low flame for up to 1 1/2 hours, but you'll have to add liquid as it sits to keep it from getting too stiff. If using steel-cut oats, you can reduce the cooking time to 15 to 20 minutes by soaking the oats overnight in cold water.*

VARIATIONS

Savory Oatmeal

For those of you out there who prefer your oatmeal savory instead of sweet, here's what to do. Substitute milk or additional water for the fruit juice above, omit the dried fruit, and simmer for 30 to 35 minutes, until it reaches the desired texture. Stir in 1 to 2 tablespoons of butter. Serve with a fancy salt, such as Maldon or fleur de sel, and buttermilk or cream to pour over.

Oatmeal Made from Rolled Oats

Old-fashioned rolled oats require less liquid and less cooking time than steel-cut oats. I like the texture of the big, chewy oat flakes. For the fruity oatmeal, reduce the amount of fruit juice to 1/2 cup and add only 1 1/2 cups water to the pot to boil. Use 1 cup rolled oats (not instant or quick-cooking) and add the dried fruit from the beginning. The oatmeal will cook in 6 to 7 minutes. Similarly, for savory oatmeal made with old-fashioned rolled oats, reduce the milk to 1/2 cup and the water to 1 1/2 cups. Cook for 7 to 10 minutes, or until the oatmeal reaches the desired consistency.

Oatmeal Mix-Ins

I like to stir all sorts of things into oatmeal once it is cooked: applesauce, buttermilk, heavy cream, ground flax seed, brown sugar, honey, and chocolate chips are but a few examples.

Lemon Blueberry Sour Cream Muffins

For a restaurant project on which I was recently a consultant, I scoured Manhattan looking for the perfect muffin to use as a model to show a couple of French pastry chefs who were not familiar with muffins but who were going to have to figure out how to make them. I bought dozens. Some tasted good but looked terrible; others looked good but tasted like they were made with a mix. In the end I had to make a batch of these blueberry muffins myself to show them what a perfect blueberry muffin should look and taste like. The delicate texture of these muffins results from cutting in the butter, the way you do for biscuits or pie crust. I use a food processor to cut it in, but you can do it by hand if you prefer.

Makes 12 muffins

3½ cups unbleached all-purpose flour
1 cup granulated or light brown sugar
1½ tablespoons baking powder
Grated zest of 1 lemon
Pinch of kosher salt
¾ cup (1½ sticks) unsalted butter, cut into cubes and chilled
1 cup milk
½ cup sour cream or plain or vanilla-flavored yogurt
Juice of ½ lemon (about 2 tablespoons)
2 large eggs, lightly beaten
2 cups fresh blueberries

Preheat the oven to 350°F. Line large muffin tins with paper muffin cups or grease the tins with softened butter.

In the work bowl of a food processor fitted with a metal chopping blade, combine the flour, sugar, baking powder, lemon zest, and salt. Pulse once or twice to combine the ingredients. Add the butter and pulse 8 to 10 times to cut the butter into the flour mixture until it resembles coarse crumbs. Transfer this mixture to a large bowl. Alternatively, you can cut the butter into the flour mixture using a pastry cut-ter or two butter knives. In a medium bowl, mix the milk, sour cream, lemon juice, and eggs. Pour this liquid mixture into the flour mixture and using a fork, stir just to combine. Do not overmix or your muffins will be tough. Stir in the blueberries.

Spoon the batter into the prepared muffin tins, filling them almost to the top. Bake for about 40 minutes, or until a knife or skewer inserted in the center comes out clean and the top of the muffin bounces back to your touch. Remove from the oven and allow the muffins to cool for about 10 minutes before unmolding them onto a wire rack to cool completely.

PREP TIME: 15 minutes
COOKING TIME: 40 minutes
TOTAL TIME: 1 hour

ADVANCE PREP *You can prepare the dry and wet ingredients and cover and refrigerate them up to a day in advance, but don't combine them until ready to bake.*
LEFTOVERS *These muffins are best right after they are made, but they can be stored at room temperature in an airtight container for two or three days or in the freezer for up to two months.*

Scones

Hot out of the oven, these scones have little in common with those hockey-puck things sold at coffee shops across the country. It isn't that the other ones are bad, necessarily. It's just that nothing beats a warm scone, and in my opinion, scones don't keep for more than a few hours after they are made.

Makes 16 scones

2 1/2 cups unbleached all-purpose flour

2 cups cake flour or additional 1 3/4 cups all-
purpose flour plus 2 tablespoons cornstarch

2 teaspoons baking powder

1/2 teaspoon baking soda

1/3 cup sugar

Pinch of kosher salt

1 cup (2 sticks) unsalted butter, cut into cubes
and chilled

1 cup heavy cream, chilled

1 large egg

1/4 cup milk

In the work bowl of a food processor fitted with a metal chopping blade, combine the flours, baking powder, baking soda, 2 tablespoons of the sugar, and salt. Pulse two or three times to blend. Add the butter and pulse 8 to 10 times, or until the mixture resembles coarse crumbs. Transfer to a large bowl. Alternatively, you can combine the dry ingredients in a large bowl and cut in the butter using a pastry cutter or two butter knives. Pour in the heavy cream and, using a fork, gently mix until the dry ingredients are moistened and the dough beings to form. Do not overmix. Add a dribble more cream if the dough seems too dry to cohere. Pat the dough into a ball, wrap in plastic, and refrigerate for about 30 minutes to rest.

Preheat the oven to 375°F.

Divide the dough into two equal portions and on a lightly floured work surface, pat each portion into an 8-inch circle about 3/4 inch thick. With a sharp knife, cut each circle into 8 equal wedges and set about 1 1/2 inches apart on an ungreased cookie sheet. In a small bowl, beat together the egg and the milk. Brush the top of each wedge with this egg mixture and sprinkle with some of the remaining sugar. Bake for

about 15 minutes, or until the scones have nicely risen and browned. Serve warm.

PREP TIME: 15 minutes
COOKING TIME: 15 minutes
TOTAL TIME: 1 hour (includes resting time)

ADVANCE PREP *You can combine the dry ingredients, cut in the butter, and store this mixture in the refrigerator for up to a day in advance, but don't add the cream and form the dough until just before baking.*

LEFTOVERS *Scones will keep for three or four days in an airtight container in the refrigerator. They can also be frozen for up to one month. I find the best way to reheat them is in the microwave for 20 seconds on high. Leftovers can be crumbled and used in stuffings or bread puddings.*

VARIATIONS

Chocolate Chip Scones

Before adding the heavy cream, stir 2/3 cup top-quality chocolate chips into the dry ingredients. Proceed with the recipe as directed.

Cranberry Orange Scones

Grate the zest of 1 orange, and then juice the orange (you should get about 2/3 cup juice). Soak 1/2 cup dried cranberries in the orange juice for about 30 minutes. Drain well. Add the orange zest to the dry ingredients and stir in the cranberries when you add the cream.

Lemon Poppy Seed Scones

Add 2 tablespoons poppy seeds and the grated zest of 1 lemon to the dry ingredients before adding the heavy cream.

FLAVORED BUTTERS AND CREAM CHEESES

Everything old is new again. Flavored butters used to be much more popular at brunches in the 1970s and 1980s than they are today, but I still like to serve them with warm scones or biscuits or bagels. They are easy enough to make. Place 1 cup (2 sticks) room-temperature unsalted butter in the work bowl of a food processor fitted with a metal chopping blade or in a medium bowl. Add 1/4 to 1/3 cup of flavoring, such as orange marmalade, strawberry jam, peach or fig preserves, honey, or chopped toasted walnuts or pecans, and a pinch of kosher salt, and pulse or mix for a minute or two until well combined. Scrape the butter out into a small, attractive dish and chill until ready to serve or for up to three weeks. Flavored butters can also be frozen for up to three months.

Flavored cream cheese can be made following the same proportions and technique as for flavored butters, omitting the salt; cream cheese is already salty enough. Favorite savory mix-ins include chopped scallion, smoked salmon, and fresh herbs.

Sesame Ginger Scones

Add 2 tablespoons toasted sesame seeds and 1/4 cup finely minced candied ginger to the dry ingredients before adding the heavy cream.

Streusel Coffee Cake

Nothing makes me think of my mother more than the aroma of a streusel coffee cake baking. The combination of cinnamon, walnuts, and butter produces an enchanting aroma. This cake has a lighter, more ethereal texture than most pound cakes owing in part to the substitution of honey for some of the sugar. It was inspired by a recipe by Emily Luchetti, the pastry chef at Farallon in San Francisco. You can use the same cake batter as a base for other types of coffee cake, too, layering sliced prune plums, quartered figs, or other fruit tossed with some brown sugar or honey between the layers of batter instead of the streusel mixture.

Makes 12 to 16 servings

1/4 cup cake, cookie, or unseasoned bread crumbs

1/3 cup light brown sugar

1/2 cup chopped toasted walnuts or pecans (see page 10)

1 tablespoon ground cinnamon

1 cup (2 sticks) unsalted butter, at room temperature

1 1/2 cups granulated sugar

1/4 cup mild honey, such as acacia or wildflower

4 large eggs

1 teaspoon pure vanilla extract

1 cup sour cream or plain yogurt

3 cups unbleached all-purpose flour

1 3/4 teaspoons baking powder

1/2 teaspoon kosher salt

Preheat the oven to 350° F. Generously butter a 10-cup, preferably nonstick, Bundt pan. Place 2 tablespoons of the crumbs in the pan and shake around to coat the pan with the crumbs. Invert and tap out any excess crumbs. Set aside. In a small bowl, combine the remaining 2 tablespoons crumbs with the brown sugar, chopped walnuts, and the cinnamon. Set the streusel mixture aside.

In the bowl of an electric mixer fitted with a paddle attachment or in a large bowl using a wooden spoon, beat the butter with the sugar until light and fluffy, about 2 minutes. Add the honey and beat in the eggs, one at a time, beating well after each addition. Beat in the vanilla. Add half of the sour cream and stir in half of the flour along with the baking powder and salt. Add the remaining sour cream and the rest of the flour and mix until combined.

Spoon one fourth of the cake batter into the bottom of the pan and spread to form an even layer. Sprinkle with one fourth of the streusel mixture. Top with another layer of batter and sprinkle with another quarter of the streusel. Repeat once more, top with the remaining cake batter, and end with the remaining streusel mixture.

Bake for about 55 minutes to 1 hour, or until the cake has risen, the top has browned and cracked, and a skewer inserted into the center of the cake comes out clean. Remove from the oven and let cool for about 30 minutes in the pan before unmolding. To unmold, run a knife along the edge and along the inner tube and invert onto a wire rack to cool completely.

PREP TIME: 20 minutes
COOKING TIME: 1 hour
TOTAL TIME: 1 1/2 hours

ADVANCE PREP *The cake is actually best if it is made a day in advance and allowed to sit, wrapped airtight, at room temperature until ready to serve.*
LEFTOVERS *The cake will keep four or five days at room temperature or it can be frozen for up to two months.*

VARIATIONS
Fig or Plum Coffee Cake
Omit the walnut-cinnamon streusel mixture and instead use 12 black Mission figs or Italian prune plums, quartered and tossed with 2 to 3 tablespoons light brown sugar and a pinch of cinnamon or 3/4 cup Fig Preserves (page 140) for the filling. Make three layers of fig and end with a layer of batter. Proceed with the recipe as directed.

Lemon Poppy Seed Coffee Cake
Omit the walnut-cinnamon streusel mixture. Stir 3 tablespoons poppy seeds and the grated zest and juice of 1 lemon into the cake batter. Bake for 55 minutes to 1 hour.

Buckwheat Buttermilk Bundt Cake with Walnuts
This cake is based on an idea for a buckwheat cake I came across in the *Fannie Farmer Baking Book*. The combination of flavors is superb. Because it isn't too sweet and the flavor is reminiscent of buckwheat pancakes, I like to serve it at brunch, but it is equally well suited for an afternoon snack. To dress it up a little, serve it with sweetened whipped cream and fruit or Orange Confectioners' Glaze, as described below.
Makes 1 Bundt cake or one 8 by 12-inch cake

1 cup buckwheat flour
1 cup unbleached all-purpose flour
3/4 cup light brown sugar
1/2 teaspoon kosher salt
4 teaspoons baking powder
Finely grated zest of 1 orange
2 large eggs
2 cups buttermilk, milk, or water
6 tablespoons unsalted butter, melted and
    cooled, or 6 tablespoons vegetable oil
1/4 cup buckwheat or other honey

½ teaspoon pure vanilla extract

¾ cup chopped toasted walnuts
   (see page 10)

Preheat the oven to 375°F. Butter and flour a 10-cup Bundt pan or an 8 by 12-inch cake pan. Set aside.

Into a large bowl, sift together the buckwheat flour, all-purpose flour, brown sugar, salt, and baking powder. Stir in the orange zest. In a separate bowl, beat together the eggs and buttermilk. Mix in the butter, honey, and vanilla. (Don't worry if the honey hardens when it's mixed into the cold liquid; keep stirring, it will dissolve.) Pour the liquid ingredients into the dry ingredients and stir just to combine. Stir in the nuts. Pour the batter into the prepared pan. Bake for 25 to 30 minutes, until the cake rises, pulls away from the center, and springs back to the touch. Remove from the oven and cool for 15 minutes before unmolding onto a wire rack to finish cooling completely.

PREP TIME: 15 minutes

COOKING TIME: 25 to 30 minutes

TOTAL TIME: 45 minutes

ADVANCE PREP *The cake is good freshly baked, but better if it is allowed to sit, wrapped airtight, at room temperature for a day before serving.*
LEFTOVERS *Well wrapped, the cake will keep four or five days at room temperature or up to two months in the freezer.*

VARIATION

Buckwheat Buttermilk Bundt Cake with Orange Glaze

Prepare the cake as directed. While it is baking, juice half an orange and strain into a bowl.

You should have about ¼ cup of juice. Stir in enough confectioners' sugar (about 2½ cups) to make a smooth, pourable, but not too thin glaze. With the cake cooled but still on the rack, drizzle the glaze back and forth over the top of the cake, letting the glaze drip down the sides. Allow the glaze to harden before serving.

Spanish Potato Omelet

This large potato omelet, similar to a potato frittata, is the national dish of Spain, where it's called *tortilla española* and you are likely to find it in every tapas bar across the country. I like to serve it as part of a brunch or as an hors d'oeuvre or appetizer before dinner because I always have the ingredients on hand and because it can be prepared in advance—it actually develops better flavor if it's allowed to cool to room temperature before serving. For a simple variation, substitute sweet potatoes for the white potatoes and add a pinch of ground nutmeg.

Makes 4 to 6 brunch servings and 8 to 10 appetizer servings

   ¾ cup extra-virgin olive oil

   1 pound (3 medium) Yukon Gold or any other
      moderately starchy potatoes, peeled

   2 teaspoons kosher salt

   ½ small yellow or white onion, or 1 large shallot,
      minced (optional)

   8 large eggs

   ¼ teaspoon freshly ground black pepper

   2 tablespoons chopped flat-leaf parsley

Heat the oil in an 8- to 10-inch nonstick frying pan over medium-high heat. Cut the potatoes lengthwise in half and then in quarters, and slice them about ⅛ to ¼ inch thick, placing them in the hot oil as you slice them. Sprinkle the potatoes with 1 teaspoon of the salt. Cook the potatoes in the oil, stirring them frequently so they cook evenly. After 5 to 6 minutes, add the onion, if using, and continue cooking for another 5 to 6 minutes or so, until the potatoes are almost cooked through. Avoid browning them.

Meanwhile, in a large bowl, beat the eggs with the remaining teaspoon salt and the pepper until blended. Beat in the parsley. When the potatoes are tender, about 12 minutes total, remove them from the oil with a slotted spoon or spatula and transfer them—in small batches to avoid cooking the egg—into the beaten egg mixture. Stir the egg mixture, then let it sit at room temperature for 15 to 30 minutes. (Cooling the potatoes in the egg mixture before frying helps prevent the omelet from sticking to the pan.) Pour the olive oil from the pan into a small bowl and reserve. Wipe out the pan with paper towels.

When ready to cook the tortilla, use some of the reserved oil to grease a rimless dinner plate or a flat pot lid large enough to cover the frying pan with an inch or so to spare. Set aside. Heat 3 tablespoons of the reserved olive oil in the frying pan over medium-high heat. When the oil is hot but not smoking, stir the egg and potato mixture and pour it into the hot pan. Use a wooden spoon or spatula to evenly distribute the potatoes in the pan. As the egg cooks, pull the edges of the omelet in toward the center of the pan with a wooden spoon or spatula, allowing the uncooked egg to flow underneath to the edges. Even out the surface of the omelet as

you work. When the omelet has firmed up enough to hold its shape and is browned on the bottom, 8 to 10 minutes, use a spatula to loosen the bottom of the egg and make sure that it hasn't stuck. (If the pan was hot enough when you put in the egg, it shouldn't.) Take the greased plate and invert it over the omelet. With oven mitts on, hold the plate firmly and turn the omelet, pan and all, over to dump it out onto the plate. If any bits stick to the pan, scrape them off and put them back on the omelet where they came from. Wipe out the pan, return it to the heat, and add another couple of tablespoons of the reserved olive oil. Slide the omelet from the plate back into the hot pan (cooked side up) and continue cooking until the underside is browned, about 8 minutes. Wipe the plate clean and use it to flip the omelet one more time. Slide the tortilla onto a serving plate and serve warm or, better yet, at room temperature.

PREP TIME: 15 minutes
COOKING TIME: 30 minutes
TOTAL TIME: 1 hour and 15 minutes (includes resting time)

ADVANCE PREP *You can fry the potatoes in advance and keep them in the eggs for about an hour at room temperature. Otherwise refrigerate the mixture until you are ready to cook it. Once cooked, the tortilla can sit uncovered at room temperature for about half a day.*
LEFTOVERS *I like the tortilla cold out of the fridge for breakfast or heated up in the microwave (in wedges) for just a minute or so. Any olive oil leftover from frying the potatoes can be used to fry other savory ingredients.*

Frittata

A frittata is a large Italian omelet that is studded with lots of vegetables or other fillings. You can make frittata out of just about any vegetable, from asparagus to zucchini. You can use seafood, prosciutto, meat, or even leftover spaghetti. Keep in mind that whatever you are using as a filling must be able to cook in the same amount of time as the eggs, which isn't very long, or else it must be precooked.

Here in America, most recipes for frittatas instruct you to bake the omelets in the oven. This is an American technique. I've never seen an Italian make a frittata this way. Instead, they cook them on top of the stove, flipping them with the aid of a large, flat, greased plate or pot lid—the same technique Spanish home cooks use to make *tortilla española* (page 118).

Makes 4 to 6 brunch servings and 8 to 10 hors d'oeuvre servings

About ²/₃ cup extra-virgin olive oil

8 large eggs

¼ cup grated Parmigiano Reggiano cheese

2 tablespoons chopped flat-leaf parsley

1 teaspoon kosher salt

¼ teaspoon freshly ground black pepper

½ small white onion, chopped

1 small garlic clove, minced

1½ pounds quick-cooking vegetables, such as thin asparagus, zucchini, or mushrooms, sliced

Pinch of crushed red pepper flakes (optional)

Use some of the olive oil to grease a large, rimless plate or flat lid at least 10 inches in diameter. In a large bowl, whisk the eggs until frothy. Whisk in the Parmigiano, parsley, salt, and pepper. Set aside.

In a 10-inch nonstick frying pan, heat ¼ cup of the olive oil over medium-high heat. Add the onion and sauté until translucent, about 5 minutes. Add the garlic and sauté for another minute or two. Add the vegetables and sauté until tender, 8 to 12 minutes, depending on the vegetable. Add the red pepper flakes, if using. Cool this mixture slightly and add it to the egg mixture. Let sit for about 15 minutes. Wipe out the pan with paper towel.

Heat ¼ cup of the olive oil in the pan over medium heat. When quite hot but not smoking, whisk the egg mixture again and pour it into the pan. As the egg cooks, pull the edges of the omelet in toward the center of the pan with a wooden spoon or spatula, allowing the uncooked egg to flow underneath to the edges. Even out the surface of the omelet as you work. When the omelet has firmed up enough to hold its shape and browned on the bottom, 8 to 10 minutes, use a spatula to loosen the bottom of the egg and make sure that it hasn't stuck. (If the pan was hot enough when you put in the egg, it shouldn't.) Take the greased plate and invert it over the omelet. With oven mitts on, hold the plate firmly and turn the omelet, pan and all, over to dump it out onto the plate. If any bits stick to the pan, scrape them off and put them back on the omelet where they came from. Wipe out the pan, return it to the heat, and add another couple of tablespoons of the reserved olive oil. Slide the omelet from the plate back into the hot pan (cooked side up) and continue cooking until the underside is browned, about 8 minutes. Wipe the plate clean and use it to flip the omelet one more time. Slide the frittata onto a serving plate and serve warm or, better yet, at room temperature.

PREP TIME: 15 minutes
COOKING TIME: 30 minutes

ADVANCE PREP *The frittata egg mixture can be made in advance, covered, and refrigerated for up to a day before cooking. You can also cook the frittata two or three hours in advance and keep it at room temperature or refrigerate it for up to one day before serving.*

LEFTOVERS *The frittata will keep four or five days in the refrigerator. You can eat it chilled, at room temperature, or heated for 45 seconds in a microwave on high.*

Smoked Sturgeon with Scrambled Eggs and Onions

On mornings when I'm in the mood for scrambled eggs with smoked sturgeon, but I don't feel like schlepping from my apartment in Chelsea all the way to Barney Greengrass on the Upper West Side for breakfast, I make them myself. I keep smoked sturgeon in my freezer for when the craving hits. This is my interpretation of the Sturgeon King's signature dish. For variety you can substitute smoked sablefish (black cod) or smoked salmon for the sturgeon.

Makes 2 to 4 servings

4 tablespoons (½ stick) unsalted butter

½ large sweet white onion (about 8 ounces), such as Vidalia, Maui, or Texas, diced

4 ounces smoked sturgeon, sablefish (black cod), or salmon, diced

8 large eggs, beaten

Freshly ground black pepper

In a heavy sauté pan set over medium heat, melt the butter. Add the onion and cook gently until

ever-so-slightly browned, about 6 minutes. Add the fish and continue cooking until the flesh of the fish turns from translucent to opaque, about 3 minutes. Add the beaten eggs and stir continuously, scraping the bottom of the pan, until the eggs begin to set. Just as all of the liquid appears to be firming up, take the pan off the heat and continue stirring for another minute or so. Season with pepper and serve immediately.

TOTAL TIME: 15 minutes

ADVANCE PREP *The eggs are best made just before serving.*

Fried Salami and Egg Sandwich

I consulted on the menu for a restaurant in Las Vegas that was supposed to recreate the taste of a New York Jewish delicatessen. The chef, John Regan, and I created a lot of recipes with traditional flavors. This sandwich was one of my favorites. My grandmother used to fry garlicky kosher salami until crisp and serve it with eggs for breakfast. We took that salami, added it along with sautéed onions to scrambled eggs, and served it on a toasted bagel spread with scallion cream cheese. The cream cheese sort of melts, making the filling super-creamy.

Makes 2 sandwiches

8 slices kosher beef salami

2 tablespoons unsalted butter

¼ medium white onion, chopped

Kosher salt and freshly ground black pepper

5 large eggs, beaten

2 sesame or poppy seed bagels, cut crosswise in half

3 ounces scallion or chive cream cheese

Thin slices ripe tomato (optional)

Poached Eggs

I think just about everything is better with a poached egg on top—salads, sandwiches, vegetables in vinaigrette, hashes of any number of things like corned beef, turkey, lobster, and potatoes. I wish I had a dollar for all the devices that have been sold to help people poach eggs on the stove or in the microwave. Working as a brunch chef in a Toronto restaurant—where I used to poach ninety eggs at a time—taught me how easy poaching eggs really is without any fancy contraptions. All you need are eggs, the fresher the better, and a pot. Here's how to do it.

Makes 4 poached eggs

> 1 tablespoon white vinegar
> Large pinch of kosher salt
> 4 large or extra-large eggs, chilled

Place about a quart of water in a medium saucepan and set it over medium-high heat. Add the vinegar and salt and bring to a boil. Have a slotted spoon, a clean dish towel, and a timing device nearby. When the water boils, take the eggs out of the fridge. Crack the first egg directly into the water, toward one side of the pot, in one quick motion. (Don't bother swirling the water to make a whirlpool or anything like that; I haven't found that particularly helpful.) Crack the other eggs into different quadrants of the pot. When the water comes back to the boil, turn down the heat so that the water simmers and time the eggs: 2½ minutes for soft poached eggs and 3 minutes for eggs that are a littler firmer but still with runny yolks.

When the time is up, turn off the heat. With a slotted spoon in one hand and a clean, folded dish towel in the other, lift each poached egg out of the pot, using the edge of the spoon pressed against the side of the pot to trim any straggling wisps of egg white. Carefully roll the egg off of the spoon onto the dish towel to pat dry, and transfer to a clean plate or directly on top of whatever you are serving with the eggs.

TOTAL TIME: 5 minutes

ADVANCE PREP *Poached eggs can be made a day or two in advance. If preparing them in advance, have a bowl of ice water ready near the stove. Proceed with the recipe, undercooking the eggs by about 30 seconds because they will cook more when you reheat them. As they are cooked, transfer them into the bowl of ice water to stop the cooking. Refrigerate the eggs in the cold water until you are ready to use them. An hour before serving, take the eggs out of the fridge to bring them to room temperature. To reheat, bring a small pot of lightly salted water to a simmer. Using a slotted spoon, transfer the poached eggs to the simmering water and heat for about a minute. Remove, pat dry, and serve. Make one or two more eggs than you need in case you break any while transferring them back and forth.*

Place a medium frying pan over medium-high heat. Put the salami in the pan and fry until browned and crisp, 3 or 4 minutes per side. Transfer the salami to a cutting board, cut each slice into quarters, and set aside. Add the butter to the pan along with the onion. Sauté until translucent, about 5 minutes. Season with salt and pepper. Add the eggs to the pan along with the fried salami. Scramble the eggs until the desired doneness and then let them sit in the pan, off the heat, undisturbed for a few minutes to cohere. Meanwhile, toast the bagels. Spread both halves of the bagels with the cream cheese. Divide the eggs and salami between the two bagels, top with tomato, if using, and serve warm.

TOTAL TIME: 15 minutes

ADVANCE PREP *The salami and the onions can be fried a day or two in advance and kept refrigerated until ready to use.*

Eggs Benedict

Though almost teetering on the edge of cliché, poached eggs on toasted English muffins with fried ham and hollandaise is just one of the all-time great combinations of flavors. On freshly baked biscuits it's even better. The most difficult part is the hollandaise, a warm, emulsified sauce similar to a mayonnaise that isn't nearly as difficult as some people lead you to believe. The secret to hollandaise is patience. If you work slowly, without getting impatient and turning up the heat or adding too much melted butter too quickly, you will have no problem. Most recipes recommend using a double boiler to make hollandaise, but most double boilers made for home use have flat bottoms, which I

find do not allow you to whisk the egg yolks sufficiently well, and therefore can cause curdling. I prefer to use a heat-proof glass (e.g., Pyrex) or metal bowl with a rounded bottom set over a pan of simmering water.

Makes 4 servings

> 1 pound (4 sticks) unsalted butter
> 3 large egg yolks
> Juice of 1 lemon (1/4 cup)
> Kosher salt
> Freshly ground white pepper
> 8 slices ham or Canadian bacon
> 4 freshly baked biscuits, split, or 4 English
>   muffins, split and toasted
> 8 poached eggs (see page 122)
> Chopped flat-leaf parsley, for garnish

Place the butter in a small saucepan and set over medium heat until melted. The butter should be warm but not hot. Set aside and keep warm without disturbing the white sediment on the bottom of the pan. Place another small saucepan with about an inch of water in it over high heat. Bring to a boil and turn down the heat so that the water is barely simmering. Place the egg yolks in a heat-proof glass or metal bowl and whisk in the lemon juice and a generous pinch of salt. Beat until pale and frothy, about 1 1/2 minutes. Holding the bowl with a pot holder or folded dish towel, place the bowl over the simmering water; the bottom shouldn't touch the water. Whisk the mixture vigorously until the mixture has doubled in volume and is warm to the touch, 4 or 5 minutes. If at any time before the mixture has doubled it feels like it is getting too hot (stick a clean finger in it to check), remove the bowl from the simmering water and beat on the counter to cool slightly.

When done, set the bowl on the counter. Whisk in 2 tablespoons of the simmering water to set the eggs. (If your arm is tired, at this point you can transfer the egg yolk mixture to the bowl of an electric mixer and beat it with a wire whip attachment.) Slowly dribble the warm butter into the egg yolk mixture while continuing to whisk. Pour or ladle the butter off the top of the saucepan, leaving the white sediment on the bottom of the pot undisturbed. The mixture will thicken as you add more butter. Add it slowly, though, and be sure you've incorporated all the butter before you add more. When the mixture has attained the consistency of a soft pudding, stop adding butter. If it is too thick to flow off a spoon, you can thin it with a few drops of water, some more lemon juice, or even some dry white wine. Season with pepper. Keep in a warm place.

To finish and assemble the Eggs Benedict, fry the ham in a dry pan over medium-high heat for 2 or 3 minutes, until browned. Arrange two biscuit halves cut side up on each of four serving plates. Place a piece of ham on each biscuit half. Top with a poached egg and spoon the hollandaise over the egg. Sprinkle with parsley and serve immediately.

PREP TIME: 25 minutes
COOKING TIME: 10 minutes
TOTAL TIME: 35 minutes

ADVANCE PREP *The hollandaise can be made up to an hour in advance. Cover it with plastic wrap and keep it in a warm place. You can also keep it over the pan with the simmering water in it but off the heat.*

Beef, Chicken, or Turkey Hash

Hash is my favorite way to use up leftover cooked meat, whether beef, chicken, or turkey. I've even been known to make lobster hash on the lucky occasions when I've got leftover lobster. With a poached egg on top, hash is a one-dish meal that will fortify you for the whole day.

Makes 4 servings

2 tablespoons unsalted butter
1 ounce bacon, pancetta, or prosciutto, finely chopped (about 2 tablespoons)
1 medium white or yellow onion, chopped
1/2 red bell pepper, cored, seeded, and chopped (optional)
1 pound all-purpose potatoes, peeled and cut into 1/2-inch cubes
Kosher salt and freshly ground black pepper
1 1/2 tablespoons all-purpose flour
1/2 cup milk or light cream
1 tablespoon finely chopped flat-leaf parsley
3 to 4 cups cooked beef, chicken, or turkey, cut into 1/2-inch dice
4 poached eggs (see page 122)

Bring a small saucepan of salted water to a simmer. In a heavy-bottomed nonstick or cast-iron frying pan, heat the butter and bacon until the fat on the meat has rendered, about 2 minutes. Add the onion and bell pepper, if using, and cook for a few minutes more, until soft. Add the potatoes and cook for 8 to 10 minutes or so, until the potatoes begin to color and soften. Season with 1 1/2 teaspoons salt and some pepper. Add the flour and stir for a minute or two to cook. Pour in the milk, parsley, and the meat. The mixture will start to thicken. Continue cooking the hash, stirring it frequently and spreading it out to cover the bottom of the

A FEW WORDS ABOUT RAW OR UNDERCOOKED EGGS

Sadly, due to a variety of factors, since the 1980s our commercial chicken and egg supply has been contaminated with the bacteria *Salmonella enteritidis*, which can cause a serious form of food poisoning. According to the Center for Disease Control, in certain parts of the country, such as the northeast, where I reside, one in fifty consumers is exposed to salmonella bacteria from eggs each year. In addition to handling eggs carefully and keeping them refrigerated, the best way to ensure the safety of your eggs is to thoroughly cook them to a temperature of between 150° and 160°F and never to hold them between 40° and 140°F for more than 2 hours.

The problem with the recommended cooking temperatures is that by the time they are reached, the eggs are hard and they can easily become rubbery. Also, preparations such as hollandaise or mayonnaise fall outside the range of safety. I choose to accept the health risk of undercooked eggs as a trade-off for gastronomic pleasure. I hedge my bets by buying eggs only from a local farmer who raises free-range chickens organically. But when feeding very young or old people or anyone with a compromised immune system, I wouldn't take the risk of serving undercooked eggs. If you can find pasteurized eggs, which have been treated to kill bacteria, use those. Otherwise choose a recipe that calls for the eggs to be fully cooked.

pan, until the potatoes are soft and the hash has browned, about 10 minutes. Adjust the seasoning with salt and pepper. Let the hash sit over the heat for a few minutes to set. Meanwhile, heat the poached eggs in the simmering water for 1 minute. Run a spatula underneath the hash to loosen it and invert onto a serving plate. Lift the eggs out of the simmering water with a slotted spoon and pat dry with paper towel or a clean dish towel. Arrange the eggs on top of the hash and serve.

PREP TIME: 15 minutes
COOKING TIME: 25 minutes
TOTAL TIME: 40 minutes

ADVANCE PREP *The ingredients can all be prepared in advance. If you dice the potatoes, be sure to keep them submerged in cold water to prevent discoloring. The hash can be made up to an hour in advance. Keep it covered on the stove. To serve, heat the hash on top of the stove for 5 minutes or so, and then proceed with the recipe as directed.*
LEFTOVERS *The hash will keep in the fridge for about a week.*

Angel Biscuits

These light, airy biscuits are flavored and risen in part with yeast. The beauty of them is that, unlike most baking soda biscuits, you can make these the night before, keep them in the refrigerator, and just cut and bake them in the morning for breakfast. They call for cake flour or soft wheat flour (e.g., White Lily), but you can substitute a combination of all-purpose flour and cornstarch as indicated.

Makes 1 dozen biscuits

MAKIN' BACON

Both for eating with eggs at breakfast and for crumbling into salads and other dishes, I think the best way to make bacon is to roast it in the oven on a wire rack. With almost no effort, roasted bacon comes out evenly cooked and perfectly crisp, without being overly greasy. Preheat the oven to 400°F. Set a wire rack on a baking sheet. Lay the strips of bacon flat across the rack. Set the pan in the oven and roast the bacon for 10 to 14 minutes, depending on the thickness of the slices, or until the fat renders and the bacon browns and crisps. Remove the pan from the oven, transfer the bacon to paper towels to pat off any excess grease, and save the rendered fat in the pan for cooking potatoes, cornbread, or eggs, for example.

2¾ cups cake flour or soft wheat flour (such as White Lily), or 2½ cups bleached all-purpose flour mixed with 3 tablespoons cornstarch

1½ tablespoons sugar

1 teaspoon instant yeast

1½ teaspoons baking powder

½ teaspoon baking soda

1 teaspoon kosher salt

4 tablespoons (½ stick) unsalted butter, cut into cubes, chilled

½ cup lard or vegetable shortening, or additional 4 tablespoons unsalted butter

Scant 1 cup buttermilk, plus extra for glazing

1 tablespoon sesame seeds (optional)

In a large bowl, whisk together the flour, sugar, yeast, baking powder, baking soda, and salt.

Using a pastry cutter or two butter knives, cut in the butter and lard. Alternatively, you can place the dry ingredients in the bowl of a food processor fitted with a metal cutting blade and cut in the fat using on/off pulses until the mixture resembles coarse crumbs; transfer the mixture to a large bowl. Add the buttermilk and, using a fork, mix to form a soft, shaggy dough. Turn out the dough onto a clean work surface, scraping out the bowl. Knead lightly five or six times, no more, just until the dough coheres, and pat it into a disk about 8 inches in diameter and ½ inch thick. Place on a clean plate, cover with plastic wrap, and refrigerate for at least 8 hours and up to two days.

Preheat the oven to 425°F. Lightly butter a baking sheet.

Remove the biscuit dough from the refrigerator and cut it into biscuits using a round biscuit cutter or a sharp knife dipped in flour. Press the scraps together into a disk and cut additional biscuits. Place the biscuits on the baking sheet, brush the tops lightly with buttermilk, and sprinkle with sesame seeds, if using. Bake for 10 to 12 minutes, until the biscuits have risen and browned. Serve warm.

PREP TIME: 10 minutes
COOKING TIME: 10 to 12 minutes
TOTAL TIME: 8 hours 20 minutes (includes rising time)

ADVANCE PREP *The dough can be made up to two days in advance and refrigerated until you are ready to bake. It can also be frozen for up to one month. Defrost in the refrigerator overnight before baking.*

Buttermilk Biscuits

Delicate buttermilk biscuits, raised with baking powder, are a great accompaniment to any meal of the day, especially brunch. Adding cheese and scallions, as described in the variations below, makes a rich, savory alternative. And smothering the biscuits with sausage gravy is a Southern breakfast tradition worth keeping!

Makes about 1 dozen biscuits

2$\frac{1}{2}$ cups bleached all-purpose flour
2$\frac{1}{2}$ teaspoons baking powder
$\frac{1}{2}$ teaspoon baking soda
$\frac{1}{2}$ teaspoon kosher salt
$\frac{1}{2}$ cup (1 stick) unsalted butter, cut into small cubes and chilled
1$\frac{1}{4}$ to 1$\frac{1}{2}$ cups buttermilk

Preheat the oven to 375°F. Line a cookie sheet with parchment paper or spray with nonstick vegetable oil spray.

In a large bowl, combine the flour, baking powder, baking soda, and salt. Using a pastry cutter, two knives, a large fork, or your fingertips, cut or rub in the butter until the mixture resembles coarse crumbs. (Alternatively, you can pulse the mixture four or five times in a food processor fitted with a metal chopping blade.)

Add about 1$\frac{1}{4}$ cups of the buttermilk and, using a fork, push around the mixture to moisten the dry ingredients just until they come together to form a dough. Don't beat or otherwise overwork the dough. Add a little more buttermilk if necessary to moisten all of the dry ingredients.

Turn the mixture out onto a clean work surface. Knead three or four times, no more, to create a mostly smooth dough. Pat or roll the dough out $\frac{3}{4}$ inch thick and cut into twelve 1$\frac{1}{2}$-inch rounds or wedges or other shapes with a floured cutter. (You can rework any scraps once, pressing them together to cut out more biscuits.) Place on the prepared cookie sheet and bake for about 15 minutes, or until the biscuits have risen and browned. The bottoms should be golden brown. Serve warm.

PREP TIME: 20 minutes
COOKING TIME: 15 minutes
TOTAL TIME: 35 minutes

LEFTOVERS *Biscuits are best straight out of the oven, but you can keep them in the fridge for a couple of days or freeze them for up to a month. Reheat in a 300°F oven for 8 to 10 minutes, or until warm. You can also heat them in a microwave for about 25 seconds apiece on high.*

VARIATION
Scallion and Cheese Biscuits
Add 3 ounces shredded sharp Cheddar cheese (about $\frac{3}{4}$ cup), 2 scallions, white and green parts, chopped, and a pinch of freshly ground black pepper to the flour and butter mixture before stirring in the buttermilk.

Sausage Gravy
One way to make biscuits even better than they already are is to split them in half and smother them with sausage gravy. In a large frying pan, melt 1 tablespoon unsalted butter over medium-high heat. Add 1 small, chopped white onion and cook until soft, about 5 minutes. Add about 1 pound sausage meat, removed from its casing, and cook, breaking it up into little bits, until the fat has rendered and the

meat is lightly browned, about 8 minutes. Add 2 tablespoons all-purpose flour and cook, stirring, for a minute or two. Pour in 1½ cups milk and keep stirring until the milk has thickened, 2 or 3 minutes. Add a drop or two of your favorite hot sauce, if desired; turn down the heat to very low; and simmer the mixture for a couple of minutes, just to make sure the flour is cooked. Adjust the gravy to the desired consistency with additional milk, if need be, before spooning over the biscuits.

Home Fries

In the small town in upstate New York where I went to college, there was a diner that put a giant pile of home fries on the griddle at 5 A.M. As the day wore on, and eggs and bacon and other items were fried on the same griddle, the home fries would get crisp and buttery. Around 11:30 A.M., they had become the best home fries in the world. At home, without a griddle, I like to use a cast-iron pan that I place in the oven to crisp up the home fries before serving.

Makes 6 to 8 servings

> 6 tablespoons (¾ stick) unsalted butter
> 2 tablespoons bacon fat, or additional unsalted butter
> 2 large yellow or white onions, peeled and thinly sliced
> 2½ pounds Yukon Gold or other all-purpose potatoes (5 large), peeled
> Kosher salt and freshly ground black pepper

Preheat the oven to 400° F.

In a large cast-iron or other ovenproof frying pan, melt the butter and bacon fat over medium-high heat. Add the onions and cook

until soft, about 10 minutes, stirring frequently. The onions should be translucent and they should have given off a lot of liquid. Let them brown only very slightly. Meanwhile, cut the potatoes in half lengthwise and then in quarters lengthwise to produce long, thin spears. Slice the quarters crosswise to produce small chunks. Add the potatoes, 4 teaspoons salt, and ½ teaspoon pepper to the onions and cook, stirring occasionally—you want to incorporate the brown bits from the bottom of the pan without breaking up the potatoes too much—for about 15 minutes or until the potatoes are beginning to become tender. Adjust the seasoning with additional salt and pepper to taste.

Spread the potatoes out in the pan, but don't pat them down; leave the surface uneven so it will crisp nicely. Place the potatoes in the oven for 20 to 25 minutes, or until browned. Serve from the pan.

PREP TIME: 10 minutes
COOKING TIME: 50 minutes
TOTAL TIME: 1 hour

ADVANCE PREP *The home fries can be made several hours ahead up to the point that they would go in the oven. Bake to crisp them up before serving.*
LEFTOVERS *The home fries will keep for about a week in the refrigerator. Reheat leftovers in a frying pan or the microwave.*

Sweet Potato Home Fries

Home fries made from sweet potatoes are a delicious alternative to those made with regular potatoes. They have the added advantage of taking less time to cook.

Makes 4 servings

4 tablespoons (½ stick) unsalted butter

1 medium white or yellow onion, chopped

1½ pounds sweet potatoes, peeled and cut into ¼-inch dice

2 teaspoons kosher salt

¼ teaspoon freshly ground black pepper

Pinch of freshly ground nutmeg

Preheat the oven to 400°F.

Melt the butter in a large cast-iron or other ovenproof frying pan over medium-high heat. Add the onion and cook until soft, about 5 minutes. Add the sweet potatoes, salt, pepper, and nutmeg. Cook, stirring, flattening them out so they cook and color evenly, for about 10 minutes, until the potatoes begin to soften. Don't let the onions burn—turn down the heat if the onions become too brown. At this point, don't pat down the potatoes; keep the surface uneven so the home fries brown nicely in the oven. Set the pan in the preheated oven for 15 minutes, or until the sweet potatoes have browned. Serve in the pan.

TOTAL TIME: 30 minutes

LEFTOVERS *The home fries will keep for a week in the fridge. Reheat leftovers in a 300°F oven or in the microwave.*

Cheese Grits

Grits is good. (Note that Southern linguists consider the word *grits* to be singular.) Like its Italian cousin, polenta, grits is made from coarsely ground dried corn. Lately there has been revived interest in what you might call "heirloom" or "artisanal" grits—that is, small-production stone-ground grits made from native varieties of corn. One bite of these special grits—which have a delightful creaminess and true corn taste—and you'll never eat another dish of bland, mushy, commercially produced grits again. Leading this artisanal grits movement is a guy named Glenn Roberts at Anson Mills in Columbia, South Carolina (www.ansonmills.com), though there are other excellent producers, too (Weisenberger Mill in Midway, Kentucky; www.weisenberger.com, is another). I recommend you order some (if you do, keep them in the freezer because, unlike commercial grits, they are perishable). Avoid instant grits at all cost. They are insipid and mushy.

This is a recipe for cheese grits, which I think makes a perfect partner to a giant Southern breakfast. One trick to making creamier grits is to leave the salt out until the grits is cooked.

Makes 6 to 8 servings

1 cup white or yellow grits, preferably stone-ground, and not instant

2 teaspoons kosher salt

5 to 8 ounces sharp aged Cheddar, aged Gouda, Fontina, or Comté cheese, shredded (about 2 cups)

¼ cup heavy cream or half-and-half

3 tablespoons unsalted butter

¼ teaspoon freshly ground white pepper

In a heavy medium pot, bring about 4½ cups of water to a boil. Slowly whisk the grits into the water in a steady stream. Bring the water back to a boil, then turn down the heat as low as it will go. At first, the grits will look like they are suspended in the water. Stir them frequently until they seem to be a thin mush, about 7 minutes. Set the cover ajar on top. Continue simmering the grits very slowly for about 35 minutes or so, stirring occasionally, until they are creamy and smooth. Using a wooden spoon, stir in the salt, and cook for another 5 minutes or so. Stir in the cheese, cream, butter, and white pepper, and stir constantly until the cheese and butter have melted and been incorporated.

TOTAL TIME: 50 minutes

ADVANCE PREP *You can have the Cheese Grits ready up to an hour before you want to serve them. Keep them covered in a double boiler or directly on the lowest heat of your stove. If the grits seem too thick, thin them with some more cream, hot milk, or hot water.*

LEFTOVERS *Grits will keep in the refrigerator for about five days. Like polenta, they firm up when chilled, and once they are hard, you can slice and fry them in butter or oil, just like polenta. Serve fried grits as a side dish to meats or other savory entrées. You can also reheat grits in the microwave for a more pudding-like revival.*

VARIATIONS

Basic Grits

After the initial 45 minutes of cooking, add the salt and pepper and serve the grits as is, without the cheese, cream, or butter.

Cheese Grits "Soufflé"

This is a fancier, richer style of cheese grits that is convenient because you can make it in advance. Since it doesn't rise, I put *soufflé* in quotes, but that's what this dish is traditionally called in the South. Prepare the Cheese Grits as directed up to the point when you have added the salt but before you add the cheese. Scald 3 cups of milk. Stir 2 cups of the warm milk into the grits and bring them back to a boil over medium-high heat. Keep stirring until the milk has been incorporated and the mixture has

thickened, about 5 minutes. Lower the heat. Add the remaining cup of milk, 6 tablespoons unsalted butter at room temperature, 1 tablespoon Worcestershire sauce, 4 beaten large eggs, 1 cup shredded extra-sharp Cheddar cheese, ¼ cup grated Parmigiano Reggiano, and ¼ teaspoon freshly ground white pepper, and stir to melt and incorporate. Pour this mixture into a buttered (2-quart) soufflé dish, cover with plastic wrap, and chill overnight. The next day, preheat the oven to 350°F. Sprinkle the grits with paprika and a little more Cheddar and Parmigiano cheese, and bake for 1 hour, or until the grits are browned and bubbly.

Cheese Soufflé

Call me old-fashioned, but I love a soufflé. I think it's exciting when, as if by magic, a soufflé rises over the rim of the baking dish and turns a deep golden brown. I love the ephemerality of it, the imperative to stop whatever you are doing and eat the soufflé *right now!* I love the delicate taste. What's more, making a soufflé is easy.

Makes 1 soufflé, enough for 4 appetizers or 2 light main courses

> 3 tablespoons finely grated Parmigiano Reggiano or other hard grating cheese
> 1 cup Cream Sauce (page 404), made with 2 tablespoons of butter and 3 tablespoons flour
> ½ teaspoon Worcestershire sauce or Dijon mustard (optional)
> 4 ounces strong cheese, such as Roquefort or feta, crumbled; or aged, imported Gruyère or Emmentaler, grated (1 cup)
> 1 tablespoon finely chopped chives (optional)

4 large eggs, separated, at room temperature
Kosher salt

Preheat the oven to 425°F. Grease a 7-cup soufflé dish or other baking dish. Place 1 tablespoon of the grated Parmigiano Reggiano in the dish and shake it around, tapping it on the counter, to coat with the cheese. Set aside.

In a small saucepan, warm the cream sauce over medium-high heat, stirring constantly as it comes to a simmer. Add the Worcestershire, if using, and stir to combine. Remove from the heat and stir in the strong cheese, the remaining 2 tablespoons of Parmigiano, and the chives, if using. When the cheese has melted, transfer the mixture to a medium bowl and cool slightly. Stir in the egg yolks and continue to let it set while you beat the egg whites.

In the bowl of an electric mixer, beat the egg whites with a pinch of salt on medium-low speed for a minute or two until frothy white. Increase the speed to high and beat until the whites hold stiff peaks. They should be shiny, not dry. Using a large rubber spatula, gently stir about one fourth of the egg whites into the cheese mixture to lighten it. Then empty the remaining egg whites onto the cheese mixture and gently fold them in to incorporate.

Transfer to the prepared baking dish. The mixture should come about halfway up the side. Gently smooth out the top. Place in the oven. Set a timer for 20 minutes—and don't open the oven door until that timer goes off. When 20 minutes are up, peek in to make sure the soufflé has risen. Carefully close the door and then turn the oven temperature down to 375°F. Bake for another 10 minutes or so, until the soufflé has browned and there are no wet, shiny patches on top, which means the soufflé has set.

Remove from the oven and serve immediately. A large spoon plunged into the center to scoop out the soufflé is the easiest way to serve it. Be sure to give everyone a piece of the browned crust.

PREP TIME: 15 minutes
COOKING TIME: 35 minutes
TOTAL TIME: 50 minutes

ADVANCE PREP You can make the cheese sauce base several hours in advance. Keep it at room temperature.

Carrot and Ginger Soufflé

A light brunch dish or side dish with a beautiful color, this carrot soufflé is as easy as pie. Easier, in fact. You can use just about any vegetable as long as you cook it and purée it. For a simple variation, add 2 teaspoons curry powder to the sautéed shallots and ginger.

Makes 6 to 8 servings

4 large carrots (about 1 pound), peeled and sliced (1½ cups)
¼ cup heavy cream, sour cream, plain yogurt, or buttermilk
Kosher salt and freshly ground white pepper
4 tablespoons (½ stick) unsalted butter
1 tablespoon grated fresh ginger
1 shallot, minced
¼ cup all-purpose flour
1 cup milk or vegetable stock
Juice of ½ lemon (about 2 tablespoons)
6 large eggs, separated

Preheat the oven to 425°F. Grease a 2-quart baking dish or six or eight individual (4-ounce) soufflé dishes or ramekins.

AND A SOUFFLÉ IS JUST EGGS . . .

A dish that even experienced cooks find intimidating, a soufflé is actually quite simple to make. The basic technique is the same no matter what flavor soufflé you are preparing, savory or sweet. You start with a thick paste, usually based on Cream Sauce (page 404) or béchamel for savory soufflés. You enrich that paste with egg yolks and whatever flavorings the recipe calls for. And then you fold in beaten egg whites. The whites are what make the soufflé rise. Pop it into a hot oven, and voilà!

Here are a few pointers that will help you make beautifully high, delicious soufflés:

• Because the flavor of the soufflé base is going to be diluted when you add the egg whites, it's important that it be strongly flavored. That's why I recommend strong cheese, such as Roquefort or feta, for cheese soufflés.
• Cool the base before folding in the whites so you don't run the risk of accidentally cooking the eggs before you bake the soufflé.
• It's important not to overbeat the egg whites. They should form stiff peaks, but still be shiny and smooth, not dry and matte. It helps to have the egg whites at room temperature before you beat them. A pinch of salt and a tiny bit of acid, such as cream of tartar or lemon juice, helps achieve glossy egg whites with a silken texture.
• Deflate the egg whites as little as possible when you are folding them into the base. It helps to first lighten the base by stirring in about one fourth of the egg whites and then folding the rest of the whites into the lightened base with a large rubber spatula. When the whites are folded in, the soufflé should have the texture of a light mousse or foam.
• Although many recipes for soufflé require you to make a collar of aluminum foil or parchment paper for the soufflé dish, I find this unnecessary. Leave at least $1/2$ inch of space at the top of the dish so the soufflé can support itself as it rises.
• Be sure there's enough room in the oven for the soufflé to rise. On more than one occasion I've made a soufflé that has crashed into the roof of my oven. Shift racks around as necessary to avoid this.
• It's important to bake the soufflé until it is done. It should have risen and browned. There should be no visible wet patches on the top. I like to err on the side of overbaking because it only reinforces the integrity of the soufflé to cook it a little longer.

Bring a pot of salted water to a boil. Add the carrots and cook until very soft, 20 to 25 minutes, depending on how thinly they are sliced. Drain and transfer to a blender or food processor. Add the cream and purée until smooth. Season with salt and pepper. You should have about $1\frac{1}{2}$ cups of purée.

In a small saucepan, melt the butter. Add the ginger and shallot and cook for a couple of minutes until the shallot is soft. Add the flour and cook, stirring, for 2 or 3 minutes, until the flour starts to smell toasted. Whisk in the milk to make a stiff paste. Stir in the carrot purée and cook for 4 or 5 minutes. Remove from the heat and set aside to cool for about 5 minutes. Stir in the lemon juice. Whisk in the egg yolks,

Homemade Yogurt

Okay, I'm crazy. Sometimes I make my own yogurt. I wasn't a hippie in the 1960s and I never owned one of those funny electric yogurt makers with little glass jars that were the rage in the 1970s. Come to think of it, I did live in a co-op/commune in college in the early 1990s, but that's not why I make yogurt today. I do it because it's hard to find plain yogurt that has any flavor. It's hard enough to find some with any fat. Sure, you can get imported yogurt from some Balkan country, but it usually comes with a price tag to prove it traveled first class. Besides, making yogurt is really easy. It doesn't require anything but a bowl, a towel, and an instant-read thermometer. Homemade yogurt impresses your friends, and it gives you the satisfaction of making something that's actually good for you. As an added bonus, the more you make it, the more flavorful your yogurt will become. Like sourdough bread starter, you use some of the yogurt culture from the previous batch in each subsequent batch. This makes the flavor develop over time. When you are making yogurt for the first time, you will have to use some plain, commercially made, preferably organic yogurt—be sure the label says it contains live, active bacteria.

Makes just under 1 quart

- 1 quart milk, preferably organic, either 2% or whole, but not skim
- 3 tablespoons plain yogurt, at room temperature

In a large nonreactive saucepan, heat the milk over medium-high heat until boiling. Turn down the heat and let simmer for 3 or 4 minutes. Whatever you do, don't turn away from the pot while the milk is heating or it may boil over and make a mess of your stove. If you are watching, you can turn down the heat before it goes over. Otherwise, if it is too late, you can plunk a cold metal utensil (ladle, spoon, or spatula, for example) into the pot and the milk froth will deflate.

Transfer the milk to a clean glass or ceramic bowl. The milk must cool to 120°F, and this will take much longer than you think—about 1 hour. Balance an instant-read thermometer on the side of the bowl and you can periodically check it to see what the temperature is. A skin will form on the surface of the milk as it cools. Don't remove it until the milk is below 150°F or it may reform. I usually just use my thermometer to gather up the skin and throw it out. When the milk has cooled to 120°F, whisk in the yogurt starter. Cover the bowl with a clean dish towel, pulled taught so it doesn't touch the milk, and then wrap this whole thing in a couple of big bath towels. The idea is to keep it warm to incubate the bacteria. I usually put the towel-wrapped bowl in the middle of my stove, where the pilot lights below the thin metal surface give off the perfect amount of heat. You could also put it in a gas oven that isn't turned on. Let the yogurt sit for a minimum of 12 hours or up to 24 if you like your yogurt particularly tangy.

When you remove the towels, you will see that the yogurt has almost solidified and there is clear liquid around the edges and on the surface. If you like thick yogurt, which I do, you can carefully pour off this liquid or dab it with a piece of paper towel. Otherwise, you can stir it back into the yogurt. Transfer to a sealable container and refrigerate until ready to use. I've kept this yogurt in the fridge for up to three weeks, and it would probably last longer, but I usually eat it before then, anyway. You can easily double the recipe to make 2 quarts of yogurt with the same effort.

COOKING TIME: 5 to 6 minutes
TOTAL TIME: 13 to 25 hours (includes curing time)

one at a time. Season with salt and pepper to taste.

In the large bowl of an electric mixer, beat the egg whites with a pinch of salt on medium-low speed until frothy white. Increase the speed to high and beat to stiff peaks. Using a large rubber spatula, fold about a quarter of the whites into the carrot mixture and then fold in the rest just until incorporated, being careful not to deflate the whites while you work. Gently transfer this mixture to the prepared baking dish. Level the top and set in the oven for 15 to 25 minutes, until the soufflé has risen, set, and browned. There should be no visible wet patches on the top of the soufflé when it is done. Serve immediately.

PREP TIME: 20 minutes
COOKING TIME: 40 to 55 minutes
TOTAL TIME: 1 hour to 1 hour 15 minutes

ADVANCE PREP *The base of the soufflé (without the egg whites) can be made several hours in advance and refrigerated. Beat and fold in the egg whites just before baking and serving.*

Brandied Apricot Jam with Vanilla Bean

The sweet, rich taste of fresh apricots makes this jam one of my favorites. I spread it on bread, stir it into yogurt, use it to fill cookies, or bake it into tarts. I prefer the reddish-skinned apricots to the pale orange ones, but either type needs to be ripe to make the jam. If the apricots are hard as rocks when you buy them, keep them on the counter for a couple of days until they soften, or use peeled peaches. For a boost of bitter-almond flavor, I crack a few apricot pits and remove the soft inner kernels. Tie the kernels in a cheesecloth satchel and add it to the pot while the jam cooks. Remove the satchel before processing or storing.

Makes 2 pints

> 2½ pounds ripe apricots (about 30), rinsed, pitted, but not peeled, cut into small dice (about 5 cups)
> 4 cups sugar
> Juice of ½ lemon (2 tablespoons)
> One 1-inch piece cinnamon stick
> ¼ cup brandy
> ½ vanilla bean
> Pinch of kosher salt

In a wide, heavy large saucepan, combine the apricots, sugar, lemon juice, cinnamon stick, and brandy. With a sharp paring knife, split the vanilla bean in half lengthwise and scrape the seeds into the pot. Add the pod, too, along with the salt. Bring the mixture to a boil over medium-high heat, stirring to encourage the sugar to dissolve. Lower the heat to a simmer and let cook for 25 to 30 minutes, until the jam has thickened, the bubbles have slowed and gotten bigger, and a candy thermometer reads between 219° and 220° F. Skim any light foam that rises to the top while it cooks. Turn off the jam and let it sit for 5 minutes. Remove the cinnamon stick and vanilla bean. Ladle the jam into hot, sterilized pint jars, seal, and process in a water bath (see page 138) or cool to room temperature and refrigerate. If processed, refrigerate after opening.

PREP TIME: 5 minutes
COOKING TIME: 25 to 30 minutes
TOTAL TIME: 40 minutes (plus processing time)

VARIATION

Brandied Peach Jam with Vanilla

Substitute 3 pounds of peaches, peeled (see page 429), pitted, and diced, for the apricots and proceed as directed.

Strawberry Jam

I add some finely grated green apple to increase the pectin and improve the texture of this simple, summery jam without adding commercial liquid pectin. (Apples are high in pectin; strawberries are low in pectin.) Grate the apple very fine on a Microplane grater and it will completely dissolve as the jam cooks.

Makes 2 pints

1 quart ripe strawberries, hulled and sliced
    (just under 4 cups)
2½ cups sugar
⅓ cup finely grated peeled green apple, such as
    Granny Smith
Juice of ½ lemon (about 2 tablespoons)
Pinch of kosher salt

In a wide, heavy, nonreactive medium saucepan, combine the strawberries with the sugar, apple, lemon juice, and salt. Set over medium-high heat and bring to a boil, stirring to dissolve the sugar and skimming any froth that accumulates on the surface. Turn down the heat and simmer until the jam thickens, the bubbles get larger and slower, and the jam reads about 219°F on a candy thermometer, 15 to 20 minutes. Remove from the heat and let sit for 5 minutes. Transfer to hot, sterilized pint jars, seal, and process in a water bath (see page 138) or cool to room temperature and refrigerate. If processed, refrigerate after opening.

JAM SESSION

Whenever I have guests for brunch, I like to decorate the table with jars of colorful homemade jams. They aren't just delicious to eat on biscuits and toast, they are also beautiful to look at. Jam is one of the easiest types of preserves to make at home. You can make it in small batches and keep it in the fridge, or you can process jars in a water bath (do not be intimidated: this is a lot easier than it sounds; see page 138) and store them for long periods, up to two years. The only trick is getting the jam to the right consistency, which is a factor of temperature, time, and the pectin content of your fruit.

For some reason I can't quite articulate, I prefer not to use commercially prepared pectin in my jams. I guess I feel like it is cheating. Pectin is a carbohydrate that occurs naturally in fruits, more in some than others. It is responsible in large part for the gelling of jams. The properties of heated sugar and evaporation also help jams reach their thickened consistency. The idea is to strike a balance between the cooked flavor of the fruit and the texture of the jam.

In my recipes for jam, I've given specific instructions for making my favorite jams. Although the traditional ratio of fruit to sugar is 1 to 1—that is, for every cup of fruit you use 1 cup of sugar—I find the result too sweet to my taste sometimes; my recipes generally call for less sugar. I use these recipes every year, but as with everything in the kitchen, sometimes because of variations in ingredients, things just work out differently. If your jams are too thin, use them as sauces for cakes and ice cream instead.

If you have too much jam to eat on toast, consider making a delicious Jam Cake (page 438).

BEFORE YOU THROW IT AWAY, CONSIDER MAKING SOME MICROWAVE JAM

If you've got some fruit that you just can't eat or it's ripened slightly beyond its prime, consider turning it into a quick jam in the microwave. I treat plums, nectarines, berries, and other fruit this way. The beauty of using the microwave for jam is that you can turn any amount of fruit, no matter how little, into jam. And you don't have to stand over a hot stove. Wash and cut up the fruit and remove any pits or blemishes. Combine an equal amount (by volume) of sugar with the fruit and a squirt of fresh lemon juice in a glass dish. Microwave on high for 8 to 15 minutes, depending on how much fruit you have. Stop the cooking and stir every minute or so, until your jam has thickened to the desired consistency (remember that it will thicken more as it cools). Store microwave jam in the fridge for no more than a week or two.

COOKING TIME: 15 to 20 minutes

TOTAL TIME: 25 minutes (plus processing time)

Strawberry Rhubarb Jam

The addition of lemon and orange to this jam helps round out the classic strawberry-rhubarb flavor.

Makes about 2½ pints

1 quart ripe strawberries, hulled and sliced (just under 4 cups)

8 ounces rhubarb (about 2 medium stalks), cut into ½-inch pieces (just under 2 cups)

2½ cups sugar

Grated zest and juice of ½ orange

Grated zest and juice of ½ lemon

Pinch of kosher salt

In a wide, heavy, nonreactive medium saucepan, combine the strawberries, rhubarb, sugar, orange zest and juice, lemon zest and juice, and salt. Set over medium-high heat and bring to a boil, skimming off any froth that accumulates on the surface. Turn down the heat and simmer the mixture until it thickens, the bubbles get bigger and slower, and the jam reaches 219°F on a candy thermometer, 20 to 25 minutes. Remove from the heat and let cool for 5 minutes. Transfer to hot, sterilized jars, seal, and process in a water bath (see page 138) or cool to room temperature and refrigerate. If processed, refrigerate after opening.

COOKING TIME: 25 minutes

TOTAL TIME: 30 minutes (plus processing time)

Spiced Blueberry Jam

This delicious jam comes out of an American tradition of sweet-and-sour spiced pickled fruits and jams. Blueberries are naturally high in pectin so this jam sets up very firm. The technique for this jam is a little different from the others in this book. If you cook the blueberries with the sugar from the beginning, they have a tendency to get hard. Instead I cook the blueberries first and then add the sugar.

Makes about 2½ pints

4½ cups fresh blueberries, stems removed

⅓ cup red or white wine vinegar

3 cups sugar

½ teaspoon pure vanilla extract

¼ teaspoon freshly grated nutmeg

¼ teaspoon ground cinnamon

⅛ teaspoon ground allspice

Pinch of ground cloves

Kosher salt and freshly ground black pepper

In a wide, heavy, nonreactive medium saucepan, combine the blueberries with the vinegar. Slowly bring to a boil, drawing out the juice of the berries as they heat. Simmer the blueberries for 10 minutes. Add the sugar, vanilla, nutmeg, cinnamon, allspice, cloves, a pinch of salt, and some pepper. Bring back to the boil, skim off any froth that accumulates on the surface, reduce the heat, and simmer for about 15 minutes, until thick and jamlike—it should register 218° F on a candy thermometer. Remove from the heat and let sit for 5 minutes. Transfer to hot, sterilized jars, seal, and process in a water bath (see page 138) or cool to room temperature and refrigerate. If processed, refrigerate after opening.

COOKING TIME: 25 minutes

TOTAL TIME: 30 minutes (plus processing time)

Sour Cherry Jam

Sour cherries, or "pie" cherries, are available for only a few weeks a year. Though not very good to eat fresh, they have a deep cherry flavor when cooked. This jam is one of my favorites. Like apricots, the kernel of the cherry pit has a delicious bitter-almond flavor. For this jam I smash some of the cherry pits, revealing the inner kernel, wrap them in cheesecloth, and add them to the pot while the jam cooks. To boost the pectin, I add some finely shredded green apple, which disintegrates as the jam cooks.

Makes 2 pints

1 quart sour cherries, washed, stems removed, and pitted; reserve one fourth of the pits

2½ cups sugar

⅓ cup finely grated green apple, such as Granny Smith

Pinch of kosher salt

Place the cherries in the bowl of a food processor fitted with a metal chopping blade. Pulse four or five times to roughly chop. You should have about 3 cups of cherry pulp. Transfer to a wide, heavy, nonreactive medium pot. Using a meat tenderizer or other heavy object, smash the reserved cherry pits to reveal the soft inner kernels. Gather the cracked pits into a 5-inch square piece of cheesecloth and tie with kitchen twine into a bundle. Add this bundle to the cherries along with the sugar, apple, and salt.

Set the pot over medium-high heat and bring to a boil, skimming any froth that accumulates on the surface. Turn down the heat and simmer the cherry mixture for about 20 minutes, or until the consistency thickens, the bubbles get bigger and slower, and the jam reads about 220° F on a candy thermometer. Remove from the heat and cool for 5 minutes. Remove the bundle of cherry pits and transfer the jam to hot, sterilized jars. Seal and process in a water bath (see page 138) or let cool completely to room temperature before storing in the refrigerator. If processed, refrigerate after opening.

PREP TIME: 10 minutes

COOKING TIME: 20 minutes

TOTAL TIME: 35 minutes (plus processing time)

CANNING JAMS

You can keep jars of jam for several weeks, even months, in the refrigerator, but if, like me, you don't have a lot of room in your fridge, you are better off canning them for longer storage. Although you will see many different techniques for preserving jams—including inverting the jars to cool or sealing with paraffin wax—the surest and the safest way is to pack the hot jam into sterilized jars and process them in a boiling water bath. Properly processed jams will keep in a cool, dark place for up to two years. Here's how I do it:

• Bring a large stockpot or canning kettle full of water with a rack in the bottom of it to a boil. Cover and turn down the heat until you are ready to process your jams. You need enough water to cover the jars by 2 inches; just in case you need more hot water, fill a tea kettle and bring it to a boil also.

• Jams should be processed while still hot in hot, clean, sterilized glass canning jars. My preferred way to sterilize jars is to heat them in the oven. This avoids having to boil the jars in large vats of water. Wash the jars well with soap and hot water and rinse them, keeping them somewhat wet. Line a baking sheet with a damp dish towel and place the wet jars on the towel. Set the sheet in a cold oven and turn the dial to 300°F. When the oven comes up to temperature, set a timer for 15 minutes. Keep the jars in the oven until you need them. Meanwhile, to sterilize and soften the metal lids that sit on top of the jars, place them in a small saucepan, cover with water, and boil for 5 minutes or so. (Note that you can reuse jars and their metal rings, but you cannot reuse the lids.)

• After the jam has finished cooking and has sat for 5 minutes off the heat (which helps keep the fruit from floating to the top), use a wide plastic canning funnel (metal can nick the glass and cause the jars to break) to transfer the jam to the jars, leaving a ½-inch headspace at the top of each jar. Dip a clean dish towel in the boiling water in the canning kettle and use it to wipe the rim of the jars clean. Using a lid lifter (a plastic stick with a magnet on the end), lift the lids out of the hot water and place on top of each jar, with the rubberized ring side facing down. Screw the metal bands tight, then unscrew them one quarter turn.

• Turn up the heat under the canning kettle to high to bring the water back to a rolling boil. Using jar tongs, lower the jam jars into the boiling water. They should be covered by at least 2 inches of water. If not, add more hot water. If there's too much water, use a small pot to scoop it out. Cover the pot. When the water comes back to a boil, start timing. Process ½-pint (1-cup) jars for 5 minutes and 1-pint (2-cup) jars for 7 minutes. After the processing time is up, lift the jars out with the tongs and set them on a dish towel or newspaper to cool completely to room temperature. You will hear distinct pops as the jars seal and the center of the lids will be sunk in. Whatever you do, don't tighten the bands, which can break the seals. When the jars are totally cool, in about 4 hours, check the seals by pushing down on the center of the top of each jar; if you hear a clicking sound, the jar isn't sealed. Wipe the jars. Store unsealed jars in the fridge for no more than a few weeks. Label, date, and store sealed jars in a cool, dark place for up to two years. Refrigerate jams after opening.

Green Tomato Ginger Jam

This unusual jam is equally delicious with sweet and savory dishes. It is lovely spread on buttered toast or used as a condiment with roasted pork. Make it at the end of the summer when green, unripened tomatoes are plentiful. Because the green tomatoes are very dry, I macerate them with the sugar for a day to draw out whatever moisture they contain. They take a lot longer to cook than other fruits, but you don't have to worry about losing the fresh fruit flavor.

Makes 2 pints

> $2\frac{1}{2}$ pounds green unripe tomatoes, cored and
>   diced (about 5 cups)
> 3 cups sugar
> Finely grated zest of 2 lemons (about $\frac{1}{4}$ cup)
> 3 tablespoons minced fresh ginger

In a wide, heavy, nonreactive medium pot, combine the tomatoes with the sugar and lemon zest. Let sit at room temperature for a full day.

Stir the ginger into the tomatoes. Set the pot over medium-high heat and bring to a boil. Skim off any froth that accumulates on the surface. Turn down the heat and simmer the jam until it thickens and the tomatoes are well cooked, $1\frac{1}{4}$ to $1\frac{1}{2}$ hours. Remove from the heat and let sit for 5 minutes. Transfer to hot sterilized jars, seal, and process in a water bath (see page 138) or cool to room temperature and store in the refrigerator. If processed, refrigerate after opening.

COOKING TIME: $1\frac{1}{4}$ to $1\frac{1}{2}$ hours
TOTAL TIME: 24 hours (includes macerating time) plus processing time

Bitter Orange Marmalade

One day in a fruit store in my neighborhood I stumbled across the most beautiful Seville (aka bitter or sour) oranges I have ever seen. They were intensely orange with deeply ridged skin and a strong orange perfume. I bought all they had, six of them, and turned them into the best marmalade I have ever made. This is a traditional recipe and technique for what is known as Scotch marmalade. It has an intense orange flavor and a delicate, almost creamy texture. You can alter the proportions for however many oranges you stumble across.

Makes 2 pints

> 6 large Seville or bitter oranges, washed
> About 4 cups sugar

Using a sharp paring knife, remove the peel and pith of the oranges (for a good technique, see page 70). Discard about two thirds of the peel, reserving the nicest-looking pieces. Lay those pieces flat on the counter, white part facing up, and with the same knife, shave off the white pith to leave only a thin layer of pith and the orange zest behind. Discard the trimmings and slice the zest into thin strips. Place the zest in a small saucepan and cover with cold water. Bring to a boil, turn down the heat, and simmer for about 5 minutes. Drain and repeat this process two or three times until the zest is soft. Drain and set aside.

Cut the peeled oranges into chunks, removing the seeds, and place in a wide, heavy, nonreactive medium saucepan. Cover with cold water and set over medium-high heat. Bring to a boil and cook until the oranges are fall-apart mushy, about 15 minutes. Using a potato masher or large spoon, mash the pulp to extract as much juice and pectin as possible. Strain this mixture through a muslin jelly bag or through a fine-mesh sieve lined with several layers of cheesecloth.

Measure the juice. For every 2 cups of juice, add 3 cups of sugar and combine the juice and sugar in the saucepan. Add the zest. Set over medium-high heat and bring to a boil, skimming off any froth that accumulates on the surface. Keep boiling and stirring until the mixture thickens to a jamlike consistency and reaches about 218°F on a candy thermometer, about 10 minutes. Remove from the heat and let sit for 5 minutes. Transfer to hot, sterilized jars, seal, and process in a water bath (see page 138) or let cool to room temperature and refrigerate. If processed, refrigerate after opening.

PREP TIME: 30 minutes

COOKING TIME: 40 minutes

TOTAL TIME: 1 hour 10 minutes (plus processing time)

Fig Preserves

In late August you start to see inexpensive pints of black Mission figs for sale on the street carts around Manhattan. That's when I put up jars of these preserves to enjoy at breakfasts and brunches all year long.

Makes 6 cups

3 pints fresh black Mission figs (about 45), stems removed, quartered lengthwise

$\frac{1}{2}$ cup brandy

$3\frac{1}{2}$ cups sugar

Grated zest and juice of 1 lemon or orange

One 2-inch piece cinnamon stick

In a wide, heavy, nonreactive medium saucepan, combine the figs, brandy, sugar, lemon zest and juice, and cinnamon stick. Set over medium-high heat. Bring to a boil, skimming any froth that accumulates on the surface. Turn down the heat so that the figs simmer, and cook for about 25 minutes, or until the mixture thickens, the bubbles get bigger and slower, and a candy thermometer reads about 217°F. Let sit for 5 minutes. Ladle into hot, sterilized jars. Wipe the jars carefully with a damp cloth because the fig seeds tend to get everywhere. Seal and process in a water bath (see page 138) or cool to room temperature and refrigerate. If processed, refrigerate after opening.

COOKING TIME: 25 minutes

TOTAL TIME: 30 minutes (plus processing time)

■ ■ ■

Vegetables, Beans, and Potatoes

T HE ARRAY OF VEGETABLES that exist in the American marketplace these days is overwhelming, especially if you include the produce sellers in ethnic neighborhoods. Even potatoes, which were once available in only two styles, boilers and bakers, now come in a variety of colors and sizes. And yet most people eat a very narrow selection of vegetables. Beans are another category of nutritious, delicious foods of which the majority of folk cook only a limited variety, if any at all. Some people complain about the amount of time it takes to prepare these ingredients. Enter instant mashed potatoes, canned baked beans, prewashed salad packs, and bags of "baby" carrots. (I use quotes because most of the carrots sold as baby carrots are actually plugs punched out of giant old tough, tasteless carrots.) But considering how important freshness is in the flavor of these items, I think a few minutes spent cleaning vegetables at the sink or peeling potatoes over the garbage can is time well spent.

This is not to say I don't use frozen and canned vegetables when and where appropriate. But one of the saddest sights to me is visible in August and September, when my local farmer's market is in full bloom, and people still pack into the produce section of the neighborhood grocery store just steps away. How can they pass by such a beautiful, bountiful assortment of vegetables in season for a tired selection of vegetables shipped into town from who knows where? The "in season" part is key. No matter how much of a vine is attached to a hothouse tomato from Holland in February, it is going to taste more like a potato than a Jersey tomato picked ripe in August. Some vegetables—such as eggplants, peppers, lettuce, potatoes, and cabbage, for example—are fine throughout the year (though even these stalwarts improve when they are consumed closer to their growing season). But other vegetables, tomatoes and asparagus come to mind as prime examples, are best eaten when they were meant to grow.

On the question of organic vegetables, I'm of two minds. Because seasonality, variety, and freshness are the most important factors in finding the best-tasting vegetables, I think locally grown, organic vegetables are the best choice, provided the farmer has planted the most delicious varieties. (Even with the recent increase in the number of varieties of organic vegetables available, there still are some gaps.) Next in my personal hierarchy of vegetable selection would be locally grown conventional vegetables, which I think are usually better than organic vegetables that have been shipped in from faraway places like California or Holland. After that, I'd choose organic vegetables from faraway lands. And finally, if there was nothing else available, I'd reach for conventionally grown vegetables from around the globe. Of course, your own ethical and gastronomic formula should determine how you shop.

Vegetable cookery is pretty simple because once you have mastered a few basic techniqes—roasting, grilling, glazing, blanching, mashing, frying, and gratinéing, for example—the vegetables do all the work. Change the vegetable and you change the dish. You can alter the texture, flavor, and overall character of a recipe simply by using a different main ingredient. The same is true of beans, all of which can be cooked the same way: boiled in liquid until they are soft. Of course, you can cook them differently, too, as these recipes show.

With deference to my vegetarian friends, all of the recipes that follow are portioned as side dishes unless otherwise stated.

■ ■ ■

Roasted Asparagus

As with most vegetables, when asparagus is roasted, the flavor intensifies. This is a quick and easy way to cook asparagus. Choose asparagus stalks less than $\frac{1}{2}$ inch in diameter. (For boiling or steaming, I prefer fatter asparagus, which should be peeled first.) A hot oven helps the asparagus to cook quickly and to brown. I like to serve my roasted asparagus with a squirt of lemon juice and a sprinkling of grated cheese, but they are delicious plain, as well.

Makes 4 servings

1$\frac{1}{4}$ to 1$\frac{1}{2}$ pounds asparagus
3 tablespoons extra-virgin olive oil
Kosher salt and freshly ground black pepper
Juice of $\frac{1}{2}$ lemon (optional)
2 tablespoons freshly grated Parmigiano
    Reggiano cheese (optional)

Preheat the oven to 450°F.

Trim the woody, fibrous ends of the asparagus with a knife or by snapping the stalks in your hands—they break at the point that the stalk becomes inedible. Pour 2 tablespoons of the olive oil onto a baking sheet or in an oven-proof cast-iron pan. Add the asparagus and roll around to coat with the oil. Season generously with salt and pepper. Roast for 10 to 12 minutes, or until the asparagus has shriveled somewhat and browned. Remove from the oven; toss with the remaining tablespoon of olive oil and the lemon juice and Parmigiano, if using.

PREP TIME: 5 minutes
COOKING TIME: 10 to 12 minutes
TOTAL TIME: 15 to 20 minutes

LEFTOVERS *Roasted asparagus will keep for about a week in the fridge. Use leftovers in pasta or salads.*

Roasted Carrots with Spices

Here's an example of how you can use ready-mixed spice blends to add a little zing to your daily cooking. I like to roast carrots with Middle Eastern spices, such as Za'atar (page 407) and Dukkah (page 408), though the same technique can be used with other spice blends, such as Indian garam masala.

Makes 4 servings

1$\frac{1}{2}$ pounds carrots (4 or 5 large), peeled and cut
    into 1-inch chunks
3 tablespoons extra-virgin olive oil
Kosher salt and freshly ground black pepper
2 garlic cloves, roughly chopped
1 tablespoon Za'atar (page 407), Dukkah (page
    408), or other spice mix

Preheat the oven to 425°F.

Place the carrot chunks on a baking sheet or in a baking dish and toss with the olive oil, about $\frac{1}{4}$ teaspoon salt, and some black pepper. Roast for 15 minutes or so, until the carrots begin to pucker a little. Add the garlic, toss, and continue roasting for another 20 minutes, tossing occasionally. The carrots should be crispy brown around the edges and tender when pricked with a fork. Sprinkle the za'atar over the carrots and toss to coat. Roast for another 5 minutes, remove from the oven, and serve.

PREP TIME: 5 minutes
COOK TIME: 40 minutes
TOTAL TIME: 45 minutes

LEFTOVERS *The cooked carrots will keep up to a week in the refrigerator. Reheat leftovers in the microwave for a minute or two on high.*

Roasted Winter Squash

I find winter squash so naturally sweet that I've never quite understood the need to drown it in honey, brown sugar, or syrup, or to smother it with marshmallows. For this recipe—more like a technique, really—choose any winter squash variety, such as acorn, butternut, delicata, or hubbard. It should feel firm, dense, and heavy for its size. There should be no soft spots, which indicate bruising. I like to roast my squash in thin slices or rings, peeled or not, rather than whole or in halves. It's quicker and the edges brown nicely, which adds texture and flavor.

Makes 6 to 8 servings

> About 2 pounds winter squash
> 6 tablespoons ($^3/_4$ stick) unsalted butter, melted
> Kosher salt and freshly ground black pepper

Preheat the oven to 425°F.

Wash the squash and pat dry. Cut it in half. Scoop out the seeds and scrape the cavity to remove any stringy flesh. With a serrated knife, cut the squash into $^1/_4$- to $^1/_2$-inch slices or wedges, depending on its shape. You can peel the slices if you wish, but I think they are more attractive with the peel left on. Brush a baking sheet or gratin dish generously with butter and arrange the squash slices on it, touching but not overlapping. Brush the squash with butter and season generously with salt and pepper. Set the squash in the oven and bake for 15 minutes. Baste with more butter and bake for another 15 minutes, or until the squash is tender when pricked with a fork and nicely browned around the edges.

PREP TIME: 10 minutes
COOKING TIME: 30 minutes
TOTAL TIME: 40 minutes

ADVANCE PREP *The squash can be sliced and seasoned up to one day in advance. Wrap tightly and store in the refrigerator until ready to bake.*
LEFTOVERS *The roasted squash will keep for about a week in the refrigerator. Reheat it in the microwave for 25 to 30 seconds per slice.*

Roasted Sweet Potato Wedges

These sweet potato wedges are all about the flavor of the vegetable—they have no added sweetness, save for what the potato brings to the dish. There's no need to peel the sweet potatoes, just scrub them well.

Makes 4 to 6 servings

> 2 pounds sweet potatoes, washed but not peeled
> 3 tablespoons extra-virgin olive oil
> 1$^1/_2$ teaspoons kosher salt
> Freshly ground black pepper
> 2 garlic cloves, smashed but not peeled

Preheat the oven to 425°F.

How you cut up the sweet potatoes depends on their size and shape. The idea is to create wedges, each with some skin on it. I usually cut very large sweet potatoes in half crosswise, and then I cut each half lengthwise in half again. From each quarter I then cut wedges radiating out from the center. Use your high school geometry and your imagination. The important thing is that the wedges be roughly the same size and thickness so they cook evenly.

Place the wedges in a large cast-iron pan or other metal baking dish. Drizzle the olive oil over the potatoes and sprinkle with the salt and a generous amount of black pepper. Add the garlic to the pan, and using a large spoon or

Roasted Peppers

Roasting sweetens peppers and intensifies their flavor. You can roast peppers in the oven, on a charcoal or gas grill, or, if you have a gas stove, over an open flame. Because the flesh of the pepper cooks less when the peppers are done over an open flame, I prefer this technique. But if you have a lot of peppers, the oven is easier. Either way, you can eat the peppers plain or use them in recipes. You can also marinate roasted peppers in a vinegary herb dressing to serve as an antipasto or use in salads.

Makes 2½ to 3 cups

2 pounds large, firm red or yellow bell peppers
Extra-virgin olive oil

To roast the peppers in the oven, preheat the oven to 425°F. Line a cookie sheet with aluminum foil (for easy cleanup). Lightly grease the aluminum foil with olive oil. Arrange the peppers on the tray and set in the oven. Roast for about 1 hour, turning the peppers every 15 minutes or so, until they are black and blistered all over.

To roast the peppers over an open flame, turn on a gas burner to high. Place a pepper on the metal grate or guard over the burner, and when the underside of the pepper begins to blacken and blister, rotate the pepper with a pair of long tongs. Continue rotating until the pepper is evenly colored. Repeat with the remaining peppers. You can also roast peppers over a hot grill in the same manner.

Whichever technique you use, when the peppers are roasted, place them in a bowl and cover with plastic wrap to trap the steam, which helps loosen the skin. Allow to cool to room temperature, 30 to 45 minutes. When cool, peel the blackened skin off of each pepper as best you can; don't worry if you can't get it all. Remove the core, seeds, and ribs. If I can avoid it, I prefer not to rinse the peppers, which removes some of their sweet flavor. But sometimes there are so many stray seeds you have to rinse them. Either way, pat dry. Toss with some olive oil or marinate in a tangy vinaigrette with herbs, and store in an airtight container in the fridge.

PREP TIME: 15 minutes
COOKING TIME: 1 hour
TOTAL TIME: 1 hour 45 minutes (includes cooling time)

ADVANCE PREP *The peppers can be made up to two weeks in advance. Refrigerate until needed.*
LEFTOVERS *The peppers will keep for two to three weeks in the refrigerator.*

your hands, toss the potatoes to coat with the oil and spices. Roast for about 30 minutes, or until the wedges are tender and nicely browned around the edges. Toss them around once or twice while they are roasting to ensure even cooking.

PREP TIME: 10 minutes
COOKING TIME: 30 minutes
TOTAL TIME: 40 minutes

ADVANCE PREP *You can cut the potatoes and toss them in the oil and spices in advance. While the po-*

tatoes are best served right from the oven, they are also good at room temperature.

LEFTOVERS *The potatoes will keep for about two weeks in the fridge. Reheat in a 300° F oven for 7 to 8 minutes. They are also good with eggs for breakfast.*

VARIATION

Roasted Sweet Potato Wedges with Herbs

If you'd like to add a handful of chopped fresh herbs, such as rosemary, thyme, marjoram, or flat-leaf parsley, to the potatoes, do so 5 to 7 minutes before the potatoes are done. Toss in the herbs, stir the pan, and finish cooking. If you put the herbs in sooner, they will burn and give the potatoes a bitter flavor.

Roasted Cauliflower

It's important to break the cauliflower into equal-size florets so that they cook evenly.

Makes 4 servings

> 1 medium head cauliflower (about 1 1/2 pounds), cut into 1 1/2- to 2-inch florets
> 1/4 cup extra-virgin olive oil
> Kosher salt and freshly ground black pepper

Preheat the oven to 400° F. Line a baking sheet with parchment.

Place the florets in a large bowl, drizzle with the olive oil, and sprinkle with about 1 teaspoon salt and a generous amount of black pepper. Toss the cauliflower to coat evenly with the oil and spices. Arrange the florets on the baking sheet, stem side down. Bake for 35 to 40 min-

utes, or until the cauliflower has browned and is tender when poked with the tip of a knife. Serve hot or at room temperature.

PREP TIME: 5 minutes
COOKING TIME: 35 to 40 minutes
TOTAL TIME: 40 to 45 minutes

ADVANCE PREP *The cauliflower can be seasoned several hours in advance and roasted just before serving.*

LEFTOVERS *The cauliflower will keep for about two weeks in the fridge. Leftovers can be reheated, but they can also be turned into a soup (page 38), cut up and added to a salad (such as Spicy Moroccan Olive Salad, page 6), or else turned into a relish, with capers, Preserved Lemon (page 409), and golden raisins plumped in white wine vinegar.*

Roasted Fennel

I love the mild licorice flavor and crunchy texture of fennel, both raw and cooked. Roasting has the opposite effect on fennel than it does on most vegetables: it softens the flavor. Although it is sometimes mislabeled anise, fennel and anise are not the same thing. Anise is a licorice-flavored seed; fennel is a vegetable.

Makes 6 servings

> 2 fennel bulbs (about 1 1/2 pounds)
> 1/4 cup extra-virgin olive oil
> Kosher salt and freshly ground pepper
> 3 garlic cloves, smashed but not peeled
> Juice of 1/2 lemon

Preheat the oven to 400° F.

Trim the fronds, stems, and root ends of the fennel bulbs. Slice the bulbs in half lengthwise and then cut the halves into wedges, three or four per half, through the core so that the wedges do not separate into layers. Place the wedges in a baking dish. Drizzle the fennel with the olive oil and season generously with salt and pepper. Add the garlic to the dish and toss to coat the fennel with the oil and seasonings. Spread out the fennel so it's in an even layer and roast for 35 to 40 minutes, until the fennel is tender and browned. Toss two or three times during the roasting period. Remove from the oven and sprinkle with the lemon juice before serving warm or at room temperature.

PREP TIME: 5 minutes
COOKING TIME: 35 to 40 minutes
TOTAL TIME: 40 to 45 minutes

ADVANCE PREP *The fennel can be cut and tossed with the oil and spices several hours before serving. It can also be roasted in advance and reheated in the oven or microwave.*
LEFTOVERS *Roasted fennel will keep for about two weeks in the refrigerator. Chop the roasted fennel and use it in other dishes, such as soup, risotto, or pasta.*

Roasted Jerusalem Artichokes

At the market I often overhear people intrigued by the way Jerusalem artichokes look, but they are unsure of what to do with them. Jerusalem artichokes are sometimes called sunchokes because they are tubers that grow on the roots of a native sunflower plant. They have a gnarled look about them, like a cross between a potato and fresh ginger. They are related to artichokes only in name. Roasting is what I suggest because it's easy—you don't even have to peel them—and it's a

SOME TIPS FOR ROASTING VEGETABLES

As you can tell from this section, roasting is one of my favorite ways to prepare vegetables. Roasting concentrates the flavors of the vegetables, and if you do it right, it produces crispy brown bits that add complexity to the flavor. Some vegetables are so good roasted that people who think they hate them will learn to love them. Brussels sprouts come to mind.

There are a few things to keep in mind when roasting vegetables. High heat is almost always better than low heat (one exception is for tomatoes, whose flavor is improved by long, slow roasting). High heat causes any liquid the vegetables give off to evaporate quickly, which encourages browning. I roast vegetables between 400° and 450° F. Cast-iron retains heat, which also helps cook and brown the vegetables quickly. You can preheat a cast-iron pan in the oven while the oven is preheating, if you like, for an even hotter roasting environment. A baking sheet or roasting pan works well, too. (Line it with aluminum foil for easy cleanup.) It's important not to overcrowd the pan. If air cannot circulate around the vegetables, they don't roast as much as they steam. Extra-virgin olive oil or butter and salt and pepper are just about the only seasonings most vegetables require. Of course, you can add other spices and flavorings as you wish. Once the vegetables are roasted, I usually dress them with a little more olive oil and a squirt of lemon juice or a splash of vinegar to bring out their best flavors.

Roasted vegetables can be used in any recipes that call for cooked vegetables: soups, salads, stuffings, and more.

Roasted or Steamed Beets

Roasting or steaming beets in the oven is the easiest way to cook them for use in other dishes. Both methods have the added benefit of concentrating the flavor of the beets, unlike boiling beets, which I think dilutes their flavor. If I'm going to use cooked beets in something that requires them to be dry—a savory tart or the filling for a ravioli, for example—I roast them; if it's better that they remain moist—in a salad or risotto, for instance—I steam them. The only difference between the two techniques is a piece of aluminum foil.

Medium beets

Preheat the oven to 400°F.

Trim the tops of the beets, leaving about 1 inch of the stems attached. Reserve the tops for another use. Trim the root end, also leaving about an inch of the thin root attached. Scrub the beets to remove any dirt.

TO ROAST

Place the beets directly on the oven rack and cook for 60 to 70 minutes, or until the skins have dried and the beets are tender when pricked with a fork. The exact time will depend on the size of the beets. Remove smaller beets when they are done. The outer skin of larger beets has a tendency to burn by the time the beets are done, but you can just cut away any dark patches when you peel them.

TO STEAM

Wrap the beets in aluminum foil and set in the oven. Cook for 1 hour 20 minutes, or until the beets are tender. Remove from the oven and cool in the foil.

When the beets are cool enough to handle, slice off the root and stem ends and peel with a paring knife. The skin should just fall off. Use these beets in any recipe that calls for cooked beets.

PREP TIME: 15 minutes
COOKING TIME: 1 hour to 1 hour 20 minutes
TOTAL TIME: 1 hour 40 minutes

ADVANCE PREP The beets can be steamed or roasted up to a week in advance of being used. Peel them and store wrapped in plastic in the refrigerator until needed.
LEFTOVERS The cooked beets will keep for a week or so in the fridge.

---

good way to highlight the artichoke-like flavor of this underappreciated vegetable. Another favorite preparation of mine is to use Jerusalem artichokes in a flan (see page 175).

Makes 4 to 6 servings

1½ pounds Jerusalem artichokes, scrubbed
¼ cup extra-virgin olive oil
3 garlic cloves, smashed but not peeled
½ teaspoon kosher salt
Freshly ground black pepper
Juice of ½ lemon (about 2 tablespoons)

Preheat the oven to 400°F.

Cut the Jerusalem artichokes into 1-inch chunks and place in a baking dish. Drizzle with the olive oil. Add the garlic to the dish, sprinkle with salt and pepper, and toss to coat the artichokes with the oil and seasoning. Roast until the edges are browned and the artichokes are tender, 40 to 50 minutes. Toss the artichokes two or three times while they are roasting. Toss with lemon juice before serving.

PREP TIME: 5 minutes
COOKING TIME: 40 to 50 minutes
TOTAL TIME: 45 to 55 minutes

ADVANCE PREP *The Jerusalem artichokes can be tossed with the olive oil and spices several hours in advance and roasted just before serving.*
LEFTOVERS *The roasted Jerusalem artichokes will keep about two weeks in the fridge. Use leftovers in soups, pasta sauces, risotto, frittatas, or cut up and stirred into hash.*

Roasted Okra

Roasted, okra has all of the flavor and none of the sliminess of other okra preparations. Serve this with cocktails, as a side dish, or as a garnish for a salad.

Makes 4 servings

> 1 pound fresh okra, preferably small, firm pods, rinsed
> 2 tablespoons extra-virgin olive oil
> 1/2 teaspoon kosher salt
> Freshly ground black pepper

Preheat the oven to 425°F. Line a baking sheet with parchment paper or aluminum foil (for easy cleanup).

Place the okra in a large bowl. Drizzle with the olive oil and sprinkle with the salt and some freshly ground black pepper. Toss the okra to coat with the oil and seasonings. Arrange the pods in a single layer, not touching, on the

parchment paper. Roast for 15 minutes. Turn the okra over and roast for another 10 minutes or so, until the pods are nicely browned and crisp. Remove from the oven and cool. If desired, toss with a little more extra-virgin olive oil and salt before serving.

PREP TIME: 5 minutes
COOKING TIME: 25 minutes
TOTAL TIME: 30 minutes

ADVANCE PREP *The okra can be made several hours in advance and stored at room temperature until serving.*
LEFTOVERS *Roasted okra can be refrigerated for up to a week. As the okra sits, it loses its initial crispness. Add roasted okra to salads, or cut them up and add them to soups or stews.*

MAKING QUICK VEGETABLE STOCKS

Although some people look at a pile of artichoke leaves or pea pods or corn cobs and see compost, I see a quick vegetable stock. Using some scraps and some aromatic vegetables, you can easily make a stock to enhance the flavor of whatever vegetable dish you are preparing. You may never again reach for a box of vegetable stock on the supermarket shelf.

The secret is to emphasize one particular vegetable so you concentrate the flavor of your finished dish. For example, if I am making a broccoli soup that calls for vegetable stock, I use the tough stems and leaves to make a stock by adding a small carrot, some onion, celery leaves, parsley stems, leek or scallion tops, and whatever else I have around. Fill a saucepan with some of these aromatics and your vegetable scraps. Add a few peppercorns, a bay leaf, and whatever other spices will complement your dish. Then fill the pot with cold water to cover the ingredients by 1 inch, bring to a boil, turn down the heat, and simmer for 30 minutes to 1 hour. Strain and you have a delicious, light stock.

Corn on the Cob

This is a very easy way to make corn on the cob that produces delicious results every time. For something different (and spicy), try slathering the hot corn with Chipotle Butter (page 407) and a squirt of fresh lime juice.

Makes 4 ears of corn, or as many as you want

    4 ears of corn, husked and cleaned of all silk,
       rinsed
    Unsalted butter
    Kosher salt

Bring a large pot of salted water to a boil. Add the corn. Once the water comes back up to a boil, time it for 2 minutes. Turn off the heat and let the corn stand in the hot water for 5 minutes. Remove from the water and serve with plenty of butter and salt.

PREP TIME: 5 to 10 minutes
COOKING TIME: 7 minutes
TOTAL TIME: 25 to 30 minutes

ADVANCE PREP *You can shuck the corn several hours before you intend to cook it and store it in cold water to keep it from drying out.*
LEFTOVERS *Keep cooked corn on the cob in a sealed plastic bag in the refrigerator for up to a week. Reheat leftovers in boiling water for 1 minute or in the microwave for 20 seconds per ear. You can remove the kernels of cooked corn from the cob with a sharp knife and use it in a variety of things, from salads, to soups, to fried rice, to fritters (see page 194).*

VARIATIONS
Microwave Corn on the Cob
To microwave corn, simply take an ear of corn, without removing the husk or the silk, and place it in a microwave on high for 4 to 5 minutes, depending on how large the corn is and how strong your microwave is. The corn actually steams insides its husk. Peel and serve.

Grilled Corn on the Cob
Soak whole ears of corn, with the husk and silk intact, in cold water. Remove the corn from the water, drain, and place on a hot gas or charcoal grill. Let the corn cook for about 7 minutes, turning it frequently, until steam escapes from the top of the husks. Cool. Peel back the husks and re-

Roasted Whole Garlic

If you've never eaten roasted garlic, you are likely to be skeptical that you would want to. But in the oven garlic undergoes a magical transformation, losing all of its pungency without losing its distinct flavor. Roasted garlic has a mild, almost sweet garlic flavor. I like to spread it on crusty bread. One thing to remember, though, is that roasted garlic isn't always a good substitute for fresh garlic. It doesn't have a strong enough flavor to stand up to other strong flavors, and you'll need a lot more of it—say, a whole head for a couple of cloves. Use roasted garlic as the accent flavor in subtly flavored dishes, such as mashed potatoes.

Although covered clay baking dishes and other devices designed to roast garlic are being marketed, don't be fooled into buying them—all you need is an oven.

Makes 4 heads garlic, about ½ cup purée

> **4 large heads of garlic**

Preheat the oven to 400°F.

Place the garlic directly on the oven rack and roast for 30 minutes, until the outer skin is brittle and browned around the edges and the cloves are soft when you press them. Remove from the oven and cool. Separate the heads into cloves and pinch the pointy end of each clove between your thumb and forefinger to squeeze out the soft garlic into a small dish. You can serve the garlic lumpy, as is, or else purée it in a food processor or blender until smooth.

TOTAL TIME: 30 minutes

ADVANCE PREP *The garlic can be roasted up to a day in advance and kept refrigerated until needed.*
LEFTOVERS *The roasted garlic will keep for a week or so in the refrigerator. Stir it into salad dressings, spreads, mashed potatoes, pasta sauces, or fresh goat cheese.*

VARIATION
Roasted Garlic for Presentation

For an hors d'oeuvre, some people prefer to serve roasted garlic as a whole head rather than a purée so that guests can squeeze the cloves onto bread themselves. To prepare roasted garlic to present this way, slice off the bottom of the heads of garlic to reveal the cloves, no more than ¼ inch up from the base. Brush the cut surface with olive oil and place the garlic in a baking dish, cut side down. Roast as directed.

move the silk. Return the corn to the grill for a minute or two to slightly char the kernels. Serve with plenty of sweet butter and salt or Chipotle Butter (page 407) and a squirt of fresh lime.

Grilled Eggplant Parmesan

Here's an easy, healthful way to prepare eggplant Parmesan that doesn't require breading and frying the eggplant first. Salting eggplant before grilling it draws out some of the bitter juices of the vegetable. Once grilled, the eggplant is dusted with cornmeal, which adds texture and absorbs some of the excess moisture.

Makes 4 servings

> **1½ to 2 pounds eggplant, sliced crosswise into ½-inch-thick disks**
> **Kosher salt**

TIPS FOR GRILLING VEGETABLES

Grilling is right up there with roasting as one of my favorite ways to cook vegetables. The high heat of a grill works quickly, cooking the vegetables without affecting their fresh, natural flavor and adding a delicate smoky flavor—especially if they are grilled over a charcoal fire. You can even get excellent results using a grill pan on the stovetop, provided you heat it very well before you begin and you have good ventilation. (I once smoked myself out of my apartment while grilling portobello mushrooms for a party.)

For grilling, choose vegetables that will cook relatively quickly and that will retain their integrity when they are done—something that turns to mush, like sliced tomato, or is tough or stringy, like leeks, doesn't have much to gain from grilling. But give it some thought before you give up; even though tomato slices fall apart, you can grill tomato halves or green tomato slices, which hold together nicely. Among my favorite vegetables for grilling are sliced zucchini, yellow squash, eggplant, thin asparagus, red onion, red and yellow bell peppers, radicchio, scallions, portobello mushroom caps, sliced green tomatoes, and corn on the cob. Even thin slices of potato, winter squash, and sweet potato turn out well on a grill.

To prepare the vegetables, cut them in equal-size pieces of equal thickness to encourage even cooking. Slices should be thin enough to cook through without burning, but not so thin that when cooked they will disappear or fall apart—somewhere between $1/4$ and $1/2$ inch is good. Before grilling, brush the vegetables lightly with extra-virgin olive or other oil. Too much oil will cause flare-ups on an outdoor grill, and will cause vegetables on a grill pan to fry. Without enough oil they may stick. The vegetables should glisten without looking wet. Season the vegetables well with salt and pepper.

Allow the grill to get good and hot. To make attractive grill marks, lay the vegetables on the grate diagonally and don't move them if you can help it. (One turn at a 90° angle about halfway through the cooking time for one side will produce a nice cross-hatch pattern, though it takes a little practice.) If you don't care about the grill marks, move the vegetables around as you wish. Turn the vegetables when the first side is browned and the flesh has begun to soften. Cook the second side until the vegetable is tender.

You can toss grilled vegetables with a squirt of fresh lemon juice and a splash of olive oil or dress them with a simple vinaigrette (see page 391) as they come off the grill. You can also use grilled vegetables in other recipes, such as the Grilled Eggplant Parmesan (page 152) or any dish that calls for the vegetables to be cooked beforehand.

---

2 or 3 tablespoons extra-virgin olive oil

Freshly ground black pepper

1 cup tomato sauce of choice (pages 250 to 252 or store-bought)

About $1/4$ cup finely ground yellow cornmeal

8 ounces fresh mozzarella, very thinly sliced

1 or 2 ounces Parmigiano Reggiano cheese, grated (about $1/2$ cup)

Arrange the eggplant slices on a large plate in a single layer. Sprinkle with about $1/2$ tablespoon of salt, turn the slices over, and sprinkle the other side with another 1/2 tablespoon or so of salt. Let the eggplant sit for 30 to 45 minutes.

Rinse the eggplant under cold water and pat dry with paper towels. Heat a grill pan over high heat or fire up a grill. Brush the eggplant slices on both sides with olive oil and set on the grill. Season the slices with black pepper. Grill until the eggplant is nicely marked and begins to become tender, 4 or 5 minutes. Turn over the slices. Season with salt and pepper, and grill for another 4 or 5 minutes. The eggplant should be almost cooked through, but not soft or mushy. Remove from the heat and set aside.

Preheat the oven to 400°F.

Spread 1/4 cup or so of tomato sauce over the bottom of a deep 2-quart baking dish. Sprinkle the grilled eggplant with a light coating of cornmeal. Arrange a layer of grilled eggplant, about one third of the slices, on top of the sauce—it's okay if some of the slices overlap. Spoon 1/4 cup of sauce on top of the eggplant and spread it out evenly to cover. Arrange about one third of the thinly sliced mozzarella in an even layer on top. Sprinkle with half of the Parmigiano. Make another layer of eggplant, sauce, mozzarella, and Parmigiano. Repeat, ending with Parmigiano.

Bake for about 30 minutes, or until the sauce is bubbling and the cheese has melted and browned. Let sit at room temperature for 10 minutes to allow the eggplant to set. Slice and serve.

PREP TIME: 30 minutes
COOKING TIME: 40 minutes
TOTAL TIME: 1 hour 10 minutes (plus resting time)

ADVANCE PREP You can grill the eggplant and assemble the dish and refrigerate it up to two days before baking.

LEFTOVERS The eggplant Parmesan will last about a week in the fridge. Reheat the eggplant in the oven or microwave. It's delicious in sandwiches, too.

VARIATIONS

Grilled Zucchini Parmesan

For the eggplant, substitute 2 to 2 1/2 pounds firm, fresh zucchini (about 4 large; you'll need more zucchini than eggplant because it contains more water and shrinks more when cooked). Slice the zucchini lengthwise into 1/4-inch-thick strips. There is no need to salt the zucchini as you do for the eggplant, so skip right to the grilling. Proceed with the recipe as directed.

Grilled Portobello Parmesan

Substitute 1 1/3 pounds portobello mushroom caps (about 4 large) for the eggplant. There is no need to salt the portobellos as you do for the eggplant, so skip right to the grilling. Proceed with the recipe, making only one layer of mushroom caps in the baking dish and topping them with the cheese and sauce.

Glazed Carrots

Glazing is a technique that's ideal for roots and other vegetables that have a little natural sweetness. Basically, you braise them with a little butter and just enough liquid so that it all but evaporates as the vegetables cook. Sometimes, a little honey or sugar is added to emphasize the flavor and make for a more sparkling glaze. I think of glazed carrots as traditional at Thanksgiving, but they are delicious throughout the year.

Makes 6 to 8 servings

4 tablespoons (½ stick) unsalted butter

10 medium carrots (about 2 pounds), peeled and
cut into 1-inch chunks

1 tablespoon mild honey, such as acacia, or
granulated or light brown sugar

½ teaspoon kosher salt

⅔ cup vegetable stock or water

1 tablespoon chopped fresh parsley, mint, or dill

Juice of ¼ lemon

Freshly ground black pepper

In a medium saucepan, melt 3 tablespoons of the butter over medium-high heat. Add the carrots and sauté for a minute or two to begin cooking. Stir in the honey and salt. Pour in the vegetable stock and bring to a simmer. Reduce the heat to medium-low, cover the pan tightly, and cook until the carrots are tender, about 25 minutes, depending on their freshness. If the carrots are not soft by the time all of the liquid has evaporated, add a couple of tablespoons of more stock or water. If the liquid hasn't evaporated by the time the carrots are done, remove the lid, raise the heat to medium-high, and let the liquid evaporate. Add the remaining tablespoon of butter and toss to coat the carrots. Add the parsley, lemon juice, and some black pepper, toss again, and serve.

TOTAL TIME: 35 minutes

ADVANCE PREP *The carrots can be made several hours ahead and kept at room temperature. Do not add the final tablespoon of butter or other seasonings until just before serving.*

LEFTOVERS *The carrots will keep for about two weeks in the refrigerator. They can also be frozen for up to one month.*

VARIATIONS

Glazed Parsnips

Substitute 4 medium parsnips (about 2 pounds) for the carrots.

Glazed Turnips

Follow the same recipe, substituting 5 medium firm turnips (about 2 pounds), peeled and cut into chunks, for the carrots, omitting the honey and substituting chopped, fresh tarragon for the parsley.

Glazed Radishes

Substitute about 2 pounds radishes (red, black, or daikon; peel all but red ones), and cut into chunks, as for the carrots. Omit the honey, and use chopped fresh thyme instead of parsley.

Glazed Rutabagas

Substitute 2 pounds (1 or 2 large) rutabagas, peeled and cut into chunks, for the carrots. Omit the honey, and substitute fresh tarragon for the parsley.

Glazed Pearl Onions

This is a recipe for sweet-and-sour glazed pearl onions that I learned while I was cooking in Italy. They are delicious with braised and stewed meats. I used to consider them a production to make until I learned that it's easy to peel small onions if you blanch them for a minute in salted water. Then the outer peel (and sometimes a layer or two of the onion) just slips right off.
Makes 6 servings

2 pounds white pearl onions

2 tablespoons extra-virgin olive oil

2 teaspoons sugar

Pinch of salt

Freshly ground black pepper

1/4 cup golden raisins (optional)

1 tablespoon unsalted butter

2 tablespoons white wine vinegar or cider vinegar

Bring a large pot of salted water to a boil. Cut both the stem and root ends off the onions, but do not peel. When the water is boiling, dump the onions into the pot and blanch for 1 minute. Drain and rinse under cold water to stop the cooking. Peel off the outer layer of the onions.

Place the olive oil in a large frying pan with a tight-fitting cover and set over medium heat. Add the onions, sugar, a pinch of salt, some pepper, raisins if using, and 1/2 cup of water. Cover, turn down the heat, and simmer for about 15 minutes, until the onions are soft and most of the water has evaporated. If the water evaporates before the onions are fully cooked, add more, a tablespoon at a time.

Remove the lid, add the butter, and cook for a minute or two to let the onions brown slightly. Add the vinegar, cover, and cook for another 3 or 4 minutes, or until most of the vinegar has evaporated and the liquid in the pan has become syrupy.

PREP TIME: 15 minutes

COOKING TIME: 25 minutes

TOTAL TIME: 40 minutes

ADVANCE PREP *The onions can be peeled up to a day in advance. They are best cooked just before serving, but you can reheat them, if necessary.*

LEFTOVERS *The onions will keep for about two weeks in the fridge. To reheat leftovers, place them in a frying pan with a tablespoon of water, cover,*

and gently heat until warm. They tend to get mushy after reheating, however.

Shredded Brussels Sprouts with Bacon

Sometimes chefs separate Brussels sprouts into leaves to sauté them quickly. The effect is to create a lighter taste and texture, eliminating much of the bitterness we associate with Brussels sprouts. It works, but since I don't have a staff of people who can do such labor-intensive prep for me, I like to just thinly slice my Brussels sprouts into thin shreds, which works well, too. This is a Brussels sprout dish for people who think they hate Brussels sprouts.

Makes 4 servings

1 1/2 pints Brussels sprouts

1 tablespoon extra-virgin olive oil or unsalted butter

1 bacon slice, finely chopped

1 large shallot or small white onion, minced

1 teaspoon kosher salt

1/4 teaspoon freshly ground black pepper

1 tablespoon sherry, red wine, or cider vinegar

1 tablespoon finely chopped flat-leaf parsley

2 scallions, green and white parts, finely chopped (optional)

Using a sharp chef's knife, cut the Brussels sprouts in half and lay the halves cut side down on the cutting board. Thinly slice the Brussels sprouts as you would a mushroom. You should have about 4 cups.

In a large frying pan, heat the oil or butter over medium-high heat. Add the bacon and sauté for a minute or two until the bacon renders some of its fat. Add the shallot and cook until soft, 3 minutes or so. Add the Brussels sprouts and stir to coat with the fat. Add about 2 tablespoons of water along with the salt and black pepper and stir to cook. As the sprouts cook, they will wilt and the water will evaporate. Add additional water, 2 tablespoons or so at a time, until the sprouts are thoroughly cooked, about 7 minutes. (You should need about ½ cup water, total.) It's okay if the sprouts brown a little bit. When they are done, stir in the vinegar, parsley, and scallions, if using. Cook a minute more and serve.

PREP TIME: 10 minutes
COOKING TIME: 15 minutes
TOTAL TIME: 25 minutes

ADVANCE PREP *The dish can be made several hours or a day or two in advance and refrigerated. Reheat in a frying pan with a couple of tablespoons of water or in a microwave.*
LEFTOVERS *The Brussels sprouts will keep for four or five days. These sprouts are good in sandwiches, stirred into scrambled eggs, tossed with pasta, or used as a vegetable layer in a baked casserole.*

Garlicky Broccoli

Blanching broccoli before you sauté it maintains the broccoli's bright green color and enables you to use less oil because the broccoli doesn't have to cook as long in the sauté pan. The broccoli has a strong garlic flavor, somewhere between Italian and Chinese.
Makes 4 servings

Kosher salt
1 bunch broccoli (about 1¼ pounds)
3 tablespoons extra-virgin olive oil

1 large garlic clove, thinly sliced
Freshly ground black pepper
2 or 3 tablespoons freshly grated Parmigiano Reggiano cheese (optional)

Bring a medium pot of heavily salted water to a boil. Use a vegetable peeler to peel the tough, dark green stalks of the broccoli down to their light green core. Trim the ends and slice the stalks on the diagonal into ½-inch-thick pieces. Cut the flowery top of the stalk into 1-inch florettes. When the water is boiling, add the broccoli and blanch for about 2 minutes. Drain and rinse under cold water to stop the cooking. Drain well.

In a large frying pan, heat the oil over medium-high heat. Add the garlic and sauté for just a minute or two, until the garlic begins to soften. Add the broccoli and sauté for 3 or 4 minutes, until it reaches the desired doneness. Watch the garlic to make sure it doesn't burn; if it darkens too much, turn down the heat. Season the broccoli with salt and pepper and sprinkle with Parmigiano, if using.

PREP TIME: 5 minutes
COOKING TIME: 10 minutes
TOTAL TIME: 15 minutes

ADVANCE PREP *You can blanch the broccoli a day or two in advance, refrigerate it, and sauté it just before serving.*
LEFTOVERS *The broccoli will keep for about a week in the fridge. Cut up leftover broccoli and use it in soup, pasta, risotto, or omelets.*

VARIATIONS
Garlicky Cauliflower
Substitute a head of cauliflower for the broccoli.

Garlicky Kohlrabi

Peel and trim 2 or 3 large kohlrabi bulbs and cut into 3/4-inch chunks. Blanch and proceed with the recipe as directed.

Chinese-Style Baby Bok Choy

This is a quick, satisfying way to prepare baby bok choy or any other Chinese-style green, such as Chinese broccoli or watercress; it's a combination of stir-frying and steaming. I keep the bok choy soaking in water until I cook it so that when I place it in the pan, there's enough water on the leaves to create steam. Serve the bok choy with steamed white rice.

Makes 4 servings

> 2 tablespoons peanut or vegetable oil
> 2 small garlic cloves, minced
> 1 tablespoon minced fresh ginger (optional)
> 6 to 8 baby bok choy (about 1 1/2 pounds), split in half, rinsed well, and soaked in cold water
> 2 tablespoons soy sauce
> 1 tablespoon oyster sauce
> 1 teaspoon toasted Asian sesame oil

Heat a large frying pan that has a tight-fitting cover over medium-high heat. Add the oil. When the oil is hot, add the garlic and ginger, if using, and stir for just a minute. Don't let it burn. Lift the bok choy out of the soaking water and lay it, still wet, into the frying pan in an even layer. Add the soy sauce, oyster sauce, and sesame oil, and turn the bok choy over once or twice to coat in the sauce. Cover and cook for about 5 minutes, until the bok choy has shrunk and the leaves have wilted, but the core and stems remain al dente. Spoon some of the cooking liquid over the greens to serve.

TOTAL TIME: 10 minutes

LEFTOVERS *The bok choy will keep for a week in the refrigerator. I also like to save the cooking liquid, strain it through a fine sieve, and add it to chicken stock to make an Asian-flavored broth. Add some chopped scallion and a few pieces of tofu, and you have a delicious Chinese soup.*

Sautéed Spinach

I like to sauté fresh spinach in one of two ways: Italian style, with garlic and olive oil; or what I think of as American style, with bacon or butter and onion. Fresh spinach needs to be washed thoroughly (see page 60), but it doesn't have to be blanched before being sautéed. Frozen spinach needs only to be defrosted and drained well before being sautéed.

Makes 4 servings

ITALIAN STYLE

> 3 tablespoons extra-virgin olive oil
> 1 large garlic clove, very thinly sliced
> 1 pound fresh spinach or 1 (10-ounce) package frozen spinach, defrosted
> Kosher salt and freshly ground black pepper

In a large skillet, heat the olive oil and garlic over medium heat. Don't let the oil get too hot or the garlic may burn. Add the spinach to the pan. If using fresh, it may not all fit initially, but in a minute or so it will wilt and you'll be able to add more. When all of the spinach is in the pan, cook it for just a couple of minutes, pushing it from side to side in the pan until most of the liquid that has run off the spinach has evaporated. Season with salt and pepper.

TOTAL TIME: 12 minutes

AMERICAN STYLE

    3 bacon slices, chopped, or 3 tablespoons
        unsalted butter
    1/2 small white onion, thinly sliced
    1 pound fresh spinach or 1 (10-ounce) package
        frozen spinach, defrosted
    Kosher salt and freshly ground black pepper

Cook the bacon in a large skillet over medium-high heat until the fat renders and the bacon begins to brown, 3 or 4 minutes. Add the onion to the pan and cook until the onion is soft, about 5 minutes. Add the spinach to the pan. If using fresh, it may not all fit initially, but in a minute or so it will wilt and you'll be able to add more. When all of the spinach is in the pan, cook it for just a couple of minutes, pushing it from side to side in the pan, until most of the liquid that has run off the spinach has evaporated. Season with salt and pepper.

ADVANCE PREP *The spinach is best made only up to an hour before serving. Keep it at room temperature (in the pan) and reheat gently.*
LEFTOVERS *Keep the spinach refrigerated for up to a week. Use any leftovers in pasta sauces, omelets, vegetable stews, what have you.*

VARIATIONS
Creamed Spinach
Prepare the spinach using the American-style recipe. When cooked, chop the spinach and re-turn it to the pan. (If using frozen spinach, start with chopped spinach.) Stir in 1/4 cup heavy cream or sour cream and a pinch of freshly grated nutmeg. Bring to a simmer over medium heat and cook until the mixture thickens, about 5 minutes. Adjust the seasoning and serve.

Sautéed Mushrooms
This is a recipe for sautéed mushrooms that can be served as a side dish or used as the base of other recipes. The secret is to keep the pan hot and not to overcrowd it, which allows the liquid to evaporate and the mushrooms to brown.
Makes 4 servings

    1/4 cup extra-virgin olive oil or unsalted butter, or
        a combination
    1 small shallot or garlic clove, minced
    1 pound button or other mushrooms, cut into
        quarters or sliced, depending on their size
    Kosher salt and freshly ground black pepper
    Juice of 1/2 lemon
    1 tablespoons chopped flat-leaf parsley

Heat 2 tablespoons of the oil in a large sauté pan over medium-high heat. Add half the shallot and cook until soft, about 2 minutes. Add half the mushrooms and cook, stirring until the mushrooms begin to give off their liquid. Keep cooking, moving the mushrooms from one side of the pan to the other to allow any liquid that accumulates to evaporate. Season with salt and pepper, transfer to a plate, and reserve. Repeat with the remaining oil, shallot, and mushrooms. When they are just about done, turn up the heat to high. Add the first batch of mushrooms back to the pan. Add a squirt of lemon juice and the chopped parsley, toss, adjust the seasoning, and serve.

TOTAL TIME: 25 minutes

LEFTOVERS Sautéed mushrooms will keep about one week in the refrigerator. Reheat them in a frying pan with a little butter or in a microwave for a minute or two on high. Stir into pasta, soup, risotto, frittata, or grains.

Sautéed Zucchini with Toasted Almonds and Mint

There's a restaurant just down the street from my apartment in New York City, The Red Cat, that serves an appetizer so simple it's almost weird to see it on a menu: sautéed shredded zucchini. And yet somehow the simplicity of it is refreshingly satisfying. Here's my version. It's best in the summer, when locally grown zucchini are fresh and at their peak of flavor.

Makes 4 servings

> 3 tablespoons whole or sliced almonds
> 1/4 cup extra-virgin olive oil
> 2 scallions (green and white parts), 1 shallot, or 1/2 garlic clove, or a combination, minced
> 1 1/2 pounds zucchini (3 medium), shredded (about 4 cups)
> Kosher salt and freshly ground black pepper
> 1 tablespoon chopped fresh flat-leaf parsley
> 1 tablespoon chopped fresh mint

Place the almonds in a dry frying pan and set over medium-high heat. Swirl the pan as it heats to toast the almonds evenly. When they are shiny and toasted, after 3 or 4 minutes, remove to a small dish to cool. If using whole almonds, finely chop them.

In the same frying pan, heat the olive oil over high heat. Add the scallions and sauté for a minute or two, until soft. Add the zucchini and salt and pepper to taste, and sauté, stirring constantly, until the zucchini has cooked and the liquid it releases has mostly evaporated, 7 or 8 minutes. Add the parsley, mint, and almonds, and cook for an additional minute. Serve immediately.

TOTAL TIME: 20 minutes

ADVANCE PREP You can grate the zucchini up to an hour before you make the dish. Before cooking, drain any liquid that collects as the zucchini sits.
LEFTOVERS Whatever's left should be refrigerated and eaten within a day or two. Reheat leftovers in a hot frying pan for a minute or two. You can also stir them into scrambled eggs.

Sautéed Cucumbers

The idea of cooking cucumbers is foreign to Americans. But it's quite popular in France and China, two countries where they know a thing or two about food. For the sheer surprise factor, not to mention their delicious taste, I like to serve sautéed cucumbers as a light summer appetizer or side dish. Seedless English cucumbers are a little too watery to sauté, but thin Japanese ones work well, as do Kirbys and your standard, medium-size waxed green cucumber.

Makes 6 servings

> 2 pounds firm, dense cucumbers (about 3 medium), peeled
> 3 tablespoons unsalted butter

½ medium sweet white onion, thinly sliced

¼ cup chopped fresh mint or fresh dill

Kosher salt and freshly ground white pepper

Remove the ends of the cucumbers and slice them lengthwise in half. Using a teaspoon, scrape out the seeds and the juicy core of the cucumber. Slice the cucumbers crosswise into ¼-inch-thick slices. In a large sauté pan, heat the butter over medium-high heat. Add the onion and sauté until soft, about 5 minutes. Add the cucumbers and sauté until they wilt, 7 or 8 minutes. Stir in the chopped mint or dill, and salt and pepper to taste. The cucumbers may give off a lot of water. If so, remove them from the pan with a slotted spoon to serve.

PREP TIME: 10 minutes

COOKING TIME: 15 minutes

TOTAL TIME: 25 minutes

LEFTOVERS *You can store the sautéed cucumbers in the fridge for two or three days, but they will give off even more water. The cucumbers reheat reasonably well in the microwave or in a sauté pan, but they do lose their pleasant crunch.*

Shredded Kohlrabi with Caraway and Bacon

The contrast in flavor and color of the dark green leaves and the light green bulbs makes this kohlrabi dish a beautiful accompaniment to just about any meal. The combination of caraway and bacon is ideal with a wintry stew.

Makes 4 servings

1 bunch kohlrabi (about 1½ pounds), with leaves

Kosher salt

1 tablespoon extra-virgin olive oil

1 tablespoon bacon fat or butter

½ small yellow or white onion, thinly sliced

¼ teaspoon caraway seeds

Freshly ground black pepper

2 tablespoons cider or white wine vinegar

Remove the stems from the kohlrabi and remove the leaves from the stems as you would for spinach or Swiss chard—peeling the dark green leaf off the thick central vein. Soak the leaves in cold water to remove any sand. Lift out of the water and drain. Bring a medium pot of water to a boil. Add 1½ teaspoons of kosher salt. Add the kohlrabi leaves and boil for about 7 minutes, or until tender. Drain and roughly chop. (If you don't have the leaves or you don't want to bother, simply omit them and proceed.)

Meanwhile, peel the bulbs of the kohlrabi and shred on a box grater or in a food processor. You should have about 2 cups. In a large frying pan, heat the olive oil and the bacon fat or butter over medium-high heat. Add the onion and cook until soft, about 5 minutes. Add the caraway seeds and cook for another minute. Add the shredded kohlrabi and sauté until it wilts and the liquid that it gives off has evaporated, 4 or 5 minutes. Add the leaves, along with ½ teaspoon salt and some freshly ground black pepper. Cook, stirring, until both the kohlrabi and the leaves are tender and the dish has sort of come together, another 2 or 3 minutes or so. Add the vinegar and cook until it evaporates, about 2 minutes. Adjust the seasoning with salt and pepper and serve.

PREP TIME: 10 minutes

COOKING TIME: 15 to 25 minutes

TOTAL TIME: 25 to 35 minutes

Burst Cherry Tomatoes

Just a quick sauté in butter turns cherry tomatoes from a salad ingredient into a side dish. By cooking them just until their skins burst, you concentrate and sweeten their flavor.

Makes 2 to 4 servings

> 3 tablespoons unsalted butter or extra-virgin olive oil
>
> 1 pint cherry tomatoes
>
> Kosher salt and freshly ground black pepper
>
> 1 tablespoon chopped flat-leaf parsley

In a medium sauté pan, heat the butter over medium-high heat. When the butter stops foaming, add the tomatoes. Cook, tossing, until the skin of the tomatoes begins to wrinkle, about 5 minutes. Add a generous pinch of salt and some pepper. Continue cooking until a few of the cherry tomatoes begin to burst. Toss in the parsley and serve.

TOTAL TIME: 10 minutes

LEFTOVERS The cherry tomatoes will keep for four or five days, but they become too mushy when reheated to serve as a side dish. Instead, stir them into a tomato sauce or toss them into rice or another grain dish.

Asparagus Mignonette

How you like to cook your asparagus—boiled, steamed, or grilled—will determine what type you should buy. If you are going to boil or steam it, buy the thickest spears you can find. Peel the stalks with a vegetable peeler to remove any tough fibers. If you are going to grill the asparagus, buy pencil-thin spears, which hold up better because they don't have to be peeled. However you cook it, asparagus is best treated simply so you don't mask its fresh, delicate flavor. Next to a buttery hollandaise (see page 123), this is one of my favorite garnishes.

Makes 4 servings

> 1 to 1½ pounds fresh asparagus, thick stalks for blanching, thin for grilling
>
> ¼ cup olive oil or 4 tablespoons unsalted butter, melted, plus extra if grilling
>
> Kosher salt and freshly ground black pepper, to taste
>
> 1 hard-cooked egg (see page 29), finely chopped
>
> 2 crisp cooked bacon slices, crumbled (see page 126)
>
> 1 small shallot or 1 small piece red onion, minced
>
> 1 tablespoon minced flat-leaf parsley
>
> ¼ cup white wine vinegar or fresh lemon juice

To blanch thick asparagus, first peel the stalks. Cut about an inch of the woody end off the bottom of each spear. Lay the asparagus flat on the work surface. With a sharp vegetable peeler, starting about one-third down from the top of the spear, peel toward the bottom, revealing the light-colored core. Rotate the spear as you work. It's okay to leave a little dark green toward the tip, but most of it should be gone. Arrange the peeled spears all facing the same direction. Bring a wide pot or deep frying pan of heavily salted water to a boil. The pot has to be large enough for the asparagus to lie flat in it. When the water's boiling, gently drop in the asparagus. Cook the asparagus no more than 4 or 5 minutes, just until it is tender but not soft. Using tongs remove the asparagus to a colander to drain. Be careful not to break the spears. Rinse with cold water to stop the cooking.

To grill thin asparagus, trim the ends off the spears, but do not peel. Brush with olive oil and season with salt and pepper. Heat a charcoal grill or grill pan until quite hot. Grill the asparagus just until they are lightly marked and somewhat limp, but not soft, 2 or 3 minutes, depending on how hot the grill is. Turn frequently with tongs while the spears cook. As the asparagus is cooked, remove it to a plate.

To assemble the dish, divide the asparagus among four serving plates, arranging the spears all in the same direction. Across the lower half of the asparagus, arrange one fourth of the chopped egg in a band. Top this with the bacon, shallot, and parsley. Drizzle a tablespoon of olive oil and a tablespoon of vinegar over each plate. Sprinkle with salt and pepper and serve warm or at room temperature.

PREP TIME: 10 minutes
COOKING TIME: 5 minutes
TOTAL TIME: 15 minutes

LEFTOVERS *Cooked asparagus will keep for about a week in the refrigerator. Use leftover asparagus in a frittata, a risotto, scrambled eggs, or a tuna casserole.*

KITCHEN SENSE

BLANCHING
Blanching refers to the simple technique of par-cooking vegetables quickly in boiling salted water. Blanching sets the bright color and preserves the crispness of most green vegetables, such as asparagus, peas, and green beans. It is usually all the cooking these vegetables need. For some vegetables, such as pearl onions and fava beans, blanching also makes peeling easier. To my taste, certain vegetables, such as broccoli and cauliflower, are better blanched than raw, especially in salads and crudités.

For blanching, I like to use heavily salted water, about 1 tablespoon of kosher salt per quart. The extra salt enhances the flavor and texture of the vegetables. Have a bowl of ice water and a strainer handy. In a nonreactive pot, bring the salted water to a boil. There should be enough water to allow for the vegetables to be fully submerged with room to move around; the more water the better. Add the vegetables to the pot and return to a boil. Cook for 1 minute and then remove the vegetables from the pot, drain them, and transfer to the ice water to stop the cooking. Drain well.

Certain white or lightly colored vegetables, such as artichokes, cardoons, fennel, and salsify, tend to discolor unless they are blanched in acidulated water. Use 1 tablespoon of fresh lemon juice or white vinegar and 1 tablespoon of kosher salt per quart of water for these vegetables. French cooks recommend using a *blanc* for these vegetables, which means they add 1 tablespoon of all-purpose flour and 1 tablespoon of vegetable oil per quart of salted, acidulated water. I can't decide if a blanc makes much difference in the finished product.

I do not advocate adding baking soda to the cooking water; I find it produces dull, mushy vegetables.

Green Beans with Potato, Onion, and Bacon

My mother's favorite vegetable was green beans, and when she cooked them, she really cooked them. This was before the impact of nouvelle cuisine reached our kitchen in north Toronto. When I make green beans to this day, I prefer to cook them just on the far side of al dente. In this dish, this extra cooking brings their texture more in line with the potatoes.

Makes 4 servings

2 tablespoons extra-virgin olive oil

2 thick-cut, double-smoked bacon slices, diced

1 small white or yellow onion, chopped

1 large all-purpose potato, such as Yukon Gold, peeled and finely diced

8 ounces green beans, ends trimmed, cut into 1/2-inch pieces

Kosher salt and freshly ground black pepper

Pinch of fresh thyme

Juice of 1/2 lemon (about 2 tablespoons)

In a large saucepan, heat the olive oil with the bacon over medium-high heat. Fry until the bacon renders its fat, about 4 minutes. Add the onion and cook until soft, 5 minutes. Add the potato and cook for about 8 minutes, stirring frequently, until the potato begins to soften. Add the green beans, salt, pepper, and thyme, and continue cooking for about 10 minutes more, or until the beans soften and the potatoes are tender. Add the lemon juice, toss, and serve.

TOTAL TIME: 30 minutes

LEFTOVERS *The dish will keep for about one week in the fridge. Reheat leftovers in the microwave.*

Curried Green Beans

This is a pseudo Indian way of cooking green beans that can be used with any number of vegetables, such as cauliflower or peas. Use any curry powder you like, or make up your own mixture of spices (see page 409).

Makes 4 servings

2 tablespoons unsalted butter

1 medium white or yellow onion, finely chopped

1 small garlic clove, minced

2 tablespoons minced fresh ginger

2 teaspoons curry powder

3 ounces fresh, ripe plum tomatoes (about 3), cut into 1/2-inch dice, or 2 or 3 canned tomatoes

12 ounces green beans, ends trimmed, cut into 1 1/2-inch lengths

1/2 teaspoon kosher salt

In a medium saucepan set over medium-high heat, melt the butter. Add the onion, garlic, and ginger, and cook, stirring frequently, until the onions start to brown nicely, 10 to 12 minutes. Add the curry powder and cook for another minute or two, stirring constantly, until you can smell the spices begin to toast. Add the tomatoes and 1/3 to 1/2 cup of water (use less water if using canned tomatoes), and cook for another minute, until the liquid is boiling and the tomatoes have given off their juice. Add the green beans and the salt. Cook for 8 to 10 minutes, until the green beans soften. The beans should be cooked through—not mushy, but not crunchy, either.

TOTAL TIME: 25 minutes

ADVANCE PREP *The beans can be made up to a day or two in advance and refrigerated. In this case,* *stop cooking the beans while they are still a little firm so that they do not overcook when you reheat them.*

LEFTOVERS *The beans will keep for at least a week in the fridge. Heat them in a pot on the stove, adding a little more water if necessary. Otherwise you can reheat them in the microwave.*

VARIATIONS
Curried Cauliflower
Follow the same technique, using ½ head of cauliflower that's been cut into small florets in place of the green beans. Once you've added the cauliflower to the spice and tomato mixture, cover the pot, reduce the heat, and let simmer for 10 to 15 minutes, until the cauliflower has cooked through.

Curried Peas
Substitute 12 ounces shelled fresh or frozen peas for the green beans. The peas will take slightly less cooking time than the beans, depending on how big they are.

Szechuan Green Beans
This simple recipe for green beans is quick and delicious, with a satisfying combination of Chinese flavors.
Makes 4 servings

2 tablespoons soy sauce
2 tablespoons ketchup
Pinch of crushed red pepper flakes
3 tablespoons peanut or vegetable oil
2 small garlic cloves, minced
2 tablespoons minced fresh ginger
1 to 1¼ pounds green beans, trimmed

In a small bowl, combine the soy sauce, ketchup, and red pepper flakes with ⅓ cup cold water. Set aside. In a large frying pan with a lid, heat the oil over medium-high heat until hot. Add the garlic and ginger and cook, stirring constantly, for a minute or two until they begin to brown. Add the green beans and fry for 3 or 4 minutes, until they begin to wilt. Pour in the soy sauce mixture, toss the beans to coat, cover the pan, and let the beans cook until tender, about 5 minutes. Remove the lid and if there is any liquid still in the bottom of the pan, continue cooking until it has evaporated. Serve immediately.

TOTAL TIME: 15 minutes

LEFTOVERS *The beans will keep for about a week in the fridge. Reheat them in the microwave on high for a minute or two until heated through.*

Southern-Style Collard Greens
Collards are big, tough greens that require extra-long cooking time to make them palatable and release their delicious flavor. I have to laugh every time I see a recipe for which collards are just quickly sautéed or otherwise delicately cooked. If you think you don't like collards, you've probably had them prepared this way. Forget your modern vegetable ideas and boil them at length as directed.
Makes 4 to 6 servings

1 small smoked ham hock or smoked turkey wing or drumstick, or 3 ounces double-smoked bacon
1 small white or yellow onion, sliced
1 small hot chile, split in half

Vegetables, Beans, and Potatoes

2 teaspoons kosher salt
1 1/2 pounds collard greens
Malt vinegar or other vinegar

Place the ham hock in a pot with the onion, pepper, and salt. Cover with 3 quarts cold water. Bring to a boil over high heat, cover, reduce the heat, and simmer while you prepare the greens.

Cut away the stems of the collard greens and rinse the greens in a basin with two changes of water, lifting them out of the water each time to drain. This will help remove any sand on the leaves. Cut the leaves lengthwise into 1-inch strips, removing any tough veins. Uncover the pot, turn the heat up to high, add the greens, and simmer, stirring frequently, for about 25 minutes, or until they are soft.

Lift the greens out with a spatula and drain. (Reserve the liquid as a base for soup.) Serve the greens with a splash of vinegar.

PREP TIME: 10 minutes
COOKING TIME: 25 minutes
TOTAL TIME: 35 minutes

ADVANCE PREP *The greens can be made in advance and reheated in a frying pan with some of the cooking liquid or in the microwave.*
LEFTOVERS *The collards will keep for about ten days in the fridge. Cut up leftovers and stir them into other dishes, such as soups, stews, succotash, or mashed potatoes.*

Ratatouille

Ratatouille is a vegetable stew from the south of France that is traditionally made in the height of summer, when the vegetables it contains—eggplant, zucchini, tomatoes, and bell peppers—are at the peak of their season. Although many recipes have you just put all the vegetables in the same pot and simmer away, I prefer the more traditional technique of sautéing the vegetables separately and mixing them after they are cooked. This allows you to better control the doneness of each vegetable. Once the ratatouille is assembled, I like to bake it—sometimes with a topping of cheese—to bring all of the flavors together.

Makes 6 servings

1/2 cup extra-virgin olive oil
1 large white or yellow onion, finely chopped
2 garlic cloves, minced
Kosher salt and freshly ground black pepper
1/2 fennel bulb, chopped
1 small eggplant, diced
1 medium zucchini, diced
4 to 5 fresh or canned plum tomatoes, chopped
1 sprig rosemary, minced
1 tablespoon chopped fresh oregano or thyme, or
   a combination
1 tablespoon chopped flat-leaf parsley
1 bay leaf
4 ounces mozzarella, grated (1 cup), optional

In a large skillet, heat 2 tablespoons of the oil over medium-high heat. Add the onion and sauté for about 5 minutes, until soft. Add the garlic and continue sautéing until the garlic gives off a strong aroma, about 2 minutes. Season with salt and pepper. Transfer one fourth of this mixture to the bottom of a 2-quart baking dish and the rest to a plate.

Return the pan to the heat. Add another 2 tablespoons of olive oil, and when hot, add the fennel. Cook until soft, about 7 minutes. Season with salt and pepper and transfer to the baking dish on top of the onion and garlic mixture. Scatter another one fourth of the onion mixture on top of the fennel. Return the pan to the heat. Add another 2 tablespoons of olive oil to the pan, and when hot, add the eggplant. Cook until the eggplant is soft, about 8 minutes. Season with salt and pepper and layer on top of the cooked fennel in the baking dish. Add another one fourth of the onion mixture to the dish. Repeat with the zucchini, cooking it for about 5 minutes and layering it on the eggplant. Pour the last 2 tablespoons of olive oil into the pan. Add the last one fourth of the onion mixture to the pan along with the tomatoes, rosemary, and oregano. Cook until the tomatoes melt into a sauce, about 8 minutes. Season with salt and pepper and add the chopped parsley. Pour this mixture over the vegetables in the baking dish. Add the bay leaf.

Preheat the oven to 400°F.

Top the ratatouille with the grated cheese, if using, and set in the oven to bake for about 25 minutes, or until the cheese has melted and the ratatouille is bubbling. Remove from the oven and serve warm or at room temperature.

PREP TIME: 15 minutes
COOKING TIME: 1 hour
TOTAL TIME: 1 hour 15 minutes

ADVANCE PREP *The ratatouille can be assembled and stored, refrigerated, for up to two days before baking. Increase the baking time by 10 to 15 minutes to ensure the ratatouille is heated through. If the top gets too browned, reduce the oven temperature to 350°F, cover the ratatouille with aluminum foil, and continue baking until heated through.*
LEFTOVERS *The ratatouille will keep for up to a week in the refrigerator. Leftovers can be used in*

sandwiches, as part of a pasta sauce, or as a base for a stuffing.

Peperonata

Though most people think of it as Italian, I first encountered this spicy stew of peppers and tomatoes in the form of *lecso*, a condiment that is served in Hungary with just about everything—cooked meats, eggs, bread—and as an ingredient in soups, stews, and other traditional Hungarian dishes. Whatever you call it, keep some in your fridge. Peperonata is good warm, at room temperature, or chilled.

Makes 6 to 8 servings

>2 tablespoons extra-virgin olive oil
>1/2 ounce pancetta or bacon, minced (optional)
>1 medium white or yellow onion, thinly sliced
>1 garlic clove, minced
>4 anchovy fillets (optional)
>2 pounds Italian frying peppers, such as cubanelle or long banana peppers, cored, seeded, and cut into 1-inch pieces
>2 or 3 green or red hot chiles, or to taste, seeded and minced
>3 ripe plum tomatoes, peeled and chopped, or 4 canned plum tomatoes with a few tablespoons of juice, chopped
>Handful of fresh herbs, such as basil, flat-leaf parsley, marjoram, or oregano, finely chopped
>Kosher salt and freshly ground black pepper

In a medium saucepan, heat the olive oil and the pancetta, if using, over medium-high heat. Add the onion and sauté until soft, about 5 minutes. Add the garlic and anchovies, if using, and sauté for another minute or two. Add the frying peppers and chile and cook until they have wilted and given off some of their liquid, about 5 minutes. Add the tomatoes, herbs, 3/4 teaspoon salt, and a generous amount of pepper. Bring to a boil, reduce the heat, cover, and simmer for about 20 minutes, or until the peppers are quite soft. The peperonata should be on the dry side. If it is watery, let it simmer uncovered to reduce the liquid a little bit. If it is too dry, add a couple of tablespoons of water or white wine. Adjust the seasoning with more salt and pepper, if necessary.

TOTAL TIME: 40 minutes

ADVANCE PREP *The peperonata can be made several days in advance and refrigerated. It is good when first made, but gets even better as it sits.*
LEFTOVERS *Peperonata will keep for two weeks in the refrigerator. Use the peperonata on, with, or in just about anything that could use a little oomph. Think of it as Italian ketchup.*

Green Tomato Caponata

Caponata is a sweet-and-sour Sicilian eggplant dish similar in concept to ratatouille. Like ratatouille, it's best if you cook each element separately and combine them when they are done. I don't make my caponata as sweet or as sour as some. One day I added a green (unripe) tomato to my caponata simply because I had one lying around and I thought the tart flavor of the green tomato would contribute a nice, subtle tang to the finished dish. I liked it very much, and ever since I add green tomato to my caponata. I like to serve caponata at room temperature as an hors d'oeuvre, spooned onto toasted rounds of bread such as Crostini (page 22), or as a sort of chunky salsa to accompany fish or other entrées.

Makes 3 cups

2 tablespoons dried currants or dark raisins
1 tablespoon Marsala or ruby Port wine
1 tablespoon red wine vinegar
2 tablespoons pine nuts
5 tablespoons extra-virgin olive oil
1 small white, yellow, or red onion, finely chopped
1 small garlic clove, minced
Kosher salt and freshly ground black pepper
8 ounces eggplant (1/2 medium), cut into 1/4-inch dice
1 red or yellow bell pepper, cored, seeded, and cut into 1/4-inch dice
1 small hot chile, seeded and minced, or pinch of crushed red pepper flakes
1 large green (unripe) tomato, cored and cut into 1/4-inch dice
2 tablespoons minced flat-leaf parsley
2 tablespoons minced fresh basil or other herb

In a small bowl, combine the currants with the Marsala and vinegar, and let soak while you cook the vegetables.

Place a large frying pan, preferably nonstick, over medium-high heat. Add the pine nuts and swirl them around and flip them to toast to an even golden brown. (They will start to look oily and then brown quickly, so don't leave the pan unattended or they might burn.) Transfer the pine nuts to a medium bowl and put the pan back on the heat. Place 1 tablespoon of the olive oil in the hot pan and add the onion and garlic. Add a pinch of salt and some pepper, and cook, stirring frequently, until the onion is soft, 4 or 5 minutes. Transfer the cooked onion and garlic to the same bowl as the pine nuts.

Add another tablespoon of oil to the pan along with half the eggplant. Add another pinch of salt and some pepper, and cook the eggplant, stirring frequently, until tender, about 5 minutes. Don't worry if the pan seems too dry. As long as the eggplant isn't sticking, it will cook fine. (I happen to like the smoky flavor of the eggplant if it burns a tiny bit.) Transfer the cooked eggplant to the same bowl as the onion and pine nuts, and repeat with the remaining eggplant, using another tablespoon of olive oil. When the second batch of eggplant is done, add another tablespoon of olive oil to the pan along with the bell pepper and the chile or red pepper flakes. Season with salt and black pepper and cook until soft, 3 or 4 minutes. Add this to the bowl. Finally, add the remaining tablespoon olive oil and the green tomato. Season with salt and pepper and cook for 4 or 5 minutes, until the tomato is soft. Add the parsley and basil and cook for just another minute. Add this to the bowl of cooked vegetables. Stir in the soaked raisins along with the liquid they are soaking in. Adjust the seasoning, if necessary, with salt and pepper. You may also wish to add more Marsala, vinegar, and/or extra-virgin olive oil, to taste.

PREP TIME: 5 minutes
COOKING TIME: 25 minutes
TOTAL TIME: 30 minutes

ADVANCE PREP *The caponata can be cooked a day or two in advance and refrigerated. Bring it to room temperature before serving to maximize flavor.*
LEFTOVERS *Keep it in the fridge for up to a week. Caponata is delicious as a condiment or side dish, and it makes a great addition to pasta sauces, lasagna, and similar Italian dishes.*

Artichoke and Fava Bean Fricassée

This is an Italian-seeming dish, although I've never really eaten anything exactly like it in Italy. Where I live, artichokes and fava beans come into the farmer's market at about the same time, and that's a good enough reason for me to prepare a recipe that contains them both. Fresh lima beans, which come in a little later than favas, are a very good substitute for favas. And of course, if you can find neither, frozen favas or limas will also work, as will fresh shelled edamame. I prefer using baby artichokes because they are easier to clean than big globe artichokes (they are tender and there's no choke to remove), but you can also prepare this dish with larger, blanched artichoke hearts or bottoms that have first been blanched (see page 174 for artichoke cleaning tips).

Makes 4 servings

> ¼ cup extra-virgin olive oil
>
> 4 shallots, sliced, or 1 small yellow onion, finely chopped
>
> 1 small hot chile, seeded and minced
>
> 1½ to 2 cups peeled fresh fava beans (see page 170), fresh shucked lima beans, or frozen fava, lima, or soy beans
>
> 12 baby artichokes, trimmed (see page 174)
>
> 1 teaspoon kosher salt
>
> Freshly ground black pepper
>
> 10 or 12 basil leaves
>
> 2 tablespoons chopped fresh mint or flat-leaf parsley

In a large sauté pan, heat the olive oil over medium-high heat. Add the shallots and hot chile, and sauté until soft, about 5 minutes. Add the fava beans, and cook until they are tender, another 4 or 5 minutes or so.

While the beans are cooking, begin slicing the artichokes (slicing them earlier will cause them to brown too much). Cut each artichoke

CLEANING FRESH FAVA BEANS

Fresh fava beans have a delicious, mild flavor and delicate texture, but they take a little prep work. To clean favas, split open the spongy pods with your fingers and remove the pale green beans inside. Bring a pot of water to a boil. Add 1 tablespoon salt. Drop in the beans. When the water comes back to a boil, time them for 1 minute 30 seconds. Drain the beans quickly and run under cold water to stop the cooking.

Now each bean has to be peeled. Using your fingernail, gently pierce the outer skin of the bean, being careful not to damage the bean inside. Pinch the skin between your thumb and forefinger and pop them out into a small bowl. Don't worry if the beans split in half. (Some stubborn beans may require you to actually peel away the outer skin.) Repeat until all of the beans are peeled.

ADVANCE PREP *The favas can be shucked and peeled up to a day or two in advance. Don't prepare the artichokes, however, until you are ready to cook them or they will discolor.*
LEFTOVERS *Once cooked, this dish will keep for about five days in the fridge. Leftovers are delicious stirred into a sauce for pasta or mixed into scrambled eggs.*

lengthwise in half and then thinly slice each half, as though you were slicing an onion. As the artichokes are sliced, add them to the pan. Season with the salt and pepper. The artichokes will shrink as they cook, so you should be able to get them all in the pan. Once they are all cut up and in the pan, cook them for 5 minutes more or so, until they have wilted. Add the basil and mint or parsley and continue cooking until the ingredients have cooked through and come together to form a lovely fricassée, another 2 or 3 minutes.

PREP TIME: 30 minutes
COOKING TIME: 20 minutes
TOTAL TIME: 50 minutes

Succotash

I love this Southern side dish, especially in September, when sweet corn and fresh lima beans are in the farmer's market. If you've never had a fresh lima bean, you don't know what you are missing. They are soft and buttery and have only the shape in common with those mushy, pasty canned things we used to be served as kids. If you can't get fresh, I would recommend using frozen. Better yet, use frozen, shelled soy beans (edamame), which have an even better texture than frozen lima beans.

Makes 4 servings

> 3 slices tasso ham (about 3 ounces), thick-sliced applewood-smoked bacon, or pancetta
> 2 tablespoons unsalted butter
> 1 small white onion, chopped
> 1¼ cups fresh or frozen corn kernels (from 2 to 3 ears if using fresh)
> 1¼ cups shelled fresh or frozen baby lima beans or frozen soy beans (edamame)
> 1 teaspoon chopped fresh thyme
> ¼ cup heavy cream
> Kosher salt and freshly grated black pepper
> ¼ teaspoon cayenne pepper

In a large sauté pan (I like to use cast-iron) set over high heat, fry the tasso until crisp, about 4 minutes. Remove and drain on paper towels. Mince very fine and set aside. Add the butter to the pan with the rendered fat and set over medium-high heat. Add the onion and sauté until translucent, 5 minutes or so. Add the corn, lima beans, and thyme and continue sautéing until the vegetables are soft and cooked through, another 5 minutes. Pour in the cream and simmer until it has evaporated somewhat and thickened slightly, about 5 minutes. Stir in 1 teaspoon salt, a generous amount of pepper, and the cayenne. Stir in the minced tasso and adjust the seasoning with additional salt and pepper.

PREP TIME: 5 minutes
COOKING TIME: 25 minutes
TOTAL TIME: 30 minutes

ADVANCE PREP *The succotash can be made several hours in advance and reheated in the pan to serve.*
LEFTOVERS *The succotash will keep for about a week in the refrigerator. Reheat leftovers in a frying pan or in a microwave, adding a touch more cream to prevent burning. I like to make omelets with succotash filling for breakfast.*

Braised Red Cabbage with Apple and Currants

This wintry vegetable dish can warm you up on the coldest day. It's particularly good served alongside smoked pork, but it also goes well with anything schnitzel-like.

Makes 4 servings

2 tablespoons duck fat, bacon fat, or butter, or a combination
1 medium white or yellow onion, thinly sliced
1 small head red cabbage, sliced (5 or 6 cups)
1 medium Granny Smith apple, peeled and shredded
2 tablespoons dried currants
4 tablespoons red wine vinegar
2 tablespoons sugar
1 bay leaf
½ teaspoon salt
½ teaspoon cracked pink or black peppercorns

In a large saucepan, heat the fat over medium-high heat. Add the onion and sauté for about 4 minutes, until wilted. Add the cabbage and sauté for a few minutes to coat with the fat and wilt. Add the apple, currants, vinegar, sugar, bay leaf, salt, and peppercorns. Mix well. Cover the pot, turn down the heat, and let simmer for about 5 minutes, until the cabbage has released some of its liquid and shrunk. Remove the cover and continue cooking for about 20 minutes, moving the cabbage from one side of the pan to the other so that any liquid that accumulates evaporates. When finished, the cabbage should be tender but not mushy. Discard the bay leaf before serving.

TOTAL TIME: 30 minutes

ADVANCE PREP *The cabbage can be made a day or two in advance, refrigerated, and reheated before serving.*
LEFTOVERS *The cabbage will keep for about two weeks in the fridge. Reheat leftovers in a pan on the stove, adding a touch of water to moisten the cabbage if necessary, or in the microwave.*

Braised Belgian Endives

You can braise Belgian endives on top of the stove or in the oven. I usually decide which technique to use based on how many burners I need to prepare the rest of the meal. This version incorporates the subtle flavors of butter, wine, and a little orange, which I like to add because I think it complements the slightly bitter taste of the endives.

Makes 4 servings

> 4 tablespoons (1/2 stick) unsalted butter
> 1 shallot, minced
> 4 to 6 Belgian endives (about 1 1/4 pounds), cut in half lengthwise through the core
> Kosher salt and freshly ground white pepper
> 1/2 cup dry white French vermouth plus 1/4 cup water or 3/4 cup dry white wine
> One 2-inch piece orange zest, made with a vegetable peeler

In a large, heavy saucepan with a tight-fitting lid over medium heat, melt the butter. Add the shallot and cook until wilted, about 3 minutes. Add the endive halves and turn over once or twice to coat with the butter. Season with about 3/4 teaspoon salt and some white pepper.

Arrange the endives in a single layer, cut side up. Add the vermouth and water. Add the orange zest, making sure it is in the liquid, not on top. Cover the pan, turn down the heat, and simmer for 10 minutes. Turn over the endive, cut side down, and simmer, covered, for another 10 minutes. Remove the cover, turn up the heat to medium-high, and cook until the wine has evaporated and the endive has browned slightly around the edges, about 5 minutes.

TOTAL TIME: 30 minutes

ADVANCE PREP *The endives are best made just before serving.*
LEFTOVERS *The endives will keep for about a week in the refrigerator. The endives reheat pretty well in the microwave, or in a covered frying pan with a splash of wine.*

VARIATION
Oven-Braised Endives

Preheat the oven to 350°F. Generously butter or oil a 2-quart baking dish. Arrange the endives in the casserole, cut side up. Sprinkle with the shallot, salt, and pepper. Add the vermouth and 1/4 cup water and the zest and dot with butter. Cover with aluminum foil. Bake for 45 minutes, or until the endives are tender. Remove the foil, turn up the heat to 400°F, and continue baking until the endives are slightly browned, about 10 minutes.

Radicchio Braised in Red Wine

As with endives, braising softens the bitter taste of radicchio. This is a delicious side dish with braised meats or stew. It's also nice served with polenta as an appetizer.

Makes 4 servings

> 4 small, compact, firm heads of radicchio
> 3 tablespoons extra-virgin olive oil
> 1 shallot or 1/4 small red onion, minced
> 1 small garlic clove, minced
> 1/2 cup dry Italian red wine, such as Barolo or Chianti
> 1 strip orange zest, made with a vegetable peeler
> 1 small sprig rosemary
> 1 small bay leaf
> Kosher salt and freshly ground black pepper

Depending on their size, slice the radicchio in half or quarters lengthwise through the core. The leaves should remain attached. In a large sauté pan with a lid, heat the olive oil over medium-high heat. Add the shallot and garlic and sauté until soft, about 4 minutes. Arrange the radicchio, cut side down, in the pan. Cook for a minute or two, until it begins to wilt. Pour in the red wine; add the orange zest, rosemary sprig, and bay leaf; and season with about ¾ teaspoon salt and a generous amount of pepper. Cover the pan, turn down the heat, and simmer for about 20 minutes, or until the radicchio is tender but not mushy. Remove the cover, turn up the heat, and let any cooking liquid evaporate until the pan is almost dry. Discard the bay leaf before serving.

PREP TIME: 5 minutes
COOKING TIME: 30 minutes
TOTAL TIME: 35 minutes

ADVANCE PREP *The radicchio can be made up to a day or two in advance and refrigerated. Reheat in a covered frying pan with a splash of red wine.*
LEFTOVERS *The radicchio will keep for about a week in the fridge. Chop up leftover radicchio and stir it into risotto or pasta.*

Braised Leeks with Cream and Tarragon

The delicate onion flavor of leeks makes them delicious braised. In this recipe, the leeks are cooked in the oven in a tarragon-infused cream that creates a rich sauce. When properly cooked, braised leeks remain fibrous— they require a sharp knife to cut—but that gives them a nice bite. Don't be tempted to overcook them to a mush.
Makes 4 servings

3 tablespoons unsalted butter, at room temperature
4 large leeks, white and light green parts only
½ cup dry white wine
¼ cup heavy cream
2 sprigs tarragon, leaves only, chopped
1 small bay leaf
Kosher salt and freshly ground white pepper

Preheat the oven to 350°F. Generously butter the bottom of a large baking dish with half of the butter. With a sharp knife, slice the leeks lengthwise in half, keeping the layers intact. Rinse each half under cold water to remove any sand, fanning the layers under the water without out separating them. Set the leeks on paper towels to dry.

Arrange the leeks, cut side down, tightly packed in a single layer on the bottom of the dish. Pour in the wine and cream. The leeks should be about three-fourths submerged; if not, add a little more liquid. Sprinkle with the tarragon, add the bay leaf, and season with about ¾ teaspoon salt and a generous amount of pepper. Dot the top with the remaining 1½ tablespoons butter. Cover the pan tightly with aluminum foil and bake for about 1 hour 15 minutes, or until the leeks are tender.

To serve, carefully lift the leeks out of the braising liquid with two forks or with tongs. Discard the bay leaf, and spoon some of the braising liquid on top of the leeks.

PREP TIME: 15 minutes
COOKING TIME: 1 hour 15 minutes
TOTAL TIME: 1 hour 30 minutes

ADVANCE PREP *The leeks are best served the day they are made. They can be braised in the morning*

TRIMMING LARGE AND SMALL ARTICHOKES

Preparing artichoke hearts for cooking requires a little time and some effort. You have to remove the tough outer leaves, trim the soft inner center, remove the choke if there is one, and peel the stalk. And while you do all of that, you have to work pretty quickly because artichokes discolor rapidly. But the payoff is worth it.

To clean a couple of dozen baby artichokes, place 2 cups of cold water in a large bowl. Squeeze the juice of 1½ lemons into the water and drop the squeezed halves in, too. Working with one artichoke at a time, being careful not to prick yourself with any thorns, hold the artichoke upright and pinch and pull off the outer leaves, working in a circular direction around the vegetable. Stop when you expose the compact, light-green leaves of the center bud. It's okay if the tips of the leaves are dark green, but the primary color of the leaves left intact should be light green. The leaves should also be tender. Using a sharp paring knife, peel away the outer layer of the stem to expose the light-colored core, leaving about an inch of stem attached if possible. Trim around the base of the artichoke to remove any dark patches. Cut off the top ½ inch or so of the artichoke bud to remove the tough part of the leaves and expose the center of the artichoke. Drop this trimmed artichoke quickly into the acidulated water. Repeat with the remaining artichokes.

To prepare 6 or 8 large globe artichoke hearts, you use a similar trimming process, but you have to remove the choke. This can be done when the artichokes are raw, but I find it comes out more easily if you blanch the trimmed hearts. Place about 3 quarts of water in a large pot. Add 1 tablespoon of salt and the juice of 3 or 4 lemons. Add the juiced lemon halves, also. Bring this pot to a boil. Meanwhile, place 2 cups of cold water in a large bowl and add the juice of 1½ lemons as directed above. Using the pinch-and-pull technique explained above, remove the outer leaves of the artichoke until only the pale green, tender leaves of the heart remain. The base will be bigger than the heart and it will be covered with the stubs of the base of the leaves that have been removed. Using a sharp paring knife, peel the base like you would peel an apple, removing any remnants of dark green, until it is smooth and neatly trimmed. If the stem is still attached, peel the stem to reveal the tender, pale-green core. When you are finished, the artichoke should look like a tulip-shaped wineglass. Slice about an inch off the top of the leaves to remove any parts that are dark green and tough. Now, slice the artichoke lengthwise in half, down the middle, right through the stem. This will reveal the hairy choke in the center of the heart. Place the halves into the acidulated water. Repeat with the remaining artichokes. (If the artichoke starts to brown while you are trimming it, you should rub a cut lemon on the surface and pick up the pace.)

When the water is boiling, drain the trimmed artichoke halves and plunge into the boiling water. When the water comes back to the boil, drain immediately and run under cold water to stop the cooking. Using a pointed teaspoon, remove the hairy choke from the center of each half. It should come out easily in clumps. Discard the choke. Clean the cavity by scraping it with the spoon. If you like, cut the artichoke halves in half lengthwise again to make quarters. Proceed with your recipe as directed.

To prepare whole artichokes, simply snip off the pointy ends of the leaves with kitchen shears or sharp scissors, slice off the tops, and boil the artichokes in the salted, acidulated water for 15 to 25 minutes, depending on size, or until tender.

and cooled in their liquid. Reheat, covered, in a 300°F oven for 15 to 20 minutes, or until warmed, before serving.

LEFTOVERS The leeks will keep for about a week in the fridge. They can be eaten chilled or reheated. They can also be used to make Leek Gratin (page 184).

VARIATION

Chilled Braised Leeks with Vinaigrette

A classic summertime dish in France, leeks with vinaigrette can be made with only a few moderations to the braised leek recipe above. Follow the directions for braising leeks, substituting ¼ cup chicken or vegetable stock or additional white wine for the cream. When the leeks are cooked, let them cool in their cooking liquid and then refrigerate. To serve, lift the leeks out of their liquid onto serving plates and dress with Basic Vinaigrette (page 391).

Jerusalem Artichoke Flan

I worked in a restaurant in Italy that used to serve this flan as a side dish with just about every dish on the menu. The delicate flavor of the Jerusalem artichokes and the smooth custardy texture of the flan really grew on me. Now I bake it in ramekins and serve it as an appetizer before dinner or as a side dish. The flan is very easy to make, but it has a richness of texture and flavor worthy of a more complicated dish. Just about any vegetable can be treated in the same way to make a flan— cauliflower, spinach, corn, and others.

Makes 6 to 8 servings

1¼ to 1½ pounds Jerusalem artichokes, peeled and cut into chunks
2 cups whole milk or light cream
Kosher salt
Pinch of freshly grated nutmeg
5 large egg yolks
Freshly ground white pepper

Preheat the oven to 350°F.

Place the Jerusalem artichokes in a small saucepan and cover with the milk. Add a pinch of salt. Set over medium-high heat, bring to a boil, turn down the heat, and simmer until the artichokes are very tender, 20 to 25 minutes. Remove from the heat. Using an immersion blender, regular blender, or food processor, purée until smooth. Add the nutmeg. In a small bowl, whisk the egg yolks. Whisk about ½ cup of the hot artichoke mixture into the egg yolks and then whisk this mixture back into the remaining artichoke purée. Adjust the seasoning with salt and white pepper.

Divide the mixture among six to eight (½-cup) ramekins. Fill them to just below the rim. Place the ramekins in a baking dish and place the baking dish in the oven. Carefully fill the baking dish with hot water to come halfway up the sides of the ramekins. (I use a pitcher to make pouring easier.) Close the oven door and bake for about 40 minutes, or until the flans have set. Gently jostle a ramekin to check if the flan is still liquidy. Carefully lift the pan out of the oven. You can serve the flans hot or at room temperature.

PREP TIME: 15 minutes
COOKING TIME: 1 hour
TOTAL TIME: 1 hour 15 minutes

The Jerusalem artichoke mixture can be made a day in advance and kept in the refrigerator before baking. The mixture can also be baked in advance and reheated for a minute in a microwave, but I prefer the texture of the just-baked flan.

LEFTOVERS *The flan will keep for about a week in the refrigerator. Spread the flan on bread or use it as a dip or a condiment for a sandwich.*

Shredded Beets with Sour Cream and Dill

This quick beet dish has a rich, buttery taste that will win over anyone who thinks he or she doesn't like beets. Although there is a decent amount of sour cream in the recipe, it melts into the beets, lightening them and adding flavor, without making them creamy. You can begin with raw or cooked beets (roasted, steamed, or boiled); adjust the cooking time accordingly.

Makes 4 servings

1 pound fresh beets, raw or cooked (see page 149), peeled

3 tablespoons unsalted butter

1 teaspoon kosher salt

Freshly ground black pepper

¼ cup sour cream

1 tablespoon chopped fresh dill (optional)

Using the large holes of a box grater or a food processor, shred the beets. You should have about 3 cups. Heat the butter in a sauté pan over medium-high heat. Add the beets and cook, stirring frequently, until they soften and give up some of their liquid, about 3 minutes for cooked beets, 6 or 7 minutes for raw. Stir in

the salt and a generous amount of freshly ground black pepper. If using raw beets, turn down the heat and cover the pan. Let the beets steam for 4 or 5 minutes to soften before proceeding. Stir in the sour cream and dill, if using. Cook for another 2 or 3 minutes, or until they've reached the desired doneness, then remove from the heat and serve.

PREP TIME: 10 minutes

COOKING TIME: 10 to 15 minutes

TOTAL TIME: 20 to 25 minutes

ADVANCE PREP *The beets can be shredded in advance and stored for up to two days in the refrigerator.*

LEFTOVERS *The beets will last for about ten days in the refrigerator. Leftover beets can be heated for a minute or two in a microwave. They also make a delicious garnish for sandwiches.*

VARIATIONS

Shredded Beets with Bacon and Sour Cream

Substitute 3 slices bacon, finely chopped, or 3 tablespoons rendered bacon fat for the butter and proceed with the recipe as directed, cooking the bacon, if using, until the fat melts and the bacon browns slightly before adding the shredded beets.

Stuffed Peppers

Here's something to do with leftover rice or other grains. I particularly like to use Tomato Rice (page 221) for the filling, but other grains, lentils, and even mashed potatoes will work well, too. The same stuffings can be used with zucchini, onions, and other vegetables; adjust the cooking time so that the vegetables are tender and the stuffing is cooked through.

Makes 2 servings

- 2 small firm red or yellow bell peppers
- 1 small white or yellow onion, thinly sliced
- 2 cups Tomato Rice (page 221) or other cooked grain, such as plain rice, couscous, bulgur, or quinoa
- 1 large egg, lightly beaten
- 1/2 cup freshly grated Parmigiano Reggiano cheese
- 1 handful chopped fresh herbs, such as basil, thyme, marjoram, or flat-leaf parsley
- Kosher salt and freshly ground black pepper
- 1/4 cup vegetable stock or water

Preheat the oven to 350°F.

Slice the peppers in half lengthwise through the center of the stem if it is still attached. Using a sharp paring knife, neatly clean out the core and the ribs, being careful not to puncture the pepper's flesh. On the bottom of an 8-inch baking dish, scatter the sliced onion. Arrange the pepper halves cut side up on top of the onion.

In a small bowl, mix the rice with the egg, Parmigiano, fresh herbs, and a generous amount of salt and pepper. Spoon this mixture into the pepper halves, mounding it up in the center. Add the stock to the pan and cover it tightly with aluminum foil. Bake for 40 minutes. Remove the foil, turn up the temperature to 425°F, and continue baking for about 20 minutes, or until the rice has browned nicely and the peppers are soft but still hold their shape.

PREP TIME: 15 minutes
COOKING TIME: 1 hour
TOTAL TIME: 1 hour 15 minutes

ADVANCE PREP *The peppers can be assembled, covered, and refrigerated for about a day. They can also be cooked in advance and reheated, covered, in a 350°F oven for about 15 minutes before serving.*

LEFTOVERS *The peppers will keep for about five days in the fridge.*

VARIATION
Stuffed Peppers with Meat
You can stuff peppers with any number of meat fillings, such as the meat mixture for Meatloaf (page 362) or Italian Meatballs (page 365). You will need about 1 1/2 cups meat mixture, which I like to lighten with 1/2 cup cooked white or brown rice, cooked couscous, or other grain. Follow the same cooking directions as for the vegetarian stuffed peppers. To be sure the meat-stuffed peppers are done, insert an instant-read thermometer in the center of the filling. It should read at least 165°F.

Baked Broccoli Rabe
For broccoli rabe I use a typical Italian technique for cooking vegetables that you'll find almost anywhere south of Rome. What makes it Italian is that the broccoli rabe is very well cooked before it's baked with olive oil, garlic, and cheese. As with most bitter greens, parboiling diminishes the bitterness.

Makes 4 servings

- 1 large bunch (1 1/2 to 2 pounds) broccoli rabe, woody stems removed
- 3 tablespoons extra-virgin olive oil
- 1 tablespoon finely chopped pancetta (optional)
- 1/2 small white or yellow onion, thinly sliced
- 1 garlic clove, minced

1 small anchovy (optional)

Kosher salt and freshly ground black pepper
   to taste

1 tablespoon chopped fresh parsley

1 tablespoon toasted unseasoned bread crumbs

1 tablespoon grated Parmigiano Reggiano or
   other imported hard grating cheese

Preheat the oven to 375°F.

Bring 4 or 5 quarts of heavily salted water to a boil. Add the trimmed broccoli rabe and cook for 10 to 13 minutes, until the stems are tender but not mushy. Drain but do not rinse.

In a small frying pan, heat 2 tablespoons of the olive oil. Add the pancetta if using and fry for a minute or so until it starts to brown. Add the onion and sauté until it softens, about 5 minutes. Add the garlic and anchovy, if using, and sauté for another couple of minutes. Transfer this mixture to a baking dish and evenly distribute the onion on the bottom. Spread the cooked broccoli rabe on top of the onion and season with salt and pepper.

In a small bowl, combine the parsley, bread crumbs, and cheese. Sprinkle this mixture evenly over the broccoli rabe. Drizzle with the remaining tablespoon olive oil and bake for about 20 minutes, or until the top begins to brown. Serve warm or at room temperature.

PREP TIME: 20 minutes

COOKING TIME: 40 minutes

TOTAL TIME: 1 hour

ADVANCE PREP *The broccoli rabe can be boiled a day or two in advance and kept in the refrigerator until you are ready to assemble and bake the dish.*
LEFTOVERS *This broccoli rabe will keep for about ten days in the refrigerator. Chop up leftovers and*

stir them into pasta sauce. Otherwise, use leftovers as a garnish for a roast pork sandwich, like my favorite Pork and Greens sandwich from Tony Luke's in Philadelphia.

Mashed Potatoes

The secret to great mashed potatoes is butter. I have some friends who cannot eat dairy products, so sometimes I make mashed potatoes with extra-virgin olive oil instead of butter (see Variations). These are quite delicious, but I have to say, if push comes to shove, butter is what I want in my mashed potatoes. And although you can put just about anything you want in them, mashed potatoes, in my opinion, are better left alone. I think the best mashed potato texture comes from using a food mill or potato ricer. For lumpier potatoes, use a masher. Whatever you do, don't use a food processor, which makes them gummy.

Makes 6 to 8 servings

5 medium all-purpose potatoes (about 2½
   pounds), on the starchy side, such as Yukon
   Gold, peeled and cut into 2-inch chunks

Kosher salt

½ cup (1 stick) unsalted butter

2 to 3 tablespoons heavy cream

Freshly ground black or white pepper

Place the potatoes in a large pot, cover with cold water, add a tablespoon of salt, and set over high heat. Bring to a boil, reduce the heat to a simmer, and cook until the potatoes are very tender, 25 to 30 minutes. Drain well.

Mash the potatoes using a food mill, ricer, or masher. Add the butter and cream and mix until the butter is melted and the potatoes are smooth. Season with about 2 teaspoons salt and some pepper.

PREP TIME: 10 minutes

COOKING TIME: 25 minutes

TOTAL TIME: 35 minutes

ADVANCE PREP *The potatoes can be cut up and kept submerged in cold water in the refrigerator for a day or so, but the mashed potatoes should be made just before serving. If necessary, you can hold them for about 20 minutes by covering the pot they are cooked in and keeping them in a warm place. If you prefer to make the mashed potatoes in advance, see Variations below.*

LEFTOVERS *Mashed potatoes will keep in the fridge for about a week. They also can be frozen for up to a month. The best way to reheat them is in the microwave with a little extra liquid mixed into them. You can also use leftover mashed potatoes as a binding agent for croquettes (see page 190) or potato cakes.*

VARIATIONS

Mediterranean Mashed Potatoes

Substitute $1/2$ cup extra-virgin olive oil for the butter and omit the cream. Heat the olive oil gently in a frying pan with a sprig of rosemary to infuse it with flavor before mixing it into the potatoes.

Make-Ahead Mashed Potatoes

This is the best way to make mashed potatoes if you want to make them in advance or if you want to use up leftover mashed potatoes. Prepare the recipe as directed, increasing the cream to $1/4$ cup. When done, set the potatoes aside to cool. Stir in 3 tablespoons sour cream and 2 large eggs. You can add $1/2$ cup grated Parmigiano Reggiano, if you like. Transfer the potatoes to a buttered 2-quart baking dish, smooth the top, and sprinkle with paprika. You

can refrigerate the potatoes at this point for up to two days or freeze them for up to a month. Before serving, bake in a preheated 350°F oven for about 45 minutes (longer if they came straight from the freezer), or until the top is browned and the potatoes are heated through.

Winter Mash

A combination of root vegetables gives this wintry side dish a deep flavor and a beautiful color. I prefer the texture when the whole thing is passed through a food mill, but if all you've got is a masher, use that instead. Do not use a food processor, which produces a gummy mess.

Makes 8 to 10 servings

> 3 medium sweet potatoes (2 pounds), peeled and cut into 2-inch chunks
>
> 2 to 3 medium all-purpose white potatoes (1 pound), such as Yukon Gold, peeled and cut into 2-inch chunks
>
> 1 medium celery root or large rutabaga (1 pound), peeled and cut into $1 1/2$-inch chunks
>
> 4 medium carrots (1 pound), peeled and cut into 1-inch chunks
>
> Kosher salt
>
> 1 small bay leaf
>
> 1 cup (2 sticks) unsalted butter
>
> $1/4$ cup heavy cream
>
> Freshly ground nutmeg (optional)

Place the sweet potatoes, white potatoes, celery root, and carrots into a large pot. Cover with cold water. Add 2 tablespoons of salt and the bay leaf and bring to a boil. Reduce the heat and simmer until the vegetables are very tender, about 35 to 40 minutes. Drain. Remove the bay leaf. Pass the vegetables through a food mill or mash well with a potato masher. Beat in the butter and cream. Season with another tablespoon or so of salt and a pinch of nutmeg, if using.

PREP TIME: 15 minutes
COOKING TIME: 35 to 40 minutes
TOTAL TIME: 1 hour

ADVANCE PREP The vegetables can be peeled and cut in advance. Only the potatoes need to be submerged in cold water until cooking. Once made, the mash will keep warm, covered in a pot near the stove, for about 30 minutes.
LEFTOVERS The mash will keep for about two weeks in the fridge. It can also be frozen for up to a month. To reheat, I find the microwave works best. Leftovers are good as a binding for croquettes (page 190) or a filling for a savory potato pie.

VARIATION
Root Vegetable Purée Baked with Cheese

For a delicious dish, and a good way to use up leftovers, layer the chilled winter mash in a baking dish with Cream Sauce (page 404) and a combination of shredded Cheddar and Swiss cheeses. End with a layer of cheese, sprinkle with paprika, and bake in a 375°F oven for 35 to 40 minutes or until the mash is heated through and the cheese has browned.

Seedy Potatoes

This Indian potato dish has a complex flavor that results from a variety of seeds: coriander, cumin, mustard, and fennel. I serve it not only with other Indian dishes but also with roasted pork, chicken, or veal. The potatoes are delicious served with a dollop of strained yogurt (see page 163).

Makes 4 to 6 servings

4 tablespoons (½ stick) unsalted butter, or
    peanut or vegetable oil, or a combination
1 large white or yellow onion, chopped
1 tablespoon minced fresh ginger
2 garlic cloves, minced
1 teaspoon coriander seeds
½ teaspoon cumin seeds
½ teaspoon brown mustard seeds
¼ teaspoon fennel seeds
1 large ripe tomato, peeled and chopped,
    or 2 canned plum tomatoes, chopped
½ teaspoon turmeric
¼ teaspoon cayenne
2 tablespoons fresh lemon juice
5 medium red-skinned potatoes (about
    1¾ pounds), peeled and cut into 1-inch cubes
2 teaspoons kosher salt

In a medium saucepan, heat the butter or oil over medium-high heat. Add the onion and cook until golden brown, 8 to 10 minutes. Add the ginger and garlic and continue cooking for a couple of minutes. Add the coriander, cumin, mustard seeds, and fennel, and cook for a minute or two more, until the mustard seeds start to pop and the other seeds toast. Add the tomato, turmeric, cayenne, and lemon juice, along with 2 cups water, and bring to a boil. Add the potatoes, stir, cover, turn down the heat, and cook until the potatoes are tender, about 20 minutes. Remove the cover, turn up the heat, and reduce the cooking liquid until thick.

TOTAL TIME: 40 minutes

Sautéed Potatoes and Turnips

There are a wide variety of dishes that combine these two root vegetables. Neeps and tatties is a common Scottish version. Mashed potatoes with turnips strikes a chord in the American South, too. This variation, a quick sauté, is perhaps more French in character. I like it best at the beginning of the summer, when fresh-dug potatoes and small, sweet turnips are available. That's usually the same time I can find garlic scapes (the green, curlicue shoots of fresh garlic), and if I can, I add them to the dish.

Makes 4 to 6 servings

6 tablespoons extra-virgin olive oil

3 or 4 garlic scapes, chopped, or 1 large shallot, minced

4 scallions, white and green parts, thinly sliced

1½ pounds new potatoes, peeled and cut into small dice

1 pound small white turnips, peeled and cut into small dice

2 teaspoons kosher salt

½ teaspoon freshly ground black pepper

2 tablespoons chopped flat-leaf parsley

Heat the oil in a large sauté pan set over high heat. Add the garlic scapes and cook for a minute or two, until they begin to soften. Add the scallions and sauté for another couple of minutes. Add the potatoes, turnips, salt, and pepper, and sauté, stirring frequently to prevent sticking, for about 10 minutes, until they begin to soften and brown. As soon as the potatoes are just cooked through (don't overcook them or they will turn to mush), stir in the parsley and serve.

TOTAL TIME: 20 minutes

Creamy Potato Gratin

The most common mistake made when preparing a potato gratin is to undercook it. There is nothing more disappointing than cutting into a beautifully browned gratin to find raw potato slices in the center. To assure proper cooking, thinly slice the potatoes, don't stack them too high, and don't take the pan out of the oven until the potatoes are tender all the way through when poked with the tip of a knife.

Makes 6 to 8 servings

3 tablespoons unsalted butter, at room temperature

1 small garlic clove, minced

5 large baking potatoes (about 2½ pounds), such as Russet or Yukon Gold, peeled and thinly sliced

1 large white onion, thinly sliced

2½ cups grated Emmentaler, Gruyère, or Fontina cheese (about 8 ounces)

1 teaspoon finely chopped fresh thyme or rosemary

Kosher salt and freshly ground black pepper

2½ to 3 cups half-and-half or milk, or a combination

1 tablespoon freshly grated Parmigiano Reggiano cheese

PREP TIME: 15 minutes

COOKING TIME: 1 hour 30 minutes

TOTAL TIME: 1 hour 45 minutes

ADVANCE PREP The gratin can be made several hours in advance and kept at room temperature until ready to serve.

LEFTOVERS Reheat leftovers in a covered frying pan with a little butter over medium heat or in a microwave on high for a couple of minutes.

Preheat the oven to 350°F. Generously grease a large gratin dish or shallow 3-quart baking dish with half of the butter.

Scatter the garlic on the bottom of the pan. Arrange about one fourth of the potato slices in a layer on the bottom of the pan. Scatter one third of the onion on the potatoes. Top with ½ cup of the Emmentaler cheese and ¼ teaspoon of the thyme. Season with about ½ teaspoon salt and a generous amount of pepper. Repeat, layering the potatoes, onion, cheese, thyme, salt, and pepper twice more. End with a layer of potatoes (you should have 1 cup cheese left). Season with salt and pepper. Pour in enough half-and-half to just about submerge the potatoes. Dot the top with the remaining 1½ tablespoons butter. Cover the dish with foil and bake for 1 hour.

When the hour is up, remove the foil. Top the potatoes with the remaining Emmentaler and the grated Parmigiano and continue baking, uncovered, for another 30 to 40 minutes, until the cheese has melted and browned and a small knife inserted in the center goes easily through the gratin. The liquid should have been absorbed or evaporated. Remove from the oven and serve.

Beer-Baked Potato Gratin

The yeasty flavor of beer gives this sliced-potato gratin a deep, rich taste. Think of it as a German version of scalloped potatoes. The key with this, as with all potato gratins, is to cook it long enough so that the potatoes are fully cooked and the liquid has mostly evaporated or been absorbed. When in doubt, let it cook a little longer. **Makes 4 to 6 servings**

1 tablespoon bacon drippings or unsalted butter, softened

1½ pounds Yukon Gold or other all-purpose potatoes (3 medium), very thinly sliced

1 medium white or yellow onion, very thinly sliced

1 large garlic clove, very thinly sliced

Kosher salt and freshly ground black pepper

1 sprig fresh rosemary or 4 sprigs fresh thyme

1 cup beer, preferably lager or ale, or chicken or vegetable stock

Preheat the oven to 400°F.

Generously grease a 1½-quart baking dish with the bacon drippings. Arrange about one third of the potatoes in a layer on the bottom of the pan. Scatter one third of the onion and the garlic on top of the potatoes and sprinkle ¾ teaspoon of salt and some black pepper over the top. Scatter a few whole leaves of fresh rosemary or thyme on the potatoes. Repeat with the remaining ingredients until they are used up, ending with a layer of potatoes. Pour in the beer. Cover the dish tightly with aluminum foil and bake for about 1 hour, until the potatoes are soft. (You will know they are almost done when you can smell their strong aroma in the kitchen.) Remove the foil and continue baking for another 15 minutes to brown the top layer. Serve warm or at room temperature.

PREP TIME: 10 minutes

COOKING TIME: 1 hour 15 minutes

TOTAL TIME: 1 hour 25 minutes

ADVANCE PREP *You can bake the potatoes up until the point that you remove the foil and keep at room temperature for a few hours or refrigerate for up to a day. Then, before serving, brown the potatoes for 15 to 20 minutes (it might take more time if they start out cold) in a preheated 400Y F oven.*

LEFTOVERS *The gratin will keep for a day at room temperature and at least a week in the fridge. Fry leftovers in butter or more bacon fat to make home fries for breakfast.*

Cauliflower Gratin

Here's a classic French recipe for cauliflower that's hard to beat. In fact, it's a technique that's good for a whole host of vegetables. First, you blanch the vegetable, then you slather it with Cream Sauce, top it with cheese and bread crumbs, and bake it until it is bubbly and browned. Delicious.

Makes 4 to 6 servings

Unsalted butter, at room temperature, for greasing the pan

1 medium head of cauliflower (about 1 1/2 pounds), cut into florets

Kosher salt

2 cups Cream Sauce (page 404), prepared with a whole clove and a pinch of nutmeg

3/4 cup shredded Swiss cheese, such as Gruyère, Emmentaler, Comté, or aged Gouda (about 3 ounces)

2 tablespoons freshly grated Parmigiano Reggiano cheese

1 tablespoon unseasoned bread crumbs

Freshly ground black pepper

Preheat the oven to 375°F. Butter a 1 1/2- to 2-quart gratin dish or other baking dish.

Bring a large pot of salted water to a boil. Add the cauliflower florets and cook for about 4 minutes, just until they begin to soften. Drain and rinse with cold water to stop the cooking. Drain well. Arrange the cauliflower in the prepared dish and season with salt. Cover the cauliflower with the cream sauce. Sprinkle with the shredded Swiss cheese, and top with the Parmigiano and bread crumbs. Sprinkle with some pepper. Bake until the cheese has melted and browned and the sauce is bubbling, 35 to 40 minutes.

PREP TIME: 5 minutes

COOKING TIME: 40 to 45 minutes

TOTAL TIME: 45 to 50 minutes

ADVANCE PREP *The cauliflower can be assembled in the baking dish and refrigerated up to two days in advance. It's best baked just before serving.*

LEFTOVERS *The gratin will keep for about ten days in the fridge.*

Leek Gratin

Leeks are delicious cooked in this same way. Cut off the dark green tops of 1 1/2 pounds leeks, leaving only the white and light green parts, and then halve them lengthwise through the root, which will help keep them intact. Rinse very well to remove any sand. Blanch in salted water until tender, about 10 minutes. Drain and cut into 3-inch pieces before proceeding with the recipe. You can also use leftover Braised Leeks (page 173) to prepare this dish.

Butternut Squash Gratin

The dense, flavorful, deep-orange flesh of butternut squash makes a surprisingly light gratin. For this recipe, the squash is roasted, mashed, and enriched with béchamel and cheese. Any dense-fleshed winter squash can be used.

Makes 6 servings

6 tablespoons (3/4 stick) unsalted butter, at room temperature

One 2- to 2 1/2-pound butternut squash, split in half lengthwise, seeds removed

1 small white onion, chopped

1/4 cup all-purpose flour

1 1/2 cups milk

Kosher salt and freshly ground white pepper

Pinch of freshly ground nutmeg

2 large egg yolks

2 tablespoons freshly grated Parmigiano Reggiano cheese

1 cup grated sharp Cheddar cheese (about 4 ounces)

Preheat the oven to 400°F. Grease a rimmed baking sheet with 1 tablespoon of the butter, and a large gratin dish or shallow baking dish with a second tablespoon of the butter.

Lay the squash cut side down on the baking sheet and roast until soft, about 1 hour 15 minutes.

Meanwhile, in a medium saucepan, heat the remaining 4 tablespoons butter over medium-high heat. Add the onion and cook until soft but not colored, about 5 minutes. Add the flour and cook, stirring, until the flour is toasted and has a rich, nutty aroma, about 3 minutes. Whisk in the milk to create a stiff sauce. Bring to a boil, reduce the heat, and simmer for 3 or 4 minutes. Stir in about 1 teaspoon salt, some pepper, and the nutmeg. Remove from the heat and let cool slightly. In a small dish, whisk the egg yolks. Whisk in 3 or 4 tablespoons of the hot sauce to temper the yolks, and then stir the mixture back into the sauce. Stir in the Parmigiano.

When the squash is tender, remove it from the oven and set aside to cool. Turn down the oven temperature to 375°F. Using a spoon, scoop out the butternut flesh into a large bowl. With a fork or potato masher, mash the flesh; you can keep it somewhat lumpy. Mix in the sauce. Adjust the seasoning with additional salt and pepper. Transfer this mixture to the prepared gratin dish and smooth out the top. Sprinkle the Cheddar cheese evenly over the squash mixture. Bake until the squash is bubbly and the cheese has melted and begun to brown, about 30 minutes.

PREP TIME: 15 minutes
COOKING TIME: 1 hour 45 minutes
TOTAL TIME: 2 hours

ADVANCE PREP *The gratin can be made up to the point that the purée is placed in the baking dish and*

refrigerated for up to two days. Sprinkle with the cheese and bake just before serving, adding a few more minutes to the baking time if the squash is going into the oven straight from the fridge.

LEFTOVERS *This squash will keep for about a week in the refrigerator. Reheat leftovers in the microwave on high for a couple of minutes.*

Turnip and Potato Galette

Here's another delicious side dish that uses two of my favorite roots, potatoes and turnips. I've called it a galette, which is just a fancy French word for "pie," because the potatoes and turnips compress as they bake to make a dense, pie-like mass with a crisp browned crust. I use a small plastic Japanese mandoline, but you can also use a food processor or a very sharp knife to get thin-as-paper slices. As for the cheese, any sharp aged Swiss-like cheese will do, such as Emmentaler or Gruyère, or even aged Gouda or Provolone.

Makes one 8-inch galette, about 6 servings

- 3 tablespoons unsalted butter, at room temperature
- 1 pound small, firm white turnips, peeled and very thinly sliced
- 1½ pounds small, firm, all-purpose potatoes, such as Yukon Gold, peeled and very thinly sliced
- 1 large white onion, thinly sliced
- 2 teaspoons kosher salt
- ½ teaspoon freshly ground black pepper
- About 10 sprigs fresh thyme
- 8 ounces aged Swiss cheese, such as Emmentaler, or aged Gouda or Provolone, grated (about 2 cups)
- 2 to 3 tablespoons grated Parmigiano Reggiano cheese

Preheat the oven to 350°F. Butter a deep, 8-inch round or square baking dish with 1 tablespoon of the butter.

Using about one fourth of the turnips and potatoes, arrange a thin layer on the bottom of the buttered dish. Scatter one fourth of the sliced onion on the vegetables in the dish. Sprinkle with a generous ¼ teaspoon salt and ⅛ teaspoon pepper. Pick the leaves off of 3 or 4 sprigs of thyme and scatter them on top. Finally, sprinkle one fourth of the grated Swiss cheese on top. Repeat this layering of turnips and potatoes, onion, salt, pepper, thyme, and cheese to make four layers. End with cheese, but do not put any thyme on the top layer (it will burn). Instead, sprinkle the grated Parmigiano on top and dot with the remaining butter. Bake for about 1 hour 30 minutes, or until the galette has browned nicely, compacted, and pulled away from the sides of the pan, and a paring knife inserted into the center meets no resistance. Remove from the oven and let cool for 10 minutes on the counter before serving.

PREP TIME: 20 minutes
COOK TIME: 1 hour 30 minutes
TOTAL TIME: 1 hour 50 minutes

LEFTOVERS *The galette can be kept for four or five days in the refrigerator. Reheat leftovers in a 300°F oven for about 20 minutes or in the microwave for just a minute or two. You can also fry leftovers in a frying pan with additional butter.*

Savory Beet and Goat Cheese Tart

I serve this shallow tart for brunches and cocktail parties. The beets are baked in a custard and the result is a lot like a quiche. It's a simple way to use up cooked vegetables, extra cheese, and other things you may have in your fridge. Because I never like to throw anything away, tarts like this one are a staple of my repertoire.

Makes one 10-inch round or 9-inch square tart, enough for about 6 people

2/3 recipe Pie Dough (page 421), Cream Cheese Pastry (page 431), or other pie crust
1 tablespoon unsalted butter
1 large shallot or 1/2 small white onion, chopped
Kosher salt and freshly ground black pepper
2 large eggs
2/3 cup heavy cream
2 tablespoons freshly grated Pecorino Romano cheese
Pinch of freshly grated nutmeg
1 medium beet, either roasted or steamed (see page 149), peeled, and cut into small dice
1/2 cup chopped cooked beet greens (see page 150), or spinach or Swiss chard
2 or 3 ounces fresh goat cheese, cut into small cubes

On a lightly floured surface, roll out the crust to a 1/4-inch thickness and transfer to a 10-inch round or 9-inch square fluted tart pan with a removable bottom. Fold any overhanging dough behind the sides of the tart to reinforce them, and press the dough to fit snugly into the tart pan. Refrigerate for 30 minutes to 1 hour.

Preheat the oven to 425°F.

Line the pan with aluminum foil and fill with about 2 cups dried beans or rice or ceramic pie weights. Bake for 20 minutes. Remove the beans, rice, or weights and the foil, return to the oven, and bake for 12 to 15 minutes more, until the crust has set and browned. Remove from the oven and cool. Turn the oven down to 400°F.

Meanwhile, in a small sauté pan, heat the butter over medium-high heat. Sauté the shallot until soft, about 5 minutes. Season with salt and pepper. In a bowl, beat together the eggs, cream, Pecorino, and nutmeg. Season this mixture with salt and freshly ground black pepper.

Place the tart pan on a baking sheet. Scatter the beet, beet greens, goat cheese, and shallot over the bottom of the prebaked tart shell. Pour the egg mixture into the shell so that it comes as close to the edge as you can get it without spilling over. Carefully transfer the baking sheet to the oven and bake for 35 to 40 minutes, or until the center has risen and set and the edges of the crust are dark golden brown. Let cool for 30 minutes or so before unmolding.

PREP TIME: 20 minutes
COOKING TIME: 1 hour 15 minutes
TOTAL TIME: 2 hours and 5 minutes (includes cooling time)

ADVANCE PREP All of the components, including the prebaked crust, can be made a day or two in advance. Finish assembling and baking the tart just a few hours before you intend to serve it. Keep it at room temperature for up to 3 hours, or until ready to serve.

LEFTOVERS The tart will keep for about a week in the fridge. The tart can be served warm, at room temperature, or cold. I think it's best just slightly warm. To reheat, place it in a 300°F oven for about 10 minutes, or until the tart is heated through. Do not microwave or the crust will become soggy.

Potato Pancakes (Latkes)

The James Beard Foundation used to hold an annual latke cook-off every Hanukkah. With this recipe, I won the People's Choice award at the first competition in 1995. I can take no credit, really: it is my mother's recipe. The secret, as she used to freely divulge to people who asked but didn't believe her, is one onion for every two potatoes. Serve these latkes as an appetizer or side dish with applesauce and sour cream.

Makes 8 to 10 three-inch latkes, enough for 3 to 4 servings

- 4 large potatoes (about 2 pounds), such as Yukon Gold or Russet, peeled and cut into large chunks
- 2 large white or yellow onions (about 1 pound), peeled and halved
- 2 large eggs, lightly beaten
- 1/4 cup matzo meal or unseasoned bread crumbs
- Kosher salt and freshly ground black pepper
- About 3/4 cup peanut or vegetable oil, for frying

Using the medium shredding disk of a food processor or the large holes of a box grater, grate a few chunks of potato. Next grate half an onion onto the potato—the onion juice helps keep the potato from turning brown. Continue alternating until all of the potatoes and onions are grated. Transfer half of this mixture to a clean dish towel, roll it up, and holding the towel over the sink, wring out as much liquid as you can. Place in a large bowl and repeat with the remaining potato-onion mixture. Add the eggs, matzo meal, 2 teaspoons salt, and about 1/2 teaspoon pepper, and mix well.

In a large, heavy cast-iron or nonstick sauté pan, heat about 1/8 inch of oil over medium-high heat. Fry a tablespoon or so of the potato mixture until crisp on both sides. Taste and adjust the seasoning with more salt or pepper, if necessary.

To form the latkes, scoop up about 1/2 cup of the potato mixture with your hands and pat it loosely into a thick patty, letting any liquid fall back into the bowl. Slip the latke into the hot oil and flatten the center slightly with your fingertips. Fill the pan but do not crowd it. Fry the latkes until the undersides are golden brown, about 10 minutes. Turn them over and cook for another 8 to 10 minutes, until browned. If the latkes begin to darken too quickly, before the centers are cooked, lower the heat. To prevent excess oil absorption, flip each latke only once. Add more oil to the pan only between batches and be sure to allow the oil to heat up before adding more latkes. As the mixture sits, liquid will collect in the bottom of the bowl. Squeeze the pancakes between your hands to remove excess liquid before placing in the hot frying pan. When done, transfer the latkes to clean paper towels or a brown paper bag to drain. Serve immediately.

PREP TIME: 20 minutes
COOKING TIME: 1 hour
TOTAL TIME: 1 hour 20 minutes

ADVANCE PREP *Once the potatoes are shredded, the latkes must be fried within 30 minutes. The latkes are best eaten out of the pan, but if you have to make them in advance, transfer them to a wire rack after they have drained on paper towels. To reheat, place the rack on a baking sheet in a 300° F oven for 10 to 15 minutes to warm.*
LEFTOVERS *The latkes will keep for about a week in the fridge. They can also be frozen for up to a month.*

Beet Pancakes

Here's an excellent appetizer or side dish for a braised roast or stew. Like a potato latke, but made primarily with beets, these pancakes have a deep red color and an earthy taste. They are delicious with a dollop of sour cream. Their flavor also complements smoked salmon and herring in wine sauce. (Mini beet pancakes with a piece of herring and dab of sour cream make a delicious hors d'oeuvre.) I add a little potato and some starch to the mixture to help hold the beets together, but they are still more fragile than potato pancakes.

Makes 12 to 14 two-inch pancakes, enough for 4 to 5 servings

3 medium beets (about 1 pound)
1 large all-purpose potato (about 8 ounces),
    such as Yukon Gold
1 medium white or yellow onion, shredded
    (about $1/2$ cup)
2 large eggs
1 large egg white
3 tablespoons bread crumbs
2 teaspoons potato starch or cornstarch
$1/4$ cup chopped fresh flat-leaf parsley or
    2 tablespoons chopped fresh dill
2 teaspoons kosher salt
$1/2$ teaspoon freshly ground black pepper
$1/2$ to $3/4$ cup peanut or vegetable oil, for frying
Sour cream, to serve

Partially cook the beets by steaming them for 40 minutes according to the directions on page 149. While they are cooking, parbake the potato in the same oven for 30 minutes. When cool enough to handle, peel the beets and the potato and shred them both on the large holes of a box grater or in a food processor. Combine the beets and potato with the onion and mix well. Add the eggs, egg white, bread crumbs, potato starch, parsley, salt, and pepper and stir to combine. In a large frying pan, heat $1/8$ inch of oil over medium-high heat. Line a clean plate with paper towels.

Using about $1/4$ cup of the beet mixture, form a small patty. Place the patty in the hot oil. Use a spatula to gently press down the pancake to compact and flatten it. Fill the pan with pancakes, leaving enough room between them so they will fry without touching. (Rinse your hands periodically so they don't turn permanently red.) As the mixture sits, liquid will collect on the bottom of the bowl. Squeeze the pancakes between your hands to remove excess liquid before placing in the hot frying pan. Cook until the underside is very nicely browned, about 5 minutes. Because of the dark color of the beets, it's a little difficult to see the pancakes brown, but you'll begin to notice the edges turning even darker than the rest of the pancake. It's important not to cook the pancakes too quickly or the insides will be raw. If the edges begin to burn, lower the heat.

Carefully flip the pancakes with a spatula without breaking them. Press them down gently again and fry for another 4 minutes or so until brown. Remove to the paper towels to drain. Add more oil to the pan only between batches and be sure to allow the oil to heat up before adding more pancakes. Serve immediately, topped with sour cream.

PREP TIME: 15 minutes
COOKING TIME: 70 minutes
TOTAL TIME: 1 hour 25 minutes

ADVANCE PREP The pancakes can be fried, kept on a wire rack for an hour or so, and reheated on the rack in a 300° F oven before serving.

Kitchen Sense

LEFTOVERS *The beet pancakes will keep in the re-*
frigerator for about one week. Reheat leftovers on a
wire rack in a preheated 300° F oven for 15 minutes
or so until the pancakes are heated through.

VARIATION

Celery Root Pancakes

Follow the same recipe, substituting 1 pound celery root (3 cups shredded) for the beets. Parbake the potato for 30 minutes at 400°F as directed, but there is no need to parbake the celery root. Simply use it raw and follow the recipe as directed.

Spinach and Feta Rolls

The spanakopita sold in Greek diners and restaurants was the inspiration for this simple vegetarian entrée, little rolls that are like small spinach and feta strudels. As with all phyllo pastries, the secret to success is moistening the dough with a generous amount of fat before baking.

Makes 4 servings

$\frac{1}{2}$ cup extra-virgin olive oil or unsalted butter, melted, plus extra for greasing the pan

1 medium white or yellow onion, chopped

1 large garlic clove, minced

1 pound fresh spinach, stems removed and cleaned, or 1 (10-ounce) package frozen spinach, defrosted and drained

Pinch of freshly grated nutmeg

1 tablespoon chopped fresh dill

1 tablespoon chopped flat-leaf parsley

4 ounces feta cheese, crumbled ($\frac{2}{3}$ cup)

1 large egg yolk

1 tablespoon unseasoned bread crumbs

2 sheets phyllo dough, cut in half crosswise

Preheat the oven to 400°F. Grease a baking sheet or line it with parchment.

In a large sauté pan, heat $\frac{1}{4}$ cup of the olive oil over medium-high heat. Add the onion and cook until soft, about 5 minutes. Add the garlic and cook for another minute or two. Add the spinach and nutmeg, and cook until the pan is dry, about 8 minutes. To help evaporate the moisture, move the spinach from side to side, exposing some surface area in the center of the pan. Remove from the heat and let cool until just warm. Stir in the dill, parsley, feta, egg yolk, and bread crumbs.

On a clean work surface, lay out $\frac{1}{2}$ sheet of phyllo, short edge facing you (see page 106). Brush the dough generously with some of the remaining olive oil and fold in half crosswise. Brush again with oil. Arrange one fourth of the spinach-feta mixture along the short edge of the dough closest to you. Fold over the long sides and roll up the dough away from you to form a log, brushing all of the exposed dough as you work. Place the roll on the prepared pan and repeat with the remaining spinach and phyllo. Brush the rolls again with oil. Bake for 20 minutes, or until the dough is nicely browned. Serve warm or at room temperature.

PREP TIME: 15 minutes
COOKING TIME: 40 minutes
TOTAL TIME: 55 minutes

ADVANCE PREP *These rolls can be made in advance and stored in the refrigerator for two or three days or frozen for up to a month. Bake directly from the freezer, increasing the cooking time by 10 minutes.*

Potato and Spinach Croquettes

Funny that potato croquettes would be one of those dishes that transcend ethnic culinary borders. I've had them in Japan, in France, in eastern Europe, in Central America—just about everywhere. When something's that popular, you know it must be good. The base is usually leftover mashed potatoes, which add texture, flavor, and binding strength. As a rule, I generally like to have less potato and more spinach or whatever else I'm putting inside.

Makes 10 to 12 croquettes, enough for 4 to 5 servings

FOR THE CROQUETTES

2 tablespoons unsalted butter

1/2 small onion or 1 small shallot, finely chopped

1 to 2 tablespoons assorted chopped fresh herbs, such as rosemary, thyme, parsley, mint, tarragon, sage

2/3 cup chopped cooked spinach (from about 5 ounces fresh or frozen), drained well

1 cup leftover mashed potatoes, or 1 large Russet or Yukon Gold potato, peeled, boiled until tender, and mashed

1 large egg

2 to 3 tablespoons freshly grated Parmigiano Reggiano or Pecorino Romano cheese

1/2 teaspoon kosher salt

Freshly ground black pepper

1 to 2 tablespoons Japanese bread crumbs (panko) or other unseasoned bread crumbs

FOR BREADING AND FRYING

2/3 cup all-purpose flour

2/3 cup Japanese bread crumbs (panko) or other unseasoned bread crumbs

1 large egg beaten with 1 teaspoon cold water

1/2 cup peanut or vegetable oil, or more as necessary, for frying

To prepare the croquettes, heat the butter in a small sauté pan over medium-high heat. Add the onion and sauté until soft, about 5 minutes. Add the herbs and sauté for another minute or so. Add the spinach and sauté for a minute to combine. Set aside to cool. In a medium bowl, combine the mashed potatoes with the egg, cheese, salt, and some pepper. Stir in the spinach mixture. If you have the time, chill this mixture for a couple of hours before shaping and frying the croquettes.

Remove the croquette mixture from the fridge. If it is too soft to hold its shape when you pinch it, add a tablespoon or two of bread crumbs to stiffen it. In three separate small bowls, place the flour, bread crumbs, and beaten egg. Heat the peanut oil in a small to medium frying pan. Wet your hands with cold water. Take about 1 1/2 to 2 tablespoons of the croquette mixture in the palm of your hand and shape it into a ball or an oblong egg shape. Roll this croquette first in flour and tap off any excess. Next, dip it in the beaten egg. Be sure the entire surface is coated with egg, and then lift up the croquette with a fork to drain off any excess egg. Finally, roll the croquette in the bread crumbs, being careful to keep its shape intact. (Reshape it in your palm if you have to.)

Place the croquette in the hot oil and repeat. Do not overcrowd the pan. When the croquettes are browned on the bottom, turn them on their side. Continue rotating until they are evenly browned, about 5 minutes total. If they start to brown too quickly or burn, lower the heat. Remove to drain on paper towels. Transfer to a wire rack to cool. Repeat until all of the croquettes are fried.

PREP TIME: 20 minutes
COOKING TIME: 25 minutes
TOTAL TIME: 45 minutes

ADVANCE PREP The croquette mixture can be made up to two days in advance and kept covered in the fridge until you are ready to fry.
LEFTOVERS The croquettes are best eaten just as they are fried or just when they come to room temperature. To reheat, place the wire rack of croquettes on a baking sheet and set in a 350° F oven for 15 to 20 minutes until heated through. This is a dish designed to use up leftovers, but if you have leftover croquettes, try putting them in a sandwich with a tangy dressing, such as a flavored mayonnaise.

VARIATION
Potato and Ham Croquettes
Substitute $^1/_2$ cup finely diced ham for the spinach and proceed with the recipe as directed. You can add $^1/_4$ cup frozen peas if you like, too.

VARIATION
Potato and Turnip, Beet, or Mustard Greens Croquettes
I happen to love using various greens in my cooking. Turnip greens have a mild bite, beet greens are soft and buttery, and mustard greens are a little sharp and spicy. Each is delicious in these croquettes. Substitute $^2/_3$ cup chopped, boiled turnip, beet, or mustard greens for the spinach and proceed with the recipe as directed. (Be sure to remove the stems and the tough large veins of the leaves of the greens before chopping them.)

VARIATION
Potato, Corn, and Mushroom Croquettes
Substitute $^1/_3$ cup sauteed finely diced mushrooms (they should be cooked in butter, seasoned with salt and pepper, and drained) and $^1/_3$ cup fresh or frozen corn kernels for the spainach and proceed with the recipe as directed.

French Fries
Since I moved to New York City in the early 1990s, there's been a sort of french fry renaissance: the quality of fries served in restaurants has improved tremendously. That's because chefs began to make their own fries from fresh potatoes instead of buying frozen, precut, preblanched fries. The secrets to making good french fries at home are (1) to choose a good, starchy potato—I like Russet or Yukon Gold and I prefer not to peel them; (2) to soak the potatoes in cold water after they are cut to bring some of the starch to the surface; and (3) to cook the fries twice: once in 325° F oil for a few minutes, just until the potatoes are limp—this is called blanching—and then, once they have cooled, a second time in 375° F oil until crisp. My preference for french fries is peanut oil, which I think makes a delicate, crisp fry, but you can use whatever vegetable oil you wish. (Don't use olive oil, which cannot take the heat of deep frying.) I like my french fries tossed with plenty of salt and served with ketchup, of course, but homemade Mayonnaise (page 405) or malt vinegar is also delicious on the side. For a different effect, toss the fries with

SHALLOW VERSUS DEEP FRYING

Although I like to think of myself as a relatively deep person, when it comes to frying I'm about as shallow as they come. Some people think this is because I do not have room on my counter for an electric deep fryer—and that's partly true. But more important, I think shallow frying is less of a hassle and in most cases I like the results better. As an added bonus, shallow frying uses much less oil, which is less wasteful and which allows me to afford better-quality oil for frying, such as peanut oil, which gives fried food a buttery flavor, or grapeseed oil, which is neutral in flavor but makes things very crisp.

I realized my affinity for shallow frying after my cooking experiences in Italy, where deep frying in not common. Even presumably deep-fried Italian dishes, such as stuffed zucchini flowers, fried risotto balls, and fried semolina fritters, are usually cooked in a shallow pan. I almost never fry anything in more than an inch of oil (exceptions would include French Fries, page 191). I use a medium cast-iron pan and work in small batches so I can control the temperature and pay close attention to ensure even cooking. Regulating the temperature is easy with cast-iron cookware, whether by lowering the heat under the pan or by periodically removing the pan from the heat to cool slightly. Any heavy pan that conducts the heat well will work fine, though.

Here are a few things to remember whether you are shallow frying or deep frying: The oil should be hot enough—usually 350°F to 375°F—when you begin frying. This avoids excess oil absorption, which can cause the food to be greasy. To test the oil, put a tiny drop of water or a piece of something you are frying in the oil. If the oil is hot enough, it should immediately bubble. Never add cold oil while something is cooking, and after you add more oil to the pan always allow the oil to come back up to temperature before frying more food. Finally, don't crowd the pan or the oil temperature will drop, and the item you are frying won't have the opportunity to

---

an assortment of fried herbs and garlic cloves, as described in the Variation, below.

Makes 1½ pounds fries, or enough for 4 to 6 servings

> 1 quart peanut or vegetable oil, for frying
> 2 pounds Russet or Yukon Gold potatoes, cut into sticks about ¼ inch across and 3 inches long, and soaked in cold water for at least an hour
> Kosher salt

Place the oil in a large, heavy saucepan or deep fryer. It should not come more than halfway up the sides of the pot. (I use a cast-iron Dutch oven, but any heavy pot will do.) Set the pan over medium-high heat and bring to 325°F. (A deep-frying thermometer is essential.)

Meanwhile, remove a large handful or two of potatoes from their soaking water and drain well on paper towels. Pat dry with more paper towels to be sure there is no excess moisture on the potatoes. When the oil is at the right temperature, drop the potatoes into the hot oil and fry for about 5 minutes, until they are shiny and limp. (The oil will bubble up at first but then subside.) Lift out the potatoes with a mesh strainer or slotted spoon, drain well, and place on a baking sheet. Repeat with the remaining potatoes. Let the potatoes cool to room temperature, at least 30 minutes.

Heat the oil to 375°F. Return the potatoes in handfuls to the hot oil and cook until dark golden brown and crisp, 8 to 10 minutes. Remove from the oil, drain on paper towels, and place in a large bowl. Toss with plenty of salt and serve immediately.

COOKING TIME: 45 minutes

TOTAL TIME: 1 hour 15 minutes (includes cooling time)

ADVANCE PREP *The potatoes can be cooked the first time—that is, blanched— and refrigerated for up to a day before frying the second time.*

VARIATION
French Fries with Garlic and Herbs

After the fries have been cooking the second time for 2 or 3 minutes, add several sliced garlic cloves to the oil. Just before the fries are done, add a handful of assorted herbs, leaves only, such as parsley, basil, sage, and rosemary. Remove the fries with the garlic and herbs, drain well, and toss with salt before serving.

Buttermilk Fried Onions

Here's a recipe for fried onions that are delicious on their own or great as a topping or accompaniment to dishes such as macaroni and cheese or stewed vegetables. On the spectrum of fried onion dishes, they'd fall somewhere between onion rings and canned fried onions, only way better. If they are fried properly, which means quickly, they are remarkably crispy, flavorful, and not greasy.

Makes about 4 cups, enough for 6 to 8 servings

1 large white or yellow onion, very thinly sliced
1 cup buttermilk, or more to cover
1 cup all-purpose flour
Kosher salt and freshly ground black pepper
2 cups peanut or vegetable oil, for frying

Separate the onion slices into rings and place them in a small bowl. Pour the buttermilk over the onions to cover and let sit at room temperature for 2 hours or refrigerate overnight.

Line a plate with paper towels. In a small pot or deep-fat fryer, bring the oil to 350°F—a thermometer immersed in the oil is the only way to be sure of the temperature. Drain the onions well, but don't rinse. Put the flour in a bowl and mix with 1 teaspoon salt and some black pepper. Dump a small handful of the onions into the flour mixture. Dredge to coat evenly with the flour. Shake off any excess flour and drop the onions into the hot oil. Stir the onions around in the oil with a fork to prevent clumping. Keep stirring occasionally while they fry to a deep golden brown, about 2 minutes. Lift the onions out of the oil with the fork, drain for a second or two, and place on the paper towels. Sprinkle with salt. Repeat with the remaining onions.

PREP TIME: 10 minutes

COOKING TIME: 6 minutes

TOTAL TIME: 2 hours 15 minutes (includes soaking time)

ADVANCE PREP *The onions can be sliced, soaked in buttermilk, covered, and stored in the fridge for up to two days before frying.*
LEFTOVERS *Once cooked, the onions should really be eaten the same day. If you must keep them around longer, line an airtight container with a paper towel, place the onions inside, and seal. Store*

at room temperature. You'd be surprised how many things are better with a handful of fried onions thrown in: mashed potatoes, salads, meatloaf, macaroni and cheese, chopped liver—you name it.

Fried Green Tomatoes

I use fried green tomatoes as a side dish for Southern meals—from breakfast through dinner—but also as a filling for sandwiches. For a simpler version, you can skip the flour-and-egg step, but I happen to like the contrast between the soft tomato center and the thicker breading that the dip produces. Granulated or coarse semolina flour makes a nice substitute for cornmeal.

Makes 4 servings

> 1 1/2 cups buttermilk
> 1 teaspoon kosher salt
> 2 large hard, green (unripe) tomatoes (about 1 pound)
> 3/4 cup all-purpose flour
> 1/4 teaspoon freshly ground black pepper
> 2 large eggs
> 3/4 cup yellow cornmeal or granulated semolina
> 1/2 cup peanut or vegetable oil, for frying

In a medium bowl, combine the buttermilk and salt. Core the tomatoes and slice crosswise into 1/4-inch-thick slices, placing the slices in the buttermilk. Let sit at room temperature for about 2 hours.

In a wide, shallow bowl, combine the flour with the pepper. Mix well. Put the eggs in a separate bowl, and beat with 1 tablespoon water. Put the cornmeal in a third bowl. Heat about 1/4 inch of oil in a heavy frying pan (cast-iron works well) over medium-high heat. Line a plate with paper towels or a brown paper bag.

Remove a slice of tomato from the buttermilk, drain it, and dredge it in the seasoned flour. Dip the floured tomato slice in the beaten egg and then dredge it in the cornmeal until thoroughly coated. Place in the hot oil. Repeat until the pan is full but the tomatoes aren't touching. Fry until the crust is golden brown and the tomato has softened, 4 to 6 minutes per side. Remove from the pan and drain on paper towels or brown paper. Repeat with the remaining slices of tomato. Serve immediately.

PREP TIME: 20 minutes
COOKING TIME: 25 to 35 minutes
TOTAL TIME: 2 hours 45 minutes (includes soaking time)

ADVANCE PREP *The tomatoes can sit in the buttermilk overnight in the refrigerator. You can also bread them and keep them on a plate in the fridge for up to six hours before you fry them.*
LEFTOVERS *The fried tomatoes will keep for about a week in the fridge. They lose their crispness, but they are still delicious, cold or hot. Use them in sandwiches, on burgers, or cut up and stirred into hash.*

Corn Fritters

This is a delicious way to prepare fresh corn when it's in season. Out of season, use frozen kernels. Serve these fritters as a side dish with grilled meat.

Makes 12 (2-inch) fritters, enough for 4 to 6 servings

> 3/4 cup unbleached all-purpose flour
> 1/3 cup yellow cornmeal
> 1/2 teaspoon baking powder

1 teaspoon kosher salt

Freshly ground black pepper

1 cup beer, such as lager or ale

1 large egg

1 large egg white

2½ cups fresh or frozen corn kernels (from about
   3 ears)

1 scallion, white and green parts, chopped

1 tablespoon chopped flat-leaf parsley or cilantro

Peanut or vegetable oil, for frying

In a large mixing bowl, combine the flour, cornmeal, baking powder, salt, and pepper. In a small bowl, beat together the beer, egg, and the egg white. Pour this mixture into the flour mixture and add the corn, scallion if using, and parsley. Stir just until mixed and there are no lumps of flour. If you have the time, let the mixture sit, uncovered, at room temperature for about 1 hour.

In a large frying pan, preferably cast iron, pour a shallow layer of oil, about ⅛ inch deep, and heat over medium-high heat. With a large tablespoon, drop the batter into the hot pan to make small pancakes. Do not crowd the pan. Cook until the edges are browned and you can see bubbles coming up through the surface of the fritters, about 5 minutes. Flip and cook the other side for 2 to 3 minutes, until browned. Watch out as the fritters cook because fresh corn kernels tend to pop, splattering hot oil. Remove the fritters to paper towels. Repeat with the remaining batter.

PREP TIME: 15 minutes

COOKING TIME: 25 minutes

TOTAL TIME: 45 minutes to 1 hour 45 minutes (includes resting time)

ADVANCE PREP *The batter can be mixed and kept for up to two hours at room temperature. For longer storage, up to two days, refrigerate. The fritters are best eaten right away, but they can be kept warm in a 250°F oven for up to 30 minutes, or until ready to serve.*

LEFTOVERS *The fritters will keep for a week in the fridge. Reheat them in a microwave on high for 30 seconds apiece.*

Fried Zucchini Flowers with Fried Sage Leaves

The romantic in me loves the idea of eating flowers. And the gourmet in me thinks fried zucchini flowers, which are available only a few weeks a year, are the height of superb, local, seasonal eating. The flowers don't travel well because they are so delicate. Fried zucchini flowers are popular all over Italy, especially Rome, but I have to say, I often find the batter the Italians use too thick and tough for the delicate flower. It is also common in Italy to stuff the flowers before they are fried, but I think the stuffing usually overpowers the blossom, too. So I make a simple beer batter and fry the flowers plain—all they need is a sprinkling of sea salt. Use the leftover batter to fry sage leaves, another treat.

Makes 4 servings

½ cup unbleached all-purpose flour

¾ cup beer, such as lager or ale

Kosher salt

Peanut or vegetable oil, for frying

12 zucchini flowers, about a pint depending on
   size, stamens removed if present

4 to 8 fresh sage leaves

In a small bowl, whisk together the flour and beer with a fork until smooth and the consistency of a thin pancake batter. Add a pinch of salt. In a medium frying pan, preferably cast iron, heat a ¼-inch layer of oil over medium-high heat. Place a paper-towel–lined plate near the pan. Holding the blossoms by the stem end, pull the flower through the batter—one side, then the other. Don't worry if the flower isn't evenly coated or there are parts that aren't coated. As you remove the flower from the batter, scrape it along the edge of the bowl to remove any excess batter, and then lay the flower in the hot oil. Repeat until the pan is full but the blossoms aren't touching.

Fry until the underside is golden brown, about 4 minutes, turn over, and fry until the second side is browned, 3 minutes more. Remove to the paper towels to drain and repeat until all of the flowers are fried. If you need more oil, only add it to an empty pan and be sure it comes back up to temperature before you add more flowers. When you are finished with the flowers, holding the stem end, run the sage leaves through the leftover batter on both sides and fry until golden brown. While still warm, sprinkle with salt, and serve.

PREP TIME: 15 minutes
COOKING TIME: 35 minutes
TOTAL TIME: 50 minutes

ADVANCE PREP *The batter can be mixed in advance and kept at room temperature for several hours until ready to use. The flowers should be fried just before they will be eaten.*

Black-Eyed Pea Fritters with Country Ham

Made small, these spicy fritters are delicious as an hors d'oeuvre dipped in your favorite salsa or dip—the spicier, the better. Larger fritters make a nice side dish for grilled or pan-fried meat.

Makes about 3 dozen fritters, enough for 8 to 10 servings

1 cup dried black-eyed peas
1 small white or yellow onion, cut into chunks
½ small hot chile, minced, or pinch of cayenne pepper
1 large egg
1 teaspoon kosher salt
Freshly ground black pepper
1 tablespoon dry white wine
¼ cup finely diced country, smoked, or boiled ham (optional)
1 tablespoon minced flat-leaf parsley
Peanut or vegetable oil, for frying

Place the black-eyed peas in a large bowl and cover with at least 3 inches of cold water. Let soak overnight at room temperature. Drain the peas and place them in a food processor fitted with a metal chopping blade. Add the onion and chile, and pulse to chop fine, then let the machine run until the mixture is puréed or as smooth as possible. Add the egg, salt, and black pepper, and pulse to blend. With the machine running, add the white wine through the feed tube along with 2 to 3 tablespoons cold water to make a batter thick enough to hold its shape but thin enough to drop off a spoon. Add the ham, if using, and parsley and pulse once or twice to blend.

Heat about ¾ inch of oil in a medium heavy frying pan, preferably cast iron, over medium-high heat to about 350°F. For hors d'oeuvres, drop teaspoonsful of the black-eyed-pea batter into the hot oil to make small blobs. For a side dish, use tablespoonfuls. Do not crowd the pan. Cook until the fritters are golden brown, 3 to 4 minutes, then flip with a fork to cook the second side, 2 to 3 minutes more, a little longer for larger fritters. Lift out of the oil with a fork or slotted spoon and let drain on paper towels. Repeat with the remaining batter. If serving as hors d'oeuvres, allow the fritters to cool for a minute or two before serving so your guests don't burn their fingers.

PREP TIME: 15 minutes

COOKING TIME: 15 to 20 minutes

TOTAL TIME: 9 hours (includes soaking time)

ADVANCE PREP *The batter can be made and re-frigerated up to two days in advance. It can also be frozen.*

LEFTOVERS *The fritters will keep for about four days in the refrigerator. Reheat in a microwave on high for 15 seconds or so until ready to serve.*

VARIATIONS

The same technique can be used with other dried beans, such as chickpeas, favas, and lentils. Substitute an equal amount (6 ounces by weight) and proceed with the recipe as directed.

Falafel

This recipe produces a delicious falafel that's crisp on the outside and moist on the inside. Serve these Middle Eastern chickpea cakes wrapped in warm pita along with assorted pickled vegetables, lettuce, and tomato, and douse with tahini sauce made by shaking tahini (sesame paste) with fresh lemon juice and water.

Makes 2 dozen falafel, enough for 6 to 8 servings

1¼ cups dried chickpeas

2 garlic cloves

1 large shallot or ¼ small red onion

2 tablespoons all-purpose flour or unseasoned bread crumbs

1½ teaspoons ground cumin

2 teaspoons kosher salt

¼ teaspoon cayenne pepper

¼ teaspoon freshly ground black pepper

¼ cup chopped fresh flat-leaf parsley

1 to 1½ cups peanut or vegetable oil, for frying

Place the chickpeas in a medium bowl, add enough cold water to cover by at least 3 inches, and let sit for 8 hours or overnight.

In the work bowl of a food processor fitted with a metal chopping blade, pulse the garlic and shallot four or five times to chop fine. Drain and rinse the chickpeas and add them to the food processor along with the flour, cumin, salt, cayenne, black pepper, and parsley. Using on/off pulses, grind the chickpeas until they resemble fine meal. Scrape down the sides and pulse two or three more times to be sure the mixture is evenly ground. Pinch the mixture to be sure it will hold its shape; if not, grind some more.

Heat about ½ inch of oil in a large, heavy frying pan over medium-high heat until quite hot. Shape about 2 tablespoons of the falafel mixture into a small ¾-inch-thick patty and place in the hot oil. Repeat, filling the pan. Fry until the falafels are dark brown, about 5 minutes, and then flip to brown the other side, about 3 minutes. Remove to paper towels to drain and repeat with the remaining falafel mixture.

PREP TIME: 15 minutes

COOKING TIME: 30 minutes

TOTAL TIME: 9 hours (includes soaking time)

SOAKING BEANS

A good soak helps lessen the time required to cook dried beans and makes for plump, tender beans that aren't mushy when cooked. Soaking also helps remove some of the complex sugars in beans—the oligosaccharides—that cause flatulence. Lentils and mung beans are two exceptions because they cook quickly enough not to require soaking.

It's important to pick over beans before soaking because, due to the way beans are sorted by size, small stones can easily end up mixed in with the beans. From 2 cups of black beans I recently removed seven small pebbles. Put the beans on one side of a baking sheet and sort through them as you move them to the other side.

The easiest way to soak beans is to put them in a bowl, cover them with plenty of cold water—enough to come at least 3 inches above the beans—and let them sit overnight on the counter. Drain, rinse, and cook them according to the directions in your recipe. Adding a teaspoon of salt to the soaking water helps encourage water absorption. If you cannot use the soaked beans right away, you can store them either in their soaking liquid or drained in an air-tight container in the refrigerator for up to two days. Do not keep them at room temperature or they will begin to germinate. It's important to drain the beans to flush away the flatulence-causing oligosaccharides.

If you forget to soak your beans the night before, you can cheat by using the quick-soaking method. Place the beans in a saucepan. Cover with cold water, bring to a boil, boil for 5 minutes, turn off the heat, and let soak for 1 hour. Drain and rinse the beans and proceed with your recipe as directed. Beans soaked this way will take a little bit longer to cook and sometimes I think they have a slightly mushier texture than beans that have soaked at room temperature overnight. I do not advise using baking soda, as some people do, because I think it leads to mushy beans.

If you are going to be making dishes that allow the beans to cook slowly for long periods of time, such as baked beans made overnight in a low oven or slow-cooker, there is no need to soak the beans first. The long cooking softens the beans and also breaks down the oligosaccharides. Simply rinse the beans and use them in the recipe as directed.

ADVANCE PREP *The falafels mixture can be made up to two days in advance and kept in the refrigerator until ready to fry.*

LEFTOVERS *The falafels are best eaten immediately, but they can be reheated on a wire rack in a 300° F oven for 8 to 10 minutes or in a microwave on high for 30 seconds apiece. Leftover falafel can be crumbled and stirred into chili.*

Giant Beans in Tomato Sauce

Giant beans—*gigantes* or butter beans—are superb, delicate, buttery-textured white beans. This preparation—stewed with tomato and dill—is a classic Greek way to prepare them, though without the dill they could be found in just about any country around the Mediterranean. Serve these beans as an appetizer or as a side dish with grilled lamb.

Makes 6 servings

1 1/2 cups dried gigantes or butter beans
   (about 1 pound)
3 tablespoons extra-virgin olive oil
1 medium white or yellow onion, finely
   chopped
2 garlic cloves, minced
1 (28-ounce) can tomatoes, cut up, with juice
5 sprigs fresh thyme, leaves only, chopped, or
   1 teaspoon dried thyme
2 bay leaves
2 teaspoons sugar
2 tablespoons chopped fresh dill or mint
2 tablespoons chopped fresh flat-leaf parsley
1 tablespoon fresh lemon juice
Kosher salt and freshly ground black pepper

Place the dried beans in a large bowl, add enough water to cover by about 3 inches, and let sit for 8 hours or overnight.

In a large saucepan, heat the olive oil over medium-high heat. Add the onion and cook until wilted, about 5 minutes. Add the garlic and continue cooking until the onion just begins to brown, another 5 minutes or so. Drain and rinse the beans and add them along with the tomatoes with their juice, the thyme, and bay leaves. Add enough water to cover the beans, 1 to 2 cups. Bring to a boil, reduce the heat so that the liquid simmers, cover loosely, and cook until the beans are tender but not mushy, 45 minutes to 1 hour, depending on how fresh the beans are. If the cooking liquid falls below the surface of the beans while they are cooking, add more water to cover.

When the beans are cooked, remove the cover. Discard the bay leaves. Stir in the sugar, dill, parsley, lemon juice, 1 teaspoon salt, and some pepper. Bring back to a simmer. Taste

and adjust the seasoning with more salt if necessary. Serve the beans hot, warm, or at room temperature.

PREP TIME: 5 minutes
COOKING TIME: 1 hour 15 minutes
TOTAL TIME: 9 hours 20 minutes (includes soaking time)

ADVANCE PREP *The beans are good when just cooked but are even better the next day. Refrigerate and then reheat on the stovetop, if desired.*
LEFTOVERS *The beans will keep for about ten days in the refrigerator.*

Boston Baked Beans with Country Bacon

There's not a whole lot of skill to making great baked beans, and that's one of the things that makes them so appealing. You throw all of the ingredients into an ovenproof dish (with a cover) or slow-cooker and let the beans cook very slowly, 7 to 8 hours, until they are soft. I do not like my beans very sweet, and this recipe produces baked beans with an old-fashioned, savory taste. If you like really sweet baked beans, double or triple your sweetener of choice.

Makes 8 cups, enough for 6 to 8 servings

2 cups dried white beans (1 pound), such as navy
   beans, soldier beans, Great Northern beans, or
   cannellini beans, rinsed in cold water
6 to 8 ounces country bacon, salt pork, or slab
   bacon, rinsed under cold water and diced
1 large white or yellow onion, chopped
2 garlic cloves, minced

2 tablespoons blackstrap (unsulphured) molasses,
   hoisin sauce, dark honey, or dark brown sugar,
   or $1/4$ cup maple syrup, or a combination of
   these
2 tablespoons Dijon mustard or 1 teaspoon dry
   mustard
1 small ripe or canned tomato, finely chopped, or
   1 tablespoon tomato paste or ketchup
1 tablespoon minced fresh ginger or $1/4$ teaspoon
   ground ginger
2 bay leaves
Pinch of cayenne pepper or a couple of drops of
   hot sauce
$1 1/2$ teaspoons kosher salt
$1/4$ teaspoon freshly ground black pepper

In a large ovenproof pot with a lid or a slow-cooker, combine the beans, bacon, onion, garlic, molasses, mustard, tomato, ginger, bay leaves, cayenne, salt, and pepper. Stir in $4 1/2$ cups cold water. Cover the pot, set in the oven, and turn the dial to 250°F, or switch the slow-cooker on to low. After about seven hours, check the beans: they should have thickened and softened. The top will look dry, but if you stir up the beans, you'll see liquid below the surface. If they aren't quite tender, keep the beans going for another hour or so. Remove from the oven or turn off the slow-cooker. Discard the bay leaves. Let the beans cool at room temperature. As they sit they will absorb any excess liquid.

TOTAL TIME: 7 to 8 hours

ADVANCE PREP *The beans can be made a day or two in advance and refrigerated. Reheat in the oven or on top of the stove before serving.*

LEFTOVERS *The beans will keep for up to one week in the fridge. Reheat leftovers in the microwave or in a pot on the stove, adding a tablespoon or two of water to prevent burning.*

Southwestern Baked Beans with Chorizo, Poblanos, and Orange

These unusually flavored baked beans have a rich, creamy texture and delicate orange flavor that blends surprisingly well with the chorizo and spices. I just love them. Be sure to use a fresh (raw) Mexican chorizo, not cured, smoked Spanish chorizo—the flavor will be good either way, but the Spanish chorizo ends up very dry.

Makes about 8 cups, enough for 8 servings

2 cups small white beans (1 pound), such as navy,
   soldier, Great Northern, cannellini, or baby
   lima beans
1 pound fresh (raw) Mexican chorizo or other
   spicy sausage, cut into $1 1/2$-inch pieces
1 large white or yellow onion, chopped
2 garlic cloves, minced
2 dark green poblano chiles, seeded and diced
1 or 2 jalapeño or serrano chiles, seeded and
   finely chopped
3 tablespoons orange juice concentrate
$1 1/2$ teaspoons kosher salt
$1/4$ teaspoon freshly ground black pepper
1 bunch fresh cilantro, chopped (about $1/3$ cup)

In a large, deep ovenproof pot with a lid or in a slow-cooker, combine the beans, chorizo, onion, garlic, poblanos, jalapeños, orange juice concentrate, salt, and black pepper. Stir in $4 1/2$ cups water. Cover the pot, set in the oven, and turn the temperature to 250°F, or switch the slow-cooker on to low. Cook for 8 hours or until the

Cooking Dried Beans

Here's a recipe you can use to cook just about any bean. The cooking time will depend on the type of beans, their freshness, and what you intend to do with them when they are done. For instance, if you are going to purée them, the beans should be cooked until very soft. If you are going to use them in another recipe, such as a bean soup, they should be slightly underdone because they will continue cooking when added to the soup. If you are going to serve them as a side dish, they should be cooked until they are soft but not mushy. You can, of course, cook beans in plain water, without any aromatic vegetables, but this way both the beans and the cooking water are more flavorful.

By adding salt to the beans while they soak, I have recently learned from kitchen scientist Harold McGee, the beans soften and absorb water more quickly. In contrast, if you cook the beans in salted water, they toughen somewhat.

Makes 5½ to 6 cups

2 to 2½ cups dried beans, such as cannellini, borlotti, chickpeas, red kidney beans, navy beans, or black beans (about 1 pound)

2 teaspoons kosher salt

½ large white or yellow onion

2 large garlic cloves

1 celery stalk, or the leafy tops of 2 or 3 celery stalks

2 medium carrots (about ¼ pound), peeled

1 bay leaf

1 or 2 sprigs rosemary, sage, or thyme (optional)

5 sprigs flat-leaf parsley

¼ teaspoon freshly ground black pepper

Best-quality extra-virgin olive oil (optional)

Pick over the beans to remove any discolored or shriveled beans or stones. Place in a deep bowl and add enough water to cover by 2 inches. Add 1 teaspoon of the salt. Let sit on the counter for 8 hours or overnight.

Drain the beans and rinse under cold water. Drain and transfer to a large saucepan. Add the onion, garlic, celery, carrots, bay leaf, rosemary, parsley, and black pepper. Add about 8 cups cold water, or enough to cover the beans by 2 or 3 inches, and bring to a boil. Turn down the heat so that the water simmers and cook until the beans are tender, but still al dente, 45 minutes to 1 hour depending on the type of beans, how fresh they are, and what you are going to do with them (see headnote above). If the liquid boils down below the level of the beans, add more water to keep them submerged. Skim off any scum that forms on top as they cook.

When the beans are cooked, remove and discard the vegetables and herbs. I like to let the beans cool in their cooking liquid, which makes them plump. Reserve the cooking liquid, which you can use later to adjust the consistency of whatever dish you are using with the beans. To serve the beans as is, season the beans with the remaining 1 teaspoon salt and serve with a very generous drizzle of the best-quality extra-virgin olive oil you can find.

PREP TIME: 10 minutes
COOKING TIME: 1 hour
TOTAL TIME: 10 hours (includes soaking time)

ADVANCE PREP Beans can be cooked up to a week before serving and stored in their cooking liquid in the refrigerator until needed.
LEFTOVERS Use them in salads, soups, or pastas.

beans are soft but still hold their shape. Remove from the oven or turn off the slow-cooker. Let the beans cool at room temperature. As they sit they will absorb any excess liquid. Stir in the cilantro before serving.

TOTAL TIME: 8 hours

ADVANCE PREP *I find the beans are actually best if they are made the day before and reheated (on the stove or in the oven) before serving.*
LEFTOVERS *The beans will keep for two weeks in the fridge or can be frozen for several months. Reheat leftovers on the stove, in the oven, or in a microwave.*

Spicy Chickpeas

This is a recipe adapted from a cookbook by my friend Madhur Jaffrey. It's a simple way to prepare chickpeas with a great Indian flavor. Dried chickpeas you cook yourself (see page 201) produce the best results, but the flavors in the dish are so pronounced that even canned chickpeas work perfectly well.

Makes about 6 cups, enough for 6 servings

  $^1/_4$ cup peanut or vegetable oil
  2 medium white or yellow onions, finely chopped
  6 garlic cloves, minced
  1 tablespoon minced fresh ginger
  2 teaspoons Hungarian sweet paprika
  1 tablespoon ground coriander
  1 tablespoon ground cumin
  1 teaspoon turmeric
  1 teaspoon garam masala
  $^1/_4$ teaspoon cayenne pepper, or to taste
  1 ripe tomato or 2 canned tomatoes, finely
    chopped

  4 cups drained cooked chickpeas, from 2 cups
    dried chickpeas (see page 201), or
    2 (20-ounce) cans, drained
  $^1/_2$ teaspoon kosher salt
  Juice of $^1/_2$ lemon (2 tablespoons)

In a medium saucepan over medium heat, heat the oil. Add the onions and cook until wilted, about 5 minutes. Add the garlic and continue cooking until the onions begin to brown evenly, without burning, about 10 minutes. Stir in the ginger. Lower the heat and add the paprika, coriander, cumin, turmeric, garam masala, and cayenne, and cook for 30 seconds, until the spices begin to toast. Add the tomato and cook until the flesh of the tomato sort of melts, forming a paste with the spices, and browns, about 10 minutes. Add 1 cup cold water and the chickpeas, and bring to a simmer. Stir in the salt and lemon juice. Reduce the heat to low, cover, and simmer for about 10 minutes. Serve hot or at room temperature.

TOTAL TIME: 65 minutes

ADVANCE PREP *The spicy chickpeas can be prepared up to two or three days in advance and stored in the refrigerator. Reheat in a saucepan with an additional tablespoon or two of water to avoid burning.*
LEFTOVERS *The chickpeas will keep in the refrigerator for up to ten days. These chickpeas make a delicious filling for wraps or other sandwiches.*

VARIATION
Spicy Chickpeas with Yogurt
Yogurt adds a pleasant creaminess to the chickpeas. Just before serving, stir a couple of table-

spoons of the hot chickpea cooking liquid into 1 cup whole-milk yogurt to temper it. Stir this mixture back into the chickpeas. Bring back to a simmer and serve.

Lentil and Root Vegetable Stew

This simple, hardy stew of lentils and root vegetables goes well with just about any meat or poultry. Even if you think you don't like turnip, I would suggest you use it. As the turnip cooks, it becomes sweet, and the flavor is particularly well suited to lentils.

Makes 6 servings

1 tablespoon extra-virgin olive oil
1 to 2 ounces bacon or pancetta, chopped, or an additional 1 to 2 tablespoons olive oil
1 medium yellow or white onion, chopped
1 leek, white and light green parts only, chopped
1 small garlic clove, minced
1 carrot, peeled and cut into medium dice
1 medium turnip, peeled and cut into medium dice
1 celery stalk, cut into medium dice
1 small parsnip, peeled and cut into medium dice
1 1/2 cups green or brown lentils, picked over
1/2 cup dry white or red wine
4 cups chicken or vegetable stock, water, or a combination
1 bay leaf
2 teaspoons kosher salt
Freshly ground black pepper
1 medium Yukon Gold or other firm, starchy potato, peeled and diced
2 tablespoons chopped fresh flat-leaf parsley

In a large saucepan, heat the olive oil with the bacon or pancetta over medium-high heat. Add the onion and leek and cook for 5 minutes or so, until they are wilted. Add the garlic, carrot, turnip, celery, and parsnip, and continue cooking until they begin to soften, about 5 minutes. Add the lentils, wine, stock, and bay leaf, and bring to a boil. Add 2 teaspoons salt and some pepper, turn down the heat so that the mixture simmers, cover loosely, and cook for 25 minutes. Add the potato and cook for another 25 to 30 minutes, or until the potato and lentils are tender but not mushy. They should remain just barely covered with liquid while they cook; if not, add a little more stock or water as needed. When the lentils and potatoes are done, the liquid should be gone (this is a stew, not a soup). Discard the bay leaf, stir in the parsley, adjust the seasoning with salt and pepper, and serve.

TOTAL TIME: 1 hour 10 minutes

ADVANCE PREP *The lentils can be made a day or two in advance and refrigerated until ready to serve. Reheat in a saucepan, adding more stock or water if necessary to prevent burning.*
LEFTOVERS *The lentils will keep for about one week in the refrigerator.*

Vegetarian Chili with Bulgur and Cashews

The combination of bulgur and cashews gives this vegetarian chili a thick, meaty texture. Red kidney beans are traditional in chili, but you can use any bean or combination of beans, including cannellini and chickpeas. Of course, if you cook your own beans (see page 201), the texture and flavor of the finished chili will be that much better, but canned beans work perfectly well, too. If cooking your own, reserve some of the bean cooking liquid to adjust the consistency of the chili.

Makes 6 servings

¼ cup extra-virgin olive oil or vegetable oil

1 large white or yellow onion, chopped

3 garlic cloves, chopped

1 celery stalk, chopped

1 green bell pepper, cored, seeded, and
    chopped

1 medium carrot, shredded

3 tablespoons chili powder

1½ teaspoons ground cumin

1 teaspoon dried oregano

½ teaspoon ground chipotle

Cayenne pepper or crushed red pepper flakes,
    to taste

1 cup tomato juice

1 (28-ounce) can tomatoes with juice, cut up
    into chunks

Kosher salt and freshly ground black pepper

2½ to 3 cups drained cooked kidney or other
    beans (see page 201), or 1 (20-ounce) can
    beans, drained, reserving about ½ cup
    cooking liquid

½ cup bulgur

½ cup cashews or pecans, toasted (see page
    10) and chopped

¼ cup chopped fresh cilantro leaves and tender
    stems

In a large saucepan, heat the oil over medium-high heat. Add the onion and cook until soft and beginning to brown, about 8 minutes. Add the garlic, celery, and green pepper, and cook for another 5 minutes or so, until the vegetables are soft. Add the carrot and cook for another couple of minutes. Stir in the chili powder, cumin, oregano, chipotle, and cayenne and cook for a minute or two, until the spices begin to toast. Add the tomato juice and tomatoes. Rinse the can or measuring cup with 1 cup water and add that, too, along with about 1 teaspoon salt and a generous amount of pepper. Bring to a boil, add the kidney beans, bring back to a boil, reduce the heat, cover, and simmer for about 15 minutes. Stir in the bulgur and simmer for another 10 minutes. If the chili becomes too thick, add some reserved bean cooking liquid or water to thin it. Stir in the cashews, bring back to a simmer, stir in the cilantro, and serve.

TOTAL TIME: 50 minutes

ADVANCE PREP *The chili is good when it is just made but even better after it has sat for a day or two in the refrigerator. Reheat on top of the stove before serving.*

LEFTOVERS *The chili will keep for about a week in the refrigerator. It can also be frozen for up to a month. Use leftovers as a filling for tacos or a mix-in for scrambled eggs.*

VARIATION

Baked Vegetarian Chili with Cheese

Transfer the chili to a baking dish and top with 1½ cups shredded Manchego, Monterey Jack, or Cheddar cheese. Bake in a preheated 400°F oven for 25 to 30 minutes, or until the chili is bubbling and the cheese has melted and browned.

"Refried" Beans

My sister's friend Patti taught us this recipe for traditional Mexican refried beans with a deep, rich flavor. The beans are not actually fried—hence, the quotation marks—which makes them lighter than most refried beans you've had before. To make the beans in a hurry, substitute 2 large cans of black beans for the dried beans and skip the soaking and cooking steps—simply purée the beans with the fried scallions and spices.

Makes about 6 cups, enough for 6 servings

2 cups dried pinto or black (turtle) beans, picked over

2 medium white onions, peeled

3 or 4 large garlic cloves, peeled

2 to 3 jalapeño chiles, stems removed

$1/4$ cup lard, bacon fat, extra-virgin olive, or corn oil

4 scallions, white and green parts, chopped

1 teaspoon ground cumin (optional)

$1/2$ cup tomato juice

Small handful of fresh cilantro, roughly chopped

Kosher salt

Soak the beans in cold water for 8 hours or overnight.

Drain and rinse the beans. Place the beans in a large saucepan and add enough water to cover the beans by about 3 inches. Add the onions, garlic, and jalapeños. Bring to a boil, turn down the heat, set a cover loosely over the pot, and simmer until the beans and vegetables are very tender, $1^{1}/2$ to 2 hours, depending on the freshness of the beans. If necessary, add more water while the beans are cooking to be sure they are completely submerged. Drain, reserving about 1 cup of the cooking liquid, and return the beans, onions, garlic, and jalapeños to the pot.

While the beans are cooking, heat the lard in a medium skillet over medium-high heat. Add the scallions and cook until soft, about 3 minutes. Add the cumin, if using, and cook to toast the spice, a minute or two more. Pour in the tomato juice, and when it begins to simmer, stir in the cilantro.

Add the tomato juice mixture to the beans along with about $1/4$ cup of the cooking liquid and $1^{1}/2$ teaspoons salt. Using an immersion blender, purée the beans so they are as lumpy or as smooth as you like them. (Alternatively, you can use a blender or food processor fitted with a metal chopping blade to purée the beans.) If necessary, adjust the consistency with more cooking liquid, and adjust the seasoning with more salt.

PREP TIME: 10 minutes
COOKING TIME: $1^{1}/2$ to 2 hours
TOTAL TIME: 10 hours (includes soaking time)

ADVANCE PREP The beans are delicious when first made, and even better after they have sat for a day or two in the refrigerator. Reheat the beans in a nonstick frying pan until warm.
LEFTOVERS The beans will keep for about a week in the refrigerator. They can also be frozen for up to two months. Use them to make burritos or tacos, or as a side dish for meat.

VARIATION
Refried Beans with Cheese
Cut about 6 ounces queso fresco, Monterey Jack, Manchego, or Cheddar into $1/2$-inch cubes. In a nonstick frying pan, mix 3 cups refried beans with the cheese. Heat over medium heat until the beans have heated through, the cheese has melted, and the whole thing has begun to brown around the edges of the pan, 8 to 10 minutes.

Peas and Rice

Here's a dish I remember from my childhood, when a Jamaican family friend used to make it occasionally. I remember wondering why she called it "peas" and rice because all I could see were red kidney beans. She said that's just what it was called. I have since learned that pigeon peas are traditional, but since I remember it with kidney beans and they are easier to find, that's how I make it today. This recipe is enriched with coconut milk, which gives it a delicate, sweet flavor.

Makes 4 to 6 servings

1 tablespoon butter or vegetable oil

$\frac{1}{2}$ small white or yellow onion, finely chopped

1 small garlic clove, minced

1 cup long-grain white or converted rice

2 cups drained cooked red kidney beans (see page 201) or 1 (20-ounce) can, drained

$\frac{3}{4}$ cup canned unsweetened coconut milk

Kosher salt

1 teaspoon fresh thyme or $\frac{1}{4}$ teaspoon dried thyme

1 Scotch bonnet, habanero, or other very hot fresh or dried chile

In a medium pot, heat the butter over medium-high heat. Add the onion and garlic and sauté until soft, about 5 minutes. Add the rice, beans, coconut milk, and $1\frac{1}{4}$ cups water. Stir in 1 teaspoon salt and the thyme and place the chile in the pot. Bring to a boil, reduce the heat so that the liquid simmers gently, cover tightly, and cook for about 25 minutes, or until all of the liquid has been absorbed and the rice is tender. Turn off the heat and let sit, covered, for about 5 minutes. Discard the chile, adjust the seasoning, and serve.

TOTAL TIME: 30 minutes

ADVANCE PREP *The rice can be made up to 45 minutes before serving and kept covered in a warm place. If made longer in advance, the rice can be reheated in a microwave for a minute or two on high.*

LEFTOVERS *The peas and rice will keep for about two weeks in the fridge and actually freezes pretty well for up to two months. Peas and rice make a good base for a stuffing for vegetables, fish, or chicken. Simply add sautéed mushrooms, herbs, and an egg.*

Baked Tofu

I find the chewy texture and delicate flavor of baked tofu a nice accompaniment to salad, a good filling for a sandwich, or a great snack. The secrets are to let the tofu marinate long enough to pick up some flavor, and to bake it long enough so that it is crunchy on the outside and soft on the inside.

Makes 4 to 6 servings

6 tablespoons soy sauce

1 tablespoon honey or sugar

1 tablespoon balsamic vinegar

1 small garlic clove, minced

2 tablespoons minced fresh ginger

1 to 2 teaspoons Asian garlic chili sauce or other hot sauce

About 1 pound firm or extra-firm tofu, drained and cut into $\frac{1}{2}$-inch-thick slices

Vegetable oil

In a small bowl, blend the soy sauce, honey, vinegar, garlic, ginger, and chili sauce. Arrange the tofu slices in a shallow dish and pour the marinade over the top. Let the tofu marinate for at least 2 hours at room temperature or up to two days in the refrigerator, turning it once or twice.

Preheat the oven to 400°F.

Lightly grease a baking sheet with vegetable oil. Brush off any garlic or ginger from the tofu slices and arrange the slices in a single layer on the sheet without touching. Bake for 25 to 35 minutes, until the tofu has browned on the edges and crisped. The time will depend on the moisture content of your tofu. I prefer not to turn the tofu over, so one side becomes well done and crispy, but feel free to flip it if you prefer a more even texture.

PREP TIME: 5 minutes

COOKING TIME: 30 to 40 minutes

TOTAL TIME: 2 hours 45 minutes (includes marinating time)

LEFTOVERS Baked tofu will keep for about ten days in the fridge. Cut leftovers into cubes and use them in stir-fries, scrambled eggs, fried rice, or other dishes.

Fresh Corn and Tomato Relish

This is a light summer relish that's good with just about anything—hamburgers, crab cakes, grilled pork chops, you name it.

Makes 3 cups

2 tablespoons extra-virgin olive oil or vegetable oil
1 small white, yellow, or red onion, finely chopped
1 garlic clove, minced
½ red, yellow, or green bell pepper, cored, seeded, and chopped
1 jalapeño chile, seeded and finely chopped
1 cup fresh or frozen corn kernels
¼ cup sherry vinegar, red wine vinegar, or cider vinegar
2 tablespoons sugar
½ teaspoon salt
Freshly ground black pepper to taste
1 large ripe tomato, chopped
2 scallions, white and green parts, chopped
1 tablespoon finely chopped fresh cilantro

Heat the oil in a medium saucepan set over medium-high heat. Add the onion and sauté for 3 or 4 minutes, until soft. Add the garlic and cook for another minute or so. Add the bell pepper and jalapeño and continue sautéing for a minute or two until soft. Add the corn and cook for another minute. Mix in the vinegar, sugar, salt, and black pepper. Cook for another minute, then remove from the heat and cool to room temperature. Stir in the tomato, scallions, and cilantro. Adjust the seasoning and let cool for 15 minutes.

TOTAL TIME: 20 minutes

ADVANCE PREP You can prepare everything up to the point that you stir in the tomato, scallion, and cilantro up to two days in advance. Keep chilled. Finish just before serving.

LEFTOVERS The relish will keep in good shape for four days in the fridge. Stir leftovers into a chicken, tuna, or potato salad.

Marinated Eggplant Relish

I worked for a time in a restaurant in Turin, Italy, for Luigi Caputo, a chef from Puglia. In the kitchen, on the windowsill, Luigi always had a jar of the spicy eggplant relish that I loved. It took me years to come up with a recipe that approximated my memory of that eggplant dish. This is it.

Makes 3½ pints

> 4 pounds firm eggplant
> ½ cup kosher salt
> 3 cups distilled white vinegar
> 5 small garlic cloves, thinly sliced
> 1 or 2 small hot red chiles, seeded and minced,
>   or 1 teaspoon crushed red pepper flakes,
>   or to taste
> 2 tablespoons chopped flat-leaf parsley, basil,
>   or mint, or a combination
> ½ teaspoon freshly ground black pepper
> 1½ cups extra-virgin olive oil

Peel and thinly slice the eggplant lengthwise. Cut the slices into ribbons about ½ inch wide, put them in a large bowl, and toss with the salt. Transfer the salted eggplant to a colander and set it in the sink. Invert a plate just smaller than the colander on top of the eggplant and place a heavy weight (such as a can or two of tomatoes or a brick) on the plate. Allow the eggplant to drain for twenty-four hours.

When the eggplant has finished draining, place the vinegar in a large nonreactive pot. Add 6 cups of water and bring to a boil. Remove the weight and the plate from the eggplant, and add the eggplant to the pot, breaking it up with your hands into ribbons again. Turn off the heat and let the eggplant sit for 3 minutes. Drain in the colander, pressing the eggplant with the back of a large spoon or your hand to remove any excess moisture. Transfer to a large bowl. Add the garlic, chiles, herbs, black pepper, and half of the oil, and mix well. Transfer the relish to clean jars, topping off with more oil to be sure the eggplant is submerged. Insert a clean chopstick or the handle of a spoon down to the bottom to be sure the oil has penetrated. Refrigerate for at least 1 week before eating.

PREP TIME: 20 minutes
COOKING TIME: 5 minutes
TOTAL TIME: 1 day, 25 minutes (includes draining time)

LEFTOVERS Covered in oil, the eggplant relish will keep for at least one month in the refrigerator. Bring to room temperature before serving. The relish is delicious on sandwiches, as part of an antipasto, as a condiment for roasted lamb.

Bread and Butter Pickles

Here's a recipe for delicious pickles—the kind you pile on hamburgers and other sandwiches or chop up and mix into potato salad. Although bread and butter pickles are traditionally made with Kirby cucumbers, they are also excellent made with small zucchini and yellow squash (see Variation, below). Using maple syrup makes the pickles less sweet than they are when made with sugar.

Makes 2 pints

> 6 Kirby cucumbers (about 2 pounds), sliced about
>   ¼ inch thick
> 1 large white or yellow onion, thinly sliced
> Kosher salt
> 1¾ cups cider vinegar
> 1¾ cups granulated sugar or pure maple syrup

IN A PICKLE

Like jam making (see page 135), pickling is a sat- isfying and delicious culinary endeavor. A little work today pays off months from now. There are two basic types of pickles, short- or quick-brine and long-brine. Short-brine pickles, like Bread and Butter Pickles (page 208) and Pickled Onions (page 211), require vinegar to contribute acidity. Long-brine pickles, such as kosher dills, ferment naturally with the aid of salt to produce their own tartness.

I think the most important and most difficult challenge in pickling is maintaining crispness. Starting with fresh, firm produce is key. If the produce is cut up, the thickness of the pieces will have an effect on the finished texture, too. Using the proper amount of salt in the brine and mini- mizing any time the pickles are heated or processed will also help maintain crispness. Over my years of pickling I've developed recipes for pickles that maximize flavor and crispness with- out sacrificing safety. I recommend you make the following recipes once, and then experiment on your own.

PRESERVING PICKLES

Although long-brine pickles will keep for a rela- tively long period of time at room temperature because the salt in the brine acts as a preserva- tive, short-brine pickles need to be refrigerated or processed in a water bath. Read Canning Jams, page 138, before you begin.

• To pack the jars, begin as for processing jams (page 138), by bringing a large canning kettle to a boil and sterilizing pint jars. I prefer narrow-mouth pint jars for cold-pack pickles (see below) because the pronounced shoulders of the jars help hold the produce down in the brine. Hot-pack pickles, which are less likely to float, can be processed in narrow- or wide-mouth pint jars. Larger jars re- quire relatively longer processing, which I find di- minishes the crunch of the finished pickles.

• Cold pack: Recipes that require you to pack the vegetables or fruits for pickling in the jar raw and then pour over a hot vinegar solution (e.g., Pickled Okra, page 211) are using what is called the cold-pack technique. Be sure to pack the jars very tightly; the more tightly they are packed, the less likely the vegetables are to float above the brine. Be careful not to bruise the produce. Leave 1 inch of headspace. Pour over the hot vinegar solution, leaving ¾ inch of headspace. Wipe the rims, seal, tighten the bands all the way, loosen them one-quarter turn, and process for the amount of time specified in the recipe.

• Hot pack: Recipes that require you to heat the produce briefly in the vinegar solution (e.g., Bread and Butter Pickles, page 208) are using what is called the hot-pack technique. Using a wide-mouth funnel, transfer the pickles into the jars, leaving about 1 inch of headspace. Top off the jars with another ¼ inch of the brine to be sure the pickles are submerged, leaving ¾ inch of headspace. Wipe the rims, watch out for seeds and spices, seal, tighten the bands all the way, then loosen them one-quarter turn, and process for the amount of time specified in the recipe.

• Allow processed pickles to cool to room tem- perature. If the seals have popped and the center of the lids has sunk, wipe off the jars, label them, and store them in a cool dry place for up to one year. Do not tighten the bands. The pickles are best after about 1 month to give the flavors time to come together and mellow. Store unsealed jars in the refrigerator and use them within 1 month.

1 teaspoon celery seeds

1 teaspoon yellow mustard seeds

1 teaspoon turmeric

In a large bowl, layer the cucumber slices and onion with about $\frac{1}{4}$ cup of kosher salt. Cover with cold water and refrigerate for 4 to 6 hours. Drain and rinse with cold water.

In a large nonreactive saucepan, combine the vinegar, sugar, celery seeds, mustard seeds, and turmeric. Set over medium-high heat and bring to a boil. Reduce the heat and simmer the mixture for 5 minutes. Turn up the heat, add the cucumbers and onion, and let come back to just below the boiling point. Using a slotted spoon, pack the pickles into two sterilized pint jars. Pour the hot liquid over the cucumbers, leaving a $\frac{1}{2}$-inch headspace. Wipe the rims, seal, and refrigerate for up to one month. (For long-term storage, process the jars for 7 minutes in a boiling water bath; see Canning Jams, page 138.) Refrigerate after opening.

PREP TIME: 10 minutes

COOKING TIME: 7 minutes

TOTAL TIME: 4 hours 20 minutes (includes soaking time; plus processing time)

ADVANCE PREP *The pickles can be eaten right away, but they are best after sitting for at least one week.*

VARIATION

Summer Squash Bread and Butter Pickles

Substitute 2 pounds assorted small zucchini and yellow squash for the cucumbers. Proceed with the recipe as directed, omitting the step of adding the zucchini to the boiling vinegar so-lution. Instead, pack the zucchini and onion raw into jars and pour the boiling solution over the top.

Pickled Beets with Caraway

I prefer pickled beets, which have a delicious sweet-and-sour taste, flavored with caraway, but if you prefer beets spiced with more traditional spices (clove, cinnamon, and allspice), see the Variation below. To cook the beets, I like to steam them in the oven rather than boil them because I think steaming concentrates the beet flavor.

Makes 5 pints

3 bunches beets, trimmed (about 4 pounds), leaving 1 inch of the stem and root attached

4 cups cider or white vinegar

1 cup granulated sugar or $1\frac{1}{2}$ cups pure maple syrup

1 tablespoon caraway seeds

5 juniper berries

1 bay leaf

1 teaspoon kosher salt

1 medium white or red onion, thinly sliced

Preheat the oven to 400°F.

Wrap the beets in aluminum foil and set in the oven to roast for 1 hour. Remove from the oven, and set aside to cool. Peel the beets; they will not be totally soft, but that's okay. Slice the beets about $\frac{1}{4}$ inch thick.

In a large saucepan, combine the vinegar, sugar, caraway, juniper, bay leaf, and salt with 1 cup water. Bring to a boil, turn down the heat, and simmer for 5 minutes. Remove the bay leaf and juniper berries and add the beets. Bring back up to a boil and remove from the heat. Using a slotted spoon, layer the beets in sterilized pint jars, alternating with the onion. Strain the hot liquid over the beets, leaving a 1/2-inch headspace in each jar. Wipe the rims and seal the jars. You can keep the beets as is in the refrigerator for up to 1 month or process them for 20 minutes in a water bath (see Canning Jams, page 138) for long-term storage. Refrigerate once opened.

PREP TIME: 30 minutes

COOKING TIME: 1 hour 15 minutes

TOTAL TIME: 1 hour 45 minutes (plus processing time)

ADVANCE PREP *The beets are best eaten after they have sat for about one week.*

VARIATION
Spiced Pickled Beets
For a more traditional flavor, omit the caraway and use instead 1/4 teaspoon allspice berries, 1 (2-inch) cinnamon stick, 1 star anise, and 1/2 teaspoon whole cloves. Proceed with the recipe as directed, straining the liquid into the jars to remove the spices.

Pickled Okra
These pickled okra are very tart, with an intense flavor, crisp texture, and none of the sliminess associated with cooked okra. I like to serve them as part of an hors d'oeuvre spread or condiment tray.
Makes 6 pints

 6 small dried hot red chiles
 1 tablespoon mustard seeds
 1 1/2 teaspoons dill seeds

 1 1/2 teaspoons coriander seeds
 1 small red onion, thinly sliced
 2 1/2 to 3 pounds small, firm okra pods
 2 cups cider vinegar
 2 cups white vinegar
 1/4 cup kosher salt

Into each sterilized canning jar, place 1 chile, 1/2 teaspoon mustard seeds, 1/4 teaspoon dill seeds, and 1/4 teaspoon coriander seeds. Alternating with the sliced onion, pack the okra into the jars, up to 3/4 inch from the top. In a large nonreactive saucepan, combine the vinegars with 2 cups water and the salt. Bring to a boil and pour the hot vinegar solution into the jars to cover the okra, leaving a 1/2-inch headspace. Wipe the rims and seal the jars. Refrigerate for up to 1 month. For long-term storage, process the jars in a boiling water bath for 5 minutes (see Canning Jams, page 138). Refrigerate once opened.

PREP TIME: 20 minutes

COOKING TIME: 3 minutes

TOTAL TIME: 30 minutes (plus processing time)

ADVANCE PREP *For the best flavor, the pickles should be made at least one month before being eaten.*

Pickled Onions with Fresh Horseradish
This is a delicious recipe for tart, crisp pickled pearl or cocktail onions, spiked with fresh horseradish to give them a little kick. These onions are equally delicious used in cocktails or cut up for salads and sandwiches.
Makes 4 pints

2 quarts white pearl onions, peeled

Kosher salt

1 teaspoon white peppercorns

1 teaspoon black peppercorns

4 bay leaves

4 whole cloves

4 cups white vinegar

$^1/_2$ cup sugar

2 tablespoons yellow mustard seeds

2 tablespoons freshly grated horseradish
or 1 tablespoon prepared white
horseradish

Place the onions in a large bowl and sprinkle them with about $^1/_2$ cup kosher salt. Cover with cold water and let sit for at least 12 hours or overnight. Drain and rinse.

Pack the onions into sterilized pint jars. Into each jar, place $^1/_4$ teaspoon of the white and black peppercorns, a bay leaf, and a clove. In a large, nonreactive saucepan, combine the vinegar, sugar, mustard seeds, and horseradish. Bring to a boil, turn down the heat, and simmer for 5 minutes. Pour the hot mixture over the onions, leaving at least a $^1/_2$-inch headspace in the jars. Wipe the rims and seal the jars. Refrigerate for up to 1 month. (For long-term storage, process in a water bath for 7 minutes; see Canning Jams, page 138). Refrigerate once opened.

PREP TIME: 10 minutes

COOKING TIME: 5 minutes

TOTAL TIME: 12 hours, 15 minutes (includes brining time; plus processing time)

ADVANCE PREP *The pickled onions can be eaten right away, but they are best after they have sat for a least a month, which allows the flavors to come together.*

KITCHEN SENSE

QUICK PICKLING

When I want to perk up a dish or a sandwich with a little spicy, crunchy tang, I often make a quick pickle. The process for making quick pickles is the same as for making pickles that sit for a longer time. Basically, you boil vinegar with some aromatic seasonings and a little sugar and salt. You pour the hot vinegar solution over whatever it is that you want to pickle. Let it sit for 30 minutes or so, and you have a quick, delicious condiment. I pickle shredded carrots, shaved fennel, sliced onions, green beans, mushrooms, and other vegetables.

LEFTOVERS *I like to use pickled onions in chicken and tuna salad and as a garnish for sandwiches. They are of course essential in a classic Gibson cocktail—a dry gin martini made with cocktail onions instead of olives.*

Kimchee

For some reason, where I live they seem to sell napa cabbage only in giant heads of 2 or 3 pounds. This is more than I usually want for any given recipe. With the leftovers, I make kimchee, the spicy Korean pickled cabbage condiment. It takes only a few days of curing. I love kimchee on sandwiches, served with a bowl of rice, cut up and stir-fried with pork, and in soup. There's a guy with a hot dog cart on Manhattan's Lower East Side who sells delicious kimchee hot dogs into the wee hours of the night. Don't be afraid to experiment.

Makes 1 quart

$^1/_2$ cup kosher salt

$1^1/_2$ pounds napa cabbage (Chinese cabbage)

1 bunch scallions, white and green parts, chopped

1 tablespoon minced fresh ginger

1 large garlic clove, minced

1 1/2 teaspoons crushed red pepper flakes, or to
   taste

1/4 cup sugar

In a large bowl, dissolve the salt in about 6 cups of warm water and let cool to room temperature. Meanwhile, cut the cabbage leaves into 2-inch pieces. Place the cabbage in the salt solution, cover with an inverted plate to weight it down, and let sit for about 3 hours at room temperature, being sure the cabbage stays submerged.

Drain the cabbage, rinse, and drain again. Return to the bowl. Add the scallions, ginger, garlic, red pepper, and sugar, and toss to distribute the seasonings. Pack the leaves neatly into a sterilized glass quart jar, and top with any seasoning left in the bowl. Cover and refrigerate for three or four days to ferment the kimchee before serving.

PREP TIME: 15 minutes

TOTAL TIME: 3 hours (includes brining time)

ADVANCE PREP The kimchee needs to be made three or four days in advance to ferment.

LEFTOVERS Kimchee will keep in the fridge for up to two months. Chop the kimchee and experiment with it in soups, omelets, stir-fries, and other dishes.

■ ■ ■

Grains

AMERICA MAY BE BEAUTIFUL for its amber waves of grain, but when it comes to American home cooking, people shy away from all but a few of the myriad cereals and grasses on the market. In addition to there being a wide variety of grains available, most of them come in a number of forms, each with its distinct taste and texture. As a country, wheat is our most important grain, but the majority of it is consumed as refined white flour. Meanwhile, bulgur, couscous, semolina, farina, wheat berries, whole-wheat flour, and other delicious (and nutritious) forms of wheat are relegated to the shelves of health food stores. Any good cook's repertoire should include a range of grain dishes.

The phrase "whole grain" means that the kernels of the grain have the bran and the germ intact. Whole-grain products are higher in nutrients and fiber than refined grain products, for which the bran and germ have been removed from the kernels before processing. Because whole-grain products contain essential oils, they turn rancid rather quickly. Once opened, whole-grain products—everything from whole-wheat flour to brown rice to stone-ground cornmeal—should be stored in the refrigerator or freezer. Refined grain products are also sometimes bleached to make them whiter, softer, and more shelf stable. Bleached products are even more devoid of nutrients, which is why most of them are enriched, and I try to use them for only the most delicate baked goods, such as biscuits or pie crust. Whole-grain and refined-grain products are not interchangeable. I prefer to think of them as separate things, and I use both in my kitchen depending on what I'm making.

Cooking grains is easy to master because there really are only three basic techniques. The simplest is what I call the "pasta" technique—that is, you cook the grains as you would cook pasta, in a generous amount of rapidly boiling water. This is the easiest technique because you don't have to measure the water or the grain. The pasta technique works well for whole grains such as wheat berries (soaked overnight first), pearl barley, wild rice, and even white rice. Whether or not to salt the water depends on the grain. Those with outer husks, such as wheat berries, tend to harden when cooked with salt, but those that have been polished to remove the husks, such as pearl barley and rice, can and should be cooked with salt in the water.

The second technique for cooking grains is sometimes called the "pilaf" method. This technique involves sautéing some aromatic vegetables in fat, adding the grain, and stirring to coat it with the fat. A measured amount of hot liquid is added to the pot and the pot is covered while the grain simmers. When the grain is done, that is to say tender, all of the liquid should have been absorbed. It is customary to remove the pan from the heat, keep it covered, and let the grain sit for 5 to 15 minutes more to steam. Then you fluff it with a fork. (This last stage of resting and fluffing is very important for the texture of the finished dish.) The pilaf method is one of my favorite ways to cook grains because it allows you to add all sorts of ingredients to the grain while it cooks, thereby infusing the grain with deep, complex flavors. You can sauté different vegetables before you add the grain—onion, carrots, leeks, beets, fennel, or spinach, for example. Then you can use different liquids for the broth—stock, milk, vegetable juice, wine, or a combination. You can also add a variety of spices—saffron, cinnamon, bay, cardamom, or cumin, to name just a few.

The third general method for cooking grains is sometimes referred to as the "porridge" technique. This is used primarily for cooking meals, such as cornmeal (polenta), semolina, and cream of wheat (farina). For this technique, a measured amount of salted water or other liquid is brought to the boil. The grain is slowly whisked into the simmering liquid. Then the porridge is allowed to simmer very slowly, stirred occasionally, until it is done. In my experience, people tend to undercook porridges. As soon as the porridge thickens, they think it is done. But long, slow cooking brings out the flavor and texture of most meals, especially cornmeal. For example, coarse stone-ground cornmeal, which makes the best polenta, should cook for 45 minutes to an hour, even though it becomes a porridge about 10 minutes after you whisk the meal into the hot liquid.

There are, of course, variations to these techniques. Risotto is actually a combination of two techniques, pilaf and porridge. The procedure for cooking basic rice is like a pilaf method without using fat or aromatics. Couscous, which is precooked and dried so that reconstituting it makes it palatable, is simply steeped, though purists will tell you that once it is steeped it should be steamed for about an hour or so to fully cook it. The permutations are endless.

Grain cookery is not an exact science. But if you buy good-quality grains and familiarize yourself with the basic cooking techniques, you will be able to make a variety of delicious grain dishes. See the Soups and Salads chapters for additional recipes.

■ ■ ■

Basic White Rice

The idea that there is a "basic rice" is kind of funny, since every culture seems to have a type of rice that is considered basic, and they are all quite different and prepared differently. But because we are here in America, long-grain Carolina rice is what I mean when I say basic rice. (The name "Carolina" is both a brand and a type of rice.) Here's a recipe (it's more of a technique, really) for white rice the way my mother always made it. On subsequent pages I have included directions on how to make other rices that are generally easy to find—such as basmati or jasmine—to expand your "basic" rice repertoire.

Makes 3½ cups, enough for 4 to 6 servings

> 1 cup long-grain white Carolina rice
> 1 teaspoon kosher salt
> 1 tablespoon unsalted butter or extra-virgin
>   olive oil

Place the rice in a small saucepan with a tight-fitting lid. Add 2 cups cold water, the salt, and butter. Bring the water to a boil, then lower the heat as low as the burner will go so that the water simmers very gently, tightly cover the pot, and cook the rice for 15 minutes. Turn off the heat (do not remove the cover) and let the rice sit for an additional 15 minutes before fluffing with a fork.

COOKING TIME: 15 minutes
TOTAL TIME: 30 minutes (includes resting time)

ADVANCE PREP *If you keep the rice covered once it is cooked, it will keep hot enough to serve for about 1 hour.*
LEFTOVERS *Cooked rice will keep in the fridge for about a week. Reheat according to the directions on page 219. Make fried rice with leftover rice, or use as a garnish in brothy soups.*

VARIATIONS
Converted White Rice

Converted rice has been processed with steam and enriched with nutrients. Uncle Ben's is the most popular brand of converted white rice. The technique for cooking it is the same as for long-grain white rice, the only difference being the amount of water and cooking time needed (the converted rice needs more water and more cooking time). Increase the amount of water to 2¼ cups and the simmering time to 20 minutes.

Yellow Rice

There are three spices you can use to make rice yellow, each with it's own distinct flavor: turmeric, saffron, and annatto (aka achiote). To use turmeric, simply add ¼ teaspoon turmeric to the saucepan and proceed with the recipe above as directed. To use saffron, soak a pinch of saffron threads in 2 cups warm water for about 15 minutes before making the rice. Proceed with the recipe above as directed, substituting the saffron and its soaking water for the water. To use annatto, see Cuban-Style Yellow Rice (page 221).

Basmati Rice

Basmati rice has a distinct flavor, the result of about a year's worth of aging, and long, fluffy grains. Because of its unique character and texture, basmati requires a unique cooking method. The following procedure is pretty much foolproof. Basmati comes in a variety of grades based on its age, flavor, and quality. The older the rice and longer, more uniform its grains, the better the quality, and the higher the price. I prefer basmati that's imported from India or Pakistan.

Makes about 3 cups, enough for 4 to 5 servings

1 cup basmati rice

½ teaspoon kosher salt (optional)

Place the rice in a medium saucepan with a tight-fitting cover. Fill the pan with water about 1 inch over the top of the rice. Swish the rice around with your fingertips until the water turns milky white. Dump the rice out into a sieve to drain. Put the rice back in the saucepan and repeat, rinsing two or three times more until the water running off is clear. Drain and return the rice to the pot.

Once again, add enough water to cover the rice by an inch or two. Let stand for 30 to 45 minutes, until the rice has swollen.

Add the salt, if using, and put the pot over high heat. As soon as it comes to a boil, set a timer for 3 minutes. When the timer goes off, taste the rice. It should be cooked, but with a slight al dente center. It may need another minute, but don't overcook it now because it isn't done yet. Drain the rice well. Put it back in the pot, cover it, and set it back over very low heat for about 4 minutes to dry. Turn off the heat, and let the rice sit for another few minutes before fluffing with a fork and serving.

PREP TIME: 10 minutes

COOKING TIME: 7 minutes

TOTAL TIME: 50 minutes (includes soaking time)

LEFTOVERS *Rice will keep for about one week in the refrigerator. Reheat it according to the directions in the box at right. You can also rejuvenate basmati rice by stirring the leftover rice into a mixture of onions sautéed in plenty of butter, along with currants or raisins, pine nuts, and/or a spoonful of brown mustard seeds for a sort of makeshift pilaf or biryani.*

KITCHEN SENSE

REHEATING RICE

As long as I'm making rice, I usually make enough to have leftovers. To reheat rice, I find the easiest and most effective technique is to use the microwave. A small bowl of rice will return to its steaming, fluffy glory in 45 seconds to 1 minute on high. (Brown rice will take a little longer.) Set it in the microwave for 30 seconds, stir it around with a fork, and then heat it in 15-second increments to be sure you don't overcook it. (Overnuked, the grains of rice turn into little inedible pellets.)

If you don't have a microwave, don't despair. You can reheat rice perfectly well on top of the stove. Place the rice in a saucepan over medium-low heat. When the pan begins to get hot, add a couple of tablespoons of water, cover the pan, and lower the heat so the rice steams, 3 to 6 minutes, depending on how much rice you are reheating. (You may also need to add a little more water if the steam dies out.) Remove from the heat and let sit for a few minutes before serving.

Jasmine Rice

Usually imported from Thailand, jasmine rice has a fragrant aroma and a light, delicate texture. The smell when you lift off the lid of the cooked rice is enchanting. A domestically produced variety, Jasmati, isn't nearly as flavorful, but it will work in a pinch.

Makes about 3 cups, enough for 4 to 5 servings

1 cup jasmine rice

½ teaspoon kosher salt (optional)

Place the rice in a small saucepan with a tight-fitting cover. Add 1¼ cups cold water and salt, if using. Set over medium-high heat. When the rice comes to a boil, lower the heat as low as it will go and cover the pot. Allow the rice to simmer, covered, for 10 minutes. Do not remove the cover and do not stir the rice. Turn off the heat and let the pot sit covered for about 15 minutes. Remove the cover and fluff the rice with a fork.

COOKING TIME: 15 minutes
TOTAL TIME: 30 minutes (includes resting time)

LEFTOVERS *The rice will keep about a week in the fridge. Reheat rice according to the directions on page 219. Leftover jasmine rice is perfect to use for Fried Rice (page 222).*

Brown Rice

Brown rice takes more water and more time to cook than regular rice. It has a distinct nutty flavor and chewiness that is a nice change from white rice, but I don't view the two as interchangeable at all. In my opinion, brown rice just doesn't work when eaten alongside Asian food, though, interestingly, it fares pretty well in fried rice. Use brown rice instead as a side to heartier dishes, such as stews and other braised meat dishes. Because brown rice doesn't become mushy, I also like to use it in rice salads. A word of caution: brown rice tends to turn rancid quickly, which gives it an off flavor. Store it in the refrigerator.

Makes 3¼ cups, enough for about 4 servings

  1 cup long-grain brown rice
  1 teaspoon kosher salt

Place the rice in a small saucepan and cover with 2½ cups water. (Don't add the salt at the beginning or it will make the rice even chewier.)

Set over high heat and bring to a boil. Cover, turn down the heat as low as the burner will go, and let simmer, undisturbed, for about 40 minutes, until the water is absorbed and the rice is cooked. Turn off the heat, and let the pot sit covered for 15 minutes. Add the salt and stir the rice with a fork to fluff.

COOKING TIME: 40 minutes
TOTAL TIME: 55 minutes (includes resting time)

LEFTOVERS *Cooked brown rice will keep in the fridge for about a week. Reheat as described on page 219. Use leftovers in fried rice or rice salads.*

Rice Pilaf

Just one step up in complexity from making basic rice, rice pilaf has a little more pizzazz. Use long-grain white rice, such as Carolina. Several of the recipes that follow in this chapter are simply variations on this basic technique. Experiment for yourself, adding vegetables, toasted nuts, spices, and other flavorings as you wish. Don't worry if a crust of rice forms on the bottom of the pot; in many cultures this crust is a delicacy and its formation is considered good luck.

Makes 5 cups, enough for 4 to 6 servings

  2¼ cups chicken or vegetable stock or water
  ½ bay leaf
  1 teaspoon kosher salt
  3 tablespoons unsalted butter or extra-virgin olive oil
  ½ medium white or yellow onion, finely chopped
  1 small garlic clove, finely minced
  1 cup long-grain white rice, such as Carolina
  Freshly ground white or black pepper

Place the stock, bay leaf, and salt in a small saucepan and bring to a boil. Reduce the heat so that the liquid simmers. In a medium, heavy saucepan, heat the butter over medium-high heat. When it sizzles, add the onion and cook until translucent, about 5 minutes. Add the garlic and cook for another 2 minutes. Add the rice and cook for 3 or 4 minutes, until the grains of rice are coated with the butter and they begin to toast very lightly. Pour in the hot stock, add a pinch of pepper, raise the heat, and bring the liquid back to a boil. Reduce the heat as low as it will go, cover the pan tightly, and cook very slowly for about 20 minutes, or until the liquid has evaporated and the rice is fully cooked. (If all of the liquid has not been absorbed or evaporated, let the rice cook uncovered for a few minutes to dry out.) Remove from the heat, keep covered, and let sit for 10 minutes. Uncover, remove the bay leaf, and fluff with a fork before serving.

COOKING TIME: 30 minutes
TOTAL TIME: 40 minutes (includes resting time)

ADVANCE PREP The pilaf is best made just before serving.
LEFTOVERS The pilaf will keep for about a week in the fridge. Reheat leftovers as you would for plain rice (page 219).

VARIATIONS
Pilaf in the Oven
Preheat the oven to 375°F. Proceed with the recipe as directed, using an ovenproof saucepan or Dutch oven. Once you have added the stock and it has come back to a boil, cover the pan tightly and set in the oven. Bake for about 45 minutes, until the liquid has been absorbed and/or evaporated and the rice is cooked. Remove from the oven, remove the cover, and fluff with a fork.

Cuban-Style Yellow Rice
Follow the recipe for Rice Pilaf using olive oil and increasing the amount to ¼ cup. Before adding the onion to the oil, add 1 tablespoon annatto (achiote) seeds. Let the seeds cook for 2 or 3 minutes, until the oil is very yellow. Remove the seeds (I use a fork with close tines), leaving the colored oil behind in the pan. Add the onion and proceed with the recipe as directed, adding a small red dried chile to the pan, if desired.

Tomato Rice
Rich with butter and sautéed vegetables, this recipe of my sister's makes a delicious side dish and a superb stuffing (see Stuffed Peppers, page 176). It's best made with a starchy, short-grain rice such as Arborio, the texture of which holds up well to the vegetables.
Makes 3½ cups, enough for 4 servings

4 tablespoons (½ stick) unsalted butter
1 large white or yellow onion, chopped
1 large garlic clove, minced
½ red bell pepper, cored, seeded, and chopped
2 celery stalks, chopped
1 medium carrot, shredded
½ pound ripe beefsteak or plum tomatoes, cored and cut into ½-inch dice, or 3 or 4 canned tomatoes, with juice, cut up
2 tablespoons chopped fresh flat-leaf parsley
Kosher salt and freshly ground black pepper
2 cups cooked rice

In a medium sauté pan, melt the butter over medium-high heat. Add the onion and garlic and sauté until soft, about 5 minutes. Add the bell pepper, celery, and carrot, and continue sautéing until the vegetables soften, another 5 minutes or so. Add the tomatoes, parsley, 2 teaspoons salt, and some black pepper, and keep cooking until the tomatoes wilt and give off their juice, another 5 minutes or so. Add the rice, and sauté for a minute or so, just until the rice and the vegetables are well blended. Taste and adjust the seasoning with additional salt and pepper, if necessary.

TOTAL TIME: 20 minutes

ADVANCE PREP *The vegetables can be sautéed and stored in the refrigerator for a day or two before you stir them into the rice.*
LEFTOVERS *The rice will keep for about one week in the refrigerator. Leftovers can be reheated in the microwave (see page 219). They can also be reheated in a frying pan—melt a little butter and add the rice. A little water will help keep the rice from sticking.*

Fried Rice

Fried rice is my favorite use for leftover rice. Just about any cooked rice will work—long-grain, short-grain, even brown. What you put in to garnish your fried rice depends on what you have around. Among my favorite garnishes are Chinese Barbecued Pork (page 380), shrimp, peas, bean sprouts, shredded carrots, celery, scallions, and water chestnuts. I particularly like to chop up and stir leftover Chinese food into my fried rice—broccoli with oyster sauce, soy sauce chicken, or anything made with pork. Though most traditional techniques for making fried rice have you cook the eggs first, shred them, and stir them into the rice at the end,

I prefer to mix my eggs with the rice and fry the rice until the eggs are cooked for a homier fried rice.
Makes 4 to 6 servings

> 3 large eggs
> 1/4 cup Chinese rice wine or dry sherry
> 1 1/2 tablespoons soy sauce
> 1/2 teaspoon toasted Asian sesame oil
> 3 tablespoons peanut or vegetable oil
> 1 medium onion, diced
> 1 large garlic clove, minced
> 2 tablespoons minced fresh ginger
> 1 celery stalk, chopped
> 1/4 cup chopped fresh water chestnuts
> 1/2 cup frozen peas
> 3/4 cup diced cooked or raw meat and/or seafood
> 3 or 4 cups cooked white or brown rice, or a combination, chilled
> 1/2 cup fresh bean sprouts
> 2 scallions, white and green parts, chopped

In a small bowl, beat the eggs with the rice wine, soy sauce, and sesame oil, and set aside. Place a large well-seasoned or nonstick wok or frying pan over high heat. When the pan is hot, add the oil. After 1 minute, add the onion and cook, stirring constantly, until the onion begins to soften, 3 or 4 minutes. Add the garlic and ginger and cook for another minute or so until their aromas are strong. Add the celery and cook for a minute or two. Add the water chestnuts, peas, and meat or seafood. If the meat or seafood is already cooked, just fry it long enough to heat through, about 3 minutes. If it is raw, continue cooking until it is thoroughly cooked, 5 to 7 minutes.

Add the rice and stir, breaking up the chunks of rice, until the rice has separated into grains and the ingredients are well blended, about 5 minutes. Beat the egg mixture again and pour over the rice. Stir quickly to coat the rice with the egg. The rice will clump up at first but then separate back into grains as the egg cooks. When the egg is almost all cooked, about 5 minutes, stir in the bean sprouts and scallions. Cook for 1 minute more, then serve.

PREP TIME: 5 minutes
COOKING TIME: 25 minutes
TOTAL TIME: 30 minutes

ADVANCE PREP *You can prepare the various ingredients in advance, but the rice should be fried just before serving.*
LEFTOVERS *Leftovers can be fried again in a hot pan with some oil or reheated in the microwave on high for a minute or two.*

Risotto

Risotto is made by gradually stirring hot broth into rice as it cooks. (One myth of risotto making is that it has to be stirred constantly. This is simply not the case. It has to be stirred regularly, but letting the rice periodically simmer in the liquid improves the final texture of the dish.) The stirring causes some of the starch to escape from the rice grains and this excess starch produces a rich, creamy dish. Risotto is really the diametric opposite of converted rice, which is characterized by the individuality of each grain. Risotto is a thick, soupy, porridge-like dish. Of course, when you add wine and butter and cheese, as you do with most *risotti* (that's how you make the plural in Italian), the result is even creamier and richer.

One master recipe for risotto is all you need because most variations just add different vegetables and flavorings to the basic recipe (see Variations). Risotto must be prepared just before it is served or it overcooks, thickens, and turns gloppy. Still one of the best things about making risotto is having leftovers, which I like to eat cold from the fridge or turn into rice balls or pancakes (see below).
Makes about 4½ cups, enough for 4 or 5 servings

> 4 cups light chicken or vegetable stock
> Kosher salt
> ¼ cup extra-virgin olive oil
> 1 small white onion or 2 large shallots, finely chopped
> 1 cup short-grain imported Italian rice, such as Arborio, Vialone Nano, or Carnaroli
> ½ cup dry white wine
> 2 tablespoons unsalted butter, at room temperature
> ⅓ cup freshly grated Parmigiano Reggiano cheese
> Freshly ground white or black pepper

Pour the stock or broth into a medium saucepan and set over medium heat to bring it to a simmer. Season it with salt. Lower the heat to keep the stock simmering very gently while you prepare the rice. (It's important to add hot liquid, not cold, to the rice as it cooks.)

In a separate medium, heavy-bottomed saucepan, heat the olive oil over medium-high heat. Add the onion or shallot and sauté until soft, about 5 minutes. Add the rice and cook for 1 or 2 minutes to coat the rice with the oil and heat it up. Do not let the onions or rice brown. Add the wine along with about ½ teaspoon salt.

When the wine is almost all absorbed and/or evaporated, add about 1 cup of the simmering stock to the rice. Stir the rice with a wooden spoon four or five times. When the liquid is thick, bubbling, and almost all absorbed, in 3 or 4 minutes, add another cup of stock. Continue adding stock in this way until the rice is almost cooked. Taste it to check. The texture should not be soft, but al dente, which means that each grain of rice has some bite to it, but it isn't so hard that it sticks in your teeth. The risotto should also be somewhat soupy because it will continue to thicken right up until the time it is eaten. The total cooking time for the rice is about 16 minutes, and you should have no more than $1/3$ cup or so of broth left.

Turn off the heat. Stir in the butter, cheese, and pepper until melted and blended. A properly made risotto should be liquidy enough to spread out in the bowl, but not thick enough to make a mound in the middle. Adjust the consistency with more stock or wine if necessary. Adjust the seasoning with salt and serve immediately in warm bowls.

TOTAL TIME: 25 minutes

LEFTOVERS *Once cooked, risotto will keep for about a week in the fridge. You can reheat leftovers in the microwave for a minute or so on high, but they have a mushy texture—comforting and delicious, but inelegant. To use up leftover risotto, I make either risotto pancakes or risotto balls. Stir 1 large egg into $1^1/2$ cups risotto. Shape into $1^1/2$-inch balls or 3-inch patties. Dredge in flour, dip in egg wash, and roll in bread crumbs (the balls or pancakes can be frozen at this point). Fry in $1/2$ inch of vegetable oil for about 4 minutes per side, or until golden brown.*

VARIATIONS
Saffron Risotto
To make the classic saffron-flavored *risotto milanese*, soak 2 or 3 generous pinches of saffron threads in the wine or a few tablespoons of the hot stock and add it to the risotto with the first addition of stock. Proceed with the recipe as directed.

Porcini Risotto
In a small bowl, soak $1/2$ to 1 ounce of dried porcini in hot water for about 15 minutes, or until soft. Remove the mushrooms and cut into small pieces, reserving the soaking liquid. With a soup spoon, lift the liquid out of the bowl without disturbing any sand on the bottom of the bowl, and transfer to another dish. After you add the first bit of hot stock to the risotto, add the soaked porcini pieces and the soaking liquid. Proceed with the recipe as directed.

Risotto with Radicchio and Barolo
Substitute $1/2$ cup Barolo or other dry red wine for the white wine. After the first addition of stock, add 2 cups (about 2 heads) thinly sliced or shredded radicchio, and proceed with the recipe as directed.

Risotto with Roasted Beets and Gorgonzola
After the first addition of stock, add 1 medium roasted beet (see page 149), finely diced (about $1^1/4$ cups) to the pot and proceed as directed. With the butter and cheese stirred in at the end, add 2 to 3 ounces Gorgonzola or other blue cheese.

Honey-Buttermilk Cornbread
This recipe produces a delicious cornbread that's somewhere between a dessert and a side dish for chili. Slathered with butter, it's perfect for breakfast or brunch. For the basis of a savory stuffing, I prefer the less-sweet Southern-Style Skillet Cornbread on page 225.

Makes an 8-inch square cake, enough for 6 to 9 servings

4 tablespoons (1/2 stick) unsalted butter or
  rendered bacon fat, melted and cooled

1 cup all-purpose flour

3/4 cup yellow cornmeal, preferably stone-ground

1 teaspoon baking powder

1 teaspoon kosher salt

1 cup buttermilk

2 large eggs

3 tablespoons mild honey, such as acacia or
  wildflower

Preheat the oven to 425°F. Using a little of the
butter, grease an 8-inch square baking pan.

In a medium bowl, combine the flour, cornmeal, baking powder, and salt, and stir to mix
well. In a separate bowl, beat the buttermilk,
eggs, honey, and melted butter or bacon fat.
Add this wet mixture to the dry ingredients
and stir with a fork just until blended. Do not
overmix. Pour the batter into the prepared pan
and bake for 20 to 25 minutes, until the cornbread has pulled away from the edges of the
pan, risen and cracked slightly, and it springs
back to the touch. Serve warm or at room temperature.

PREP TIME: 10 minutes

COOKING TIME: 25 minutes

TOTAL TIME: 35 minutes

LEFTOVERS *The cornbread will keep for about four
days wrapped airtight at room temperature. It can
also be frozen for up to two months. Slice leftovers
and toast them or fry them in butter.*

VARIATIONS

Cornbread with Fresh Corn

Stir 1 1/2 cups (from 3 ears fresh corn or frozen)
kernels into the batter. Bake as directed.

Savory Cornbread with Ham, Cheese, and Jalapeño

Sauté some chopped onion and/or scallion and a
jalapeño or other chile in butter until soft. Season with salt and pepper; stir this into the cornbread along with 3/4 cup grated sharp Cheddar or
Jack cheese and 1/4 cup cubed, cooked ham. Proceed with the recipe as directed, increasing the
cooking time by 5 minutes or so, until the cornbread pulls away from the sides as described.

Southern-Style Skillet Cornbread

In my freshman year of college I went to my friend
Brian's home in Dayton, Ohio, for Thanksgiving. That
was the first time I stayed in a household that ate
cornbread with every meal. Southern cornbread isn't
sweet and it's a little dry and crumbly—Brian used to
dismiss my Honey-Buttermilk Cornbread (page 224) as
"cake." If you want to make a delicious cornbread
stuffing, this is what you should use. It's best made with
bacon fat, but it's also pretty good with schmaltz (rendered chicken fat), especially if the cornbread is destined for a turkey stuffing. Butter and oil work fine, too.

Makes one 10-inch cornbread, enough for 6 to 8 people

3 tablespoons rendered bacon fat, chicken fat
  (schmaltz), or a combination of 1 tablespoon
  butter and 2 tablespoons peanut or
  vegetable oil

2 cups yellow cornmeal, preferably stone-ground

1 tablespoon sugar

1 teaspoon kosher salt

2 teaspoons baking powder

1/2 teaspoon baking soda

2 large eggs

2/3 cup milk

1 1/2 cups buttermilk

Preheat the oven to 450°F. Place the fat in a well-seasoned 10-inch cast-iron skillet and set in the oven to heat while you prepare the batter.

In a large bowl, combine the cornmeal, sugar, salt, baking powder, and baking soda, and blend well. In a medium bowl, beat the eggs. Stir in the milk and buttermilk. Pour the liquid ingredients into the dry ingredients and mix with a fork, wooden spoon, or whisk until smooth (because there's no flour, which means there's no gluten, you don't have to worry about overbeating). Carefully remove the hot pan from the oven. Swirl the fat to coat the pan, then pour the fat into the batter and mix it in. Pour the batter into the pan and set back in the oven for 20 minutes, or until the center has risen and set, the sides have pulled away from the pan, and the edges have browned. Remove from the oven, cool on the stove top or rack for 5 minutes or so, cut into wedges, and serve in the skillet.

PREP TIME: 10 minutes
COOKING TIME: 20 minutes
TOTAL TIME: 30 minutes

LEFTOVERS Cornbread will keep at room temperature for a couple of days, in the fridge for up to a week or more, or in the freezer for up to two months. Reheat in the microwave. Stale cornbread is perfect for cornbread stuffing (page 229) or Cornbread Pudding below.

Cornbread Pudding

This is a hearty Southern-inspired side dish that's an excellent use for leftover cornbread. It's like a cornbread stuffing, only more custardy. If you don't want to bother making your own cornbread (pages 224 to 225), buy some and let it sit out for a day or two to go stale.

Makes 6 servings

1 to 1½ pounds stale cornbread, crumbled or cut into ½-inch chunks (2½ to 3½ cups)
3 tablespoons unsalted butter, plus extra for greasing the dish
1 small yellow or white onion, finely chopped
1 medium red bell pepper, cored, seeded, and chopped
1 garlic clove, minced
1 small red or green hot chile, such as jalapeño, seeded and minced
1½ cups corn kernels (from 3 ears or frozen)
1 cup cooked greens, such as spinach, chard, or collards, chopped (optional)
1 cup milk
1 cup buttermilk or additional whole milk
3 large eggs
⅓ cup grated Parmigiano Reggiano or aged Manchego cheese

Preheat the oven to 350°F. Butter a 2-quart baking dish.

Put the cornbread in a large bowl and set aside. Heat the butter in a medium sauté pan over medium heat. Add the onion and sauté for 3 or 4 minutes, until soft. Add the bell pepper, garlic, and chile, and continue sautéing until wilted, about 5 minutes. Add the corn and greens, if using. Cook just to heat through, 2 or 3 minutes. Transfer this mixture to the bowl with the cornbread and let cool.

In a small bowl, combine the milk, buttermilk, and eggs and whisk until blended. Stir in the grated cheese. Pour this mixture into the bowl with the cornbread and vegetables and stir gently to mix. Try not to break all of the corn-bread into mush.

Pour the cornbread mixture into the prepared pan. Bake for about 1 hour, or until the pudding has risen, browned, and set. A bamboo skewer or knife inserted in the center should come out clean. Remove from the oven and serve. As the pudding cools, it will sink.

PREP TIME: 15 minutes
COOKING TIME: 1 hour 15 minutes
TOTAL TIME: 1 hour 30 minutes

ADVANCE PREP *The vegetables can be made several hours in advance. Do not combine the liquid ingredients with the cornbread mixture until just before you are ready to bake.*
LEFTOVERS *The pudding will keep in the fridge for up to a week. Heat leftovers in the microwave or on top of the stove in a covered pan with a little water or milk to create some steam.*

Savory Pumpkin Bread Pudding

A stuffing-like savory bread pudding, this dish has a deep, fall taste because of the pumpkin and herbs. It also has a beautiful fall color. Far be it from me to discourage anyone from roasting or steaming a fresh pumpkin and puréeing it, but rest assured that canned pumpkin is fine here.

Makes 8 servings

Butter, for greasing the dish
1 (15-ounce) can pure pumpkin purée, or 2 cups fresh pumpkin or squash purée
4 large eggs
1 shallot or a small piece of red onion, minced
1 small garlic clove, minced

1 tablespoon chopped fresh marjoram or thyme
1 tablespoon chopped fresh rosemary
2 teaspoons kosher salt
Freshly ground black pepper
Pinch of freshly grated nutmeg
3 cups milk
1/2 pound stale bread, cut into 1-inch cubes (about 4 cups)

Preheat the oven to 350°F. Generously grease a 2-quart baking dish.

Put the pumpkin in the bowl of a food processor fitted with the metal blade. Add the eggs and blend until smooth. Add the shallot, garlic, fresh herbs, salt, pepper, and nutmeg and process until blended. Add a cup or two of the milk, depending on the size of your work bowl, and process until smooth. Transfer to a large bowl. Stir in the remaining milk. Add the bread cubes and stir to coat. Transfer this mixture to the prepared baking dish. (If you have the time, it's best to let the bread pudding sit at room temperature for an hour or so to soak up the pumpkin mixture.) Bake for 1 hour, or until the pudding has risen slightly, set, and browned. Serve warm.

PREP TIME: 10 minutes
COOKING TIME: 1 hour
TOTAL TIME: 1 hour 10 minutes

ADVANCE PREP *Ideally, the pudding should be assembled and left to sit for at least an hour before baking. It can be baked up to 24 hours in advance, cooled, covered, and refrigerated. Reheat in a 300Y F oven for 15 to 20 minutes.*
LEFTOVERS *The pudding will keep for up to one week in the refrigerator. Reheat leftovers for a minute or so in the microwave. It's delicious sliced*

and fried in butter and served as a breakfast side or with a poached egg.

Sausage and Bread Stuffing with Apples and Sage

The combination of flavors in this stuffing is classic. Bake inside a 14- to 16-pound turkey or in a dish on the side. See page 331 for turkey stuffing advice.

Makes about 10 cups, enough for 10 to 12 servings

1/2 cup (1 stick) unsalted butter, plus extra for greasing the dish

1 loaf stale bakery white bread (about 1 1/4 pounds), cut into 1-inch cubes (10 cups)

1 pound sausage meat, bulk or removed from the casings (from about 4 large sausages)

1 large yellow or white onion, chopped

2 celery stalks, chopped

2 medium carrots, shredded

2 medium firm apples, peeled, cored, and diced

4 teaspoons kosher salt

1/2 teaspoon freshly ground black pepper

2 tablespoons minced fresh sage (about 10 leaves) or 2 teaspoons dried sage

2 tablespoons chopped flat-leaf parsley

6 large eggs

2 cups chicken, turkey, or vegetable stock, or roast turkey or chicken pan juices, or water

Preheat the oven to 400°F. If not stuffing a turkey, generously butter a 2 1/2- to 3-quart baking dish and set aside.

Put the bread in a large bowl and set aside.

In a large frying pan over medium-high heat, cook the sausage meat, breaking up the meat as it cooks, until browned and crumbled, about 10 minutes. Scrape the sausage, along with the cooking fat, into the bowl with the bread.

Return the pan to the heat. Melt the butter in the pan. Add the onion and sauté until soft, about 5 minutes. Add the celery and cook for another 2 to 3 minutes. Add the shredded carrots and diced apples and continue cooking for 3 or 4 minutes, until the apples are tender. Stir in 2 teaspoons of the salt, 1/4 teaspoon of the pepper, and the sage and parsley. Cook for another minute, and then transfer this mixture to the bowl with the sausage and bread.

In a medium bowl, beat the eggs with the stock or pan juices until blended. Beat in the remaining 2 teaspoons salt and 1/4 teaspoon pepper. Pour this mixture into the bread bowl, and mix to thoroughly moisten the bread and distribute the vegetables and sausage meat.

Transfer this mixture to the prepared pan. (Alternatively, at this point use it to stuff a Roast Turkey, page 328.) Bake for about 25 minutes, until the surface starts to brown. Turn down the oven temperature to 375YF and continue baking another 20 minutes or so, until the stuffing is set, risen, and browned. Serve hot.

PREP TIME: 15 minutes
COOKING TIME: 1 hour 10 minutes
TOTAL TIME: 1 hour 25 minutes

ADVANCE PREP You can prepare the stuffing right to the point that you bake it and cover and refrigerate it up to a day in advance. Add 15 minutes to the baking time if going straight from fridge to oven.
LEFTOVERS The stuffing will keep in the refrigerator for up to one week. Reheat it in the microwave or in a covered pan with a little stock or gravy to keep it moist. I like to fry leftover stuffing in butter and serve it like hash with a poached egg on top for breakfast.

Cornbread Stuffing with Fennel, Cranberries, and Toasted Pecans

This is a light, fall stuffing that's a perfect accompaniment for turkey, especially at Thanksgiving, when cranberries are everywhere. I prefer to bake my stuffing on the side of the bird, but there's more than enough here to stuff a 12- to 14-pound turkey and still have some left to bake in a small dish. To lighten the texture I cut the cornbread with white bread, but if you prefer a purer cornbread flavor and denser texture, go ahead and use all cornbread. Use a Southern-style cornbread (see page 225), that is, one that isn't too sweet. For advice on stuffing a turkey, see page 331.

Makes 10 cups, enough for 10 to 12 servings

1/2 cup (1 stick) unsalted butter, plus extra for greasing the dish

1 1/2 pounds stale cornbread, cubed (about 4 cups)

1/2 loaf stale white bread (about 1/2 pound), crust removed, cubed (about 5 cups)

2 medium yellow or white onions, chopped

2 celery stalks, finely chopped

1 fennel bulb, finely chopped

1 medium carrot, shredded

5 teaspoons kosher salt

1/2 teaspoon freshly ground black pepper

1 tablespoon chopped fresh sage or thyme (optional)

1 cup pecan halves, toasted and chopped

1 generous cup fresh cranberries

7 large eggs

2 cups chicken, turkey, or vegetable stock, or roast turkey or chicken pan juices

Preheat the oven to 350°F. Generously butter a 2 1/2- or 3-quart baking dish.

Combine the cornbread and white bread in a large bowl.

In a large sauté pan, melt the butter over medium-high heat. Add the onions and sauté until soft, about 5 minutes. Add the celery and fennel and keep sautéing until soft, an additional 5 to 8 minutes. Add the carrot along with 1 tablespoon of the salt and all of the pepper. Stir and cook until the vegetables are tender, and only slightly browned, another 3 or 4 minutes. Stir in the sage, if using.

Add the cooked vegetables to the bread, along with the pecans and cranberries. In another bowl, whisk the eggs with the stock and the remaining 2 teaspoons salt. Pour this mixture over the bread. Using a large spoon or rubber spatula, mix the stuffing to evenly distribute the ingredients, but be careful not to mix it so much that you break up all the bread and cornbread.

Transfer to the prepared dish. Bake for about 1 hour, until the stuffing has set and browned.

PREP TIME: 15 minutes
COOKING TIME: 1 hour 15 minutes
TOTAL TIME: 1 1/2 hours

ADVANCE PREP *The stuffing can be assembled up to one day in advance. Cover and refrigerate until ready to bake. Allow an extra 15 minutes or so baking time if you place it in the oven directly from the fridge.*

LEFTOVERS *Store the cooked stuffing in the refrigerator for up to a week. Reheat leftovers in the microwave for 1 or 2 minutes on high. Alternatively, you can reheat leftovers in a covered frying pan over low heat, adding a little butter and some stock or turkey gravy or water to the pan keep the stuffing moist. I like to serve leftover stuffing like a hash with poached eggs for breakfast.*

Mushroom and Wild Rice Stuffing with Orange and Pine Nuts

The woodsy flavor of mushrooms and nutty taste of wild rice complement each other nicely in this light stuffing. Use it to stuff chicken, Cornish hens, or even vegetables. For directions on how to cook wild rice, see page 232.

Makes 8 cups, enough for 8 servings

3 tablespoons unsalted butter
3 tablespoons extra-virgin olive oil
1 large white or yellow onion, chopped
1 celery stalk, chopped
1 medium carrot, shredded
1 pound assorted fresh mushrooms, such as portobellos, button mushrooms, chanterelles, porcini, or morels, chopped
$1/2$ cup dry sherry
Kosher salt and freshly ground black pepper
3 cups cooked wild rice
3 cups cooked white rice
$1/2$ cup pine nuts or chopped pecans, toasted
Grated zest and juice of 1 orange
1 tablespoon chopped fresh thyme
1 tablespoon chopped fresh flat-leaf parsley

Preheat the oven to 400°F. Use some of the butter to grease a 2-quart baking dish.

Heat the remaining butter and the olive oil in a large skillet over medium-high heat. Add the onion and cook for 5 or 6 minutes, until soft. Add the celery and carrot and continue cooking for another 4 or 5 minutes, until tender. Add the mushrooms and cook for about 10 minutes, until the mushrooms have given off their water. Pour in the sherry, bring to a boil, and let reduce for 2 to 3 minutes. Season with about 2 teaspoons salt and a generous amount of freshly ground pepper.

In a large bowl, combine the wild rice, white rice, pine nuts, orange zest and juice, thyme, parsley, and the mushroom mixture. Add another teaspoon salt and some more pepper and mix. Transfer the stuffing to the buttered baking dish, cover with foil, and bake for 25 to 30 minutes, until the mixture is heated through. (Alternatively, use the mixture to stuff a chicken or other small bird.)

PREP TIME: 10 minutes
COOKING TIME: 1 hour
TOTAL TIME: 1 hour 10 minutes

ADVANCE PREP *The stuffing can be prepared up to two days in advance. Store in the refrigerator until ready to use. It can also be frozen for up to one month.*
LEFTOVERS *The stuffing will keep in the refrigerator for one week. Use it in burritos, scramble it into eggs, or use it to stuff vegetables.*

Polenta with Herbs

Several years ago I was assigned by GQ magazine to get the recipe for the perfect polenta. I knew that meant I had to get the recipe from Cibrèo, my favorite restaurant in Florence, where chef/owner Fabio Picchi makes the creamiest, tastiest, most corn-flavored polenta I have ever eaten.

It turns out that the secret to great polenta is the cornmeal itself. Although you can produce a perfectly respectable polenta with ordinary yellow cornmeal, using better stone-ground cornmeal produces better polenta. And the best cornmeal I've found comes from Anson Mills (www.ansonmills.com). Do not use instant polenta.

Makes 6 cups, enough for 5 to 6 servings

1 cup whole milk

Kosher salt

1 cup polenta or yellow cornmeal, preferably
stone-ground

1 small leaf fresh sage, minced

1/2 teaspoon minced fresh rosemary

1 small garlic clove, minced

1/2 teaspoon freshly ground white pepper

Pinch of freshly grated nutmeg

2 tablespoons unsalted butter, melted

1 ounce Parmigiano Reggiano cheese, freshly
grated (1/4 cup)

In a large, heavy saucepan (*not* nonstick) combine 4 cups water with the milk and 1 tablespoon of salt. Set over high heat and bring to a boil. Pay attention as it nears the boiling point because the milk has a tendency to boil over. In a steady stream, slowly whisk the polenta into the boiling liquid. Whisk in the sage, rosemary, garlic, pepper, and nutmeg. As soon as this mixture comes back to a boil, lower the heat as low as it will go. The polenta should be barely simmering.

Stirring only occasionally (many Italian cooks say you shouldn't stir it at all), allow the polenta to cook very slowly for 40 minutes or so. It will stick to the bottom and form a crust, which is desirable. Being careful not to disturb this crust, stir the polenta to smooth out the texture. Adjust the seasoning with salt and pepper. Cook for another 15 minutes or so until the polenta is thick and creamy. If the polenta is too thick—it should be custardy—thin it by stirring in hot water or milk. If it is too thin, keep cooking until it is thick.

To serve, spoon the polenta onto warm plates or shallow bowls, making a slight indentation with the back of the spoon. Pour the warm melted butter into the depressions and sprinkle with grated cheese.

TOTAL TIME: 1 hour

ADVANCE PREP *The polenta can be made up to 2 hours in advance and kept over very low heat until ready to serve. If it thickens too much while it sits, add hot water or milk to thin.*
LEFTOVERS *Once polenta cools it will harden. Pour warm polenta into a dish greased with olive oil or lined with plastic wrap. It will keep for up to two weeks in the refrigerator. Use it for Fried or Grilled Polenta or Polenta Parmigiana—see Variations.*

VARIATIONS
Fried Polenta
Fry 1/2-inch-thick slices of polenta in butter, olive oil, or a combination until golden brown. If you prefer, you can bread the polenta, dipping the pieces in flour, beaten egg, and bread crumbs before frying it.

Grilled Polenta
Brush 1/2-inch-thick slices of polenta with olive oil and set on a hot grill or grill pan. When the polenta is nicely marked with grill marks, flip and grill the second side until the polenta is heated through.

Polenta Parmigiana
Using either fried or grilled pieces of polenta, you can make a delicious polenta parmigiana. Arrange the slices of polenta on a baking sheet. Spoon tomato sauce over the polenta and top with shredded mozzarella and grated Parmigiano Reggiano. Bake in a 400° F oven until the cheese is melted and browned and the sauce is bubbly, 25 to 30 minutes.

Buttermilk Polenta with Fresh Corn

This is a delicious, light polenta to make in the summer, when corn is in season. Buttermilk gives this polenta a delicate tang and a creamy texture. Serve with grilled or barbecued meats.

Makes 6 cups, enough for 6 servings

2 cups buttermilk

2 teaspoons kosher salt

1 1/2 cups polenta or yellow cornmeal, preferably stone-ground

1 teaspoon minced fresh rosemary

1 teaspoon minced fresh thyme

2 cups fresh corn kernels (from 4 ears corn)

Freshly ground black pepper

4 tablespoons (1/2 stick) unsalted butter

1/3 cup freshly grated Parmigiano Reggiano cheese

In a large pot, combine 1 1/2 cups of the buttermilk with 5 cups water and the salt and bring to a boil. (Don't worry if the buttermilk looks like it is curdling in the water; whisk it and it will be fine.) In a slow stream, whisk the cornmeal into the water. Keep stirring until the polenta begins to thicken into a porridge, about 6 minutes. Add the rosemary and thyme and bring the polenta to a boil. Turn down the heat as low as the burner will go and simmer for 30 minutes, stirring periodically, until the polenta has become a smooth porridge. Don't worry if a crust forms on the bottom of the pan. Stir in the corn and the remaining 1/2 cup buttermilk and cook for another 10 minutes or so, until the corn has heated through. Season with pepper. Stir in the butter and Parmigiano until melted, and serve immediately.

TOTAL TIME: 45 minutes

ADVANCE PREP *Polenta needs to be made just before serving. You can keep it warm for about an hour on a low burner. Adjust the consistency with hot water or milk, if needed.*

LEFTOVERS *See the suggestions for Polenta with Herbs (page 230).*

Wild Rice with Apples, Dried Cranberries, and Buttered Almonds

Though technically not a relative of rice, wild rice is nevertheless a nutty, flavorful ricelike grass. Wild rice is available in several grades, which have to do with the length and uniformity of the individual grains. Giant, or long, is the top of the line and the most expensive, but extra-fancy, which is one step down, is perfectly fine, too. This is a lovely side dish for roast poultry or pork.

Makes about 4 1/2 cups, enough for 6 servings

1 cup giant or extra-fancy wild rice

1 tablespoon kosher salt

1/4 cup dried cranberries, chopped

1/3 cup dry red wine

2 tablespoons red wine vinegar

5 tablespoons unsalted butter

1/2 cup slivered almonds

1 large green apple, such as Granny Smith, peeled, cored, and diced

4 or 5 scallions, white and green parts, chopped

1 or 2 leaves fresh sage, minced

Freshly ground black pepper

Bring about 4 quarts of water to a boil. Add the wild rice and salt. Boil the rice for 40 to 50 minutes, until tender (you'll have to taste it to know for sure). Some of the grains will burst, but that's okay. Drain well and place in a large bowl.

Meanwhile, in a small bowl, combine the cranberries with the red wine and vinegar. Heat this mixture in a microwave on high for 1 minute and let sit for 15 to 20 minutes to plump. Alternatively, you can heat the wine and vinegar together and pour it over the cranberries.

In a medium frying pan, heat 2 tablespoons of the butter over medium-high heat. Add the almonds and toast for 3 or 4 minutes until golden brown, swirling the pan frequently to prevent burning. Add the toasted almonds to the cooked wild rice. Place the remaining 3 tablespoons butter in the pan and set back over the heat. Add the apple and sauté for 3 or 4 minutes, until soft. Add the scallions and sage, and cook just until wilted, a minute or two. Season with salt and pepper and add to the wild rice. Add the cranberries and their soaking liquid to the wild rice. Toss well. Adjust the seasoning with salt and freshly ground pepper, and serve warm.

PREP TIME: 10 minutes
COOKING TIME: 50 minutes
TOTAL TIME: 1 hour

ADVANCE PREP *You can cook the wild rice a day or two in advance and refrigerate until needed. The whole dish can be made a day or two in advance and reheated in the microwave or a nonstick frying pan before serving.*
LEFTOVERS *The wild rice will keep for up to ten days in the fridge. Wild rice can also be frozen.*

Spiced Millet with Cauliflower, Currants, and Pistachios

The nutty taste and texture of millet blends nicely with the Indian-inspired spices in this millet pilaf. You can use any vegetables you like instead of the cauliflower, such as zucchini or green beans. Serve as a vegetarian main course or as a side dish for grilled lamb.
Makes 5 cups, enough for 4 to 6 servings

2 teaspoons kosher salt
1 bay leaf
2 whole cloves
1/2 teaspoon ground cumin
1/4 teaspoon ground coriander
1/4 teaspoon ground cardamom
4 tablespoons (1/2 stick) unsalted butter
1 large yellow or white onion, finely chopped
2 garlic cloves, minced
1/2 small head of cauliflower, diced (2 1/2 to 3 cups)
1 cup millet
2 tablespoons dried currants
1/4 cup pistachios or almonds, toasted (page 10) and chopped
Freshly ground black pepper

Place about 4 cups cold water in a small saucepan. Add the salt, bay leaf, cloves, cumin, coriander, and cardamom and bring to a boil. Reduce the heat to low and simmer for 5 minutes. Remove the bay leaf and cloves and keep warm.

In a large, deep frying pan, heat the butter over medium-high heat. Add the onion and cook until wilted, about 5 minutes. Add the garlic and cauliflower and cook, stirring frequently, until the cauliflower begins to brown, about 10 minutes. Don't worry if the bottom of the pan starts to brown also, that's desirable—just don't let the garlic burn. Add the millet and let toast for about 2 minutes, just until it begins to color. Pour in enough of the hot, spiced water mixture to cover the cauliflower and millet. You should have about a cup or so left behind. Reserve. Stir in the currants. Turn down the heat so that the mixture simmers gently. Set a lid loosely over the frying pan and cook for about 10 minutes, stirring occasionally. Stir in the nuts. Cook for an additional 10 minutes until the grains of millet have swollen and softened. If the liquid evaporates before the millet is thoroughly cooked, add some of the reserved spiced water.

Cover the pan tightly, remove from the heat, and let sit for 10 minutes to steam. Fluff with a fork. Adjust the seasoning with salt and pepper.

PREP TIME: 10 minutes
COOKING TIME: 50 minutes
TOTAL TIME: 1 hour

ADVANCE PREP *The dish is best eaten just after it is made, but it can be reheated in a pan with the addition of a little water to prevent burning, or in the microwave.*
LEFTOVERS *The millet will keep for about a week in the fridge. Leftovers are good used as a stuffing for vegetables. Stir in an egg and some cheese and stuff peppers or zucchini before roasting.*

Bulgur Pilaf with Pine Nuts

Bulgur is a quick-cooking grain made from steamed cracked wheat. It cooks quickly because it is precooked when it is processed. (Note: bulgur is not interchangeable with cracked wheat, which isn't precooked.) This simple pilaf is ready in 15 minutes. Play around with your own combinations of flavorings. I like to stir in mushrooms, spinach, peas, or various herbs for variety. Makes 3½ cups, enough for 6 servings

4 tablespoons (½ stick) unsalted butter
2 to 3 tablespoons pine nuts
1 small yellow or white onion, finely chopped

1 small garlic clove, minced
1 cup bulgur, medium granulation (no. 2)
2 cups simmering chicken or vegetable stock
    or water
Kosher salt and freshly ground black pepper

Melt 1 tablespoon of the butter in a medium saucepan over medium heat. Add the pine nuts and swirl and toss for 2 or 3 minutes, until golden brown. Don't let the nuts burn. Remove the nuts from the pan and set aside.

Add the remaining 3 tablespoons butter to the saucepan and set back over medium heat. Add the onion and sauté for 5 or 6 minutes, until soft. Add the garlic and cook for another minute or two. Add the bulgur and stir for a minute to coat with the butter and to lightly toast. Add the stock or water along with 1 teaspoon salt. Bring to a simmer, turn down the heat as low as possible, cover, and simmer for 15 minutes until the bulgur is tender and the liquid has been absorbed. Stir the pine nuts back into the bulgur, fluff with a fork, and season with pepper before serving.

PREP TIME: 5 minutes
COOKING TIME: 25 minutes
TOTAL TIME: 30 minutes

ADVANCE PREP *The pilaf can be made up to a day or two in advance, refrigerated, and reheated though it's best served as soon as it is finished cooking.*
LEFTOVERS *The bulgur will keep for up to ten days in the refrigerator. Reheat in a microwave or on top of the stove in a covered saucepan. To make bulgur cakes from leftovers, stir 1 beaten large egg into 1 cup of the bulgur pilaf. Shape into patties and fry in butter in a nonstick pan. Leftover bulgur can also be used as a binder in meatloaf instead of bread crumbs.*

Kasha with Wild Mushrooms and Walnuts

Kasha, or toasted buckwheat groats, is a Central European staple that people either love or hate. I love it, especially with braised meats, such as short ribs or brisket. This is a hearty preparation with a deep wintry flavor that comes from the addition of dried porcini to heighten the mushroom flavor and walnuts, which I think complement the nutty taste of the grain itself. Kasha is available in fine and medium granulation and whole kernels; my preference for texture and flavor is medium granulation. To prepare the lightest, fluffiest kasha, you coat the grains with egg and toast them before adding liquid. It's an unusual technique, but the results are delicious.

Makes 4½ cups, enough for 6 servings

- ½ ounce dried porcini
- ½ cup dry red wine
- 5 tablespoons unsalted butter
- 1 medium yellow or white onion, finely chopped
- 10 ounces assorted fresh mushrooms, such as chanterelles, portobellos, cremini, or button, chopped (2½ to 3 cups)
- 2 cups stock, broth, or water
- 1 teaspoon kosher salt
- 1 cup kasha, medium granulation
- 1 large egg, beaten
- ½ cup walnut halves, toasted (page 10) and chopped
- Freshly ground black pepper

In a small bowl, combine the porcini and wine and microwave on high for 1 minute to heat. (Alternatively, you can heat the porcini and wine in a small saucepan.) Let sit for 15 minutes, or until the mushrooms have softened.

In a large frying pan, melt the butter over medium-high heat. Add the onion and sauté for 5 minutes or so, until wilted. Add the fresh mushrooms and continue sautéing until they have released their water and wilted, an additional 5 to 7 minutes. Lift the porcini out of their soaking liquid and cut them into small pieces. Add to the mushrooms and onion. Using a soup spoon, scoop the porcini soaking liquid out of the small bowl or saucepan and add it to the mushrooms, being careful not to disturb any sand that might have sunk to the bottom. Keep cooking the mushroom and onion mixture until about half of the liquid has evaporated. Transfer to a large bowl.

In a small saucepan, heat the stock with the salt. Place the kasha in the pan you used to cook the mushrooms, keeping it off the heat. Add the egg and stir the kasha until the grains are evenly coated with it; the kasha should have the texture of wet sand. Place the pan over medium-high heat and cook, stirring constantly, until the kasha has toasted and the grains have dried and separated, about 4 minutes. Pour in the hot stock. Turn down the heat so that the mixture simmers gently, cover, and cook for 7 to 9 minutes, until all of the liquid has evaporated and the kasha is soft. Turn off the heat and let sit covered for 5 minutes or so. Fluff the kasha with a fork and add it to the bowl with the sautéed mushrooms and onion. Add the walnuts, season with pepper, and serve.

PREP TIME: 10 minutes
COOKING TIME: 25 minutes
TOTAL TIME: 1 hour (includes soaking time)

ADVANCE PREP *The kasha can be made two or three days in advance and reheated in the microwave or in the oven to serve. If using an oven,* preheat it to 325° F. Place the kasha in a buttered baking dish and dot the top with more butter. If the kasha is very dry, you may also want to add a few tablespoons of broth to it. Cover with foil and bake for 20 to 25 minutes, or until heated through.

LEFTOVERS *The kasha will keep for about ten days in the fridge. It can also be frozen for up to two months. The kasha makes an excellent stuffing for poultry or vegetables. Mixed with mashed potatoes, kasha also makes a delicious filling for knishes. (See my last book,* The Mensch Chef, *for details on how to make them!)*

VARIATIONS

Plain Kasha

Omit the walnuts, mushrooms, and onion and simply prepare the kasha by toasting it with the egg and adding the hot stock as directed.

Kasha Varnishkes

Increase the butter for sautéing the mushrooms and onion to 7 tablespoons and add 2 cups cooked bowtie pasta (farfalle) or egg noodles to the kasha when you stir in the mushrooms and onions.

Barley with Orange and Dates

I think the fluffy-chewy texture and delicate taste of pearl barley make it a perfect candidate for a comfort food. Serve this as a side dish to spiced, grilled lamb or zesty Moroccan food, or just eat it plain, like a cereal.
Makes 4 cups, enough for 4 to 6 servings

3 tablespoons unsalted butter
1 small white or yellow onion, finely chopped
5 or 6 dates, pitted and chopped
Finely grated zest of 1 orange
1 cup pearl barley

3 cups chicken or vegetable stock, or water
Kosher salt
5 or 6 sprigs fresh thyme, leaves only, minced
1/2 small bay leaf
Freshly ground black pepper

In a medium nonstick saucepan, melt the butter over medium-high heat. Add the onion and cook until soft, about 5 minutes. Add the dates and orange zest and sauté for a minute or two longer. Add the barley and stir to coat with the butter. Pour in the stock and add 1 teaspoon salt, the thyme, and bay leaf. Bring to a boil, reduce the heat so that the liquid simmers, cover, and cook until the barley is tender and the liquid has been absorbed, about 30 minutes. Remove from the heat and let sit, covered, for 5 to 10 minutes. Remove the bay leaf, season with pepper, fluff with a fork, and serve.

TOTAL TIME: 50 minutes

ADVANCE PREP *The dish can be prepared in advance and reheated in a baking dish in the oven. Dot the top with butter, cover with aluminum foil, and bake at 350° F for 20 minutes or until warmed through.*
LEFTOVERS *The barley will keep for about two weeks in the fridge.*

Quinoa with Roasted Poblanos, Cilantro, and Lime

Quinoa is a tiny, ancient Aztec grain that's so rich in protein and other good things for you that some health gurus have called it a super grain. Regardless of its salubrious effects, I think it is delicious. Perhaps because of the high protein content, the tiny grains have a pleasantly chewy texture that is both substantial and light. Quinoa should be rinsed once or twice with cold water before using.

Makes 4½ cups, enough for 4 to 6 servings

- 1 cup quinoa
- 2 cups chicken or vegetable stock, or water
- ½ bay leaf
- 1 teaspoon kosher salt
- 1 lime, zest cut with a vegetable peeler
- ¼ cup extra-virgin olive oil
- 1 medium white or yellow onion, finely chopped
- 2 garlic cloves, minced
- ¼ teaspoon ground cumin
- 4 large poblano peppers or other mild chiles or bell peppers, roasted (page 146), seeded, and diced
- ½ large bunch cilantro, chopped
- Freshly ground black pepper

Place the quinoa in a mesh sieve and rinse once or twice with cold running water. Set aside to drain.

In a medium saucepan, combine the stock, bay leaf, and salt. Add 2 or 3 strips of lime zest and the juice of the lime. Bring to a boil over high heat, reduce the heat, and keep simmering for 5 to 10 minutes.

In a medium saucepan or large skillet, heat the oil over medium-high heat. Add the onion and sauté until translucent, about 5 minutes. Add the garlic and continue cooking 2 or 3 minutes, just until the garlic is soft. Add the quinoa and stir to coat with the fat. Cook for 2 or 3 minutes, until the quinoa begins to toast. Add the cumin and cook for a minute more. Strain the simmering stock mixture into the quinoa, stir, and bring to a boil. With a rubber spatula, scrape any stray quinoa off the sides of the pot. Reduce the heat to very low, cover the pan, and cook for 13 to 15 minutes, or until the liquid has been absorbed or evaporated and the quinoa is cooked. Remove from the heat and let stand, covered, for 5 minutes. Stir in the roasted peppers, cilantro, and a generous amount of black pepper.

PREP TIME: 20 minutes
COOKING TIME: 20 minutes
TOTAL TIME: 40 minutes

ADVANCE PREP *The quinoa can be made several hours in advance and reheated in the microwave before serving. It is best eaten the day it is made.*
LEFTOVERS *The quinoa will keep for about a week in the refrigerator. Reheat leftovers in the microwave on high for a minute or two.*

VARIATION
Plain Quinoa
To cook plain quinoa as a simple side dish or a base for salads or other dishes, simply stir 1 cup of rinsed quinoa into 2 cups of boiling salted water. Bring back to a boil, reduce the heat to low, cover, and simmer for 12 to 15 minutes, until the liquid is gone and the quinoa is cooked. Let stand, covered, for 5 minutes, then fluff with a fork.

Pasta, Noodles, and Dumplings

LTHOUGH MOST CLOSELY ASSOCIATED with Italian and Chinese cuisines, pasta and noodles are universally loved, whether we're talking macaroni and cheese in America, yakisoba in Japan, or spätzle in Austria. Noodles are cheap, satisfying, and fun to eat. Made from wheat, rice, bean, potato, or other starches, the whole world loves them.

In this chapter I've given directions for making a few different types of noodles, but truth be told, making noodles at home can be a bit of a production. The more you do it, the easier it becomes. But there's nothing wrong with buying sheets of ready-made fresh pasta from a reputable shop or using a good-quality dried pasta, which is delicious in its own right.

I've given two very basic recipes for cooking pasta: dried (page 241) and fresh (page 244). For both, the only things to remember are to use a lot of boiling water and plenty of salt. You probably know by now that you should cook pasta until it is "al dente." But what does that mean? *Al dente* literally means "to the tooth"—tender but still with a little bite to it. Al dente is only applicable when you are talking about dried pasta. Fresh pasta starts out softer than the al dente stage (see page 243 for a discussion of dried versus fresh pasta). Al dente is not only a factor of how long a dried pasta is cooked but also of the quality of the pasta to begin with. Good imported dried pasta retains a resilience when cooked, meaning that it holds the proper al dente stage. Cheap domestic pasta—often sold simply as macaroni—goes from hard to mushy without ever passing through the al dente stage. You can almost tell the doneness by looking at the pasta as it cooks. As dried pasta goes from hard to soft, it turns from translucent to opaque, a sign that the starch in the noodles has gelatinized.

Other types of noodles require different cooking techniques. Starchy Asian noodles, such as rice sticks or bean threads, require soaking before they are cooked. They do not need to be boiled. Instead, they can be stir-fried after soaking. Austrian spätzle are shaped by dropping them into boiling water, and after they cook they are often fried. Suffice it to say the world of noodles is vast. This chapter presents an international selection of some of my favorite noodle dishes—complete with a modern Fresh Tuna Casserole (page 262).

Second only to noodles as a comfort-food favorite, dumplings are another category of foods beloved around the world. Chinese potstickers, German cheese dumplings, and American chicken and dumplings have a quality about them that warms, soothes, and satisfies your stomach and your soul. It seems to me that, except in certain pockets across the country, Americans have lost their dumpling traditions. When's the last time you came upon a delicious dish of Chicken and Dumplings (page 324)? Although the few recipes for dumplings I've included in this chapter and elsewhere in the book barely scratch the surface of the dumpling recipes out there, my hope is they pique your interest in making dumplings. Everyone will be happier for it.

■ ■ ■

Cooking Dried Pasta

Water and salt are all you need to cook dried pasta perfectly. You can never have too much water so that shouldn't be a fear. As a rule, figure at least 5 quarts of water to cook 1 pound of pasta. Increase the amount of water proportionately if you can.

Into 5 quarts of water I usually put a handful of kosher salt—2 or 3 heaping tablespoons, or a scant 1/4 cup. I know that several of you will balk at so much salt, but for the best flavor you have to season the pasta while it cooks so the salt penetrates the pasta; you cannot get the same result by sprinkling the pasta with salt once it is done. And remember, most of the salt just goes down the drain anyway. You'll also need less salt in the sauce because the noodles themselves will be adequately seasoned.

You will note that I didn't mention oil in the water, which does nothing but float on top of the water.

Italians figure 100 grams of dried pasta per portion, which is about 3 1/2 ounces. To make measuring easier, I round off to 4 ounces, which means a pound of dry pasta will make four servings or so. While that's the rule, I know that personally I could easily eat a whole pound of pasta myself. Normal eaters might be able to squeeze five or six servings out of a pound. Know your audience and prepare accordingly.

Makes 4 to 6 servings

> Scant 1/4 cup kosher salt
> 1 pound dried pasta made from 100% durum
>   wheat (semolina)

Fill a large, deep pot with 5 quarts of water and set on a large burner over high heat. Add the salt to the water, cover the pot, and bring to a rapid boil. When the water is boiling, remove the lid. Dump the pasta into the boiling water and stir well to prevent the noodles from sticking together or from sticking to the bottom of the pot. For short pasta, a wooden spoon is fine for stirring; for long pasta, use a large fork or tongs so you can keep separating the noodles as you stir. During the first minute or so of cooking, it is important to stir the noodles frequently. After that, just stir them periodically while they cook.

Allow the pasta to cook uncovered at a rapid boil until al dente. After about 7 or 8 minutes, start to check the noodles for doneness. If you are making an Italian-style pan sauce that you intend to toss with the noodles, when they are finished cooking, remove a cup or two of the cooking water to finish the sauce before dumping the noodles into a colander or strainer to drain. Do not rinse the pasta with water, which only washes away the flavor and changes the texture.

TOTAL TIME: 8 to 12 minutes

ADVANCE PREP *Though the texture won't be perfect, pasta can be precooked to serve a large crowd. Stop the noodles from cooking 2 or 3 minutes before they are done. (It's better to err on the side of underdone.) Drain, toss with olive or other oil to prevent sticking, and store in an airtight container in the refrigerator until ready to use. To finish, bring another large pot of water to a boil, this time only lightly salted, and plunge the noodles into the boiling water to heat through.*

LEFTOVERS *Though it softens, cooked pasta will keep in the fridge in an airtight container for up to a week. Use it in baked noodle casseroles, such as Fresh Tuna Casserole (page 262) or macaroni and cheese (pages 258 and 259), or in a frittata or Yakisoba (page 266).*

Fresh Pasta Dough (Egg Noodles)

All the energy people spend on trying to find the best fresh pasta to buy might be put to better use mastering pasta making at home. Making pasta isn't that hard, though it does take a little practice. And as long as you are making pasta for four people or fewer, it doesn't even take much time.

You can roll noodles by hand without a machine, but a pasta machine makes the whole process quick and painless. Forget the machines you see on T.V. into which you dump flour and water or eggs and out come fresh noodles. These are extruders. Extrusion is good only for commercial pasta. Don't bother with it at home. Instead, invest in a small hand-crank stainless steel pasta machine ($50 or less) that clamps onto the counter or buy an attachment of pasta rollers for your stand mixer. Then be sure to throw away the recipe booklet included with the machine. These booklets have caused more people I know to end up with sticky pasta messes. They often suggest using only semolina flour, which is great for commercial pasta, but difficult to use for home pasta and totally unnecessary. All-purpose flour, eggs, and salt are all you need.

Here's the recipe and technique I use to make delicate homemade *pasta al'uovo* (i.e., egg noodles). It's a versatile noodle dough that is delicious many ways: rolled into long, thin sheets for Lasagna (page 260), cut into circles or squares and used as a wrapper for Asian dumplings (see page 270), or cooked and served with Beef Stew (page 358) or topped with a classic Italian ragù.

Makes 1¼ pounds, enough for 4 servings

> About 3¼ cups unbleached all-purpose flour
> Pinch of salt
> 4 large eggs and 2 large egg yolks, beaten
> Semolina (in flour or granule form) or additional
> flour, for dusting

MIXING THE DOUGH BY HAND

On a clean, smooth work surface, mound the flour. Mix in the salt and push in the top of the mound to make a well in the center. Pour the eggs into the well. Using a fork, stir the eggs, slowly incorporating flour from the sides of the well into the eggs to begin to form a dough. With the hand that isn't stirring, reinforce the sides of the well so they don't collapse (it's bad luck if they do). Keep incorporating more and more flour as you stir until the dough is too stiff and sticky to mix. At this point, trade the fork for a bench or pastry scraper, and work the dough with your hands, using the scraper to lift it off the surface and to help incorporate some of the flour as you work. Knead the dough into a stiff, not sticky dough. Don't worry if all of the flour is not incorporated. Scrape off and discard the excess flour on the work surface. Wrap the dough in plastic and set aside for 30 minutes.

MIXING THE DOUGH IN AN ELECTRIC MIXER

Place about 2⅔ cups of the flour in the bowl of an electric mixer fitted with a dough hook. Add the salt and mix on low for a second. Pour in the eggs and run the mixer on low until floury clumps of dough form, about 2 minutes. With a spatula, knock down the flour from the sides of the bowl so it is incorporated into the dough. Turn the machine up to medium and let it run for a minute or so to make a more cohesive dough, though it will still seem rather clumpy and dry. Turn out the dough from the bowl onto a clean work surface and knead with your hands, incorporating just as much of the stray, dry, floury bits as the dough will take. After 4 or 5 minutes of kneading, the dough should be smooth and elastic, and you should have a few

FRESH VERSUS DRIED PASTA

Somehow in America a cult of fresh pasta has developed, positioning dried pasta as a second-rate cousin. The truth is that good pasta is good pasta, fresh or dried, and most fresh pasta in the marketplace here is dreadful, gummy stuff, so you are often better off using dried, anyway.

Dried pasta is hardly a cheap, quick substitute for fresh pasta; it is a delicacy in its own right. Many traditional Italian pasta dishes are best matched with dried pasta, which stands up better to dense, chunky sauces. It is important to buy a top-quality dried pasta, and for my taste that usually means one from Italy. Good dried pasta is made from 100 percent durum wheat (also known as semolina). Durum wheat is "harder," meaning it has a higher protein content than other wheat, so the pasta made with it has more integrity once it is cooked. Of the expensive imported dried pastas, the brands Rustichella d'Abruzzo and Martelli are perhaps the best available here in the United States. Of the medium-priced pastas, I prefer Del Verde and De Cecco. If those are still too expensive, opt for Barilla. Domestic pastas just don't compare.

Fresh pasta is richer and more delicate, and it is better suited to richer, more delicate sauces than dried pasta. Good fresh pasta should be made with eggs and all-purpose flour and little else. It should have a nice golden hue from egg yolks, and be very thin, almost transparent, but resilient. It is much harder to find good fresh pasta than it is to find good dried pasta. I am fortunate to live near an old Greenwich Village pasta shop, Raffetto's, that sells sheets of good fresh pasta that they cut to order. If I didn't, I'd probably have to make it myself.

tablespoons worth of floury bits on the counter. Discard the bits, wrap the dough in plastic, and set aside for 30 minutes.

MIXING THE DOUGH IN A FOOD PROCESSOR

Place about $2\frac{2}{3}$ cups of the flour in the bowl of a food processor fitted with the metal chopping blade. Add the salt and pulse once or twice to mix. Add the eggs and pulse on/off until a dough begins to form around the blade. At that point let the machine run until the dough forms a ball that rolls around the blade. Turn the dough out of the processor bowl onto the counter and knead for a minute or two, adding more flour as necessary to make a smooth, elastic dough. Wrap in plastic and set aside for 30 minutes.

FORMING NOODLES BY HAND

Divide the dough into quarters. Rewrap in plastic all but one quarter. Lightly flour the work surface and the dough. Press the dough into a small disk. Using a long, thin rolling pin, roll the dough out as even and as thin as possible— the thinner the better. I like to press down very hard on the rolling pin as I make short, jerky passes over the surface of the dough, stretching it and flattening it until it is almost so thin you can read through it. If it's too difficult to work, let it sit for a minute or two (up to 10) and then roll again. Repeat with the remaining dough.

If you are going to use the dough for ravioli or wrappers, you can cut it immediately, as directed in the recipe. The soft texture of the freshly rolled dough will seal beautifully at the edges. If you are going to cut the dough into noodles, such as fettuccine or pappardelle,

Cooking Fresh Pasta

The rules for cooking fresh pasta are similar to those for cooking dried pasta: lots of water and lots of salt. In fact, I find fresh pasta requires even more water because it is usually coated with excess semolina or flour to keep the noodles from sticking, and this can goop up and cloud the cooking water.

The major difference between cooking fresh and dried pasta is the timing. Fresh pasta cooks in about 2 minutes. (Stuffed fresh pastas, such as ravioli and agnolotti, will take a little longer so that the fillings heat through.) Fresh pasta will never be al dente, but it shouldn't be mushy, either. Properly made and cooked fresh pasta has a good bite that can stand up to a rich sauce. In my opinion, *pasta al'uovo*—that is, pasta made with nothing but flour and eggs—has the best texture. Stuffed fresh pasta should have a delicate texture, too; one of my pet peeves is fresh ravioli that have a tough edge, as though they have been sealed with cement.

Because fresh pasta doesn't absorb as much water and therefore doesn't expand as much as dried pasta, 1 pound of fresh pasta, cooked, produces less than 1 pound of dried pasta, cooked. But fresh pasta is also richer than dried pasta, so a portion of it is generally smaller. To be safe, figure about 5 ounces fresh pasta per person. If you make the pasta yourself, it will probably be so delicious you'll want to figure on more.

Makes 4 servings

¼ cup kosher salt
1¼ pounds fresh pasta, preferably pasta
 al'uovo (made with only eggs and flour)

Fill a large, deep pot with 6 quarts of water and set on a large burner over high heat. Add the salt to the water, cover the pot, and bring to a rapid boil. When the water is boiling, remove the lid. Shake off any excess flour or semolina from the pasta and add the pasta to the water by scattering it into the pot, making sure the noodles haven't clumped together. With a long fork or tongs, stir the noodles, being careful not to break them.

Allow the pasta to cook, uncovered, stirring the noodles from time to time. Depending on how delicate your noodles are, they will be cooked through in 2 or 3 minutes. This is true even if the water doesn't come back up to a boil—which is often the case if you don't have a super-powerful burner. When cooked, the noodles should still have a bit of a bite and not be mushy. Reserve a cup or so of the cooking water for finishing a sauce, if desired, and drain the noodles in a colander. Shake well, as fresh noodles hold water more than dried noodles. Do not rinse.

TOTAL TIME: 2 or 3 minutes

LEFTOVERS *Cooked fresh pasta does not keep as well as cooked dried pasta. Toss it with olive or other oil and store in the refrigerator to use as a garnish in soup, in Fresh Tuna Casserole (page 262), or in Kasha Varnishkes (page 236).*

however, you will have to let it dry first, for 20 minutes or so, or the noodles will stick together. To dry it, lift the dough off the work surface and lay it on a clean dish towel or tablecloth. Turn the dough over after 10 minutes or so to ensure it dries evenly.

For long noodles, lightly dust the sheets of dough with semolina or additional all-purpose flour. Loosely roll up the dough into a log and, using a sharp knife, cut the log into even strips. Unroll the strips into noodles and toss with additional semolina or flour. Alternatively, use a sharp knife to cut the dough into the desired shape.

FORMING NOODLES WITH A PASTA MACHINE

A hand-crank or automatic pasta machine makes it easy to achieve a thin, delicate noodle. Begin with the machine on its widest setting (usually #1 on the dial). Divide the dough into quarters and rewrap all but one quarter. Flatten the dough and feed it through the rollers as you crank the handle. Fold the flattened dough into thirds, turn it in the opposite direction, and feed it through the rollers again. Repeat until the dough comes out smooth—usually four or five passes, total. After the last pass, do not fold the dough. Move the rollers one click closer (i.e., to #2 on the dial) and feed it through the machine. Once the dough catches, let it fall down the back of the machine and grab it out of the rollers on the other hand to stretch it evenly as it comes out. Move the rollers one notch closer again and repeat. When the dough gets too long and unwieldy to handle easily, cut it in half—noting the number on the machine at which you made the cut. Proceed with half the dough to the last or second-to-last setting of the machine,

depending on how thick you want your pasta—for noodles, I usually stop one notch from the end; for ravioli or other stuffed pasta, which will be double the thickness in parts, I usually go to the last notch.

Lay out the long strip of dough to dry on a clean dish towel or tablecloth while you finish rolling the other piece of the dough, returning the machine to the notch you left off at. Then repeat from the beginning with the remaining quarters of dough. When finished rolling the dough, cut it into noodle-length sheets and let them dry for 10 to 15 minutes on a clean dish towel or tablecloth.

If your pasta machine has a noodle-cutting attachment, use it by feeding the sheets of dough through the cutters as you crank them with the handle. Gather the noodles as they come out of the cutters. Toss with a generous amount of semolina or additional all-purpose flour, arrange in a nest-like pile on a tray and repeat with the remaining dough. If you don't have a noodle-cutting attachment for your machine, roll and cut the sheets into noodles as described above in the "by hand" method.

PREP TIME: 30 minutes to 1 hour
TOTAL TIME: 1 to 1½ hours (includes resting time)

ADVANCE PREP *The fresh noodles can be covered with a damp-ish dish towel and stored in the refrigerator for up to one day. They can also be frozen for up to two months. To freeze them, gather the noodles into little nests on a tray and freeze for 12 hours or so. When they are hard, transfer the nests to a resealable bag and keep frozen until ready to use. Use them straight from the freezer, increasing the cooking time by a couple of minutes.*

You can also dry these noodles for long-term storage. As they come out of the cutters, hang the long, thin noodles over clean broom handles that are suspended across two kitchen chairs. (Put a clean towel underneath, as the noodles tend to break off when they dry.) After about a day in the open air, the noodles will be hard. Gather them up and place them in a brown paper bag to keep drying. After a couple of days, transfer them to a resealable plastic bag. The dried noodles will last for several months, though their color will darken as they age.

VARIATION

Flavored Pasta Dough

Once you get good at making noodles, and you have memorized the feel of the dough, there are any number of variations you can make. Adding puréed roasted beets, spinach, or tomato paste to the dough makes for pretty colors. A saffron solution, made by dissolving saffron in warm water or wine, adds a beautiful color and flavor. Chopped fresh herbs are also pretty and tasty when incorporated into pasta dough. The only thing to remember is that the addition of any moisture will require additional flour to achieve the right consistency of the dough (you can also compensate by adding less egg).

Spätzle

This is a quick way to make homemade egg noodles without the fuss of kneading and rolling out dough. They are Austrian or German in origin, but my mother made free-form egg noodles like this, for which she used the Yiddish word *lokshen*. This recipe is based on my friend Dano's. There are a couple of different ways to form these noodles, the easiest of which is to use a spätzle maker—a metal device that looks either like a grater or a giant garlic press with big holes. You hold the device over the boiling water and push the batter through the holes into the boiling water. My mother used to make her batter a little thicker than I do, and then to form the noodles she would put some of the batter on a cutting board, hold it over a pot, and cut the dough with a sharp knife off the board into the boiling water.

Makes 6 to 8 servings

Kosher salt
1 1/2 cups unbleached all-purpose flour
6 to 7 large eggs
Vegetable oil
Butter, salt, and pepper, for serving

In a large pot, bring about 5 quarts of water with 3 tablespoons of kosher salt to a boil. Using a strong whisk or an electric mixer fitted with a paddle attachment, beat together the flour and 6 eggs until smooth. If you are using a spätzle maker, the mixture should be somewhat loose, slightly thicker than pancake batter. If it is too thick to pour, add another egg and beat until smooth. If you are going to cut the noodles off a board, keep it on the thicker side, more like a paste than batter. Let the batter sit for 30 minutes at room temperature to relax.

Fill a large bowl with ice water and keep it somewhere near the stove. Position a spätzle maker or a colander with large holes over the pot of boiling water and pour about one fourth of the batter through it so that it drips slowly into the boiling water. If necessary, use the back of a wooden spoon to help force the batter through the holes. The drips will form misshapen noodles.

To cut the noodles off a board, spoon a blob of the thicker paste onto a cutting board, toward an edge of the board. Hold the board in one hand over the pot and a knife in the other. Cut the dough into small, thinnish strips and scrape them off the board with the knife into the water. Repeat until you've got a potful of noodles.

Whichever method you use, don't overcrowd the pot. The noodles will sink to the bottom of the pot and float to the top and puff up when they start cooking. Once the water comes back to a boil, cook for 2 minutes. With a slotted spoon or mesh strainer, lift the noodles out of the boiling water, drain, and place into the ice water to stop the cooking. Repeat with the remaining batter.

When all of the noodles are cooked, drain them from the ice water and toss with a little oil to keep them from sticking together. To serve, sauté briefly in butter and season with salt and pepper.

PREP TIME: 15 minutes

COOKING TIME: 15 minutes

TOTAL TIME: 1 hour (includes resting time)

ADVANCE PREP The batter can be made in advance and kept at room temperature for up to 4 hours. The spätzle can be cooked, tossed in oil, and stored in the refrigerator for up to ten days.
LEFTOVERS The cooked noodles will keep in the refrigerator for about ten days. Use them in soups, stews, scrambled eggs, or as a substitute for pasta.

Pasta with Garlic and Olive Oil

There is nothing simpler than this classic Italian pasta preparation, called *pasta aglio e olio*. It's a staple in my house, especially when I get home late and I can't face cooking anything more complicated. Cook the garlic slowly so that it sweetens and to avoid browning it too much, which creates a bitter taste.

Makes 4 servings

1 pound spaghetti or other pasta
5 tablespoons extra-virgin olive oil
2 or 3 garlic cloves, minced
Pinch of crushed red pepper flakes (optional)
Kosher salt and freshly ground black pepper
Freshly grated Parmigiano Reggiano or other hard grating cheese

In a large pot of heavily salted water, cook the pasta until just al dente, about 8 minutes. Reserve about 1 cup of the cooking water and drain the pasta in a colander.

Meanwhile, in a large sauté pan, heat the olive oil over medium heat. Add the garlic and cook, stirring, until the garlic is soft and the aroma has changed from pungent to mild, 3 to 4 minutes. Do not let the garlic brown much at all. If it seems to be sizzling too quickly, lower the heat. Add the red pepper flakes, if using, and cook for another 30 seconds or so. Add the pasta to the pan, along with 3 or 4 tablespoons of the cooking water and some salt and pepper. Toss and let the pasta cook for a couple of minutes so that the garlic flavor permeates the noodles. Add a couple more tablespoons of the cooking liquid, toss, and just cook for another minute or so until the liquid evaporates. Serve with grated cheese on the side.

TOTAL TIME: 15 minutes

LEFTOVERS The pasta will keep for about a week in the refrigerator, but it's best freshly made. Use

USING PASTA COOKING WATER TO FINISH A SAUCE

One of the secrets great cooks forget to tell you that makes all the difference is the common Italian practice of finishing pasta sauces with a little of the pasta cooking water. The pasta cooking water contains salt, which helps flavor the sauce, and starch, which helps bind the sauce to the noodles. If you have also used the cooking water to cook some of the vegetables that will be added to the pasta, the cooking water has even more flavor. Just about every pasta that is finished in a pan—which in Italy is just about every pasta—gets tossed with $1/4$ to $1/2$ cup of pasta cooking water, along with a little olive oil or butter and some cheese. When the pasta is finished cooking, remove about 1 cup of water from the pot before draining the noodles, just to be sure to have enough. Finding the right amount to add to the sauce takes a tiny bit of practice; better to err on the side of adding too little water rather than too much. But when you get it right, you will be amazed how silky smooth your pasta sauces become and how well they cling to the noodles.

leftovers in dishes that call for cooked noodles and that would benefit from the additional umphf of garlic and olive oil, such as the Spaghetti Frittata (page 255).

Pasta with Broccoli Rabe

A classic dish from Sicily, Pasta with Broccoli Rabe is traditionally made with orecchiette ("little ears"), but any small pasta, such as shells, will work fine. I like to cook the broccoli rabe until it is pretty soft because I

find it is less bitter and it behaves more like a sauce. I put it in the water before the pasta and then finish cooking the two of them together.

Makes 4 to 6 servings

> Kosher salt
> 1 large bunch broccoli rabe (about 2 pounds), tough ends trimmed, and chopped into 1-inch pieces
> 1 pound orecchiette or other small pasta
> $1/2$ cup extra-virgin olive oil
> 1 medium white or yellow onion, chopped
> 3 garlic cloves, minced
> 1 small red chile, seeded and minced, or a generous pinch of red pepper flakes
> 3 or 4 anchovy fillets (optional)
> 1 tablespoon chopped flat-leaf parsley
> Freshly grated Pecorino Romano or Parmigiano Reggiano cheese

Bring 6 or 7 quarts of water to a rapid boil with $1/4$ cup kosher salt. Add the broccoli rabe and cook for about 4 minutes. Add the pasta, stir, and cook until the pasta is al dente, about 8 minutes. Reserve about $3/4$ cup of the cooking liquid and then drain the pasta well.

Meanwhile, in a large frying pan, heat $1/4$ cup of the olive oil over medium heat. Add the onion and cook slowly until soft, about 7 minutes. Do not let the onion brown. Add the garlic and cook it slowly, too, without coloring, another minute or two. Add the chile and cook for a minute, then add the anchovies, if using, and cook for 2 or 3 minutes, until they disintegrate. Add the drained pasta and broccoli rabe to the pan along with about $1/2$ cup of the reserved cooking water. Toss the pasta so that it is coated with the oil, and drizzle the remaining $1/4$ cup olive oil over the dish.

Add the parsley and toss again, adding more of the cooking water if necessary to make a light "sauce." Serve in large bowls with plenty of grated Pecorino Romano or Parmigiano Reggiano.

TOTAL TIME: 30 minutes

LEFTOVERS *The pasta with broccoli rabe will keep for about a week in the fridge, though it's best freshly made. Reheat in a nonstick frying pan with a little water or in a microwave. Leftovers can be turned into a Spaghetti Frittata (page 255).*

VARIATION
Pasta with Broccoli Rabe and Sausage
Follow the same technique, but before cooking the onion, fry about 12 ounces hot or sweet Italian sausage meat taken out of the casings. Break the sausage meat into small bits as it cooks. When it is browned, remove from the pan. Proceed with the recipe as directed, without cleaning the pan. Add the cooked sausage back into the pan when you add the cooked pasta and broccoli rabe.

Spaghetti with Tomato Sauce
Just about everyone in this country thinks he or she knows how to make spaghetti with tomato sauce. Most are wrong. You can't just spoon the sauce on top of the noodles and think you are done. In order for the whole dish to come together, the sauce and the noodles have to be heated together. Adding a little butter or olive oil, some pasta cooking water, and some grated cheese turns an ordinary dish of spaghetti with tomato sauce into something sublime.
Makes 4 servings

1 pound thin spaghetti, spaghettini, or other pasta
3 cups tomato sauce of choice (see pages 250 to 252)
3 or 4 tablespoons best-quality extra-virgin olive oil or unsalted butter, at room temperature
2 to 4 ounces freshly grated Parmigiano Reggiano, Grana Padano, Pecorino Romano, or other firm grating cheese

In a large pot of heavily salted water, cook the pasta until just al dente, about 8 minutes. Reserve about 1 cup of the cooking water and drain the pasta in a colander.

Meanwhile, in a large, deep frying pan, heat the tomato sauce over medium heat. Ladle about ½ to ¾ cup of the reserved cooking water into the frying pan with the tomato sauce and stir the sauce to incorporate. Add the pasta to the pan along with the olive oil and toss to coat the noodles evenly with the sauce. Add the cheese and keep tossing until the sauce thickens. If the pasta seems too dry, add a little more of the reserved cooking water. When the sauce starts to sizzle and the pasta is well coated with the sauce, serve.

TOTAL TIME: 15 minutes

LEFTOVERS *Once sauced, the pasta will keep in the fridge for four or five days, but it's never the same as when it is first prepared. I like cold spaghetti for breakfast like the next guy, but I wouldn't serve it to guests. Take it to work for lunch and reheat it in the microwave for 1 ½ minutes on high.*

Pasta with Uncooked Tomato Sauce
In my opinion, this is the only way to serve pasta with tomato sauce in August, when tomatoes are at the peak

of their season. Because the tomatoes and cheese stay chunky, you don't need as much pasta. If you can't find tomatoes that are deep red (or yellow or purple or green) and at their ripest, flip to another recipe for a sauce that calls for canned tomatoes.

Makes 4 servings

3 very ripe medium tomatoes (about 1 pound)
8 ounces fresh mozzarella, cut into small dice
Handful of fresh basil leaves (about 15), sliced into fine shreds
$\frac{1}{4}$ to $\frac{1}{2}$ cup extra-virgin olive oil
1 teaspoon kosher salt
$\frac{1}{2}$ teaspoon freshly ground black pepper
$\frac{1}{2}$ pound dry pasta, such as farfalle (bowties), spaghettini, orecchiette, or shells

Cut the tomatoes crosswise in half. Over a small bowl, hold a half in your hand, cut side facing down, and squeeze gently to remove the seeds. Repeat with the remaining halves. Cut the flesh into small cubes. Place the tomatoes in a serving bowl. Add the mozzarella, basil, $\frac{1}{4}$ cup olive oil, salt, and black pepper, and mix to combine. (If you have the time, let this mixture sit on the counter for a couple of hours so the flavors meld.)

In a large pot of heavily salted water, cook the pasta until just al dente, about 8 minutes. Just when it is ready, remove about $\frac{1}{2}$ cup of the cooking water and then drain the pasta in a colander. Dump the hot pasta into the tomato mixture. Add 2 or 3 tablespoons of the hot cooking water and toss the whole mixture. The hot pasta should melt the mozzarella somewhat. Taste the sauce to adjust the seasoning. If you need more liquid, add more olive oil and/or cooking water, and serve.

PREP TIME: 15 minutes
COOKING TIME: 15 minutes
TOTAL TIME: 30 minutes

ADVANCE PREP *You can prepare the sauce up to 4 hours in advance.*

Quick Tomato Sauce

This fast, chunky tomato pan sauce is delicious on fresh or dried pasta, and even better on Potato Gnocchi (page 267) or Naked Ravioli (page 268). If you start the sauce when you put up the water for your pasta to boil, both will be done at about the same time. I'm usually in a hurry when I make it, so I don't peel the tomatoes, but you can if you prefer a smoother sauce (see page 429). If all you can find are anemic-looking fresh tomatoes, you are better off substituting a can of plum tomatoes, preferably imported from Italy.

Makes 3 cups, enough for 4 servings

$\frac{1}{4}$ cup extra-virgin olive oil
1 small white onion, finely chopped
2 garlic cloves, minced
8 very ripe tomatoes, red or yellow, cored and diced (about 2 pounds), or 1 (28-ounce) can plum tomatoes, diced, with juice
$\frac{1}{3}$ cup dry white wine, tomato juice, or water
1 tablespoon chopped fresh marjoram, oregano, or thyme or a combination, or 1 teaspoon dried
1 bay leaf
Kosher salt and freshly ground black pepper
1 tablespoon chopped flat-leaf parsley

In a large skillet, heat the oil over medium-high heat. Add the onion and cook until translucent, about 5 minutes. Add the garlic and continue

Kitchen Sense

cooking for another couple of minutes, until the garlic softens; do not let it brown. Add the tomatoes and the wine and bring to a simmer. Stir in the marjoram, add the bay leaf, and season with about 1 teaspoon salt and a generous amount of black pepper. Cover the pan, lower the heat, and let the sauce simmer slowly for about 15 minutes, until the tomatoes have melted and the perfume of the herbs is strong. Remove the bay leaf, stir in the parsley, and adjust the seasoning.

TOTAL TIME: 25 minutes

ADVANCE PREP *The tomato sauce can be made a day or two in advance and refrigerated, though the beauty of this type of sauce is that you can make it in a jiffy and it has a just-made, fresh taste.*
LEFTOVERS *The sauce will keep for about a week in the refrigerator. It can also be frozen for up to two months.*

Spaghetti Sauce

This is the tomato sauce I make most often for pasta, lasagna, and other Italian preparations. It's quick, I always have the ingredients on hand, and it has a clean tomato taste. Imported Italian tomatoes produce the best sauce.

Makes 8 to 9 cups, enough for 4 to 6 servings

1/2 cup extra-virgin olive oil
2 medium white or yellow onions, finely chopped
3 garlic cloves, minced
1/2 teaspoon crushed red pepper flakes (optional)
1 to 2 tablespoons assorted chopped fresh herbs, such as oregano, basil, rosemary, thyme, marjoram, or flat-leaf parsley, or 1 teaspoon dried

2 (28-ounce) cans whole tomatoes, cut up with juice, or chopped or crushed tomatoes
Kosher salt and freshly ground black pepper
1 bay leaf

In a large saucepan or frying pan, heat the oil over medium-high heat. Add the onions and cook until soft, about 5 minutes. Add the garlic and continue cooking for another 3 or 4 minutes, until the smell of garlic is strong. Add the red pepper flakes, if using, and the herbs, and cook for 30 seconds more. Add the tomatoes along with 1 teaspoon salt, a generous amount of pepper, and the bay leaf. Bring to a boil, cover, turn down the heat, and simmer for about 20 minutes, until the flavors come together. Remove the bay leaf. You can leave the sauce chunky, or for a smooth sauce, pass the sauce through a food mill or purée it with an immersion blender or in a food processor fitted with a metal chopping blade. Adjust the seasoning before serving.

PREP TIME: 5 to 10 minutes
COOKING TIME: 30 minutes
TOTAL TIME: 35 to 40 minutes

ADVANCE PREP *The sauce can be made several days in advance and refrigerated or frozen for up to three months.*
LEFTOVERS *The sauce will keep in the refrigerator for up to two weeks and in the freezer for up to six months.*

Tomato Sauce with Meat (Red Gravy)

This is a classic Italian-American tomato sauce with meat, the kind they would serve on *The Sopranos*.

It's delicious on spaghetti, in lasagna, on eggplant parmesan. It takes at least 3 hours of gentle simmering to achieve the nice, meaty taste—but it's even better after 4 hours. You can use a variety of meats, depending on your taste preferences and what you have on hand. This recipe is merely a suggestion, but it's a really good one.

This recipe makes a lot of sauce but it freezes beautifully, and once you're going to the trouble, you might as well get a few meals out of it.

Makes 4 quarts, enough for 10 to 12 servings

1/2 cup extra-virgin olive oil

2 large white or yellow onions, chopped

3 large garlic cloves, minced

1 or 2 fresh, dried, or pickled chiles, seeded and minced, or 1/2 teaspoon crushed red pepper flakes, or to taste

1 (6-ounce) can tomato paste

1 (15-ounce) can tomato sauce

1 (28-ounce) can crushed tomatoes

1 (28-ounce) can whole plum tomatoes, cut into chunks

1 pound boneless pork butt or veal shoulder, cut into 1 1/2-inch pieces

2 small bay leaves

1/4 cup chopped fresh oregano, or 2 teaspoons dried oregano

1/4 cup chopped fresh flat-leaf parsley

2 teaspoons finely chopped fresh rosemary

2 tablespoons finely chopped fresh basil

2 teaspoons fresh thyme, or 1 teaspoon dried thyme

Kosher salt and freshly ground black pepper

1 pound Italian sausages, cut into 1 1/2-inch chunks, or Italian sausage meat, sweet or hot, or a combination

1 pound ground beef, pork, or veal

In a large, heavy stockpot, heat the olive oil over high heat. Add the onions and garlic and cook for about 10 minutes, until the onions start to brown very slightly. Do not allow the garlic to burn. Add the chile and cook for another minute or so. Add the tomato paste, and rinse out the can with a full can of water into the pot. Add the tomato sauce, and also add a full can of water. Add the crushed tomatoes and cut-up tomatoes. Add the pork butt, bay leaves, oregano, parsley, rosemary, basil, thyme, 1 tablespoon salt, and 1 teaspoon black pepper. Bring to a boil.

Meanwhile, in a dry nonstick or cast-iron frying pan set over high heat, fry the sausage meat, whether in the casings or not, until nicely browned. Using a slotted spoon, lift the meat out of the fat and put it in the pot with the sauce. Fry the ground meat in the same manner, lifting it out of the fat with a slotted spoon to add it to the sauce. When the sauce starts to boil, lower the heat as low as the burner will go. Set a cover slightly ajar on the pot. Simmer the sauce, stirring occasionally to prevent scorching, for at least 3 hours and up to 4 hours. It will take on a rich, heady flavor. If it gets too thick, add some water and continue simmering. When it is done, the pieces of pork should fall apart when prodded with a fork. Remove the bay leaves. Adjust the seasoning with salt, pepper, and additional herbs to taste.

TOTAL TIME: 4 to 5 hours

ADVANCE PREP *The whole sauce should be made at least a day or two before you intend to serve it and refrigerated because it gets better as it sits. It will keep for about two weeks in the fridge and can be frozen for up to six months. Freeze it in small portions so you can defrost only what you need.*

Vegetarian Red Gravy

Omit all of the meat. Add an extra can or two of water and simmer the sauce for only 1 hour 30 minutes, just until the flavors blend together. It isn't as rich, but it's delicious.

Spaghetti alla Carbonara

Spaghetti alla carbonara is a classic Roman dish made with eggs, cheese, and guanciale, a meaty, cured (not smoked) pork product made from the cheek of a pig. Guanciale is virtually impossible to find in America, so instead I use lean pancetta or country bacon, which are also cured but not smoked. In a pinch, you can use regular breakfast bacon, too. The trick to making carbonara is to heat the sauce just to the point that the eggs become creamy but do not curdle.

Makes 4 servings

Kosher salt

1 pound spaghetti

4 large eggs

$1/4$ cup freshly grated Pecorino Romano cheese

$1/4$ cup freshly grated Parmigiano Reggiano cheese

Freshly grated black pepper

1 tablespoon extra-virgin olive oil

6 ounces lean pancetta, country bacon, or breakfast bacon, cut into $1/2$-inch cubes or strips

2 tablespoons unsalted butter

Bring about 5 quarts of water to a rapid boil with a scant $1/4$ cup salt. Add the spaghetti and cook until al dente, about 8 minutes. Reserve $1/2$ cup of the cooking water and drain the pasta.

Meanwhile, in a large bowl, beat the eggs with 2 tablespoons of the Pecorino, 2 tablespoons of the Parmigiano, $3/4$ teaspoon salt, and a generous amount of black pepper. In a large frying pan, heat the olive oil over medium-high heat. Add the pancetta and fry until the fat renders and the pancetta begins to brown, about 6 minutes. Add the butter and cook until the butter begins to brown, about 2 minutes. Add the pasta and toss to coat with the fat. Remove the pan from the heat. Beat the $1/2$ cup of hot pasta cooking water into the egg mixture and pour this mixture slowly into the pan with the pasta, stirring the noodles constantly to coat with the egg. Toss until the egg begins to thicken and coat the noodles; avoid scrambling the egg. Divide among warm serving bowls and top with the remaining cheese. Serve immediately.

PREP TIME: 5 minutes

COOKING TIME: 15 minutes

TOTAL TIME: 20 minutes

ADVANCE PREP *The pancetta can be fried in advance but the dish needs to be finished and assembled immediately before serving.*

Pasta with Sheep's Milk Cheese and Black Pepper

This simple pasta dish is a staple in Rome, where it's known as *cacio e pepe* ("cheese and pepper"). A real synergy results between the pasta, the cheese, and the pepper, with the pasta cooking water holding everything together.

Makes 4 servings

Kosher salt

1 pound spaghetti or other pasta

¾ cup grated imported Pecorino Romano cheese
(be sure it is made from sheep's milk)

1 tablespoon coarsely ground black pepper

Bring about 5 quarts of water with a scant ¼ cup salt to a boil. Add the pasta and cook until al dente, about 8 minutes. Reserve ½ cup of the pasta cooking water and drain the noodles in a colander.

Meanwhile, combine the Pecorino and pepper and mix well. Place the drained pasta back in the pot. Sprinkle with the cheese and pepper mixture, a pinch of salt, and 3 or 4 tablespoons of the reserved cooking liquid. Toss, adding more pasta water if necessary to form a light sauce with the melted cheese. Serve immediately.

PREP TIME: 2 minutes
COOKING TIME: 10 minutes
TOTAL TIME: 12 minutes

LEFTOVERS *The pasta will keep for about one week in the fridge. Reheat leftovers in a microwave for a minute or two on high.*

Seafood Pasta

One of the best things about cooking seafood is that it cooks quickly. This pasta sauce for spaghetti or linguine takes no longer to cook than the pasta itself; it should be part of every cook's repertoire.

Makes 4 servings

1 pound dried, long, thin pasta, such as
spaghettini, spaghetti, or linguine

¼ cup extra-virgin olive oil

3 garlic cloves, minced

¼ cup unseasoned bread crumbs

2 tablespoons finely chopped flat-leaf
parsley

Finely grated zest and juice of ½ lemon

Kosher salt and freshly ground black pepper

2 pancetta, prosciutto, or bacon slices (about
1 ounce), finely chopped, or 1 additional
tablespoon of extra-virgin olive oil

1 small white or yellow onion, finely
chopped

3 anchovies

2 tablespoons capers, minced

1½ pounds assorted shelled seafood, such as
cleaned shrimp, scallops, or squid

½ cup dry white wine or dry white
vermouth

1 or 2 tablespoons unsalted butter or additional
extra-virgin olive oil

In a large pot of heavily salted water, cook the pasta until al dente, about 8 minutes.

While the pasta is cooking, prepare the sauce. In a large frying pan, heat 2 tablespoons of the olive oil over medium-high heat. Add about one third of the garlic and cook for a minute or two, until soft. Add the bread crumbs, stir to coat with the oil, and cook until the crumbs are lightly toasted. Be careful not to let them burn. Stir in 1½ tablespoons of the chopped parsley and the lemon zest. Season with salt and pepper. Transfer to a small bowl and set aside.

Return the pan to the heat and add the remaining 2 tablespoons oil and the pancetta. Cook until the fat has rendered from the meat, about 2 minutes. Add the onion and cook until translucent, about 5 minutes. Add the remaining garlic and cook for another minute. Add the anchovies and capers, and cook, mashing the anchovies with your spoon until they dissolve, about 2 minutes. Add the seafood, sauté for a minute or two, then pour in the wine and lemon juice and bring to a simmer. Cook just until the seafood turns opaque, 4 or 5 minutes.

Add a ladleful of the pasta cooking water ($\frac{1}{2}$ cup or so) to the pan. Drain the cooked pasta and transfer it to the frying pan along with the butter and the remaining $\frac{1}{2}$ tablespoon parsley. Toss to coat the noodles with the sauce. Simmer for a minute or two, until the sauce thickens and adheres to the pasta. Adjust the seasoning with salt and pepper. Transfer to serving bowls and sprinkle with the toasted bread crumb mixture.

TOTAL TIME: 30 minutes

LEFTOVERS *The pasta will keep for about four days, but the seafood inevitably gets overcooked when it's reheated.*

VARIATIONS
Pasta with Clams
To prepare pasta with clam sauce, follow the recipe up until the point that you add the seafood. Add about $1\frac{1}{4}$ pounds of scrubbed clams, along with the wine and lemon juice, and cover the pan. Simmer for 3 or 4 minutes, just until the clams open. Discard any that didn't. Add the pasta cooking water, pasta, and other ingredients as directed.

Pasta with Sardine Cream Sauce
Substitute 1 (6.5-ounce) can skinless and boneless sardines packed in olive oil, drained well, for the anchovies and omit the seafood. Instead of

the pasta cooking water, add $\frac{1}{2}$ cup heavy cream and bring to a simmer before adding the pasta. As with anchovies, much of the sardines' sharp, fishy taste dissipates as they cook.

Spaghetti Frittata
Though it sounds funny to American ears, a frittata (or omelet) is a traditional use for leftover pasta in Italy. I've added Italian sausage and spinach to this recipe to make a complete, satisfying entrée for lunch or dinner. Although most American frittata recipes call for finishing the omelet in the oven, the traditional technique of flipping the omelet onto a plate and then sliding it back into the pan produces better results.

Makes 4 servings

> $\frac{1}{2}$ cup extra-virgin olive oil, plus extra for greasing the plate
> 8 ounces hot or sweet Italian sausage (about 2 links), removed from the casings
> 1 medium yellow or white onion, finely chopped
> 1 garlic clove, minced
> 6 ounces fresh spinach, roughly chopped, or $\frac{1}{2}$ (10 ounce) package frozen spinach, defrosted and drained
> $1\frac{1}{2}$ teaspoons kosher salt
> Freshly ground black pepper
> 2 tablespoons dry white wine, vegetable stock, or water
> 7 large eggs
> About 3 cups leftover cooked spaghetti or other pasta, or 8 ounces dried pasta, cooked
> $\frac{1}{4}$ cup grated Parmigiano Reggiano or other hard Italian grating cheese

In a medium (8-inch) nonstick or well-seasoned frying pan, heat 1 tablespoon of the olive oil over medium-high heat. Add the sausage and cook, breaking up the meat as it cooks, until browned, about 5 minutes. Remove the meat to a medium bowl and set aside. Add 2 more tablespoons of the olive oil to the pan and heat. Add the onion and sauté for a couple of minutes until soft. Add the garlic and keep sautéing until the onion begins to color ever so slightly, about 7 minutes total. Add the spinach, 1/2 teaspoon of the salt, and some pepper and cook until the spinach is completely wilted, about 2 minutes. Add the wine, and using a wooden spoon, scrape off any browned bits that have stuck to the bottom of the pan. Add this mixture to the bowl with the sausage and let cool. Wipe out the pan with paper towels.

In a large bowl, beat the eggs until frothy. Add the sausage and spinach mixture and mix well. Season with the remaining teaspoon kosher salt and some more freshly ground pepper. Add the pasta and cheese and mix well with a large fork. (If you have the time, let this mixture sit for 30 minutes to an hour at room temperature.)

Lightly grease a large flat plate or pot lid, without a lip, with olive oil. Heat the same frying pan you were using over medium-high heat. Add the remaining 5 tablespoons olive oil and heat until the oil is hot. Pour the egg mixture into the pan all at once and pat it down with a large wooden spoon or heatproof rubber spatula into an even layer. As the omelet cooks and bubbles up on the side, use the spoon to draw the egg mixture from the edges of the pan into the center, patting the omelet back down into an even layer each time. Continue doing this until the omelet has almost solidified into a solid mass, 6 or 7 minutes. Let sit and cook for another minute without disturbing it. The eggs should be firmly set.

Place the greased large plate over the pan, and using oven mitts, invert the pan onto the plate so the omelet falls out of it. If anything sticks to the bottom of the pan, scrape it off and patch it on top of the omelet. Slide the omelet off the plate and back into the pan, cooked side up. Cook for 3 or 4 minutes, until browned on the bottom. Slide onto a large plate and serve hot or at room temperature.

PREP TIME: 10 minutes
COOKING TIME: 30 minutes
TOTAL TIME: 40 minutes

ADVANCE PREP *The omelet can be made several hours in advance and served at room temperature.*
LEFTOVERS *The omelet will keep for about a week in the fridge. Leftovers are delicious cold and make a nice sandwich filling.*

Pastitsio

This Greek noodle and meat "pie" is a cross between Shepherd's Pie (page 387) and baked ziti. It's up there in the "ultimate comfort food" category, which I think explains why it's pretty much a staple on Greek diner menus across the United States. I prefer a 50-50 combination of beef and lamb for the meat, but just about any ground meat will work. The spicing of the meat in this recipe is particularly nice, with the subtle sweet flavor of cinnamon, cumin, and cloves. It's a great dish to feed a crowd.

Makes 8 servings

> Olive oil or unsalted butter, for greasing the baking dish
> 1 pound long tubular pasta, such as ziti, penne, or macaroni
> 6 tablespoons extra-virgin olive oil

Kosher salt and freshly ground black pepper

12 ounces ground beef

12 ounces ground lamb or additional
  ground beef

1 large yellow or white onion, chopped

2 garlic cloves, minced

3 long Italian cooking peppers, seeded and
  chopped

2 tablespoons tomato paste

1 cup dry white wine

$\frac{1}{4}$ cup finely chopped fresh flat-leaf
  parsley

$\frac{1}{4}$ teaspoon ground cinnamon

$\frac{1}{4}$ teaspoon ground cumin

Pinch of ground cloves

5 tablespoons unsalted butter

5 tablespoons all-purpose flour

3 cups milk

$\frac{1}{4}$ teaspoon freshly grated nutmeg

$\frac{3}{4}$ cup grated Parmigiano Reggiano cheese
  (about 3 ounces)

Preheat the oven to 375°F. Grease a deep $2\frac{1}{2}$- to 3-quart baking dish with olive oil or butter. In a large pot of boiling, heavily salted water, cook the pasta until just al dente, 7 or 8 minutes. Drain. Toss the pasta with about 2 tablespoons of the olive oil, a pinch of salt, and some freshly ground black pepper. Set aside to cool.

In a large frying pan, heat 1 tablespoon of the olive oil over medium-high heat. Add the ground beef and lamb and cook, breaking the meat up with a wooden spoon, until it is browned and crumbly, about 8 minutes. Drain the meat and set aside. Pour the remaining 3 tablespoons olive oil into the pan. Add the onion and cook for 3 or 4 minutes, until softened. Add the garlic and peppers and continue

cooking for another 3 or 4 minutes, until the peppers are soft. Add the meat back to the pan along with the tomato paste, white wine, about 2 teaspoons salt, some freshly ground pepper, the parsley, cinnamon, cumin, and cloves and cook for another couple of minutes until the wine evaporates. Adjust the seasoning with additional salt and pepper if necessary. Remove from the heat.

Heat the butter in a medium saucepan over medium-high heat. Add the flour and stir to blend into a paste (a roux). Cook for 2 or 3 minutes, until the aroma of toasted flour wafts up from the pan. Whisk in the milk to form a smooth sauce. Bring the sauce to a simmer and cook, stirring, for about 7 minutes, until it thickens and there's no taste of raw flour. Add about $1\frac{1}{2}$ teaspoons salt, some freshly ground black pepper, and the nutmeg. Remove from the heat and set aside to cool for a few minutes.

Toss the pasta with about $\frac{1}{4}$ cup of the grated cheese. Arrange half of the noodles in an even layer on the bottom of the greased baking dish. Spoon the meat mixture in an even layer on top of the noodles. Top the meat with another $\frac{1}{4}$ cup or so of cheese, and then arrange the remaining noodles on top of that. Finally, pour the white sauce over the noodles, making sure the sauce penetrates down through the noodles. Sprinkle the top evenly with the remaining $\frac{1}{4}$ cup cheese. Bake for 35 to 40 minutes, until the pastitsio is bubbly and browned. Remove from the oven and let cool for about 10 minutes before serving.

PREP TIME: 10 minutes

COOKING TIME: 1 hour

TOTAL TIME: 1 hour 10 minutes (plus cooling time)

ADVANCE PREP The whole pastitsio can be assembled, covered, and refrigerated up to a day before baking.
LEFTOVERS The pastitsio will keep for about one week in the refrigerator. Heat leftovers in the oven, in a frying pan, or in a microwave, until warmed through.

Baked Macaroni and Cheese with Tomatoes

When I wrote my first cookbook about ten years ago, *Cook Something*, my family's "cheese thing"—a baked macaroni and cheese dish with tomatoes that never had a real name—became a metaphor for my easy, casual but delicious approach to home cooking. I'm including the recipe again in this book for two reasons. The first is that my sister Carrie pointed out that I made a small mistake in the ingredients list by calling for twice as much butter as the original recipe called for. Now, my mother was an excellent cook of the school "if some butter is good, twice as much butter is twice as good." And she was also known to lie sometimes about just how much butter she put into things. So even though I was pretty sure that I used to see her use a whole stick of butter in her Cheese Thing, I thought I would right the public record and republish the recipe with the original proportions, or at least the proportions Carrie remembers. The second reason I'm including the recipe in this book is that it is still one of my favorite foods to eat—with or without the extra butter.

Note that the recipe calls for two types of Cheddar—mild and extra-sharp, because combining the two produces the best texture and cheesy flavor. Of course, in a pinch you can use all of one or the other or something in the middle. Also, don't be tempted to shred the cheese instead of cube it. The

cubes leave big globs of melted cheese that are preferable.

Makes 4 main-course servings or 8 side-dish servings

1 pound penne rigate, ziti, or rigatoni
4 tablespoons ($^1/_2$ stick) unsalted butter
8 ounces extra-sharp Cheddar cheese, cut into $^1/_2$-inch cubes
8 ounces mild Cheddar cheese, cut into $^1/_2$-inch cubes
1 (28-ounce) can whole peeled plum tomatoes, cut into chunks, with juice
2 tablespoons sugar
1 teaspoon kosher salt
Freshly ground black pepper

Preheat the oven to 375°F.

Cook the penne in at least 5 quarts of heavily salted boiling water until al dente, about 9 minutes. Drain. Return the hot pasta to the pot. Add the butter and stir to melt. Add the two types of Cheddar, the tomatoes and their juice, the sugar, salt, and pepper to taste, and stir to combine.

Transfer to a 2-quart baking dish. Bake for 50 minutes to 1 hour, until the sauce is bubbly and the noodles that are sticking out of the top have turned dark brown and crisp.

PREP TIME: 5 minutes
COOKING TIME: 1 hour
TOTAL TIME: 1 hour 5 minutes

ADVANCE PREP This dish is best if it is made and allowed to sit for several hours before baking. It can stay covered in the refrigerator for up to two days. You can also freeze it for up to a month before baking. There is no need to defrost it; simply increase the cooking time by 20 to 30 minutes.

The Ultimate Macaroni and Cheese

The name says it all. I've concocted many recipes for this artery-clogging classic and this one is, in my humble opinion, by far the best. The idea to use cream cheese came from a conversation with my friend Emily, and it's an idea for which I will be eternally grateful. The cream cheese adds a rich, cheesy background flavor that holds the whole thing together. I have used Italian mascarpone or fresh goat cheese instead of the cream cheese and the results have been equally delicious. On the occasions that I'm afraid there aren't enough calories from fat in a meal of macaroni and cheese, I serve it with Buttermilk Fried Onions (page 193) or crumbled bacon (see page 126) on top, or both.

Makes 6 to 8 servings

    5 tablespoons unsalted butter
    ¼ cup unseasoned bread crumbs
    1 cup freshly grated Parmigiano Reggiano, Grana
        Padano, or other strongly flavored hard
        grating cheese (3 or 4 ounces)
    1 pound curly pasta, such as elbow macaroni,
        cavatappi (corkscrews), or fusilli
    3 tablespoons all-purpose flour
    2 cups milk
    2 teaspoons Dijon mustard or ½ teaspoon dry
        mustard
    ½ teaspoon Worcestershire sauce
    Pinch of cayenne pepper
    Pinch of freshly ground white pepper
    ½ teaspoon kosher salt
    8 ounces cream cheese, mascarpone, or fresh
        goat cheese
    8 ounces extra-sharp Cheddar cheese, shredded
        (2 cups)
    8 ounces extra-aged Gouda, Emmantaler, or
        Appenzeller, shredded (2 cups)

Preheat the oven to 400° F. Using 1 tablespoon of the butter, grease a 2-quart baking dish. Place 2 tablespoons of the bread crumbs in the buttered dish and shake it around to evenly coat. Leave any excess bread crumbs in the bottom of the baking dish. Combine the remaining 2 tablespoons of bread crumbs with 2 tablespoons of the Parmigiano and set aside.

In a very large pot, cook the pasta in about 5 quarts boiling salted water until al dente, about 9 minutes. Drain.

Meanwhile, make the sauce. In a medium saucepan over medium-high heat, melt 3 tablespoons of the butter. Add the flour and stir with a wooden spoon to make a paste (called a roux). Cook the roux for a minute or two, stirring often, until it is very lightly browned and you can smell the nutty aroma of toasted flour. Switch to a whisk. Whisk in the milk and continue whisking until the mixture comes to a boil and thickens, about 4 minutes. Turn down the heat to low. Whisk in the mustard, Worcestershire sauce, cayenne, pepper, and salt. Add the cream cheese and stir until thoroughly melted.

Place the pasta back in the pot it was cooked in. Add the Cheddar, Gouda, and remaining Parmigiano. Pour the hot cream sauce on top. Stir the mixture until all the cheese is melted and the sauce is well combined with the noodles. (If you are in a hurry to eat, you can actually serve the macaroni and cheese at this point, but I prefer it baked.) Transfer this mixture to the prepared baking dish. Sprinkle the bread crumb and Parmigiano mixture evenly over the top. Dot with the remaining tablespoon of butter. Bake for about 40 minutes, until the top is nicely browned, the bread crumbs are toasted, and the sauce is bubbling.

PREP TIME: 5 minutes
COOKING TIME: 50 minutes
TOTAL TIME: 1 hour

ADVANCE PREP *The macaroni and cheese can be made in advance. Before topping with the bread crumb mixture, cool the mac 'n' cheese to room temperature in the baking dish, cover with plastic wrap, and refrigerate for a day or two. Proceed with the recipe, adding an additional 10 minutes or so to the baking time. You can also freeze the macaroni and cheese for up to a month. Defrost it overnight in the refrigerator before baking.*

LEFTOVERS *The macaroni and cheese will keep for up to two weeks in the refrigerator. You can also freeze it for up to two months. Defrost before reheating. Reheat leftovers in the microwave for a minute or two on high, or in a 300°F oven for 20 minutes or so, until heated through.*

Although it seems like it should be illegal, in a restaurant in New York I recently encountered another thing to do with leftover macaroni and cheese: deep-fry it. The restaurant cut chilled macaroni and cheese into chunks, dipped the chunks in beaten egg, rolled them in bread crumbs, and deep-fried them until golden brown.

Lasagna

Here's a recipe for a classic lasagna that calls for both a cream sauce (béchamel) and a tomato sauce. I use the cream sauce to lighten the texture of the ricotta. You could also add sautéed mushrooms, onions, or spinach, for example. Use this recipe as a starting point.

Makes 6 to 8 servings

> Kosher salt
> 10 ounces fresh lasagna noodles or 8 ounces dried lasagna noodles
> 1 1/2 cups Cream Sauce (page 404), at room temperature
> 1 pound fresh ricotta
> 1 large egg
> 1/4 cup finely chopped fresh flat-leaf parsley
> Freshly ground black pepper
> 3/4 cup freshly grated Parmigiano Reggiano cheese (about 3 ounces)
> 2 to 3 cups homemade tomato sauce (choose one from pages 250 to 252), or jarred sauce
> 8 ounces fresh mozzarella, grated (1 1/2 cups)

In a large, wide pot, bring 6 quarts of water with 1/4 cup kosher salt to a boil. Add the noodles. If using fresh pasta, boil the noodles for just under 2 minutes, if using dried pasta, cook the noodles until al dente, about 8 minutes. Drain the noodles in a colander and rinse with cold running water to stop the cooking. Separate any noodles that may have stuck together.

Preheat the oven to 375°F. In a bowl, combine the Cream Sauce with the ricotta, egg, parsley, salt and pepper to taste, and all but 3 tablespoons of the grated Parmigiano, and mix well.

In a deep, 2-quart baking dish, place a couple of spoonfuls of the tomato sauce. Arrange a layer of noodles, slightly overlapping, on the bottom of the dish with the noodles all going in one direction. Cover the noodles with a thin layer of tomato sauce. Then spread about one quarter of the ricotta mixture in a thin layer over the sauce. Sprinkle with some freshly ground pepper. Arrange another layer of noodles perpendicular to the first. (This will make the lasagna more stable when you go to slice it.) Repeat with the tomato sauce, ricotta mixture, and pepper. Continue layering, alternating the direction of the noodles, until you have reached the top of the dish, ending with a layer of noodles. I usually get four layers. Spread a final layer of tomato sauce on top of the noodles. Sprinkle the grated mozzarella evenly over the top along with the remaining 3 tablespoons grated Parmigiano.

Bake for about 40 minutes, or until the lasagna is bubbly and the cheese on top has browned nicely. To test if the lasagna is done, insert a knife in the center and hold it there for a few seconds. Remove it and feel the blade on the back of your hand. If it is very hot, it is good to go. If it is warm or cool, it needs more time. Remove from the oven and let sit at room temperature for 10 minutes or so to settle before slicing and serving.

PREP TIME: 15 minutes
COOKING TIME: 50 minutes
TOTAL TIME: 1 hour 5 minutes (plus resting time)

ADVANCE PREP *The sauces can be prepared several days in advance and refrigerated for up to a week or frozen for several months. The lasagna can be assembled and refrigerated up to two days in advance or frozen for about one month (provided you didn't freeze the other ingredients first). Bake it directly from the freezer, increasing the cooking time to 1 hour or more. If the cheese on top starts to brown too much before the center is warmed, cover the lasagna with aluminum foil, lower the temperature to 350° F, and return to the oven.*

LEFTOVERS *The lasagna will keep for about ten days in the fridge. You can reheat the leftovers in the oven, in a frying pan, or in a microwave. Add a few spoonfuls of tomato sauce to keep the lasagna moist while it reheats.*

VARIATIONS
Vegetable Lasagna
You can layer cooked vegetables in the lasagna for a little variety. For instance, sauté some onions, garlic, and lots of mushrooms and layer them along with the noodles and cheese. Add cooked spinach, wrung out until really dry and then finely chopped, to the ricotta. You can also sneak in thin slices of grilled or fried eggplant or zucchini. The only thing to be careful of is to not add anything that has too much moisture and that will make the lasagna wet.

Chicken and Artichoke Lasagna
This is an especially delicious lasagna that's more in the French tradition than the Italian. There's no tomato sauce, only white sauce. Cook the noodles as directed. Combine 3 cups thin white sauce or béchamel, 1/4 cup chopped parsley, and finely grated zest of 1 lemon. Adjust the seasoning with salt and pepper. In a buttered baking dish, place a couple of spoonfuls of the white sauce mixture and spread evenly over the bottom. Arrange a layer of noodles, then spoon on about one fourth of the white sauce mixture and scatter 2/3 cup cubed cooked chicken and 1/3 cup thinly sliced Marinated Artichoke Hearts (page 7). Sprinkle on 1/3 cup shredded Gruyère and 1 tablespoon grated Parmigiano over that.

Repeat layers two more times, ending with a layer of noodles. Top the noodles with the last bit of the white sauce mixture, and sprinkle with the additional Gruyère and Parmigiano. Bake the lasagna for about 40 minutes, as directed.

Fresh Tuna Casserole

If down-home macaroni and cheese can cross over to the realm of gourmet comfort food, why not tuna casserole? To elevate the dish, I use fresh tuna (although you can of course substitute canned) and imported Gruyère. The results are delicious.

Makes 6 to 8 servings

6 tablespoons (¾ stick) unsalted butter, plus extra for greasing the baking dish

8 ounces dry broad egg noodles, elbow macaroni, or other noodles

1 ounce bacon or ham, finely chopped (optional)

1 medium white or yellow onion, finely chopped

12 ounces fresh tuna steak, cut into ½-inch cubes or 2 (6½-ounce) cans tuna packed in oil, drained well and flaked

4 ounces white mushrooms, thinly sliced

½ cup fresh or defrosted frozen peas

2 tablespoons minced flat-leaf parsley

Kosher salt and freshly ground black pepper

3 tablespoons all-purpose flour

2 cups milk

½ teaspoon dry mustard

½ teaspoon Worcestershire sauce

1 cup shredded imported Gruyère (about 4 ounces)

1 tablespoon bread crumbs

1 tablespoon freshly grated Parmigiano Reggiano cheese

¼ teaspoon paprika

Preheat the oven to 375°F. Butter a 2-quart baking dish or casserole.

Cook the egg noodles in a large pot of heavily salted, boiling water until al dente, about 8 minutes. Drain.

Meanwhile, in a large frying pan over medium-high heat, melt 3 tablespoons of the butter. Add the bacon, if using, and fry until the fat is rendered, about 4 minutes. Add the onion and cook until soft, about 5 minutes. If using fresh tuna, add the cubes to the onion and cook, stirring, just until the flesh turns opaque, about 4 minutes. Add the mushrooms and cook until they are soft and have given up their water, about 5 more minutes. Add the peas and cook until heated through, a minute or two. Stir in the parsley and season with about 1 teaspoon kosher salt and plenty of freshly ground black pepper. Set aside.

In a medium saucepan over medium-high heat, melt the remaining 3 tablespoons of butter. Add the flour and stir to form a smooth paste (a roux). Cook this mixture for 2 minutes or so, until it gives off the nutty aroma of toasted flour. Whisk in the milk to form a smooth cream sauce (or béchamel). Stir in the mustard and Worcestershire. Bring to a simmer, turn down the heat, and cook for 7 or 8 minutes, until the sauce has thickened and there is no floury taste. Season with about 1 teaspoon salt and pepper.

In a large bowl, combine the white sauce with the sautéed mushroom and tuna mixture or canned tuna, the pasta, and Gruyère. Adjust the seasoning with salt and pepper. Transfer this mixture to the prepared baking dish.

In a small bowl, combine the bread crumbs, Parmigiano Reggiano, and paprika until blended. Sprinkle this mixture over the top of the casserole. Bake until the casserole is bubbling and the top has browned, about 30 minutes.

PREP TIME: 15 minutes
COOKING TIME: 1 hour
TOTAL TIME: 1 hour 15 minutes

ADVANCE PREP The casserole can be assembled up to two days in advance, covered, refrigerated, and baked just before serving. If baking it directly from the fridge, add about 10 minutes to the cooking time.
LEFTOVERS The tuna casserole will keep for about a week in the refrigerator. Reheat leftovers in a 325° F oven, in a nonstick frying pan, or in the microwave.

VARIATION
Chicken Casserole
Substitute 12 ounces cooked chicken, skin removed, cubed, for the cooked tuna and proceed with the recipe as directed.

Curried Rice Noodles with Peanuts
This is a quick, satisfying noodle dish with Southeast Asian flavors. Have all of the ingredients measured and ready when you start, and in minutes you'll have a delicious lunch or dinner.
Makes 2 servings

8 ounces dried rice noodles (rice "sticks"), size M (about ¼ inch wide)

3 tablespoons peanut or vegetable oil
2 garlic cloves, minced
2 tablespoons minced fresh ginger
½ teaspoon curry powder
½ teaspoon cayenne pepper, or to taste
2 tablespoons salted peanuts, ground or very finely chopped
1 tablespoon Asian fish sauce, such as Thai *nam pla* or Vietnamese *nuoc nam*
1 cup fresh bean sprouts or shredded napa cabbage
Juice of ½ lime (about 1½ tablespoons)
3 scallions, white and green parts, chopped
Handful of fresh cilantro leaves

Place the rice noodles in a large bowl and cover with hot tap water. Let soak for 20 to 30 minutes to soften.

Heat a large frying pan or wok over high heat. Add the oil and when it is hot, add the garlic and ginger. Stir for 30 seconds. Add the curry powder, cayenne, and peanuts, and stir for 30 seconds or a minute, until you smell the aroma of toasted spices. Don't let them burn. Lift the soaked rice noodles out of the water into the wok or frying pan—they should be quite wet. With a large spoon or tongs, toss and stir the noodles as they fry. They will soften and start to clump, but keep breaking them up, and swirling them around, to cook evenly.

After about 5 minutes, the noodles should be almost soft enough to eat. Add the fish sauce and cook for a minute more. Add the bean sprouts and lime juice and keep cooking for a minute or two, until the bean sprouts have wilted. If the noodles are still too al dente, add a few tablespoons of water and cook for another minute. Transfer the noodles to serving bowls or plates and sprinkle with the scallions and cilantro.

PREP TIME: 10 minutes

COOKING TIME: 10 minutes

TOTAL TIME: 40 minutes (includes soaking time)

ADVANCE PREP *The noodles can be soaked in advance and kept in the water for several hours at room temperature or up to a day in the refrigerator.* **LEFTOVERS** *The noodles will keep for a week or so in the fridge. Reheat them in the microwave for a minute on high.*

VARIATION
Curried Rice Noodles with Beef, Chicken, or Shrimp

To make a heartier dish, you can easily add 8 ounces sirloin or top round thinly sliced against the grain, boneless and skinless chicken breast sliced on the bias, or peeled raw shrimp. Before you begin the recipe as directed above, heat the wok over high heat and add 2 tablespoons of peanut or vegetable oil. Fry the beef, chicken, or shrimp for 2 minutes or until just barely cooked through. Toss with a teaspoon or so of fish sauce and a squirt of lime juice, cook for another minute, and transfer to a plate. Proceed with the recipe, and at the point that you add the tablespoon of fish sauce, return the cooked beef, chicken, or shrimp to the pan. Finish the recipe as directed.

Rice Noodle Bowl with Ginger and Watercress

Here's an easy, satisfying soup with clean Asian flavors. The only unusual thing is the addition of a touch of baking soda, which is a Chinese technique that causes the watercress to take on a silken texture. Experiment with other related flavorings, such as Asian toasted sesame oil, fresh cilantro, or chili sauce. You can also add julienned carrot, daikon, cucumber, or napa cabbage. Makes 4 servings

8 ounces dried rice noodles (rice "sticks"), size M (about 1/4 inch wide)

2 quarts chicken stock

One 2-inch piece fresh ginger, peeled and cut into thick slices

2 garlic cloves, smashed

1 small piece white or yellow onion

1 tablespoon light soy sauce

Scant 1/4 teaspoon baking soda

2 bunches (about 8 ounces) watercress, tough stems removed

1 teaspoon sugar (optional)

Kosher salt

2 scallions, white and green parts, chopped

Place the dried noodles in a wide bowl and cover with warm water. Let soak for at least 20 minutes to soften.

In a large pot, combine the chicken stock, ginger, garlic, and onion. Bring to a boil, turn down the heat, and simmer for about 15 minutes. Strain the soup into a clean pot and bring back to a boil. Add the soy sauce and baking soda and stir. Add the watercress and cook until it wilts, about 2 minutes. Drain the noodles, add them to the pot, and cook for a minute or two, until they become soft and supple. Taste the stock and adjust the seasoning with the sugar, if you find the ginger taste bitter, and a pinch of salt. Divide among four large bowls and sprinkle with the scallions.

PREP TIME: 10 minutes

COOKING TIME: 10 minutes

TOTAL TIME: 40 minutes (includes soaking time)

Fraud Thai

Here's a recipe for a quick, inauthentic pad Thai that's easy to make at home and that provides an excellent approximation of Thailand's national dish. I use ketchup to simulate tamarind, and I throw in soybeans to avoid having to deep-fry tofu. You can vary the ingredients based on what you've got on hand.

Makes 4 servings

8 ounces rice noodles (rice "sticks"), size M (about 1/4 inch wide), or 6 ounces thin rice threads

1 large egg

3 tablespoons plus 1 teaspoon Asian fish sauce, such as Thai *nam pla* or Vietnamese *nuoc nam*

2 tablespoons soy sauce

2 tablespoons ketchup

1 tablespoon hoisin

1 tablespoon rice, cider, or white vinegar

2 teaspoons garlic chili sauce or other hot sauce

1/3 cup chicken or vegetable stock or water

3 tablespoons peanut or vegetable oil

1/2 small white onion, thinly sliced

2 garlic cloves, minced

2 tablespoons minced fresh ginger

1 (6-ounce) skinless and boneless chicken breast, cut crosswise on the bias into thin strips

8 ounces peeled medium shrimp

1/4 cup frozen shelled edamame (soybeans)

1/2 cup bean sprouts

2 or 3 scallions, white and green parts, chopped

2 tablespoons dry-roasted, salted peanuts, toasted (page 10) and chopped

1 lime, cut into wedges

Place the rice noodles in a large bowl or container and cover with hot tap water. Let sit for at least 20 minutes to soften.

In a small bowl, beat the egg with 1 teaspoon of the fish sauce and set aside. In another small bowl, mix the remaining 3 tablespoons fish sauce, the soy sauce, ketchup, hoisin, vinegar, chili sauce, and stock. Set aside.

Heat a well-seasoned large cast-iron frying pan or wok over very high heat. Add 1 tablespoon of the oil, and when it is very hot, pour in the egg. Cook the egg, stirring, to make a thin omelet, about 2 minutes. Remove the egg to a cutting board and let cool. Roll up the omelet and thinly slice it into strips, like fine noodles. Set aside.

Return the wok or cast-iron pan to the heat. Add the remaining 2 tablespoons oil and heat until almost smoking. Add the onion and cook until soft, about 2 minutes. Add the garlic and ginger and cook for another minute or so, until fragrant. Add the chicken and cook, stirring constantly, until the chicken has turned opaque and begun to brown, about 5 minutes. Add the shrimp and soybeans, and cook, tossing, until the shrimp have curled, turned opaque white, and are cooked through, about 4 minutes. Remove everything to a plate and set aside.

Return the pan to the heat. Add the soy sauce mixture and heat for a minute. Lift the noodles out of their soaking water, and while still wet, add them to the pan. Cook, stirring and tossing, until the noodles soften and are evenly coated with the sauce. If you need more liquid, add a little more stock or water. Once the noodles have softened up, about 5 minutes, return the chicken and shrimp mixture to the pan along with the egg. When the ingredients are all heated through, remove the noodles to a serving platter. Sprinkle with the bean sprouts, scallions, and peanuts, and serve with wedges of lime on the side.

PREP TIME: 15 minutes
COOKING TIME: 25 minutes
TOTAL TIME: 1 hour (includes soaking time)

ADVANCE PREP The noodles can be soaked up to a day in advance. Keep them in their water at room temperature or in the refrigerator for up to 12 hours. After that, drain and refrigerate until needed. You can prepare the egg and the chicken and shrimp mixture several hours in advance.
LEFTOVERS The noodles will keep for about a week in the refrigerator. Reheat leftovers in the microwave for a minute or two on high.

Yakisoba

Almost everywhere you go in Japan you can find some version of yakisoba, or fried noodles, for sale on the street. Here is my version of this dish, redolent of garlic and fresh ginger, which may be inauthentic but is nevertheless delicious. Before you gasp at the addition of ketchup and Worcestershire, however, rest assured that these are authentic (and beloved) Japanese ingredients.
Makes 4 to 6 servings

12 ounces fresh or dried Chinese ramen or
   lo mein noodles or Italian spaghetti

1 tablespoon Asian toasted sesame oil
¼ cup oyster sauce
¼ cup dashi or chicken or vegetable stock
3 tablespoons mirin or dry sherry
1 tablespoon ketchup
1 tablespoon Worcestershire sauce
1 tablespoon soy sauce
½ teaspoon chili oil or hot sauce, or to taste
   (optional)
3 tablespoons peanut or vegetable oil
1 medium white onion, thinly sliced
2 large garlic cloves, minced
2 tablespoons finely minced fresh ginger
2½ cups thinly sliced green or Chinese (napa)
   cabbage
1 medium carrot, shredded
1 red bell pepper, cored, seeded, and thinly sliced
8 ounces skinless and boneless chicken breast,
   thinly sliced, or 8 ounces peeled and deveined
   shrimp, or a combination
2 scallions, white and green parts, chopped

Bring a large pot of heavily salted water to a boil. Cook the noodles until just slightly past al dente, 2½ minutes for fresh noodles, about 9 minutes for dried. Drain. While still warm, toss the noodles with the sesame oil to coat. Set aside.

Meanwhile, in a small bowl, blend the oyster sauce, dashi, mirin, ketchup, Worcestershire, soy sauce, and chili oil, if using. Set aside.

Heat a large wok or frying pan over high heat. Add 1½ tablespoons of the peanut oil and when it is really hot, add the onion. Cook, stirring and tossing frequently, for 2 or 3 minutes, until the onion is soft. Add the garlic and ginger and cook for another 2 minutes or so, until the aromas are strong. Add the cabbage, carrot, and bell pepper, and cook just until the vegetables have wilted, about 2 minutes. Remove the vegetables to a plate and return the pan to the heat. Add the remaining $1\frac{1}{2}$ tablespoons peanut oil and let it get very hot. (Don't worry about any bits browning on the bottom of the pan; they will add flavor.) Add the chicken and cook, tossing frequently, for 3 or 4 minutes, until the flesh turns opaque. Return the vegetables to the pan along with the noodles and sauce. Continue cooking until the noodles absorb and are evenly coated with the sauce and are shiny, 3 or 4 minutes more. Serve garnished with scallions.

PREP TIME: 10 minutes
COOKING TIME: 20 minutes
TOTAL TIME: 30 minutes

ADVANCE PREP *The noodles can be cooked up to a day in advance and refrigerated until ready to proceed.*
LEFTOVERS *The yakisoba will keep for about a week in the fridge. It can be reheated with additional oil in a frying pan or in a microwave for a few minutes on high.*

Potato Gnocchi

Lying somewhere between pasta and dumplings, potato gnocchi (pronounced NYO-kee) are a good transition to take this chapter into dumplings. Every Italian cook has a secret when it comes to making gnocchi light. Some say not to add flour. Others say not to add eggs.

To my taste, the best gnocchi are made with both flour and eggs, though sparingly. Just about every gnocchi maker agrees that if the potatoes are too wet, the gnocchi will be gummy. I bake rather than boil the potatoes to avoid that possibility. To mash them I use a ricer (like a giant garlic press), which produces the finest texture. And I freeze gnocchi before I cook them

so they hold their shape better. There, my secrets are out. Good luck.

Makes about $1\frac{1}{2}$ pounds, enough for 6 to 8 servings

> 4 large starchy baking potatoes (about 2 pounds), such as Russet Burbank
> $\frac{1}{2}$ cup all-purpose flour, plus more for dusting
> 2 large eggs
> 1 tablespoon kosher salt
> Freshly ground black pepper
> $\frac{1}{2}$ cup (1 stick) unsalted butter
> 10 leaves sage
> Freshly shaved or grated Parmigiano Reggiano cheese

Preheat the oven to 375°F. Place the potatoes on a baking tray and bake until soft, 50 minutes to 1 hour. Remove from the oven and cool. When cool enough to handle, peel the potatoes. Pass them through a ricer or food mill into a large bowl. Let cool completely. Sprinkle the potatoes with the flour and crack the eggs into the bowl. Add the salt and a generous amount of black pepper. Gently mix the potato mixture with a wooden spoon or your hands, being careful not to overmix. The dough should have the texture of soft Play-Doh.

Dust a baking sheet with flour. Lightly flour a work surface and dust your hands with flour, also. Take about a cup of the potato mixture, and using the palms of your hand, roll it out on the work surface into a thin dowel or rope, about $\frac{1}{2}$ inch in diameter. Using a knife dipped in flour, cut the rope into $\frac{3}{4}$-inch lengths. They should be a little pinched on each end, resembling tiny pillows. Carefully transfer the cut gnocchi onto the prepared pan and set it in the freezer while you shape the remaining potato mixture. When all of the gnocchi are shaped, return the pan to the freezer until the gnocchi are firm.

Meanwhile, bring a large pot of salted water to a boil. In a large frying pan, heat the butter with the sage leaves just until the butter starts to brown. Remove quickly from the heat to prevent burning, but keep warm.

Take a handful of the gnocchi, tap to remove any excess flour, and place in the boiling water. Repeat, being careful not to overcrowd the pot. Bring the water back to a simmer, reduce the heat, and let cook for 8 to 10 minutes; the gnocchi will float to the top. Return the pan with the butter to a burner set to low. When the gnocchi are done, remove them from the water with a slotted spoon and drain well. Place in the pan with the butter. Carefully toss to coat with the butter and transfer to warm serving bowls. Cover with a blanket of shaved Parmigiano and serve immediately.

PREP TIME: 45 minutes

COOK TIME: 1 hour 15 minutes

TOTAL TIME: 2 hours

ADVANCE PREP The gnocchi can be formed and kept frozen for up to a month. Once they are firm, transfer them from the baking sheet to a resealable plastic bag or other container.

LEFTOVERS The gnocchi will keep for four or five days in the refrigerator. Leftover cooked gnocchi are delicious as a side dish fried in butter until crisp or scrambled into eggs for breakfast.

VARIATION

Potato Gnocchi in Fresh Tomato Sauce

Place 3 cups Quick Tomato Sauce (page 250) in a skillet and add 2 or 3 tablespoons of butter or extra-virgin olive oil. Bring to a simmer. As the gnocchi are done, lift them out of the cooking water, drain well, and place them in the tomato sauce. Bring back to a simmer, spoon into warm bowls, and top with shaved Parmigiano.

Naked Ravioli with Browned Butter, Sage, and Toasted Walnuts

These Italian dumplings are called *gnudi*—pronounced "nudie," which means "naked"—because they are essentially ravioli filling that's been disrobed of its pasta clothes. They are also sometimes called ricotta gnocchi. The mixture is very forgiving so that you can stir in all kinds of yummy flavorful things—herbs, various greens, or ground nuts, for example—to make your own variations. Be sure whatever you add is well drained: the drier the mixture, the lighter the dumplings will be. (Conversely, if you add too much flour, they become gummy.)

Serves 8 to 10 as an appetizer, 6 as an entrée

FOR THE DUMPLINGS

$2\frac{1}{2}$ cups fresh ricotta (about $1\frac{1}{4}$ pounds)

Kosher salt

3 bunches Swiss chard, fresh spinach, beet greens, turnip tops, or a combination (about 3 pounds), stems removed, or 2 (10-ounce) packages frozen chopped spinach

4 tablespoons ($\frac{1}{2}$ stick) unsalted butter, melted and cooled

3 large eggs

$\frac{1}{4}$ cup all-purpose flour, plus additional flour for coating

$\frac{1}{4}$ cup freshly grated Parmigiano Reggiano, Grana Padano, or other hard grating cheese

2 tablespoons chopped fresh flat-leaf parsley

¼ teaspoon freshly ground black pepper
Pinch of freshly grated nutmeg

FOR THE SAUCE
4 tablespoons (½ stick) unsalted butter
20 sage leaves
⅓ cup freshly grated Parmigiano Reggiano cheese
3 tablespoons finely ground toasted walnuts (see pages 10 and 435)

Make the dumplings. Dump the ricotta into a mesh strainer and set it over a bowl to drain. If your ricotta is very soft, you may have to let it drain for a couple of hours.

If using fresh greens, bring a large pot of water, about 4 quarts, to a boil. Add 1 tablespoon of salt. Boil the greens for about 7 minutes, until they are tender and their bitterness is toned down. Drain and rinse with cold water. Drain again. Taking small handfuls of fresh or frozen and defrosted greens at a time, squeeze them over the sink in your fist until every bit of moisture is released. Finely chop the greens. You should have about 2 cups.

In a bowl, combine the greens with the ricotta, butter, eggs, flour, cheese, parsley, pepper, nutmeg, and 1 teaspoon salt. Stir well with a wooden spoon to combine. Chill this mixture for an hour or two until firm.

Bring another large pot of water to a boil. Add a tablespoon of salt. Fill a small bowl with flour. Wet your hands with cold water and shape 2 tablespoons or so of the ricotta mixture into an egg shape. Roll this dumpling in the flour, knocking off any excess with a slight tap. Plop the dumpling in the boiling water and repeat. (You'll have to rinse your hands occasionally.) When all of the mixture has been shaped, dusted with flour, and dropped in the water

(you should have about 30), bring the pot back to a boil. Turn down the heat so that the water simmers, cover the pot, and cook for 5 to 7 minutes, until all of the naked ravioli have floated to the top.

Meanwhile, prepare the sauce. Melt the butter with the sage leaves in a large frying pan over medium-high heat until the butter starts to brown and the sage leaves crisp up, about 5 minutes. The butter should darken but not burn. Set aside.

When the ravioli are done, hold a clean dish towel in one hand. Using a slotted spoon, remove the dumplings from the boiling water, one at a time, and blot quickly on the towel to remove any excess moisture. Arrange them on warm serving plates and spoon the sage butter on top. Dust with Parmigiano, sprinkle with walnuts, and serve immediately.

PREP TIME: 20 minutes
COOKING TIME: 10 minutes
TOTAL TIME: 4 to 6 hours (includes draining and chilling time)

ADVANCE PREP *You can drain the ricotta and prepare the greens a day or two in advance. Refrigerate. Once the mixture for the dumplings is made, it will keep overnight in the fridge, but not longer. You can also shape the dumplings, roll them in flour, and freeze them individually on a cookie sheet. Transfer to a resealable plastic bag and freeze for up to one month. To cook the frozen dumplings, drop them directly into the boiling salted water without defrosting. Increase the cooking time by 3 or 4 minutes.*
LEFTOVERS *The cooked dumplings will keep for a couple of days in the fridge. Reheat in the microwave for just under a minute on high.*

Naked Ravioli with Tomato Sauce

Substitute 2 cups Quick Tomato Sauce (page 250) heated with 2 tablespoons butter for the browned butter and sage. Sprinkle with chopped flat-leaf parsley.

Semolina Dumplings

When served in beef broth, these light dumplings are a tradition of Bavaria. I serve them in almost any brothy soup. They have a delicate texture and creamy flavor and I can eat a whole batch myself. Without the parsley, the dumplings are also traditionally (and deliciously) served in chilled Sour Cherry Soup (page 414).

Makes 24 dumplings, enough for 6 to 8 servings

> 1 cup milk
> 2 tablespoons unsalted butter
> ½ teaspoon kosher salt
> ¼ cup granulated semolina
> 1 large egg, lightly beaten
> 1 tablespoon finely chopped flat-leaf parsley
> Pinch of freshly grated nutmeg (optional)

In a small saucepan over medium heat, bring the milk and butter with the salt to a simmer. Watch closely to be sure the milk doesn't boil over. While stirring with a wooden spoon, slowly add the semolina to form a smooth mixture. Keep cooking for 3 or 4 minutes, until the mixture thickens to a porridge and pulls away from the sides of the pan. Remove from the heat and cool for about 5 minutes. Stir in the beaten egg, parsley, and nutmeg, if using. Chill for 30 minutes to 1 hour.

Bring a medium pot of salted water to a boil. Turn down the heat so the water simmers. Using two teaspoons or your palms moistened with cold water, shape 1-inch balls of the dumpling mixture and drop into the hot water. Cover and simmer, without boiling, for 15 minutes, until the dumplings have swollen to almost double in size. Lift out of the water with a slotted spoon, drain, and transfer to your soup.

PREP TIME: 10 minutes
COOK TIME: 15 minutes
TOTAL TIME: 25 minutes

ADVANCE PREP *The dumpling mixture can be made a day or two in advance and refrigerated.*

Potstickers

Here's a recipe for your basic Chinese dumpling. Similar dumplings in Japan are called *gyoza;* in Korea they are known as *mandoo.*

Makes about 3 dozen dumplings, enough for 6 servings

FOR THE DUMPLINGS

> 6 tablespoons peanut or vegetable oil
> ½ small white onion, finely chopped
> 1 large garlic clove, minced
> 1 tablespoon minced fresh ginger
> 1 cup shredded Chinese (napa) cabbage
> 10 ounces ground pork
> 1 fresh or canned water chestnut, finely chopped
> 2 scallions, white and green parts, finely chopped
> 1 tablespoon dry sherry
> 1 tablespoon soy sauce
> 2 teaspoons Asian toasted sesame oil
> 1 large egg yolk or white
> 1 tablespoon oyster sauce

CHINESE DUMPLINGS

Each time I embark on a Chinese dumpling production, I'm amazed by how easy they are to make and how delicious the results are. And because they freeze perfectly well, you can make a ton of dumplings and always have a bag of them ready in the freezer. You can take a couple of dumplings out of the freezer at a time for a snack or use them as hors d'oeuvres at a party.

You can find dumpling (or wonton) wrappers in an Asian specialty store or any good grocery store. Better yet, you can make your own. I use the Fresh Pasta Dough recipe on page 242, rolling the dough very thin and dusting it with cornstarch instead of semolina or flour. Cut it into circles or squares as your recipe requires.

I provide recipes for the two classic Chinese dumplings: Potstickers (page 270) and Shu Mai (pork and shrimp dumplings; page 272). Experiment with different ingredients in the fillings and a whole world of dumplings will open its doors for you.

1 teaspoon sugar

1 1/2 tablespoons cornstarch

Freshly ground white pepper

36 (3-inch) round dumpling wrappers

FOR THE DIPPING SAUCE

1/4 cup chicken or vegetable stock or water

2 tablespoons soy sauce

2 tablespoons rice or white vinegar

1 scallion, white and green parts, chopped

1 tablespoon minced fresh ginger

Make the dumplings. In a large frying pan or wok, heat 2 tablespoons of the oil over medium-high heat until very hot. Add the onion and cook for 2 or 3 minutes, until soft. Add the garlic and ginger and continue cooking for another minute or two, until they give off a strong aroma. Add the cabbage and cook until wilted and most of the moisture in the pan has evaporated, about 4 minutes. Remove from the heat and set aside to cool.

In a bowl, combine the pork, water chestnut, scallions, sherry, soy sauce, sesame oil, egg yolk, oyster sauce, sugar, cornstarch, a pinch of white pepper, and the onion mixture. Mix well. (I find using two chopsticks in a circular motion works best to break up the pork and distribute the ingredients evenly.)

Have a small bowl of cold water nearby. Line a baking sheet with parchment paper. While you work, keep the wrappers covered with a damp cloth so they don't dry out. Place a wrapper in the palm of your left hand (or right hand if you are left-handed). Dip a clean finger in the cold water and moisten the edges of the circle of dough. Spoon about 2 teaspoons of filling into the center of the dough and fold the circle in half, pinching to seal and to envelope the filling. Place the dumpling on the parchment, pleat side up, cover with another damp dishcloth, and repeat until all of the dumplings are filled.

Make the dipping sauce. Combine all of the ingredients in a small bowl. Set aside.

Place a large frying pan, preferably nonstick with a tight-fitting cover, over medium-high heat. Add 2 tablespoons of the oil, and when it is good and hot, arrange half of the dumplings in the hot oil so they are not touching. Add about 1/3 cup cold water to the pan and cover immediately. Let the dumplings cook until the water evaporates, about 10 minutes. The tops of the dumplings should be translucent and the bottoms should be nicely browned. If not, add a couple of tablespoons more of water, cover, and steam a few minutes more. Remove from the pan and serve with the dipping sauce. Repeat with the remaining oil and dumplings.

PREP TIME: 30 minutes
COOKING TIME: 20 minutes
TOTAL TIME: 50 minutes

ADVANCE PREP *You can prepare the filling a day or two before you intend to form the dumplings and keep it refrigerated. The dumplings themselves can be made up to a day in advance and refrigerated until ready to cook, or else they can be frozen. To freeze, place the tray of freshly made dumplings in the freezer for about 4 hours, until they are frozen solid. Transfer to a resealable plastic bag and keep frozen for up to four months. There is no need to defrost the dumplings before cooking. Simply increase the water by a couple of tablespoons and the cooking time by a few minutes. The dipping sauce is best made several hours in advance so the flavors have a chance to meld.*

VARIATIONS
Steamed Dumplings
Bring an inch or two of water in a wok or large pot to a boil. Line a bamboo or other flat steamer with leaves of Chinese cabbage or parchment paper with holes punched out of it. Arrange the dumplings on top. Place the steamer over the boiling water (not touching it), cover, and let steam for 10 minutes or so, until the wrappers are translucent and the filling has set.

Vegetarian Potstickers
To prepare a vegetarian filling, follow the recipe for the filling above, omitting the pork.

To the sautéed onion, garlic, and ginger mixture, add 2½ cups shredded Chinese cabbage and 1 shredded small carrot and cook until wilted, about 5 minutes. Add 3 or 4 reconstituted dried shiitake mushroom caps, chopped, and cook until most of the moisture has evaporated. Combine this mixture with the remaining ingredients, using a whole egg instead of just the yolk or white, and adding 1 cup cooked white rice. Mix well. Proceed with stuffing and cooking the dumplings as directed.

Shu Mai
These traditional dim sum dumplings have a delicate filling of shrimp and pork that is enhanced with sesame paste. They are addictive.

Makes about 3 dozen dumplings, enough for 6 servings

> 6 dried black Chinese (shiitake) mushrooms
> 12 ounces ground pork
> 8 ounces fresh shrimp, shelled and finely chopped
> 1 water chestnut, fresh or canned, finely chopped
> 1 scallion, white and green parts, finely chopped
> 1 tablespoon minced fresh ginger
> 1 teaspoon sugar
> 1 tablespoon soy sauce
> 1 tablespoon Asian toasted sesame paste, tahini, or smooth natural peanut butter
> 1 tablespoon peanut or vegetable oil
> 1 teaspoon Asian toasted sesame oil
> 1½ tablespoons cornstarch
> Pinch of freshly ground white pepper
> 36 (3-inch) dumpling wrappers
> Dipping Sauce (page 271)

Place the dried mushrooms in a bowl and cover with about ¾ cup boiling water. (Alternatively you can cover them with cold water and microwave them for 2 minutes on high.) Let sit for 20 minutes or so, until the mushroom caps are soft. Drain, reserving the soaking liquid. Remove and discard the mushroom stems, and finely chop the caps. Set aside.

In a medium bowl, combine the mushrooms, pork, shrimp, water chestnut, scallion, ginger, sugar, soy sauce, sesame paste, peanut oil, sesame oil, cornstarch, and pepper. Mix well. (I find using two chopsticks gripped firmly together to stir in a circular motion helps break up the pork and distribute the ingredients.)

Have a small bowl of cold water nearby. Line a baking sheet with parchment. Keep the wrappers under a damp cloth so they don't dry out while you work. Hold a round of dough flat in your left hand (or your right hand if you are left-handed). With a clean finger, moisten the edges with cold water. Place a mound of about $1\frac{1}{2}$ tablespoons of the filling in the center of the dough. Forming a circle with your thumb and forefinger, bring up the sides of the dough to create a sort of open basket shape. Gently squeeze the center of the dumpling horizontally to create a "waist" while you press down on the top of the dumpling (the filling) with your opposite hand to flatten and compact the filling. Tap the bottom of the dumpling on the work surface to flatten so the dumplings will stand upright. When you are done, the dumpling should resemble the bottom of a tiny, squat Russian doll.

Bring an inch or two of water in a wok or large pot to a boil. Line a bamboo or other flat steamer with leaves of Chinese cabbage or parchment paper with holes punched out of it. Arrange the dumplings on top. Place the steamer over the boiling water (not touching it), cover, and let steam for 10 minutes or so, until the wrappers are translucent and the filling has set. Serve with dipping sauce.

PREP TIME: 30 minutes

COOKING TIME: 10 minutes

TOTAL TIME: 1 hour (includes soaking time)

ADVANCE PREP You can prepare the filling a day or two before you intend to form the dumplings and keep it refrigerated. The dumplings themselves can be made up to a day in advance and refrigerated until ready to cook, or else they can be frozen. To freeze, place the tray of freshly made dumplings in the freezer for about 4 hours, until they are frozen solid. Transfer to a resealable plastic bag and keep frozen for up to four months, until ready to use. There is no need to defrost the dumplings before cooking. Simply increase the water by a couple of tablespoons and the cooking time by a few minutes.

■ ■ ■

Pasta, Noodles, and Dumplings

Fish and Shellfish

A LTHOUGH THERE ARE A NUMBER of traditional American dishes based on foods from the sea—from New England clam chowder to Pacific planked salmon to Cajun cornmeal-crusted catfish— over the last fifty years or so we developed a squeamishness toward seafood. It's no wonder, given the general quality of what was available in the marketplace. I can still remember my mother buying rectangular blocks of frozen bluefish that were better suited to doorstops than dinner. Though it is unlikely that creatures of the sea will ever be as integral to our diet as they are in, say, Japan, the rise in popularity of, well, Japanese food in America speaks to an increasing openness for us to try to experiment with fish and seafood once again.

The benefits of eating fish and shellfish go beyond the gastronomic. Fish and shellfish are rich in omega-3 fatty acids, which studies show can help prevent heart disease. Because it is low in fat and calories, seafood is also an excellent source of protein. Doctors and nutritionists are almost always telling people to eat more seafood.

But there are complications. Just when consumer interest in seafood is on the rise and the distribution network in America has improved to the point that you can find decent quality fresh fish in most areas of the country, the fishing industry itself is in flux. Polluted waters and overfishing have severely depleted the stocks in oceans and lakes. Fish farming or aquaculture, which was once considered the only viable, sustainable solution to the diminishing supply, has proved an environmental hazard with mixed results in terms of the quality and safety of the end product. Even more distressing, because of these complications, the healthfulness of some seafood has come into question. And the prices of quality fish and seafood continue to rise.

Fish farming is here to stay, and my guess is that the techniques and technologies employed by fish farmers will continue to improve. Right now most salmon and shrimp in the world are produced on farms. Although to my taste wild salmon has a much better flavor and texture than most farmed salmon, and environmentalists are advocating selecting wild over farmed, I can't help but think that if everyone were to stop eating farmed entirely it would be only a matter of minutes before all the wild salmon in the world were gone. It seems inevitable that the ocean ecology will change, and not just because rising global temperatures are altering underwater environments. As I write, swordfish, shark, Chilean sea bass (aka Patagonian toothfish), orange roughy, and caviar produced from sturgeon in the Caspian sea are considered the most endangered seafood products on the market. The list keeps changing, in part because when a new species is added to the endangered list or a new fish is brought to market, demand for what's left—or for the next new thing—is so great that consumption soon outpaces sustainable production.

Despite these serious mitigating factors, the general consensus is that it is still a good idea to eat seafood. The health benefits outweigh the risks. And with thoughtful management, experts believe that the supply can in fact be maintained, though not without the cooperation of consumers, governments, fishermen, chefs, and everyone else involved in seafood production and consumption to make systematic change work.

All this is really to say that now, more than ever, *where* you buy your fish and seafood is perhaps the most important consideration in the success of your seafood cookery. Find a knowledgeable source that can help you make good purchasing decisions based on freshness, quality, taste, and environmental friendliness. Because of the sporadic availability of different fish, you need a fishmonger who can say, "We don't have any fresh cod today, but I'd recommend the tilefish, which has a similar texture and flavor." You need to be able to trust that when you mention you will be serving your fish raw, the fish you are given will be of supreme quality and freshness.

If you are already a lover of seafood, I think you will find a few new and delicious ideas on how to cook it in the recipes that follow. And if you don't like seafood at all, I ask you to please give it one more try. If you don't like My Mother's Breaded Sole (page 303), which is just an excuse to eat butter, I'll believe you—skip to the chapter on meat.

■ ■ ■

SELECTING FRESH FISH AND SEAFOOD

Your most important tool in selecting fresh fish and seafood is your nose. Before you even get up to the counter, if you smell a strong, fishy smell, consider going somewhere else. Fresh fish and seafood (and a store that sells them) should smell clean, like the ocean or a lake.

Buying Whole Fish

As a rule, whole fish should be on ice. They should be firm and glistening, with a clear sheen, clear eyes, firmly attached scales, taut skin, and bright red gills. A poke to the flesh should meet resistance and not leave an indentation.

Buying Fillets and Steaks

In contrast to whole fish, cleaned and filleted fish should not be in direct contact with ice, which is too cold and can burn the flesh. Instead they should be kept on trays set on ice. Fillets and steaks should glisten and look moist. If not white-fleshed, the color should be deep and vibrant, without evidence of splotches, which might indi-cate bruising. There should be a translucence to the flesh and the flakes should be tight.

Buying Seafood

Seafood should smell sweet and fresh. If alive, such as crab and lobster, they should be sprightly. Mollusks, such as clams, oysters, and mussels, should be tightly closed. Cleaned shellfish, such as shrimp and scallops, should have shiny, translucent, firm flesh.

Whatever fish or shellfish you buy, it's important to get it home and into the refrigerator quickly. Make the fish store or counter the last stop on your shopping path—or second to last if you are buying ice cream, which you should put with the fish to keep it cold. It's best to buy what you need the same day or the day before you are going to use it. Home refrigerators usually aren't cold enough to keep fish at its best. If you can, avoid freezing fish, which for optimal results also requires a colder environment than most home freezers can provide.

Grilled Shrimp

I like to marinate and grill whole shrimp, head on and in the shell, because they have the best flavor that way. If you just can't deal with the heads, at least use unpeeled shrimp. I bunch them up on bamboo skewers to make grilling easier. Serve with Aïoli (page 406) or just a squirt of lemon juice.

Makes 4 to 6 servings

3 pounds large shrimp, heads on and in the shell, or 2 pounds large headless shrimp in the shell, brined if desired (see page 280)
1 lemon

2 large garlic cloves, thinly sliced
1/2 cup extra-virgin olive oil
Handful of assorted fresh herbs, such as rosemary, thyme, flat-leaf parsley
Freshly ground black pepper

Rinse the shrimp, pat dry with paper towels, and place in a large container. Using a vegetable peeler, peel four or five strips of zest from the lemon and place in the container with the shrimp. Add the garlic, olive oil, herbs, and a generous sprinkling of pepper. Gently toss

Simple Cooked Shrimp

Although it is always tempting to buy shrimp cooked, cleaned, and ready to eat because they are easy, the truth is that most pre-cooked shrimp for sale in the marketplace are tasteless and overcooked to the point of being rubbery. For shrimp cocktails, salads, or other recipes that require cooked shrimp, you are better off cooking them yourself. Look for bright, shiny fresh shrimp in the shells, head on or off, your choice. The shells should be brittle, the flesh firm. To save some prep time, you can try to find shrimp without a dark vein down the back, although often the vein will disappear when the shrimp are cooked, and the need to remove it is purely aesthetic. Most shrimp have been frozen before you buy them, so don't be fooled by marketing or price gimmicks that say your shrimp are fresh; they rarely really are.

Shrimp are sized and sold by "count"—that is, the number of shrimp of that size that are in a pound. The lower the count, the bigger the shrimp. Each count corresponds to a category. I find 26/30s (that's 26 to 30 shrimp per pound), or "extra-large," or 31/35s, or "large," versatile enough for just about everything. A pound of headless shrimp in the shell will yield 8 to 10 ounces when cooked and cleaned. A pound of shrimp with heads in the shell will yield about 4 ounces when cooked and cleaned.

Makes 1 to 1¼ pounds cleaned, cooked shrimp, enough for 4 servings

2 celery stalks, with leaves, cut into chunks
1 small onion, peeled and cut into quarters
1 carrot, cut into chunks
1 lemon, cut in half
1 tablespoon black peppercorns
2 bay leaves
½ to 1 cup dry white wine (optional)
5 teaspoons kosher salt
2 pounds headless large (31/35 count) to jumbo (21/25 count) shrimp in the shell, rinsed and drained

In a large, wide pot, place 2½ quarts cold water. Add the celery, onion, and carrot. Squeeze the lemon halves into the water and add both halves. Add the peppercorns, bay leaves, white wine, if using, and salt. Set over high heat. Bring to a boil, reduce the heat, cover, and simmer for 5 minutes. Turn the heat back up to high. Add the shrimp, stir, cover, and set a timer for 2 minutes. At the end of 2 minutes, turn off the heat, do not uncover, and let the pot sit for 2 minutes for smallish shrimp, up to 5 minutes for larger shrimp. Remove the cover. The shrimp shells should be reddish and the flesh opaque white. Lift the shrimp out with a strainer or slotted spoon and rinse with cold water to stop the cooking. Strain and reserve the cooking liquid as a light broth for a seafood soup or risotto, if desired (but remember that it's salted, so adjust the seasoning in your recipe accordingly).

With your fingertips, starting at the head end, peel the shrimp, removing the shell in sections toward the tail. If you are serving the shrimp as a cocktail, leave the last section of the shell and tail intact. If you are using the shrimp in salad, remove the last section by pinching the tail to release the meat. If there is a dark vein down the back of the cooked shrimp, use a small, sharp paring knife to make an incision along the length of the shrimp and scrape out the vein, if desired. Rinse under cold water. When all of the shrimp are cleaned, chill.

PREP TIME: 30 minutes
COOKING TIME: 10 minutes
TOTAL TIME: 40 minutes

ADVANCE PREP The shrimp can be cooked two or three days in advance of serving.
LEFTOVERS Keep the shrimp in an airtight container in the fridge for two or three days.

BRINING SHRIMP

While everyone's going gaga about brining turkeys for Thanksgiving, more people ought to be brining shrimp. Brined shrimp have a snappy texture and excellent flavor and are perfect for sautéing or grilling. If you've ever remarked how crunchy and delicious shrimp are in a good Chinese restaurant, it is because they were brined. To brine shrimp, dissolve 1/4 cup kosher salt and 1/4 cup sugar in 1 cup of boiling water. Add 2 cups of ice and 2 cups of cold water to cool the liquid. Add 2 pounds of shrimp, and let sit, refrigerated, for 30 minutes if the shrimp are peeled and 1 hour if they are in the shell. Drain, rinse, and proceed with your recipe as directed.

CLEANING SQUID

Just about every day of the three months I worked in a restaurant in Italy began with me cleaning squid. And although most squid I've seen for sale in the United States comes already cleaned, knowing how to clean squid is a good skill to have—just in case.

To clean a whole squid, pull on the tentacles to separate the head and tentacles from the body. With the head will come most of the guts. Remove and discard the plastic-like quill. Cut through the top of the tentacles, just below the eyes, to remove and discard the head and guts. In the center of the ring of tentacles is a hard ball, called the beak. Squeeze on the tentacles to pop out the beak and discard. (You may need to cut through the ring of tentacles to dislodge the beak.) Peel any purplish skin off the body and scrape out any residue of the guts from inside. Rinse well, pat dry, and proceed with your recipe as directed.

the shrimp. Cover and refrigerate for 4 or 5 hours or overnight.

Soak 12 or more bamboo skewers in cold water for about 30 minutes. Fire up a hot grill. Lay 4 shrimp in the same direction flat on a clean work surface in a line. Insert one skewer through all 4 shrimp bodies toward the tail end, and then insert a second skewer nearer the head. Repeat with the remaining shrimp. Grill the shrimp for 2 or 3 minutes per side, just until the shells change color and the flesh turns from translucent to opaque white. Serve on the skewers or separate the shrimp, as you wish.

PREP TIME: 10 minutes

COOKING TIME: 4 to 6 minutes

TOTAL TIME: 4 1/2 hours (includes marinating time)

ADVANCE PREP *The shrimp can be marinated and skewered up to a day in advance. Keep in the refrigerator until ready to use.*

LEFTOVERS *The grilled shrimp will keep for two or three days in the refrigerator. Use leftovers in a salad or in pasta.*

Fried Calamari

A dusting of rice flour makes for an especially light and crisp coating on this American favorite. You can substitute fine cornmeal or semolina for a crunchy alternative to the rice flour; all-purpose flour or cornstarch also work perfectly well. Serve the squid with a tomato sauce (pages 250 to 252), Aïoli (page 106), or just a squirt of lemon juice.

Makes 4 to 6 servings

1 1/2 pounds cleaned medium squid (see box, above)
1 quart vegetable oil or peanut oil

¾ cup rice flour, fine cornmeal, or semolina
¼ to ½ teaspoon cayenne pepper, to taste
   (optional)
Kosher salt
1 lemon, cut into wedges

Cut the bodies into ¼-inch-wide rings and cut the tentacles through the center into two or three pieces, depending on how big they are. Rinse the squid in cold water and pat dry with paper towels.

In a deep, heavy pot, heat the oil to about 360°F. Place the rice flour in a wide bowl. Stir in the cayenne, if using. Line a plate with paper towels.

If you don't have a deep-frying thermometer, dip a squid ring in rice flour and put it into the oil. It should float and sizzle immediately if the oil is hot enough. Take a handful of the squid, about a third, and dredge it in the rice flour. Put the floured squid in a strainer or colander and shake off any excess flour back into the bowl. Place the squid in the hot oil, and using a long fork, break up the squid so it doesn't clump. Fry, turning the squid over in the oil, until it is evenly golden brown, 2 or 3 minutes. Avoid overcooking or the squid will be rubbery. Using a slotted spoon or small strainer, quickly remove the squid and place it on the paper towels to drain. Repeat with the remaining squid. Toss the fried squid with salt and squirt with lemon juice to serve.

PREP TIME: 15 minutes
COOKING TIME: 10 minutes
TOTAL TIME: 25 minutes

ADVANCE PREP *The squid can be cut a day in advance and refrigerated, but don't flour or fry it until just before serving.*

Stewed Octopus

I'm not sure why it is that squid has become mainstream in America but octopus remains obscure. Perhaps the Italian word *calamari* is a powerful euphemism and nobody knows how to say octopus in Italian (it's *polpo*). Maybe it's just because nobody knows what to do with this cephalopod. I've assumed the last, and that's why I'm giving you this simple, delicious, Mediterranean-inspired recipe. You can add potatoes and/or olives to the mix and make it a one-pot meal. Or else serve it over rice or some other starch that will soak up the flavorful stewing liquid. It's also good as a sauce for pasta. There are as many secrets to making octopus tender as there are octopus cooks—including cooking the octopus with a wine cork in the pot. I find that freezing the octopus before cooking is consistently effective in producing tender octopus.

Makes 4 servings

Kosher salt
2 small to medium octopuses (about
   2 pounds total), cleaned, frozen, and
   defrosted
¼ cup extra-virgin olive oil
1 medium onion, chopped
2 garlic cloves, chopped
2 anchovies, chopped (optional)
1 tablespoon drained capers, rinsed
1 small fresh, dried, or marinated hot red chile,
   chopped
4 ripe or canned plum tomatoes with some juice,
   chopped, or 1 cup tomato purée or tomato
   sauce
2 cups dry white wine
One 2-inch strip lemon zest
1 pound potatoes, peeled and diced
   (optional)
½ cup small black olives (optional)

Handful of flat-leaf parsley, chopped

Freshly ground black pepper

Bring a medium pot of water to a boil. Add a tablespoon of salt. Add the octopuses. Bring the water back to a boil and blanch for 1 minute. Drain and rinse the octopuses under cold water. To cut up the octopuses, slice through the center of the tentacles and body, dividing it in half. With the tip of a knife, remove the dark hard ball (the beak) in the middle of each body and discard. Separate the tentacles, and if they are large, cut them into 1½-inch pieces. Cut the head into bite-size pieces also. Set aside.

In the same pot, heat the olive oil over medium heat. Add the onion and garlic and cook until soft, about 8 minutes. Add the anchovies, if using, capers, and chile and cook for a minute or two more, until the anchovies break up and the chile softens. Add the octopus pieces, and cook, stirring, for a minute or two. Add the tomatoes, white wine, and lemon zest. The octopus pieces should be covered in cooking liquid. Bring to a boil, turn down the heat, cover, and simmer for about 1 hour, until the octopus is tender. (Depending on how big the octopus is, it may take more or less time.) About 30 minutes into the cooking, add the diced potatoes, if using. After 45 minutes, add the black olives, if using. When the octopus is tender, remove from the heat, stir in the parsley, and adjust the seasoning with salt and pepper.

PREP TIME: 10 minutes

COOKING TIME: 1 hour 10 minutes

TOTAL TIME: 1 hour 20 minutes

KITCHEN SENSE

CLEANING CLAMS AND MUSSELS

Because they live in sandy places, it's important to clean clams and mussels before opening or cooking them to avoid getting sand in your food. I find a stiff brush the best way to clean the shells. Scrub the shells under cold, running water. If your mussels have a beard—a hairy, ropelike protrusion dangling outside the shell—grab it between your thumb and forefinger and yank it out. Clams benefit from a salt-water soak, which encourages them to open up and discharge any sand they have trapped inside. Add about ½ cup kosher salt to 2 quarts water and let the clams soak in the refrigerator for 4 hours or overnight before using. Whichever mollusks you are using, they should be tightly closed. Discard any that don't close after you prod or poke them.

LEFTOVERS *This dish will keep in the refrigerator for about five days. Serve chilled or at room temperature, or reheat in a small pot or in a dish in the microwave. You can also use leftovers as the base of a seafood sauce for pasta.*

Buttermilk Fried Clams

It's hard to beat the taste of a freshly fried clam belly from a shack on the side of the road in Maine. The secret to making good fried clams at home is choosing fresh soft-shell, or "steamer," clams, then shucking them just before you are ready to cook them and frying them quickly so they don't dry out.

Makes 4 servings

2 pounds soft-shell clams, soaked (see box, above) and shucked (see page 284)

Steamed Clams

A bucket of fresh clams served with melted butter for dipping transports me to the coast of New England. The same simple steaming technique can be used to prepare clams for chowder, pasta, or anything that calls for cooked and/or chopped clam meat. As an added bonus, you can use the cooking broth as the base for your soup or sauce, provided you strain it well through cheesecloth to remove any sand.

Makes 2 servings of clams or 2 cups chopped clams plus 8 cups clam stock

> 2 celery stalks, with leaves, cut into chunks
> 1 large carrot, unpeeled, cut into chunks
> 5 sprigs parsley
> 2 bay leaves
> 1/2 teaspoon black peppercorns
> 6 dozen steamer, Manilla, or other small clams (about 4 pounds), or 2 dozen large chowder clams (about 10 pounds), scrubbed and soaked (page 282)

In a large, wide, heavy pot, place the celery, carrot, parsley, bay leaves, black peppercorns, and 6 cups of cold water. Bring to a boil, turn down the heat to a simmer, cover, and let cook about 5 minutes, until you can smell the bay leaf. Add the clams, cover, turn up the heat, and let boil until the clams open, 2 or 3 minutes for the smaller Manilla clams, 10 to 15 minutes for the larger chowder clams. With tongs, lift out the clams (reserve the cooking liquid) and place them in a large bowl or basin to cool. Discard any clams that didn't open.

Remove the clams from the shells and discard the shells. If your recipe calls for chopped clams, with a sharp knife, chop the clams to small, 1/4-inch pieces. You should have about 2 cups.

Line a sieve with several layers of cheesecloth. Strain the clam cooking liquid, being careful to leave any sandy sediment in the pot, and reserve. You should have about 8 cups.

TOTAL TIME: 10 to 15 minutes

ADVANCE PREP *If the clams are going to be served in the shell, they should be cooked just before serving. If they are going to be used in chowder or sauce, they can be steamed a day or two in advance and refrigerated until needed.*
LEFTOVERS *The clams will keep up to two or three days in the refrigerator.*

---

1 1/4 cups buttermilk
Peanut or vegetable oil, for frying
1 1/2 cups fine yellow cornmeal or semolina
1/2 cup rice or all-purpose flour
Kosher salt and freshly ground black pepper
Pinch of cayenne pepper
Lemon wedges, for garnish

Place the clams in a bowl and cover with the buttermilk. Let sit for 15 minutes.

Meanwhile, in a large, heavy pot or deep-fryer, heat 3 to 4 inches of oil to 360°F. In a medium bowl, combine the cornmeal, flour, 2 teaspoons kosher salt, a generous amount of black pepper, and the cayenne, and mix well.

Drain the clams in a mesh strainer. Dredge them in the cornmeal mixture and set on a wire rack. Let dry for 5 minutes or so. When the oil is hot, add a handful of clams, being careful not to overcrowd the pan. Fry until golden brown, about 3 minutes, turning the clams over from time to time so they cook evenly. Lift the clams

SHUCKING CLAMS

Steamers and other soft-shell clams are the easiest to shuck because they do not close completely—that's why they are also known as "gapers." Hard-shell clams, such as littlenecks and quahogs, which should be closed tight, take a little more force and skill. (If the recipe allows, I prefer to steam them open.) A clam knife is longer and thinner than an oyster knife, like a short, squat butter knife. To use it, cup the clam in the palm of your left hand (or your right hand, if you are left-handed), with the edge of the shell that opens facing your fingers. With your other hand, place the blade of the clam knife along the seam of the clam, and with the fingers of the hand holding the clam, try to force the knife into the shell. As soon as the blade goes in, the clam will open. Scrape the knife along the top of the shell to loosen the muscle—don't force the knife into the center of the clam or you'll rupture the flesh. Scrape the clam off the bottom of the shell and collect the clams in a bowl with the clam juice.

out of the oil with a slotted spoon, drain, and transfer to paper towels or a brown paper bag to drain. Repeat until all of the clams are fried. Serve with wedges of lemon.

PREP TIME: 10 minutes

COOKING TIME: 15 minutes

TOTAL TIME: 50 minutes (includes soaking time)

ADVANCE PREP *The clams can be shucked up to 4 hours before frying; cover and refrigerate. They can be breaded up to an hour before frying. Keep refrigerated.*

LEFTOVERS *Fried clams are best hot out of the oil. Leftovers will keep for a couple of days in the fridge.*

They can be served on sandwiches or used in salads (with plenty of mayonnaise).

VARIATIONS

Buttermilk Fried Oysters

Follow the same recipe, substituting 2 dozen shucked oysters for the clams.

Buttermilk Fried Shrimp or Calamari

Follow the same recipe, substituting 1½ pounds cleaned shrimp or calamari for the clams.

Steamed Mussels

As with other seafood, the beauty of mussels is that they are ready in a matter of minutes. Figure 1 to 1½ pounds per person for a main-course serving.

BELGIAN MUSSELS

The combination of white wine, butter, and parsley produces the classic flavor of these mussels.

Makes 2 servings

> 2 to 3 tablespoons unsalted butter
> 2 shallots, thinly sliced
> 1 cup dry white wine
> ¼ cup dry white vermouth or additional white wine
> 1 bay leaf
> ½ teaspoon kosher salt
> Freshly ground black pepper
> 3 pounds mussels, scrubbed and debearded (see page 282)
> 2 tablespoons chopped flat-leaf parsley

In a large pot, heat the butter over medium-high heat. Add the shallots and cook until translucent, about 5 minutes. Add the wine, vermouth, bay leaf, salt, and pepper, and bring to a simmer. Cover the pot and cook for about 5 minutes, until the shallots are soft.

Turn the heat to high. Add the mussels to the pot, cover, and cook for about 5 minutes, or until the mussels have opened. Discard any that didn't. Divide the mussels between two bowls and spoon the broth on top, being careful not to spoon out any of the sand that may have settled on the bottom of the pot. Sprinkle with parsley.

SOUTHEAST ASIAN MUSSELS

There's plenty of extra spicy broth with these mussels. Serve them with rice and eat the broth like a soup.

Makes 2 servings

   2 tablespoons vegetable or peanut oil
   1 small onion, sliced
   1 garlic clove, minced
   1 cup coconut milk
   2 to 3 tablespoons canned Thai red or green
      spice paste
   2 tablespoons Asian fish sauce, such as Thai *nam
      pla* or Vietnamese *nuoc nam*
   2 tablespoons sugar
   1 lime, cut in half
   3 pounds mussels, scrubbed and debearded (see
      page 282)
   2 scallions, white and green parts, sliced

In a large pot, heat the oil over medium-high heat. Add the onion and cook until translucent, about 5 minutes. Add the garlic and cook for a minute or two more. Add the coconut milk along with 1 cup of water. Add the spice paste, fish sauce, and sugar, and stir to dissolve the paste. Squeeze the lime juice into the pan and

add the lime halves. Bring to a boil, turn down the heat so that the mixture simmers, cover, and cook for 5 minutes.

Turn the heat back up to high. Add the mussels, cover, and steam for 5 minutes, or until the shells have opened. Discard any that didn't. Divide the mussels between two bowls and spoon the broth on top, being careful not to spoon out any of the sand that may have settled on the bottom of the pot. Sprinkle with the scallions.

ITALIAN MUSSELS

A broth of tomato that's redolent with fresh herbs and garlic makes these mussels taste decidedly Italian.

   3 tablespoons extra-virgin olive oil
   1/2 small onion, chopped
   1 garlic clove, thinly sliced
   1 1/2 cups tomato sauce (choose one from pages
      250 to 252), simmering
   1/2 cup dry white wine or dry white
      vermouth
   Kosher salt and freshly ground black pepper
   3 pounds mussels, scrubbed and debearded (see
      page 282)
   2 tablespoons chopped flat-leaf parsley

In a large pot, heat the olive oil over medium-high heat. Add the onion and garlic and cook until soft, about 5 minutes. Add the tomato sauce, white wine, a pinch of salt and a generous amount of pepper, and bring to a simmer. Turn the heat to high, add the mussels, cover, and let steam for about 5 minutes, until the mussels have opened. Discard any that didn't.

Divide the mussels between two serving bowls. Sprinkle with parsley and serve.

LEFTOVERS *Remove any leftover mussels from the shells and add them to the cooking liquid. Use the liquid as a base for seafood pasta or a soup.*

Scalloped Oysters

This classic Southern appetizer bears no relationship to scallops, or scalloped potatoes, for that matter. Instead, some suggest the name comes from the tradition of serving the oyster and buttery cracker-crumb mixture in scallop shells. However you serve them, they are delicious.

Makes 6 servings

> 1/2 cup (1 stick) unsalted butter, plus extra for greasing the baking dishes
>
> 20 to 22 oysters, shucked (see box, right; about 1 pint)
>
> 7 to 8 ounces plain oyster crackers, saltines, or other white crackers, or 2 cups cracker crumbs or meal
>
> 2 lemons, 1 cut into 6 wedges, 1 left whole
>
> 1/4 teaspoon ground black pepper
>
> 1/4 teaspoon cayenne pepper
>
> Pinch of freshly grated nutmeg
>
> 1/4 cup finely chopped flat-leaf parsley

Position a rack 6 inches beneath the broiler and preheat the broiler. Butter six 4-inch individual gratin or baking dishes, or cleaned scallop shells. Set aside.

Drain the oysters in a sieve, reserving the liquor for another dish (such as Clam Chowder, page 47). If using whole crackers, place

SHUCKING OYSTERS

There are a number of devices that are supposed to make shucking oysters easy. I find a simple, short, squat, pointy oyster knife (with or without a guard) to be the easiest tool. Clean the shells with a stiff brush under cold running water. Discard any oysters that won't close. With your left hand wrapped in a dish towel (use your right hand if you are left-handed) and the oyster on a cutting board, press down flat on the oyster to hold it firmly in place. Carefully but forcefully insert the tip of the knife at the point of the hinge—the hinge is opposite the flat, rounded end of the shell. As soon as you manage to wiggle the knife in, the shell will open. Scrape the oyster muscle from the top of the shell and discard the top shell, leaving the oyster sitting in the bottom shell. Clean away any bits of shell or sand that are visible. Be careful not to displace the flavorful liquid (called the liquor). Some people like to separate the oyster from the bottom of the shell; others believe that doing so risks ruining the integrity of the flesh. I usually leave mine attached until just before serving.

them in the bowl of a food processor fitted with a metal chopping blade. Use on/off pulses to grind the crackers into crumbs. You should have about 2 cups. Alternatively, you can crush the crackers in a resealable plastic bag with a rolling pin.

In a large sauté pan, melt the butter over medium heat. Add the cracker crumbs and stir for a minute or so, just until all of the crumbs are coated with the butter. Remove from the heat. Finely grate the zest of the whole lemon into the crumbs. Add the black pepper, cayenne pepper, and nutmeg. Stir in the parsley. Reserve about half of the crumb mixture in a bowl and set aside.

Squeeze the juice of the zested lemon over the oysters and toss. Add the oysters to one half of the crumb mixture and stir to coat the oysters with mixture. Divide the oysters in the crumbs among the six prepared baking dishes. Generously cover the oysters with the reserved crumbs. Broil until the crumbs are nicely browned and the oysters have visibly curled, about 5 minutes. Serve with lemon wedges.

PREP TIME: 15 minutes
COOKING TIME: 7 to 10 minutes
TOTAL TIME: 25 minutes

ADVANCE PREP *The crumbs can be buttered and seasoned several hours in advance and left at room temperature, but don't combine them with the oysters until you are ready to bake and serve.*
LEFTOVERS *Once cooked, the oysters keep for a day or two in the refrigerator. While best when freshly made, they can be reheated in a 325°F oven for about 7 minutes or in a microwave for 2 minutes. They are good for breakfast, served with scrambled or poached eggs.*

Seafood Pouches

Cooking seafood in a parchment pouch—that is, *en papillote*—produces elegant and delicious results in a matter of minutes. The idea to keep in mind is that everything in the pouch has to be able to cook in the same amount of time as the fish or seafood—15 minutes, tops. That's why I cook onions, mushrooms, or other vegetables before I enclose them in the paper. If you can't get parchment (or silicon) paper, use alu-minum foil instead, but be sure to grease it with butter or olive oil so the fish doesn't stick.

Makes 4 servings

> 6 tablespoons extra-virgin olive oil or unsalted butter
> 1 medium onion or 2 large shallots, thinly sliced
> Kosher salt and freshly ground black pepper
> 1½ to 2 pounds cleaned, moderately firm, low-fat, white fish fillets, such as sole or cod, and/or shelled seafood, such as scallops or shrimp
> 1 lemon
> ¼ cup dry white wine
> Handful of chopped fresh herbs, such as marjoram, chervil, tarragon, thyme, or flat-leaf parsley, or a combination

Preheat the oven to 425°F. Cut parchment paper into four 12-inch squares or circles.

In a medium sauté pan, heat ¼ cup of the olive oil over medium-high heat. Add the onion and cook until soft, about 8 minutes. Season with salt and pepper.

Lay out the four squares or circles of parchment on a work surface. Place a quarter of the cooked onion just off center on each piece of paper. Spread out the onion a little to make a bed for the seafood. Lay first the fish, then the shellfish, if using, on top. Season with salt and pepper. Using a vegetable peeler, peel off four strips of the zest of the lemon and put one on each pile of seafood. Cut the lemon into quarters and squirt the juice of one quarter on top of each portion. Sprinkle 1 tablespoon of wine on top of each portion, too, then sprinkle with herbs. Drizzle ½ tablespoon or so of the remaining olive oil on each portion. Fold the paper in half so the edges meet and make small

Cooked and Shelled Lobster

When a recipe calls for lobster meat that will then be cooked in the recipe, I steam live lobsters in a small amount of heavily salted water for a very short period of time—just long enough to kill them mercifully so they can be shelled but not long enough to cook the meat. To cook lobsters through completely, such as for Lobster Rolls (page 89), just increase the cooking time.

Makes about 1½ cups lobster meat, plus claws

2 tablespoons kosher salt
Two 1¼- to 1½-pound lobsters

In a wide, heavy pot with a tight-fitting lid, bring 1½ inches of water to a rolling boil. Add the salt. To prepare the lobsters if the meat will be cooked in a separate recipe, place 1 lobster in the pot, cover, and set a timer for 2 minutes. Remove the cover. The shell should have turned bright red. If there are still patches of the shell that haven't turned, cover and cook for another 30 seconds. With tongs, remove the lobster and rinse under cold, running water. Repeat with the remaining lobster.

Alternatively, to cook the lobster through, place the lobster in the pot, cover, and set the timer for 5 minutes. For larger lobsters, increase the cooking time by 45 seconds for every ¼ pound. If serving the lobster whole, do not rinse with cold water.

To shell a lobster, grasp the tail in one hand and the body and head in the other and twist the tail off. If you see any soft slimy green, that is the tomalley; any reddish sacks hanging out of the body of the lobster are the coral (eggs). Carefully remove both and set aside or discard, depending on what you are making. To get the tail meat out of the shell in one piece, use kitchen shears to cut along both sides of the soft undershell. Gently pull out the meat.

Twist off the front legs with the claws. With the back of a knife or a lobster cracker, crack each joint of the legs to remove the knuckle meat. You can also use kitchen shears. A lobster pick or bamboo or metal skewer helps get the meat out. Try to keep the chunks of meat as big as possible.

Finally, remove the claw meat. I try to keep the claw meat in one piece, but it isn't always possible. Separate the small side of the pincher by bending it back and pulling it off, leaving the little piece of meat inside attached to the whole claw, if possible. Sometimes, this part of the shell comes off with a wide, flat piece of white cartilage that's buried in the flesh of the claw. Carefully crack the shell on the large part of the claw with the back of a knife or a lobster cracker. Peel off the shell as you break it. Then, holding the bulbous part of the flesh, tug it out of the shell. If the cartilage didn't come out before, grab it from the joint of the pincher and pull it out carefully.

PREP TIME: 5 to 15 minutes
COOKING TIME: 5 to 15 minutes
TOTAL TIME: 10 to 30 minutes

ADVANCE PREP The shelled meat can be kept in the refrigerator for a day or two. If you are going to cook the meat through and eat the lobsters whole, they should be cooked just before serving.

LEFTOVERS Fully cooked lobster meat will keep for about four days in the refrigerator. Use it in Lobster Rolls (page 89), scrambled eggs, or as a substitute for crab in Crab Cakes (page 294).

(1½-inch or so) overlapping folds all around the edge to seal the pouch.

Carefully transfer the pouches to one or two baking sheets. Bake for 12 minutes (for dense fish, such as monkfish, increase the cooking time to 15 minutes). Remove from the oven, transfer the pouches to serving plates, and serve immediately, allowing your guests to open the pouches at the table so they get the full benefit of the beautiful aroma when the steam from inside is released.

PREP TIME: 15 minutes
COOKING TIME: 30 minutes
TOTAL TIME: 45 minutes

ADVANCE PREP *The pouches can be assembled up to a day in advance and stored in the refrigerator until ready to cook.*
LEFTOVERS *The fish will keep for three or four days.*

Simple Seafood Sausage

This is a deceptively simple recipe; it's quick and easy enough for any home cook to make because I don't actually use sausage casing, preferring instead to cheat with plastic wrap. The only equipment you need is a food processor. The results are simply delicious.

I like to use a combination of seafood and fish for the filling that will add flavor and texture. For a special occasion, I'll add lobster, but you don't need it to make a satisfying sausage. Serve the sausage with a little melted butter, an herbed butter sauce (page 403), or Pomegranate Vinaigrette (page 290).

Makes 6 servings

2 tablespoons unsalted butter, at room
    temperature

1 large shallot or ¼ of a small onion, finely
    chopped
2 large button mushrooms, finely chopped
½ cup packed fresh spinach, cleaned, stems
    removed, chopped, or frozen, defrosted spinach
2 tablespoons finely chopped fresh flat-leaf
    parsley
1½ teaspoons kosher salt
Freshly ground black pepper
1 pound fresh sea scallops, adductor muscle
    removed (see box, page 291), cut into
    ½-inch slices
¾ pound shrimp, shelled and deveined, cut into
    ½-inch dice
½ pound medium to firm, low-fat, white, salt-
    water fish, such as cod, flounder, fluke, or
    monkfish, or a combination, cut into ½-inch
    dice
½ cup heavy cream

In a frying pan set over medium heat, melt the butter. Add the shallot and cook for a couple of minutes to soften. Add the mushrooms and continue cooking a minute or two until they give off their liquid. Add the spinach and keep cooking for 2 minutes to wilt. Cook off any liquid that has formed. Stir in the parsley, ½ teaspoon of the salt, and some pepper. Set aside to cool completely to room temperature.

Place half of the scallops in a large mixing bowl. To that bowl, add the shrimp and half of the diced fish. Add ½ teaspoon of the salt and some black pepper and toss. Set aside.

In the bowl of a food processor fitted with a metal chopping blade, place the remaining scallops. Use on/off pulses to grind the scallops to a purée, scraping down the sides once or twice. Let the machine run steadily for 2 or 3 minutes to make a smooth paste. Add the remaining white fish, and purée that, too, for 2 or 3 minutes. Add the remaining $\frac{1}{2}$ teaspoon kosher salt. With the machine running, pour the cream slowly through the feed tube just until it is incorporated into the puréed scallop mixture. Scrape down the sides and purée some more. You should have a bright white paste.

To finish the sausage, add the sautéed mushroom and spinach mixture and the scallop and cream paste to the mixed, diced seafood. Stir well to combine. On a clean work surface lay out a small piece of plastic wrap. In the center of the plastic place about $\frac{1}{2}$ cup of the seafood mixture. Roll up the plastic like a candy or bonbon wrapper, shaping the filling into a short, squat sausage, about 3 inches long and 1 to $1\frac{1}{2}$ inches wide. Twist the ends and fold them in toward the center. Wrap the sausage in a small piece of aluminum foil, set on a plate, and refrigerate. Repeat with the remaining filling; you should have about six sausages total.

To cook, bring a large pot of unsalted water to a boil. Plop the chilled sausages into the water (still wrapped in foil and plastic). Cover, turn off the heat, and let sit for 30 minutes. When the time is up, remove the sausages from the water and carefully unwrap.

PREP TIME: 40 minutes

COOKING TIME: 30 minutes

TOTAL TIME: 1 hour 10 minutes

ADVANCE PREP *The sausages can be made in advance and stored in the refrigerator for two days or in the freezer for up to one month. To cook the frozen sausages, do not defrost. Add them to the boiling water and simmer for 5 minutes before cov-*

ering the pot and turning off the heat to let them sit for 30 minutes as directed.

LEFTOVERS *The seafood sausages will keep about three days in the refrigerator. They are delicious with scrambled eggs for breakfast.*

VARIATION
Simple Seafood Terrine
The same mixture used for the sausage filling can be molded and cooked as a loaf or terrine. Double the recipe and you have the perfect amount to fill a standard 6-cup terrine mold, which will feed 10 to 12 people. Preheat the oven to 325°F. Butter the mold and press the filling mixture into the terrine. Smooth out the top with a spatula. Cover with a piece of buttered foil. Set the terrine in a deep roasting pan and fill the roasting pan with hot water so that it comes $\frac{3}{4}$ of the way up the sides of the terrine. Place the pan in the oven and cook for 35 to 40 minutes, or until the terrine has set and risen—when you touch it with your fingertips it should spring back. Remove from the oven and let cool for about 10 minutes. To unmold, run a thin knife around the sides of the terrine and invert the whole thing onto a cutting board. Wipe up any liquid that runs off. Cut the terrine with a sharp knife into $\frac{3}{4}$-inch-thick slices and serve with Pomegranate Vinaigrette (below) or hollandaise sauce (see page 123).

Seared Scallops with Warm Pomegranate Vinaigrette
Whenever I stumble across large scallops in the shell, I buy them. I think the shells are pretty, and the scallops within them are usually fresher and sweeter than others you find in the market. If you can't find scallops

HOW TO PREPARE SCALLOPS FOR COOKING

If your scallops are in the shell, be sure to check they are alive. If they are open, poke a knife inside the shell to see if it closes. If it doesn't close, discard the scallop. To shuck, carefully insert a long, thin, flexible knife in between the two halves of the shell. Work the knife inside along the flatter, top half of the shell. Be sure to keep the blade as close to the shell as possible so that you lose as little of the flesh as possible. As soon as you sever the scallop, the shell will open up. Scrape the scallop off the other side of the shell. Pull away and discard everything but the scallop and the bright orange sack, which is the coral. (The coral can be seared and served along with the scallop.) Be careful not to tear the flesh as you discard the stuff around the scallop. Rinse with cold water.

Whether you have shucked your own scallops or purchased them already shucked, be sure to remove the small, tough aductor muscle on the side of each scallop. You can find it because it is a little whiter, more opaque, and tougher than the other scallop flesh. Also remove the thin membrane that holds it on.

in the shell, you can use already-shucked scallops, but be sure they are as fresh as possible and if possible, find ones that haven't been treated with any preservative chemicals (tripolyphosphate is most common).

Makes 4 appetizer servings

1 large pomegranate
2 tablespoons red or white wine vinegar
Kosher salt and freshly ground black pepper
4 tablespoons unsalted butter, chilled
2 tablespoons vegetable oil

4 to 6 large sea scallops, preferably in the shell, cleaned (see box, left)
1 ounce baby spinach, mâche, mesclun, or other small, delicate green
2 scallions, white parts only, sliced thinly on the bias

Cut the pomegranate crosswise in half. Pull out and reserve about 20 juicy seeds for garnish. Using a large grapefruit or citrus juicer, juice the pomegranate as you would a grapefruit half. Strain the juice. You should have ¼ to ⅓ cup of juice. Place this juice in a small saucepan and set over medium heat. Bring to a boil and let reduce until only 2 tablespoons of juice remains, 3 or 4 minutes. Add the vinegar, and season with salt and pepper. Add 2 tablespoons of the butter, remove from the heat, and whisk to form a smooth emulsion. Set aside and keep warm.

Heat the remaining 2 tablespoons of butter and the vegetable oil in a frying pan over high heat. Season the scallops generously with salt and pepper. When the oil is hot, add the scallops and their coral, if there is any, and sear until browned around the edges, 2 minutes.

To serve, arrange the spinach or other greens in a nice pattern on four small, chilled plates. Arrange the seared scallop on top. Drizzle the scallops and greens with a teaspoonful or two of the pomegranate dressing. Scatter the scallions and reserved pomegranate seeds on the plates as garnish.

PREP TIME: 15 minutes
COOKING TIME: 5 minutes
TOTAL TIME: 20 minutes

ADVANCE PREP The pomegranate dressing can be made several hours before serving.

Tuna Tartare with Toasted Sesame

Ubiquitous on fancy restaurant menus, tuna tartare is delicious and easy to make. Buy the best, sushi-quality yellowfin tuna you can find. And be sure to tell the fishmonger you intend to serve it raw. See the box at the right for more information.

Makes 1½ cups, enough for 6 appetizer servings

8 ounces sushi-grade yellowfin tuna, finely diced

2 tablespoons finely chopped scallion, white part only

2 teaspoons sesame seeds, toasted (see page 10)

2 teaspoons minced crystallized ginger

2 teaspoons toasted Asian sesame oil

1 teaspoon light soy sauce

Kosher salt and freshly ground black pepper

Cucumber slices, for garnish

In a medium bowl, combine the tuna with the scallion, sesame seeds, ginger, sesame oil, and soy sauce. Season with salt and pepper and mix well. Cover and chill for 1 hour before serving.

Arrange a bed of cucumber slices on a serving plate in an attractive pattern and mound the tuna tartare on top to serve.

PREP TIME: 10 minutes

TOTAL TIME: 1 hour and 10 minutes (includes chilling time)

ADVANCE PREP *The tartare can be made and refrigerated up to 4 hours in advance, but no more.*
LEFTOVERS *Don't keep the tartare around for more than a few hours. If you have any leftover tuna, sear it in a hot frying pan and use it for a salad.*

KITCHEN SENSE

RAW FISH AND SEAFOOD

There was a time when the idea of raw fish and seafood was anathema to most Americans. But now that Japanese sushi and Latin American ceviches have caught on across the country, raw fish is becoming increasingly popular. Although it is important that all fish and seafood is fresh, when it is going to be served raw freshness is even more vital. To serve raw, buy fish and seafood only from a reputable fish shop or fish counter, and buy only the best quality. Sometimes you will see tuna marketed as "sushi-grade," which has come to mean the best quality and freshest tuna you can buy. Be sure to mention to the fishmonger that you are going to be serving what you are buying raw. Buy what you need the day you intend to serve it and keep it chilled until just before you set it in front of your guests.

Some fish experts recommend freezing fish that is going to be served raw for 24 hours to kill parasites. Although you might think it odd to buy fresh fish and then stick it in the freezer, the truth is that, to preserve freshness, most fish and seafood used for sushi has already been frozen on the boats when it was caught. Still, because of the poor quality of most home freezers, I find freezing the fish diminishes the texture of its flesh. I trust my fishmonger to steer me to the best fish to eat raw. If you'd feel better freezing or even cooking your fish, go right ahead.

Salmon Tartare with Preserved Lemon and Olives

This is a bright-tasting dish that's perfect for an hors d'oeuvre or appetizer. Use very fresh wild salmon (not farmed) and delicate brined black and green olives (not canned). Serve the tartare with Crostini (page 22) or toast points and crème fraîche. For tips on buying fish to eat raw, see page 292.

Makes 1½ cups, enough for 6 to 8 appetizer servings

- 8 ounces best-quality fresh salmon fillets, preferably wild, skin and pin bones removed
- 1½ tablespoons finely chopped black olives, or black olive paste or tapenade
- 1½ tablespoons finely chopped green olives, or green olive paste or tapenade
- 1½ teaspoons capers, rinsed, drained, and minced
- 1 tablespoon finely chopped chives
- 1 tablespoon minced shallot
- 1 teaspoon minced Preserved Lemon (page 409) or ½ teaspoon minced lemon zest and a squirt of lemon juice
- 4 teaspoons extra-virgin olive oil
- Freshly ground black pepper
- Kosher salt

Using a very sharp knife, finely chop the salmon into a tiny dice. In a medium bowl, combine the salmon with the black and green olives, capers, chives, shallot, preserved lemon, olive oil, and some pepper. Taste and adjust the seasoning, adding salt if necessary (be careful with the salt because the olives and capers are salty). Cover and chill for about 1 hour before serving.

TOTAL TIME: 15 minutes (plus chilling time)

ADVANCE PREP The tartare can be made and refrigerated up to 4 hours in advance, but no more.
LEFTOVERS The salmon doesn't keep well for more than a day; use it in salmon cakes or in a salmon quiche.

VARIATION
Spicy Salmon Tartare
For a little kick, stir 1 teaspoon of Tunisian harissa (spice paste) or other hot sauce into the tartare.

Ceviche

The cuisines of Latin America, especially Peru and Ecuador, are full of different types of citrusy marinated raw fish dishes called ceviche (also spelled seviche or cebiche). Served chilled with slices of ripe avocado, spicy and colorful ceviches make superb appetizers on hot summer days. Although the acid in the marinade changes the texture of the protein to make it seem cooked, the fish really is raw, so use care when making ceviche (see page 292).

Makes 4 servings

- 1 pound firm, fresh white fish, such as grouper or snapper
- ½ cup fresh lime juice (from about 3 limes)
- ½ cup fresh lemon juice (from about 2 lemons)
- ½ cup fresh sour or regular orange juice (from 1 orange)
- Kosher salt
- ½ red bell pepper, cored, seeded, and thinly sliced
- ½ yellow bell pepper, cored, seeded, and thinly sliced
- 1 ripe tomato, cored and diced

½ small red onion, thinly sliced

1 jalapeño chile, seeded and finely chopped

2 scallions, white and green parts, finely chopped

¼ cup fresh cilantro leaves

½ cup tomato juice

2 tablespoons ketchup

Freshly ground black pepper

Cut the fish into ½-inch cubes and place it in a bowl. Combine the lime juice, lemon juice, and orange juice with ½ teaspoon kosher salt and pour 1 cup of this mixture over the fish. Cover and refrigerate the fish for 4 to 6 hours, until the flesh goes from translucent to opaque. Drain the fish.

In a large bowl, combine the bell peppers, tomato, onion, jalapeño, scallions, cilantro, tomato juice, ketchup, and the remaining ½ cup citrus juices. Season with salt and pepper. Add the fish and toss, being careful not to break up the chunks of fish. Chill for about 1 hour before serving.

PREP TIME: 15 minutes

TOTAL TIME: 4 to 6 hours (includes marinating time; plus chilling time)

ADVANCE PREP *The fish can be marinated in the citrus juice, drained, and refrigerated for up to two days before finishing the ceviche. Once tossed with the vegetables, the ceviche should be served within 4 hours.*

VARIATION

Shrimp or Calamari Ceviche

The same basic ceviche can be made with shrimp or other seafood, such as calamari or scallops, or a combination of seafood and fish, but the seafood has to be blanched in salted water before it is combined with the other ingredients. To use shrimp or calamari, omit the step of marinating the fish in citrus and reduce the amount of juice to 3 tablespoons each of lime, lemon, and orange. Bring a large pot of salted water to a boil. Add ½ to 2 pounds of shrimp in the shell and let blanch for 2 or 3 minutes, just until the flesh begins to turn opaque. (Blanch 1 pound cleaned calamari for 30 seconds.) Quickly remove the shrimp and rinse under cold water to stop the cooking. Peel and clean the shrimp. Combine with the other ingredients as directed, using the reduced amount of citrus juice.

Crab Cakes

The sweet, buttery taste of fresh crab is the predominant flavor of these classic crab cakes. They are delicious served with a summery Grilled Tomato and Corn Salsa (page 16).

Makes 4 servings

2 slices stale white bread, crusts removed, cut into ½-inch cubes

½ cup milk

12 ounces lump crab meat (about 2 cups)

1 small shallot, minced

1 tablespoon finely chopped flat-leaf parsley

1 tablespoon unsalted butter, at room temperature

1 teaspoon fresh lemon juice

1 large egg

½ teaspoon kosher salt

Freshly ground black pepper

Peanut or vegetable oil, for frying

½ to ¾ cup Japanese bread crumbs (panko) or
    unseasoned bread crumbs

Place the bread cubes in a small bowl and pour the milk over them. Let sit for at least 15 minutes, until the bread is soft and wet.

In a medium bowl, combine the crab meat, shallot, parsley, butter, lemon juice, egg, salt, and pepper. Squeeze the bread in your fist to remove the excess milk. Add the bread to the crab mixture and stir gently with a fork to combine. (You don't want to break up the lumps of meat.) In the palm of your hands, shape the mixture into six or eight small patties, about ½ inch thick. Place on a clean plate and chill for 1 hour, until firm.

Preheat the oven to 350°F. Set a wire rack on a baking sheet.

Heat less than ¼ inch of the oil in the bottom of a heavy sauté pan; cast iron works well. Carefully coat the crab cakes with the bread crumbs, patting the crumbs into the cake to coat lightly. Place in the hot oil. Fry until golden, 3 or 4 minutes, carefully flip, and fry the other side. Transfer the crab cakes to the wire rack and bake for 8 to 10 minutes, until heated through.

PREP TIME: 10 minutes

COOKING TIME: 25 minutes

TOTAL TIME: 1 hour 35 minutes (includes chilling)

ADVANCE PREP *The crab cakes can be refrigerated for up to a day before they are coated in the bread crumbs.*

LEFTOVERS *The crab cakes will keep in the fridge for two or three days. To crisp them up, reheat them on a wire rack on a cookie sheet in a 325°F*

oven. Leftover crab cakes make great fillings for sandwiches.

Steamed Fish with Ginger, Scallion, and Soy

The Chinese way of steaming fish is so simple and delicious that it will make a fish cooker and eater out of just about anyone. The only limit to how much fish you can steam is the size of your steamer.

Makes 2 servings

4 leaves white, green, or napa cabbage

One 1- to 1½-pound whole soft, white-fleshed
    fish, such as sea bass or red snapper, gutted,
    scaled, and rinsed

5 scallions, 3 cut in half, 2 thinly sliced

6 to 7 sprigs fresh cilantro

2 garlic cloves, 1 thinly sliced, 1 minced

2 walnut-size pieces of fresh peeled ginger,
    1 thinly sliced, 1 minced

2 tablespoons soy sauce

In a wok or large pot, bring an inch or two of water to a simmer over medium heat. Line a Chinese bamboo or other type of steamer with the cabbage leaves and lay the fish on top of the cabbage. Inside the cavity of the fish arrange the halved scallions, the cilantro, the sliced garlic, and the sliced ginger. Set the steamer over the wok and cover. Steam the fish for 15 to 20 minutes, depending on how thick the flesh is. The fish is done when the flesh is opaque white and it doesn't spring back when you press it. Turn off the heat and let sit for another 5 minutes.

Meanwhile, prepare the sauce. Combine the soy sauce with the sliced scallions, the

ONE FISH, TWO FISH, RED FISH, BLUE FISH

Owing to a complicated and often inadequate distribution network and sporadic catches these days, it isn't always easy to find the particular type of fish you are looking for. Even within supermarket chains, such as Whole Foods, what's available in Florida is different from what you'll find in Seattle. Luckily, within certain parameters, similar types of fish can be used interchangeably. For most intents and purposes, from a culinary standpoint there are really only four parameters to consider: (1) *flavor*, which can often be determined by the color of the flesh—the more intense its color, usually the stronger the flavor. Delicately flavored fish are always white; (2) *texture of the flesh*, in part a function of the size, shape, and arrangement of the flakes; (3) *fat content*, which affects flavor, texture, and the flesh's ability to withstand certain cooking techniques; and (4) whether the fish comes from *fresh or salt water*, which also affects flavor and texture.

Thus, were you to approach a fish counter and ask for "a firm, white, saltwater fish, with low to moderate fat content," what you would be offered, provided your fishmonger knows his stuff, could likely be used in any recipe that calls for monkfish, pompano, or sturgeon. Similarly, a request for "something like cod" should produce another moderately firm, white, low-fat, saltwater fish such as haddock, grouper, or tilefish. Want a rich, moderately firm, saltwater fish? Then salmon, arctic char, or Chilean sea bass might do. Change that to firm and say you don't mind a strong flavor, and you'd get tuna, swordfish, or shark. Freshwater fish? How about trout, tilapia, or walleye?

Identifying and categorizing every fish at the fish counter, let alone in the sea, is beyond the scope of this book. But to help, in the recipes that follow, I've given you the descriptors you need if you can't find the fish called for and you have to make a substitution with something similar.

minced garlic, and the minced ginger. Add 5 or 6 tablespoons of the hot steaming liquid from under the fish. Using the cabbage leaves as support, carefully transfer the cooked fish to a warm serving plate and pour the sauce over the fish. Bone the fish at the table (see page 297).

PREP TIME: 15 minutes
COOKING TIME: 20 minutes
TOTAL TIME: 35 minutes

LEFTOVERS *The fish will keep for a day or two in the refrigerator. Reheat gently over steam or in the microwave for the best texture. If you don't have* *enough fish left for an entire portion, you can use the leftovers as a filling for omelets or as an addition to any seafood salad.*

VARIATION

Steamed Fish, Mediterranean Style

Omit the ginger and fill the fish cavity with the garlic and a handful of fresh herbs, such as parsley, rosemary, marjoram, or fresh thyme. Also place 2 or 3 thin slices of lemon in the cavity. Rub the outside of the fish with extra-virgin olive oil and season the fish with salt. Steam it on a bed of spinach or fresh herbs instead of the napa cabbage. For a sauce, combine $1/4$ cup extra-virgin olive oil with the juice of $\frac{1}{2}$ lemon and a pinch of salt and freshly ground pepper.

Whole Fish Baked in Salt

All around the Mediterranean there's a version of fish baked in salt. This is one of my favorite techniques for cooking whole fish. Even though the fish is well done when it's finished, the flesh has a silken, juicy texture. And it's remarkably not salty. Depending on the size of your oven and how much salt you can get your hands on, you can cook any size fish this way, but for home cooking I usually stick to a fish that weighs between $1\frac{1}{2}$ and 3 pounds. There is no need to scale the fish because you don't eat the skin, but if the fish is scaled already, that's fine, too.

Makes 2 to 4 servings

1 whole fish, such as black sea bass, red or
    yellow snapper, John Dory, or sea bream,
    between $1\frac{1}{2}$ and 3 pounds, cleaned,
    head on
1 garlic clove, thinly sliced
3 or 4 sprigs fresh herbs, such as rosemary,
    thyme, marjoram, or flat-leaf parsley, or a
    combination
2 or 3 very thin slices of lemon, cut in half
2 to 3 pounds kosher or other coarse salt

Preheat the oven to 450°F.

Rinse the fish in cold water and pat dry with paper towels. Place the garlic, herbs, and lemon slices in the cavity of the fish. On a baking sheet or in a baking dish just slightly longer than the fish, place about one third of the salt, or enough to make an even $\frac{1}{2}$-inch-thick layer an inch or so wider than the body

of the fish. Lay the fish on top of the salt base. Pat the remaining salt over the fish to enclose it completely in salt, $\frac{1}{4}$ to $\frac{1}{2}$ inch thick all around.

Bake for 20 to 25 minutes, depending on the size of the fish. As it bakes, the crust will harden and trap the moisture and steam given off by the fish. You can tell the fish is done when the crust cracks (from the pressure of the steam) and browns in patches. Remove from the oven and let sit for a minute or two. With a spatula, carefully remove the top crust in large pieces. Lift the fish off the bottom crust onto a serving plate and bone the fish at the table as described in the box above.

PREP TIME: 20 minutes
COOKING TIME: 20 to 25 minutes
TOTAL TIME: 40 to 45 minutes

LEFTOVERS *The fish will keep for three or four days in the refrigerator.*

Baked Salmon

This is a simple way to prepare a side of salmon for a large group of people. I like to serve it at room temperature as an entrée for a light dinner or for brunch with bagels, cream cheese, and all the fixin's. By curing the fish first, you preserve its moistness when cooked.

Makes 6 to 8 servings

> One 3-pound side of salmon, preferably wild,
>   bones removed, skin on
> 3 tablespoons kosher salt
> 3 tablespoons sugar
> 1½ tablespoons coarsely ground black
>   pepper
> Finely grated zest of 1 lemon

Lay a large sheet of plastic wrap over a cookie sheet or plate big enough to hold the fish flat. Lay the salmon, skin side down, on the plastic wrap. Run your fingers over the surface to feel for any pin bones that were not removed. Using needle-nose pliers or tweezers, yank out those pin bones, tugging in the direction of the grain of the flesh. In a small bowl, mix the salt and sugar. Rub this mixture on both the flesh and skin side of the salmon. Wrap up the fish and refrigerate overnight or up to a full day.

The next day, preheat the oven to 425°F. Lay a wire rack on a baking sheet and grease the rack or spray it with nonstick cooking spray. Unwrap the salmon, rinse it briefly with cold water, and pat it dry with paper towels. Lay the salmon, skin side down, on the rack. Sprinkle the black pepper and lemon zest in an even layer over the flesh side of the salmon. Bake for 20 to 25 minutes, or until the flesh is just barely cooked through—the fish will continue cooking when you remove it from the oven. You can tell the flesh is near done when small dots of white liquid appear on the surface. Remove from the oven and cool to room temperature before serving.

PREP TIME: 10 minutes
COOKING TIME: 20 to 25 minutes
TOTAL TIME: 8½ hours (includes marinating time)

ADVANCE PREP *The fish can be made a day or two in advance, wrapped, refrigerated, and brought back to room temperature before serving.*
LEFTOVERS *The fish will keep four or five days in the refrigerator. Use leftovers in any recipe that calls for cooked or canned salmon, such as salmon salad or salmon croquettes.*

Baked Fish Fillets with Lemon and Olive Oil

Any delicate white fish, such as flounder, snapper, or sea bass, can be prepared deliciously in a matter of minutes with a splash of olive oil and a squirt of lemon juice. I like to add caper or olive juice for a little extra flavor boost.

Makes 4 servings

¼ cup extra-virgin olive oil

1½ pounds delicate white fish fillets, such as
    flounder, snapper, or sea bass

Juice of ½ lemon (2 tablespoons)

1 tablespoon brine from capers or olives

Kosher salt and freshly ground black
    pepper

Finely chopped flat-leaf parsley

Preheat the oven to 425°F.

Lightly grease a baking sheet with some of the olive oil and lay the fish fillets on the pan. Rub the rest of the olive oil into the fillets and sprinkle with the lemon juice and the caper brine. Season lightly with salt and with a generous amount of fresh pepper. Bake for 10 to 15 minutes, depending on the thickness of the fillets. The fish is done when the flesh has turned opaque white, the edges have browned, and the fish flakes apart when pricked with the tines of a fork. Remove from the oven and carefully transfer to serving plates. Spoon any pan juices over the fish and sprinkle with the parsley.

PREP TIME: 5 minutes
COOKING TIME: 10 to 15 minutes
TOTAL TIME: 15 to 20 minutes

LEFTOVERS *Leftover fish will keep three or four days. Use it in sandwiches or flaked and turned into a salad.*

VARIATION
Baked Fish Fillets with an Herbed Crust
Mix together ⅓ cup unseasoned bread crumbs, 1 tablespoon chopped fresh herbs, and the grated zest of 1 lemon. Sprinkle this mixture over the fish before baking.

Spiced-Yogurt Grilled Fish Steaks

Tuna, salmon, halibut, turbot, and swordfish are often sold in steaks—like fillets, only thicker and chunkier (and often with a bone). Because they are generally made from rich, firm-fleshed fish, fish steaks are excellent for grilling. They hold their shape well and they tend not to stick. If you don't have a grill, you can broil the steaks or sear them in a hot cast-iron skillet.

Makes 4 servings

4 large 1-inch-thick tuna, salmon, or swordfish
    steaks (1¾ pounds total)

2 cups plain yogurt

2 garlic cloves, minced

1 tablespoon minced fresh ginger

1 tablespoon extra-virgin olive or vegetable oil

Finely grated zest of ½ lemon

2 tablespoons curry powder (page 409)

1 tablespoon garam masala

½ teaspoon kosher salt

Freshly ground black pepper

Arrange the fish in a single layer in a wide, shallow dish. In a bowl, combine the yogurt, garlic, ginger, oil, lemon zest, curry powder, garam masala, salt, and some pepper. Pour this mixture over the fish, cover, and let marinate for at least 2 hours or overnight in the refrigerator, turning the fish over once or twice while it marinates.

Heat a charcoal grill, broiler, or cast-iron pan. The yogurt has a tendency to stick so if using a fish grilling basket, spray it with non-stick cooking spray. Alternatively, oil the grill grates or pan. Remove the fish from the marinade, scraping off all but a thin coating of the yogurt mixture, and place on the hot grill. Grill for 4 or 5 minutes, depending on the thickness of the fish, then carefully flip with a spatula to grill the second side until the fish reaches the desired doneness.

PREP TIME: 5 minutes
COOKING TIME: 10 to 12 minutes
TOTAL TIME: 2 hours 15 minutes (includes marinating time)

ADVANCE PREP *The fish can be refrigerated in the yogurt marinade for up to 24 hours.*
LEFTOVERS *Leftover fish will keep for about three days in the refrigerator. Use leftovers as the base of a curried fish salad.*

Orange–Soy Sauce Salmon

This quick flavorful marinade for salmon can be used whether you are going to grill, broil, or pan-sear the fish. The ingredients are combined in equal proportion so you can adjust the recipe for however much salmon you wish to cook.
Makes 2 servings

12 ounces salmon fillets
1/2 cup light soy sauce
1/2 cup fresh orange juice (from 1 large orange)
1/2 cup dry white wine
Peanut or vegetable oil

Lay the salmon in a single layer in a container. In a small bowl, mix the soy sauce, orange juice, and wine. Pour this mixture over the fish. The marinade should come about halfway up the side of the fillets. Cover and marinate in the refrigerator for at least 6 hours, turning the

fish over periodically to coat evenly with the marinade.

When ready to cook, heat the grill, broiler, or a heavy frying pan, such as cast iron. Brush the grill or broiler pan with oil, or if you are pan-searing the fish, heat about 1/8 inch of oil in the frying pan. Cook the fish on the skin side first, until the skin is brown and crisp, about 5 minutes. Turn over and brown the other side for 3 to 5 minutes, depending on how thick the fillets are. The fish should be just cooked through, flaky but still moist in the middle.

PREP TIME: 5 minutes
COOKING TIME: 10 minutes
TOTAL TIME: 6 hours 15 minutes (includes marinating time)

ADVANCE PREP *The salmon can be marinated up to 24 hours in advance, but it should be cooked just before serving.*
LEFTOVERS *The salmon will keep for four or five days. Eat as is or flake it and use it in a salmon salad or salmon cakes.*

VARIATION
Orange–Soy Sauce Tuna
The same marinade can be used with tuna steaks. Substitute an equal amount of fresh tuna for the salmon and proceed with the recipe as directed.

Chardonnay-Poached Salmon with Mustard Tarragon Sauce
Here's a recipe for a simple but satisfying poached salmon dish that can be served either hot or cold. I use

the poaching liquid to thin down the sauce to add a little extra flavor.

Makes 4 servings

FOR THE FISH

- 1 (750 ml) bottle Chardonnay or other dry white wine
- 1 white onion or leek, roughly chopped
- 1 medium carrot, roughly chopped
- 2 celery stalks, with leaves, roughly chopped
- 1/2 lemon
- 2 sprigs fresh tarragon
- 5 or 6 sprigs flat-leaf parsley
- 1 bay leaf
- 1 teaspoon black peppercorns
- 1 1/2 teaspoons kosher salt
- 4 skinless fillets salmon, preferably wild (about 1 3/4 pounds)

FOR THE SAUCE

- 2 tablespoons unsalted butter or extra-virgin olive oil
- 1 large shallot, minced
- 1 tablespoon grainy Pommery-style mustard
- 2/3 cup plain yogurt or sour cream
- 1 tablespoon minced fresh tarragon

In a wide, deep skillet or pot with a lid combine the wine, onion, carrot, celery, lemon juice and the squeezed half of the lemon, tarragon, parsley, bay leaf, peppercorns, and salt. Add enough cold water to cover the salmon fillets, about 2 cups. Bring the liquid to a boil. Reduce the heat so that the liquid simmers very slowly, cover, and cook for about 15 minutes to develop the flavors of the poaching liquid.

Meanwhile, feel the cut surface of the fish

KITCHEN SENSE

POACHING FISH IN STOCK OR OIL

Although poaching fish seems to have fallen somewhat out of favor these days, I think a nice piece of poached salmon or other type of fish, served hot or cold, still makes a lovely, light entrée. *Poaching* just means to simmer in liquid. I like to use a flavorful liquid, such as a quick stock made from aromatic vegetables, wine, and herbs (called a court bouillon). Although you've likely seen images of impressive whole poached salmon chilled and decorated with scales of cucumber slices or aspic, I find it much easier to poach individual fillets than a whole fish. I simmer the fish for a few minutes, and then let it sit off the heat in the poaching liquid to finish cooking. This helps avoid overcooked, tough, dry fish.

Recently, there has been a trend among chefs to poach fish, especially salmon or tuna, very slowly in olive oil. The result is almost translucent flesh with a delicate, rich texture that is very appealing. To prepare fish this way, in a wide pot over very low heat, heat to 150°F enough extra-virgin olive oil to submerge the fish along with 2 or 3 strips of lemon zest and 1 teaspoon of black peppercorns. Add the fish and cook, maintaining a steady temperature of no more than 155°F for about 15 minutes, or until the flesh is firm when pressed with a fork and it separates into flakes.

for any pin bones and using tweezers or needle-nose pliers, remove them with a yank in the direction of the grain of the flesh. Lower the salmon fillets into the hot liquid. Cover and continue simmering gently for about 5 minutes. Keep the pan covered and remove from the heat. Let the salmon sit undisturbed for 5 to 7 minutes, until the fish is cooked through. Test the fish with the point of a paring knife—you should be able to separate the fish into flakes if it is cooked properly.

Meanwhile, prepare the sauce. In a small saucepan, melt the butter over medium heat. Add the shallot and cook until soft, about 5 minutes. Add about ½ cup of the poaching liquid from the salmon along with the mustard and bring to a simmer. Stir in the yogurt and tarragon and heat just until warm.

With a slotted spatula, carefully lift the fish out of the cooking water, drain, and place on warm serving plates. Spoon the sauce on top of the fish and serve.

PREP TIME: 10 minutes
COOKING TIME: 25 minutes
TOTAL TIME: 35 minutes

ADVANCE PREP *The poaching liquid can be made a day or two in advance and refrigerated.*
LEFTOVERS *The poached salmon is delicious chilled with the same sauce. The poaching liquid can be strained and reused to poach more salmon or other fish. Leftovers will keep three or four days.*

Cornmeal-Crusted Catfish

A Southern classic, this crispy catfish is best, in my opinion, when fried in a combination of bacon fat and vegetable oil, which adds flavor and richness to the fish. I cut the cornmeal with bread crumbs or cracker crumbs so the crust isn't too tough, and I add a little cayenne pepper for some zing.

Makes 4 servings

1½ **pounds catfish fillets**
¾ **cup fine yellow cornmeal**
¼ **cup toasted unseasoned fine bread crumbs or cracker crumbs**
Kosher salt and freshly ground black pepper
Pinch of cayenne pepper
2 **large eggs**
½ **cup all-purpose flour**
½ **cup bacon fat, lard, unsalted butter, vegetable oil, or a combination**

Rinse the catfish with cold water and pat dry with paper towels. On a plate, combine the cornmeal, crumbs, ¾ teaspoon salt, ¼ teaspoon pepper, and cayenne, and mix well. In a small bowl, beat the eggs with 2 tablespoons cold water and a pinch of salt. On another plate, blend the flour with a pinch of salt. Dredge the catfish fillets in the flour and tap off any excess. Now dip them in the egg and drain. Finally, coat in the seasoned cornmeal mixture. Set on a plate.

In a large cast-iron or other heavy frying pan, heat the bacon fat over medium-high heat. When the fat is quite hot, add the catfish. Do not crowd the pan. Fry until the undersides of the fillets are nicely browned around the edges and crisp, 6 or 7 minutes. With a large spatula, carefully flip the fish and fry until brown and cooked through, another 5 minutes or so. When done, carefully lift the fish out of the pan and set on a wire rack. Repeat until all of the fish is fried.

PREP TIME: 10 minutes
COOKING TIME: 30 minutes
TOTAL TIME: 40 minutes

ADVANCE PREP *The fish can be breaded and chilled a couple of hours ahead before frying. Once fried, it's best eaten right away, but it can be reheated on a wire rack—which will keep it crisp—in a 300° F oven for 10 minutes or so, until heated through.*

My Mother's Breaded Sole

My mother always fried thin pieces of sole in the morning, overcooking them, and reheated them for dinner. Somehow, they were still delicious. The secret, my siblings and I think, was that she fried the fish in tons of butter, which kept the flesh moist. Needless to say, the same fillets are even better cooked just before they are eaten.

Makes 6 servings

½ cup all-purpose flour

2 large eggs

1 cup matzo meal or unflavored bread crumbs

2 teaspoons kosher salt

½ teaspoon freshly ground black pepper

1½ to 2 pounds sole or flounder fillets

6 tablespoons (¾ stick) unsalted butter

2 tablespoons peanut or vegetable oil

Place the flour on a plate. In a wide, shallow bowl, beat the eggs with a tablespoon of cold water. On another plate combine the matzo meal with the salt and pepper. Dredge the fillets in the flour, tapping off any excess. Dip in the egg, drain, and coat with the seasoned matzo meal. Set aside on a plate.

Preheat the oven to 250° F. Place a wire rack on a baking sheet near the stove.

In a large skillet over medium heat, heat 3 tablespoons of the butter with 1 tablespoon of the oil. When the butter is sizzling, add half of the fillets to the pan, leaving enough space so the fish can brown evenly. Fry the fish until the underside is golden brown, 7 or 8 minutes. Using a wide spatula, carefully flip the fillets and fry the second side until browned and cooked through, 5 to 6 minutes. Remove the fish to the wire rack and transfer to the oven to keep warm while you cook the rest of the fillets. Add the remaining butter and oil to the pan and repeat with the remaining fish.

PREP TIME: 10 minutes

COOKING TIME: 25 minutes

TOTAL TIME: 35 minutes

ADVANCE PREP *The fish can be made in the morning and reheated in a 325° F oven for 10 minutes before serving.*

Beer Batter–Fried Fish

Here's how I like to make my fish for fish and chips. (For the chips, see French Fries, page 191.) I use a simple beer batter, which I think makes for a crunchy but delicate crust. My favorite fish for this is cod, though haddock, dogfish, and even halibut are also fine. My preference is to use peanut oil, which has a buttery taste and texture, but any oil with a high enough smoke point for frying will work.

Makes 4 servings

1 cup all-purpose flour

½ teaspoon baking powder

¼ teaspoon baking soda

1 teaspoon kosher salt

½ teaspoon freshly ground black pepper

1 cup beer, such as lager or ale

1 large egg

Peanut or vegetable oil, for frying

1½ pounds skinless firm, thick white fish fillets, rinsed, patted dry, and cut into 2-inch pieces

½ cup cornstarch

In a small bowl, combine the flour, baking powder, baking soda, salt, and pepper. In another bowl, beat together the beer and the egg. Add this mixture to the flour and stir just to form a smooth batter. Let sit at room temperature for at least 1 hour.

Meanwhile, heat about 3 inches of oil in a large, heavy pot or in a deep-fryer to 370°F. Place a plate lined with paper towels or a brown paper bag near the stove. Dredge the fish in cornstarch to coat lightly. Tap off any excess. Dip a piece of fish in the batter, and scraping off any excess batter on the side of the bowl, place the fish in the hot oil. Add two or three more pieces, depending on how large the fryer is. Cook the fish until the coating is golden brown, 4 or 5 minutes. Turn the fish over and cook until the second side is evenly brown, another 2 minutes or so. Remove the fish with a slotted spatula or tongs and let drain on the paper while you fry the remaining fish.

PREP TIME: 10 minutes

COOKING TIME: 20 minutes

TOTAL TIME: 1½ hours (includes resting time)

ADVANCE PREP *The batter can be made several hours in advance and kept at room temperature until ready to use.*

Cod in the Basque Style

With its big flakes and moist texture, cod is one of my favorite fish. Its flavor stands up to some serious prepa-rations, such as this one, my take on the traditional Basque-style stewed pepper sauce. Halibut or monkfish will also work well.

Makes 4 servings

1 pound skinless cod, halibut, or monkfish fillets, cut into 4 pieces

2 tablespoons all-purpose flour

½ teaspoon kosher salt

Freshly ground black pepper

¼ cup extra-virgin olive oil

1 or 2 ounces pancetta, bacon, or prosciutto, finely chopped

1 small onion, chopped

2 garlic cloves, finely minced

12 ounces sweet cooking peppers, such as cubanelle, or red bell peppers, cored, seeded, and roughly chopped

2 or 3 small hot chiles, seeded and minced

2 anchovies, rinsed

2 tablespoons capers, rinsed and finely chopped

4 ripe plum tomatoes, peeled, or 4 canned tomatoes, with a few tablespoons of their juice, chopped

¼ cup dry white wine or water

2 tablespoons finely chopped flat-leaf parsley

Run your fingers over the surface of the cod fillets to be sure there are no pin bones left in the flesh. If you find any, use tweezers or needle-nose pliers to yank them out in the direction of the grain of the flesh of the fish. Very lightly dust both sides of the fillets with flour and tap off any excess. Season both sides with salt and pepper. In a large, nonstick frying pan, heat the olive oil over high heat. When it is very hot, add the cod. Sear for about 2 minutes, just until the fish is lightly browned. Carefully flip and sear for another 2 minutes. Remove to a plate.

Return the pan to the stove and lower the heat to medium. Add the pancetta and let the fat render for a minute or two. Add the onion and garlic and cook until the onion is soft, about 8 minutes. Add the sweet peppers and chiles and cook until they have wilted and given off their water, about 10 minutes. Add the anchovies and capers and cook for 1 minute, mashing the anchovies until they dissolve. Add the tomatoes and wine. Bring to a simmer and cook until the peppers are soft, about 10 minutes. Carefully transfer the cod back to the pan, jostling it gently to be sure it is almost covered by the sauce. Cover the pan and simmer until the fish is cooked through, 10 to 15 minutes, depending on the thickness of the fillets. Transfer to a serving plate and sprinkle with the parsley.

PREP TIME: 5 minutes
COOKING TIME: 40 minutes
TOTAL TIME: 45 minutes

ADVANCE PREP *You can sear the fish and prepare the sauce a full day in advance and refrigerate. To finish the dish, reheat the sauce, add the fish, and simmer until done as directed.*
LEFTOVERS *The dish will keep for two or three days in the fridge. Reheat in a frying pan over low heat.*

Crisp Skate with Brown Butter and Capers

I think skate is an underappreciated fish. This classic preparation takes minutes to prepare and is a great match for the delicate flavor and juiciness of the flesh. For a little textural contrast, I use a light dusting of granulated semolina (you can use cornmeal, too). If you'd rather not use butter, I've also given a variation with olive oil that's got some other Mediterranean flavorings.

Makes 4 servings

1 to 1½ pounds trimmed skate pieces
2 to 3 tablespoons granulated semolina or cornmeal
Kosher salt and freshly ground black pepper
4 tablespoons (½ stick) unsalted butter
3 tablespoons vegetable oil
1 large shallot, minced
3 tablespoons small capers, preferably salted, rinsed and drained
½ cup dry white wine or dry white vermouth
Juice of ½ lemon
1 to 2 tablespoons chopped flat-leaf parsley

Lay the skate out flat on a clean plate. Cover with a light dusting of semolina, pressing it into the flesh with your fingertips. Season to taste with salt and pepper. Turn over and repeat, dusting off any excess semolina or cornmeal that doesn't stick.

In a large frying pan, heat 2 tablespoons of the butter and the vegetable oil over high heat. When hot, lay the skate into the pan. Fry for 4 or 5 minutes, until the underside is lightly browned. With a long spatula, carefully turn over the skate and fry the second side until browned, about 4 minutes. Transfer the pieces to serving plates—this time they will be even more difficult to lift in one piece. Pour the fat out of the frying pan and wipe clean with a paper towel.

Add the remaining 2 tablespoons butter to the pan and set back over the heat. Add the shallot and cook for a minute or two, until soft. Add the capers and fry for another minute. Pour in the wine and lemon juice. Simmer until the sauce reduces and thickens slightly. Adjust the seasoning with salt and pepper, add the parsley, and spoon this mixture over the skate pieces.

PREP TIME: 5 minutes
COOKING TIME: 15 minutes
TOTAL TIME: 20 minutes

LEFTOVERS *The fish will keep for three or four days in the refrigerator, but the texture changes and it loses its fresh taste.*

VARIATION

Mediterranean-Style Skate with Capers

Substitute extra-virgin olive oil for the butter and vegetable oil. Add ½ minced garlic clove and a teaspoon of minced herbs (such as rosemary, marjoram, or thyme) along with the shallot. Proceed as directed.

■ ■ ■

Poultry

CHICKEN AND TURKEY have become America's default proteins. They are viewed as low in fat and neutral in a way that I think does a disservice to both the poultry and the people eating it. For starters, all chicken and turkey are not created equal. Despite what most people think, chicken and turkey should not be flavorless—they should have a distinct, albeit subtle, flavor. Although prices can vary tremendously, when possible you should search out a brand or source of top-quality, naturally raised poultry because the flavor, texture, and healthfulness of these birds is almost always better than factory-produced chicken or turkey. I am also a fan of kosher chickens and turkeys. Because of the salting involved in the koshering process, kosher poultry is like already brined poultry (more on that in a second). Of course, you can make a pretty tasty dish from just about any bird, provided you don't overcook it and you use a great recipe. Not being able to find—or not having the budget for—a free-range chicken, shouldn't stop you from cooking a chicken properly.

Once you've got the chicken or turkey, the question is what to do with it. Although brining—that is, soaking the meat in a salt or salt and sugar solution—has become a bit of a fad, with people swearing that the only way to cook a moist bird is to brine it, in my opinion the most common reason for dryness is overcooking. Everyone is so paranoid about salmonella and other bacteria and food-borne illnesses associated with poultry that we overcook all of our birds just to be safe. The truth is that these bacteria are killed at 160°F, so as long as you cook your meat to that temperature, and you clean your work area and utensils after handling raw poultry to avoid cross-contamination, you shouldn't have anything to worry about.

Don't get me wrong, I do think brining is a useful technique for cooking poultry as it assures a certain juiciness (see Chipotle-Rubbed Turkey Breast, page 330, for example). But I'm not a fanatic about it. Sometimes a simple advance salting, seasoning, or marinating can serve the same purpose as a full-fledged soak in brine. Brining not only affects juiciness but also the texture of the meat, and sometimes that altered texture—a little firmer, less falling-off-the-bone tender—is not desirable in a particular dish. And sometimes you just don't have time.

We shouldn't forget that chicken and turkey are only two of our friends from the poultry world. Duck and goose are also delicious birds that are readily available. Both are fattier and gamier than chicken or turkey and they have dark-meat breasts. I've included several recipes that I hope will make these other birds a part of your repertoire.

■ ■ ■

WHEN IS YOUR POULTRY DONE?

The most effective way to avoid dry poultry is not to overcook it. At the temperatures below your poultry should remain moist. Use an instant-read thermometer and poke it both in the center of the muscle and near the bone to be sure the meat is evenly cooked.

COOKING TEMPERATURES FOR POULTRY

Poultry	Temperature
White-meat chicken or turkey	160°F
Dark-meat chicken or turkey	175°F
Duck or goose, roasted	175°F
Boneless duck breast, medium rare	140°F to 150°F

As a rule, white meat is cooked and still moist at 160°F and dark meat is cooked and moist at 175°F. The difference in temperatures has to do with the structure of the meat. Dark meat is high in intramuscular fat and connective tissue, which break down after longer cooking and give the meat more flavor and a moist texture. Much beyond 160°F, white meat is chokingly dry. This difference in temperatures of doneness means that for some methods, like whole roasting, you have to manipulate the bird to be sure the dark meat cooks properly while the white meat is protected. An example would be turning a chicken over while it cooks. Note that duck is safe to eat at a lower temperature.

Although a thermometer is the only true way to test for doneness, you can also check by inserting the long tines of a roasting fork into the flesh of the bird. If the meat is done, the fork should penetrate easily and the juices that run out should be clear.

My Mother's Roast Chicken

This is how my mother roasted chickens. For all the various techniques I've tried—high temperature, brining, drying the skin, etc.—I think this is still one of the best ways to make a moist, flavorful bird. Although the skin isn't wafer-crisp, it browns well and imparts a nice flavor.

Makes 4 to 5 servings

2 large onions, chopped

1 large garlic clove, minced

One 4½-pound roasting chicken, rinsed and patted dry

1 tablespoon kosher salt

½ teaspoon freshly ground black pepper

½ teaspoon granulated garlic

½ teaspoon paprika

4 medium all-purpose potatoes, such as Yukon Gold, peeled and cut into chunks (optional)

Preheat the oven to 350°F.

Place the onions and minced garlic in the bottom of a roasting pan just slightly bigger than the chicken. Set the chicken, breast side up, on the onions. (Be sure to remove the neck and giblets from the cavity.) Season inside and out with half of the salt, half of the pepper, half of the granulated garlic, and half of the paprika. Turn the bird over—that is, breast side down—and season with the remaining spices. Cover the roasting pan with a tight-fitting lid or aluminum foil and set in the oven for 1 hour.

Remove the cover and scatter the potatoes, if using, around the base of the chicken. Raise the oven temperature to 400°F and continue roasting until the skin begins to brown, 20 to 25 minutes. Using two large forks or a pair of tongs, turn the chicken over so the breast is facing up. Move the potatoes around. Continue roasting for an additional 30 minutes, until the skin has browned and crisped. When done an instant-read thermometer inserted into the center of the breast should read at least 160°F, the thigh should register 175°F, and the thigh juices should run clear. The potatoes should be fork-tender. Remove from the oven and let rest for about 10 minutes before cutting up the chicken with poultry shears as explained on page 313. Strain the onions and pan juices through a fine-mesh sieve, pressing the onions to extract as much of their sweet juice as possible. Serve with the chicken.

PREP TIME: 10 minutes

COOKING TIME: 2 hours

TOTAL TIME: 2 hours 10 minutes (includes resting time)

ADVANCE PREP *The chicken can be seasoned, covered, and refrigerated a day or two in advance. In fact, preseasoning makes for a more flavorful, more succulent bird.*

LEFTOVERS *The chicken will keep for up to a week in the fridge. Use leftover roast chicken in any recipe that calls for cooked chicken, such as Chicken Pot Pie (page 322), Chicken Salad (page 78), or Chicken Hash (page 124).*

VARIATION

Roast Chicken with Fresh Herbs

Follow the same recipe, omitting the paprika and instead using 1 or 2 tablespoons of chopped assorted fresh herbs, such as rosemary, thyme, marjoram, or flat-leaf parsley. Also, place a handful of fresh herbs in the cavity. A squirt of fresh lemon juice on the skin (place the squeezed lemon halves in the cavity, too) also adds a nice flavor.

Crisp Roast Chicken with Herbs Under the Skin

This is a recipe for the sort of chicken that San Francisco's Zuni Café is famous for. At Zuni, they cook the chicken in an extremely hot wood-burning oven. The quick, high-heat cooking makes their birds crisp and juicy. At home, 475° to 500°F is as hot as most ovens get. At that temperature, for best results, it helps to use a smallish chicken—in the 3-pound range rather than the 5-pound. In addition to the high heat, the secret to good, crisp bistro-style chicken is a lot of salt. On a 3-pound bird I use a little more than a tablespoon of kosher salt. The salt helps dry out the skin, which makes it crisp. If you have time to salt the bird in advance and refrigerate it for a day or two—in effect brining the chicken—your results will be even better. Finally, for a little flavor and flourish, I put fresh herbs under the skin—not a lot, just enough to perfume the meat as it cooks. At such a high temperature, herbs sprinkled on the outside of the chicken would burn.

Makes 2 to 4 servings

One 3-pound chicken, rinsed and patted dry
4 or 5 sprigs fresh herbs, such as rosemary, thyme, marjoram, or sage, leaves only
Juice of ½ lemon
Kosher salt and freshly ground black pepper

Preheat the oven to 475°F. Place a cast-iron pan or other baking dish just big enough to hold the chicken in the oven while it preheats.

With the bird sitting breast side up, legs pointing toward you, carefully insert first your fingers and then your hand between the skin and the flesh of the chicken to loosen the skin on the breast and also on the legs and thighs. Be careful not to tear the skin. Insert the fresh herbs under the skin as far in as you can go. Pull the skin back over the flesh to keep it covered. Squeeze the lemon juice over the chicken. Season the chicken generously with salt, using about a tablespoon or so, and with pepper. Sprinkle some salt and pepper in the cavity and under the chicken, too. (Be sure to remove the neck and giblets from the cavity.)

Place the chicken, breast side up, in the hot pan in the oven. Roast for about 30 minutes, until the skin is blistered and somewhat browned. Turn the chicken over and roast the underside for 15 minutes or so, until browned. Return the chicken to the upright position and finish roasting until the skin over the breast is evenly browned and crisp, another 10 minutes or so. When done, an instant-read thermometer inserted into the center of the breast should read at least 160°F, the thigh should register 175°F; and the thigh juices should run clear. Remove the chicken and let it sit at room temperature for 10 minutes or so to relax. To serve, cut the chicken into halves or quarters.

PREP TIME: 5 minutes
COOKING TIME: 1 hour
TOTAL TIME: 1 hour 15 minutes (includes resting time)

ADVANCE PREP *The chicken is actually juicier and more flavorful if you can season it with herbs and salt in advance and let it sit in the refrigerator for*

KITCHEN SENSE

TO TRUSS OR NOT TO TRUSS
Occasionally I like to truss chickens because of the tradition of it—it makes me feel like I'm back working in a butcher shop in high school or that I'm really cooking like a classically trained French chef—but the truth is I usually don't truss anything. If you want to try it anyway, and you have a couple of feet of butcher's twine lying around, here's what you do. Sit a chicken on a clean work surface, breast up, cavity facing you. Place the string under the tail of the chicken and pull both ends up around the legs, looping them around the ankles, and crossing the string to form an X in front of the cavity. Holding the string taut, turn the chicken over and run both ends of the string along the back to the wings, looping them over the elbows. Turn the chicken right side up again and tie the string together over the shoulders and the front of the breast, pulling the wings and legs tightly into the body.

Because of the way they are processed, turkeys don't usually require trussing. There should be a loop of skin by the tail into which you can tuck the ends of the drumsticks to hold any stuffing inside the cavity and essentially truss the bird. If you can't find that loop of skin, follow the directions for trussing a chicken, only double the length of string to about 4 feet.

up to two days before you roast it. Season with pepper just before roasting.
LEFTOVERS *Leftovers will keep for about a week in the fridge. Use in any recipe that calls for cooked chicken.*

CUTTING UP A COOKED CHICKEN

Although whole roasted chickens are infinitely more flavorful than roasted chicken parts, I think people are intimidated by the idea of having to deal with a whole bird when it is done. But cutting up a cooked chicken to serve doesn't require nearly the amount of skill of carving a turkey. First, unlike turkey carving, chicken portioning happens in the kitchen, not the dining room, so you don't have to deal with the pressure of having to perform in front of an audience. Second, if you have a good pair of kitchen shears, whether specialized for cutting poultry or not, you can't go wrong.

I like to cut up my chickens while they are sitting in the roasting pan so all of their flavorful juices are captured in the pan. (Strain the juices to serve with the meat.) Depending on how large a bird you have cooked and how many people you are serving, you can cut a chicken into halves, quarters, eighths, or tenths. With the bird sitting, breast up, legs pointing toward you, use your poultry or kitchen shears to cut through the center of the breast bone from the cavity straight up to the neck. The carcass will fall open to the sides. In front of you, at the bottom of the cavity, you will see the ridge of bone that is the back or spine. Cut along both sides of the back bone to separate the bird into halves; discard the back bone. You now have two halves. Each half will separate easily into two pieces, the leg and thigh forming one piece, the breast and wing, the other. Cut the skin if necessary to separate them. Wiggle the leg to find the joint, and use the shears to snip through the cartilage, separating the leg from the thigh. Remove the wing from the breast in the same way. If the breasts are very large, you can snip them in half also, right through the center. You should end up with eight to ten pieces.

Spice-Rubbed Roast Chicken

I once improvised a Peruvian-style roast chicken based on a very brief conversation with a friend who frequented a small Peruvian restaurant. It was delicious. When I finally had the Peruvian chicken served at the restaurant, it was completely different but also quite delicious. You can alter the spices in this not-so-Peruvian chicken, but hold onto the marinating step, which will make your chicken delicious, too.

Makes 4 servings

> 2 medium onions, roughly chopped
> One 4- to 4½-pound chicken, rinsed and
>   patted dry
> 1 head of fresh garlic, cut in half crosswise
> 2 lemons, cut in half crosswise
> 1 tablespoon kosher salt
> 1 teaspoon freshly ground black pepper
> 1 teaspoon ground cumin
> ½ teaspoon ground cinnamon
> ½ teaspoon cayenne pepper
> ½ teaspoon granulated garlic
> 1 handful of fresh cilantro

Place the onions on the bottom of a roasting pan or baking dish that's just large enough to hold the chicken. Set the chicken on top of the onions. (Be sure to remove the packet of giblets and neck from the cavity.) Rub the skin of the chicken all around with the cut side of the garlic. Place the garlic inside the cavity of the bird. Squeeze the lemon juice from both lemons over the chicken and rub it into the skin with the cut side of the lemon. Place 1 or 2 of the squeezed lemon halves inside the cavity, too. In a small bowl, mix the salt, black pepper, cumin, cinnamon, cayenne, and granulated garlic. With your fingertips, rub this mixture into the skin, being sure to get the mixture onto every part of the bird. Place the cilantro in the cavity with everything else. Cover the chicken and refrigerate it for at least a couple of hours, but preferably overnight.

Preheat the oven to 350°F.

Turn the chicken breast side down on top of the onions. Roast for about 45 minutes. Your kitchen should fill with a beautiful bouquet of aromas. Turn the chicken breast side up. Raise the oven temperature to 425°F and continue roasting for 30 to 45 minutes, until the chicken is browned and the meat is cooked through. An instant-read thermometer inserted close to the breast bone should read 160°F, and in the thigh should read 175°F; the thigh juices should run clear. Remove the chicken and let sit at room temperature for about 10 minutes before cutting into pieces to serve.

PREP TIME: 10 minutes

COOKING TIME: 1 hour 15 minutes

TOTAL TIME: 4 hours 45 minutes (includes marinating time and resting time)

ADVANCE PREP The chicken is actually best if it is seasoned and refrigerated for up to two days before roasting.

LEFTOVERS The chicken will keep in the refrigerator for about five days. Use the meat for a chicken salad, hash, or any recipe that calls for cooked chicken.

VARIATION

Grilled Spice-Rubbed Chicken

Use chicken pieces instead of a whole bird. Omit the onions. Follow the same marinating procedure—save for stuffing things in the cavity, obviously. Grill the chicken over hot coals. It usually takes longer to cook chicken on a grill than you think it will, about 30 min-

utes total. Check the internal temperature with an instant-read thermometer as you would for a whole chicken (see page 310).

Cold Poached Chicken Breast

This recipe is based on a Chinese technique for making cold poached chicken that has a delicate, almost silken, juicy texture. You can serve the chicken in a salad or sandwich or with any sauce, but I recommend either Spicy Asian Chili Sauce (page 397) or garlicky Spanish Romesco Sauce (page 401).

Makes 4 to 6 servings

> 4 medium bone-in chicken breasts, skin on (2 to 2½ pounds), rinsed
> Three ½-inch-thick slices fresh ginger, smashed
> 4 scallions, white and green parts, cut into 2-inch pieces, or 1 shallot, sliced
> 2 garlic cloves, smashed
> 1 bay leaf
> 1 tablespoon kosher salt
> 1 teaspoon white or black peppercorns

Place the chicken breasts in a pot and cover with enough cold water to come 2 or 3 inches above the breasts. Remove the breasts and set aside. To the water in the pot add the ginger, scallions, garlic, bay leaf, salt, and peppercorns. Bring to a boil, cover, turn down the heat, and simmer for about 5 minutes.

Turn the heat back up to high. Remove the cover and add the chicken to the pot. Bring back to a simmer, cover, and cook for 5 minutes. Remove the pot from the heat, still covered, and let sit, undisturbed for about 2 hours, or until the chicken is cool enough to handle.

CUTTING UP A RAW CHICKEN

Don't underestimate the value of knowing how to cut up a chicken. When I was a freshman in high school, my mother told the owner of her local butcher shop that I wanted a job. He handed me the largest, sharpest knife I had ever seen in my life and said, "Here, cut this chicken into eighths." I did just an okay job cutting up that bird, but it was good enough to get me the gig. Even though today's grocery stores are filled with an impressive number of different configurations of chicken parts, I think it is preferable to cut up your own chicken if you can. Whole chickens tend to be fresher and juicier than chicken parts. Plus, for aesthetic reasons, the best-quality chickens are usually sold whole, which means you stand to get better-quality pieces if you start with a whole bird.

Cutting up a raw chicken is not that much different from cutting up a cooked chicken (see page 313), except that the bones of a raw chicken are a little tougher, so you can't use shears. Instead, you need a sharp knife.

Wash and pat dry the chicken. Stand the chicken up on a cutting board, neck side down, tail and legs in the air, with the underside or back of the chicken facing you. The chicken should balance pretty well on its wings. Hold the chicken up by one of the legs. With the tip of a sharp chef's knife, cleaver, or Japanese-style knife, cut along one side of the back bone from the tail to the cutting board. Keeping the chicken upright, run the knife down the other side of the back bone to remove it, along with the neck. (Save the back and neck for chicken soup, stock, or broth.) Now lay the chicken splayed open flat on the cutting board, skin side down. Using the entire blade of the knife, cut straight through the breast bone and cartilage to divide the chicken into two even halves.

Turn one half of the chicken over. Pull the leg and thigh away from the breast, pulling apart the two sections as much as possible, and then cut through the skin, following the outline of the breast to separate. Holding the leg and thigh upright to form a V, cut through the cartilage of the joint to separate the two pieces. Separate the wing from the breast in a similar way, wiggling the wing to find the joint closest to the breast and then cutting through the cartilage to remove it. If the breast is large, you can cut it in half right through the center. Repeat with the second side. If you are successful, you should have eight to ten pieces, depending on whether you cut the breast in half.

Take the chicken out of the pot, and remove the skin and discard. With your fingers, carefully lift the meat off the bone in one piece. Slice crosswise into ½-inch-thick slices.

PREP TIME: 15 minutes

COOKING TIME: 10 minutes

TOTAL TIME: 2 hours 20 minutes (includes resting time)

ADVANCE PREP The chicken can be made up to two days in advance. Reserve the whole breasts in the cooking liquid until ready to serve.

LEFTOVERS The chicken will keep for a week in the refrigerator. Use leftovers in anything that calls for cooked chicken. Save the poaching liquid to use as a light chicken broth for cooking.

Sautéed Chicken Breasts with Mushrooms

Skinless and boneless chicken breasts need help in the flavor department. Mushrooms, which have a deep, woody flavor, come to the rescue in this quick, delicious entrée. The same dish can be made with veal or pork cutlets.

Makes 4 servings

1¾ pounds skinless and boneless chicken breasts

½ cup all-purpose flour

Kosher salt and freshly ground black pepper

½ cup (1 stick) unsalted butter

1 shallot, minced

12 ounces assorted mushrooms, such as cremini, portobello, chanterelle, black trumpet, or button, sliced

¼ cup mushroom or chicken broth

½ cup dry sherry, Marsala, or Madeira

1 tablespoon chopped flat-leaf parsley

Rinse the chicken breasts and pat dry with paper towels. If they are very thick, more than ¾ inch, you should pound them between two sheets of plastic wrap with a mallet or the bottom of a frying pan to an even ½-inch thickness.

In a wide bowl, combine the flour with 1 teaspoon salt and ¼ teaspoon pepper.

Heat the butter in a large frying pan over medium heat. Dredge the breasts in the flour, tap off any excess, and set half in the hot butter. Fry the breasts until the undersides are light golden brown, about 6 minutes, and then flip and fry the second side for 4 or 5 minutes more until cooked through. Remove from the pan to a plate. Repeat with remaining breasts.

Turn up the heat to medium-high. Add the shallot and sauté until soft, about 3 minutes. Add the mushrooms and sauté until they have wilted and given off some of their water, 4 or 5 minutes. Pour in the mushroom broth and cook until the liquid is almost evaporated, about 5 minutes. Add the sherry and bring to a simmer. Return all the chicken to the pan and bury in the mushrooms to heat through. Stir in the parsley. Adjust the seasoning with additional salt and pepper, if necessary, and serve.

PREP TIME: 10 minutes
COOKING TIME: 30 minutes
TOTAL TIME: 40 minutes

LEFTOVERS *The chicken will keep for about one week in the fridge. Reheat leftovers in a frying pan, adding a tablespoon or so of water, if necessary, to avoid burning.*

Jerk Chicken

Along the side of the roads in Jamaica you see people selling jerk chicken grilled on makeshift oil-drum grills. It is vinegary, painfully spicy, and delicious. Scotch Bonnet chiles (similar to habaneros) are impressively hot. You should wear rubber gloves when you handle them. If the sauce is too spicy for your taste, substitute a jalapeño instead. The same jerk spice paste is also delicious on pork.

Makes 6 to 8 servings

1 small white onion, chopped

3 garlic cloves

1 Scotch Bonnet, habanero, or jalapeño chile, seeded and chopped

3 scallions, white and green parts, chopped

1 tablespoon ground allspice

1 tablespoon dried thyme

1 tablespoon dried sage

1 tablespoon dry mustard

1 tablespoon sugar

1 tablespoon kosher salt

1 teaspoon freshly ground black pepper

3/4 teaspoon freshly grated nutmeg

3/4 teaspoon ground cinnamon

1/2 teaspoon ground cloves

1/2 teaspoon cayenne pepper

Juice of 2 limes (about 1/3 cup)

Juice of 1 orange (about 1/2 cup)

1/4 cup peanut or vegetable oil

1/4 cup cider or white vinegar

2 tablespoons ketchup

8 pieces bone-in chicken with the skin (about 4 pounds), rinsed and patted dry

In a blender or food processor fitted with a metal blade, combine the onion, garlic, Scotch Bonnet, scallions, allspice, thyme, sage, mustard, sugar, salt, pepper, nutmeg, cinnamon, cloves, cayenne pepper, lime juice, orange juice, peanut oil, vinegar, and ketchup. Blend, using on/off pulses, to form a smooth paste. Place the chicken in a nonreactive container, and spoon enough of the spicy paste over the meat to coat. Reserve extra jerk rub aside. If you have the time, let the chicken marinate in the refrigerator overnight.

Heat a grill. If using charcoal, the coals should be medium-hot and set a little off to one side. Place the chicken on the grill, bone side down, almost directly over the coals, and grill for about 10 minutes to begin to cook the meat. Turn it over and continue grilling for 10 to 15 minutes, until the meat looks opaque and almost cooked through. Turn it over

again, skin side up, and baste the chicken with more of the spice mixture. Move it to an area of the grill that isn't directly over the coals or the heat. Cover the grill and let cook until the meat is falling off the bone, another 30 minutes or more, depending on the size of the chicken parts and the temperature of the grill. As individual pieces are done, remove them from the grill and wrap them in aluminum foil to keep warm.

PREP TIME: 10 minutes

COOKING TIME: 50 minutes to 1 hour

TOTAL TIME: 1 hour

ADVANCE PREP *The chicken is best after it has marinated for at least 12 hours and up to two days. If you don't have the time, though, you can go ahead and cook it right away—just keep basting the chicken with the spice mixture as it cooks.*
LEFTOVERS *The chicken will keep for about a week in the fridge and it is delicious cold. In fact, if you find the chicken overly spicy when it is first made, the spice is less pronounced when chilled.*

Cracker-Crumb Chicken Fingers

Chicken fingers breaded with cracker crumbs have a delicate, crunchy crust. I'm an advocate of grinding your own crackers, since they are fresher tasting than already ground cracker crumbs. Allowing the chicken to soak for several hours in a saltwater brine before breading makes the chicken juicy and flavorful.

Makes 4 to 6 servings

3 tablespoons kosher salt

1 1/2 pounds skinless and boneless chicken breasts

8 ounces plain crackers, such as saltines or oyster crackers, or 1 1/2 cups Japanese bread crumbs (panko)

1/2 cup all-purpose flour

1/4 teaspoon freshly ground black pepper

2 large eggs

1 to 1 1/2 cups peanut or vegetable oil, for frying

1/4 cup grainy French mustard

1/4 cup honey

Dissolve the salt in 1 cup hot water. Add 3 cups cold water. Put the chicken breasts in a shallow bowl, pour the saltwater over the chicken, and refrigerate for 2 hours. Drain, rinse, and pat the chicken dry. Slice the chicken on a slight diagonal into long, thin strips about 1 inch wide and 1/2 inch thick.

Place the crackers in a resealable plastic bag and crush with a rolling pin to make fine crumbs. (Alternatively, you can use a food processor fitted with a metal blade to pulse the crackers to crumbs.) You should have about 1 1/2 cups. Place the crumbs on a plate.

In a bowl, combine the flour with the pepper and mix well. (You don't need any extra salt because of the brine and the salty crackers.) In a wide bowl, beat the eggs with 3 tablespoons water until frothy.

Heat about 1/4 inch of oil in a heavy frying pan, such as cast iron, over medium-high heat. Dredge the chicken in flour. Tap off any excess. Dip it in the egg. Using a fork, pick up the pieces, let drain for a second, and roll in the cracker crumbs to coat. Place half of the chicken in the hot oil, filling the pan without overcrowding. The chicken should sizzle instantly. If not, the oil isn't hot enough. Fry the chicken until golden brown on the underside, 3 or 4 minutes, then turn over and fry the second side, another 3 or 4 minutes. Remove to a paper-towel-lined plate to drain. Add more oil if necessary, let it heat up, and then repeat with the remaining chicken.

Blend the mustard and honey with $\frac{1}{4}$ cup cold water to make a thin sauce. Serve with the hot chicken fingers.

PREP TIME: 15 minutes
COOKING TIME: 20 minutes
TOTAL TIME: 35 minutes

LEFTOVERS *The chicken fingers will keep for about five days in the fridge. Reheat leftovers on a wire rack in a 350° F oven for 10 minutes. Or cut them up and use them cold in salads.*

Barbecued Chicken, With or Without a Grill

As with ribs (see page 379), I like to bake my chicken before I put it on the grill and slather it with barbecue sauce. This ensures that the chicken cooks through and doesn't burn as the fat drips onto the fire. In lieu of brining, I coat the chicken with a spice mixture and let it marinate overnight in the fridge, which makes it extra juicy and flavorful. If you don't have access to a grill, you can finish the barbecued chicken under a broiler. Use your favorite homemade or store-bought barbecue sauce. Wrapping the chicken in aluminum foil and letting it continue to cook/steam on the grill makes the chicken falling-off-the-bone tender.

Makes 4 servings

1 tablespoon grainy French or Dijon mustard
1 tablespoon honey
1 tablespoon smoked paprika or 1 teaspoon ground chipotle pepper and 2 teaspoons sweet Hungarian paprika
2 tablespoons vegetable oil
1 tablespoon kosher salt
$\frac{1}{4}$ teaspoon freshly ground black pepper
$\frac{1}{4}$ teaspoon ground cumin
1 large garlic clove, minced
2 tablespoons minced fresh ginger
One 4- to 4$\frac{1}{2}$-pound chicken, cut into 10 pieces (see page 315), or 3$\frac{1}{2}$ to 4 pounds chicken parts, rinsed and patted dry
1$\frac{1}{2}$ cups Evelynne's Barbecue Sauce (page 406) or your own favorite sauce

In a small bowl, combine the mustard, honey, paprika, oil, salt, pepper, cumin, garlic, and ginger and mix to form a smooth paste. Rub this mixture all over the surface of the chicken, pack the chicken into a bowl or container, pour any excess spice mixture on top, cover the chicken, and let marinate in the refrigerator for at least 2 hours, and preferably overnight.

Preheat the oven to 400° F. Line a baking sheet with parchment paper or aluminum foil (for easy clean-up).

Arrange the chicken on the baking sheet, skin side up, and set in the oven to roast for about 30 minutes, or until the meat is just about cooked through.

While the chicken is cooking, preheat a grill to medium-hot.

Remove the chicken from the oven and brush with a generous amount of barbecue sauce. Grill the chicken, turning and basting regularly with more sauce, until the chicken is browned and crisped, 10 to 15 minutes, depending on the heat of the grill. An instant-read thermometer should register 160°F when inserted into the center of the flesh of a breast and near a bone, and 175°F in a leg or thigh. As chicken pieces are done, you can smother them with more sauce, wrap them in aluminum foil, and keep them warm on a cooler part of the grill until everything is done. (Alternatively, you can finish the chicken under a hot broiler, turning and basting the chicken with the barbecue sauce until it is evenly browned and crisp.) Serve the chicken with additional barbecue sauce on the side.

PREP TIME: 15 minutes
COOKING TIME: 45 to 50 minutes
TOTAL TIME: 3 hours (includes marinating time)

ADVANCE PREP *The chicken can sit in its spice rub for up to two days in the fridge before being cooked.*
LEFTOVERS *The chicken will keep for about one week in the fridge.*

Chicken and Pepper Casserole

I like to think of this dish as an Italian pot pie, only the "crust"—really toasted slices of bread—is on the bottom instead of the top.

Makes 4 to 6 servings

4 or 5 (½-inch-thick) slices crusty country bread
6 tablespoons extra-virgin olive oil
Kosher salt and freshly ground black pepper
1 medium onion, sliced
2 garlic cloves, minced
5 or 6 cubanelle or Italian frying peppers (about 1 pound), seeded and cut into 1-inch chunks

1¼ pounds boneless and skinless chicken breasts, cut into 1-inch chunks
1 teaspoon fresh thyme or ½ teaspoon dried
¼ teaspoon dried oregano
Pinch of crushed red pepper flakes
1½ cups canned plum tomatoes with juice, cut into chunks
4 ounces sharp provolone cheese, grated (1 cup)

Preheat the oven to 400°F.

Lay out the bread on a baking sheet. Using about 2 tablespoons of the olive oil, brush the bread with oil on both sides. Season with salt and pepper. Place the bread in the preheating oven to toast for about 10 minutes, or until nicely browned, turning once or twice.

Meanwhile, in a large frying pan, heat the remaining ¼ cup olive oil over medium-high heat. Add the onion and cook until soft, about 5 minutes. Add the garlic and cook for another minute or so. Add the peppers, and fry until they have wilted, about 7 minutes. Add the chicken and cook until it turns opaque white, about 5 minutes. Add the thyme, oregano, red pepper flakes, and canned tomatoes and juice, along with about 1 teaspoon kosher salt and a generous amount of black pepper. Bring to a simmer, and cook until some of the liquid in the pan has evaporated and the chicken is cooked through, another 4 or 5 minutes or so.

Line the bottom of a 1½- or 2-quart baking dish with the toasted bread. Spoon the chicken and pepper mixture over the bread to fill the dish and pour the pan juices evenly over the top. Sprinkle the chicken with an even layer of provolone. Bake for about 35 minutes, until the cheese has melted and browned and the chicken is bubbling.

PREP TIME: 30 minutes

COOKING TIME: 50 minutes

TOTAL TIME: 1 hour 20 minutes

ADVANCE PREP *The casserole can be assembled up to a day in advance, refrigerated, and baked before serving.*

LEFTOVERS *The casserole will keep for about a week in the fridge. Reheat leftovers in a frying pan or in the microwave. They make delicious fillings for hero sandwiches on Italian bread with a little extra tomato sauce and additional melted cheese.*

Summertime Chicken Cacciatore

Traditionally, this Italian "hunter's" chicken is loaded with wild mushrooms, which give it a woodsy, wintry flavor. My sister uses eggplant or zucchini instead, which makes this recipe lighter and more summery, with a garden-fresh taste.

Makes 4 to 6 servings

> One 4- to 4½-pound chicken, cut into 10 pieces (see page 315), or 3½ to 4 pounds chicken parts, rinsed and patted dry
>
> Kosher salt and freshly ground black pepper
>
> ¼ cup extra-virgin olive oil
>
> 1 medium onion, sliced
>
> 1 large garlic clove, minced
>
> 1 pound eggplant, peeled and cubed, or zucchini, cubed
>
> 1 tablespoon fresh oregano, minced, or 1 teaspoon dried
>
> ½ cup dry red wine or dry sherry
>
> 1 red bell pepper, seeded and cubed
>
> 1 (28-ounce) can plum tomatoes, cut into chunks, with juice
>
> Pinch of crushed red pepper flakes (optional)
>
> 2 bay leaves

Season the chicken pieces generously with salt and black pepper. In a Dutch oven or other wide pot, heat the olive oil over medium-high heat. Add the chicken pieces and cook for 7 or 8 minutes, turning frequently, until the chicken has browned. Remove to a plate. To the pot add the onion and garlic, and cook until wilted, about 5 minutes. Add the eggplant and oregano and cook until soft, another 5 minutes or so. Add the red wine and scrape off any bits stuck to the bottom of the pan. Add the bell pepper, tomatoes with their juice, red pepper flakes, if using, and bay leaves. Return the chicken to the pan and bury it under the tomato mixture. Cover the pan, turn down the heat, and simmer for 30 minutes. Remove the cover and continue simmering for another 30 minutes, until the sauce has reduced and the meat falls off the bone. Discard the bay leaves.

PREP TIME: 15 minutes

COOKING TIME: 1 hour 30 minutes

TOTAL TIME: 1 hour 45 minutes

ADVANCE PREP *The chicken can be made a day in advance, refrigerated, and reheated—covered, over low heat—to serve.*

LEFTOVERS *The cacciatore will keep for about one week in the fridge. It can also be frozen for up to two months. Reheat leftovers in a small, covered pan. You can also take the meat off the bones, cut it into chunks, and use as the base for a pasta sauce.*

Chicken Paprikash

Although this is a traditional Hungarian dish, to me it has a retro 1950s American connotation. Regardless, it's delicious. Because the principal flavor is paprika, making

Chicken Paprikash is a good excuse to throw out your old stale jar of paprika and buy a new, fresh one. Serve it over buttered egg noodles or Spätzle (page 246).

Makes 4 to 6 servings

One 4- to 4½-pound chicken, cut into 10 pieces (see page 315), or 3½ to 4 pounds chicken parts, rinsed and patted dry
Kosher salt and freshly ground black pepper
2 tablespoons peanut or vegetable oil
2 tablespoons lard, bacon fat, or additional oil
½ cup all-purpose flour
1 medium onion, chopped
1 large garlic clove, minced
1 or 2 cubanelle or Italian frying peppers, seeded and chopped
2 tablespoons sweet Hungarian paprika
1 cup chicken stock or water
½ cup white wine
1 large ripe tomato, peeled and cut into chunks, or 2 canned tomatoes, cut up
½ cup sour cream

Season the chicken pieces generously with salt and pepper. Heat the oil and lard in a heavy, wide pot over medium-high heat. Dredge the chicken in the flour, tap off any excess, and place in the hot oil. Fry the chicken until it is nicely browned on all sides, 7 or 8 minutes. Remove the chicken to a plate. Add the onion and garlic to the pot and cook until soft, about 5 minutes. Add the peppers and cook for 3 or 4 minutes, until the peppers are soft. Add the paprika and cook for a minute or two, until lightly toasted. Add the stock, wine, and tomato and stir to combine. Return the chicken to the pot along with any juices that have accumulated on the plate, cover, turn down the heat to low, and simmer for about 30 minutes, stirring occasionally.

Remove the cover, turn up the heat slightly, and let the chicken simmer for about 20 minutes, or until the cooking liquid has reduced by about half and the chicken starts to fall off the bone. Stir 3 or 4 tablespoons of the hot cooking liquid into the sour cream to temper it and then carefully stir that mixture back into the pan to blend. Adjust the seasoning with salt and pepper and serve.

PREP TIME: 10 minutes
COOKING TIME: 65 minutes
TOTAL TIME: 1 hour 15 minutes

ADVANCE PREP *The chicken can be made a day in advance, refrigerated, and reheated on a low burner to serve.*
LEFTOVERS *The chicken will keep for about a week in the fridge. It can also be frozen.*

Chicken or Turkey Pot Pie

Although chicken pot pie is a recipe designed to use up leftover cooked chicken, it is so good I usually make it from scratch with boneless chicken breasts instead of waiting for leftovers. Either way, it is a homey, satisfying, American dish. For a flaky, puff-pastry-like crust, use Cream Cheese Pastry (page 435); for a biscuit topping, use Angel Biscuits (page 125) or Buttermilk Biscuits (page 127). You can also use a regular pie crust (page 421) or store-bought puff pastry.

Makes 4 to 6 servings

Kosher salt
1½ pounds skinless and boneless chicken or turkey breasts, or 3½ cups cubed cooked chicken or turkey
½ cup (1 stick) unsalted butter

1 medium onion, chopped

1 medium carrot, diced

1 celery stalk, chopped

4 ounces mushrooms, sliced

1 teaspoon chopped fresh thyme or ¼ teaspoon
   dried, or other herbs

⅓ cup frozen peas

Freshly ground black pepper

½ cup dry sherry or dry white wine

5 tablespoons all-purpose flour

2 cups chicken stock

1 bay leaf

1 tablespoon chopped flat-leaf parsley

½ recipe Cream Cheese Pastry (page 431) or
   ½ recipe Angel Biscuits (page 125) or
   Buttermilk Biscuits (page 127), made with a
   handful of chopped fresh herbs mixed into
   the biscuit dough; regular pie dough (page
   421); or store-bought, frozen all-butter puff
   pastry, defrosted

1 large egg

If I'm using raw chicken breasts, I first like to brine them, although this step is optional. Dissolve 2 tablespoons kosher salt in 2 cups warm water. Cool to room temperature and pour over the chicken. Refrigerate for at least 1 hour and up to 4 hours. Remove the chicken from the brine and rinse before cutting into 1-inch chunks.

Preheat the oven to 425°F.

In a large frying pan, melt 3 tablespoons of the butter over medium-high heat. Add the onion and cook until soft, about 4 minutes. Add the carrot and celery and continue cooking until soft, about 4 more minutes. Add the mushrooms and thyme and cook until the mushrooms wilt and give off their water, 5 minutes. Add the peas, 1 teaspoon salt, and pepper

to taste, and stir for a minute or so. Pour in ¼ cup of the sherry and scrape the bottom of the pan to remove any bits that might have stuck. Set aside.

Meanwhile, in a large saucepan, melt the remaining 5 tablespoons butter. Stir in the flour to make a paste or roux. Cook the roux for 2 minutes or so until it gives off a nutty, toasted aroma. Whisk in the stock, add the remaining ¼ cup sherry, the bay leaf and parsley, 1 teaspoon salt, and pepper to taste, and simmer for 3 or 4 minutes, until thickened. If using the raw chicken, add it to the pot now, bring to a boil, cover, turn down the heat, and simmer for 5 or 6 minutes, until cooked through. Remove the bay leaf. Add the cooked vegetables. If using cooked chicken, add it to the pot now. Transfer this mixture to a 1½-quart round baking dish and let cool while you prepare the crust.

Roll out the dough to a circle about 1 inch larger in diameter than the baking dish. Pastry dough should be rolled out about ¼ inch thick; biscuit dough about ½ inch thick. Transfer the dough to the top of the baking dish, pressing the overhang onto the outside lip of the dish. Beat the egg with 1 tablespoon of cold water and brush egg wash on the surface of the dough. With a sharp knife, make four or five small slits in the dough to allow steam to escape.

Bake for 20 minutes, until the dough has risen and begun to brown. Turn down the heat to 350°F and bake for another 15 to 20 minutes, until the dough has turned a deep brown and cooked through. Remove from the oven and serve immediately.

PREP TIME: 20 minutes
COOKING TIME: 1 hour
TOTAL TIME: 2 hours 20 minutes

ADVANCE PREP *The filling and crust can be made up to a day in advance and refrigerated separately. Before baking, warm the filling in a saucepan or in the microwave before you place the crust on top. Heating the filling helps the crust bake more quickly and more evenly.*

LEFTOVERS *The pie will keep for about a week in the fridge. Reheat leftovers in a frying pan or in a dish in a 350° F oven.*

VARIATION
Chicken or Turkey Gratin

If you would rather not bother rolling out a crust, simply pour the filling into a buttered baking dish. Top with ³/₄ cup (about 3 ounces) grated Swiss cheese, such as Emmentaler or Gruyère, and 3 tablespoons grated parmesan mixed with 1 tablespoon bread crumbs. Bake in a preheated 375° F oven for about 30 minutes, or until the cheese has melted and browned.

Chicken and Dumplings

This classic American dish—a sort of fricassée covered with soft dumplings—is about as satisfying as any dish could be. For the full effect, I like to make it in a cast-iron Dutch oven with a glass lid that I carry to the table. You can see the puffy dumplings inside the gurgling pot, and then when you lift the lid, the table fills with the irresistible aroma of the dish.

Makes 4 to 6 servings

FOR THE CHICKEN
- One 3¹/₂- to 4-pound chicken, cut into 10 pieces (see page 315), or 3¹/₂ pounds chicken parts
- 4 teaspoons kosher salt
- ¹/₂ teaspoon freshly ground black pepper
- 2 tablespoons unsalted butter, bacon fat, or vegetable oil
- 1 large onion, sliced
- 1 large garlic clove, minced
- About 4 cups chicken stock
- 1 bay leaf
- ¹/₄ cup dry sherry or dry white wine
- 4 ounces button or cremini mushrooms, sliced

FOR THE DUMPLINGS
- 1¹/₂ cups all-purpose flour
- 1 tablespoon baking powder
- ³/₄ teaspoon kosher salt
- ¹/₄ cup vegetable shortening, lard, rendered chicken fat (schmaltz), or butter, chilled
- 2 tablespoons finely chopped flat-leaf parsley
- ³/₄ cup buttermilk, sour milk, or regular milk

Remove and reserve the skin and any excess fat from each piece of chicken. Season the chicken pieces with half of the salt and black pepper, then turn the pieces over and season with the remaining salt and pepper. Set aside.

Over medium-high heat, heat a 6-quart Dutch oven or other wide, heavy pot that is deep enough to hold the chicken with 2 or 3 inches of space left above it. Place the chicken skin and fat and butter in the pot. Cook until the chicken fat renders and the skin curls and starts to brown, about 4 minutes. Remove and discard the skin. Add the onion and cook for 4 or 5 minutes, until it softens. Add the garlic and cook for an additional 4 or 5 minutes or so, until the onion begins to brown.

Add the chicken pieces to the pot. Pour over just enough stock to almost cover all the chicken. Add the bay leaf. Turn down the heat, cover, and simmer for about 30 minutes. Add the sherry and the mushrooms and simmer, covered, for another 10 minutes or so, until the chicken is almost fully cooked.

Meanwhile, prepare the dumpling batter. In a large bowl, combine the flour, baking powder, and salt. Mix well. Add the shortening or other fat and using a pastry cutter, two knives, or your fingertips, cut in the fat until the mixture resembles coarse crumbs. (Alternatively, you can combine the dry ingredients in the bowl of a food processor, pulse to blend, add the chilled shortening or fat, and pulse three or four times to cut in the fat.) Stir in the parsley. Chill this mixture.

Remove the lid from the chicken. Ladle out about a cup or so of the cooking liquid to expose the chicken pieces. Reserve this liquid for another use, such as gravy or stock. Discard the bay leaf. To help the dumplings cook evenly, you are going to place them on the chicken, so be sure there's enough exposed meat or bone to hold them. Turn up the heat slightly. Take the dumpling mixture out of the fridge. Pour the buttermilk into the mixture and using a fork, mix just to moisten the ingredients without overmixing, which would cause the dumplings to be tough. The mixture should have the consistency of a soft, sticky dough or a very stiff batter. Drop the batter by heaping tablespoonfuls into the pot on top of the exposed chicken pieces. (Any dumpling batter that falls into the cooking liquid will thicken it nicely.) Simmer, uncovered, for 10 minutes or so, until the dumplings begin to puff. Cover the pot and continue cooking for 10 to 15 minutes, until the dumplings have risen and set. To be sure they are done, you can poke a knife in the center of a dumpling and see if it is cooked through. Serve directly from the pot.

PREP TIME: 20 minutes
COOKING TIME: 1 hour 15 minutes
TOTAL TIME: 1 hour 35 minutes

ADVANCE PREP *Up to a day in advance, the dish can be prepared to the point that you add the dumplings to the pot and refrigerate. To finish the dish, bring the chicken mixture back to a simmer, add the dumplings, and proceed as directed.*

LEFTOVERS *The chicken will keep for about a week in the fridge. Reheat leftovers, covered, on top of the stove.*

Buttermilk Fried Chicken with Cream Gravy

This pan-fried chicken has a deep mahogany crust that is crisp on the outside and moist on the inside. It is traditional to serve the chicken with cream gravy, made from the pan drippings.

Makes 4 to 6 servings

FOR THE CHICKEN
One 3½- to 4-pound chicken, cut into 8 to 10 pieces (see page 315), or 3½ pounds chicken parts
2½ tablespoons kosher salt
About 1 quart buttermilk
About 1½ cups peanut oil, vegetable shortening, or a combination
2 cups all-purpose flour
1¼ teaspoons freshly ground black pepper

FOR THE CREAM GRAVY
2 tablespoons unsalted butter
3 tablespoons all-purpose flour
1½ cups milk

1 teaspoon chopped fresh sage or thyme or
  ¼ teaspoon dried
Kosher salt and freshly ground pepper

Place the chicken in a large bowl. Sprinkle with 2 tablespoons of the salt and pour over the buttermilk to cover. Let sit in the refrigerator for at least 1 hour and as long as overnight.

In a large, heavy frying pan, preferably cast iron or electric, heat a little less than ½ inch of oil over medium-high heat to 365°F. Put a wire rack on a rimmed baking sheet and keep it near the pan.

Place the flour in a large plastic bag. (Depending on the size of your chicken and your bag, it may work best to divide the flour between two bags.) Add the remaining ½ tablespoon salt and the pepper to the flour and mix well. Lift one piece of chicken out of the buttermilk and allow it to drain for a few seconds. (Alternatively, you can drain the chicken in a colander.) Place the chicken in the seasoned flour and move the bag around to be sure the chicken is well coated. Repeat until all of the chicken is in the bag. Remove a piece of chicken from the flour, tap off any excess flour, and place in the hot oil. Repeat to fill the pan with chicken, being careful not to overcrowd the pan (which will prevent the chicken from getting crisp).

Fry half of the chicken, turning it once or twice, until it is a deep mahogany brown color on all sides, about 20 minutes. The wings and drumsticks should be finished first, then the thighs and breasts. When done, an instant-read thermometer, inserted near a bone, should read at least 160°F in the breast and 175°F in the leg and thigh. Remove from the fat and place on the wire rack. Add more oil as necessary to maintain an even depth and heat it before adding the remaining chicken. After the chicken cools a few minutes on the rack, pat it with paper towels to remove any excess oil. After frying the chicken, cool the oil for a few minutes. Pour it off into a can or some other container, leaving behind the brown bits stuck to the bottom of the pan.

To make the gravy, add the butter and melt over medium heat. Add the flour and stir to make a paste, cooking the flour for a minute or two. Whisk in the milk and add the sage. Simmer for 4 or 5 minutes, until the sauce thickens. Season with salt and pepper. Serve with the chicken.

PREP TIME: 20 minutes
COOK TIME: 40 minutes
TOTAL TIME: 2 hours (includes soaking time)

ADVANCE PREP *Although the chicken is best served hot from the pan, it can be made in advance and reheated on a wire rack in a 325°F oven until heated through and crisp, about 15 minutes. It can also be served at room temperature or even cold.*
LEFTOVERS *Fried chicken will keep for about a week in the fridge. Layer it with paper towels and put it in a resealable plastic bag or container. Reheat leftovers in the oven as described above in Advance Prep.*

Indian-Spiced Chicken

I can't claim that this dish is authentic anything. It's my personal combination of spices that approximates an Indian curry dish. I make it all the time because it doesn't require much effort, it's got a deep satisfying flavor, and it's done in only an hour—just enough time to make some rice and clean up the kitchen before dinner's ready. I use dark-meat chicken—thighs and drumsticks—because I prefer their moist texture and because I think the flavor stands up better to the heavy spices. But feel free to substitute white meat if you desire.

Makes 3 to 4 servings

1 teaspoon ground coriander
1 teaspoon ground cumin
1 teaspoon yellow mustard seeds
1 teaspoon turmeric
1 teaspoon garam masala
¼ teaspoon ground cinnamon
2 pounds chicken drumsticks and thighs, separated
Kosher salt and freshly ground black pepper
3 tablespoons peanut or vegetable oil
1 medium onion, chopped
1 large garlic clove, minced
2 tablespoons minced fresh ginger
4 canned tomatoes, cut into chunks, plus 2 or 3 tablespoons juice (about 1 cup total)
2 medium all-purpose potatoes (about 12 ounces), such as Yukon Gold, peeled and cut into chunks
¼ cup frozen peas
⅔ cup plain full-fat yogurt (optional)

In a small bowl, combine the coriander, cumin, mustard seeds, turmeric, garam masala, and cinnamon. Set aside.

Season the chicken generously with salt and pepper. In a medium, wide, shallow saucepan, heat the oil over high heat. When the oil is hot, add the chicken and brown well on all sides, about 7 minutes. Remove the chicken to a plate. Turn down the heat to medium.

Add the onion to the pan and sauté for 4 or 5 minutes, until the onion begins to brown. Add the garlic and ginger and sauté for another minute or so. Add the spices and cook, stirring constantly, until you can smell their strong aroma, about a minute. Pour in 2 cups of water and scrape the bottom of the pan with a wooden spoon. Add the tomatoes along with a teaspoon of kosher salt and bring the mixture back up to a boil. Return the chicken to the pot along with any juice that has accumulated on the plate, turn down the heat, set the cover ajar, and simmer for 30 minutes.

Add the potatoes and simmer for another 20 minutes, until the potatoes are soft. Add the peas and simmer for 5 minutes or so more. If you'd like the broth a little thicker, smash some of the potatoes on the side of the pot. Otherwise, if you are using the yogurt, spoon 2 or 3 tablespoons of the hot chicken cooking liquid into the yogurt to temper it and then pour it back into the pot to combine. Bring the chicken back up to a simmer and serve.

PREP TIME: 5 minutes
COOKING TIME: 70 minutes
TOTAL TIME: 1 hour 15 minutes

ADVANCE PREP *The chicken can be made a day in advance and reheated on the stove. If you are using yogurt, don't add it to the broth until just before serving.*
LEFTOVERS *The chicken will keep for about a week in the fridge.*

Mock Tandoori Chicken

You can't really make tandoori chicken without a 1,000-degree tandoor oven, but why should that stop you? The spicy yogurt marinade for this chicken produces a juicy, flavorful chicken. It is a delicious, low-fat entrée that's extremely satisfying. The longer it can marinate, up to two days, the better.

Makes 4 servings

2 cups plain yogurt, full- or low-fat
2 tablespoons minced fresh ginger
2 garlic cloves, minced
2 teaspoons kosher salt
1 tablespoon garam masala
1 tablespoon curry powder
Pinch of cayenne pepper, or to taste (optional)
4 skinless and boneless chicken breasts or 8 skinless and boneless chicken thighs (about 2 pounds)

In a medium bowl, combine the yogurt with the ginger, garlic, salt, garam masala, curry powder, and cayenne, if using. Mix well. Add the chicken and be sure the meat is covered with the yogurt mixture. Cover with plastic wrap and refrigerate for at least 3 hours.

Preheat the oven to 450°F. Place a wire rack on a roasting pan or baking sheet.

Remove the chicken from the yogurt mixture, but don't scrape off any excess. Lay the meat on the wire rack. Bake for 20 to 30 minutes, depending on how thick the chicken is, or until the yogurt has dried and the edges of the meat have browned. When done, an instant-read thermometer inserted into the center of the flesh, near the bone should read 175°F in the thigh (or 160°F in the breast).

PREP TIME: 5 minutes
COOKING TIME: 20 to 30 minutes
TOTAL TIME: 3 hours 30 minutes (includes marinating time)

ADVANCE PREP *The chicken can be kept in the yogurt mixture in the fridge for up to two days.*
LEFTOVERS *The chicken will keep for about a week. Use leftovers in a Chicken Salad (page 78) or other dish that calls for cooked chicken.*

Roast Turkey with Gravy

There are a lot of theories about roasting a turkey. Some say brine, others say don't bother. Some say stuff the cavity, others say if you do you're taking your life into your hands. Some say baste regularly, others say basting doesn't do anything. For all the talk, I think the biggest problem is that most people terribly overcook their birds. That's why they are so dry and tough. Giant turkeys, above 20 pounds, are another problem. Although they make an impressive presentation, they are rarely very good eating, whether because they are pumped up on fake foods that don't give them much flavor or because they are so big it's almost impossible not to overcook them. In my opinion, you are always better off cooking two 10- to 12-pound turkeys than one huge one.

When it comes to brining, I have mixed feelings. Brining does make the flesh juicy, but at holiday time there's not a lot of extra room in my fridge for a couple of turkeys to be sitting in tubs of salted water. Also, if you stuff a brined turkey, the stuffing can get very salty. Instead of brining, I salt the bird in advance and let it sit in the fridge overnight. Then I butter it up and bake it to a delicious, golden brown, basting occasionally with more butter. To stuff, see page 331.

Makes 8 to 10 servings

One 12- to 14-pound turkey, fresh or defrosted
   (not self-basting)
Kosher salt
4 medium onions (about 2 pounds), peeled
1 large carrot, peeled and cut into chunks
2 celery stalks, peeled and cut into chunks
1 whole head of garlic, cut crosswise in half
1 cup (2 sticks) unsalted butter, at room
   temperature
Freshly ground black pepper
$\frac{1}{2}$ cup dry white wine or dry sherry
About 1 cup chicken or vegetable stock, if needed
$\frac{1}{4}$ cup all-purpose flour

The night before you intend to roast the turkey, remove and reserve the neck and giblets from the cavity. Rinse the bird with cold water, inside and out, and pat dry with paper towels. Sprinkle 2 tablespoons of salt all over the exterior and interior of the bird. Wrap in plastic wrap and refrigerate overnight.

The next day, preheat the oven to 325°F.

Chop 3 of the onions into 1-inch chunks and scatter on the bottom of a roasting pan. Add all but a chunk or two of the carrot and celery to the pan. Place the turkey neck and giblets in the pan, too. Place a wire rack on the onions and set the turkey, breast side up, on the rack. Into the cavity place the remaining onion, cut in half, the garlic, and the reserved carrot and celery. Spread $\frac{3}{4}$ cup of the butter all over the turkey and massage it into the skin. Sprinkle the turkey with a generous amount of black pepper.

Pour $\frac{1}{2}$ cup water into the pan and set it in the oven. Roast, basting with the pan juices every 20 minutes or so, for about 15 minutes a pound. For a 12-pound turkey, that's 3 hours; for a 14-pound turkey, that's $3\frac{1}{2}$ hours. To test if it's done, prick the breast and thigh and the

juices should run clear. An instant-read thermometer inserted in the center of the muscle and near the bone should register 160°F in the breast and 175°F in the thigh. If the bird isn't brown enough for your taste, crank up the oven to 425°F for 10 minutes.

Remove the turkey from the oven, transfer to a carving board, cover loosely with foil, and let rest for at least 20 minutes.

While the turkey is resting, make the gravy.

Remove the rack from the roasting pan and set the pan over a burner turned to low. When the juices start to simmer, pour in the wine. Scrape the bottom of the roasting pan with a wooden spoon to remove any browned bits that have stuck. Simmer for about 5 minutes. If there doesn't appear to be at least a cup or two of liquid in the pan, add some chicken or vegetable stock and simmer for another 5 minutes or so. Strain the contents of the pan into a small saucepan, pressing the onions and other bits with the back of a spoon to extract as much juice as possible. You should have about 2 cups. Make a paste by combining the remaining $\frac{1}{4}$ cup butter with the flour. Bring the strained cooking juices to a simmer. Using a wire whisk, pick up some of the butter-flour paste and whisk it into the simmering liquid. Let cook for 4 or 5 minutes to thicken, adding more of the paste until the gravy reaches the desired consistency. Adjust the seasoning with salt and pepper. Simmer until there is no trace of the flavor of raw flour, 4 or 5 minutes more.

Carve the turkey (see page 331) and serve with the gravy.

PREP TIME: 20 minutes
COOKING TIME: 3 to $3\frac{1}{2}$ hours
TOTAL TIME: 12 hours (includes salting time)

ADVANCE PREP The turkey should be roasted just before it is served. While I know people who cook their turkeys days in advance and reheat them before serving, they get the chokingly dry meat they deserve.

LEFTOVERS The turkey will keep for one week in the fridge. Use in any recipe that calls for cooked turkey or chicken, such as Turkey Hash (page 124), or Turkey Pot Pie (page 322), or in sandwiches. Use the carcass to make a turkey stock (see page 51).

VARIATION
Orange Glazed Turkey

Follow the recipe for Roast Turkey as directed, but beat the ¾ cup butter with ⅓ cup defrosted orange juice concentrate before you rub it into the bird's skin.

SLATHERED TURKEY

By using any of the slathers on pages 351 and 352, you can create an unexpectedly delicious roast turkey. Double or triple the recipes as written, depending on the size of your bird, and rub the slather evenly into the skin. Let the turkey marinate, refrigerated, for at least one and up to two days prior to roasting. Proceed with the recipe as indicated.

Chipotle-Rubbed Turkey Breast

The once-a-year Thanksgiving turkey is usually more than enough turkey for me, but a turkey breast is less of a production and takes very well to brining, ensuring moist meat. I use sugar in this brine to balance the spiciness of the chiles, but you can substitute additional salt if you prefer.

Makes 4 to 8 servings

TURKEY NOTES

Here's some advice on how to handle a turkey. Because many people cook one just once a year, at Thanksgiving, you can never have too much turkey advice. Just ask the people who answer the phone at the Butterball turkey hotline (800-323-4848).

• **Defrosting.** If you've purchased a frozen turkey, you must defrost it before you cook it, and you should defrost it in the refrigerator. This takes a very long time, so plan accordingly. Figure about three full days for a 12-pound turkey. A bigger turkey will take four or five days. If you are in a rush, put the turkey in a large basin in the sink and place it under running cold water. Depending on the size, the turkey will be defrosted this way in about 12 hours, but you waste a lot of water. Do not defrost a turkey by leaving it out at room temperature.

• **Brining.** If you are going to brine a turkey, you should think of getting an insulated cooler. The brine should be made in the proportion of $1/4$ cup kosher salt for every quart of water or 2 pounds of ice. You can add aromatics to the brine, such as garlic, herbs, or spices, as you wish. To keep the turkey chilled, figure equal parts water and ice. For example, depending on the size of the cooler, to submerge a 14-pound turkey I would use 3 quarts water, 6 pounds of ice, and $1^1/2$ cups kosher salt. Brine the turkey for 12 to 24 hours.

• **Stuffing.** The beauty of stuffing a turkey is that the juices run into the stuffing, making it rich and flavorful. (Note that if you brine the turkey, these juices are quite salty, so you should underseason the stuffing accordingly.) If you bake the stuffing in a dish on the side, you don't get the same flavor or moist texture. To compensate, I baste the stuffing baked in a dish with pan juices from the turkey or with chicken stock.

To avoid any chance of food-borne illness, you have to be sure to cook and handle a stuffed turkey properly. Before you stuff the bird, the stuffing should be hot. If you have made the stuffing in advance, reheat it. (Remember to leave out the eggs until you reheat it so the stuffing doesn't set prematurely.) Pack the stuffing into the cavity, leaving a little room for it to expand. You can also stuff the cavity around the neck. Where the tail of the bird was, there is usually a flap of skin, under which you can tuck the drumsticks to hold them and the stuffing in place. Roast the bird as described in the recipe on page 328, roasting for about 18 minutes a pound and making sure the stuffing reaches 165˚F when you insert an instant-read thermometer into the center of the stuffing. If the bird is done before the stuffing comes up to temperature, transfer the stuffing to a baking dish and return it to the oven to finish cooking.

• **Carving.** Carving takes a little practice. If there is a surgeon at the table, you might want to solicit his or her services. If you've stuffed the bird, first scoop out all of the stuffing. Remove the legs, thighs, and wings by cutting through the cartilage at the joints. (I like to use poultry or kitchen shears.) Carve the meat off the leg and thigh, removing any tough tendon, and arrange on a platter. To make carving the breast easier, from around the neck you should remove the wish bone, which forms the shoulders of the bird. Carefully dig in behind the neck with the point of a knife until you find the bone then cut around it to remove it. Just above where you removed the wing, cut horizontally into the breast, holding the knife parallel to the work surface. Follow the contour of the carcass to make the cut. Then slice the breast vertically on a slight, outward angle, into thin slices, until you hit bone. Repeat on the other side.

(box continues on next page)

• **Gravy.** A good gravy makes even a dry turkey more palatable (but be sure you have plenty of it). Follow the directions on page 331. If you are worried that you won't have enough pan juices or you know your crowd likes a lot of gravy, while the turkey roasts you can make a stock from the neck and giblets, and/or additional turkey parts (see page 51). Otherwise, you can doctor up store-bought chicken stock by simmering it with onions, carrots, celery, and other vegetables. Use the stock for the base of the gravy, adding it to the roasting pan when you take the turkey out.

¼ cup kosher salt

¼ cup sugar or additional kosher salt

One 4-pound whole turkey breast, on the bone, rinsed in cold water and patted dry

2 large garlic cloves, peeled

3 tablespoons extra-virgin olive oil

2 chipotle chiles in adobo, plus 2 teaspoons of the adobo sauce

½ teaspoon freshly ground black pepper

Dissolve the salt and sugar in a cup of hot water. Place this solution in a container large enough to hold the turkey breast submerged in water. Add about 8 cups cold water. Place the turkey breast in the container with the brine. If you need more brine to submerge the turkey completely, add it in the proportion of 1 tablespoon salt and 1 tablespoon sugar per cup of water. Cover and refrigerate overnight or for up to 12 hours.

The next day, preheat the oven to 425°F.

In the bowl of a food processor fitted with a metal chopping blade or in a blender, mince the garlic with quick on/off pulses. Add the olive oil and let the machine run to purée the garlic.

Add the chipotles with the adobo sauce and the black pepper and continue running the machine until the mixture is smooth.

Remove the turkey from the brine. Rinse under cold water and pat dry with paper towels. Place the turkey breast skin side up on a roasting rack in a roasting pan. Using a small rubber spatula or your hands, rub all of the chipotle purée over the surface of the breast and the bone. Roast for about 1 hour and 15 minutes, or until an instant-read thermometer inserted into the center of the thickest part of the breast near the bone reads between 160° and 165°F. The skin should have browned nicely. Remove from the oven and let the turkey breast rest for about 15 minutes before slicing. If using for cold sandwiches, let it cool to room temperature, then wrap, and chill.

PREP TIME: 20 minutes

COOKING TIME: 1 hour 15 minutes

TOTAL TIME: 9½ hours (includes brining time)

LEFTOVERS *The turkey will keep, wrapped in the fridge, for about a week. I frequently make this dish to have leftovers for sandwiches. You can also use it in Turkey Hash (page 124) or as a substitute for chicken in Chicken Salad (page 78).*

Grilled Turkey Cutlets on Cabbage and Snow Pea Slaw

Although it is certainly not my predilection, I occasionally have to write simple, low-fat recipes for various assignments. Without fat, the flavor has to come from elsewhere—and here a great Asian marinade does the trick. Originally created for a fitness magazine, this recipe has remained a favorite of mine. You can substitute pounded chicken breasts, if desired.

Makes 2 servings

- 1 pound turkey breast cutlets or scaloppine
- 3 tablespoons fresh orange juice
- 2 tablespoons soy sauce
- 1 tablespoon hoisin sauce
- 1 tablespoon honey
- $\frac{1}{2}$ teaspoon toasted Asian sesame oil
- 1 teaspoon minced fresh ginger
- $\frac{1}{2}$ teaspoon minced garlic
- 2 cups finely sliced napa cabbage
- 20 snow peas, thinly sliced
- 4 scallions, white and green parts, chopped
- 1 cup bean sprouts
- $\frac{3}{4}$ teaspoon sesame seeds, toasted (page 10)
- 2 tablespoons unseasoned rice vinegar

Place the turkey cutlets in a shallow bowl. In a separate bowl or jar with a lid, combine the orange juice, soy sauce, hoisin sauce, honey, sesame oil, ginger, and garlic. Pour half of this mixture over the turkey and turn the meat to coat evenly with the marinade. Marinate in the refrigerator for at least 1 hour. Reserve the remaining marinade at room temperature for the slaw.

Preheat the grill.

Grill the turkey cutlets until cooked through, 2 to 3 minutes per side.

Meanwhile, in a large bowl, combine the cabbage, snow peas, scallions, bean sprouts, and $\frac{1}{2}$ teaspoon of the sesame seeds. Pour the reserved marinade over the vegetables, add the vinegar, and toss. Divide this slaw among four plates. Place the cooked turkey on top of the salad and sprinkle with the remaining $\frac{1}{4}$ teaspoon sesame seeds.

PREP TIME: 20 minutes
COOKING TIME: 6 minutes
TOTAL TIME: 1 hour 25 minutes (includes marinating time)

ADVANCE PREP *The marinade can be made in advance and stored in the refrigerator for up to one week. You can marinate the meat in the fridge for up to 12 hours.*
LEFTOVERS *The turkey will keep in an airtight container in the refrigerator for up to one week. Use for sandwiches or salads.*

Ground Turkey with Scallion and Chili

This quick Chinese-style dish has a lot of flavor and a moist texture. Serve with fragrant Jasmine Rice (page 219) and Chinese-Style Baby Bok Choy (page 158) and you have a fast, lovely, healthful, and cheap Chinese meal.

Makes 4 servings

- 1$\frac{1}{2}$ pounds ground turkey, chicken, pork, or veal
- 2 tablespoons soy sauce
- 2 tablespoons Chinese cooking rice wine, gin, or dry sherry
- 2 to 3 teaspoons Asian garlic chili sauce, or $\frac{1}{2}$ teaspoon crushed red pepper flakes, or to taste
- 1 tablespoon toasted Asian sesame oil
- 1 tablespoon peanut oil
- 2 tablespoons minced fresh ginger
- 1 large garlic clove, minced

1½ teaspoons cornstarch

2 tablespoons bacon fat or additional
   peanut oil

½ cup Chinese Stock (page 52), Poultry Stock
   (page 51), Vegetable Stock (page 53), or
   water

4 scallions, thinly sliced

2 tablespoons minced fresh cilantro

Place the meat in a medium bowl and add the soy sauce, rice wine, chili sauce, sesame oil, peanut oil, ginger, garlic, and cornstarch. Mix well to distribute the seasonings. (I find two chopsticks gripped together the easiest way to stir the meat.)

Place a large nonstick or cast-iron pan over high heat. Add the bacon fat. When it is very hot, dump in the marinated meat along with any juice that has accumulated in the bowl. Using chopsticks, a wooden spoon, or a spatula, move the meat around in the pan to brown it. Break up the larger pieces as the meat cooks. When all of the meat appears to be browning, about 8 minutes, add the stock, scallions, and cilantro and continue cooking until the liquid thickens, about 2 minutes.

PREP TIME: 5 minutes
COOKING TIME: 10 minutes
TOTAL TIME: 15 minutes

ADVANCE PREP *You can marinate the meat in the refrigerator up to 2 hours in advance, but the dish should be cooked just before serving.*

LEFTOVERS *The turkey will last for about five days in the refrigerator. Reheat leftovers gently in the microwave. They are also good stirred into rice noodles or mixed in with scrambled eggs.*

Grilled Duck Breast

In texture and flavor, duck is not far from steak. Grilling really brings out the meatiness of duck. The difficulty is that the excess fat melts onto the coals and causes an impossible number of flare-ups. I find it easiest to remove the skin and fat and marinate the meat before grilling it. The texture and flavor of grilled duck is best medium rare, but you can cook it through to medium if you prefer. If you don't have or don't want to bother with a grill, you can prepare the same recipe and cook the duck in the broiler or in a hot skillet. *Magret* (pronounced mah-GRAY) is the French term for the big, meaty breast of foie gras ducks, which have become more common here in the United States; you can also use regular duck breast.

Makes 4 servings

4 duck magrets or boneless breasts (about
   2 pounds)

¼ cup extra-virgin olive oil

2 garlic cloves, minced

Handful of rosemary, thyme, marjoram, or other
   fresh herbs, chopped

Kosher salt and freshly ground black pepper

Remove the skin and fat from the breasts, using a sharp paring knife if necessary to separate any connective tissue. (Reserve the fat for rendering; see page 336.) Place the breasts in a bowl or container. Drizzle with the oil, scatter the garlic and herbs over the meat, and season generously with salt and pepper. Cover and refrigerate for at least 2 hours.

Preheat a grill, broiler, or heavy skillet.

Remove the duck from the marinade, dragging it along the edge of the container to remove any excess oil, garlic, or herbs that might burn as the duck cooks. Grill or otherwise cook the duck for 3 or 4 minutes per side, to reach medium rare or the desired doneness. To serve, slice crosswise on the bias.

PREP TIME: 10 minutes
COOKING TIME: 6 to 8 minutes
TOTAL TIME: 2 hours 20 minutes (includes marinating time)

ADVANCE PREP *The duck can be marinated for up to a day.*
LEFTOVERS *The duck will keep for five days in the fridge. Use in a duck salad or hash (see page 124).*

Duck Stew

Here's perhaps the simplest way to prepare a duck. It's got a delicious, full flavor, rich with garlic, herbs, tomatoes, and olives. If you don't have a butcher who can cut the duck into pieces for you, follow the directions for cutting up a chicken (see page 315), cutting the elongated breasts in half. You should end up with two wings (tips removed), two drumsticks, two thighs, and four pieces of breast. Serve with polenta, fresh noodles, rice, or boiled potatoes.

Makes 4 servings

> One 4- to 5-pound duckling, cut into 10 pieces
> Kosher salt and freshly ground black pepper
> 1/4 cup extra-virgin olive oil
> 2 medium red onions, sliced
> 4 small garlic cloves, thinly sliced
> One 6-inch sprig rosemary
> 4 bay leaves
> 1 cup dry red wine
> 1/2 cup tomato paste
> 1 cup small black olives, such as niçoise, brined, not canned

Pull the skin and fat off the duck pieces. If necessary, use a sharp knife to cut any connective tissue or membrane so you can loosen the skin. Trim any remaining visible fat. (Render the fat and skin to use for cooking; see page 336.) Rinse the duck pieces and pat dry with paper towels. Season generously with salt and pepper. Over medium-high heat, heat the oil in a Dutch oven or similar pan large enough to hold the duck pieces without too much extra room. Add the duck to the pan and brown the pieces on all sides. Add the onions and garlic and sauté with the duck for 7 to 10 minutes, until soft. Add the rosemary, bay leaves, red wine, tomato paste, and 1 1/2 cups water, and bring to a boil. Lower the heat, cover loosely, and let simmer for about 1 1/2 hours, until the duck is tender.

Add the olives, remove the bay leaves, adjust the seasoning with salt and pepper, and simmer for another 10 minutes.

PREP TIME: 10 minutes
COOKING TIME: 2 hours
TOTAL TIME: 2 hours 10 minutes

ADVANCE PREP *The stew can be made a day in advance, refrigerated, and reheated. It's almost better that way.*
LEFTOVERS *The stew will keep for about a week in the fridge. Use leftovers as a sauce for pasta: Remove the bones, cut up the meat, thin down the sauce with additional wine or tomato sauce, and adjust the seasoning before tossing with cooked pasta.*

Duck Confit

Confit is an old French technique for preserving duck legs in fat. Although most people no longer have to keep duck through the winter without refrigeration, the technique is still used a lot because it makes for delicious eating. The only difficult part is coming across enough luscious duck fat—you can order it from www.hudsonvalleyfoiegras.com or www.dartagnan.com. You can render duck fat yourself (see box, right), or you can substitute lard (page 423). Once you make confit, you can keep it in the fridge for months.

Makes 4 servings

1/2 cup kosher salt

2 tablespoons sugar

4 large duck legs and thighs (attached), about
  3 pounds

1 teaspoon black peppercorns

1/2 teaspoon juniper berries

15 sprigs fresh thyme

About 4 cups rendered duck fat (see box, right) or
  lard (page 423)

Place the salt in a bowl and blend with the sugar. Holding one duck leg at a time over the bowl, rub a generous amount of the salt-sugar mixture all over the leg, into the skin and flesh. Repeat with the remaining legs. In the bowl or another container, pack the salted legs on top of each other, layering them with the peppercorns, juniper berries, and thyme. Sprinkle with any remaining salt mixture. Cover with plastic wrap and refrigerate for 12 to 24 hours.

The next day, unpack the duck legs and rub off any salt and spices with paper towels. Pat dry. Melt the fat or lard in a wide heavy-bottomed pot just big enough to hold the legs. Add the duck to the fat; it should be submerged. Simmer the duck very slowly for 1 1/4 to 1 1/2 hours, or until the meat browns, shrinks off the bone, and is very tender when pricked with the point of a knife. The fat should never go much above

KITCHEN SENSE

RENDERED DUCK FAT
Duck fat is delicious for cooking potatoes and other dishes. To render, that is, melt, the fat off the skin, put it in a pot with 1/4 cup water and set over medium-low heat. Cook until the fat has melted, the water has evaporated, and the skin has lightly browned, about 40 minutes. Strain and discard the skin. The rendered fat will keep in the fridge or freezer for months.

220°F during the cooking time. Remove the pot from the heat and let the duck cool in the fat to room temperature. You can eat the duck as is or transfer it to a storage container, cover with the strained fat, and chill until ready to use.

To serve the duck, pull a leg piece out of the fat, being careful not to pull out the bone and leave the meat behind. If you can't get the piece out, you can let the fat come to room temperature, heat it in a microwave, or warm it in a water bath in a large pot on the stove. Scrape any excess fat off the meat. Heat a dry frying pan, preferably cast iron, over medium-high heat and place the leg in the pan, skin side down, to crisp up and heat through before serving, about 6 minutes. (Alternatively, you can brown and crisp the duck, skin side up, under a broiler for about 8 minutes.)

PREP TIME: 15 minutes

COOKING TIME: 1 1/2 hours

TOTAL TIME: 9 1/2 hours (includes salting time; plus curing time)

ADVANCE PREP *The confit is best if it is made well in advance—up to a month or more. But it can be eaten as soon as it is made.*

LEFTOVERS *The confit will keep covered in fat for months in the refrigerator. Leftovers can be used in anything that calls for cooked meat, such as a duck salad, hash, or stuffing. I use duck confit and duck fat instead of bacon for a variation of Frisée aux Lardons (page 80). Don't waste the fat, either. It's delicious for cooking just about anything, especially roasted potatoes. And it can be melted and strained to use for making more confit, of course.*

Duck Prosciutto

This is an easy cold cut you can make at home by curing duck breast in a combination of salt and sugar. Magret—the big, fatty breasts of foie gras ducks—make the best prosciutto. Cured this way, the fat on the breasts is delicious and keeps the meat moist. Serve this duck prosciutto sliced paper thin with fresh figs or ripe melon as an hors d'oeuvre, or use it as you would regular prosciutto or bacon, as a flavoring ingredient in stews and sauces.

Makes 1½ pounds, enough for 10 to 12 servings

1½ cups dark brown sugar
1½ cups kosher salt
5 juniper berries
1 bay leaf, crumbled
1 teaspoon black peppercorns
1 teaspoon coriander seeds

2 duck magrets or breasts (about 1½ pounds), rinsed and patted dry

In a small bowl, combine the brown sugar, salt, juniper berries, bay leaf, peppercorns, and coriander seeds. Place about one third of this mixture in the bottom of a nonreactive loaf pan. Lay one breast, fat side up, on top of the salt and sugar mixture. Cover with another third of the mixture and lay the second magret on top of that. Top with the remaining salt and sugar mixture, being sure that the duck breasts are well coated. Cover with plastic wrap and refrigerate for six to eight days, until the meat is cured throughout. The prosciutto is done when the duck breasts are firm to the touch, with the stiff texture and dark color of cooked meat. The fat should be a creamy, off-white color. Completely wipe off the seasoning and wrap the breasts in plastic. Refrigerate until ready to use

To serve, with a very sharp knife or electric meat slicer, slice the duck very thinly crosswise, being sure to keep the fat attached to the meat.

PREP TIME: 5 minutes
TOTAL TIME: 6 days (includes curing time)

LEFTOVERS *The duck will keep for a month or so once cured.*

■ ■ ■

Meat

WHEN I WAS JUST STARTING my freshman year of high school, my mother told our butcher that I wanted a job. After I demonstrated that I knew how to hold a knife and could cut a chicken into eighths, I spent every Wednesday afternoon and all day Sunday for the next two years working behind the counter at a butcher shop in north Toronto. It was a large, expensive, very busy, kosher-style butcher shop; kosher-*style* meaning the meat was not salted or blessed as dictated by the laws of kashrut, but that we didn't sell pork or carry any cuts that couldn't be kosher (only meat from the forequarters of the animal are permitted). Of course, that didn't stop us from selling the popular and pricey New York strip steaks, which could never be kosher, or a special brand of meat pie I was convinced was so delicious because the crust was made with lard.

My time behind the counter Frenching racks of lamb and cutting pockets into breasts of veal for demanding clients obviously taught me a lot about meat. The most important thing I learned was to not be intimidated by it. So many of my friends who like to cook and bake go into a panic when they have to prepare a large roast for a special dinner. Because meat is generally more expensive than other ingredients, I think the value of what they are handling is part of the intimidation factor. But mostly I think there is something deeper, more visceral, more anthropological about our connection to meat and the ritual or celebration that is supposed to surround the cooking and eating of it. The irony is that meat is one of the easiest things to prepare. Of course, recipes for meat can get extremely elaborate—it is after all often the focal point of dinner, and people like to show off. However, if you buy good-quality beef, or veal, or pork, or lamb, all you have to do is season it with salt and pepper and apply heat and you will have a satisfying meal.

One thing you do have to pay attention to is that various cuts require different treatments to bring out their best qualities. There was a time when you could rely on knowledgeable butchers to guide you to the right piece of meat for various preparations, but butchering is a dying art. Now most meat arrives at the meat counter already cut up, prepackaged, and ready for sale. Most people working in the meat section of the grocery store have never seen a primal cut (the large pieces of meat that are broken down into steaks and roasts), let alone a whole animal carcass. Throughout the recipes and the informative boxes in this chapter I have given you plenty of advice on which cuts of meat to cook how and what substitutions you can make.

When it comes to quality, I cannot emphasize enough how important it is to start with good meat. Well-marbled, properly aged, and expertly cut meat is a pleasure to cook, and the higher price you will pay for it is worth the payoff on the plate in the end. These days, when fear of bacterial contamination and mad cow disease looms, some people are more anxious about meat than ever before. Buying the best quality is one way to handle the problem. Producers such as Niman Ranch in California and Coleman Purely Natural in Colorado have made naturally raised, hormone-free meat more readily available and more affordable. Small-scale, organic local producers have also taken up the charge, and farmer's markets across the country are increasingly welcoming producers and purveyors of meat from heirloom breeds.

Meat is less perishable than fish or poultry, and the larger the cut, the longer it will last. Depending on how fresh it was when you bought it, ground meat should be kept in the refrigerator only for a couple of days; steaks will keep for a few more; and roasts will last for up to a week. If you are going to keep meat in the fridge for a bit, consider marinating it in spices and aromatic herbs so it gains flavor while it sits. Meat also fares pretty well in the freezer. Properly wrapped it will keep three to four months. And although I prefer to grill or roast fresh meat, you can't tell the difference between braised frozen or fresh meat.

My goal in this chapter is to familiarize you with different types and cuts of meat and different ways to handle them. My hope is that these recipes will alleviate some of the intimidation factor. The only way to really become proficient in meat cookery—as in all cookery—is to do it. My mother used to cook a large piece of meat for our family practically every day of the year. It's no wonder her rib roast was delicious. So go ahead—roast, braise, grill, tie, stuff, brine, and sauté and you will be amazed how quickly you master meat.

■ ■ ■

Standing or Prime Rib Roast

Although the days are long gone when the only decision about what to have in a fine restaurant was whether to order the queen- or the king-size cut of prime rib, a succulent standing rib roast is still my favorite cut of beef. Nicely browned and glistening with fat and juices, a rib roast is a regal entrée. It is also versatile: you can cook a small roast—two to three ribs—for a gathering of four to six people, or a large one—five or six ribs—for a crowd of 12 or 16 or more.

Choosing the right roast is important. *Standing rib* and *prime rib* are used interchangeably to refer to the cut of meat between the shoulder and the loin of the cow. (Although Prime is also the USDA's top grade of beef, in the case of prime rib, *prime* refers to the cut, not the grade—technically, you could buy a prime prime rib roast.) If the roast is cut from the loin end—often called the first ribs even though they come last in the animal—the roast will have a large center muscle of meat (called the eye). If cut from the shoulder end—called the last ribs, even though they come first in the animal—the center muscle is less distinct, the surface of the roast is bigger, and there is generally more fat and intramuscular tissue. Roasts from both ends are delicious, but a roast from the loin end is better quality. Specify which you would like when you order.

When it comes to seasoning a rib roast, I think the meat itself is so flavorful that all you need is salt and pepper. But a coating of garlic, herbs, and mustard makes a pretty delicious roast, too (see Variations). If you want to serve the roast with a *jus* (a light meat juice), add an onion to the pan and deglaze the pan with stock or wine as directed below.

Makes 12 servings

> One 4-rib standing rib roast (about 8 pounds)
> Kosher salt and freshly ground black pepper
> 1 small onion, chopped (optional)

> 1 cup beef, veal, or chicken stock, dry red wine, or a combination (optional)

Remove the roast from the refrigerator about 1 hour before you intend to cook it. Preheat the oven to 425°F.

Place the roast in a shallow roasting pan standing up on its bones (hence the name), the fat facing up. Season the roast generously with salt and pepper and, if you intend to make a jus, place the onion in the pan. Set the meat in the middle of the oven and roast it for 20 minutes. Turn down the heat to 325°F. For medium rare, the roast should take about 15 minutes per pound, or about 2 hours. (For rare, subtract 1 or 2 minutes per pound; for medium, add 2; for well, add 5.) After about 1 hour and 45 minutes, start checking the internal temperature of the roast with an instant-read thermometer. When you are within 10 degrees of the temperature you want the roast to be at (see page 345), start to check every 5 minutes or so. Remove the roast when it hits the right temperature. Transfer the roast to a large cutting board, cover loosely with aluminum foil, and let sit for 20 to 30 minutes to rest. The internal temperature will continue to rise while it sits.

If you like, make a jus while the roast rests. Drain most of the fat from the roasting pan, but keep the browned bits and the onion on the bottom. Set the pan on the stove over low heat. Pour in the stock and simmer, scraping the bits off the bottom of the pan, until the stock has reduced by half or even three quarters. Strain, season with salt and pepper to taste, and keep warm.

To carve the roast, turn it over so the bones are facing up. If your roast was tied, remove any string. Using a long carving knife and a large fork, remove the entire rack of rib bones by cutting between the bones and the meat. Separate the bones to make individual ribs and serve them alongside the meat. Turn the roast over so the roast is sitting on the side from which you removed the bones and slice it crosswise 1/4 inch thick, perpendicular to the work surface. Because the meat on the smaller, loin end of the roast will be more cooked than the meat on the larger, shoulder end of the roast, cut from both sides so there will be meat of varying degrees of doneness to please your guests. Spoon the hot jus over the meat and serve.

PREP TIME: 10 minutes

COOKING TIME: 2 hours

TOTAL TIME: 3 1/2 hours (includes warming time and resting time)

LEFTOVERS *The roast beef will keep for about five days in the refrigerator. Use it in roast beef sandwiches or hash (page 124).*

VARIATIONS

Standing Rib Roast with a Garlic and Herb Mustard Crust

Prepare the Garlic and Herb Mustard Slather (page 351) and spread the mixture over the entire surface of the roast before placing it in the oven. Proceed with the recipe as directed.

Rib-Eye Roast

A boneless standing rib roast is called a rib-eye roast. Prepare as for Standing Rib Roast, seasoning it simply with salt and pepper or coating it with the mustard and herb mixture, as described above. Roast the rib-eye on a wire rack in a roasting pan. The boneless roast will take approximately 18 minutes per pound. Figure 2 1/2 servings per pound.

Grilled or Broiled Rib Steaks

In my opinion, rib steaks are the next best thing to a rib roast. They are, in fact, cut from the same section of the animal. I prefer rib steaks on the bone to boneless rib-eyes because they have more flavor and because I like to chew on the bone, but both are tasty grilled or broiled. You can take two approaches with portioning rib steak: Have the steaks cut 3/4 to 1 inch thick and prepare one steak per person; or have the steaks cut 2 inches thick and slice the steak to serve it. Because I grew up eating my own rib steak, I prefer the first option, but feel free to do what you like. As with a rib roast, I think a simple seasoning of salt and pepper is preferable to any complex seasoning that might mask the delicious flavor of the beef.

Makes 4 to 6 servings

> 4 rib steaks, cut 1 inch thick, or 2 rib steaks, cut 2 inches thick, on the bone (4 to 5 pounds)
> Kosher salt and freshly ground black pepper

Preheat a charcoal or gas grill or a broiler.

Season the steaks with salt and pepper. Place the steaks on the hot grill or under the broiler, and cook until they reach the desired doneness. For 1-inch-thick steaks, figure 4 minutes per side for medium rare and 6 minutes per side for medium. For 2-inch-thick steaks, figure 9 minutes per side for medium rare and 12 minutes per side for medium. Refer to page 345 for advice on testing for doneness. Let the steak sit for a few minutes before serving.

TOTAL TIME: 8 to 25 minutes

Grilled Rib-Eyes

Cut boneless rib-eye steaks 1 to $1\frac{1}{2}$ inches thick and plan on 1 to $1\frac{1}{2}$ steaks per person (or about $\frac{3}{4}$ pound per person). Grill or broil them as directed above, decreasing the cooking time by a minute or two per side.

Soy-Marinated Hanger Steaks

Almost forgotten, the hanger steak has made an amazing, and deserved, comeback in the last few years. Sometimes called the "butcher's tender" because only butchers knew how good it was and they saved it for their families, the hanger steak comes from the cow's diaphragm. It has a deep, beefy taste and resilient but not tough texture, similar in some ways to a skirt steak, only thicker and better tasting. Each animal has only two hanger steaks, about a pound each. Two full hangers are more than enough for four people, though they are sometimes sold cut into smaller pieces.

The hanger is flavorful enough to stand on its own with just a little salt and pepper, or you can marinate it, as I recently did for a big surf 'n' turf feast at a friend's country house. It is best charcoal grilled or broiled.

Makes 4 servings

2 whole hanger steaks (about 2 pounds)

2 tablespoons minced fresh ginger

2 garlic cloves, minced

$\frac{1}{4}$ cup soy sauce

2 tablespoons hoisin sauce or other Asian bean paste

2 tablespoons peanut or vegetable oil

1 tablespoon Asian fish sauce, such as Thai *nam pla* or Vietnamese *nuoc nam* (optional)

Freshly ground black pepper

Lay the hanger steaks in a snug container. In a small bowl, blend the ginger, garlic, soy sauce, hoisin sauce, oil, and fish sauce, if using. Pour this mixture over the steaks, moving them around to coat. Refrigerate and let marinate for at least 1 hour, turning the steaks once.

Fire up a charcoal or gas grill or broiler, or heat a dry grill pan on the stove. Remove the steaks from the marinade, letting any excess drain off, season with black pepper, and place over the heat. The steaks should sear on the first side for about 5 minutes. If the steaks are more than 1 inch thick, close the barbecue or cover the pan after the initial searing and let them continue cooking for another 4 minutes or so. Either way, turn the steaks over and sear the second side. Depending on their thickness, the steaks should be ready in 10 to 12 minutes for rare. Luckily, hanger steaks are best served sliced, so you can see how done they are in the center when you cut them. If they need more time to attain your desired doneness, just put them back on the heat.

Remove the steaks from the heat and slice them crosswise on a slight bias into pieces about $\frac{1}{2}$ inch thick.

PREP TIME: 5 minutes

COOKING TIME: 10 to 12 minutes

TOTAL TIME: 1 hour 20 minutes (includes marinating time)

ADVANCE PREP *The steaks can marinate for up to two days before cooking.*

LEFTOVERS *The steaks will keep three or four days in the fridge. Sliced steak is delicious in a salad, such as Vietnamese Beef Salad with Watercress (page 81). It is also good on sandwiches.*

COOKING MEAT TO THE PROPER DONENESS

One of the most common causes for concern about cooking meat—and with good reason—is knowing when it is done. And although you can time and poke and touch a piece of meat to ascertain whether it is cooked properly or not, the only surefire way to know is to use an instant-read thermometer. Every cook should have one. To use an instant-read thermometer, you insert it deep into the meat in a few different places—near a bone or in the center of a large muscle, for instance—and take a reading. (Clean the thermometer between tests.) Pretty simple.

There are a few things to keep in mind. First, meat continues cooking once it has been removed from the heat source. And most meat, especially roasts, should rest at room temperature for about 15 minutes after being cooked, during which time the internal temperature can rise 5 to 10 degrees as the meat sits. In the chart below, one temperature indicates what the reading should be on the thermometer when you remove your meat from the oven or other heat source. The other temperature is the one at which the meat will be properly cooked. The former is lower to allow for this latent rise in internal temperature.

When estimating cooking times, note that meat with bones cooks faster than meat without bones because the bones actually conduct heat through the roast. Also, for reasons that no one seems willing or able to explain, organic, pasture-raised meat cooks faster than regular store-bought meat. Change your timing accordingly, but still use an instant-read thermometer to be sure whatever meat you are making will be perfectly cooked.

Note that when braising or using other long, slow-cooking methods for tougher pieces of meat, the goal is not to get to a specific temperature—whatever you are cooking will be very well done—it is to cook your meat long enough to break down the collagen, connective tissue, and other tough components of the cut. Cooking such meat to one of the temperatures below will make it done, but it won't make it palatable.

(box continues on next page)

Type of Meat	Desired Doneness	Stop Cooking at	Final Temperature
Beef	Rare	120°–125°F	125°–130°F
	Medium rare	125°–130°F	130°–135°F
	Medium	135°–145°F	140°–150°F
	Medium well	150°–160°F	155°–165°F
	Well done	165°–175°F	170°–180°F
Veal	Medium	135°–145°F	140°–150°F
	Medium well	150°–155°F	155°–160°F
Pork	Medium	145°–155°F	150°–160°F
	Medium well	160°–170°F	165°–175°F
Lamb	Rare	120°–125°F	125°–130°F
	Medium	135°–145°F	140°–150°F
	Well done	165°–175°F	170°–180°F

It's usually too difficult to take an accurate temperature of steaks and chops that are less than 2 inches thick. Some experienced grillers can tell by touch whether a steak is properly cooked, but I think a visual test is your best option. With a sharp knife, make a small incision in the center of the thickest part of the steak. A properly cooked medium-rare steak should be reddish in the center, a medium steak should be pinkish, and a well-done steak should be gray all the way through, but still moist.

Chicken-Fried Steak

Chicken-fried steak is just that—steak that is fried as though it were chicken, served with a little cream gravy. It is a delicious preparation that is popular in the South and especially in Texas. For the steak, most people suggest bottom round or rump steak, but sometimes I like to splurge on rib-eye, which I pound thin.

Makes 4 servings

Eight $\frac{1}{2}$-inch-thick rib-eye steaks (about
   $1\frac{1}{2}$ pounds), or $1\frac{1}{2}$ pounds bottom round or
   rump steaks
2 cups buttermilk
1 cup all-purpose flour
Kosher salt and freshly ground black pepper
$\frac{1}{4}$ cup lard, bacon fat, peanut or vegetable oil, or
   a combination
$\frac{3}{4}$ cup milk

Trim away any excess fat from the steaks, including the nugget of fat in the center of the rib-eye steak. Place the meat between two sheets of plastic wrap or waxed paper and pound them to an even $\frac{1}{4}$-inch thickness with a mallet or the bottom of a heavy frying pan. Transfer the steaks to a bowl or container and add the buttermilk. Let soak for at least 2 hours in the refrigerator.

Reserve aside about 1 tablespoon of the flour and dump the rest onto a plate. Stir in 1 tablespoon salt and $\frac{1}{2}$ teaspoon pepper. Place the lard in a large frying pan, preferably cast iron, and set over medium-high heat to melt. When the lard is hot, lift a steak out of the buttermilk, drag both sides along the side of the bowl to remove any excess, and dredge in the seasoned flour to coat. Tap off any excess flour and set the steak in the hot fat. Repeat until the pan is full. Don't overcrowd it. Fry the steaks until they are golden brown and crisp, about 5 minutes, then flip and fry the second side, another 3 or 4 minutes or so. Remove from the pan and drain the steaks on paper towels. Cover the steaks with foil to keep warm. (You can also put them on a wire rack in a 250°F oven.) Repeat until all of the steaks are fried.

Pour the fat out of the frying pan, leaving the browned bits stuck to the bottom. Return the pan to the heat. Add the reserved flour and cook, stirring, for a minute or two to make a paste. Whisk in the milk, stirring to make a smooth sauce. Bring the sauce to a simmer and let cook 4 or 5 minutes to thicken and to cook the flour. Adjust the seasoning with salt and pepper and pour the hot sauce over the steaks to serve.

PREP TIME: 10 minutes
COOKING TIME: 20 minutes
TOTAL TIME: 2 hours 30 minutes (includes marinating time)

ADVANCE PREP The steaks can soak in the buttermilk for up to one day.

MEAT TERMINOLOGY

Beef, veal, and lamb are graded by the USDA to give some indication of quality, flavor, and tenderness. (Pork is also graded by the USDA, but the grades are not carried through to the market.) If you've ever seen purple ink stripes of shields on the fat of a roast, you've seen how the grade is indicated. To judge the quality of meat, an inspector considers the age of the animal, the amount of intramuscular fat or marbling in the muscle, the color and the overall appearance of the flesh, and other factors that affect flavor, texture, and taste. Of course, the judgment is made quickly, by inspection and not tasting, so just because something is graded one way or another doesn't mean it is certain to be good or bad—it is only an indication.

Grading is optional and it adds an expense to production since the producer has to pay the USDA inspectors. Consequently, some producers, including many boutique producers of organic or naturally raised meats, opt out of the grading system. Therefore, ungraded meat isn't necessarily better or worse than graded meat; you just have to learn more about it by asking your butcher or visiting the producer's website.

Although there are other commercial grades used by the USDA, below are the most common consumer-quality grades of meat. I've also defined some other terms you may see on meat packages.

Grade/Designation	Qualities
USDA Prime	The best quality and most expensive beef, veal, and lamb, from the youngest animals, with the most marbling. Prime meat is the best candidate for dry-aging. Not much Prime meat makes it to the consumer market because restaurants and hotels buy the bulk of whatever is produced.
USDA Choice	The bulk of the beef, veal, and lamb available to the consumer falls into this category. It is still from young animals, though there is less marbling and a wider range of acceptable variation of various quality criteria in this category than in Prime.
USDA Select	Unique to beef grading, this category has grown in popularity over the last few years as consumers have sought out leaner beef. Select has the least amount of intramuscular fat of the three common grades. Though fat is an indication of good quality, it is also obviously caloric. Owing to increased demand, ironically, Select beef will often be more expensive than Choice, which is technically of better quality.
Certified Angus Beef	If beef meets certain criteria, including that the animal it came from contains at least 51% of the Black Angus breed in its genetic makeup, Prime and some Choice beef can also qualify to become Certified Angus Beef (CAB). Though not a grade per se, CAB is a branding and marketing program of the USDA and various organizations of beef producers. It generally represents very good-quality beef.
Organic	The certification program for organic meat—administered by various governmental agencies, including the USDA and the National Organic Standards Board—scrutinizes the process of production rather than the meat itself. That entire process, from the rearing of the livestock to their feed to the processing of the carcass, must be conducted without the use of chemicals, hormones, or antibiotics in order to earn an organic designation.
Naturally Raised	There are no binding definitions of the terms "natural" or "naturally raised," so the parameters are left to the discretion of the producers. As a result, they vary considerably from one producer to the next, and nothing is regulated or enforced. Generally, naturally raised beef is free of hormones and antibiotics, and the animals are not fed any meat byproducts. But you have to check with the individual producers and take their word.

LEFTOVERS Chicken-fried steak should be reheated on a wire rack in a 325° F oven for about 12 minutes or until warmed through. It's never as good as when first made, but reheated it makes a tasty sandwich.

Roast Tenderloin of Beef

Whereas my mother used to serve standing rib roast for company, her mother, my grandmother, preferred to roast a whole tenderloin for guests. As its name suggests, tenderloin—which sometimes goes by its French name, *filet*—is the most tender piece of meat on a cow. Although I'm not a big fan of steaks made from the tenderloin, which I find are missing good, meaty flavor and texture, a roast made from a tenderloin is a different matter, especially if it is slathered with herbs and/or spices and allowed to marinate as recommended in the variations below.

A whole, trimmed, tied, ready-to-roast tenderloin weighs between 4 and 5 pounds, and because it is solid, rich meat, it will serve eight to ten people. The trimming is important because there's a strip of tough, fatty meat that runs down the side of the main muscle, and some shiny membrane (called silverskin) along the surface, both of which can make the tenderloin tough. These should be removed with a sharp knife. Because the tenderloin tapers, tying is also important to ensure even cooking—tuck the thin tail underneath and tie it up to even out the thickness of the roast.

In the summer, I like to serve sliced roast tenderloin at room temperature with a flavorful sauce, such as garlicky Spanish Romesco (page 401), Aïoli (page 406), or Chimichurri (page 400).

Makes 10 to 12 servings

> 1 whole beef tenderloin, trimmed and tied (4 to 5 pounds)

¼ to ½ cup extra-virgin olive oil or melted butter
Kosher salt and freshly ground black pepper
1 small white onion (optional)
1 cup beef, veal, or chicken stock, dry red wine, or a combination (optional)

Preheat the oven to 400° F.

Place the tenderloin on a wire rack in a roasting pan. Brush all over with olive oil and season generously with salt and pepper. If you want to make a jus to serve with the roast, place the onion in the pan. Set the tenderloin in the oven and let roast for about 10 minutes. Baste with more oil, turn over the meat, and baste again. Return to the oven and cook for another 10 minutes. Baste the meat, turn it over, and baste again. Cook for another 20 minutes or so, basting once or twice more, and then take the internal temperature in the thickest part of the tenderloin. Consult the doneness chart on page 345, and when the meat reaches the desired temperature, remove it from the oven, cover lightly with aluminum foil, and let rest for 15 minutes.

While the roast sits, make a jus. Pour out any excess fat in the roasting pan and set over low heat. Add the stock and simmer, scraping any bits off the bottom, until the liquid reduces by half or even three quarters. Season with salt and pepper, and keep warm.

To carve, remove the string from the roast and cut the meat on a slight angle into slices about ¼ inch thick. Spoon the hot au jus on top, if desired.

PREP TIME: 5 minutes
COOKING TIME: 40 to 50 minutes
TOTAL TIME: 45 to 55 minutes

LEFTOVERS *Leftover roast tenderloin will keep for about five days in the refrigerator. Use leftovers as part of a beef salad, hash, or in any recipe that calls for cooked beef.*

VARIATIONS

Mustard and Herb-Roasted Tenderloin

Prepare the Garlic and Herb Mustard Slather (page 351) and spread it over the tenderloin before roasting and proceed with the recipe as directed, basting the tenderloin with olive oil as it roasts.

Spiced Yogurt-Roasted Tenderloin

Coat the tenderloin with the Spiced Yogurt Slather (page 351) and roast as directed, basting the tenderloin with butter as it roasts.

Sliced Steak Smothered with Mushrooms and Onions

Because of their arrangement of fibers and other structural components, certain steaks are best when quickly grilled or broiled and thinly sliced. Though each comes from a different part of the animal, flank steak, skirt steak, and cuts used for London broil (a thick-cut steak usually made from sirloin tip or top round) all fall into this category. All three have good, meaty flavor, but they are all a little tough, and none has enough fat or collagen to make it a good candidate for braising. These types of steaks are, however, good candidates for marinating, and any of the seasoning slathers on pages 351 to 352 would nicely enhance their flavor.

That said, my mother made all three of these steaks exactly the same way: she seasoned them with salt and plenty of pepper, grilled or broiled them, sliced them thinly, and covered the slices with tons of mushrooms and onions steeped in a shocking amount butter. This is still my favorite way to prepare this type of steak.

Makes 4 servings

> 1/2 cup (1 stick) unsalted butter
> 2 medium onions, chopped
> 1 pound fresh button mushrooms, sliced (about 5 cups)
> Kosher salt and freshly ground black pepper
> 1 tablespoon chopped flat-leaf parsley
> 2 pounds flank steak, skirt steak, or London broil, rinsed and patted dry
> 2 tablespoons vegetable oil

Preheat a charcoal or gas grill or broiler. (Alternatively, you can use a heavy skillet or griddle, preferably cast iron, set over high heat.)

In a medium saucepan, melt the butter over medium-high heat. Add the onions and cook until soft, about 6 minutes. Add the mushrooms, season generously with salt and pepper, and cook until the mushrooms have softened, shrunk, and given off their water, about 8 minutes. The mixture should be quite soupy. Stir in the parsley, adjust the seasoning, and set aside.

Brush both sides of the steak with oil and season liberally with salt and pepper. Grill, broil, or sear for about 4 or 5 minutes, until slightly charred; turn the steak over and grill another 3 or 4 minutes. Make a small cut into the center of the steak to check doneness. Continue cooking until the steak is just slightly underdone for your taste—it will finish cooking away from the heat. Remove the steak and let it sit on a cutting board, covered lightly with foil, for 5 to 10 minutes.

Reheat the mushroom and onion mixture. Slice the steak crosswise against the grain into very thin slices, holding your knife at about a 45 degree angle to the cutting board to make broad slices. Arrange the slices on a serving platter. Pour any of the steak juices that have run off the meat into the mushroom and onion mixture, and spoon this mixture over the sliced steak to serve.

PREP TIME: 5 minutes
COOKING TIME: 35 minutes
TOTAL TIME: 40 minutes

ADVANCE PREP *The mushroom and onion mixture can be made up to two days in advance. Reheat it in a saucepan.*
LEFTOVERS *Leftover sliced steak will keep for four or five days in the refrigerator. It is delicious in sandwiches and salads.*

VARIATION
Marinated Flank Steak
Use any of the slathers on pages 351 to 352 and let the steak sit in the marinade, refrigerated, for at least 2 hours and up to 12 hours before cooking.

Grilled T-Bone or Porterhouse Steaks

T-bone and porterhouse steaks are virtually the same cut of meat. They come from the loin section of the cow and they are easy to identify because they have a bone at the top that runs down the center of the steak in the shape of the letter T. On one side of the bone is a piece of the strip loin (also called a New York strip) and on the other side is a portion of the tenderloin (also called the filet). The only difference between the two steaks is that on the porterhouse, the diameter of the tenderloin portion is larger.

KITCHEN SENSE

WHAT'S THE DEAL WITH DRY AGING?
Dry aging is a process by which large cuts of top-quality beef are aged for three or four weeks in a controlled environment to encourage certain enzymatic activity that increases the flavor and tenderness of the meat. Dry aging is what gives the best steakhouse steaks their buttery texture and strong, meaty, mineral flavor. But because dry aging takes time and space and is costly—the meat shrinks during the process and you have to trim away nasty, gnarly bits, so the yield is low—it's hard for a consumer to find dry-aged meat except at the most exclusive butcher shops. Instead, now the beef industry touts "wet aging," by which they mean they seal small cuts of meat in vacuum bags (Cryovac) and let them sit around for a while before they sell them. I am not a fan of wet-aged meat, which is slightly more tender than regular meat, but which has an off, sour taste I find unpleasant. If I find myself in an expensive steakhouse and I detect the sour taste of wet-aged meat, I'll send it back and order a piece of fish.

Unfortunately, you can't really dry-age your own meat at home—the cuts on the market are too small and you need to be able to control the humidity and temperature of the aging environment. If I can't find dry-aged meat that I can afford, I stick to ordinary fresh meat, which, provided you are buying good-quality meat from a good butcher or supermarket, is pretty darn good as is.

Dry aging is only desirable for meat that is going to be cooked at high temperatures, such as roasting or grilling. And in fact only the best cuts of meat are ever dry aged. For stews or other braised meat dishes, regular, unaged meat is perfect.

Seasoned Slathers for Meat

Certain combinations of herbs, spices, and other flavoring make delicious, versatile condiments for grilled and roasted meats. Whether they take the form of rubs, pastes, or marinades, most can be used interchangeably on beef, veal, lamb, or pork. Although you can make the mixtures and season your meat with them just before cooking, if you have the time, you should let the meat marinate with the spices in the refrigerator for at least 2 hours and up to 12 so the flavors penetrate deep into the flesh. Rather than drown my meat, I prefer to coat it with a paste or marinade and turn it frequently while it sits so it absorbs the flavors evenly—that's why I call them slatherings. Remember to discard any marinade that has not been cooked to avoid the chance of cross-contamination.

Spiced Yogurt Slather

Slather this curry-flavored paste on beef or lamb destined to be grilled or roasted. It is also good on chicken.

Into $\frac{1}{2}$ cup plain yogurt, stir 2 tablespoons extra-virgin olive oil, 1 minced garlic clove, 1 tablespoon minced fresh ginger, 1 tablespoon curry powder, 1 teaspoon garam masala, 1 teaspoon kosher salt, $\frac{1}{4}$ teaspoon ground coriander, $\frac{1}{4}$ teaspoon cayenne pepper, and a pinch of freshly grated nutmeg.

Garlic and Herb Mustard Slather

Use this Mediterranean-flavored paste on a rib roast or a rack or leg of lamb.

Using a blender, food processor, or by hand, make a paste by combining $\frac{1}{4}$ cup Dijon mustard, 2 tablespoons extra-virgin olive oil, 2 teaspoons anchovy paste (optional), 2 minced garlic cloves, 2 tablespoons chopped fresh

herbs such as rosemary or thyme, and a generous amount of freshly ground black pepper.

Cilantro Chili Slather

This spicy paste with a hint of lime is delicious on beef or pork.

In a food processor or blender, combine 2 seeded and chopped jalapeños, 3 garlic cloves, $\frac{1}{4}$ cup extra-virgin olive oil, the finely grated zest of 1 lime, $\frac{1}{2}$ bunch of fresh cilantro (leaves and tender stems), $\frac{3}{4}$ teaspoon ground cumin, 1 teaspoon dried oregano, 1 teaspoon kosher salt, and a pinch of ground chipotle (optional) to make a paste.

Soy Sauce Slather

This Asian-flavored marinade is delicious on beef, pork, or chicken.

Mix $\frac{1}{4}$ cup soy sauce, 2 chopped scallions, 2 minced garlic cloves, 2 tablespoons minced fresh ginger, 1 tablespoon hoisin sauce or Asian bean paste, 1 teaspoon toasted Asian sesame oil, 2 tablespoons peanut or vegetable oil, 1 tablespoon Thai or Vietnamese fish sauce (optional), and 1 teaspoon chili sauce (optional).

Red Wine Slather

This marinade is delicious on beef, lamb, and pork.

Combine $\frac{1}{2}$ cup dry red wine, 2 tablespoons balsamic vinegar, 2 tablespoons extra-virgin olive oil, 3 or 4 strips orange zest, 1 minced garlic clove, 1 tablespoon finely chopped rosemary, 1 teaspoon kosher salt, a pinch of grated nutmeg, and a generous amount of freshly ground black pepper.

(box continues on next page)

White Wine Slather

An excellent flavoring for veal, chicken, and seafood.

Combine ½ cup dry white wine, 1 tablespoon minced capers or 2 tablespoons olive juice, 2 tablespoons extra-virgin olive oil, 3 or 4 strips of lemon zest, 1 minced shallot or garlic clove, 1 teaspoon kosher salt, and some freshly ground white pepper.

Pomegranate Slather

This Middle Eastern–inspired combination of flavors is delicious on lamb and chicken.

Combine ½ cup pomegranate juice, 2 tablespoons extra-virgin olive oil, 2 minced garlic cloves, ¾ teaspoon ground cumin, ¾ teaspoon ground coriander, 1 teaspoon kosher salt, some freshly ground black pepper, and a pinch of cayenne pepper.

Tea Slather

The flavor of tea nicely complements beef and lamb.

Combine ½ cup very strongly brewed Oolong or Lapsang Souchong tea, 2 tablespoons peanut or vegetable oil, 2 chopped scallions, 1 tablespoon minced fresh ginger, ¼ cup chopped cilantro, 1 teaspoon kosher salt, and some freshly ground white pepper.

Thai Slather

The pungent Thai flavors in this marinade turn ordinary strips of chicken, beef, or lamb into fragrant satay. Use it on roasts, too. And it's yummy on shrimp.

Mix ½ cup coconut milk with 1 to 2 tablespoons Thai red or green curry paste (depending on how hot you can stand it; available in small cans in the ethnic food section of the grocery store), 1 tablespoon minced fresh ginger, 1 minced garlic clove, and 3 tablespoons Thai or Vietnamese fish sauce, such as *nam pla* or *nuoc nam*.

Tunisian Slather

Harissa is a Tunisian spice paste available in small tubes and cans. Adjust the heat of this marinade for lamb or chicken by using more or less harissa.

Mix together ½ cup extra-virgin olive oil, 2 tablespoons minced black olive, 1 tablespoon minced preserved lemon rind (page 409), 1 to 3 teaspoons harissa, 1 minced garlic clove, ¾ teaspoon ground cumin, ¾ teaspoon ground coriander, and a pinch of ground cinnamon.

These steaks are costly. They are the preferred steak of New York steakhouses—my favorite, Peter Luger's in Brooklyn, serves only one cut of meat, the porterhouse. So if you are planning to go to the expense of making a porterhouse, you might as well find a butcher or other source that dry-ages its meat (see page 350). The thicker the steak, the juicier it will be—up to a point. I think a 1¾-inch steak is about the right size, so that when it is cooked through, the outside will be nicely charred and the inside will still be rare. You can serve it with some sort of sauce, such as Grilled Tomato and Corn Salsa (page 16) or Chimichurri (page 400), but keep in mind that you don't want to mess with the integrity of the steak's delicious, beefy flavor. A 2-pound steak will serve two to three people.

Makes 4 to 6 servings

> Two 1¾-inch-thick T-bone or porterhouse
> steaks
> Kosher salt and freshly ground black pepper

MARINATING MEAT

It's hard to find concensus on the effect of marinating meat. By marinating, I mean covering meat with spices and other aromatics, whether dry or in some sort of liquid, and letting the meat sit for several hours or even days in the fridge. If there's acid in the marinating mixture, some think the acid penetrates the meat and makes it tender; others see no proof of this. If there's salt in the marinade, some think it draws out the moisture of the meat and makes it dry; others think that's only true on the surface. Everyone agrees that fresh ginger has an enzyme in it that helps tenderize meat, but no one can decide how much is needed to have a significant impact.

Without any scientific experimentation to back me up, my sense after years of cooking meat is that the most important factor in the tenderness of the meat is the animal itself. I look at marinating as pure flavor enhancement, and because of that I think the longer, the better. Though I believe many cuts of meat are just fine simply seasoned with salt and pepper, once I've made the decision to marinate, I don't want to hold back. Based on my experience in the kitchen, if you season a good piece of meat and cook it right away, it is delicious. If you season it and let it sit for a couple of hours, it is even better. If you season it and let it sit overnight, it has even more flavor. The biggest factor in how long I marinate something is how much time I have before I have to cook it. Some cuts of meat, like pork butt for Pulled Pork (page 376), I like to marinate for three or four days to get the full benefit of the seasonings.

There is one issue to consider, and that's the moisture marinating causes on the surface of the meat. If you want a crisp, char-broiled crust on your meat, the surface shouldn't be wet. In fact, one of the drawbacks of pre-salting meat is not necessarily that the juices it draws out make the meat dry, but rather that the juices it draws out make the surface moist, which can inhibit browning and thereby affect flavor. This is true mostly when grilling, broiling, or pan-frying small cuts of meat, which will cook so quickly the moisture won't have time to evaporate. The simple way to overcome this problem is to pat the meat dry before you cook it and reseason it lightly with salt and pepper to compensate just before you apply heat.

Throughout this chapter I've suggested you marinate certain meats for certain periods of time based on my experience preparing them. If your experience proves otherwise, please feel free to change them.

Preheat a gas or charcoal grill, or a broiler and broiler pan.

Season the steaks quite generously on both sides with salt and pepper. Place the steaks on the hot grill or broiler pan and for medium rare, cook for about 9 minutes, until the side facing the heat is nicely charred. Flip the steaks and cook for another 7 or 8 minutes. Make a small cut into the steak to check the doneness.

Be sure to pull the steak off the heat just before it is finished cooking because it will continue to cook as it sits.

Transfer the steak to a cutting board and let rest for 5 to 10 minutes. To carve, cut the meat off both sides of the bone and then cut straight through the meat crosswise to make ½-inch-thick slices. Be sure to serve each person some slices from both sides of the steak—the strip loin and the tenderloin, each of which have a different flavor and texture.

TOTAL TIME: 20 minutes

LEFTOVERS *Leftover steak will keep for about five days in the refrigerator. The problem with most leftover steak is that to eat it you have to heat it up, which overcooks it. But leftover slices of a thick, juicy steak are still pretty good if you pan-fry them for just a minute or two in a dry pan. Otherwise, use the steak in a recipe that calls for cooked beef, such as hash (page 124).*

Pepper Steak

This is a delicious steak dish with a sort of retro 1950s feel to it. Because you cut the steak into strips and cook it slowly for a long period of time, it's an excellent way to prepare a steak that's on the tough side, such as shoulder steak or top round. Using a top-quality, tender steak would be a waste.

Makes 4 servings

> 1/4 cup peanut or vegetable oil
> Three 1/2-inch-thick shoulder or top round steaks (about 1 1/2 pounds)
> Kosher salt and freshly ground black pepper
> 1 large onion, chopped
> 2 to 3 pounds cubanelle or Italian frying peppers, seeded and cut into 1/2-inch-wide strips
> 2 teaspoons Worcestershire or soy sauce

In a large skillet, preferably cast iron or nonstick, heat the oil over high heat. Season the steaks generously with salt and pepper. When the oil is quite hot, add the steaks and brown on both sides, for a total of 5 or 6 minutes. Re-

move the steak (reserving the pan), and slice the meat crosswise on the diagonal into 3/4-inch-wide strips. Catch any juice that runs off the steak.

Return the pan to medium-high heat. Add the onion and sauté until translucent, about 5 minutes. Return the steak to the pan along with any juice and 2 or 3 tablespoons of water, turn down the heat to very low, cover, and cook for 40 to 45 minutes, stirring regularly, until the meat is very browned and tender. If the pan goes dry, add another tablespoon or two of water. As you stir, scrape the bottom of the pan to remove any browned bits. Remove the cover, add the peppers and the Worcestershire sauce, stir to distribute the meat among the peppers, cover, and continue cooking for another 20 minutes or so, until the peppers have wilted and browned. Adjust the seasoning with salt and pepper, and serve.

PREP TIME: 5 minutes
COOKING TIME: 1 hour 10 minutes
TOTAL TIME: 1 hour 15 minutes

ADVANCE PREP *The pepper steak can be made several hours in advance and reheated before serving. If necessary, add a tablespoon or so of water to the pan so the steak doesn't burn as it reheats.*
LEFTOVERS *Leftovers will keep for about one week in the fridge. They are delicious on sandwiches.*

Brisket

Among the recipes in my previous book, *The Mensch Chef*, was this one for brisket, which has a rich, mildly

PAN-FRYING, SAUTÉING, AND STIR-FRYING MEAT

It is in fact possible to cook a perfectly tasty piece of meat on top of the stove, without a grill or broiler—though, to be honest, the flavor will never be quite as delicious as if it had been cooked over fire. The terms *pan-frying*, *pan-searing*, and *pan-roasting* refer to cooking meat in a very hot, dry pan so that it sears to form a crisp browned crust and cooks quickly enough to remain tender and juicy inside. The best device to use for pan-cooking is a well-seasoned cast-iron pan, griddle, or grill pan. The two most important things to keep in mind are to get the pan good and hot and to make sure the meat is dry when it goes into that pan. Both will help ensure that the surface of the meat browns to develop more flavor and create a more appetizing appearance— the pale gray color of improperly pan-seared meat is unattractive. In fact, the reason grill pans have ridges is to allow any juices that come out of the meat to run off, keeping the surface of the pan touching the meat dry. To further ensure that the surface of the meat is dry, season it with salt just before it goes in the pan. If the meat has been marinated or pre-seasoned, pat it dry and salt it again just before it goes in the pan.

In my experience, the best cuts of meat for pan-searing are either thin tender steaks or big, fat, juicy ones. Thin steaks, such as rib-eyes, strip steaks, or medallions of veal, or pork pounded thin, cook quickly enough to sear and be done with it. Thick juicy steaks and chops, such as T-bones, loin chops, rib steaks, or rib chops cut 1½ inches thick, cook long enough to get a good crust and remain juicy. Thin lean steaks or medallions should be brushed with a little oil before frying, but steaks and chops with a good amount of fat on them don't need anything but salt and pepper. I've also had success pan-roasting larger cuts of meat, such as a boneless tied shoulder of pork (see page 372). For larger cuts, the technique is to brown the outside well, and then cover the pan to dry-roast the meat, turning it frequently, until it is done. One thing to keep in mind is that pan-searing causes a lot of smoke, especially if it is properly done. Turn on the hood fan to high, open the windows, and sear away.

Other stove-top techniques for quickly cooking meat include sautéing and stir-frying. Both are similar to pan-searing in that they are quick high-heat cooking methods. But neither is done in a dry pan. Instead, some sort of fat, such as oil, clarified butter, bacon fat, duck fat, lard, or a combination, is used. The goal is still to brown the meat for flavor and keep it moist. Sautéing is usually reserved for lean thin pieces of meat, such as pounded medallions (e.g., veal scaloppine). To help encourage browning, meat for sautéing is usually dusted with a light coating of flour. Though stir-frying is mostly done in a wok, it is similar to sautéing save that the meat is generally cut up into small pieces or thin strips and it is not dusted with flour (though cornstarch is sometimes used).

Whether you pan-fry, sauté, or stir-fry your meat, remember that when you are done, a lot of flavor is left in the pan in the form of little brown bits stuck to the bottom. Don't let that flavor go to waste. Pour off any excess fat and add some stock, wine, or other liquid to deglaze the pan to make a sauce. As the liquid simmers, scrape off the bits. Strain and finish the sauce however your recipe directs.

spicy, barbecue-flavored sauce and was given to me by my friend Adam's mother, Maxine. Since I wrote the book, a slightly modified version of her recipe has become the only brisket I make.

Brisket, for those of you who do not know, is the cut of meat from the shoulder of a cow that is used to make corned beef. It is big, meaty, and flavorful, but it's tough, so you have to braise it a long time to make it tender. Be sure you don't buy a corned beef brisket, which some butchers try to pass off as regular brisket. There are two parts to a whole brisket—the leaner front end, called the "single" brisket, and the thicker, fattier back end, called the "double" brisket. (Note that even though a small brisket looks like a giant piece of meat, it can shrink by as much as half when it is cooked.) Although my local butcher ties my briskets because they just can't leave a piece of meat alone, there is no need to tie a brisket because the structure of the muscle fibers holds the meat together in a nice shape. If you have the time, the easiest way to handle slicing the brisket is to cook the meat halfway, let it cool, slice it (always against the grain), and finish cooking the slices in the braising liquid.

Makes 10 to 12 servings

One 6- to 7-pound whole beef brisket, trimmed of excess fat

1 (14-ounce) bottle ketchup

2 large onions, chopped

2 tablespoons dark brown sugar

2 tablespoons Worcestershire sauce

1 tablespoon dry mustard

1 tablespoon white vinegar

1 teaspoon chili powder

$1/2$ teaspoon paprika or smoked paprika

2 teaspoons kosher salt

1 teaspoon freshly ground black pepper

2 large bay leaves

Preheat the oven to 350°F.

Place the brisket, fat side up, in a roasting pan large enough to hold it flat. In a bowl, combine the ketchup, onions, brown sugar, Worcestershire, mustard, vinegar, chili powder, paprika, salt, and pepper, along with $1\frac{1}{4}$ cups water. Use some of the water to clean out the ketchup bottle. Blend well. Pour the ketchup mixture over the brisket to coat. Place the bay leaves on top of the meat. Cover the roasting pan (use aluminum foil if your pan doesn't have a lid) and set in the oven to roast for 2 hours.

Remove the brisket from the oven and cool. If you have the time, chill the brisket in its cooking liquid overnight. This makes slicing easier and allows you to remove the fat that congeals.

Preheat the oven to 350°F. Remove the brisket from the liquid and slice the meat on an angle across the grain (perpendicular to the striations of the meat) into $1/4$- to $1/2$-inch-thick slices. Place the slices back into the cooking liquid. They should be submerged. Cover the pan again and return to the oven for $1\frac{1}{4}$ to $1\frac{3}{4}$ hours, until the meat is tender enough to cut with a fork. Remove the bay leaves from the liquid and discard. Serve the sliced brisket with plenty of the pan sauce on the side, handling the slices carefully because they break apart easily.

PREP TIME: 10 minutes
COOKING TIME: $3\frac{1}{2}$ hours
TOTAL TIME: 12 hours (includes resting time)

ADVANCE PREP *The brisket can be cooked halfway, sliced, and stored in its cooking liquid up to four days in advance. It can also be frozen. Finish cooking the meat before you serve it.*

Barolo-Braised Short Ribs

When I was growing up I had never heard of beef short ribs; we ate flanken. Of course I later learned that *flanken* is Yiddish for beef short ribs. Since I was a kid, admiration for the rich beefy taste and fall-apart tenderness of short ribs has swept the nation. Now you find them on the menu at just about every upscale restaurant—ironic, since the tough short rib is a peasant cut that requires long braising to reveal its true, tasty self. This recipe echoes a simple, classic braising technique of browning the meat, adding aromatic vegetables, and covering with liquid, in this case dry red wine. Though my preference is for Barolo, it can be pricey, and truth be told, any dry red wine will produce a delicious braised short rib. If you don't have enough wine to almost cover the ribs, cut it with some stock or even water. The only thing to keep in mind is that you don't want to undercook short ribs, which makes them tough; since you can hardly overcook them, better to err on the side of overdone.

Makes 6 servings

6 pounds bone-in, square-cut (English-style), short ribs
3 tablespoons extra-virgin olive oil
2 tablespoons unsalted butter
Kosher salt and freshly ground black pepper
2 large onions, chopped
1 large carrot, chopped
1 celery stalk, chopped
1 small parsnip, chopped
1 small turnip, diced

3 garlic cloves, minced
2 (750-milliliter) bottles dry red wine
1 tablespoon tomato paste
Two 2-inch pieces orange zest (use a vegetable peeler)
One 4-inch sprig fresh rosemary
5 or 6 sprigs fresh thyme
5 sprigs fresh flat-leaf parsley

Preheat the oven to 325°F.

With butcher's twine, tie each short rib once or twice crosswise so the meat doesn't fall off the bone as it cooks. In a large, covered Dutch oven or roasting pan that can hold the meat with a few inches of extra space around it, heat the olive oil and butter. Season the short ribs generously with salt and pepper. Brown the short ribs in the hot fat until seared on all sides, about 10 minutes. (Alternatively, you can use a separate frying pan to brown the meat and transfer it to a roasting pan.) Take the pan off the heat. Add the onions, carrot, celery, parsnip, turnip, and garlic to the pan. Pour over enough of the red wine to almost cover the meat. Add the tomato paste, orange zest, rosemary, thyme, parsley, salt, and pepper to the pan. Cover and set in the oven to roast for 3 to 3½ hours, turning the pieces over once or twice, until the meat is fall-apart tender. The meat will have shrunk by about one third.

When cooked, remove the string and bones from the short ribs and discard. Transfer the meat to shallow bowls. Strain the cooking liquid, discarding the solids, and skim off the fat from the surface. If desired, simmer the cooking liquid to thicken it and concentrate the flavor. Serve the cooking liquid with the short ribs.

TOTAL TIME: 3½ hours

ADVANCE PREP This dish is ideal to prepare in advance. You can cook and bone the meat and keep it for a week in the fridge. It can also be frozen for up to one month. Reheat the meat in its cooking liquid on the stovetop or in a covered baking dish in a 300°F oven until the meat is warmed through.

LEFTOVERS The short ribs will keep for up to about a week in the refrigerator, covered in their cooking liquid (which will solidify). They can also be frozen for up to two months. The leftover meat and the braising liquid make a delicious base for a pasta sauce for pappardelle, or other noodles.

Beef Stew

Beef stew is another one of those dishes that's more like a technique than a recipe, and that technique is a basic braise (see Osso Buco, page 360, and Barolo-Braised Short Ribs, page 357, for other braises). You brown the meat, add some aromatic vegetables and some liquid, cook the meat over low heat for a long period until it is just about tender, and then add some vegetables for garnish. Here's a basic recipe or outline that should be a starting point for your creativity.

Although you will always see something labeled "stewing meat" in the meat case of the grocery store, I prefer to cut my own stewing beef so that I know exactly what's going into it. My preference is for chuck, but you can also use shoulder, short ribs, brisket, shank, or rump. Buy steaks or roasts at least 1 1/2 inches thick and cut the meat into cubes, removing sinew and excess fat.

Makes 6 to 8 servings

2 pounds beef chuck, shoulder, short ribs, brisket, shank, or rump, cut into 1 1/2-inch cubes, or stewing beef

1/2 cup all-purpose flour

Kosher salt and freshly ground black pepper

1/2 teaspoon dried thyme

1/4 cup extra-virgin olive oil, vegetable oil, bacon fat, or unsalted butter, or a combination

1 small onion, chopped

2 carrots, 1 chopped, 1 cut into small chunks

1 celery stalk, chopped

1 garlic clove, chopped

1 cup dry red or white wine

2 to 3 cups beef, chicken, or vegetable stock, or water

1 tablespoon Dijon mustard or Worcestershire sauce

1 bay leaf

12 ounces new or boiling potatoes (about 8), peeled and cut into small chunks

1 medium parsnip, cut into small chunks

1 small turnip, cut into small chunks

4 ounces pearl onions (about 8), peeled

4 ounces fresh button mushrooms, stem ends trimmed, left whole or cut in half, depending on their size

1 tablespoon finely chopped flat-leaf parsley

Rinse the meat and pat dry with paper towels. In a plastic bag, combine the flour with about 1 tablespoon salt, 1/2 teaspoon freshly ground black pepper, and the thyme. Dump the meat into the bag and move it around to coat the meat with the flour. Set aside.

In a wide, heavy pot, heat the fat over medium-high heat. Remove the pieces of meat from the flour, tapping off any excess, and place them into the hot fat to sear and brown on all sides, about 10 minutes. Remove the meat from the pan and set on a plate.

To the pan add the onion, chopped carrot, celery, and garlic. Cook for 5 or 6 minutes, until soft. Return the meat to the pan along with any juice that has accumulated on the plate. Pour in the wine and stock, adding just enough to come about two thirds of the way up the meat. Add the mustard and bay leaf, along with about 1 teaspoon kosher salt and $\frac{1}{4}$ teaspoon freshly ground pepper. Bring the liquid to a boil, reduce the heat as low as the burner will go, cover, and simmer the beef for about $1\frac{1}{2}$ hours, or until the meat is almost tender when you poke it with a fork. At this point you can stop the cooking if you are making the stew in advance.

Raise the heat to medium. If there's very little liquid left in the pan, add $\frac{1}{2}$ to 1 cup or so of more stock or wine. Add the chunks of carrot, the potatoes, parsnip, turnip, and pearl onions; cover and let cook for about 25 minutes, stirring often, until the vegetables are almost soft. Add the mushrooms, stir, cover, and simmer for another 10 minutes or so, until the mushrooms are cooked through. Remove the lid and continue simmering for 5 minutes or so, until the cooking liquid thickens slightly. Adjust the seasoning with more salt and pepper, remove and discard the bay leaf, and serve with a sprinkling of parsley.

PREP TIME: 10 minutes
COOKING TIME: 3 hours
TOTAL TIME: 3 hours 10 minutes

ADVANCE PREP *The stew can be made up to the point that you add the diced vegetables, refrigerated, and then finished one or two days later as directed. It actually gets better as it sits.*
LEFTOVERS *The stew will keep for about a week in the fridge. It will also freeze well for up to two months, provided you don't add the potatoes. If you have a lot of leftovers, use them to make a beef pot pie by placing the stew in a baking dish, topping it with pie crust or puff pastry, and baking in a 425°F oven until the pastry is browned and the meat is heated through.*

VARIATION
Irish Stew
By substituting lamb for beef and adding some pearl barley, you can make a delicious version of Irish stew. Use 2 pounds lamb stew meat cut into $1\frac{1}{2}$-inch cubes. Omit the wine and increase the amount of stock to 4 cups. Along with the chunks of carrot, potato, and other vegetables at the end, add 3 tablespoons pearl barley. Continue simmering until the vegetables and the barley are soft.

Beer-Braised Pot Roast

Pot roast is like brisket or other braised meat dishes, only it is cooked entirely on top of the stove. Use a boneless chuck or rump roast, tied so that it holds its shape. And keep the roast gently simmering so the meat doesn't toughen.
Makes 8 to 10 servings

$\frac{1}{4}$ cup peanut or vegetable oil, bacon fat, or lard
One 4- to 5-pound boneless chuck or rump roast, tied
Kosher salt and freshly ground black pepper
1 large onion, chopped
1 garlic clove, minced
1 celery stalk, chopped
1 medium carrot, chopped
1 small turnip, chopped
1 (12-ounce) bottle beer, such as lager or ale
$\frac{1}{2}$ cup beef, veal, chicken, or vegetable stock or water
1 tablespoon tomato paste

1 bay leaf
3 or 4 sprigs fresh thyme, leaves only,
   or 1/2 teaspoon dried
2 tablespoons unsalted butter

In a stove-top Dutch oven that is large enough to hold the roast but without much extra room, heat the oil over high heat. Season the roast generously with salt and pepper. Brown the roast in the hot oil on all sides, until nicely browned, 15 to 20 minutes total. Remove the roast to a plate.

Remove all but 2 tablespoons of fat from the bottom of the pan and reduce the heat to medium-high. Add the onion and cook until translucent, about 5 minutes. Add the garlic, celery, carrot, and turnip, and continue cooking until the vegetables have begun to wilt and brown, about 7 minutes. Add the beer, stock, tomato paste, bay leaf, and thyme, and bring to a boil. Return the roast to the pan along with any juice that has accumulated on the plate. Reduce the heat as low as it will go and cover the pan. Let the roast cook, turning it occasionally, for about 3 hours, or until the meat is fall-apart tender (it may take more or less time, depending on the toughness of the meat). Be sure there is always at least an inch of liquid in the pan while the roast is cooking; if not add more stock, beer, or water.

When the meat is done, remove it to a dish and cover with foil to keep warm. Remove the bay leaf from the pot. Skim off any visible fat on the surface of the sauce (if you have time to chill the meat in the cooking liquid, skimming will be very easy). Using an immersion blender, food processor, food mill, or blender, purée the vegetables in the sauce. Pass this mixture through a fine-mesh sieve into a clean pot. Bring the strained liquid to

a gentle simmer, whisk in the butter, and adjust the seasoning with salt and pepper. Keep warm. Slice the roast into 1/4- to 1/2-inch pieces and spoon the sauce over the top to serve.

PREP TIME: 30 minutes
COOKING TIME: 3 1/2 hours
TOTAL TIME: 4 hours

ADVANCE PREP *The pot roast is actually better made a day or two in advance, and chilling makes skimming the sauce and slicing the meat easier. When the meat is finished cooking, cool it to room temperature in the braising liquid and chill. When ready to serve, remove the meat and slice while still cold. Place the slices in a skillet or baking dish. Skim any congealed fat off the surface of the cooking liquid. Heat the liquid, purée it, and pass it through a fine-mesh sieve as directed above. Whisk in the butter and pour the sauce over the meat. Cover and heat on top of the stove or in a 300°F oven until warm.*

LEFTOVERS *The pot roast will keep for up to two weeks in the refrigerator. It can also be frozen for up to two months. Reheat leftovers as described above. Pot roast can also be used in any recipe that calls for cooked beef, such as hash (page 124).*

VARIATION
Wine-Braised Pot Roast
Follow the same recipe, substituting 1 1/2 cups dry red or white wine for the beer.

Osso Buco
Since I started cooking, shanks—the lower part of the animal's leg—have gone from being undesirable cuts

of meat that were ground for chopped meat to trendy, center-of-the-plate delicacies. This classic Lombardian veal shank dish, Osso Buco, which literally means "bone with a hole," is probably the reason for that transformation.

Osso Buco is traditionally served with Saffron Risotto (page 224), and a sprinkling of gremolata—a parsley, garlic, and citrus zest condiment—a recipe for which is included below. The hole is filled with marrow, and if you really like your dinner guests, you'll give them a little spoon so they can scoop out that marrow and enjoy it with the succulent meat.

Makes 6 servings

6 large pieces osso buco or veal shank cross-
    sections, about 1 1/2 to 2 inches thick (4 to 5
    pounds)
1/2 cup all-purpose flour
Kosher salt and freshly ground black pepper
6 tablespoons extra-virgin olive oil
2 large onions, chopped
1 medium carrot, chopped
1 large celery stalk, chopped
1 small parsnip, chopped (optional)
3 garlic cloves, minced
1 to 2 anchovies, packed in olive oil
3 small ripe or canned tomatoes, cut up into
    chunks
2 tablespoons canned tomato juice or 1 teaspoon
    tomato paste
1 cup dry white wine
1 cup veal, chicken, or vegetable stock
    or water
2 bay leaves
One 4-inch sprig fresh rosemary
2 sprigs fresh flat-leaf parsley
1 sprig fresh thyme
1/2 lemon, seeded
1 small hot chile, left whole (optional)

FOR THE GREMOLATA
1 garlic clove, minced
2 tablespoons finely chopped flat-leaf parsley
1 teaspoon finely grated or minced lemon zest
1 teaspoon finely grated or minced orange zest

Preheat the oven to 325°F.

Rinse the veal shank and pat dry with paper towels. To make serving easier, you may want to tie a piece of kitchen string tightly around each shank to hold the meat to the bone. Combine the flour with 1 tablespoon salt and 1/2 teaspoon pepper and place in a shallow bowl. Over medium-high heat, heat the olive oil in the bottom of a covered stove-top Dutch oven large enough to hold the shanks side by side in one layer. (Alternatively, you can brown the shanks in a frying pan and transfer them to a covered ovenproof dish.) Dredge 3 of the shanks in the seasoned flour, tap off the excess, and place in the hot oil. Brown the shanks on all sides, 10 to 15 minutes total. Remove them to a plate and reserve. Repeat with the remaining shanks.

Keep the pan on the heat. Add the onions and sauté until soft, about 5 minutes. Add the carrot, celery, and parsnip, if using, and continue cooking for another 3 or 4 minutes or so, just until they wilt. Add the garlic and anchovies and cook for a minute or two more. Add the tomatoes and juice or paste, along with the white wine, stock, bay leaves, rosemary, parsley, and thyme. Stir in about 2 teaspoons kosher salt and a generous amount of freshly ground black pepper. Place the shanks back in the pan and arrange them side by side, cut side up. Pour any veal juice that has accumulated on the plate into the pan. Add the lemon and chile, if using, to the pot, cover tightly, and transfer to the oven for 2 hours and 15 to 30 minutes, until the meat is falling off the bone.

While the osso buco is braising, make the gremolata by combining the garlic, parsley, lemon zest, and orange zest. Set aside. If you tied the veal, remove the string. Remove and discard the bay leaves. To serve, I like to present the osso buco in the baking dish. When you lift off the lid, the dining room fills with a beautiful aroma. Carefully lift the osso buco out of the pan with a wide spatula. If it falls apart, just try to reassemble the nuggets of meat around the bone on the plate. Spoon some of the cooking liquid and vegetables over the top and sprinkle with the gremolata.

PREP TIME: 30 minutes
COOKING TIME: 3 hours
TOTAL TIME: 3½ hours

ADVANCE PREP *The osso buco can be braised up to a day in advance. Undercook the meat slightly, taking it out of the oven after 1½ hours of braising. Let cool in the pan and refrigerate until the next day. Then allow an hour to reheat the dish and finish cooking the meat before serving.*

LEFTOVERS *The osso buco will keep for about a week in the fridge. It can also be frozen for up to one month. Take the leftover meat off the bone, removing any sinew or connective tissue, cut it up, and stir it into the cooking liquid to use as a sauce for pasta.*

Meatloaf

Unlike hamburgers (see page 95), which I believe should be left as pure and simple as possible, meatloaf needs some help in the way of some seasoning and a binding agent or two. I think of meatloaf as an everyday pâté, only it's good hot or cold, with mashed potatoes and gravy, or sliced thin on sandwiches with ketchup. This is a simple recipe, but consider it a starting point. You can bake it in a loaf pan, for a more compact texture, or shape it into a free-form loaf for a more crumbly texture.

Makes 4 to 6 servings

> Unsalted butter or oil, for greasing the pan
> 2 pounds ground beef, regular, not lean, such as chuck (85% lean), or a combination of ground beef, veal, and/or pork
> 1 large egg
> 1 small onion, grated
> 1 small garlic clove, minced
> 1 tablespoon Dijon mustard or Worcestershire sauce
> 3 tablespoons ketchup
> ¼ cup unflavored bread crumbs
> 1 tablespoon finely chopped flat-leaf parsley
> 2 teaspoons kosher salt
> ¼ teaspoon freshly ground black pepper
> 2 bacon strips (optional)

Preheat the oven to 375°F.

Grease a loaf pan, roasting pan, or sheet pan.

In a large bowl, combine the ground meat, egg, onion, garlic, mustard, ketchup, bread crumbs, parsley, salt, and black pepper. Mix well with a wooden spoon or your hands to distribute all of the ingredients. Either pack the meat mixture into the prepared loaf pan, rounding the top to form a nicely shaped loaf, or shape the meat into a loaf about 4 inches wide and 8 inches long in the roasting pan or on the sheet pan. If using bacon, lay the strips along the top of the loaf.

GRINDING YOUR OWN MEAT

If you aren't fortunate enough to live near a butcher who grinds meat to order, the only way to know what is in your ground meat is to grind it yourself. Freshly ground beef made from chuck or round has a superior texture and flavor to anything that you buy already ground. (The same is true for ground veal, pork, or lamb.) Given the current issues with the contamination of ground meat, if you like your hamburgers rare or you are making steak tartare, I would advise you to grind your own meat.

One of the most important considerations is how much fat to use. Fat provides flavor and juiciness to ground meat, and although you might be tempted to trim away everything but the lean muscle, if you are making hamburgers, meatballs, or meatloaf, I would recommend you leave a decent amount of fat attached, 15 to 20 percent by weight. In fact, if your meat is especially lean, you might consider buying some beef fat to add to it. (Sometimes I add ground bacon or pancetta.) Trim the meat of all connective tissue, sinew, gristle, or other impurities. Cut the meat into 1-inch cubes and chill it well before you grind it. Then choose one of the three techniques explained below:

By Hand

Chopping meat by hand produces ground meat with the best texture and most juiciness, ideal for steak tartare and hamburgers. It is easiest to do with two large, sharp chef's knives of equal size and weight and a large, sturdy cutting board. Place the cubes of trimmed meat in a pile on the board, and using one of the knives, chop it coarsely back and forth into smallish pieces the way you would chop fresh herbs. Pick up the second knife, and holding one knife in each hand by the handles, chop the meat with a drumming motion and rhythm, moving back and forth over the flesh until it is finely and evenly chopped. Occasionally scrape the meat up and turn it over itself while you work.

In a Food Processor

Using a food processor to chop meat is fast and efficient. The texture is somewhere between hand chopped and commercial ground. Work in small batches and use on/off pulses, so the machine doesn't heat up the meat too much and to be sure the texture is even. Working with no more than 8 ounces of trimmed, cubed meat at a time, place the meat in the work bowl of a processor fitted with the metal chopping blade. Using 3- or 4-second on/off pulses, grind the meat to an even, fine texture. If necessary, scrape down the sides and around the bottom edge of the bowl with a rubber spatula. When all the meat is ground, mix the batches to even out the texture.

With a Meat Grinder

An electric or hand-crank meat grinder produces ground meat closest to the texture of store-bought hamburger. To keep the grinder from heating up, I chill the grinder in the freezer. Use a grinding disk with medium-size holes and be sure the X-shaped blade of the grinder is sharp and properly assembled with the sharp edge of the blade against the grinding disk. Feed the meat into the grinder one or two pieces at a time, and use the wooden plunger to push the meat through at a steady pace. To be sure all of the meat has come out of the grinder, I use a trick I learned while working at a butcher shop in high school. Take a foot-long piece of plastic wrap, scrunch it up like a rope, and feed it into the grinder while it is still running. The plastic will force through any meat left in the grinder and bunch up around the blade without coming through. Be sure to clean all parts of the grinder thoroughly before putting it away.

Bake for about 1 hour, or until the meatloaf has browned and an instant-read thermometer inserted into the center of the loaf reads 160°F. While it bakes, the meat will release some liquid; it will subside and brown, giving the meatloaf a nice crust. Remove from the oven and let cool for 15 minutes in the pan before unmolding and slicing.

PREP TIME: 10 minutes

COOKING TIME: 1 hour

TOTAL TIME: 1 hour 10 minutes (plus resting time)

ADVANCE PREP *The meatloaf can be mixed and shaped up to one day in advance. Wrap and refrigerate until ready to bake.*

LEFTOVERS *The meatloaf will keep for about a week in the refrigerator. Leftovers are delicious thinly sliced and used in sandwiches or crumbled and added to spaghetti sauce, chili, or sloppy joes.*

VARIATIONS

Meatloaf with Roasted Potatoes

If you bake the meatloaf in a roasting pan, you can add 2 or 3 peeled Russet or Yukon Gold potatoes cut up into 1- or 2-inch chunks to the pan. As the meatloaf bakes, the potatoes will roast in the pan juices. Turn them once or twice during baking to evenly coat them with the juices.

Meat and Vegetable Loaf

My sister Leslie adds shredded vegetables to her meatloaf to give it a lighter texture. Follow the same recipe, grating a medium zucchini and a medium carrot into the meat mixture before mixing and shaping.

Buffalo Chili

Unlike Buffalo chicken wings, which are named for the city in northwestern New York State where they were "invented," this chili is called Buffalo Chili because it is made with buffalo (aka bison) meat. Of course you can substitute beef, but buffalo has a deep, beefy flavor and pleasantly chewy texture that enhances the chili. It's also very lean. As an added bonus, I think making chili with buffalo meat has some historical resonance—you can imagine cowboys eating this chili from metal bowls next to a fire on the plains of the Wild West.

Whether to use ground meat or finely diced meat is an age-old chili debate. I prefer the final texture of a chili made with diced meat, but if you would rather use ground meat, go ahead; you can cook the chili a little less. If you substitute beef for the buffalo, you have to cook the chili a few minutes longer, until the meat is tender.

I would urge you to cook your own kidney beans for this recipe; the flavor and texture of the final chili will benefit from the extra effort. If you must use canned, drain them and substitute a good stock for the bean cooking liquid in the recipe.

Makes 6 servings

2 tablespoons peanut or vegetable oil

2 slices bacon or pancetta, finely minced, or an additional 2 tablespoons oil

1 medium onion, chopped

1 large garlic clove, minced

1 pound buffalo (bison) or beef chuck, round, rump, or stewing meat, finely diced (about 2½ cups), or ground

1 medium parsnip, peeled and finely diced

1 small, fresh hot chile, such as jalapeño, seeded and minced, or 1 chipotle chile in adobo, minced

3 tablespoons chili powder

5 cups cooked kidney beans (from 2 cups dried, page 201, or 2 (20-ounce) cans kidney beans, drained) with 1 1/2 cups cooking liquid or beef, chicken, or vegetable stock
1 tablespoon tomato paste
2 teaspoons kosher salt
1/2 teaspoon freshly ground black pepper
1/4 teaspoon ground chipotle chile or paprika

Heat the oil and bacon, if using, in a large pot over medium-high heat. Add the onion and garlic, and cook, stirring often, until translucent, about 5 minutes. Add the meat, parsnip, and chile, and cook until the meat begins to brown, about 10 minutes. The meat will give off some liquid initially, but as it cooks this liquid will evaporate and the meat will begin to color. Add the chili powder and continue cooking until the mixture gives off a strong, fragrant aroma of spices, a couple of minutes. Add the bean cooking liquid, tomato paste, salt, pepper, and ground chipotle, and stir to combine. Lower the heat, cover, and simmer gently for about 15 minutes, until the meat begins to break up. Stir in the beans and continue simmering, covered, for about 20 minutes, until the meat is tender.

TOTAL TIME: 1 hour

ADVANCE PREP *The chili's actually better if you make it a day in advance, refrigerate it, and reheat it.*
LEFTOVERS *This chili will keep for about a week in the fridge. It can be frozen for up to two months.*

VARIATION
Chili Dogs
Prick good, garlicky hot dogs with the point of a knife (to prevent bursting) and simmer in water for about 10 minutes, or until heated through. Warm the buns in a 325°F oven. (You can also grill the hot dogs and buns.) Place the hot dogs in the buns, spoon hot chili on top, and sprinkle with shredded Monterey Jack cheese (with or without jalapeños).

Italian Meatballs
Here's a recipe for basic meatballs that are delicious when they are first fried, but even better when they are allowed to simmer in a tomato sauce for an hour or two. Use them for sandwiches, or put them on top of spaghetti—just to annoy your Italophile friends, who will no doubt point out that in Italy nobody eats spaghetti and meatballs.

Makes about 24 meatballs, enough for 4 to 6 servings

2 pounds ground chuck, or a combination of ground beef, pork, and/or veal
3 large eggs
1/2 cup fine, unseasoned bread crumbs
1 garlic clove, minced
1 medium onion, grated
2 tablespoons heavy cream, milk, or water
1/2 cup freshly grated Parmigiano Reggiano cheese
1/4 cup finely chopped fresh flat-leaf parsley
2 teaspoons dried oregano
1/2 teaspoon dried marjoram or thyme
1/2 teaspoon granulated garlic
2 1/2 teaspoons kosher salt
1/2 teaspoon freshly ground black pepper
2 tablespoons extra-virgin olive oil, plus about 1/2 cup for frying

Place the ground meat in a large bowl. Add the eggs, bread crumbs, garlic, onion, cream,

Parmigiano Reggiano, parsley, oregano, marjoram, granulated garlic, salt, pepper, and 2 tablespoons of olive oil. Using a wooden spoon or your hands, mix the ingredients until they are evenly distributed and well combined.

Heat about ¼ inch of olive oil in a large cast-iron or nonstick frying pan over medium-high heat. I like to fry a small patty of the meat mixture to test the seasoning and make adjustments before I fry up the whole batch. When you have adjusted the seasoning to your satisfaction, wet your hands with cold water. Pick up 2 or 3 tablespoons of the meat mixture (you can use more if you prefer your meatballs supersized) and roll it into a smooth, compact ball in the palm of your hand. Place the meatball into the hot oil. Repeat with the remaining mixture, being careful not to overcrowd the pan, which would prevent even browning. (Rinse your hands with cold water every two or three balls and keep them moist to prevent sticking.)

Cook the meatballs until they have browned nicely on the bottom and then turn them so that they brown evenly on all sides. They should take 8 to 10 minutes total frying time. I like my meatballs to have a nice, thick, brown crust on them so they have more texture and flavor. To be sure they are cooked through, you can cut one in half. Transfer them to a plate lined with paper towels to drain. Repeat with the remaining meat mixture.

PREP TIME: 20 minutes

COOKING TIME: 25 minutes

TOTAL TIME: 45 minutes

ADVANCE PREP *The meatball mixture can be made up to a day in advance and stored in the fridge. You can also shape the meatballs several hours in ad-vance, cover them with plastic wrap to prevent drying, and refrigerate them until you are ready to fry them.*

LEFTOVERS *Keep the meatballs in a plastic bag in the refrigerator for up to a week or in the freezer for up to a month. It's best to store them in tomato sauce, which helps preserve the texture and prevent them from drying out. It also makes reheating simpler. Slice leftovers up and make meatball sandwiches. Or cut them into small pieces for sloppy joes.*

VARIATION

Sicilian Meatballs with Raisins and Pine Nuts

Substitute ground lamb for all or part of the ground beef and add ½ cup chopped raisins and ½ cup toasted pine nuts to the meat mixture. Proceed with the recipe as directed.

Moroccan-Spiced Meatballs with Preserved Lemon, Tomato, and Olive

Here's a delicious dish made with ground lamb enriched with Moroccan spices. It looks complicated because there are a lot of ingredients, but it's really quite easy; most of the ingredients are likely already on your spice shelf. If you don't have any preserved lemon in your fridge, I would encourage you to make it and keep it on hand (page 409). It is an excellent condiment for meat, fish, and vegetables. Serve these meatballs with Minted Yogurt Sauce (page 402) for a superb summertime meal.

Makes about 18 meatballs, enough for 4 to 6 servings

FOR THE MEATBALLS
    1½ pounds ground lamb
    ½ small yellow or white onion, minced

1 medium garlic clove, minced

½ teaspoon finely minced Preserved Lemon peel
(page 409) or grated lemon zest

2 tablespoons finely chopped flat-leaf parsley

1 large egg

2 tablespoons extra-virgin olive oil, plus extra
for frying

¼ cup unseasoned bread crumbs

1½ teaspoons ground cumin

½ teaspoon ground coriander

¼ teaspoon ground cinnamon

1½ teaspoons kosher salt

¼ teaspoon freshly ground black pepper

FOR THE BRAISING LIQUID

¼ cup extra-virgin olive oil

½ small yellow or white onion, sliced

½ medium garlic clove, minced

1 small hot chile pepper, seeded and minced

2 tablespoons tomato paste

⅔ cup lamb, chicken, or vegetable stock,
or water

1 teaspoon finely minced Preserved Lemon peel
(see page 409) or grated lemon zest

½ teaspoon kosher salt

¼ teaspoon freshly ground black pepper

½ cup small brined black olives, such
as niçoise

Preheat the oven to 350°F.

To prepare the meatballs, in a large mixing bowl combine the lamb, onion, garlic, lemon peel, parsley, egg, olive oil, bread crumbs, cumin, coriander, cinnamon, salt, and black pepper, and mix very well with a wooden spoon to evenly distribute the spices.

Heat about ¼ inch of olive oil in a heavy frying pan over medium-high heat. Taking a heaping tablespoon or so of the meat mixture at a time, shape meatballs, wetting your hands with cold water occasionally to prevent the meat from sticking. Fry the meatballs in batches in the hot oil until they are browned on all sides, about 7 minutes total. Let drain on paper towels. When all of the meatballs have been browned, arrange them in a baking dish that's just big enough to hold them in a single layer.

Pour out the oil and wipe the pan. Return to medium heat to prepare the braising liquid. Add the olive oil and, when hot, add the onion and garlic. Sauté until soft, about 5 minutes. Add the chile and sauté for another minute or two until soft. Add the tomato paste, stock, lemon peel, salt, and pepper and bring to a simmer. Cook for about 3 or 4 minutes, just until the sauce coheres. Stir in the olives and pour this mixture over the meatballs to cover. Cover the dish with aluminum foil and bake in the oven for 25 to 30 minutes, until bubbling. For the last 5 minutes or so, remove the foil. Serve hot.

PREP TIME: 45 minutes
COOKING TIME: 45 minutes
TOTAL TIME: 1½ hours

ADVANCE PREP The meatball mixture can be made and refrigerated up to a day before the meatballs are shaped and fried. The whole dish can be prepared up to the point of the final baking and held for a day in the refrigerator.

LEFTOVERS The meatballs will last for a week in the refrigerator. Leftovers reheat very well on top of the stove. Add a little water to prevent burning. The meatballs also make delicious sandwiches.

LEARNING YOUR CHOPS

For some reason, beef (and some fish) is cut into steaks, while all other meat is cut into chops. Like steaks, veal, lamb, and pork chops are cut from various parts of the animal that correspond to various levels of quality. Loin chops, which are akin to T-bone steaks, are generally considered the best quality. Consequently, they are also the most expensive. Rib chops, which correspond to rib steaks, are also pricey. As I prefer rib steaks to T-bones, I also prefer rib chops to loin chops. I find the meat juicier and more flavorful as a result of more intramuscular fat characteristic of the rib section of the animal. Shoulder chops are similar to shoulder or blade steaks. They are made up of several different muscles and usually have one or two bones. But because veal, lamb, and pork come from smaller, younger animals than beef, the meat of a shoulder chop is not as tough as the meat on a blade steak, and these lower-priced chops can be perfectly delicious, even when quickly grilled or broiled.

There's been a lot of talk recently about pork, and anyone who is old enough to have cooked pork over the last three or four decades will tell you that the current state of pork chops is pretty sad. In an effort to make pork more attractive to consumers, pigs have been bred to have less fat. The result is a pork chop that is fine if you cook it quickly at a high temperature, such as grilling or broiling—it's better still if you brine it first—but that doesn't hold up to slow-cooking methods, such as braising, stuffing, and smothering. These lean chops become dry and tough. (Thankfully, other cuts of pork, such as the shoulder or butt and fresh ham are naturally fattier and haven't suffered as much from the trend to leaner pigs.) Luckily some pork producers are now raising special breeds of pigs that produce rich, fatty pork chops. In my area, a company called When Pigs Fly has delicious pork chops and other pork parts. While pricey and not always easy to find, special chops from heirloom breeds are worth seeking out. They are still cheaper than the best veal and lamb chops, and the difference is remarkable.

Like steaks, chops are best cooked quickly at a high temperature. I occasionally marinate them before grilling, broiling, or pan-frying, but in general I like to leave them simply seasoned so the taste of the meat comes through. I prefer to serve them with a flavorful sauce that guests can use as much or as little of as they like.

Grilled Veal Chops with Charmoula

Charmoula is a Moroccan sauce that's often served on grilled fish. I also like it on grilled meat. The combination of herbs and citrus makes everything this sauce touches light and refreshing.

Makes 4 servings

4 veal loin or rib chops, cut about 1 inch thick
(about 3 pounds), rinsed and patted dry

Kosher salt and freshly ground black pepper
¾ cup Charmoula (page 400)

Preheat a gas or charcoal grill or a broiler and broiler pan.

Season the veal generously with salt and pepper. Grill or broil to medium rare, about 6 minutes per side. Make a small cut in the center of one of the chops to check the doneness. Remove the veal from the grill and let rest for 5 minutes. Serve with the charmoula on the side.

TOTAL TIME: 15 minutes

LEFTOVERS *The veal will keep for four or five days in the fridge, but it is best just after it is made. Use in hash (see page 124), or Shepherd's Pie (page 387).*

Veal Parmesan

I know that this is an old-fashioned Italian-American dish that some people think is best left to spaghetti joints in Little Italy. But when made with good-quality veal and cheese and a fresh tomato sauce, there's nothing like it. The same preparation can be used with chicken, turkey, pork, eggplant, zucchini, or portobello mushrooms, or anything else you think might be delicious breaded, fried, bathed with tomato sauce, and topped with melted cheese—which would be just about anything!

Makes 4 or 5 servings

  1/2 cup all-purpose flour
  1 cup fine, unseasoned bread crumbs (page 370)
  2 teaspoons kosher salt
  1/2 teaspoon freshly ground black pepper
  1 large egg
  1 pound veal scaloppine, pounded thin
  1/4 cup extra-virgin olive oil
  1/4 cup peanut or vegetable oil
  2 cups tomato sauce (pages 250 to 252)
  6 to 8 ounces fresh mozzarella cheese, very thinly sliced
  1 to 2 ounces Parmigiano Reggiano cheese, finely grated (about 1/4 cup)

Place the flour in a wide, shallow bowl or on a plate with a deep rim, and place the bread crumbs in another. Divide the salt and the black pepper between the two, and mix well. Put the egg in a shallow bowl and beat it with 1 tablespoon cold water. Dredge the first piece of veal in the flour to coat; dust off any excess. Next dip in the egg to coat. Use a fork to hold up the meat and allow the excess egg to drain off. Place the veal on the bread crumbs, and cover both sides with crumbs, pressing to be sure the crumbs adhere. Brush off any extra crumbs with your fingertips and place the veal on a plate. Repeat with the remaining veal.

Meanwhile, in a medium sauté pan set over medium-high heat, combine the olive oil with the peanut oil. When the oil is hot, add two or three pieces of veal, depending on their size. Don't overcrowd the pan. Turn down the heat slightly to moderate the temperature of the oil. When the first side is golden brown, 3 or 4 minutes, use tongs, a spatula, or a fork to turn over the veal. Cook the second side for 2 or 3 minutes, until brown. Remove to drain on paper towels or brown paper. Repeat with the remaining veal.

Preheat the oven to 400° F.

To assemble, spoon about 3/4 cup of the tomato sauce on the bottom of a baking dish and spread it out evenly to coat. Arrange the veal in one layer like a jigsaw puzzle so that it is touching but not overlapping. Spoon the rest of the sauce on top of the veal. Arrange the mozzarella on top of the sauce and sprinkle with the Parmigiano Reggiano. Bake for about 25 minutes, or until the sauce is bubbling and the cheese has melted and begun to brown.

Bread Crumbs

Making bread crumbs is the most basic and most obvious thing to do with old bread, and yet people are forever buying them. Not only are homemade bread crumbs essentially free, they're also preservative- and additive-free. They are also usually fresher than store-bought bread crumbs. As a rule, I prefer dried bread crumbs for breading foods that will be fried—they make a crisper coating. Fresh bread crumbs are better to stir into stuffing and meat mixtures to absorb excess moisture. The recipe below is for dried bread crumbs. For fresh, skip the oven step and simply chop fresh bread in the food processor.

Makes 2 1/2 cups

1 pound stale white bread with about 1/3 of the crust removed

Preheat the oven to 250°F, or as low as it will go.

If the bread isn't sliced already, cut it up into chunks or slices. Lay it out in a single layer on a baking sheet or two and place in the oven. Bake, turning the pieces over once or twice, until the bread is completely dried out and very lightly toasted, 2 to 2 1/2 hours. I like to do this after dinner, then I turn off the oven and let the bread continue to dry out overnight with just the heat of the pilot light.

Remove the bread and cool to room temperature. Place a few pieces of the bread in the bowl of a food processor fitted with a metal chopping blade. Using on/off pulses, pulverize the bread to crumbs. (Be prepared for a really loud grinding noise.) Once you've got crumbs, let the machine run continuously for a minute or two to be sure they are as fine as can be. Turn off the machine and dump the crumbs into a sieve that's sitting in a baking dish or on a cookie sheet. Sift the crumbs through the sieve, using your fingertips to rub them through, until only the larger pieces remain. Return the large pieces to the food processor, add more bread, and repeat until all of the bread is ground and sieved.

PREP TIME: 25 minutes
TOTAL TIME: 2 hours 25 minutes

ADVANCE PREP *Toasted bread crumbs will keep at room temperature for a month or so, or in the freezer, carefully wrapped or in an airtight container, for up to a year.*

PREP TIME: 20 minutes
COOKING TIME: 35 minutes
TOTAL TIME: 55 minutes

ADVANCE PREP *I often assemble the dish in the morning to bake at night. Cover it with plastic wrap and store it in the refrigerator. You can also assemble it a day or two in advance, but the texture of the breading suffers a little bit. You can also assemble*

the dish, wrap it well, and freeze it for up to one month. To bake it, remove it from the freezer, don't defrost, and bake an additional 20 minutes or so, until the sauce is bubbling and the cheese is melted. To check that the veal is heated through, insert a knife in the middle of a piece of veal and then feel the tip of the knife to see if it is hot or cold.
LEFTOVERS *The veal parmesan will keep for up to a week in the fridge. Reheat leftovers in the oven,*

covered with aluminum foil. Better yet, turn them into veal parmesan hero sandwiches with extra sauce and cheese.

VARIATION

Wiener Schnitzel or Veal alla Milanese

Both of these dishes amount to breaded and fried veal scaloppine. Just proceed with the veal parmesan recipe to the point that you've fried all of the veal and skip the sauce and cheese. Serve with wedges of fresh lemon. The veal is best hot out of the pan, but if necessary it can be made several hours in advance and reheated on a wire rack in a 325°F oven until warm.

Sautéed Veal Scaloppine with Capers and Lemon

This is a classic sautéed veal dish, at one time a staple on Continental restaurant menus around the world. I think it is still delicious. Pounded chicken, turkey, or pork cutlets can be substituted for the veal.

Makes 4 servings

- 1 pound veal scaloppine (8 to 10 pieces)
- ½ cup all-purpose flour
- Kosher salt and freshly ground black pepper
- 4 tablespoons (½ stick) unsalted butter
- 2 tablespoons extra-virgin olive oil or peanut oil
- 1 small garlic clove, minced
- 2 tablespoons salted or brined capers, rinsed
- ½ cup dry white wine or vermouth
- Juice of ½ lemon
- 1 tablespoon chopped fresh herbs, such as chervil, tarragon, lemon balm, or flat-leaf parsley

If your butcher has pounded the veal, there is no need to pound it further. If not, lay the meat out between two sheets of plastic wrap or waxed paper and pound with a rubber mallet, cleaver, or the bottom of a heavy frying pan until thin. Be careful not to pound the meat too much so that it falls apart. It should be an even ¼-inch thickness.

Dredge the veal in the flour to coat. Tap off any excess flour. Season both sides of the veal with salt and pepper. Heat 1 tablespoon of the butter and 1 tablespoon of the olive oil in a large sauté pan over medium-high heat. When the fat is hot, add about half the veal to the pan in a single layer (there should be no overlapping). It's okay if the pan is a little crowded because the meat will shrink as it cooks. Sauté for 3 or 4 minutes, until lightly browned. Turn over and brown the second side. Remove the veal from the pan to a plate and repeat, heating another tablespoon each of butter and oil before cooking the remaining pieces.

Add the garlic and capers to the pan and sauté for a minute or two. Add the white wine and lemon juice and simmer for another minute or two. The sauce should thicken a little bit because of the flour left in the pan. Stir in the herbs and swirl in the remaining 2 tablespoons butter. Adjust the seasoning with salt and pepper, if necessary. Return the sautéed veal to the pan and simmer for just a minute or so until hot. Serve immediately.

PREP TIME: 10 minutes
COOKING TIME: 12 to 20 minutes
TOTAL TIME: 25 minutes

LEFTOVERS You can keep leftover veal in the sauce in the fridge for two or three days. I don't love this dish reheated and prefer using the veal and sauce cold in sandwiches.

Sausages with Kale

Based on a classic German preparation, this simple dish is quick and delicious. Use any German or Italian sausage you can find, such as bratwurst or sweet fennel sausage. Turkey and chicken sausages also work well.

Makes 4 servings

    1 pound sausages
    Olive oil or vegetable oil, if needed
    1 large onion, thinly sliced
    $\frac{1}{2}$ teaspoon yellow mustard seeds
    $\frac{1}{4}$ cup beer, hard cider, or dry white wine
    2 bunches kale or mustard greens (about $1\frac{1}{2}$
        pounds), stems removed
    Kosher salt and freshly ground black pepper

Heat a large frying pan, preferably with a tight-fitting cover, over medium-high heat until hot. Place the sausages in the dry pan and brown well on all sides, about 7 minutes; transfer to a plate and reserve.

Keep the pan on the heat. If there aren't a couple of tablespoons of rendered fat in the pan, add a little olive or vegetable oil. Add the onion and sauté in the fat until soft, about 5 minutes. Add the mustard seeds and sauté for another minute or two. Pour in the beer, and using a wooden spoon or heat-proof rubber spatula, scrape up any browned bits of sausage stuck to the bottom of the pan.

Add the kale, still wet from washing. Cover the frying pan and let the kale wilt for a few minutes. Remove the lid and stir the kale to distribute the onion. Season with salt and pepper. Cover again and let steam for about 8 minutes. If the liquid evaporates, add a couple of tablespoons of water. Meanwhile, slice the sausages into chunks. When the greens are cooked through, return the chunks of sausage to the pan. Re-cover and cook for another 8 minutes or so, until the sausage is cooked through.

TOTAL TIME: 35 minutes

ADVANCE PREP *You can prepare the whole dish several hours in advance. Leave the frying pan covered at room temperature. Reheat, covered, over medium heat until hot, about 5 minutes.*
LEFTOVERS *The sausage and kale will keep, refrigerated, for up to one week.*

Roast Pork, Tuscan Style

Here's a recipe for a delicious pork roast—*arista*, in Italian—that cooks on top of the stove. I like to make it

---

KITCHEN SENSE

PAN SAUCES

Sauces for meat and poultry don't have to be complicated. If you've sautéed medallions, cutlets, or chops in a skillet, the foundation of a delicious sauce is already in the pan. Once the meat is cooked, remove it from the pan, cover with foil, and keep warm. Pour off any excess fat from the pan. Add some minced onion, shallot, garlic, or a combination, and sauté for a minute or two over medium-high heat until soft. You can add mushrooms or other vegetables, too, if you wish. Pour in some liquid—whether dry red or white wine, dry white vermouth, dry sherry, brandy, Cognac, Marsala, Madeira, or stock, or a combination. While the liquid simmers, scrape off any browned bits on the bottom of the pan (this is called deglazing). Allow the liquid to reduce until it has thickened slightly. Season with salt and pepper. If desired, swirl in a tablespoon or two of chilled butter off the heat before serving.

in the summer because it keeps the kitchen cooler than if you turn on the oven. My preference is to use a boned, tied loin of pork, which cooks pretty quickly, is tender and flavorful, and makes beautiful, thin slices. Serve the roast hot, room temperature, or chilled, as your mood or the climate fits.

Makes 6 servings

1 or 2 leaves fresh sage

Leaves from 1 sprig rosemary

Leaves from 3 or 4 sprigs fresh marjoram, thyme, or oregano

4 garlic cloves

1 tablespoon kosher salt

1 teaspoon fennel seeds

One 2½-pound pork loin roast, tied

3 or 4 tablespoons extra-virgin olive oil

Freshly ground black pepper

¼ cup dry white wine (optional)

Mince the sage, rosemary, and marjoram together. Mince the garlic. Pour the salt over the garlic and mince some more. Add the herbs to the garlic mixture along with the fennel seeds and keep chopping to make a sort of dry paste. Rub this paste all over the pork roast. Wrap the roast in plastic and let chill for at least an hour, preferably longer.

Heat the olive oil in a deep frying pan or Dutch oven over medium-high heat. Remove the roast from its wrapping and season generously with black pepper. Place the roast in the hot oil and brown well on all sides, about 8 minutes. Turn down the heat as low as the burner will go, cover the pan tightly, and roast the pork for about 1 hour, turning it occasionally, until an instant-read thermometer inserted in the center of the roast reads between 155° and 160° F. The roast should be nicely browned

and there should be some rich liquid on the bottom of the pan.

Remove the roast from the pan and let rest 15 minutes. Add the white wine to the pan, if using, turn up the heat, and let simmer for a minute or two to reduce. Strain the pan juices. Slice the roast and serve with its juices.

PREP TIME: 10 minutes

COOKING TIME: 1 hour 15 minutes

TOTAL TIME: 2 hours 25 minutes (includes chilling time)

ADVANCE PREP *The roast can marinate with the spices for up to two days.*

LEFTOVERS *The roast will keep for a little more than a week in the fridge. It is excellent chilled, either as an entrée or sliced thinly for sandwiches.*

VARIATION
Oven-Roasted Pork
Prepare the roast with the garlic and herb rub, and sear it in olive oil to brown on all sides. Then, instead of finishing it on the stove, transfer it to a preheated 375° F oven for 1½ to 1¾ hours, basting it with white wine every 20 minutes or so.

Pork Cutlets with Marsala and Wild Mushroom Sauce
A classic combination of flavors, this recipe is also low in fat and easy to prepare. The same preparation can be used for veal scaloppine or chicken or turkey cutlets.

Makes 3 to 4 servings

4 or 5 small pieces dried porcini (scant ¼ ounce)

1 pound pork tenderloin, trimmed of fat, cut into 8 equal medallions

¼ cup all-purpose flour

Kosher salt and freshly ground black pepper

2 tablespoons extra-virgin olive oil

1 large shallot or a small piece of white onion, minced

8 ounces assorted fresh mushrooms, such as chanterelle, black trumpet, portobello, cremini, or button mushrooms, sliced

½ cup vegetable broth

½ cup Marsala or dry fino sherry

1 teaspoon fresh thyme

Place the dried porcini in a small bowl and cover with ½ cup cold water. Microwave on high for 2 minutes and let sit in the water to soften, about 15 minutes. (Alternatively, you can boil the water and pour it over the mushrooms.) When soft, cut the porcini into small pieces and reserve the soaking liquid.

Meanwhile, butterfly the pork medallions to make thin cutlets: with a sharp knife, slice each medallion crosswise through the center, as though you are going to split it in half, but don't cut all the way through. Open up the medallion and flatten it to make a cutlet. Using a mallet or the back of a frying pan, pound the cutlets between two pieces of plastic wrap so they are about ¼ inch thick. Dredge the cutlets in the flour and tap off any excess. Season both sides with salt and pepper.

In a large, nonstick frying pan, heat the oil over medium-high heat. Swirl the pan to distribute the oil evenly on the bottom. When hot, add half the cutlets. Cook until browned, about 4 minutes, then turn over and brown the other side, about 3 minutes. Remove the cutlets to a plate. Repeat with remaining cutlets.

Add the shallot to the pan and cook for 1 minute. Add the fresh mushrooms as well as the porcini. Cook for a minute or two, stirring frequently. Add the broth and about 4 tablespoons of the porcini soaking liquid: lift the liquid out of the bowl with a spoon without disturbing the sediment on the bottom. Using a wooden spoon, scrape off any bits that have stuck to the bottom of the pan. When the mushrooms have wilted, about 5 minutes, add the Marsala and thyme. Keep cooking, stirring, for 2 or 3 minutes, until some of the liquid has evaporated and the sauce has begun to thicken.

Return the pork to the pan along with any juice that has accumulated on the plate. Simmer for 3 or 4 minutes until the pork is hot and the sauce has thickened.

PREP TIME: 25 minutes
COOKING TIME: 20 minutes
TOTAL TIME: 45 minutes

LEFTOVERS *The pork will keep for up to a week in the refrigerator. It makes a delicious sandwich.*

Pork Chops with Apples and Prunes

This is a classic combination of flavors that makes for a delicious entrée. Serve it with plenty of mashed potatoes.

Makes 4 servings

½ cup pitted prunes

½ cup dry white wine

Peanut or vegetable oil, for frying

4 rib or loin pork chops, about ¾ to 1 inch thick (1¾ pounds)

¼ cup all-purpose flour

Kosher salt and freshly ground black pepper

4 tablespoons (½ stick) unsalted butter

1 small onion, finely chopped

1 large apple, such as Golden Delicious or Gala,
  peeled, cored, and chopped
1 teaspoon chopped fresh sage, rosemary, or
  thyme, or a pinch of dried
½ cup apple cider
1 tablespoon cider vinegar
½ teaspoon Dijon mustard

Place the prunes in a small bowl and cover with the wine. Heat in a microwave for a minute on high and let sit for 20 minutes or so to plump. (Alternatively, you can heat the wine in a saucepan and pour the wine over the prunes.)

Heat about ¼ inch oil in a large frying pan. Dredge the pork chops in flour to lightly coat; tap off any excess flour. Season generously with salt and pepper. Place the chops in the hot oil and fry until nicely browned, 4 or 5 minutes per side. Remove the chops to a plate and drain the oil from the pan without disturbing any browned bits on the bottom of the pan.

Add the butter to the pan and sauté the onion until it softens, about 5 minutes. Add the apple and sage and sauté until the apple is soft, another 5 minutes. The onion should begin to lightly brown. Add the apple cider, cider vinegar, mustard, and the prunes along with their soaking liquid. Bring to a simmer, scraping any browned bits off the bottom of the pan, until the sauce thickens slightly.

Return the pork chops to the pan along with any juice that has accumulated on the plate. Simmer for a few minutes to heat through. Adjust the seasoning with salt and pepper.

PREP TIME: 10 minutes
COOKING TIME: 25 minutes
TOTAL TIME: 35 minutes

LEFTOVERS The chops will keep for four or five days in the refrigerator. Reheat in a skillet, adding more cider if necessary to thin down the sauce.

Smoked Pork Chops with Mustard and Bread Crumbs

My friend Dano, a chef in upstate New York, serves smoked pork chops with Braised Red Cabbage (page 171), and Spätzle (page 246). It's one of my favorite combinations of flavors. Because smoked pork chops are brined before smoking, the meat is juicy and tender. They are fully cooked when you buy them so they just need to be heated up.

Makes 4 servings

¼ cup Dijon mustard
3 tablespoons beer (lager or ale) or dry white wine
1 cup fine, unseasoned bread crumbs
4 smoked pork loin chops, cut ¾ to 1 inch thick
  (about 1¾ pounds)
Peanut or vegetable oil, or lard, or a combination,
  for frying

In a small bowl, mix the mustard and beer. Place the bread crumbs on a plate. Using a brush, coat the pork chops all over with the mustard mixture, then dredge them in the bread crumbs to coat. Place the chops on a wire rack for about 10 minutes or so to allow the coating to dry.

In a large pan, heat about ¼ inch oil over medium-high heat. Place the chops in the hot oil and fry until nicely browned on all sides and heated through, 5 or 6 minutes per side.

PREP TIME: 10 minutes
COOKING TIME: 10 minutes
TOTAL TIME: 30 minutes (includes resting time)

ADVANCE PREP The pork chops can be breaded up to a day in advance and refrigerated.

Pulled Pork

They call this "pulled" pork because once the meat is finished cooking and it is cool enough to handle, you literally pull it apart into juicy strands. Don't be tempted to cut it up instead because it just won't have the right texture. The best cut for making pulled pork is a pork shoulder (sometimes called the butt or a picnic shoulder). I prefer a whole one with the skin and bones, which make for extra flavor. But if that's too large—they run from 7 to 10 pounds—use a boneless shoulder roast.

Makes 8 to 10 servings

2 tablespoons kosher salt

1 teaspoon freshly ground black pepper

1 tablespoon sweet Hungarian or smoked Spanish paprika

1 teaspoon Bell's Seasoning, herbes de Provence, or another spice mix you like (optional)

Cayenne pepper (optional)

¼ cup brown sugar

6 to 8 large garlic cloves, peeled and split in half

One 7- to 8-pound pork shoulder, with skin

1 quart of Evelynne's Barbecue Sauce (page 406) or your favorite barbecue sauce

In a small bowl, combine the salt, pepper, paprika, seasoning mix, if using, cayenne pepper to taste, if using, and brown sugar. Roll the garlic in this spice mixture and set aside. Rub the sugar-spice mixture all over the pork shoulder, getting it deep into any grooves you can find between layers of muscle and around the bone. Poke the seasoned garlic cloves deep into the meat anywhere you can. Place the seasoned pork into a plastic bag, tie it tight, and refrigerate for at least one day.

Preheat the oven to 500°F.

Place a wire rack in a large roasting pan. Take the pork out of the bag and set it on the rack skin side up. Pour any juices in the bag over the meat. Pour about ½ inch of water in the bottom of the roasting pan and set in the oven. (Alternatively, you can place a separate pan of water in the oven along with the roast.) The key is that the oven stay humid, which will keep the meat moist—this should not be a dry roast. Roast the shoulder for about 20 minutes, then turn down the heat to 325°F, and continue roasting for 4 to 5 hours, until the meat is obviously very well done and begins to fall off the bone. Make sure there is always water in the bottom of the pan. If not, add more during the roasting process.

When the meat is done, remove the roast from the oven. Lay out one or two sheets of heavy-duty aluminum foil, big enough to wrap the roast. Place the roast on the foil and wrap it tightly to seal. Now wrap the whole thing in several layers of newspaper to insulate it and put it in a brown paper bag. Let the pork steam inside this wrapping for at least 1 hour and up to 2 hours.

Preheat the oven again to 500°F.

Heat the barbecue sauce to a simmer. Remove the roast from its wrapping and set it back on the roasting rack, skin side up. Set in the hot oven for 20 minutes or so to crisp the skin. Remove the pork from the oven and, with tongs, lift off the skin. Cut the skin into small pieces. Now pull the meat apart into long, juicy strands along the grain of the meat. Place the meat in a baking dish or ovenproof serving dish. Be sure to leave plenty of fat on the meat.

Pour about half of the hot sauce over the meat and serve the rest on the side along with the pieces of crispy skin.

PREP TIME: 20 minutes
COOKING TIME: 5 to 6 hours
TOTAL TIME: 1 1/2 days (includes marinating and resting times)

ADVANCE PREP *The longer you let the pork marinate before cooking, up to three days, the better.*
LEFTOVERS *The pork will keep for about a week in the fridge, but it's never the same delicious texture as it is just after it is pulled. Substitute pulled pork, without the barbecue sauce on it, for roast pork on a Cuban Sandwich (page 88).*

VARIATIONS
Less Pulled Pork

If a whole shoulder is just too much meat, you can follow the same recipe using a boned and tied pork shoulder roast. The only difference is that such a roast won't have the crisp skin or the extra fat that comes with the larger piece. To compensate, here's what I do. Wrap a 2 1/2- to 3-pound roast in thin slices of pancetta or bacon. Cut the spices and sugar in half but follow the same technique and cooking instructions, instead roasting for only 2 hours after turning down the oven temperature to 325°F and omitting the step of crisping the skin.

Glazed Ham

This is a recipe for the sort of ham you should bring to the table at Christmas or Easter. It's easy to prepare since the curing and smoking of ham makes it very forgiving—all you really have to do is heat it through and

it's good to go. In my experience, come holiday time, German and Polish butchers have the most beautiful hams for sale, and they are usually less sweet and less processed tasting than regular commercially prepared hams. You can use any size ham, from a whole leg to a small piece of boneless meat. Figure about 8 ounces of meat per serving.

Makes 12 to 16 servings

> 1 cup apple cider, orange juice, pineapple juice, pomegranate juice, black coffee, or cola
> 1/4 cup honey or maple syrup
> One 10- to 15-pound ham
> 1 cup brown sugar
> 1/4 cup cider vinegar
> 2 tablespoons Dijon mustard or 2 teaspoons dry mustard
> 1/2 teaspoon freshly ground white pepper

Preheat the oven to 350°F. Place a small baking dish with about 1 inch of water in it in the bottom of the oven. In a small bowl, combine the cider and honey.

Set the ham on a wire rack in a shallow roasting pan. Place the ham in the oven and roast, basting every 15 minutes or so with the cider mixture, until the meat is heated through—it should read between 140° and 150°F on an instant-read thermometer—figure between 13 and 15 minutes per pound. If at any time the water in the small baking dish evaporates, add more.

Meanwhile, mix the brown sugar, vinegar, mustard, and pepper to form a wet paste.

When the ham has reached the proper temperature, remove it from the oven. Raise the oven temperature to 375°F. Using a serrated or very sharp knife, score the skin of the ham in a cross-hatch pattern, cutting about 1/4 inch deep.

HAMMING IT UP

There are many different types of ham. Technically, ham is made from the hind leg of a pig (called the fresh ham before it is cured). But these days ham is also made from the shoulder (sometimes called the picnic shoulder or picnic ham) and other fatty parts of the pig. Fully cooked and partially cooked hams sold in America are first cured with plenty of sugar and salt and then smoked. They have a familiar bright pink color, usually the result of nitrates and nitrites. These are the hams you see in commercials glazed with brown sugar and decorated with pineapple rings and Maraschino cherries.

Country, or Virginia ham, of which Smithfield ham is probably the most famous, is made from specially fed pigs. The meat is heavily salted, not smoked, and air-dried for at least a year. Before being eaten, country ham is usually soaked for up to three days to remove the excess salt and braised for hours to make it palatable. I've made a couple of country hams in my day, and although I love the idea and the tradition of them, I've never found country ham particularly pleasant to eat, especially considering the effort it takes to make it. Maybe it's just because I'm a Yankee.

Air-dried European hams, such as prosciutto di Parma or San Daniele from Italy, jambon de Bayonne from France, or jamon Serrano or Iberico from Spain, are also salted and air-dried for a year or more, but the techniques Europeans use keep the flesh moist and sweet. These hams are eaten raw, usually sliced very thin on bread or with fresh fruit, such as figs or melon. They are my favorite form of ham. And they can also be used in cooking, chopped up and stirred into the mix for a meatloaf or a pasta sauce, for example.

Other types of quality ham include smoked Westphalian and Black Forest hams from Germany. Boiled or cooked ham is more a luncheon meat than anything else. Don't confuse prosciutto cotto (cooked ham) from Italy for prosciutto di Parma; prosciutto cotto is Italy's equivalent to boiled ham.

Spread the brown sugar mixture evenly over the surface of the ham. Return it to the oven and let roast for about 45 minutes, until the ham is browned and glistening. Remove from the oven, cover loosely with foil to keep warm, and let sit for 15 minutes before carving.

PREP TIME: 5 minutes
COOKING TIME: 2 to 3 hours
TOTAL TIME: 2½ to 3½ hours (plus resting time)

LEFTOVERS *Leftover ham will keep for about two weeks in the refrigerator. It can be used in all sorts of dishes, such as Macaroni Salad (page 75), Potato and Ham Croquettes (page 191), Boston Baked Beans (page 199), or sliced in sandwiches. It can also be used as a substitute for pancetta, bacon, mortadella, or other cured meat products. If there is a bone, save it for Split Pea Soup (page 40).*

Ham Steaks with Red-Eye Gravy

Ham steaks are cross-section slices of cooked, partially cooked, or country ham cut about ½ inch thick. They can be pan-seared, baked, or grilled. Made with coffee, red-eye gravy is a specialty of the South. At cafés in the southern United States, you'll find giant, salty pan-fried country ham steaks with red-eye gravy served as a breakfast side dish with eggs and grits. Although I've seen several references to the name coming from the reddish color of the ham fat, I believe it's called red-eye gravy because the caffeine in the coffee keeps you awake. One regional variation I've encountered in my travels that strikes me as particularly authentic calls for replacing the coffee with Coca-Cola—which many Southerners drink for their morning pick-me-up. Though perhaps a little Northern of me, I also think red-eye gravy is tasty made with a strongly brewed English breakfast tea.

Makes 4 servings

1 tablespoon ham fat, bacon fat, or unsalted butter
4 ham steaks (about 1 1/2 pounds total), cut from cooked, partially cooked, or country ham
1/2 cup strong black coffee, cola, or strong English breakfast tea
2 tablespoons heavy cream (optional)

In a large skillet, melt the fat over medium-high heat. Fry the ham steaks until nicely browned on both sides, 3 or 4 minutes per side. Remove the ham from the pan and cover loosely with foil to keep warm.

Pour the coffee into the hot pan and simmer, scraping the bottom of the pan to loosen any browned bits. Add the cream, if using, and simmer for 4 or 5 minutes to thicken. Pour the gravy over the ham and serve.

TOTAL TIME: 10 minutes

Barbecued Spareribs

I live in New York City, a great food town, but for some reason it's almost impossible to find a decent rack of barbecued ribs. I can't explain it. I don't think it's that difficult to make them. The secret is the technique of roasting them in advance, wrapping them while hot in aluminum foil, and letting them sit for at least an hour to steam, and then finishing them either in the oven or on the grill with the sauce. Although baby back ribs are more delicate and more expensive than other types of ribs, I think they are a waste of money. Big, fat, meaty, juicy, flavorful spareribs or even meatier country ribs are my preference.

Makes 2 racks of ribs, enough for 4 to 6 servings

2 tablespoons kosher salt
2 tablespoons sugar
1 teaspoon granulated garlic
2 teaspoons sweet or smoked paprika
2 teaspoons dried thyme
1/2 teaspoon ground cumin
1/4 teaspoon ground allspice
1 teaspoon freshly ground black pepper
2 large racks spareribs or country ribs (4 to 5 pounds)
1 quart Evelynne's Barbecue Sauce (page 406) or other barbecue sauce

Make a dry rub for the ribs by combining the salt, sugar, granulated garlic, paprika, thyme, cumin, allspice, and black pepper in a small bowl. Rub this mixture all over the surface of both sides of the ribs. Wrap the ribs in plastic wrap and set in the fridge for at least 6 hours.

Preheat the oven to 350°F. Set a small baking dish with about 1 inch of water in it on the bottom of the oven. Place a large roasting rack on a rimmed sheet pan. Spray the rack and the pan with nonstick cooking spray.

Set the ribs on the rack meat side up. Roast for 1 hour. (Make sure there is always some water in the baking dish.) Remove the ribs from the oven, and while still very hot, wrap the ribs tightly in aluminum foil. Place the ribs in a brown paper bag, or wrap in newspaper to retain the heat. Let the ribs sit at room temperature for at least 1 hour.

Preheat the oven to 425°F or fire up the grill.

Unwrap the ribs. Place them meat side up on the same roasting rack you used for the initial roasting or on the grill. Slather the ribs with a generous amount of barbecue sauce. With tongs, turn them over and slather the bone side. Place the ribs in the oven or on the grill and roast until they begin to brown, 15 to 20 minutes, basting periodically with the sauce. Turn them over, slather with more sauce, and continue cooking for another 15 to 20 minutes, still basting, until this side is also well browned. Remove from the oven, slice the racks into individual portions, and serve with more sauce for dipping.

PREP TIME: 15 minutes

COOKING TIME: 1 hour 40 minutes

TOTAL TIME: About 9 hours (includes seasoning and resting times)

ADVANCE PREP *The ribs can keep marinating in their spice rub for up to two days. You can give the ribs their initial roasting, wrap them, and let them sit for up to 1 hour before you finish them in the oven or on the grill.*

LEFTOVERS *The ribs will keep refrigerated for about a week.*

VARIATION
Braised Barbecued Ribs

Instead of roasting or barbecuing the ribs, you can braise them slowly in a slow-cooker. Country ribs work best for this technique. After the ribs have marinated in their dry rub, place them in the slow-cooker. Pour over the barbecue sauce, cover, and set on low. After 7 or 8 hours, the meat will literally fall off the bone.

Chinese Barbecued Pork

Here's a recipe for the barbecued or roasted pork you see hanging in restaurant windows in Chinatown. It's called *char shiu*, and all I can say is that it is really delicious and quite simple. Making it yourself means you can cut out the nitrates, MSG, and food coloring that is typically part of the recipe. The marinade requires a few Chinese sauces, such as hoisin and oyster sauce, but these days they are available in just about every grocery store.

Makes 4 to 6 servings

2$\frac{1}{2}$ pounds boneless pork butt (aka shoulder)

1$\frac{1}{2}$ tablespoons regular soy sauce

1$\frac{1}{2}$ tablespoons dark soy sauce or additional
    1$\frac{1}{2}$ tablespoons regular soy sauce

1$\frac{1}{2}$ tablespoons Chinese oyster sauce

1$\frac{1}{2}$ tablespoons hoisin sauce

2 tablespoons Chinese rice wine, gin,
    or dry sherry

$\frac{1}{4}$ cup granulated, light brown, or dark brown
    sugar (if you don't have dark soy sauce, be
    sure to use dark brown sugar)

$\frac{1}{2}$ teaspoon Chinese five-spice powder

$\frac{1}{2}$ teaspoon kosher salt

Pinch of freshly ground white pepper

With a sharp knife, slice the pork butt into long, thin strips about 2 inches wide and 1 inch thick. Place the pork strips in a glass or ceramic baking dish just large enough to hold the pork in an even layer. In a small bowl, combine the soy sauce, dark soy sauce, oyster sauce, hoisin sauce, rice wine, sugar, five-spice powder, salt, and white pepper. Pour this mixture over the pork in the baking dish. Turn the pork strips over to coat with this marinade. Cover the dish and set in the refrigerator overnight to marinate.

Preheat the oven to 400°F.

Uncover the dish and set it in the oven. Roast for 30 to 40 minutes, basting the strips and turning them over frequently to keep them moist. The pork is done when it reaches about 170°F on an instant-read thermometer. If you slice through a piece, it should be moist but cooked through. (The pork can be served at this point, either hot or at room temperature, but I prefer to broil it for a few minutes before serving to crisp it up so that it's closer to the way it is made in Chinese restaurants.)

Preheat the broiler. Lay the strips of pork out on a broiling tray (reserve the cooking liquid) and set under the broiler. Broil for 4 to 6 minutes, until the pork becomes dark on the edges—the sugar helps crisp the surface. Turn the strips over and repeat on the other side. To serve, slice the pork about ¼ inch thick on the diagonal. Heat up some of the cooking liquid and pour over the sliced pork.

PREP TIME: 15 minutes

COOKING TIME: 40 minutes

TOTAL TIME: 9 hours (includes marinating time)

ADVANCE PREP *The pork can sit, refrigerated, in its marinade for up to four days.*

LEFTOVERS *If I am going to serve the pork soon after it is made, I will keep it at room temperature (as is done in Chinatown). This will help preserve the juiciness of the meat. Otherwise, the pork can be stored for up to a week in the refrigerator. Separate it from the cooking juices (but save them) and wrap the meat in plastic wrap. The pork can also be frozen for up to a month or so. Use in a variety of ways: thinly sliced in soup, cut into cubes in fried rice, ground in fillings for dumplings, etc.*

Pork in Adobo

This is a Spanish take on the tradition of marinating and braising pork in a vinegary liquid, which is also common in Italy. It's a spicy, vinegary stew. Filipino recipes for adobo add soy sauce. Latin American recipes add plenty of hot chiles. This recipe has a light tang and decent kick. Pieces of chicken can be treated in the same way. Serve it over white rice.

Makes 4 to 6 servings

½ cup white wine vinegar or cider vinegar

½ cup tomato juice

3 large garlic cloves, peeled and
    smashed

2 fresh poblano chiles or 2 rehydrated
    ancho chiles, seeded and chopped

1 small jalapeño or other hot chile, seeded and
    chopped

1 teaspoon cumin seeds

1 teaspoon dried oregano

¼ teaspoon ground coriander

¼ teaspoon ground cinnamon

Kosher salt and freshly ground black pepper

3 pounds boneless pork shoulder or butt,
    cut into 2-inch cubes

3 tablespoons lard, bacon fat, extra-virgin olive
   oil, or vegetable oil
1 large onion, chopped
1/2 red bell pepper, cored, seeded, and chopped
1/2 yellow bell pepper, cored, seeded, and
   chopped

In a blender or food processor fitted with a
metal chopping blade, combine the vinegar,
tomato juice, garlic, poblanos, jalapeño, cumin,
oregano, coriander, cinnamon, 2 teaspoons
salt, and a generous amount of freshly ground
pepper. Pulse to purée until smooth. Place the
pork in a nonreactive container or bowl and
pour the vinegar mixture on top. Toss the
cubes of meat around to coat, then cover, and
refrigerate overnight.

In a large saucepan or Dutch oven, melt the
lard over medium-high heat. Add the onion
and cook until soft, about 5 minutes. Add the
red and yellow bell peppers and cook until
wilted, another 3 or 4 minutes. Add the pork
along with its marinade. Bring to a simmer,
cover the pot, and let cook, stirring often, until
the pork is fall-apart tender, about 2 hours. If at
any time it looks like the liquid might evaporate, add a few tablespoons of water to keep
from burning. Adjust the seasoning with salt
and pepper.

PREP TIME: 10 minutes
COOKING TIME: 2 hours 10 minutes
TOTAL TIME: 10 1/2 hours (includes marinating time)

*ADVANCE PREP The pork can marinate for up to
three days in the refrigerator. The dish can be made
up to two days in advance, refrigerated, and reheated gently on top of the stove, adding a little bit
of water to prevent burning.*

*LEFTOVERS The pork will keep for four or five days
in the refrigerator. Reheat it on the stove, adding
some water if necessary to prevent burning.*

VARIATION
Chicken in Adobo
Substitute 3 or 4 pounds of chicken pieces for
the pork. Remove the skin but keep the meat
on the bones. Reduce the cooking time by
about 45 minutes.

Provençal Roasted Lamb
Because lamb comes from young animals, virtually all
of the cuts are tender enough to roast. The leg is the
most popular, whether on or off the bone. But a whole
leg can weigh up to 10 pounds, which is an awful lot of
meat. If I don't want so many leftovers, I sometimes
roast a boneless shoulder roast, tied by my butcher (be
sure to ask for the bones for stock or sauce). A boned
roast weighs between 3 and 4 pounds, a boned leg of
lamb weighs 6 to 8 pounds. Follow the same directions
for both, doubling the amount of the seasoning for the
latter.
Makes 6 to 8 servings

2 or 3 tablespoons chopped fresh herbs, such
   as thyme, rosemary, oregano, chervil, or
   marjoram, or a combination
2 large garlic cloves, minced
1 tablespoon kosher salt
1/2 teaspoon freshly ground black pepper
2 or 3 tablespoons extra-virgin olive oil
One 3 1/2-pound boneless lamb roast, tied
1 or 2 medium onions, roughly chopped
1/2 cup dry white or red wine
1/2 cup lamb, veal, chicken, or vegetable stock
   or water

In a small bowl, combine the chopped herbs, garlic, salt, and pepper. With your hands, rub the olive oil all over the surface of the roast, and then rub the herb mixture all over the surface. Poke the herb mixture inside the muscle any place you can. Place in a resealable plastic bag or wrap in plastic and let sit for a few hours in the refrigerator.

Preheat the oven to 375°F.

Lay the onions on the bottom of a roasting pan. Place a roasting rack on top of the onions and set the lamb on the rack. If you have any bones, put them in the pan. Roast for 1½ hours to 2 hours, or until the meat has reached your desired doneness (see chart, page 345). The lamb should still be pink inside. Remove from the oven and let it sit on the counter for 15 minutes or so before slicing.

To make a jus, add the wine and the stock to the roasting pan and set over medium heat. Simmer, scraping the bottom of the pan, until the liquid reduces by about one third. Strain, season with salt and pepper, and serve with the lamb.

PREP TIME: 10 minutes
COOKING TIME: 2 hours
TOTAL TIME: 10 hours (includes marinating time)

ADVANCE PREP *The roast can be seasoned and refrigerated for up to two days.*
LEFTOVERS *The lamb will keep for about a week. Use leftovers in a Shepherd's Pie (page 387). Cold lamb also makes delicious sandwiches.*

VARIATION
Moroccan-Spiced Roasted Lamb
Make a spice rub by combining 1 tablespoon kosher salt, 2 teaspoons paprika, 1 teaspoon ground cumin, 2 tablespoons chopped fresh mint, 2 minced garlic cloves, and ½ teaspoon freshly ground black pepper. Substitute for the herb and garlic mixture in Provençal Roasted Lamb.

Grilled Lamb Chops with Salsa Verde

For grilling, select loin or rib chops that are on the thicker side, around 1 inch or more. If the lamb is very young and delicate, double rib chops (with two bones) will grill better than single ones. Salsa Verde (page 401) is a garlicky Italian herb sauce that is traditionally served on boiled meat, but that I also like on grilled meat, especially lamb.

Makes 4 servings

> 2½ pounds lamb chops, cut from the rib or loin
> Olive oil
> Kosher salt and freshly ground black pepper
> Fresh lemon wedges
> Salsa Verde (page 401)

Fire up a gas or charcoal grill or preheat a broiler or grill pan.

Using your hands, rub the chops lightly with olive oil and season generously with salt and pepper. Grill or broil the chops for 3 to 5 minutes per side, depending on their thickness and the desired degree of doneness. Serve with a squirt of fresh lemon and a spoonful of Salsa Verde on the side.

TOTAL TIME: 10 minutes

VARIATION
Grilled Leg of Lamb
To grill a leg of lamb, it is best to butterfly the leg first—that is, remove the bone and open up

the muscles so the leg lays almost flat. A butcher can do this. The lamb fat has a tendency to cause flare-ups, so have a squirt bottle of water nearby to control the flames. Grill the herb or spice-coated lamb over medium-hot coals for 40 to 45 minutes.

LEFTOVERS *The grilled lamb will keep for four or five days in the refrigerator.*

Greek Souvlaki

Many cultures grill cubes of marinated meat on skewers. Satay, shish kebabs, and souvlaki are but a few. Here's a simple recipe for marinating and grilling meat that gives it a distinct Greek flavor. I've suggested using lamb or pork or chicken because I haven't found a cut of beef that I think lends itself well to the same treatment. I have, however, found several different, effective ways to cook them, giving you options. Serve with warm pita, either as a sandwich wrapped in the pita with lettuce, tomato, spices (such as Dukkah, page 408), and yogurt sauce, or as a "platter" (in Greek diner parlance) with rice, salad, and roasted potatoes.

Makes 2 to 4 servings

1 pound boneless lamb shoulder or pork butt, or
1½ pounds chicken thighs
Juice of 2 lemons or ½ cup dry white or red wine
½ cup extra-virgin olive oil
1 to 2 tablespoons chopped fresh oregano or
   fresh thyme or 1½ teaspoons dried oregano
   or dried thyme, or a combination
1 tablespoon kosher salt
1 teaspoon freshly ground black pepper

Cut the lamb or pork into 1-inch cubes, removing any excess fat or sinew. If using chicken thighs, remove the skin and cut the meat off the bone into cubes. Place the cubed meat in a container. Add the lemon juice, olive oil, herbs, salt, and pepper. Mix the meat around to evenly distribute the marinade. Cover and set in the refrigerator overnight.

If you are going to grill the skewers over charcoal, soak wooden skewers in cold water for 1 hour or so to prevent them from burning. Thread the meat onto skewers.

Fire up a gas or charcoal grill to high, preheat your broiler, or heat a pan, preferably a cast-iron grill pan, over high heat. Grill or broil, turning once, until nicely browned, 5 to 8 minutes.

PREP TIME: 25 minutes
COOKING TIME: 5 to 8 minutes
TOTAL TIME: 8 hours 30 minutes (includes marinating time)

ADVANCE PREP *The souvlaki can be marinated for about two days.*
LEFTOVERS *The meat will keep in the fridge for three or four days. If you have a lot of cooked meat left, you can add it to any number of dishes, such as chili, tomato sauce, or hash.*

Morrocan Couscous with Lamb

Here's my version of this regal North African dish—one of the great dishes of the world, I'd venture to say. There are a few things to note about couscous the grain and couscous the dish. The first is, couscous isn't a grain. It's really a pasta made from the same ingredient as Italian spaghetti, durum wheat (semolina). The second is that regardless of whether your box or bag of couscous says "instant," it isn't. All couscous should be steamed after it has soaked up its water and been fluffed with a fork in order for it to be fully cooked. If you've ever eaten a spoonful of couscous and had it sit like lead in your stomach, it's because it wasn't fully cooked. To steam the couscous, you just need a metal strainer or colander or a vegetable steamer. Even though it looks like the tiny grains of couscous will fall through the holes of a colander, once they are moistened, they don't.

As for couscous the dish, it's a rich, fragrant stew of meat and vegetables served on top of the steamed couscous. I love it with lamb, but it's good with chicken and merguez sausage or just vegetables, too.

Don't be put off by the long list of ingredients in this recipe. You can use just about any combination of vegetables and spices you want. And since you just keep adding them to the pot as the couscous cooks, it's really quite simple.

Makes 8 to 10 servings

2 to 3 pounds boneless lamb shoulder or beef stew meat, trimmed of fat and cut into 2-inch chunks

½ cup dried chickpeas, soaked overnight in cold water, or 1 (15-ounce) can chickpeas, drained

1 large onion, thinly sliced

3 or 4 garlic cloves, minced

Two 2-inch cinnamon sticks or ½ teaspoon ground cinnamon

2 tablespoons minced fresh ginger or 1 teaspoon ground ginger

1 small hot red chile, seeded and minced, or ½ teaspoon cayenne pepper, or to taste

1 teaspoon paprika

¾ teaspoon ground cumin

½ teaspoon freshly ground black pepper

Kosher salt

1 pound white potatoes, peeled and cut into 2-inch chunks

1 pound carrots, peeled and cut into 2-inch chunks

1 pound green cabbage, cut into wedges through the core so the leaves don't fall apart

1 pound eggplant, cut into chunks

12 ounces white turnips, peeled and cut into chunks

1 pound sweet potatoes, butternut squash, or pumpkin, peeled and cut into chunks

12 ounces pattypan or yellow (summer) squash, cut into chunks

12 ounces zucchini, cut into chunks

1½ pounds ripe fresh tomatoes, cut into quarters, or 6 canned tomatoes cut in half

½ cup raisins

1 bunch flat-leaf parsley, chopped

1 bunch cilantro or fresh mint, chopped

2¼ cups couscous

¼ cup extra-virgin olive oil

2 to 3 tablespoons harissa, to taste (optional)

In a large, heavy pot, place the lamb and cover with 6 to 8 cups of cold water. Bring to a boil and skim off any foam or froth on the surface of the water. Add the soaked dried chickpeas, if using, the onion, garlic, cinnamon, ginger, chile, paprika, cumin, and black pepper. Bring back up to a boil, turn down the heat, set the cover ajar, and simmer for 45 minutes. Add 1 tablespoon of salt, the potatoes, carrots, and cabbage and let simmer for about 20 minutes. Add the eggplant, turnips, and sweet potatoes or squash, and let cook for another 20 minutes. Add a cup or so of water if necessary to ensure the vegetables are submerged. Add the pattypan or yellow squash, zucchini, tomatoes, raisins, and canned chickpeas, if using, and let simmer for 20 minutes. Stir in the parsley and cilantro and cook for an additional 5 minutes or so, until the flavors come together. Taste and adjust the seasoning.

While the stew is cooking, prepare the couscous. Place the couscous in a large bowl. Bring 2½ cups of water to a boil with 1 teaspoon kosher salt. As soon as the water boils, pour it over the couscous. Cover the bowl with a plate or plastic wrap, and let it steam for 5 minutes, until all of the water is absorbed.

Remove the cover and use a fork to break up the couscous. Dump the couscous onto a cookie sheet or into a roasting pan. Drizzle the olive oil over the couscous. Rub the couscous between your palms to break it up and distribute the oil. There should be no lumps when you are done. Place the couscous into a steamer, colander, or sieve and set it over (but not touching) simmering water. You can put it over the stew as it cooks if your pot is deep enough so that the couscous doesn't touch the simmering liquid. Cover the pot with a tight-fitting lid to trap the steam. Steam the couscous for 45 minutes to 1 hour, making sure there is always simmering water beneath it.

When the stew and the couscous are done, transfer the couscous to a large, wide serving bowl and make a big well in the center. If serving with harissa, put the spice paste in a small bowl and ladle ¾ cup broth into the bowl. Ladle the stew into the center of the couscous, and spoon some of the cooking juices over the couscous around the edges. Pass the harissa-spiked broth at the table.

PREP TIME: 30 minutes
COOKING TIME: 2 hours
TOTAL TIME: 2½ hours

ADVANCE PREP *You can make the stew a day or two in advance and refrigerate it. If doing so, stop*

after the second addition of vegetables. The last vegetables added are the most delicate and are best cooked just before serving.

LEFTOVERS *Both the stew and the steamed couscous will keep for about a week in the refrigerator. Reheat leftover stew in a pot on the stove. You can reheat the couscous in a steamer, or you can do it in the microwave. If you intend to have a lot of leftovers, serve the two components in separate bowls so they are easier to handle when you go to reheat them later.*

VARIATIONS

Couscous with Chicken

You can easily make the stew with chicken on the bone. The chicken doesn't have to cook as long as the lamb, but you have to be sure to give enough time for the soaked dried chickpeas to cook, if that's what you are using. Substitute a 4-pound chicken cut into eight or ten pieces, or 3½ pounds chicken parts, for the lamb. Remove the skin. Place the chicken and soaked chickpeas, if using, in the pot. Cover with the cold water as indicated and bring to a boil. Skim off any froth that forms on the surface. Skip the 45 minutes of simmering indicated for the lamb. Add the onion, garlic, spices, except for the salt, and the first batch of vegetables. Proceed with the recipe as indicated, adding the salt about 45 minutes into the total cooking time.

Vegetarian Couscous

Lighter, but every bit as satisfying, vegetarian couscous can be made using virtually the same recipe. The only thing to remember is that if you are using soaked dried chickpeas, you have to give them enough time to cook; I start them in a separate pot. (If you are using canned chickpeas, skip the next sentence.) Combine the chickpeas with 4 cups of cold water, bring to a boil, turn down the heat, and simmer for about 30 minutes. Meanwhile, in a large pot, heat ¼ cup olive oil over medium heat. Add the onion and garlic and sauté until soft, about 5 minutes. Add the cinnamon, ginger, chile, paprika, cumin, black pepper, and salt, and cook for a minute or two, until the spices give off a good, strong aroma. Add the chickpeas along with their cooking water, if using, or 4 cups of cold water. Proceed with the recipe, picking up from the point when you add the potatoes.

Couscous with Merguez

You can add a few links of spicy merguez sausage to any of the variations of couscous recipes above. I use about 12 ounces sausage and fry it in a pan to remove some fat and to crisp up the skin before adding it to the stew with the last bunch of vegetables.

Couscous with Almonds and Dates

Mixing almonds and dates into the steamed couscous makes it even more delicious. Just before the couscous is finished steaming, heat 3 or 4 tablespoons extra-virgin olive oil in a small sauté pan. Add ¼ to ½ cup blanched slivered almonds and sauté until the almonds turn golden brown, about 5 minutes. Pit 4 or 5 plump fresh dates and cut them into slivers. Stir them into the almonds. Blend this mixture into the couscous before serving.

Shepherd's Pie

Here's one of the best ways to use up leftover cooked lamb or beef. Although shepherd's pie is still enjoyed in pubs in England and Ireland, in America it has a 1950s housewife connotation. Well prepared, it's delicious, however. If you don't have leftover meat, you can use fresh ground lamb or beef.

Makes 8 servings

> 5 medium all-purpose potatoes, such as Yukon Gold (about 2½ pounds), peeled and cut into chunks
> Kosher salt
> ¼ cup (½ stick) unsalted butter
> 2 tablespoons heavy or sour cream
> Freshly ground white pepper
> 2 tablespoons bacon fat, lard, unsalted butter, or vegetable oil
> 1 large onion, finely chopped
> 1 large carrot, peeled and finely chopped
> 1 large celery stalk, finely chopped
> 2 pounds cooked lamb or beef, finely chopped, or 2¾ pounds raw ground lamb or beef
> 6 ounces fresh button mushrooms, finely chopped
> 1 cup tomato sauce or tomato juice
> ½ cup fresh or frozen peas
> 1 tablespoon chopped fresh thyme
> 1 tablespoon chopped fresh rosemary
> Freshly ground black pepper
> 1 large egg

Preheat the oven to 400°F.

Place the potatoes in a large saucepan, cover with water, add a tablespoon of salt, set over high heat, and boil until they are very soft, about 25 minutes. Drain well and mash with the butter and cream. Season with salt and white pepper, and set aside.

In a large skillet, heat the bacon fat over medium-high heat. Add the onion and cook until translucent, about 5 minutes. Add the carrot and celery and cook until the vegetables are soft and the onion begins to brown, another 5 minutes. Add the meat and cook for a few minutes more, until heated through. (If using raw meat, continue cooking until the meat is brown and crumbly. Pour off the fat in the pan.)

Add the mushrooms and cook until they have wilted and given off their liquid. Pour in the tomato sauce and add the peas, thyme, rosemary, about 2 teaspoons salt, and a generous amount of black pepper. Cook until the liquid evaporates somewhat and the mixture comes together, another 5 minutes. Stir in about $\frac{1}{2}$ cup of the mashed potato mixture to give the meat some body and adjust the seasoning with additional salt and pepper. Transfer this mixture to a deep 2-quart baking dish that is nice enough to come to the table.

Beat the egg into the potato mixture and spread this evenly over the top of the meat. Smooth out the surface with a flexible spatula and sprinkle lightly with paprika. Bake for 35 to 40 minutes, until the potatoes have browned on top and the meat is heated through (if you use a clear glass baking dish, you can see it bubbling). Let cool for 5 minutes before serving.

PREP TIME: 20 minutes
COOKING TIME: 1 hour 15 minutes
TOTAL TIME: 1 hour 35 minutes (plus resting time)

ADVANCE PREP *The Shepherd's Pie can be assembled, covered, and refrigerated up to two days in advance. Uncover and bake it straight from the fridge, increasing the baking time by 5 or 10 minutes.*

■ ■ ■

Kitchen Sense

Sauces and Condiments

I
T SEEMS AS THOUGH every year food manufac-
turers come out with hundreds of new condiments. Hot sauces, olive pastes, roasted garlic spreads,
infused oils and vinegars, spice blends, and all sorts of
flavor-enhancing mixtures line the aisles of gourmet
shops and supermarkets alike. Clearly people are looking for new, simple ways to add flavor to their food.
And while I'm just as tempted by a pretty label and a
catchy name as the next guy, I think all good cooks
ought to have a few of their own condiment tricks up
their sleeves. When you make your own, you can be

sure they are preservative- and additive-free and you can make them only as sweet, salty, spicy, or sour as you like them.

Throughout this book there are sauces, spice mixes, condiments, and other flavor enhancers that I've recommended for certain recipes that can be used in others. In this chapter I've added a few more standards that are great to have on hand. Once you can master a Basic Vinaigrette (page 391) or Mayonnaise (page 405), you have unlimited salad potential at your disposal. Keeping a simple jar of a spice mix such as Dukkah (page 408) in the cupboard lets you turn an ordinary piece of bread into an exotic hors d'oeuvre. With a jarful of Preserved Lemons (page 409) at the ready, you can add a little oomph to a weeknight chicken or fish dish. The beauty of these condiments is that most of them keep well for a long time and you can jazz up an otherwise ordinary meal in minutes if you have them already prepared.

Don't get me wrong. I have nothing against ready-made condiments of every stripe. I'm always putting new and delicious-sounding jars and tubs and tubes of things in my shopping cart, even when I know I'm just buying into the marketing hype. But why should some spice manufacturer or celebrity chef have all the fun and satisfaction of creating these flavorings when they are easy to make at home?

■ ■ ■

Basic Vinaigrette

You don't need much more to dress a salad than this simple vinaigrette made from mustard, vinegar, and oil. If you vary the ingredients—by using a grainy mustard, a garlic-flavored oil, or an herb-infused vinegar, for example—you can produce an entirely different dressing. Mix-ins, such as garlic, shallots, chopped herbs, a dab of tomato paste, or crumbled blue cheese, will provide an unlimited number of variations (see page 393). This dressing is the base for many other dressings throughout the book.

I find a ratio of one part vinegar to three parts oil produces a pleasing vinaigrette. Of course, the acidity of the vinegar component is key, and if you use any of the vinegar substitutions I have suggested on page 393, or one of your own, you may have to adjust the tang of the finished dressing. A few drops of cider vinegar or water are helpful to bring the acidity of a dressing into balance without affecting the overall flavor.

Makes 1½ cups

> 2 tablespoons Dijon mustard
> ⅓ cup vinegar
> 1 cup extra-virgin olive oil or ½ cup extra-virgin olive oil and ½ cup vegetable or canola oil
> Kosher salt and freshly ground black pepper

Place the mustard in a small bowl or the bottom of a large salad bowl and mix in the vinegar. While beating with a fork or small whisk, slowly dribble in the oil to produce a creamy emulsion. You should be pouring the oil slowly enough and beating the dressing fast enough that the oil barely has time to pool in the bowl. The more oil you add, the thicker the dressing will become. If the dressing is too thick, dribble in a few droplets of water to thin it. When all of the oil has been added, season the dressing with salt and pepper.

TOTAL TIME: 5 minutes

ADVANCE PREP *The vinaigrette can be made several hours or even days in advance. Cover tightly and store at room temperature.*

VARIATIONS

Garlic or Shallot Vinaigrette

Stir 1 medium minced shallot or 1 large minced garlic clove into the mustard and vinegar mixture before beating in the oil.

Herbed Vinaigrette

Stir 1 to 2 tablespoons chopped fresh herbs into the vinaigrette.

Beet Vinaigrette

My friend Clive, who is a masterful salad-dressing maker, uses the juice from pickled beets and other vegetables in his dressings. I not only love the frugality of the concept, I also love the taste. Though I'm not always a fan of truffle oil, which is almost always artificially flavored and is overused in restaurants, in this recipe the flavor complements the earthiness of the beets. If you don't have truffle oil, leave it out. The dressing is particularly delicious on a salad that contains Gorgonzola or other blue cheese.

Makes 1 cup

> ¼ cup pickled beet juice (see page 210)
> 1 or 2 tablespoons white or red wine vinegar, depending on how sour your beet juice is
> 1 tablespoon Dijon mustard

1 teaspoon chopped fresh thyme or ¼ teaspoon
   dried

Pinch of rubbed sage

1 tablespoon minced shallot or sweet white onion

1 large garlic clove, minced

2 tablespoons chopped flat-leaf parsley

1 teaspoon sugar (optional)

½ cup extra-virgin olive oil

1 teaspoon truffle oil (optional)

Kosher salt and freshly ground black pepper

In a small bowl, combine the beet juice, vinegar, mustard, thyme, sage, shallot, garlic, parsley, and sugar, if using, and blend well. Slowly whisk in the oil in a steady stream to make a creamy emulsion. Beat in the truffle oil, if using. Adjust the seasoning with salt and pepper.

TOTAL TIME: 10 minutes

ADVANCE PREP *The dressing can be made several hours in advance. Store at room temperature until ready to use.*

LEFTOVERS *The dressing will keep for a week in the refrigerator. Bring the dressing back to room temperature and beat it again before serving.*

Roasted Shallot and Fig Dressing

Roasted figs and shallots give this dressing a delicious, deep flavor. It is especially good on warm green beans.

Makes 1 cup

8 shallots, peeled

2 black Mission figs, hard tips removed, cut in half

3 tablespoons extra-virgin olive oil

Kosher salt and freshly ground black pepper

¼ cup red wine vinegar

2 tablespoons dry white wine

¼ to ½ cup peanut or vegetable oil

Preheat the oven to 400°F.

Place the shallots and figs in a small baking dish. Drizzle with 1 tablespoon of the oil and season with salt and pepper. Toss to coat with the oil. Roast in the oven for about 40 minutes, or until the shallots are very soft and slightly browned around the edges. Set aside to cool.

Transfer the shallots and figs to a blender. Add the vinegar and wine and purée until smooth. With the machine running, slowly drizzle in the remaining 2 tablespoons olive oil and enough peanut oil to make a smooth, pourable dressing. Adjust the seasoning with salt and pepper.

PREP TIME: 10 minutes
COOKING TIME: 40 minutes
TOTAL TIME: 50 minutes

ADVANCE PREP *The dressing can be made several hours or days before serving. Keep refrigerated. If the dressing breaks, whip it in a blender again before using.*

Blueberry Vinaigrette

By using a fruit purée, such as of blueberries or raspberries, you can cut down on the amount of fat in a dressing without sacrificing flavor. This dressing has nice body that makes it suitable for a vegetable dip, too. I recommend using frozen blueberries because they purée finer than fresh and because when fresh blueberry purée comes into contact with acid, it gels and sets firm.

Makes 1½ cups

VINAIGRETTE VARIATIONS

Here are some suggestions to vary the components of a basic vinaigrette, but don't stop here.

For the Vinegar (all or part)
White wine vinegar
Red wine vinegar
Balsamic vinegar
Rice vinegar
Tarragon-infused vinegar
Raspberry vinegar
Lemon juice
Lime juice
Pomegranate juice
Tamarind juice
Sour (bitter or Seville) orange juice
Pickled beet juice (page 210)
Pickled onion juice (page 211)
Marinated artichoke juice (page 7)
Marinated roasted pepper juice
Olive brine

For the Oil (all or part)
Extra-virgin olive oil
Walnut oil
Hazelnut oil
Peanut oil
Canola oil
Vegetable oil
Grapeseed oil
Toasted pumpkin seed oil
Toasted sesame oil

Bacon fat
Duck fat

To Add to the Mustard (in part)
Tomato paste or juice
Fig purée
Anchovy paste
Green or black olive paste (tapenade)
Hot pepper jelly
Honey

To Mince and Mix In
Garlic
Roasted garlic
Shallot
Green onion
Chives
Fresh herbs
Capers
Olives
Pickles
Blue cheese
Parmesan cheese
Roasted peppers
Toasted nuts
Hard-cooked egg
Pine nuts
Crumbled bacon
Toasted sesame seeds
Toasted sunflower seeds
Toasted pumpkin seeds

1 cup frozen blueberries, defrosted

1 medium shallot, roughly chopped

1 teaspoon Dijon mustard

$1/4$ cup red wine vinegar

$1/3$ cup extra-virgin olive oil

Kosher salt and freshly ground black pepper

In a blender, combine the blueberries, shallot, mustard, vinegar, and olive oil with $1/4$ cup cold water, a pinch of salt, and some pepper. Purée until creamy and smooth, about 1 minute. For a thinner dressing, you can pass it through a fine-mesh sieve.

TOTAL TIME: 5 minutes

LEFTOVERS *The dressing will keep for about two weeks in the refrigerator. Bring it back to room temperature before serving.*

VARIATION
Raspberry Vinaigrette
Substitute 1 cup defrosted frozen or fresh raspberries for the blueberries and strain the dressing through a fine-mesh sieve to remove the seeds.

Gorgonzola Dressing
Based on a vinaigrette rather than a buttermilk or cream dressing, this gorgonzola dressing has a slightly lighter consistency than most. Use it on strong flavorful lettuces, such as arugula or mizuna. And toss in some crumbled bacon. You can make the dressing smooth or lumpy, as you prefer.

Makes $1^1/3$ cups

1 large shallot, minced

$1/4$ cup red wine vinegar

1 tablespoon Dijon mustard

$1/4$ teaspoon freshly ground black pepper

$2/3$ cup extra-virgin olive oil

4 ounces soft, creamy gorgonzola, or other strong, creamy blue cheese, such as Fourme d'Ambert, Cabrales, or Danish Blue, at room temperature

In a small bowl, combine the shallot, red wine vinegar, mustard, and pepper, and blend with a fork until smooth. While you beat continuously with the fork, slowly dribble in the olive oil, emulsifying it into a creamy mixture.

For a lumpy dressing, add the gorgonzola in crumbled pieces and continue beating while you break it up with the fork. For a smooth, creamy dressing, transfer the vinaigrette to a blender or food processor. Add the cheese and blend until smooth.

TOTAL TIME: 5 minutes

ADVANCE PREP *The dressing can be made several hours in advance and kept at room temperature until you are ready to toss the salad.*
LEFTOVERS *The dressing will keep in the refrigerator for up to two weeks, but be sure to bring it to room temperature before you toss the salad.*

Creamy Cracked Pepper Dressing
This spicy yet cool dressing is best if you toast and crack the peppercorns yourself, but you can use ordinary freshly ground black pepper, too. The dressing is delicious on firm, crisp lettuce, such as romaine hearts or iceberg. Because of the saltiness of the cheese, you don't really need to add any additional salt.

Makes 2 cups

EMULSIFYING DEMYSTIFIED

Emulsification is a scientific word that has found its way into common kitchen parlance. The process of emulsification refers to the unlikely combination of two liquids—in the case of salad dressing, oil and vinegar—which would not otherwise combine. In fact, when emulsified, they are not combined. Instead, tiny droplets of each liquid are suspended next to each other in some medium, known as the emulsifying agent. The most common and most successful emulsion in the kitchen is mayonnaise because egg yolk happens to be a terrific emulsifying agent. For the same reason, hollandaise is a successful emulsion, too. These are called permanent emulsions because unless they are broken—by adding too much fat or by changing the temperature too drastically—they will stay emulsified for a very long time.

Vinaigrette, on the other hand, is a temporary emulsion. If you stop mixing it and let it sit, the two liquids will separate again (i.e., break). In a Basic Vinaigrette (page 391), the mustard acts as the emulsifying agent, the medium in which the droplets of oil and vinegar are suspended. While mustard isn't nearly as good at this job as egg yolk, provided you add the oil slowly enough and beat it in quickly enough, you can make a creamy dressing that will last long enough for you to toss your salad. Adding other ingredients to the mustard, such as cheese, pastes, and the like, can also help stabilize the emulsion. Broken vinaigrettes, like mayonnaise, can be fixed by beating the broken dressing into more of the mustard, but this can change the proportion of ingredients and throw off the balance of flavors. Vigorous shaking, or better yet, placing a dressing in a blender, is my preferred way to fix a temporary emulsion just long enough to be able to toss a salad.

Of course, when you dress a salad simply with oil and vinegar, you are not forming any sort of emulsion, and the salad can be perfectly delicious. So there is no need to stress out over your salad dressing.

---

2 tablespoons black peppercorns

1 cup Hellmann's or Best Foods mayonnaise

1/2 cup white wine vinegar

1/4 cup fresh lemon juice

1 large garlic clove, minced

1 tablespoon minced fresh oregano or 1 teaspoon dried

1 tablespoon minced fresh flat-leaf parsley

1/2 cup freshly grated Parmigiano Reggiano cheese

Place the peppercorns in a small, dry frying pan and swirl over medium-high heat until you smell them and they begin to toast, 3 or 4 minutes. Transfer to a cutting board. With a meat-tenderizing mallet or the bottom of a heavy frying pan, coarsely crack the pepper.

In a small bowl, combine the mayonnaise, vinegar, lemon juice, cracked pepper, garlic, oregano, parsley, and cheese and mix to blend. (If you have the time, let the dressing sit at room temperature for an hour or so before serving so the flavors have a chance to meld.)

TOTAL TIME: 10 minutes

LEFTOVERS *This dressing will keep for up to two weeks in the refrigerator. It is delicious on all sorts of salads, such as potato salad and chicken salad.*

Sesame Dressing

This is a classic Japanese dressing for cooked spinach and other blanched vegetables. Dashi is a Japanese stock made from kombu seaweed and bonito flakes (see right); it is available in instant form in the Japanese section of many grocery stores. In a pinch, you can use a light vegetable or chicken stock instead of dashi.

Makes about ¼ cup

> ¼ cup white sesame seeds, toasted (see page 10)
> 1 teaspoon sugar or mirin
> 2 teaspoons Japanese soy sauce (shoyu) or light Chinese soy sauce
> 3 to 4 tablespoons dashi (see box, right), or light chicken or vegetable stock

Grind the sesame seeds in a mortar or a clean coffee grinder until they are powdery but not completely uniform. Add the sugar and grind to distribute evenly. (If using a coffee grinder, transfer to a small bowl at this point.) Dribble in the soy sauce and work the mixture to a thick paste. Dribble in enough dashi to make a pourable emulsion that's thick enough to coat vegetables.

TOTAL TIME: 10 minutes

ADVANCE PREP The dressing can be made several hours in advance.
LEFTOVERS Keep in an airtight container at room temperature for a couple of days.

BASICS

Dashi

Dashi is a simple, mild Japanese seafood stock made from kelp (kombu in Japanese) and dried flakes (katsuobushi). It is used in everything from stews to salad dressings. It lasts a very long time if you keep it in the fridge, and it adds an authentic flavor to Japanese dishes that you can't really get without it. I use it in non-Asian dishes sometimes instead of fish stock. Kelp and bonito flakes are available in Asian markets and some health-food stores. You can also find instant dashi in the Japanese section of many supermarkets.

Makes 1 quart

> One 4-inch piece of dried kelp (about 1 ounce), wiped clean with a dry cloth
> ½ cup bonito flakes (about 1 ounce)

Place 1 quart water in a medium saucepan and set over medium-low heat. Add the kelp. Bring the water very slowly to a boil, taking 7 to 10 minutes to do so. Just when the water boils, remove the kelp. Turn up the heat to high to bring the water to a rapid boil. Add ¼ cup cold water and the bonito flakes. When the liquid comes back to a boil, remove from the heat. Let sit until the bonito sinks to the bottom. Pour through a mesh sieve lined with two layers of cheesecloth. Cool the dashi to room temperature and refrigerate until needed.

Spicy Asian Chili Sauce

This pungent sauce is excellent on cold chicken and other meats.

Makes about 1 cup

- 2 scallions, white and green parts, very thinly sliced
- 2 tablespoons minced fresh ginger
- 2 small garlic cloves, minced
- 3 tablespoons soy sauce
- 1 tablespoon black Chinese vinegar or balsamic vinegar
- 1 tablespoon chicken stock or water
- 2 tablespoons chili oil
- 2 teaspoons toasted Asian sesame oil
- 1 tablespoon Vietnamese garlic chili paste or hot sauce
- 1 tablespoon sugar

In a small bowl, combine all of the ingredients.

TOTAL TIME: 5 minutes

ADVANCE PREP *The sauce can be made two or three days in advance and refrigerated until needed. Bring back to room temperature before serving.*
LEFTOVERS *The sauce will keep refrigerated up to two weeks.*

Spicy Peanut Sauce

Peanut sauce is a delicious Southeast Asian condiment traditionally served with satay (grilled meat on skewers) and other appetizers. It is also yummy thinned with water and used as a salad dressing. For the curry paste in this recipe, you can use a commercially prepared red (Penang) curry paste, which is usually available in small jars in the ethnic food section of grocery stores and in specialty Asian markets.

Makes about 2 cups

- 1 (14-ounce) can unsweetened coconut milk
- 1 tablespoon store-bought red curry paste
- 1/3 cup all-natural peanut butter
- 2 tablespoons lemon or lime juice
- 2 tablespoons Asian fish sauce, such as Thai *nam pla* or Vietnamese *nuoc nam*
- 1 tablespoon sugar
- Freshly ground white pepper
- Chicken or vegetable stock or water

Pour 1 cup of the coconut milk into a small saucepan and stir in the curry paste. Heat to a simmer, stirring, and let cook for about 10 minutes, until the oil from the coconut milk has separated and risen to the top. Stir in the remaining coconut milk and the peanut butter, and bring back to a simmer. Cook, stirring, until the peanut butter dissolves, 2 to 3 minutes. Stir in the lemon juice, fish sauce, and sugar. Turn down the heat and simmer gently for about 15 minutes, until the sauce thickens somewhat. Season with white pepper. The sauce should be the consistency of heavy cream. If necessary, thin it with stock and adjust the seasoning.

TOTAL TIME: 30 minutes

ADVANCE PREP *The peanut sauce is best if it is made about an hour in advance and allowed to sit so the flavors blend. It's even better served the next day.*
LEFTOVERS *The sauce will keep for several weeks in the refrigerator and it can be frozen for longer. It*

solidifies when it chills. To reheat, set in a pan over low heat, with some water or more coconut milk to thin it down. You can also reheat it in the microwave on high for a minute or two.

Pesto

Pesto—a sauce of fresh basil, pine nuts, garlic, olive oil, and cheese—is so popular in the United States that we assume everywhere you go in Italy you must be able to find it. But pesto is a specialty of the region of Liguria, which runs along the Mediterranean (the capital is Genova), and it's never as good anywhere else. Traditionally, the pasta for Ligurian pesto is cooked with potatoes and green beans, and then everything is tossed with the pesto sauce and parmesan cheese. Pesto can also be used as a condiment or sauce for various fish and meats, or as a spread on bread for sandwiches.

The flavor and texture of pesto is best if it is made the traditional way—that is, in a mortar and pestle. If you have one, give it a try. Otherwise, the food processor is the most suitable alternative.

Makes 1 cup

1/4 cup pine nuts, toasted (see page 10)
1 large or 2 small garlic cloves, roughly
    chopped
1 large bunch basil, leaves only (about
    2 cups)
Kosher salt and freshly ground black pepper
1/2 cup grated Parmigiano Reggiano or
    Pecorino cheese (2 ounces), or a
    combination
1/2 cup extra-virgin olive oil

In the bowl of a food processor fitted with a metal chopping blade, combine the pine nuts and the garlic. Using on/off pulses, chop finely. Add the basil, season with salt and pepper, and pulse to chop, scraping down the sides occasionally. Add the cheese, pulse to blend, and scrape down the sides again. With the machine running, slowly drizzle the olive oil through the tube to produce a creamy emulsion. The mixture should have the consistency of a thick sauce.

To prepare the pesto in a mortar and pestle, begin by pounding the garlic and salt into a paste. Add the nuts, a tablespoonful or so at a time, working the mixture to a peanut butter–like texture. Add the cheese. Chop the basil and add it a small handful at a time, pounding and grinding to make a paste. When the mixture is somewhat creamy, start adding the olive oil in dribbles, working the mixture to an emulsion after each addition.

TOTAL TIME: 10 minutes

ADVANCE PREP *The pesto sauce can be made a day or two in advance and refrigerated or frozen for one month.*
LEFTOVERS *Put pesto everywhere: in pastas, in salad dressings, in soups, on sandwiches.*

VARIATION
Walnut and Arugula Pesto
Substitute 1/3 cup walnut halves (or 1/4 cup chopped walnuts) for the pine nuts and 2 bunches fresh arugula, tough stems removed and leaves torn into small pieces (about 3 cups), for the basil. If desired, add 1 or 2 anchovies or 2 teaspoons rinsed capers to the mixture before adding the olive oil. Proceed with the recipe as directed.

Sicilian Pesto with Almonds, Tomato, and Mint

Sicilian pesto is milder than Genovese pesto. It is delicious tossed with warm pasta.

Makes 2 cups

2 tablespoons blanched almonds, toasted (see page 10)

2 tablespoons pine nuts, toasted (see page 10)

1 cup loosely packed basil leaves

1/2 cup loosely packed mint leaves

1/2 cup loosely packed flat-leaf parsley leaves

1 large garlic clove, coarsely chopped

1/2 cup grated ricotta salata, Pecorino, or Parmigiano Reggiano cheese (about 2 ounces), or a combination

2 or 3 small ripe tomatoes, peeled and seeded, or canned tomatoes

Kosher salt

2/3 cup extra-virgin olive oil

Freshly ground black pepper

In a food processor fitted with a metal chopping blade, pulse the almonds and pine nuts until chopped. Add the basil, mint, parsley, and garlic, and continue pulsing, scraping down the sides, to grind very finely. Blend in the grated cheese and scrape down the sides again. Add the tomatoes and 1 teaspoon salt and purée until smooth. With the machine running, pour the olive oil slowly through the feed tube to create a rich emulsion. Adjust the seasoning with black pepper and additional salt, if necessary.

TOTAL TIME: 10 minutes

ADVANCE PREP *The pesto can be made a day or two in advance and refrigerated or frozen for one month.*

Cilantro-Mint Sauce with Tomato

Here's a delicious sauce for lamb, chicken, even grilled vegetables. It's got a very green taste with just a hint of spice.

Makes about 1 cup

1 large garlic clove, chopped

1 small jalapeño or other hot chile, seeded and chopped

1 cup loosely packed cilantro leaves and tender stems

1 cup loosely packed fresh mint leaves

1 large ripe tomato, seeded and chopped, or 2 canned plum tomatoes, or 1/3 cup tomato juice

1 to 2 tablespoons fresh lemon or lime juice

1 tablespoon extra-virgin olive or vegetable oil

Kosher salt and freshly ground black pepper

In the bowl of a food processor fitted with a metal chopping blade, combine the garlic and jalapeño. Pulse on/off to chop finely. Add the cilantro and mint and pulse to chop. Add the tomato, lemon juice, and oil along with a generous pinch of salt and a good amount of freshly ground black pepper. Pulse and then purée the mixture until smooth, scraping down the sides occasionally, as necessary. Adjust the seasoning.

TOTAL TIME: 10 minutes

LEFTOVERS *The sauce only keeps well, refrigerated, for a couple of days before the herbs lose their fresh taste.*

Mojo

Mojo (pronounced MO-ho) is a garlicky citrus sauce fundamental to Cuban food. It's also popular in Puerto Rico. Mojo is usually made with the juice of sour (bitter) oranges, but it can be made with any sour fruit juice, such as lemon, lime, grapefruit, or even pineapple or pomegranate juice. I like to serve it with braised or roasted chicken and other meat dishes.

Makes about 2 cups

> ¾ cup extra-virgin olive oil
> 7 large garlic cloves, minced
> 2 teaspoons cumin seeds
> ¾ cup fresh juice: lemon, lime, sour orange,
>   grapefruit, pineapple, or pomegranate,
>   or a combination
> 2 jalapeño chiles, seeded and minced
> 2 scallions, white and green parts, chopped
> ¼ cup fresh cilantro leaves, chopped
> Kosher salt and freshly ground black pepper

In a small saucepan, combine the olive oil with the garlic and cumin. Set over medium heat and simmer until the garlic has become fragrant, but not browned, 1 minute or so. Cool to room temperature.

Stir the juice, jalapeños, scallions, and cilantro into the garlic oil, and season with salt and pepper.

COOKING TIME: 2 minutes
TOTAL TIME: 45 minutes (includes cooling time)

ADVANCE PREP *The mojo is best if it is made several hours in advance and allowed to sit at room temperature to let the flavors blend.*
LEFTOVERS *The mojo will keep for about a week in the refrigerator, but bring it back to room temperature before serving.*

Chimichurri

Chimichurri is a tart onion sauce that is a popular condiment for meat in Argentina—where they *love* their meat. It is similar to the onion and vinegar salsa served at Brazilian churrascaria (barbecued meat) restaurants. I like to serve chimichurri with grilled steak because the vinegar cuts through the richness of the meat.

Makes about 1 cup

> ⅓ cup extra-virgin olive oil
> ⅓ cup white or red wine or sherry vinegar
> 1 small white or red onion, finely chopped
> 1 small jalapeño or other hot chile, seeded and
>   chopped
> 2 garlic cloves, minced
> 2 tablespoons flat-leaf parsley, chopped
> 2 tablespoons fresh cilantro or mint,
>   chopped
> Kosher salt and freshly ground black pepper

In a small bowl, mix the olive oil, vinegar, onion, jalapeño, garlic, parsley, and cilantro. Season with salt and a generous amount of black pepper.

TOTAL TIME: 10 minutes

ADVANCE PREP *The sauce is best when it's allowed to sit for an hour at room temperature before serving.*
LEFTOVERS *Store the chimichurri in the refrigerator for up to one week.*

Charmoula

Charmoula is another tangy, fresh-tasting citrus sauce that's good on meat or fish.

Makes 2¾ cups

1 bunch cilantro, leaves and tender stems only
1 bunch flat-leaf parsley, leaves and tender stems only
2 large garlic cloves
Juice of 2 lemons (about $\frac{1}{2}$ cup)
Juice of 2 limes (about $\frac{1}{3}$ cup)
Juice of 1 orange (about $\frac{1}{3}$ cup)
1 cup extra-virgin olive oil
2 teaspoons ground cumin
1 tablespoon paprika
$\frac{1}{4}$ teaspoon cayenne pepper
Kosher salt and freshly ground black pepper

In the bowl of a food processor fitted with a metal chopping blade, combine the cilantro, parsley, and garlic. Using on/off pulses, finely chop the herbs, scraping the sides down once or twice. Add the lemon juice, lime juice, orange juice, olive oil, cumin, paprika, cayenne pepper, a pinch of salt, and some freshly ground black pepper. Pulse several times to blend. The sauce should be slightly chunky.

TOTAL TIME: 5 minutes

ADVANCE PREP *The charmoula can be made a day or two in advance and refrigerated.*
LEFTOVERS *The sauce will keep about one week in the refrigerator.*

Spanish Romesco Sauce

Serve this sauce with cold chicken or seafood. It is also delicious with boiled potatoes.
Makes about 1$\frac{1}{2}$ cups

$\frac{1}{2}$ cup extra-virgin olive oil
2 thick slices crusty French bread

3 tablespoons whole blanched almonds (about 30), toasted (page 10)
1 very ripe plum tomato, peeled, or 1 canned whole tomato
4 small garlic cloves, roughly chopped
2 roasted red peppers (see page 146), seeded, and roughly chopped
1 small fresh hot chile, such as serrano, seeded and roughly chopped, or a pinch of cayenne pepper
2 tablespoons sherry vinegar or red wine vinegar
2 tablespoons chicken or vegetable stock or water
Kosher salt and freshly ground black pepper

Heat $\frac{1}{4}$ cup of the oil in a frying pan over medium-high heat. Add the bread and fry until golden brown on both sides, about 6 minutes. Remove the bread and any oil in the pan to a blender or the work bowl of a food processor. Add the remaining $\frac{1}{4}$ cup olive oil along with the almonds, tomato, garlic, peppers, chile, vinegar, and chicken stock. Using on/off pulses, purée to form a rich, thick, smooth sauce. Adjust the seasoning with salt and pepper.

TOTAL TIME: 15 minutes

ADVANCE PREP *The sauce can be made a day or two in advance and refrigerated until needed. Bring back to room temperature before serving.*
LEFTOVERS *The sauce will keep one week in the refrigerator.*

Salsa Verde

The name of this flavorful condiment simply means "green sauce," so it's not surprising that there are many different versions of salsa verde in the world. This one I learned while I was cooking in a restaurant in the Piedmont region of Italy, where it is traditionally served with boiled beef. I love it with just about any meat, especially grilled lamb.

Makes 1½ cups

1 large bunch flat-leaf parsley (about 5 ounces), with stems
2 garlic cloves, peeled
5 or 6 anchovies
¼ cup drained capers, rinsed
1 small shallot, peeled and cut in half
1 small fresh or dried hot chile, seeded and chopped
3 tablespoons white wine vinegar
½ cup extra-virgin olive oil
Freshly ground black pepper

In a blender or food processor, combine the parsley, garlic, anchovies, capers, shallot, chile, and vinegar, and pulse for a couple of minutes to grind the ingredients to a paste. Scrape down the sides occasionally. With the machine running, pour in about ⅓ cup of the olive oil in a slow, steady stream and continue processing until you have a smooth paste. Add more olive oil if necessary. Season with plenty of black pepper.

TOTAL TIME: 5 minutes

ADVANCE PREP *The sauce is best after it has sat for a day so the flavors have time to blend and mellow. It can be made a week in advance and refrigerated. Bring to room temperature before serving.*

Minted Yogurt Sauce

Delicious drizzled on Greek, Middle Eastern, or Indian foods, this refreshing sauce has a pleasant tang.

Makes about 1 cup

½ cup plain yogurt
½ cup buttermilk
1 tablespoon finely minced white or yellow onion
½ medium garlic clove, minced
1 tablespoon finely chopped fresh mint
1 tablespoon finely chopped fresh flat-leaf parsley
¼ teaspoon kosher salt
Freshly ground black pepper

In a mixing bowl beat together the yogurt, buttermilk, onion, garlic, mint, parsley, salt, and pepper.

TOTAL TIME: 5 minutes

Madhur Jaffrey's Carrot and Raisin Raita

Raita is a category of cool, creamy Indian condiments made with yogurt and spices. They are traditionally served with curries, but I also like them with roasted pork, ham, or smoked meats. Popular combinations include cucumber and mint or apple and raisins. This carrot-raisin version was devised by my friend Madhur Jaffrey, and it works well with apple, too. Use yogurt that has been strained for 2 hours or less (see page 63), so the raita has a loose, saucelike consistency.

Makes about 2¼ cups

¼ cup golden raisins
1½ cups loose strained yogurt (see page 63)
2 medium carrots or 1 large tart, crisp apple, such as Macoun or Granny Smith, peeled and shredded (about 1¼ cups)

½ teaspoon ground cumin
½ teaspoon kosher salt
¼ teaspoon cayenne pepper
Pinch of freshly ground black pepper

Place the raisins in a small bowl and cover with about 1 cup of boiling water. Let sit for 20 minutes or so to plump.

Strain the raisins and add the yogurt, carrots, cumin, salt, cayenne, and black pepper. Mix well to combine.

PREP TIME: 5 minutes
TOTAL TIME: 30 minutes (includes soaking time)

ADVANCE PREP The sauce can be eaten right away but it is best after it has sat for about 1 hour. It can be made several days in advance and refrigerated until needed.
LEFTOVERS Store the sauce in an airtight container in the refrigerator for two or three days. It will keep longer if it is made with carrots rather than apples; the apples will eventually discolor and become mushy. Use the raita on grilled meats, with spicy foods, or as a creamy sauce on dishes, such as Fish Tacos (page 93).

Butter Sauce

A classic *beurre blanc*, or butter sauce, is a versatile sauce that you can flavor with any number of things—tarragon, chives, or orange, for example—to make a delicious, delicate sauce for seafood, vegetables, or chicken. There are only a few ingredients, but the sum is greater than the parts.

The trick is to create the emulsion (see page 395) that makes the sauce creamy. I'll never forget the first *beurre blanc* I made; I was 12 years old and I was using a recipe of Julia Child's. Having no idea what I was aiming for, I made what amounted to melted butter. Years later, while working at a restaurant in Toronto, a chef showed me how to make one of the sauces for the menu. I had an *aha!* moment when I realized that this creamy, delicious thing was in fact what I had been striving for years earlier. If you follow the directions below, I think you'll get closer than I did on my first try.
Makes about 1¼ cups

1 small shallot, minced
¼ cup white wine vinegar or 2 tablespoons white wine vinegar and 2 tablespoons fresh lemon juice
¼ cup dry white wine or Champagne
1 cup (2 sticks) unsalted butter, cut into cubes, chilled
1 or 2 tablespoons chopped fresh herbs, such as tarragon, thyme, chive, marjoram, or a combination (optional)
Kosher salt and freshly ground black pepper

In a small saucepan, combine the shallot, vinegar, and wine. Bring to a boil and reduce the liquid until only 1 or 2 tablespoons remain. Remove from the heat.

Add about half of the butter and whisk the butter into the liquid, creating a creamy emulsion as the butter melts. Return the pot to very low heat and continue whisking. When almost all of the butter has melted, add a cube or two of the remaining butter, and continue whisking until almost all of it is melted. Repeat until all of the butter is incorporated. The sauce should be warm, but not boiling, or it will break. It should be pale yellow and creamy.

Stir in the herbs, if using, and adjust the seasoning with salt, white pepper, and additional vinegar.

TOTAL TIME: 25 minutes

ADVANCE PREP *The sauce should be made as close to serving time as possible. Keep it warm at the back of or near the stove.*
LEFTOVERS *You can store the sauce in the refrigerator for a week or so, but to bring it back to life you will have to re-form the emulsion. Heat a couple of tablespoons of water in a saucepan until simmering. Beat in chunks of the chilled sauce as though you are beating in the butter in the original recipe. If you get the emulsion right, like magic, the sauce will come back together. If you do not want to go to the bother of re-forming the emulsion, use leftover sauce as a flavored butter to melt over grilled steaks, to finish other sauces, or even to stir into mashed potatoes or risotto.*

VARIATIONS

Pink Butter Sauce

Substitute red wine vinegar or balsamic vinegar for the white wine vinegar and use dry red wine for the dry white wine. Proceed as directed.

Orange Butter Sauce

Substitute 2 tablespoons of defrosted frozen orange juice concentrate for 2 tablespoons of the white wine vinegar and proceed with the recipe as directed.

Cream Sauce

Here is another classic that's due for a comeback. Despite all of the wallpaper-pasty cream sauces out there, I love a simple cream sauce—that is, a white sauce or béchamel. It's an ingredient in some of my favorite dishes, such as Croque Monsieur (page 86), The Ultimate Macaroni and Cheese (page 183), Cauliflower Gratin (page 259), and Lasagna (page 260). For a thicker or thinner sauce, adjust the butter and flour in equal proportions, adding more for a thicker sauce and less for a thinner one.
Makes 2 cups

> 3 tablespoons unsalted butter
> 3 tablespoons all-purpose flour
> 2 cups milk
> 1 teaspoon kosher salt
> Freshly ground white pepper
> Pinch of freshly grated nutmeg

In a medium saucepan, melt the butter over medium-high heat. Add the flour, and using a wooden spoon, stir to form a paste (called a roux). Cook for 2 or 3 minutes, until the roux has smoothed out and turned ever so lightly golden brown, and it gives off the nutty aroma of toasted flour. Switch to a whisk, and beat in the milk, beating out any lumps. Bring to a boil. Turn down the heat and simmer for 5 or 7 minutes, stirring, until the sauce has thickened and there's no perceptible taste of raw flour. Add the salt, pepper to taste, and nutmeg and cook for another minute. Remove from the heat and adjust the seasoning.

TOTAL TIME: 10 minutes

ADVANCE PREP *Cream sauce can be made in advance and stored for about a week in the refrigerator. To prevent a skin from forming when the sauce cools, you can rub the surface with a pat of butter. Reheat over low heat, adding addi-*

tional milk if necessary to attain the desired consistency.

Mayonnaise

Although I do not think homemade mayonnaise and commercial mayonnaise are always interchangeable—American-style potato salad and coleslaw taste right to me only when they are made with Hellmann's or Best Foods mayonnaise, for instance—homemade mayonnaise can be a delicious, delicate base for many salads, dressings, and sauces. I love plain mayonnaise as a dip for French Fries (page 191), or flavored with garlic and fresh herbs, for fresh vegetables or Fried Calamari (page 280).

Mayonnaise is a permanent emulsion (see page 395) that can be made by hand or in a food processor (the food processor produces a thicker, more durable mayonnaise that is less likely to break; see Variations). You can vary the flavor by varying the ingredients—use lime juice or flavored vinegar instead of lemon juice, for instance. A very garlicky aïoli can stand up to a full-bodied extra-virgin olive oil. A delicate summer vegetable salad requires a more neutral oil, perhaps grapeseed oil or a combination of vegetable oil and olive oil. For information about eating raw eggs, see page 125.

Makes 1 1/2 cups

3 large egg yolks, at room temperature

Juice of 1/2 lemon (about 2 tablespoons)

1 tablespoon white wine vinegar

1 teaspoon Dijon mustard

Kosher salt

3/4 cup canola, grapeseed, vegetable, or other neutral oil

3/4 cup extra-virgin olive oil

Freshly ground white pepper

In a large bowl, preferably with a rounded bottom, whisk together the egg yolks, lemon juice, vinegar, mustard, and a pinch of salt. You will need to be able to whisk with one hand, so if your bowl is dancing around the counter, set it on a damp dish towel to secure it in place. In a liquid measuring cup or small pitcher, combine the oils. Continuously whisk the egg yolk mixture while you start to dribble in droplets of oil. You should be incorporating the oil into the yolks almost as quickly as you are adding it to the bowl. As the mixture begins to thicken, increase the dribbles to a slow, steady stream. Periodically stop adding oil and whisk the mayonnaise for a minute or so to reinforce the emulsion. When about half of the oil is incorporated, you can start to add it a little more quickly. When you are done, the mayonnaise should be thick and creamy, somewhere between the consistency of cake batter and icing. Adjust the seasoning with salt and pepper.

TOTAL TIME: 5 to 10 minutes

ADVANCE PREP *Mayonnaise can be made a day or two in advance and refrigerated.*
LEFTOVERS *Fresh mayonnaise will keep for four or five days in the refrigerator.*

VARIATIONS
Blender or Food Processor Mayonnaise
Use 1 whole large egg and 1 egg yolk for the blender mayonnaise and keep the remaining ingredients the same. In a blender or the work bowl of a food processor fitted with either the plastic whipping blade or metal chopping blade, combine the egg, egg yolk, lemon juice, vinegar, mustard, and salt. Pulse two or three times to combine. With the machine running,

FIXING BROKEN MAYONNAISE

Mayonnaise can break—that is, the oil separates out of the emulsion—for a number of reasons. You may have added the oil too quickly or added too much of it. Perhaps you weren't beating the mayonnaise vigorously enough. It's also possible that a change in temperature during storage caused the sauce to break. Whatever the reason, it isn't difficult to fix. Beat a room-temperature egg yolk in a bowl or food processor and slowly dribble the broken mayonnaise into the yolk while beating as though you were adding the oil. The mayonnaise will begin to emulsify again. Stop when the mayonnaise has reached the right consistency.

pour the oil through the feed tube, very slowly at first and adding it more quickly at the end.

Aïoli

This garlicky mayonnaise from Provence makes a delicious dip for fresh vegetables or fried seafood and is an excellent condiment for grilled meat. I prefer to make it in a food processor. Follow the recipe for Blender or Food Processor Mayonnaise, adding to the egg mixture 2 or 3 minced large garlic cloves and processing until puréed. Use only extra-virgin olive oil and proceed with the recipe as directed. You may also want to add 1 tablespoon of anchovy paste or minced capers to the mayonnaise for additional flavor.

Lime Cilantro Mayonnaise

Substitute fresh lime juice for the lemon juice and proceed with the recipe as directed. Beat ¼ cup chopped cilantro leaves into the finished mayonnaise.

Roasted Garlic and Basil Mayonnaise

Roast 2 heads of garlic (about 14 cloves) as directed on page 152. Add the roasted garlic pulp to the egg yolk mixture and proceed with the recipe as directed. Beat ¼ cup chopped fresh basil leaves into the finished mayonnaise.

Curried Mayonnaise

Mix 2 tablespoons curry powder and 2 tablespoons water to a paste. Heat 1 tablespoon vegetable oil in a small nonstick pan. Add the curry paste, watch out for splatters, and fry for a minute or two, until the water evaporates and the spices are toasted. Cool to room temperature. Beat this mixture into the finished mayonnaise.

Evelynne's Barbecue Sauce

Here's an approximation of the secret weapon of my friend Evelynne, the reason her pulled pork and spareribs are so delicious. It's a barbecue sauce so beloved that she and her daughter actually started a company to market it. It's really just an adaptation because every time I've asked for the recipe over the years, I've been given slightly different instructions. What follows is what has become my house BBQ sauce. As the sauce cooks, it will smell and taste pretty bad. In fact, don't bother tasting it until it has finished cooking. Even then, it still tastes weird until it is spread on barbecued meat or mixed into pulled pork, and then it's delicious.

Makes about 1 quart

> ½ cup (1 stick) unsalted butter
> 1 large onion, chopped
> 1 garlic clove, minced (optional)
> 1 (24-ounce) bottle ketchup (about 2¼ cups)
> 1 (12-ounce) can ginger ale (1½ cups)

½ cup cider vinegar or white vinegar

¼ cup granulated or brown sugar

¼ cup Worcestershire sauce

Juice of 1 lemon (about 3 tablespoons)

2 tablespoons brown or Dijon mustard

1 tablespoon molasses

2 whole cloves

One 1-inch piece of cinnamon stick

1 bay leaf

1 teaspoon kosher salt

¼ teaspoon freshly ground black pepper

In a large saucepan, melt the butter over medium-high heat. Add the onion and garlic and cook until soft, about 5 minutes. Add the ketchup and rinse out the bottle with about ½ cup water and add that, too. Add the ginger ale, vinegar, sugar, Worcestershire sauce, lemon juice, mustard, molasses, cloves, cinnamon stick, bay leaf, salt, and pepper. Bring to a boil, turn down the heat to very low, and simmer, half-covered, for about 1 hour, until the sauce becomes thick and rich. Stir occasionally to prevent scorching. If the sauce gets too thick too quickly, thin it with a little water and keep simmering. Remove the cloves, cinnamon stick, and bay leaf; cool the sauce and store until ready to use.

TOTAL TIME: 1 hour 10 minutes

ADVANCE PREP *The sauce can be made in advance and stored in the refrigerator in a glass jar or other tightly covered container for at least one month.*

Chipotle Butter

This is a simple, very flavorful, and very spicy butter that is good on corn on the cob, popcorn, and grilled or broiled steak. Chipotles are smoked jalapeño chiles that are available in a spicy adobo sauce, sold in small cans in the Latino foods section of the grocery store.

Makes 1 cup

1 or 2 chipotle chiles in adobo plus a teaspoon or so of their sauce

Juice of ½ lime or lemon (about 1 tablespoon)

1 cup (2 sticks) unsalted butter, at room temperature

Combine the chipotle and sauce with the lime juice in the bowl of a food processor fitted with a metal chopping blade or in a blender. Purée with on/off pulses until smooth. Add the butter and process until well blended. Chill until ready to serve.

TOTAL TIME: 5 minutes

ADVANCE PREP *The butter will keep in the refrigerator for up to two weeks or in the freezer indefinitely.*
LEFTOVERS *Melt the chipotle butter and pour it on popcorn. You can also use it as a seasoning to finish spicy dishes such as chili. Stir a spoonful or two into mashed potatoes or pasta to spice things up a little.*

Za'atar

Like Dukkah (page 408), this Middle Eastern spice mix is a good thing to have in your cupboard. A little sprinkle takes an ordinary hummus, even store-bought, to a higher level. Dusted with za'atar, suddenly grilled pita goes gourmet. Za'atar is both the name of an herb in the hyssop family and the name of this spice mix, the base of which is supposed to be that herb.

Since we can't get za'atar—the herb—here, I substitute dried thyme or a combination of thyme and marjoram. Sumac is made by grinding the reddish, slightly sour berry of a wild bush of the same name. It is available in good spice shops and specialty Middle Eastern markets.

Makes 6 tablespoons (about ⅓ cup)

2 tablespoons sesame seeds

1 teaspoon cumin seeds

1 tablespoon dried thyme

1 tablespoon dried marjoram or additional dried thyme

1 tablespoon ground sumac

¼ teaspoon kosher salt

Preheat the oven to 350°F.

Place the sesame seeds in a small baking dish. Toast in the oven for 8 to 10 minutes, until the sesame seeds have puffed and browned slightly. Remove from the oven, transfer to a plate, and set aside to cool.

In the same dish, place the cumin seeds and toast for 5 minutes, until you smell the faint aroma of toasted cumin.

Combine the cumin with the thyme and marjoram. Transfer to a clean coffee grinder or a mortar and grind not too finely until the cumin seeds are broken up. Transfer to a bowl or jar. Stir in the sesame seeds, sumac, and salt and blend well.

PREP TIME: 5 minutes

COOKING TIME: 20 minutes

TOTAL TIME: 25 minutes

ADVANCE PREP *The za'atar can be stored in an airtight container for up to six months.*

Dukkah

Like Za'atar (page 407), dukkah is an Egyptian spice mixture with nuts that was introduced to me by my friend Bonnie. I serve it as a bar snack or hors d'oeuvre with warm bread and excellent olive oil. You dip the bread in the oil and then in the dukkah. It's also great on salads, sprinkled on grilled meats, or on anything that could use a little nutty, spicy zing. There are as many recipes for dukkah, I suspect, as there are Egyptian spice sellers. This recipe is just a guideline. Use it as a jumping-off point for your own house blend.

Makes 2½ cups

¾ cup shelled blanched pistachios or hazelnuts

¾ cup blanched almonds

¼ cup sesame seeds

¼ cup coriander seeds

3 tablespoons cumin seeds

4 teaspoons fennel seeds

1½ teaspoons black peppercorns

2 teaspoons kosher salt

Pinch of sweet or hot paprika, or cayenne pepper

Preheat the oven to 350°F.

Spread the pistachios and almonds on a cookie sheet and toast in the oven for 10 minutes. Remove from the oven, transfer to a plate, and set aside to cool. Toast the sesame seeds for 10 minutes and transfer them to a separate plate to cool.

Turn down the oven temperature to 325°F. Combine the coriander, cumin, and fennel seeds on the cookie sheet and toast for 5 minutes until you can smell their strong aroma. Set aside to cool.

Place the pistachios and almonds in a food processor fitted with a metal chopping blade and pulse on/off until coarsely ground. Some larger pieces are fine. Dump the chopped nuts into a bowl and add the sesame seeds. Place the spices in a clean coffee grinder or mortar and grind coarsely. (The spices should not be a fine powder.) Add the ground spices to the nuts and seeds. Grind the peppercorns the same way. Stir in the salt and paprika.

PREP TIME: 10 minutes

COOKING TIME: 25 minutes

TOTAL TIME: 35 minutes

ADVANCE PREP *Store in an airtight jar in a dark, cool place for at least six months.*

Curry Powder

Several of the recipes in this book call for curry powder. Although I am aware that such a mixture was popularized by colonialist cooks looking for a way to simplify the Indian pantry, I find curry powder a convenient way to add a jolt of flavor to things like salad dressings and noodles. There are as many different curry powders as there are Indian cooks. They vary by region, with marked differences between East Indian and West Indian styles of curry powder, for example. I use this combination of spices proposed by Indian cookbook author Julie Sahni as my house curry powder blend. Experiment to find your own.

Makes about ¼ cup

2 teaspoons cumin seeds

2 teaspoons coriander seeds

2 teaspoons black mustard seeds

1 teaspoon fennel seeds

½ teaspoon dill seeds

1 teaspoon black peppercorns

3 whole cloves

One 1½-inch cinnamon stick, broken into pieces

1 teaspoon cayenne pepper

2 teaspoons turmeric

Place the cumin, coriander, mustard, fennel, and dill seeds in a dry frying pan along with the peppercorns, cloves, and cinnamon stick. Set over medium-high heat, and swirl the pan to evenly toast the seeds until you begin to smell the aroma of the spices and the mustard seeds begin to pop, 3 or 4 minutes. Be careful not to let the spices burn. Remove from the heat. Cool.

Transfer the spices to a clean coffee grinder or a mortar and pestle. Grind to a fine powder. Add the cayenne and turmeric and blend.

PREP TIME: 15 minutes

COOKING TIME: 5 minutes

TOTAL TIME: 20 minutes

ADVANCE PREP *The curry powder will keep in an airtight jar in a dark, cool place for up to three months.*

Preserved Lemons

These salted and cured lemons are a delicious seasoning and condiment from North Africa, ubiquitous in the foods of Morocco and Tunisia. (In French they are sometimes referred to as confit lemons.) I always have them in my fridge because they jazz up a variety of dishes, both meat and fish. An ordinary tuna salad becomes a special treat with a tiny bit of preserved lemon mixed in. Although you can find preserved lemons for sale in some specialty markets (they are often kept near barrels of olives), they are so cheap and easy to make,

I think you are better off preserving your own. The whole lemon is edible, but you usually discard the flesh and eat only the finely chopped rind. I have tried recipes that say to cover the lemons with olive oil, but I find this makes an unpleasant, unappetizing mess, and is unnecessary.

Makes 1 pint

8 to 10 lemons, depending on the size
1/3 cup kosher salt

Juice 4 of the lemons to produce about 1/2 cup juice. Rinse the remaining lemons (remove any stickers) and pat dry. Cut the lemons lengthwise into 6 wedges. (Traditionally, the lemons are kept attached at one end, but I find them easier to use later if I cut the wedges right through.) Place the lemon wedges in a bowl. Toss with the salt to coat. Tightly pack the lemons with the salt and any juice that has run off into a sterilized pint jar. Fill the jar with the reserved lemon juice to cover the lemons. Cover tightly and let sit at room temperature for about three weeks, turning the jar upside down each day, until they have softened, darkened, and begun to ferment.

To use, remove a wedge of lemon and rinse under cold water. Cut away the fleshy center and finely mince the rind.

PREP TIME: 10 minutes
TOTAL TIME: 3 weeks (includes curing time)

ADVANCE PREP Store the lemons in the fridge for up to one year.

VARIATIONS
Preserved Lemons with Spices
For a more complex flavor you can add a combination of spices, such as cinnamon stick, whole cloves, peppercorns, and/or coriander seeds, to the jar to cure with the salted lemons.

Preserved Limes
The same technique can be used to make preserved limes, which are delicious with lamb. You can fit 1 or 2 more in the jar because of their smaller size. Juice a few limes to make 1/2 cup juice. Slice the remaining limes lengthwise into quarters and proceed with the salting and curing as directed above.

■ ■ ■

Desserts

IF ANY CHAPTER NEEDS no introduction, it's Desserts, the one you've been waiting for, the reward for having finished your meal. Often that reward is best when you've made it yourself. I will never cease to be baffled by how difficult it is sometimes to find a delicious dessert in a restaurant when it is so easy to make one at home. In an ever-accelerating, ego-driven effort to make something never before baked, some pastry chefs can't leave well enough alone. Home desserts are not restaurant desserts, and nor do I think they should try to be. There may be nothing more satisfying than a bowl of chocolate pudding or a piece of pound cake, and you don't need a raspberry tuile or caramel squiggle to make it more so. Quite the opposite, in fact. What else would explain the popularity of cupcakes at bakeries across the nation?

A dessert can be as simple as a bowl of cherries or as complicated as a multitiered torte. Both have their place. When choosing what to make or serve for dessert, remember to think of the context of the meal. A big slab of dense Chocolate Cheesecake (page 441) is overkill after a rich meal of lasagna, for instance. Whenever possible, try to think seasonally, using fruit when it's at its best and saving nuts and other timeless ingredients for the months when there's less to work with. Whatever your time constraints and inclinations, you'll find plenty of recipes for all types of homey, irresistible desserts in the pages that follow.

As with all cooking, in the realm of desserts you put in good, you get out good. Buy the best fruit, chocolate, nuts, and staples you can find and afford, and your desserts will improve considerably. Not all butter or flour is created equal. Using stale, rancid nuts instead of sweet fresh ones can ruin an entire batch of cookies. If your baking powder is dead, your cake won't rise. It's that simple.

Finally, I know a lot of people, some good cooks among them, who are intimidated by baking and dessert making in general. The sweet shop has been characterized as a sort of scientific laboratory where uptight people work with precise measurements (see page 447). The reality, especially at home, is quite different. Like the savory side of the kitchen, baking is an art, with plenty of room to experiment with style and creativity. For me, baking is therapy, and when you relax and go with the flow, you'll find out just how much truth there is to the phrases "easy as pie" and "a piece of cake." And, oh, what delicious truths they can be.

Fruit Salad

I'm a purist when it comes to fruit salad. I like fruit, plain and simple. On the odd occasion when the fruit isn't at its peak, I may add a little sugar or a touch of orange juice or apple cider to liven things up. But there's not much more that's necessary. Utterly unripe fruit makes a bad fruit salad. Try to use whatever's local and in season, and buy your fruit far enough in advance so you have time to ripen it (see page 415). In summer I tend more toward melons, stone fruits, and berries; in winter my fruit salads are citrus and pineapple and mango. I'm never happy with bananas or apples in fruit salad, both of which discolor and turn to mush.

Makes 2 quarts, enough for 10 servings

> $1/2$ ripe cantaloupe, honeydew, or pineapple, peeled and cut into chunks
> $1 1/2$ cups red or green seedless grapes
> 1 cup blueberries
> 1 ripe mango, peeled and diced
> $1/2$ cup blackberries
> 2 oranges, peeled and sectioned
> 2 to 3 tablespoons sugar (optional)
> 2 to 3 tablespoons fresh orange juice or apple cider (optional)

In a large bowl, combine the fruit, adding the orange sections last because they are the most delicate. If the fruit isn't very sweet, add the sugar and/or orange juice and let sit for about 10 minutes before serving.

TOTAL TIME: 5 minutes (plus resting time)

ADVANCE PREP *Depending on the fruit and how ripe it is, fruit salad shouldn't be made more than a day or two in advance. Refrigerate.*

LEFTOVERS *The leftovers will keep for three to four days in the refrigerator.*

VARIATION
Fruit Salad with Lavender or Rosemary
Instead of sugar, add a couple of tablespoons lavender or rosemary syrup (see page 416) to sweeten and moisten the fruit salad.

Honeydew Soup

Here's a recipe for a delicious, quick summertime fruit soup that's light and refreshing, but somehow still very satisfying. The same technique can be used with any ripe, fleshy melon, including cantaloupes and watermelon, or sweet, fleshy fruit, such as peaches or nectarines (see Variations).

Makes $4 1/2$ cups, enough for 4 or 5 servings

> 2 pounds very ripe honeydew melon, flesh only (from 3-pound melon), cut into cubes (2 to 3 cups)
> Juice of 1 lime (2 tablespoons)
> 2 teaspoons brandy
> $1/4$ teaspoon vanilla extract
> 1 tablespoon chopped fresh mint
> Pinch of salt
> 1 to 2 tablespoons honey, maple syrup, corn syrup, simple sugar syrup, or superfine sugar, to taste (optional)

Place the honeydew in a blender or food processor fitted with a metal chopping blade along with $3/4$ cup water, the lime juice, brandy, vanilla, mint, and salt. Purée using on/off pulses, until smooth, and then let the blender run for a minute or so to produce a light, frothy soup. If the melon isn't very sweet, adjust the sweetness with honey. Serve in chilled bowls.

TOTAL TIME: 10 minutes

ADVANCE PREP *The soup can be made a day or two in advance and refrigerated, but to attain the pleasant, frothy texture, it should be whizzed in the blender again before serving.*
LEFTOVERS *Keep the soup in an airtight container in the fridge for up to two days. Drink for breakfast!*

VARIATIONS
Cantaloupe Soup
Substitute cantaloupe for the honeydew and lemon or orange juice for the lime juice.

Watermelon Soup
Substitute for the honeydew 2½ pounds ripe seedless watermelon flesh (from a 4-pound piece of melon). Lime juice and fresh black peppermint are a nice flavor combination with the taste of watermelon.

Peach or Nectarine Soup
Substitute 2 pounds ripe peaches or nectarines, peeled, pitted, and cut into cubes, for the honeydew. Because of the denser texture of the fruit, you may need an additional tablespoon or two of water to achieve a nice liquid consistency.

Sour Cherry Soup
In the Northeast, sour cherries are in season for only a few weeks each summer. Also called "pie cherries," they are too tart to eat like other cherries, but they are the best cherries for cooking because they have the strongest cherry flavor. Serve this soup hot or cold, garnished with whipped cream or sour cream, if desired. Semolina Dumplings (page 270) are a traditional garnish to this soup in Germany. When I can't find sour cherries, I make the same soup using blueberries.
Makes 4 cups, enough for 4 servings

> 1 quart fresh or frozen sour cherries, washed, stemmed, and pitted
> 1 cup dry full-bodied red wine, such as Shiraz or Zinfandel
> ½ cup sugar
> One 2-inch strip lemon zest, made with a vegetable peeler
> One 1-inch piece of cinnamon stick or 2 sprigs fresh mint
> 4 black peppercorns
> 1 small bay leaf

In a medium, nonreactive saucepan, combine the cherries, wine, sugar, lemon zest, cinnamon, peppercorns, and bay leaf along with 2 cups cold water. Bring to a boil, turn down the heat, cover loosely, and simmer for 15 minutes. Remove the bay leaf and continue simmering for another 15 minutes.

Remove the lemon zest, cinnamon or mint, and peppercorns. Using a food mill, purée the soup. Alternatively, you can use a food processor fitted with a metal chopping blade, blender, or immersion blender to purée the soup and then pass it through a fine-mesh strainer. Serve warm or chilled, being sure to stir the soup before serving so the cherry pulp doesn't sink to the bottom.

PREP TIME: 10 minutes
COOKING TIME: 30 minutes
TOTAL TIME: 40 minutes

BUYING FRUIT AND RIPENING IT

For most people, choosing fruit is an enigma. One apple is crisp and tart; another is mealy and insipid. One melon tastes sweet like summer; another tastes like a potato. Next to, "How do I know when something is done?" the culinary question I am most often asked is, "How can I pick a good piece of fruit?" The answer isn't easy, and it has only gotten more complicated now that fruit is grown to look perfect and ripe long before it is ready—if ever—and good to eat. If only all fruit were as simple as bananas, which you know are ripe when the skin turns yellow and brown spots appear. Here are some general guidelines for selecting and ripening fruit.

• Your most important tool for picking fruit is your nose. When I walk through the produce section of a grocery store or a farmer's market, I'm always picking up pieces of fruit and smelling them. A peach, even if it isn't ripe, should smell of peach, a pineapple should smell of pineapple (put your nose to the bottom), a cantaloupe should smell—you guessed it—like cantaloupe (smell it on the ends where the stem and blossom used to be). If I walk by a display of apples or strawberries or apricots and the aroma is strong enough that I notice them in passing, I'm going to buy them, that's for sure.

• Next is texture. As fruits ripen, they soften (although it must be noted that no amount of ripening will make a tasteless specimen flavorful, which is why smelling them is so important). Fruits should be firm yet give a little when you squeeze them gently. The softening that results from bruising or mishandling should not be mis-

taken for ripeness. Hachiya persimmons are one of the few fruits that turn totally mushy when ready to be eaten (Fuyu persimmons remain firm). Weight is another factor to consider. Stone fruits, citrus fruits, melons, and other fruits for which juiciness is desirable should feel heavy for their size. If you pick up two oranges of the same size and one feels heavier than the other, take the heavier one.

Once you've chosen your fruit, chances are you are going to have to let it ripen a little. Melons, stone fruits, pears, pineapples, and other fruits that are picked early so they can be shipped without damage almost always require up to three or four days to soften after you bring them home. Place the fruit on a counter at room temperature, or better, in a brown paper bag. Certain fruits, such as peaches and pears, ripen faster if you put an apple in the bag because the apple gives off ethylene gas, which hastens the process. If you have ripened fruit at room temperature and you can't manage to eat or cook it, place it in the fridge to stop the ripening—you'll add another day or two to its life.

Sadly, even if you properly ripen the fruit you buy, it never tastes as good as if it had been picked from a tree when it was ready to eat. And even if you follow my advice, you still won't be guaranteed that the fruit you buy will always be delicious. If you are faced with some unfortunate fruit, consider cooking it before you chuck it. By adding sugar, spices, and other ingredients sometimes you can salvage less than ideal fruit. You could also bake it into a cake (see Green Tomato Cake, page 440) or turn it into jam (see Brandied Apricot Jam, page 134).

ADVANCE PREP *The soup can be made up to a week in advance and refrigerated.*

LEFTOVERS *The soup will last for up to two weeks in the fridge.*

VARIATION

Blueberry Soup

Substitute 1 quart fresh blueberries, stemmed and rinsed, or 2½ (10-ounce) packages frozen blueberries for the cherries.

Chunky Applesauce

Nothing could be simpler than making applesauce. To give it a good apple flavor and a chunky texture I use a combination of apples—whatever I can find—and chop the apples by hand before cooking. If you prefer your applesauce smooth, or you are making a large batch (the recipe doubles or triples well), use a food mill to purée the apples.

Makes about 2½ cups, enough for 5 to 6 servings

> 4 or 5 cooking apples, such as Northern Spy,
>   Golden Delicious, Cortland, Rome, Braeburn,
>   Gala, McIntosh, or a combination (about
>   2 pounds), peeled, cored, and cut into ¼- to
>   ½-inch dice
> ¼ cup apple cider, cranberry juice, pomegranate
>   juice, orange juice, or water
> 2 tablespoons granulated or brown sugar (optional)
> Juice of ½ lemon (about 1½ tablespoons)
> ¾ teaspoon pure vanilla extract
> ¼ teaspoon ground cinnamon
> Pinch of kosher salt

In a medium saucepan, combine the apples, cider, sugar, if using, lemon juice, vanilla, cinnamon, and salt. Cover and set over low heat.

Herbed Syrups

I like using syrups infused with various herbs—such as lavender, bay, rosemary, and basil in my desserts. They keep for a long time, and a spoonful tossed with fruit, stirred into yogurt, whipped into cream, or used to moisten a cake adds a level of sophistication to even the most home-style dessert. I also like to use them to sweeten iced tea.

Makes about 1 cup

> ¾ cup sugar
> 1½ tablespoons chopped fresh herbs, such as
>   mint, rosemary, basil, and lavender

In a small saucepan, combine the sugar with ¾ cup water and the herbs. Bring to a boil over medium-high heat, stirring to dissolve the sugar. Lower the heat and simmer for about 7 minutes, until the syrup has thickened slightly and the aroma of herbs is strong. Cool, strain into a jar, and store in the refrigerator.

TOTAL TIME: 10 minutes

LEFTOVERS *The syrup can be kept in the refrigerator for several months.*

Simmer slowly for 20 to 25 minutes, until the apples are soft.

Mash with a fork to a chunky purée. Adjust the seasoning with salt, lemon juice, and cinnamon, to taste. Serve warm or chilled.

TOTAL TIME: 30 minutes

ADVANCE PREP *Applesauce can be made up to a week in advance and refrigerated. For long-term* storage, applesauce can be canned as for jam (see page 138). Pack sterilized pint jars with hot applesauce, leaving 1/2 inch head room, and process for 15 minutes. The canned applesauce will keep up to a year.

LEFTOVERS The applesauce will keep for about ten days in the refrigerator. It can also be frozen for up to a month.

VARIATION

Pear Sauce

Similar to applesauce, pear sauce is delicious on its own or served as an accompaniment to other desserts. Follow the recipe for applesauce, substituting 4 very ripe pears and 1 apple, both peeled, cored, and cut into chunks, for the apples, and adding the optional sugar.

Baked Apples

The complexity of baked apple recipes ranges from simply putting an apple in the oven and baking it until it is soft, to coring, stuffing, and basting the apple while it bakes. This recipe falls somewhere in between. Serve the apples warm or at room temperature with ice cream.

Makes 6 servings

6 medium, tart apples (2 1/2 to 3 pounds), such as
  Golden Delicious, Jonagold, Braeburn,
  Gravenstein, or Cortland, rinsed
3 tablespoons unsalted butter, at room
  temperature
1/3 cup light brown sugar
1/4 cup chopped walnuts or pecans, toasted (page
  10)
1/4 cup dark or golden raisins, currants, or dried
  cranberries

Grated zest of 1/2 orange
1/4 teaspoon ground cinnamon
1/2 cup apple cider, orange juice, or water
1 tablespoon brandy or rum
1/2 teaspoon pure vanilla extract

Preheat the oven to 375°F.

Slice off the top of each apple, exposing a ring of flesh. With an apple corer or paring knife, dig out the core of the apple, stopping about 1/2 inch from the bottom so you don't go all the way through. Arrange the apples in a shallow baking dish so they are close but not touching.

In a small bowl, cream the butter and brown sugar into a paste. Work in the walnuts, raisins, orange zest, and cinnamon. Spoon this mixture into the center of each apple and place any that's left in the bottom of the dish. Pour the cider, brandy, and vanilla into the dish. Cover with aluminum foil and bake for 20 minutes, until the apples begin to soften.

Remove the foil, baste the apples with the pan juices, and continue baking until they are very soft, another 15 to 20 minutes, basting frequently. (If you forget about the apples, they will explode; they are still delicious, but they look a little funny.) Serve with a spoonful of the pan juices drizzled on top.

PREP TIME: 15 minutes
COOKING TIME: 35 minutes
TOTAL TIME: 50 minutes

ADVANCE PREP The apples can be baked several hours before serving and kept at room temperature.

LEFTOVERS Baked apples will keep for four or five days in the refrigerator.

Quince Paste

Here's a recipe for one of my favorite sweets, quince paste, known more commonly by its Spanish name, *membrillo*. Like a small bite of exquisite bittersweet chocolate after dinner, a small piece of fragrant quince paste satisfies my need for dessert. It is also traditional (and delicious) to serve small pieces of quince paste as an accompaniment to a cheese platter.

Makes about 2 pounds

> Vegetable oil
> 5 large quince (about 2½ pounds), cut into quarters and cored
> 3 tablespoons frozen orange juice concentrate
> One 2-inch cinnamon stick
> 1 tablespoon grated fresh ginger (optional)
> About 3½ cups sugar, plus extra for coating

Lightly grease an 8-inch square heatproof dish with vegetable oil and set aside.

Place the quince in a medium pot along with the orange juice concentrate, cinnamon stick, ginger, if using, and ⅓ cup water. Set over medium-high heat, bring to a boil, cover tightly, lower the heat, and simmer for about 30 minutes, until the flesh is very soft.

Pass the quince and any liquid in the pan through a food mill, which will remove the peel, and into a bowl. Measure the purée; there should be about 4 cups. Return the quince to the pot and add the sugar, adjusting the amount of sugar slightly more or less depending on whether you have more or less quince purée. Stir the sugar and quince to make a stiff paste. Set the pot over medium-high heat and bring to a boil. Turn down the burner as low as it will go and continue cooking the quince, uncovered, for about 1½ hours, stirring frequently, until it has darkened, thickened, and reduced by about half. As the quince cooks, it will gurgle and splatter. At a certain point it will seem like the paste is sticking to the bottom of the pot, but that's really just the sugar caramelizing. Keep stirring. When the paste is ready, it has an almost translucent quality and pulls away from the sides and bottom of the pot with a rubber-like snap.

Dump the paste into the greased pan and spread it out to an even thickness. Let the paste sit out uncovered at room temperature for about 24 hours to dry out and harden.

With your fingertips, gently pull the sides of the paste away from the pan and invert onto a cutting board to unmold; it should thump out of the pan after a good shake or two. Cut the paste into four 2-inch-wide strips and cut each strip in half to form a brick. Place the bricks on a wire rack and let them dry out for another day or so.

Roll each brick in granulated sugar.

PREP TIME: 20 minutes
COOKING TIME: 2 hours
TOTAL TIME: 1 day 2½ hours (includes drying time)

ADVANCE PREP *The quince paste keeps well, stored in an airtight container, for many months.*
LEFTOVERS *I reconstitute the paste in a little Gewürztraminer or Riesling to make a filling for thumbprint or sandwich cookies.*

Wine-poached Pears

Poached pears make a delicious, light dessert on their own, or they can be gussied up with Vanilla Custard Sauce (page 472) or Vanilla Ice Cream (page 473), if you wish. Red wine turns the fruit a deep crimson color, but you can use white wine if you prefer.

Makes 4 to 6 servings

> 2 cups dry red or white wine
> 1 1/2 cups sugar
> One 2-inch strip lemon zest, made with a
>   vegetable peeler
> Juice of 1/2 lemon (about 1 1/2 tablespoons)
> 2 or 3 whole cloves or allspice berries
> One 2-inch cinnamon stick
> 1/2 vanilla bean, split in half lengthwise
> 4 to 6 firm, ripe pears, either Bartlett, Anjou,
>   or Bosc

In a medium, nonreactive saucepan, combine the wine, sugar, lemon zest, lemon juice, cloves, cinnamon stick, and vanilla bean. Bring to a boil, stirring to dissolve the sugar, turn down the heat, and simmer for about 5 minutes.

While the poaching syrup is simmering, peel and core the pears. Place the pears in the syrup and simmer for about 10 minutes, until the flesh is tender but not mushy. (Poke it with the tip of a paring knife to test.) The less ripe the pears, the longer they will take to cook, sometimes up to 20 or 25 minutes.

Transfer the pears to a container and strain the syrup over them. Set aside to cool.

PREP TIME: 10 minutes
COOKING TIME: 15 minutes
TOTAL TIME: 25 minutes

ADVANCE PREP *Poached pears can be made up to a week in advance. Keep them in the refrigerator until ready to serve.*
LEFTOVERS *Stored in their poaching syrup, the pears will keep for about two weeks in the refrigerator.*

Roasted Figs with Mascarpone Mousse

This is a simple dessert for when fresh figs are in season. The delicate flavor and sweetness of figs are intensified by roasting. The mascarpone mousse contains raw eggs (see page 125); if this makes you nervous, serve the figs with vanilla ice cream instead.

Makes 4 to 6 servings

> 3 large eggs, separated
> 1/2 cup granulated sugar
> 1 cup (about 1/2 pound) mascarpone, at room
>   temperature
> 3/4 teaspoon pure vanilla extract
> 1/2 cup heavy cream, chilled
> 2 tablespoons light brown sugar
> 2 tablespoons orange juice
> 2 tablespoons unsalted butter, melted
> Pinch of ground cinnamon
> Pinch of kosher salt
> 12 medium black Mission figs, tips removed, cut
>   in half, or 6 large figs, cut in quarters

Using an electric mixer, beat the egg yolks with 3 tablespoons of the granulated sugar on high for 4 or 5 minutes, until the yolks have turned pale yellow, thickened, and almost tripled in volume. Beat in the mascarpone and 1/2 teaspoon of the vanilla until smooth. Transfer to another bowl and set in the refrigerator to chill.

Thoroughly clean and dry the mixing bowl and the beaters. Now whip the egg whites on high until frothy. Gradually add the remaining 5 tablespoons granulated sugar and continue beating until the egg whites are firm and glossy, 4 or 5 minutes.

Remove the egg yolk mixture from the refrigerator. With a rubber spatula, gently fold in about one fourth of the egg white mixture to lighten the yolks, and then fold in the remaining egg whites. Return to the fridge.

Whip the heavy cream until stiff. Fold the whipped cream into the mascarpone mixture. Spoon the mousse into serving dishes and chill for at least 1 hour.

Preheat the oven to 425°F.

In a medium bowl, combine the brown sugar, orange juice, butter, remaining ¼ teaspoon vanilla, the cinnamon, and salt. Add the figs and toss to coat. Dump the figs into a shallow baking dish and arrange them cut side up. Roast for about 20 minutes, or until the figs are nicely glazed.

Remove from the oven, and let cool for 5 to 10 minutes. Spoon the figs over the mousse and serve.

PREP TIME: 30 minutes

COOKING TIME: 20 minutes

TOTAL TIME: 2 hours (includes chilling time)

ADVANCE PREP *The mascarpone mousse and the figs can be made a day or two in advance. Reheat the figs in a 300°F oven or in a microwave before serving.*

LEFTOVERS *The figs and the mousse will keep for four or five days in the refrigerator.*

Apple Pie

A good apple pie has a flavorful filling of thoroughly cooked apples that isn't too wet. The crust isn't soggy, and the pastry is delicate and flavorful. I always have success with this recipe, which requires you to parbake the bottom crust to be sure it is cooked through. My favorite apples for pie are Northern Spy, but since they aren't always available, you can also use Golden Delicious, Braeburn, Gravensteins, or any other firm, flavorful apple.

Makes one 9-inch covered deep-dish pie, enough for 8 to 10 servings

1 batch pie dough (see page 421), chilled

6 or 7 large firm, tart apples (2½ to 3 pounds), peeled, cored, and sliced ¼ inch thick (6 to 7 cups)

½ cup light brown sugar

¼ cup all-purpose flour or 2 tablespoons cornstarch, arrowroot starch, or quick-cooking tapioca

½ teaspoon ground cinnamon

½ teaspoon pure vanilla extract

⅓ cup raisins or dried cranberries (optional)

¼ cup chopped walnuts or pecans, toasted (see page 10), optional

3 tablespoons unsalted butter

1 large egg beaten with 1 tablespoon cold water

Center a rack in the oven and preheat the oven to 425°F.

On a lightly floured work surface, roll a little less than two thirds of the dough into a circle about 12 inches in diameter and ¼ inch thick. Using the rolling pin, carefully transfer the dough to a deep-dish 9-inch pie plate. Press the dough to line the plate and trim off any overhang to less than ½ inch. Fold the overhang under the edge of the crust to reinforce it. Line the dough with aluminum foil, allowing the foil to overhang to cover the crust, fill with dried beans, rice, or pie weights, and bake for about 10 minutes to set. Remove the beans and foil and bake for another 10 minutes, just until the crust begins to brown lightly. Remove from the oven and cool. Lower the oven temperature to 400°F.

Meanwhile, prepare the filling. In a large

Pie Dough

Here is my foolproof recipe for flaky, buttery pie dough, inspired by a recipe and technique created by the late Julia Child. Although you could certainly make it by hand by cutting the fat into the flours and stirring in the water, it comes out so perfectly from the processor that I never make it another way. Cake flour is a delicate, low-protein flour available in the baking section of most grocery stores. If you can't find it, substitute 2 cups minus 1 tablespoon bleached all-purpose flour for both flours.

Makes enough dough for 2 single 9-inch crusts

- 1 1/2 cups unbleached all-purpose flour
- 1/2 cup cake flour
- 1/2 teaspoon kosher salt
- 3/4 cup (1 1/2 sticks) unsalted butter, diced, chilled
- 1/4 cup lard or vegetable shortening (see page 423), chilled
- 1 teaspoon white vinegar (use only if using lard)
- 1/2 cup very cold water

In the work bowl of a food processor fitted with a metal chopping blade, combine the flours and salt. Pulse once or twice to blend. Add the butter and lard and pulse five or six times to cut the fat into the flour. The mixture should resemble coarse crumbs. Combine the vinegar with the cold water (if using shortening, use just the water alone). With the processor running continuously, pour the liquid down the feed tube all at once. As soon as the dough begins to form a ball around the blade, stop the machine. Lay a piece of plastic wrap on a work surface and dump out the dough onto the plastic, scraping the bowl and the blade with a rubber spatula. Pat the dough into a ball, wrap tightly, and refrigerate for at least 1 hour before using.

TOTAL TIME: 10 minutes

ADVANCE PREP *The pie dough can be refrigerated for up to two days or frozen for up to two months. Defrost in the refrigerator overnight before using.*

bowl, toss the apples with the brown sugar, flour, cinnamon, vanilla, raisins, and walnuts, if using. Transfer the mixture to the prebaked crust and dot the top of the apples with the butter. Brush the edges of the crust with the egg mixture. Set aside.

On a lightly floured surface, roll the remaining pie dough into a 10-inch circle. Using the rolling pin, carefully lay this crust on top of the pie. Trim all but a 3/4-inch overhang from around the edges. Fold and tuck the overhang between the bottom crust and the pie plate and press the edges to seal. Pinch the edges to form a decorative rim. Cut three or four slits in the center of the top crust to let out steam. Brush the crust with the beaten egg.

Bake for 25 minutes. Lower the temperature to 350°F and continue baking for another 40 to 45 minutes or so, until the crust is nicely browned and the apples are soft—poke the point of a paring knife in one of the slits to test the texture of the apples. If the crust starts to brown too much, cover it with aluminum foil. Remove from the oven and let cool for at least 45 minutes so the filling can settle before serving.

LARD VERSUS SHORTENING

How lucky for us that recent studies have shown trans fats to be worse for your arteries than saturated fats. Trans fats are compounds created by the processes that turn liquid fats, such as vegetable oils, into solids, such as shortening and margarine. What that means in the kitchen is that lard is in fact no worse for you than shortening. In fact, if your lard was made from pigs that roamed freely and ate grass and other good vegetable matter—which would mean their fat would be high in omega-3 fatty acids—certain studies suggest it might even be health promoting!

I like to use a combination of lard and butter in baked goods such as pie dough (see page 421) and Strawberry Shortcake (page 434). Lard adds flavor and also gives baked goods a tender but pleasant chewy texture. For the best-tasting (and the most healthful) baked goods, use lard you have made yourself from the fat of organic, pasture-raised pigs (see page 423). Of course, you should certainly feel free to continue to use vegetable shortening. I always have both lard and shortening on hand, in case a vegetarian or an abstainer of pork products is coming over. But health-conscious cooks need no longer dismiss lard outright.

PREP TIME: 20 minutes

COOKING TIME: 1 1/2 hours

TOTAL TIME: 1 hour 50 minutes (plus cooling time)

ADVANCE PREP Apple pie is best eaten the day it is made. Serve warm or at room temperature.
LEFTOVERS Leftovers will keep refrigerated for about a week. To warm and crisp the crust, reheat in a 325°F oven for a few minutes. Whatever you do, don't microwave it, which makes the crust soggy.

Shaker Lemon Pie

Made with whole lemons, this traditional Shaker pie has an intense lemon flavor. The trick is to slice the lemons as thin as possible so that they almost disintegrate. I use a sharp mandoline and slice the lemons crosswise into rounds, removing the seeds as I go along. But if you don't have one, use a very sharp knife, cut the lemons lengthwise in half, place them cut side down on the cutting board, and slice them crosswise as thin as possible. If you can find fragrant Meyer lemons, they make a superb pie.

Makes one 9-inch covered pie, enough for 8 to 10 servings

> 2 lemons, rinsed, dried, ends removed, and sliced paper thin, seeds removed
> 2 cups sugar
> 1 batch pie dough (see page 421)
> 4 large eggs

Place the lemon slices in a medium bowl and toss with the sugar. Allow them to sit and macerate at room temperature for at least 2 hours.

Preheat the oven to 425°F.

On a lightly floured work surface, roll about two thirds of the dough into an 11-inch circle, about 1/4 inch thick. Carefully transfer this dough to line an 8- or 9-inch pie plate. Trim the dough, leaving a 1/2-inch overhang. Fold this overhang under the edge of the crust to reinforce it. Line the crust with aluminum foil, fill with dried beans, rice, or pie weights, and bake for 10 minutes, until the crust begins to set. Remove the beans and foil and continue baking for another 10 minutes, just until the

Homemade Lard

Why bother? A little lard makes pie crust and short-cakes and biscuits taste delicious. And most commercial lard you can buy is partially hydrogenated, which means it contains unhealthy trans fats. Besides, lard is really easy to make and it keeps in the fridge or freezer forever.

If you can find it, use leaf lard, which is the fine, rich fat that's found in clumps around the pig's kidneys and is prized for its whiteness and pure flavor. If you can't find it, fatback will also work fine to make lard. The fatback comes from the back and belly of the animal. Trim any skin and/or meat from it before you cube it. Don't mistake salt pork for fatback. Salt pork is cured with salt and sugar. It will not produce good lard.

Makes about 2 pounds or 4 cups

    4 pounds leaf lard or fatback, cut into 1/2-inch
       cubes
    1 teaspoon kosher salt

Place the cubed fat in a large, heavy pot and add the salt and 1/4 cup cold water, which helps to keep the fat from sticking and burn-ing. Set over medium-high heat. The fat will start to melt in a couple of minutes. Turn the heat down to low and stir to encourage even melting. Set a cover ajar over the pot and let simmer for 2 to 2 1/2 hours, until all of the fat has rendered. Stir the lard occasionally to make sure it doesn't stick to the bottom of the pot. If the fat or the meat attached to the cubes starts to brown, lower the heat; the lard should remain white. Alternatively, you can render the lard in the oven: cover the pot and bake in a 275°F oven for 2 to 3 hours.

When all that's left are shriveled cubes of translucent fat, remove the lard from the heat. Let cool until it is comfortable to handle. Line a fine sieve with several layers of cheesecloth and strain the lard into a ceramic, earthenware, or glass container. Store in the refrigerator or freezer until needed.

TOTAL TIME: 2 1/2 hours

LEFTOVERS Lard will keep in the refrigerator or freezer for about a year.

---

crust is set. Remove from the oven and cool completely. Turn down the oven temperature to 400°F.

Meanwhile, whisk the eggs with 1/4 cup water until light and frothy, 2 or 3 minutes. Pour the eggs over the lemon and sugar mixture and mix well. Roll the remaining crust on a lightly floured work surface into a circle 10 inches in diameter. Pour the lemon mixture into the prebaked pie crust. Transfer the dough to the top of the pie and trim so that there's less than 1/2 inch of dough overhanging. Tuck the overhang between the pie plate and the edge of the crust. Poke two or three holes in the top crust to allow steam to escape, and set the pie in the oven to bake for 25 minutes. Lower the oven temperature to 350°F and continue baking for 25 to 30 more minutes, or until the crust is very nicely browned. Remove from the oven and cool completely before serving.

PREP TIME: 10 minutes

COOKING TIME: 1 1/2 hours

TOTAL TIME: 3 hours 40 minutes (includes macerating time)

VARIATION

Lemon and Ginger Pie

For a spicy variation, stir 1/4 cup finely minced crystallized ginger into the filling and proceed with the recipe as directed.

Anya's Ground Pecan Pie

One day I brought a failed linzer torte to work and my colleague, Anya, thought it tasted more like a pecan pie made with ground pecans than anything from Austria. That got us to thinking. Would grinding the pecans for a pecan pie alleviate that unappetizingly sweet, goopy filling characteristic of most pecan pies? The answer is yes. I use a little cream in place of some of the syrup to make the pie less sweet and a little creamier than usual, but for a more traditional sweetness, you can use all syrup, too. Of course, any self-respecting Southerner wouldn't call pecan pie made with ground pecans pecan pie. In fact, everyone I've served it to thinks it seems more European than American. But they all think it is delicious.

Makes one 9-inch deep-dish pie, enough for 8 to 10 servings

2/3 recipe pie dough (see page 421)

1 1/2 cups pecan halves

1 cup sugar

2 tablespoons all-purpose flour

4 large eggs, slightly beaten

1/2 cup heavy cream

1/2 cup pure maple syrup, cane syrup, golden syrup, or dark corn syrup

1 teaspoon pure vanilla extract

Pinch of kosher salt

1/2 cup (1 stick) unsalted butter, melted and cooled

Roll out the pie dough on a lightly floured surface into a circle 11 to 12 inches in diameter, about 1/4 inch thick, and line a 9-inch deep-dish pie plate. Trim the crust to leave a 1/2-inch overhang. Fold the overhang under the edge and pinch the edge around the pie to shape. Set in the refrigerator to chill and relax for about 20 minutes.

Preheat the oven to 425°F.

Press a piece of aluminum foil into the pan and mold to the shape of the crust. Fill with dried beans, rice, or pie weights and bake for 15 minutes. Remove the weights and the foil and bake for another 10 minutes, until the crust is bubbling and ever-so-slightly browned.

While the crust is baking, toast the nuts. Place the pecans on a baking sheet and toast in the oven for 7 or 8 minutes, or until they have darkened slightly and they give off a strong pecan scent. Set the nuts and crust aside to cool. Lower the oven temperature to 375°F.

Place the pecans in the bowl of a food processor fitted with a metal chopping blade. Add the sugar and process with on/off pulses until the pecans are finely ground. Add the flour and pulse once or twice to combine. In a bowl, beat the eggs with the cream. Add the maple syrup, vanilla, and salt. Stir in the ground pecan mixture along with the butter.

Pour the pecan mixture into the prebaked pie crust. Bake in the oven for 45 minutes, or until the filling has risen, browned, and set. Remove from the oven and cool (the filling will fall somewhat). Serve slightly warm or at room temperature.

PREP TIME: 10 minutes
COOKING TIME: 1 hour 15 minutes
TOTAL TIME: 1 hour 25 minutes

ADVANCE PREP *You can mix the filling a day or two before baking the pie and refrigerate. Don't pour it into the pie shell until just before baking.*
LEFTOVERS *The pie will keep for three or four days at room temperature or for a week in the fridge.*

VARIATIONS

Chocolate Pecan Pie
Into the filling stir 1 cup semisweet or bittersweet chocolate chips or chunks.

Traditional Pecan Pie
The ingredients are the same, but the technique of making the filling is a little different. Toast the nuts as directed, but do not grind them. Beat together the eggs and cream. Add the sugar, flour, vanilla, and salt. Beat in the syrup and melted butter. Stir in the pecans. Pour into the shell and bake as directed.

Peanut Pie
Follow the directions for Traditional Pecan Pie, but substitute 1¼ cups dry-roasted, salted peanuts for the pecans, and add ¼ cup creamy peanut butter (melted with the butter) to the filling mixture. Omit the salt. This is a surprisingly delicious alternative to pecan pie.

Creamsicle Pie
The idea for this pie came from my sister Carrie, who was making a lot of Key lime pies one summer and thought the same recipe would be good made with other citrus. Oranges are not as strongly flavored as Key limes, so I use frozen orange concentrate that's been defrosted but not diluted.

Makes one 9-inch pie, enough for 6 to 8 servings

> 1 (14-ounce) can sweetened condensed milk
> 4 large egg yolks
> 1 teaspoon grated orange zest
> ½ teaspoon pure vanilla extract
> ¼ cup frozen orange juice concentrate, defrosted
> One 9-inch graham cracker crust (see page 427) or chocolate cookie crust (see page 427)
> 1 cup heavy cream, chilled

Preheat the oven to 350°F.

In a small bowl, beat together the condensed milk, egg yolks, orange zest, and vanilla. Add the orange juice concentrate and mix well. Pour this mixture into the pie crust and bake for 15 minutes or so, until the filling has set. Remove from the oven, cool to room temperature, and chill for several hours before serving.

To serve, beat the cream to stiff peaks, and spread attractively over the top of the pie. (There is no need to sweeten the cream as the pie is sweet enough.) As you move the knife or spatula around the surface with the cream, be careful not to run right up to the edge. If you do, you'll pick up cracker crumbs that will then scatter into the cream. It's still delicious this way, but it doesn't look as pretty.

PREP TIME: 15 minutes
COOKING TIME: 15 minutes
TOTAL TIME: 30 minutes (plus chilling time)

LEFTOVERS *The pie is best after it has chilled initially, but it's still pretty good four or five days later.*

VARIATIONS

Key Lime Pie

Substitute ½ cup fresh (from 8 to 10 limes) or bottled Key lime juice for the orange juice concentrate. Omit the vanilla and orange zest but add 1 teaspoon grated lime zest to the filling.

Mock Key Lime Pie

If you want a lime pie but you don't have Key limes, substitute ½ cup fresh lime juice plus 1 tablespoon fresh lemon juice for the orange juice concentrate. Add 1 teaspoon grated lemon or lime zest.

Lemon Pie

Substitute ½ cup fresh lemon juice for the orange juice concentrate. Add 1 teaspoon grated lemon zest.

Pumpkin Chiffon Pie

So few people seem to really like traditional pumpkin pie that, to everyone's relief, I started making this pumpkin chiffon pie at Thanksgiving. The recipe was given to me by my friend Adam's mom, Maxine. It has a light texture and delicate spiced flavor, not nearly as heavy or over-powering as the original. If you would prefer to avoid raw egg whites (see page 125), substitute pasteurized or powdered egg whites according to the proportions on the package and whip to stiff peaks as directed.
Makes one 10-inch pie, enough for 8 to 10 servings

¾ cup milk

3 large eggs, separated

1 cup sugar

1 envelope unflavored gelatin (1 tablespoon)

1 teaspoon ground cinnamon

¼ teaspoon freshly grated nutmeg

KITCHEN SENSE

PREBAKING PIE CRUSTS

One of my pet peeves is soggy pie crust. Crusts get soggy when their fillings are wet; the dough boils in the juices rather than bakes. The only surefire way to prevent soggy crust is to prebake it, a technique called blind baking. You will notice in most of my pie recipes, even those for covered pies, I have you prebake the bottom crust. Get in the habit. To do so, roll out the pie dough and line a pie plate as directed in the recipe. Trim any overhang to ½ inch. Do not prick the crust with a fork. For an open-face pie, roll the overhang under the edge between the pie plate and the crust to reinforce the sides and make a pretty decoration by pinching the dough between your thumb and forefinger or by pressing it with the floured tines of a fork. For a covered pie, tuck the overhang between the sides of the pie and the pie plate. Chill the crust for 20 to 30 minutes to allow the dough to relax before you bake it.

Preheat the oven to 425°F. Line the pie crust with aluminum foil and fill with dried beans, rice, or pie weights to hold the crust in place while it sets. Bake for 12 minutes, until the dough begins to firm up. Remove the weights and the foil. For an open-face pie, continue baking for 10 minutes, until the crust begins to brown lightly. Remove from the oven and cool before filling.

To place a top crust for a covered pie on a prebaked shell, roll the dough for the top about 1 inch larger than the pie. Center the crust on top over the filling and trim any overhang to ½ inch. Tuck the overhang between the bottom crust and the pie plate and press around the edges to seal, crimping them to make an attractive edge. Bake as directed in the recipe. Your pie may not be as pretty, perhaps, as if you didn't bake the bottom crust first, but it will taste better, trust me.

Graham Cracker Crust

This is a delicious crust for cheesecakes and pies that don't require baking. It's best to grind your own graham crackers, which are usually fresher than already-ground crumbs.

Makes one 9-inch pie crust

- 1 cup graham cracker crumbs (from about 10 large graham crackers, about 4½ ounces)
- 1 tablespoon sugar
- 2 tablespoons unsalted butter, melted

Preheat the oven to 350°F.

Place the cracker crumbs in a 9-inch glass, ceramic, or metal pie plate. Mix in the sugar and the melted butter. The crumbs should take on the consistency of wet sand. With your fingertips, press the crumbs to the edge of the pie plate to make an even and smooth crust. Bake for 10 minutes, until lightly browned. Cool before filling.

TOTAL TIME: 15 minutes

ADVANCE PREP *The crust can be made a day or two in advance, wrapped, and refrigerated until needed.*

VARIATIONS

A 10-inch Graham Cracker Crust

Increase the graham cracker crumbs to 1½ cups (about 14 whole crackers) and increase the butter to 3 tablespoons. Follow the recipe as directed.

Chocolate Cookie Crust

Substitute 1 cup chocolate cookie crumbs (from about 22 chocolate wafers, about 4½ ounces) for the graham crackers and proceed with the recipe as directed.

- ½ teaspoon kosher salt
- 1½ cups canned pumpkin purée (one 15-ounce can)
- One 10-inch graham cracker crust (see box, left)

In a small saucepan, whisk together the milk and the egg yolks. Whisk in ⅔ cup of the sugar, the gelatin, cinnamon, nutmeg, and salt. Set over low heat, and cook, stirring constantly, until the gelatin and sugar have dissolved (rub a drop between your fingertips to check) and the mixture begins to thicken, 3 or 4 minutes. Stir in the pumpkin and remove from the heat. Transfer to a large bowl and chill for at least 45 minutes, or until the mixture is lightly set.

Using an electric mixer, beat the egg whites until they form soft peaks. Slowly add the remaining ⅓ cup sugar and continue beating for 3 or 4 minutes, until the whites are stiff and glossy. Using a rubber spatula, fold about one fourth of the egg whites into the pumpkin mixture to lighten it, and then fold in the remaining whites, making sure no blobs of egg white remain. Pour this mixture into the crust, mounding it to a peak in the middle. Chill for at least 3 hours.

TOTAL TIME: 30 minutes (plus chilling time)

ADVANCE PREP *Well wrapped, the pie can be refrigerated up to two days in advance.*
LEFTOVERS *The pie will keep for about a week in the refrigerator.*

Peach Galette

This free-form tart is a good recipe for someone who likes pie but who doesn't like to fuss too much with pie crust.

Makes one 12-inch galette, enough for 8 to 10 servings

²⁄₃ batch pie dough (see page 421) or Cream
Cheese Pastry (see page 431)

¹⁄₃ cup sugar

¼ cup unbleached all-purpose flour

3 tablespoons blanched almonds or hazelnuts

8 firm, ripe peaches (2¹⁄₂ pounds), peeled (see
page 429) and sliced

3 tablespoons unsalted butter

2 tablespoons apricot jam (optional)

2 tablespoons sliced almonds, toasted (optional)

Preheat the oven to 425°F.

On a lightly floured surface, roll out the pie
dough to a circle of about 15 inches in diameter
and ¹⁄₈ inch thick. Transfer the dough to a large
baking sheet and set in the refrigerator to rest.

Meanwhile, in the bowl of a food processor
fitted with a metal chopping blade, combine
2 tablespoons of the sugar with the flour and
blanched almonds. Pulse on/off six or seven
times to grind the nuts finely.

Remove the dough from the refrigerator.
Sprinkle the nut mixture evenly over the dough,
leaving a 2-inch border. Arrange the sliced
peaches attractively in a single layer on top of
the nut mixture. Sprinkle the fruit with the remaining sugar. Carefully fold up the edges of
the dough (1¹⁄₂ to 2 inches worth), overlapping
the dough where necessary to make an attractive, free-form tart. Be careful to patch any
holes or tears in the dough or the juice will run
out of the crust. Dot the top of the fruit with the
butter. Bake for about 1 hour, or until the
peaches are soft and the crust is a deep, golden
brown. Remove from the oven and cool for at
least 30 minutes or so.

If desired, to make a nice decoration, heat
the apricot jam in the microwave or a small
saucepan until it is liquid. Brush the jam on
the dough ring and decorate with the sliced
almonds, gluing them on with the jam in an attractive manner.

PREP TIME: 30 minutes
COOKING TIME: 1 hour
TOTAL TIME: 1¹⁄₂ hours (plus cooling time)

ADVANCE PREP *The galette is best made the same
day you intend to serve it. Keep it at room temperature until ready to eat.*
LEFTOVERS *The galette will keep for two or three
days at room temperature or up to a week in the
refrigerator.*

VARIATIONS
Rhubarb Galette
Follow the same recipe, substituting 2¹⁄₂ pounds
fresh rhubarb cut into 2-inch pieces, for the
peaches. Increase the sugar to ²⁄₃ cup.

Summer Berry Galette
Follow the same recipe, substituting 1 quart
summer berries, such as raspberries, black berries, or gooseberries, for the peaches. Increase
the sugar to ³⁄₄ cup.

Plum Tart
I have Eric Ripert, chef of Le Bernardin in New York
City, to thank for the inspiration of this simple, elegant,
delicious dessert. This open-face plum tart is so easy to
make it's almost ridiculous. For a beautiful, dramatic
presentation, the most important thing is to slice the
plums as thin as possible. I use a mandoline, but you
can also use a very sharp knife.
Makes 1 tart, serving 6 to 8 people

½ batch Cream Cheese Pastry (page 431) or ½
   pound store-bought, frozen all-butter puff
   pastry, defrosted
⅓ cup plum, peach, or apricot jam
5 or 6 firm, ripe black plums (1½ to 2 pounds),
   rinsed and very thinly sliced
4 tablespoons (½ stick) unsalted butter, melted
1 to 2 tablespoons sugar

Position a rack in the upper third of the oven
and preheat the oven to 425°F.

On a lightly floured surface, roll out the pastry to a rectangle about 12 by 8 inches and ¼
inch thick. Transfer the pastry to a baking sheet,
preferably lined with parchment paper. Prick the
pastry all over with a fork to prevent it from rising. Spread the jam evenly over the surface of the
pastry. Arrange the plum slices in an attractive
pattern on top of the jam, overlapping and inter-
locking the slices to cover the crust completely.
Brush the plums generously with the melted
butter and sprinkle evenly with sugar, using
slightly more sugar if the plums are very tart.

Bake for 25 to 30 minutes, until the plums are
glazed and the crust is nicely browned (peek underneath to check). Remove from the oven and
cool for 15 minutes or so before transferring to a
serving plate. Be careful lifting the tart because
the jam that has dripped off the edge may have
caused it to stick in places. Run a thin, flexible
knife under the edges to be sure it is free.

PREP TIME: 20 minutes
COOKING TIME: 25 to 30 minutes
TOTAL TIME: 45 minutes (plus cooling time)

ADVANCE PREP *The tart can be made several
hours in advance and kept at room temperature
until serving. I like to brush it with melted butter,*

*sprinkle it with more sugar, and glaze it in a hot
oven or under the broiler before serving.*
LEFTOVERS *The tart will keep four or five days in
the refrigerator.*

Tarte Tatin

Tarte Tatin is a classic French caramelized apple tart
that is cooked upside down. Although I have had many
a tarte Tatin, the best one I ever ate was prepared by
my friend Oliver, who says the only secret is lots of butter. Because the apples are cut into big chunks, it is
also important to make sure the apples are properly
cooked—that is, soft but not mushy. The apples should

poach in the caramel, infusing them with the flavor of caramel and giving them a pleasing custard-like texture. You need a pan that can both go on top of the stove and in the oven, and that is easy to invert onto a serving plate. I use cast iron, but if that's too heavy, you can use whatever you like as long as it's about 9 inches across the bottom and 10 inches across the top.

Makes one 9-inch tart, enough for 8 servings

> 1/2 batch pie dough (see page 421) or Cream
> Cheese Pastry (page 431), or 8 ounces store-
> bought, frozen all-butter puff pastry,
> defrosted
> 1/2 cup (1 stick) unsalted butter
> 3/4 cup sugar
> 1 tablespoon fresh lemon juice
> 1/2 teaspoon pure vanilla extract
> 7 or 8 medium Golden Delicious apples (about
> 3 1/2 pounds), peeled, quartered, and cored
> Crème fraîche, whipped cream, or vanilla ice cream

On a lightly floured work surface, roll out the pastry into a 10-inch circle, about 1/4 inch thick. Transfer to a lightly floured baking sheet, prick all over with a fork, and set in the refrigerator to rest.

Meanwhile, in a cast-iron, nonstick, or other ovenproof skillet or pan, melt the butter over medium-high heat. When frothy, add the sugar, lemon juice, and vanilla and stir just until the sugar is melted. Remove from the heat. Preheat the oven to 400°F.

Arrange the apple quarters in the pan with the sugar mixture in an attractive, tightly packed layer. (I like to stand the quarters up, peeled side facing out, and arrange them in concentric circles, starting from the edge of the pan. This takes more apple, but it gives you a thick, dense apple layer when it is baked.) Return the pan to

medium heat and cook the apples, covered, until the apples are somewhat tender and there's a decent amount of juice visible, about 10 minutes. Remove the lid, raise the heat to high, and continue cooking for another 10 minutes, until the juices in the pan turn a deep caramel color. Set the pan in the oven and bake for about 10 minutes, until the apples are tender when pricked with a knife.

Remove the pan from the oven and remove the dough from the refrigerator. Transfer the dough to the top of the pan, tucking any overhang underneath the edge. Press the dough down to conform to the apples and return the pan to the oven. Bake until the crust is a deep golden brown, 25 to 30 minutes.

Remove the pan from the oven and cool for 20 minutes or so. Place the pan on the stove over medium-high heat for just a minute or two to loosen the caramelized apples. Turn off the heat. Place a serving dish on top of the pan and carefully invert the pan so the pie comes out onto the plate. Don't worry if any apples stick on the bottom; loosen them and replace them where they came from. If any caramel is stuck on the bottom of the pan, heat the pan to melt it and spoon the caramel on top of the apples. Serve with the cream or ice cream.

PREP TIME: 20 minutes
COOKING TIME: 45 minutes
TOTAL TIME: 1 hour 25 minutes (includes cooling time)

ADVANCE PREP *The tart can be made several hours in advance and served at room temperature or reheated in a 300°F oven until warm.*
LEFTOVERS *The tart will keep for four or five days in the refrigerator.*

Cream Cheese Pastry

This is one of my favorite doughs because it is so easy and so versatile. It's like a mock puff pastry. The three-ingredient recipe originated with my Great Aunt May, who used it to make her famous cream cheese cookies filled with apricot-pineapple jam, but it's similar to most cream-cheese rugelach doughs out there. There's no need to cut in the fat because the ratio of fat to flour is so high that the crust is always light and flaky. And for the same reason you don't have to worry too much about using too much flour to roll it out or overworking the dough. I use Cream Cheese Pastry for just about everything—sweet and savory.

Makes 1 pound dough, enough for two 9-inch tarts or 42 hors d'oeuvres

> 1 cup (2 sticks) unsalted butter, at room
> temperature
> ¾ cup (6 ounces) cream cheese, at room
> temperature
> 1½ cups all-purpose flour

In a bowl, blend the butter and cream cheese with a wooden spoon until combined. Alternatively, you can use the paddle attachment of an electric mixer. Add the flour and work to a smooth dough. Form into a ball, wrap in plastic, and refrigerate for at least 1 hour, or until firm enough to roll out.

TOTAL TIME: 10 minutes

ADVANCE PREP *The dough will keep in the refrigerator for three days or in the freezer for up to six months. Defrost overnight in the refrigerator before using.*
LEFTOVERS *Roll out any scraps, cut into squares, dab with jam, fold the corners into the center, glaze with beaten egg, and bake at 425° F for 15 minutes to make delicious cookies.*

Esther's Special Linzer Tart

This buttery, nutty, meringue-topped linzer tart is the signature of my friend Alexandra's Aunt Esther, an excellent baker in Mexico City. I've adapted her recipe a little to simplify the method, but the results are still delicious. For different effects, I vary the nuts and the jam filling: walnuts and raspberry jam, almonds and lemon marmalade, hazelnuts and blackberry jam, for example. Because the volume measurements of different nuts vary considerably, I specify the amount in weight. For reference, 6 ounces of walnut halves is about 1¾ cups; 6 ounces of whole almonds or hazelnuts is about 1¼ cups.

Makes one 9-inch tart, enough for 8 to 10 servings

> 6 ounces almonds, walnuts, or hazelnuts, toasted
> (see page 10)
> ¾ cup plus ⅓ cup sugar
> ⅔ cup all-purpose flour
> 2 large egg yolks
> About 2 tablespoons dark rum, brandy, Cognac,
> or whisky
> Pinch of kosher salt
> ½ cup (1 stick) unsalted butter, at room
> temperature
> ¾ cup jam, such as raspberry, strawberry,
> blackberry, or marmalade
> 3 large egg whites

Place the nuts and ¾ cup of the sugar in the bowl of a food processor fitted with a metal chopping blade. Process with on/off pulses until the nuts are finely ground. Scoop out a scant cup of this mixture and reserve for the topping. Add the flour to the food processor and pulse two or three times to blend. In a small bowl, beat the egg yolks with the rum and a pinch of salt. Add to the food processor along with the softened butter. Pulse three or four times, just until the mixture comes together and a soft dough forms a ball around the blade. If the dough is too dry, add a little more alcohol.

Transfer the dough to a 9-inch round baking dish or tart pan or an 8-inch square pan. Moisten your fingertips with cold water and pat or spread the dough to form an even layer on the bottom of the pan. Chill for 30 minutes.

Preheat the oven to 350°F.

Spread the jam evenly over the crust.

In the bowl of an electric mixer, beat the egg whites until frothy. Add the remaining $1/3$ cup sugar and continue beating on high until stiff peaks form, 3 or 4 minutes. With a large rubber spatula, fold in the reserved nut mixture. Spread this meringue topping in an even layer over the jam. Bake for 45 minutes, or until the meringue is browned, the jam is bubbling, and the crust is cooked through. Remove from the oven and cool completely before unmolding. The meringue will fall a little as it cools, but don't worry about it.

PREP TIME: 15 minutes
COOKING TIME: 45 minutes
TOTAL TIME: $1 1/2$ hours (includes chilling time)

ADVANCE PREP *The bottom crust can be made and placed in the pan a day or two in advance. Wrap in plastic and keep chilled until ready to assemble and bake. Alternatively, the dough can be made and frozen for up to two months. (Freeze the reserved nut mixture in a resealable plastic bag attached to the dough.) Defrost in the refrigerator overnight before pressing into the baking pan.*
LEFTOVERS *The linzer tart will keep for two or three days at room temperature before the topping begins to sweat. It may shrink and recede a little as it sits.*

Summer Fruit Cobbler

A cobbler (or slump or grunt) is a deep-dish dessert of fruit pie filling topped with biscuit dough or drop biscuits in lieu of being baked in a crust. You can use just about any summer fruit as long as it is ripe and in season.
Makes 6 to 8 servings

FOR THE FRUIT
    2 tablespoons unsalted butter, at room
        temperature
    6 cups ripe summer fruit, such as blueberries,
        raspberries, strawberries, rhubarb, pitted sour
        cherries, sliced peaches, sliced nectarines,
        sliced plums, or a combination
    $1/3$ cup all-purpose flour or 3 tablespoons
        cornstarch or arrowroot starch
    $1/2$ to $3/4$ cup sugar, depending on the sweetness
        of the fruit
    Grated zest of $1/2$ lemon or orange
    $1/2$ teaspoon pure vanilla extract
    $1/4$ teaspoon ground cinnamon

FOR THE TOPPING
    $1 1/2$ cups all-purpose flour
    $1/4$ cup sugar
    1 tablespoon baking powder
    Grated zest of $1/2$ lemon or orange
    $1/2$ teaspoon kosher salt
    5 tablespoons unsalted butter or a combination of
        butter and lard or vegetable shortening, cut
        into cubes and chilled
    $3/4$ cup buttermilk, heavy cream, or milk

Preheat the oven to 375°F.

To prepare the fruit filling, use a tablespoon or so of the butter to generously grease a deep 2-quart glass, ceramic, or enameled cast-iron baking dish. In the dish, combine the fruit, flour, sugar, zest, vanilla, and cinnamon, and toss to coat. Dot the top with another table-spoon of butter and set in the oven to bake for about 25 minutes, until the juices are bubbling.

Meanwhile, prepare the topping. In a bowl or a food processor fitted with a metal blade, combine the flour, sugar, baking powder, zest, and salt. Cut in the chilled butter until the mixture resembles coarse crumbs. Add the buttermilk and stir gently with a fork to form a wet, clumpy dough.

When the time is up on the fruit, remove the baking dish from the oven. Turn the heat up to 425°F. Drop heaping tablespoonfuls of the biscuit batter across the top of the hot fruit, leaving some spaces so the juices can bubble up over the biscuits. Return to the oven and bake for 30 minutes, or until the biscuits have risen and browned nicely and the fruit is bubbling vigorously. Remove from the oven, let cool for 15 minutes or so, and serve.

PREP TIME: 15 minutes
COOKING TIME: 1 hour
TOTAL TIME: 1 hour 15 minutes (plus cooling time)

ADVANCE PREP Cobblers are best served the day they are made. They can be made several hours in advance and kept at room temperature until ready to serve. Warm the cobbler in a 300°F oven for 15 minutes or so before serving, if desired.
LEFTOVERS Cobbler will keep for four or five days in the refrigerator.

Apple Cranberry Crisp

In the same family as cobblers, crisps (also crumbles) consist of a fruit bottom and a crumbly topping, which often contains oats and nuts. Crisps are equally delicious with summer fruits, such as berries and peaches, and fall fruits, such as apples and quince.

Makes 6 to 8 servings

FOR THE FILLING
6 to 7 large cooking apples (about 2½ pounds), such as Northern Spy, Gala, Braeburn, Jonagold, or Empire, or a combination
2 tablespoons all-purpose flour
¼ cup light brown sugar
½ cup dried cranberries or raisins
1 tablespoon brandy, rum, or fresh lemon juice
1 teaspoon pure vanilla extract
½ teaspoon ground cinnamon

FOR THE TOPPING
¾ cup all-purpose flour
½ cup rolled oats, granola, or cookie crumbs
⅔ cup granulated sugar
¼ cup finely chopped toasted walnuts (optional)
½ teaspoon ground cinnamon
Pinch of freshly grated nutmeg
Pinch of kosher salt
½ cup (1 stick) unsalted butter, at room temperature, plus extra for greasing the baking dish

Preheat the oven to 375°F. Grease a 2½-quart oblong or rectangular baking dish.

Peel, core, and cut the apples into slices or chunks and place in the baking dish. Add the flour, brown sugar, cranberries, brandy, vanilla, and cinnamon and toss to coat. Even out the apples in the dish.

To prepare the topping, in a medium bowl, combine the flour, oats, sugar, nuts, if using, cinnamon, nutmeg, and salt, and mix well with a fork. Add the butter and mix to form a coarse, crumbly mixture. Sprinkle this mixture evenly over the apples. Place the dish in the oven and bake for 55 minutes to 1 hour, until the apples are soft, the top has browned, and the juices are bubbling. Remove from the oven and let cool for 10 minutes before serving.

PREP TIME: 15 minutes
COOKING TIME: 1 hour
TOTAL TIME: 1 hour 15 minutes (plus cooling time)

ADVANCE PREP *The crisp can be made several hours in advance and served at room temperature or reheated in a 300° F oven until warm.*
LEFTOVERS *The crisp will keep for about a week in the fridge.*

Strawberry Shortcake

No dessert says summer has arrived to me as much as this Southern classic of warm biscuit shortcakes topped with ripe strawberries and whipped cream. For added flavor, brush the shortcakes or toss the fruit with a little herbed syrup (page 416). You can easily double or triple the recipe, as needed.

Makes 4 servings

FOR THE SHORTCAKES
¾ cup all-purpose flour
¼ cup sifted cake flour
1 teaspoon baking powder
2 tablespoons granulated sugar, plus a little extra for sprinkling
Pinch of kosher salt
2 tablespoons unsalted butter, chilled
1 tablespoon lard (see page 423), vegetable shortening, or additional butter, chilled
⅓ to ½ cup buttermilk, plus a little extra for glazing

FOR THE TOPPING
1 pint ripe strawberries, hulled and sliced
1 to 2 tablespoons granulated sugar, to taste
1 teaspoon fresh lemon juice
⅔ cup heavy cream, chilled
¼ teaspoon pure vanilla extract
1 tablespoon confectioners' sugar
2 to 3 tablespoons strawberry jam

Preheat the oven to 450° F.

To make the shortcakes, in a medium bowl, combine the flours, baking powder, sugar, and salt. Cut in the butter and lard so the mixture resembles coarse crumbs. Add ⅓ cup of the buttermilk and mix with a fork just until the mixture comes together into a moist dough, adding more milk if necessary to make it cohere. Turn out onto a lightly floured surface and knead the dough by folding it over onto itself just three or four times until it coheres and is smooth. Do not overwork it. Pinch off about one fourth of the dough and gently and quickly pat and coax it into a disk about ¾ inch thick. Place on an ungreased baking sheet. Repeat with the remaining dough to make four cakes. Place the pan in the refrigerator so the shortcakes can rest while you prepare the topping.

In a medium bowl, combine the strawberries with the sugar and lemon juice and set aside to macerate. In another bowl, using either an electric mixer or a wire whisk, beat the heavy cream until it begins to thicken. Add the vanilla and confectioners' sugar and continue beating until the cream is stiff enough to hold its shape when you lift the beaters. Chill the whipped cream until ready to use.

Remove the shortcakes from the refrigerator. Brush the tops with some buttermilk and

GRINDING NUTS

Many recipes call for ground nuts. You can sometimes buy nuts already ground, but because I like to toast my nuts, I prefer to grind them myself. You also never know how fresh already-ground nuts are, and once they are ground, nuts go rancid very quickly. The most effective tool for grinding toasted nuts is a cheese grater, the plastic kind with a hand crank designed for grating parmesan and other hard cheeses. The grater produces finely ground nuts that are light and fluffy without any risk of the nuts releasing their oils and turning into a paste.

The next most effective appliance is a food processor fitted with a metal chopping blade. If you grind the nuts in the food processor on their own, you risk turning them into paste. Instead, it's best to grind nuts along with some sugar or flour, which absorb whatever oils come out of the nuts as they are chopped finer and finer. I usually look at a recipe that requires ground nuts and decide whether I can use some or all of the sugar or flour to help grind the nuts (for the recipes in this book, I've done that already for you). Then I toast the nuts (see page 10), let them cool completely, place them in the food processor with the sugar or flour, and pulse the machine on and off until the nuts are finely and evenly ground. You simply incorporate this mixture back into the recipe at the appropriate stage.

sprinkle with sugar. Bake for about 8 minutes, until they have risen and browned, on both top and bottom. Remove from the oven and let cool slightly.

When the shortcakes are cool enough to handle but still warm, carefully slice off the tops (don't worry if they break; just keep the pieces together). Place the bottoms on serving plates. Spread the jam on the bottoms, top with some strawberries, spoon on some whipped cream, top with a few more strawberries, and drizzle some of the strawberry juice from the bowl on top of that. Place the tops askew on the shortcakes and serve quickly.

PREP TIME: 20 minutes
COOKING TIME: 10 minutes
TOTAL TIME: 40 minutes (includes cooling time)

ADVANCE PREP *You can prepare the dough and shape the shortcakes up to an hour or two in advance.*

VARIATIONS
Peach Shortcake
Follow the same recipe, substituting 4 very ripe peaches, peeled and diced, for the strawberries and 1 tablespoon bourbon for the lemon juice. Also, use peach or apricot jam instead of strawberry jam.

Herbed Strawberry Shortcake
Omit the sugar and lemon juice from the topping and toss the berries with 1 or 2 tablespoons of lavender, rosemary, or bay syrup (page 416) instead. Brush the split shortcakes with the same syrup before spreading the jam and assembling the shortcakes as directed.

Pineapple Upside Down Cake
Forget about the canned pineapple rings and maraschino cherries that used to top this favorite cake. When you use fresh pineapple, the results are superior.
Makes one 9-inch cake, enough for about 8 servings

FOR THE TOPPING

6 tablespoons (¾ stick) unsalted butter

½ cup light brown sugar

1 ripe small pineapple, peeled and cored

3 tablespoons coarsely chopped toasted pecans (see page 10), optional

FOR THE CAKE

1½ cups all-purpose flour

2 teaspoons baking powder

½ teaspoon kosher salt

½ cup (1 stick) unsalted butter, at room temperature

⅔ cup granulated sugar

2 large eggs

1 teaspoon pure vanilla extract

¾ cup buttermilk, milk, or a combination of milk and pineapple juice

Preheat the oven to 350°F.

To prepare the topping, in a small saucepan, combine the butter and brown sugar and set over medium heat, stirring until the butter has melted and the sugar has dissolved. Pour this mixture into the bottom of a 9-inch round cake pan and spread it out in an even layer. (Alternatively, you can use a 9-inch cast-iron pan to bake the cake and melt the butter and sugar directly in it.)

Slice the pineapple into ¼-inch-thick rings or spears and arrange in an attractive pattern on the bottom of the pan. If using pecans, scatter them around the pineapple. Set aside.

To prepare the cake, sift together the flour, baking powder, and salt, and set aside in a small bowl. In a large bowl, beat together the butter and sugar until light and fluffy. Beat in the eggs, one at a time, and add the vanilla. Stir in one third of the buttermilk, then one third of the dry ingredients, and repeat twice, mixing

just until the ingredients are incorporated and the batter is smooth. Do not overmix. Pour the batter over the pineapple in the prepared pan and even out the top of the cake with a spatula. Bake for 45 to 50 minutes, or until a toothpick or skewer inserted in the center of the cake comes out clean and the edges of the cake have pulled away from the sides of the pan. Remove from the oven and let cool on a wire rack for 15 minutes. Run a thin knife around the edge and invert onto a serving plate while still warm.

PREP TIME: 25 minutes

COOKING TIME: 50 to 55 minutes

TOTAL TIME: 1 hour 15 minutes (plus cooling time)

ADVANCE PREP *The pineapple cake is best eaten the day it is made and can be served warm or at room temperature.*

LEFTOVERS *Pineapple upside down cake should be eaten within a couple of days because the fruit makes the cake soggy.*

VARIATION

Cranberry Upside Down Cake

Add ¼ teaspoon ground cinnamon to the melted butter–brown sugar mixture and substitute 2 cups fresh cranberries (about ½ pound) for the pineapple. Arrange the cranberries in an even layer on the brown sugar mixture and proceed with the recipe as directed.

Date–Nut Cake

My mother, who loved to bake, had four fabulous cakes in her repertoire that she rotated depending on her mood. This was one of my favorites. It is a superbly moist and buttery cake that's addictive.

Makes one 9 by 13-inch cake, enough for 10 to 12 servings

8 ounces pitted dates, chopped (about 1⅓ cups)

1 teaspoon baking soda

1 cup (2 sticks) unsalted butter, plus extra for greasing the pan, at room temperature

1 cup sugar

3 large eggs

1 teaspoon pure vanilla extract

2 cups all-purpose flour

¾ cup chopped walnuts, toasted (see page 10)

Place the dates in a small bowl and pour over about 1 cup warm water. Stir in the baking soda and let soak about 1 hour, until the dates are very soft.

Preheat the oven to 375°F. Butter a 9 by 13-inch cake pan. Beat together the butter and sugar until light and fluffy. Beat in the eggs, one at a time, and add the vanilla. Stir in the flour in thirds, alternating with the date mixture. Stir in the nuts. Pour the batter into the prepared pan and bake for 30 to 35 minutes, until the cake has risen and pulled away from the sides of the pan. It should spring back to the touch. Remove from the oven and let cool for 20 minutes in the pan. Unmold onto a wire rack to cool completely.

PREP TIME: 15 minutes
COOKING TIME: 30 minutes
TOTAL TIME: 1 hour 45 minutes (plus cooling time)

ADVANCE PREP *The cake can be made a day or two in advance and wrapped well. The dates keep it very moist.*
LEFTOVERS *The cake will keep for about a week or it can be frozen for up to two months.*

Applesauce Spice Cake

Here's a recipe for a traditional American spice cake that's super moist and an excellent way to use up leftover Chunky Applesauce (page 416), Pear Sauce (page 417), or even any jam or marmalade you have lying around. (You can also use up any jam that has crystallized.)

Makes one 8-inch square cake, about 9 servings

½ cup (1 stick) unsalted butter, plus extra for greasing the pan, at room temperature

2 cups unbleached all-purpose flour

1 teaspoon baking soda

1 teaspoon ground cinnamon

½ teaspoon ground allspice

½ teaspoon freshly grated nutmeg

¼ teaspoon ground cloves

½ teaspoon kosher salt

1 cup sugar

3 large eggs

½ teaspoon pure vanilla extract

1 cup Chunky Applesauce (page 416) or Pear Sauce (page 417)

¼ cup buttermilk, regular milk, thin yogurt, or cream

½ cup chopped walnuts, toasted (see page 10, optional)

½ cup raisins (optional)

Preheat the oven to 375°F. Grease and flour an 8-inch square baking pan and set aside.

Sift together the flour, baking soda, cinnamon, allspice, nutmeg, cloves, and salt. Set aside. In an electric mixer fitted with the paddle attachment or by hand, beat the butter and sugar until light and fluffy. Add the eggs, one at a time, beating well after each addition. Add the vanilla and the applesauce and beat until smooth. Mix in about half of the dry ingredients, and just before they are blended, add the buttermilk. Stir in the remaining dry ingredients and the walnuts and/or raisins, if using. Be sure the batter is well blended, but don't overmix.

Transfer the batter to the prepared pan, smooth out the top, and bake for 25 to 30 minutes, until the cake has risen, set, browned, and pulled away from the sides of the pan. The top should spring back when pressed with your fingertips. Remove from the oven, let cool in the pan for 15 minutes, and then unmold onto a rack to finish cooling completely.

PREP TIME: 15 minutes
COOKING TIME: 25 minutes
TOTAL TIME: 40 minutes (plus cooling time)

ADVANCE PREP *The cake can be made a day or two in advance and wrapped well.*
LEFTOVERS *The cake will keep for about a week or it can be frozen for up to two months.*

VARIATION
Jam Cake
Substitute 1 cup jam—such as raspberry, strawberry, blackberry, or orange marmalade—for the applesauce and proceed with the recipe as directed. The cake may take an extra few minutes to bake.

Carrot Cake with Cream Cheese Frosting
This is a simple, classic recipe for carrot cake. It is moist and delicious. If you make the cake in layers, you will need the full amount of icing. If you make the cake in a rectangular pan and you are just frosting the top, half

the icing will suffice. For a slightly different effect, use the Caramel Cream Cheese Frosting on page 450. Makes two 9-inch layers or one 9 by 13-inch cake, enough for 12 to 16 servings

FOR THE CAKE
Unsalted butter, for greasing the pans
2 cups unbleached all-purpose flour
2 teaspoons baking powder
½ teaspoon baking soda
1 teaspoon ground cinnamon
½ teaspoon freshly grated nutmeg (optional)
1½ cups peanut or vegetable oil
2 cups granulated sugar
4 large eggs
2 cups grated carrots (from about 4 medium)
1 cup chopped toasted pecans or walnuts (see page 10)
1 cup raisins or currants

FOR THE FROSTING
12 ounces (1½ cups) cream cheese, at room temperature
½ cup (1 stick) unsalted butter, at room temperature
3 cups confectioners' sugar
2 teaspoons pure vanilla extract

Preheat the oven to 350°F. Grease two 9-inch round cake pans or one 9 by 13-inch rectangular pan.

To make the cake, sift together the flour, baking powder, baking soda, cinnamon, and nutmeg, if using. In a large bowl, beat together the oil and sugar. Beat in the eggs, one at a time. Stir in the flour mixture, along with the carrots, pecans, and raisins. Pour into the prepared pan(s). Bake the rounds for about 35 minutes and the rectangular cake for about

45 minutes, or until the cake has risen, browned, pulled away from the sides, and springs back to the touch.

Remove from the oven and let cool for 20 minutes on a wire rack. Run a knife around the edges, invert on the rack to unmold, and cool completely. (If frosting the cake, I like to chill the layers.)

To prepare the frosting, beat together the cream cheese and butter until blended. Beat in the confectioners' sugar and vanilla until smooth. The frosting should be spreadable (it will harden when it chills). If it is too soft, you can add more sugar to stiffen it or chill it somewhat before frosting the cake. Use a generous amount of frosting to cover the cake, a good ¼-inch layer.

PREP TIME: 20 minutes
COOKING TIME: 35 to 45 minutes
TOTAL TIME: 2 hours (includes cooling time)

ADVANCE PREP *The cake is delicious freshly made, and even better the next day. Frosted, well wrapped, and uncut, it will keep moist for three or four days in the refrigerator. You can freeze the layers for up to two months and, separately, the icing for up to six months.*
LEFTOVERS *The cake will keep for about a week in the refrigerator.*

Parsnip Cake

Parsnips aren't such a stretch from carrots, and this cake has a light texture and delicious flavor that no one can quite put a finger on until you say what it is. (You can substitute shredded celery root for the parsnips to make another intriguingly delicious cake.) Parsnip cake is good plain and even better frosted with Caramel Cream Cheese Frosting (page 450). The flavor of the parsnips is beautifully complemented by a spoonful of Pear Sauce (page 417), on the side.

Makes one 9 by 13-inch cake or two 9-inch round layers, enough for 12 to 16 servings

1 cup (2 sticks) unsalted butter, plus extra for greasing the pan, at room temperature
1 cup granulated sugar
1 cup light brown sugar
4 large eggs
1 teaspoon pure vanilla extract
Pinch of salt
2 cups unbleached all-purpose flour
1 teaspoon baking powder
1 teaspoon baking soda
1 teaspoon ground cinnamon
3 cups shredded parsnips (about 2 large)
1 cup chopped toasted walnuts or pecans (see page 10)

Preheat the oven to 350°F. Butter one 9 by 13-inch rectangular pan or two 9-inch round cake pans.

In the bowl of an electric mixer fitted with the paddle attachment, beat the butter with the sugars until light and fluffy. Beat in the eggs, one at a time. Beat in the vanilla and salt. Switch to a wooden spoon. Add 1 cup of the flour along with the baking powder, baking soda, and cinnamon, and stir to combine. Add the second cup of flour, and just when it is almost incorporated, stir in the parsnips and toasted walnuts.

Transfer the batter to the prepared pan(s) and even out to fill the pan(s). Bake until the cake(s) have risen, set, browned, and pulled away from the sides, about 30 minutes for the layers, 35 to 40 minutes for the 9 by 13-inch cake. The cake should spring back to the touch.

Remove from the oven and cool for 15 minutes in the pan(s). Unmold onto wire racks and cool completely.

PREP TIME: 10 minutes

COOKING TIME: 30 to 40 minutes

TOTAL TIME: 40 to 50 minutes (plus cooling time)

ADVANCE PREP *The cake is good fresh but is better the next day. Wrap and leave at room temperature overnight.*

LEFTOVERS *The cake will keep for about three days at room temperature wrapped airtight, or it can be frozen for up to two months.*

Green Tomato Cake

I'm a huge fan of putting things into cakes that people don't expect. I make cakes with parsnips, olive oil, bread, blue cheese—you name it. Near the top of my favorite cake list is this Green Tomato Cake. I first came across the recipe in a cookbook by Paula Deen, proprietor of The Lady & Sons restaurant in Savannah. With a few tweaks and personal touches, it's been part of my repertoire ever since. No one has ever guessed that the secret to the cake's moistness is unripened tomatoes.

Makes one 9 by 13-inch cake, two 8-inch square cakes, or two 4½ by 8½-inch loaves, enough for 12 to 16 servings

1 cup (2 sticks) unsalted butter, melted and cooled, plus extra for greasing the pan

2 cups sugar

3 large eggs

2 teaspoons pure vanilla extract

3 cups unbleached all-purpose flour

1 teaspoon kosher salt

1 teaspoon baking soda

1 teaspoon ground cinnamon

¼ teaspoon freshly grated nutmeg

1 cup raisins or ¾ cup dried currants

2 to 3 green tomatoes, cored and cut into ¼-inch cubes (about 2½ cups)

1 cup chopped toasted walnuts (see page 10)

1 cup shredded sweetened coconut

Preheat the oven to 350°F. Butter one 9 by 13-inch cake pan, two 8-inch square cake pans, or two 4½ by 8½-inch loaf pans.

In a large bowl, beat together the sugar, butter, and eggs until blended. Beat in the vanilla. Slowly mix in the flour, salt, baking soda, cinnamon, and nutmeg. The batter will be quite stiff, like a paste. Using a wooden spoon, stir in the raisins, tomatoes, chopped walnuts, and shredded coconut. Transfer the batter to the prepared pan(s) and smooth out the top to make it even. Bake for about 1 hour, or until the cake has risen, set, pulled away from the sides, and springs back to the touch (the loaves will take about 15 minutes more). Cool for 20 minutes before unmolding.

PREP TIME: 10 minutes

COOKING TIME: 1 hour

TOTAL TIME: 1 hour 10 minutes (plus cooling time)

LEFTOVERS *The cake will keep for about five days at room temperature, wrapped tightly, and freezes well for about three months.*

Flourless Almond and Orange Cake

This is an unusual flourless cake, likely of Middle Eastern origin, that incorporates whole citrus (peel, pith, and all). I've seen variations of it in books by James Beard, Claudia Roden, and Nigella Lawson. This version is especially good for Passover, when observant Jews are usually looking for a new flourless cake recipe. The flavor is subtle and the texture is very moist.

Makes one 8-inch round cake, enough for 8 to 10 servings

2 juice oranges or large lemons, or 4 or 5
    clementines, or a combination (about
    12 ounces total)
Unsalted butter, for greasing the pan
2 cups whole blanched almonds or hazelnuts
    (about 9 ounces), toasted (see page 10)
1 cup sugar (if using lemons, increase to
    1 ⅓ cups)
6 large eggs
½ teaspoon pure vanilla extract
Pinch of kosher salt

Place the citrus in a small saucepan and cover with cold water. Bring to a boil, turn down the heat, and simmer, uncovered, until the fruit is completely soft, 1½ to 2 hours, depending on how thick the skin is. If necessary, add more water to be sure the fruit remains submerged while cooking. Drain and cool. Cut the fruit into halves or quarters and using the point of a knife or a fork, remove and discard any seeds.

Preheat the oven to 375°F. Prepare an 8-inch springform pan by buttering it, lining the bottom with a round of parchment, and buttering it again (see page 442).

Place the nuts in the bowl of a food processor fitted with a metal chopping blade. Add the sugar and pulse on/off six to eight times to grind the nuts to a fine flour. Transfer this nut mixture to a small bowl and set aside. Place the cooked fruit, peel, pith, and all, in the food processor and purée to a smooth pulp, scraping down the sides once or twice. Add the eggs to the fruit, two at a time, blending well with on/off pulses after each addition. Scrape down the sides. Add the vanilla and salt and blend. Add the nut mixture all at once and blend, scraping down the sides. Pour this batter into the prepared pan.

Bake for 45 minutes to 1 hour, or until the cake has risen somewhat, browned, pulled away from the sides, and a skewer inserted in the center comes out clean. Remove to a rack and cool completely to room temperature before unmolding. The cake will sink a little as it cools.

PREP TIME: 20 minutes
COOKING TIME: 2 hours 15 minutes
TOTAL TIME: 2 hours 35 minutes (plus cooling time)

ADVANCE PREP *The citrus can be cooked a day or two before you make the cake. Keep in the refrigerator until ready to use. The cake itself is best made a day in advance, too, so the texture and flavor have time to settle. Wrap it and keep it at room temperature before serving.*
LEFTOVERS *The cake will keep tightly wrapped at room temperature for four days and up to a week in the refrigerator. It also freezes pretty well for up to two months.*

Chocolate Cheesecake

A deep chocolate flavor and rich, creamy texture make this cake an indulgent favorite. Several friends have told me it tastes more like a chocolate mousse cake than a cheesecake, but that's all the more reason to love it.

Makes one 9-inch round cake, enough for about 10 servings

½ cup peeled hazelnuts or walnut halves, toasted (see page 10)

22 chocolate wafers (about 4½ ounces)

5 tablespoons unsalted butter, melted and cooled

1½ pounds (about 3 cups) cream cheese, at room temperature

1 cup sugar

3 large eggs

1 tablespoon pure vanilla extract

12 ounces semisweet or bittersweet chocolate, melted and cooled

Preheat the oven to 350°F.

Place the nuts and chocolate wafers in the bowl of a food processor and process with on/off pulses until finely ground, about 2 minutes. Add the melted butter and pulse once or twice to moisten the crumbs. Dump this mixture into a 9-inch springform pan, and using your fingertips, pat it out into an even layer to form the crust. Bake for about 7 minutes to warm and set. Remove to a rack and cool.

Place the cream cheese in the bowl of an electric mixer and beat using the paddle attachment until smooth. Add the sugar and beat to blend. Add the eggs, beating after each addition. Beat in the vanilla. Add the chocolate and beat until smooth. Be sure there are no lumps of cream cheese visible. Pour this mixture into the prepared pan and smooth out the top with a rubber spatula.

Bake for 45 minutes, or until the cheesecake has risen and set, and an instant-read thermometer reaches 185°F when poked in the center. Don't worry if there are one or two small cracks. Remove from the oven and cool to room temperature.

Chill for 4 to 6 hours before serving. Slice

WHEN AND HOW TO LINE A CAKE PAN WITH PARCHMENT PAPER

Parchment paper—and its close relative, silicone paper—is very useful in the kitchen, especially for baking. Most cookies and cakes are sure not to stick if they are baked on either of these surfaces, and as far as most cookies are concerned, the papers alleviate the need to grease the pans. They also make cleanup easier. For a surprisingly little amount of money, I bought 1,000 sheets of silicone paper at a restaurant supply store that will last me for the rest of my life, even though I give sheets to all my friends whenever they need them.

I advise using parchment or silicone paper to line cake pans for particularly dense or moist cakes, which don't always come out of the pan easily, or for very delicate cakes, which have a tendency to break. To line a square or rectangular pan with either paper, I find it works best to cut the paper to fit the bottom of the pan with a couple of inches coming up two opposite sides, which facilitates removal of the cake. Butter the pan, lay down the paper, pressing it into the pan to adhere to the butter, and then butter the paper again. For round pans, take a square of paper the size of the pan. Fold it in half, corner to corner, to make a triangle. Keep folding the triangle in half to make a long, skinny triangle, about 1½ inches wide at its base. Hold the point of the triangle in the center of the pan and the base against the edge. Cut the base end to be even with the pan and unfold the paper. It should be close enough to the size and shape of your pan. Of course, now they sell parchment cut to various sizes and shapes of pans, which saves you a few steps, if not money.

with a thin knife dipped in warm water and wiped clean before each cut is made.

PREP TIME: 20 minutes
COOKING TIME: 45 minutes
TOTAL TIME: 65 minutes (plus chilling time)

ADVANCE PREP *The cheesecake can be made two or three days in advance and refrigerated. The cake can also be made and frozen for up to a month. Defrost in the refrigerator overnight.*
LEFTOVERS *The cake will keep in the fridge for up to one week (wrap it well so it doesn't pick up any other odors in the fridge), or it can be frozen for up to a month.*

Devil's Food Cake

This is my sister Carrie's recipe, but I make it all the time. It is hands down the moistest, chocolatiest, easiest, bestest devil's food cake you will ever have. It is delicious topped with Caramel Cream Cheese Frosting (page 450) or Chocolate Ganache (page 449).

Makes two 9-inch layers, one 9 by 13-inch cake, or two 4½ by 8½-inch loaves, enough for 12 to 16 servings

Unsalted butter, for greasing the pan
1¾ cups unbleached all-purpose flour
¾ cup unsweetened cocoa powder (not Dutch-processed)
2 teaspoons baking soda
1 teaspoon baking powder
¼ teaspoon kosher salt
1 cup granulated sugar
1 cup light brown sugar, packed
1 cup buttermilk or sour milk, or a mixture of ½ cup milk and ½ cup plain yogurt
1 cup strong coffee or espresso, cooled
½ cup vegetable oil
2 large eggs
2 teaspoons pure vanilla extract

Position the rack in the center of the oven and preheat to 350°F. Butter two 9-inch round cake pans, one 9 by 13-inch rectangular cake pan, or two 4½ by 8½-inch loaf pans. For foolproof removal, line the bottom with parchment paper and butter again.

Into a large bowl, sift together the flour, cocoa, baking soda, baking powder, salt, and sugars (force any lumps of brown sugar through the sifter with your fingertips, if necessary). In a medium bowl, beat together the buttermilk, coffee, oil, eggs, and vanilla. Pour the liquid mixture into the dry mixture, and using a whisk, mix to form a smooth batter. Don't overbeat. Pour this mixture into the prepared pan(s).

Bake for 25 to 30 minutes (40 minutes for loaf pans), until the center has risen and set firm, the sides have pulled away from the pan, and a toothpick inserted into the center comes out clean. Remove from the oven and cool on a rack for 15 minutes. Run a knife around the edges and invert onto the rack. Carefully lift off the pan and let cool completely.

PREP TIME: 10 minutes
COOKING TIME: 25 minutes
TOTAL TIME: 35 minutes (plus cooling time)

ADVANCE PREP *The cake is even better after it sits, well wrapped, at room temperature for a day.*
LEFTOVERS *This cake will keep fresh and moist at room temperature for four or five days. It can be wrapped and frozen for up to two months.*

Earl Grey's Devil's Food Cake

The flavor of Earl Grey tea—bergamot— makes a delicious addition to this cake. Substitute 1 cup of very strongly brewed Earl Grey tea for the coffee.

Chocolate Cupcakes

To make cupcakes, prepare the batter as directed. Use nonstick muffin tins, with 12 medium to large cups, sprayed with nonstick cooking spray, or generously butter and flour regular muffin tins. Fill the tins with batter almost to the top. Bake at 350°F for about 20 minutes, or until set.

Banana Cake

Lighter, and to my taste, more delicious than banana bread, this cake has a delicate texture and a strong banana flavor—the riper the bananas the stronger. If you have bananas that have turned totally spotted or black and you can't get around to making a cake, stick them in the freezer and defrost them when you are ready to bake (add any liquid that forms when they defrost to the cake). I like to ice banana cake with Deep Dark Chocolate Frosting (page 448) or Caramel Cream Cheese Frosting (page 450).

Makes one 9 by 13-inch cake or two 9-inch round cake layers, enough for 8 to 10 servings

- ½ cup (1 stick) unsalted butter, plus extra for greasing the pan, at room temperature
- ¾ cup buttermilk, sour milk, or regular milk
- 1 teaspoon baking soda
- 2 cups all-purpose flour
- 1 teaspoon baking powder
- ½ teaspoon ground cinnamon
- 1½ cups sugar
- 3 large eggs
- ½ teaspoon pure vanilla extract
- 3 large, very ripe bananas, mashed with a fork (about 1¼ cups)

Preheat the oven to 350°F. Butter and flour one 9 by 13-inch rectangular pan or two 9-inch round cake pans.

In a small bowl, combine the buttermilk with the baking soda and set aside—it will froth. In another bowl, combine the flour, baking powder, and cinnamon and mix well.

In a large bowl, beat the butter and sugar together to form a smooth paste. Beat in the eggs, one at a time, and stir in the vanilla. Stir in half the bananas, half the milk mixture, and half the dry ingredients, and mix until incorporated. Add the remaining bananas, milk mixture, and dry ingredients and mix just until blended. Pour into the prepared pan(s).

Bake for about 30 minutes, until the cake has risen, browned, pulled away from the edges, and springs back to the touch. Remove from the oven and let cool for 20 minutes on a wire rack. Run a knife around the edges, invert on the rack to unmold, and let cool completely.

PREP TIME: 10 minutes
COOKING TIME: 30 minutes
TOTAL TIME: 40 minutes (plus cooling time)

LEFTOVERS *Well wrapped, banana cake will keep for four or five days at room temperature or in the refrigerator. It can also be frozen for up to two months.*

Butter Cake

Here's a delicious, all-purpose butter or yellow cake, with a delicate texture and strong vanilla flavor that's ideal for a birthday cake, cupcakes, or just to have around to munch on. The cornstarch gives the cake a softer texture than just using straight flour.

Makes two 9-inch round layers or one 9 by 13-inch cake, enough for 12 to 16 servings

> ⅔ cup (10 tablespoons) unsalted butter, plus extra for greasing the pans, at room temperature
> 1¾ cups all-purpose flour
> ¼ cup cornstarch
> 2 teaspoons baking powder
> ½ teaspoon kosher salt
> 1½ cups sugar
> 2 large eggs
> 1 large egg yolk
> 1½ teaspoons pure vanilla extract
> ¾ cup buttermilk or ⅔ cup sour or regular milk

Preheat the oven to 350°F. Butter and flour two 9-inch round cake pans or one 9 by 13-inch cake pan.

Sift together the flour, cornstarch, baking powder, and salt. Using the paddle attachment of an electric mixer, beat the butter with the sugar until light and fluffy, a good 5 minutes. Add the eggs, one at a time, beating after each, and the egg yolk. Beat in the vanilla. Stir in the dry ingredients in thirds, alternating with the buttermilk, just until incorporated. Do not overmix. Dump into the prepared pan(s) and even out the surface with a spatula.

Bake for 30 to 35 minutes, or until the cake has risen, browned, pulled away from the sides of the pan, and a toothpick inserted into the center comes out clean.

Remove from the oven and let cool on a wire rack for 15 minutes. Run a knife along the edge, invert on the rack to unmold, and let cool completely before serving.

PREP TIME: 10 minutes
COOKING TIME: 30 minutes
TOTAL TIME: 40 minutes (plus cooling time)

LEFTOVERS *Well wrapped, leftovers will keep for four days at room temperature. The cake can also be frozen for up to two months.*

VARIATION
Vanilla Cupcakes

To make cupcakes, spray 12 nonstick muffin tins, medium to large, with nonstick cooking spray, or generously butter and flour regular muffin tins. Fill the tins with batter almost to the top. Bake at 350°F for about 20 minutes, or until set.

Coconut Layer Cake

I love the look and taste of a shaggy white coconut layer cake. Filled with lemon curd, coconut cake is one of my all-time favorite birthday cakes.

Makes 2-layer 9-inch round layer cake, enough for 12 to 16 servings

FOR THE CAKE
> ¾ cup (1½ sticks) unsalted butter, plus extra for greasing the pans, at room temperature
> 1¼ cups all-purpose flour
> 1½ cups sifted cake flour

MEASURING INGREDIENTS

While I don't believe that baking is an exact science (see page 447), if you want to get the same results as I do from the recipes in this chapter, we should measure our ingredients the same way.

Measuring spoons are easy because they work well enough for both liquid and dry measurements. For dry, dip the spoon into whatever you are measuring and level it off with the back of a knife. For liquid, simply pour until it's about to overflow. For thick pastes that are somewhere in the middle—the texture of mustard, say—use the dip and level technique.

Individual measuring cups, the kind with ¼, ⅓, and ½ graduations, are intended for dry ingredients and pastes. Little clear pitchers with markings on the side are intended for liquid ingredients. To measure dry ingredients, spoon them into the cups until they are overflowing and then level them off with the back of a knife. Do the same for pastes. For liquids, you have to hold the cup up to eye level (or bend down to meet it). Pour in the liquid until it is even with the marking you need. A new type of liquid measuring cup, with the graduations marked on an angled plane inside the cup, is even easier to use because you can just look down into the cup and see how much you've got.

There are a few tricks about measuring you should keep in the back of your mind. If you are measuring honey, a drop of oil or a thin film of nonstick cooking spray in the cup before you pour it in will make the honey slide out without fuss. Measurements for brown sugar always mean for you to pack it down tightly. Generally, I look at a recipe and try to measure the ingredients in an order that will allow me to use the same spoons and cups without having to clean them between measurements—that usually means dry ingredients first.

Truth be told, the only truly accurate way to measure ingredients is by weight, but until every American cook runs out and buys a scale, we'll have to stick with the quirky volume measurements we've got.

---

    1 tablespoon baking powder
    ½ teaspoon kosher salt
    1½ cups granulated sugar
    3 large eggs, separated
    1 teaspoon pure vanilla extract
    ¾ cup canned unsweetened coconut milk
        (not cream)
    ¾ cup sweetened flaked coconut

FOR THE ICING AND FILLING
    1 cup (2 sticks) unsalted butter, at room
        temperature
    1 tablespoon cane or light corn syrup
    1 tablespoon pure vanilla extract
    Pinch of kosher salt

    4 cups confectioners' sugar (about
        1 pound)
    ⅓ cup canned unsweetened coconut milk
        (not cream)
    1 cup Lemon Curd (page 451)
    1½ cups sweetened flaked coconut

Preheat the oven to 350°F. Butter two 9-inch round cake pans.

Sift together the flours, baking powder, and salt. In a large bowl, beat the butter and the sugar until light and fluffy. Add the egg yolks and vanilla and beat well. Stir in the dry ingredients, alternating with the coconut milk, until just about blended. Add the flaked coconut and

THE "SCIENCE" OF BAKING

I know that it is commonly believed that baking is an exact science, and that unlike cooking, which is a realm of unbridled creativity, baking requires careful attention to rules and recipes, and especially to measuring. I disagree. True, if you are a professional pastry chef or baker, your clientele will expect that every cake, cookie, pie, or bread you bake will be exactly the same, but there's no such pressure at home. All you have to do is compare different recipes for the same thing—pie crust, say, or chocolate cake—and you'll see immediately how much leeway there is with baking.

Unless you line up a bunch of cakes made from the same recipe with slight variations to taste them side by side—a little more sugar here, another egg there, an extra ½ teaspoon of baking powder over there—you will hardly be able to tell the difference from one to the next. Trust me, I've done it. What's more, the variation in ingredients, owing to humidity, temperature, ripeness, and other factors, means rarely are you baking the exact same thing twice, even if you adhere to the recipe to the letter.

So follow these recipes, but don't fret if you have yogurt on hand instead of sour cream or all-purpose flour instead of cake flour. I never would have come up with any of my delicious cakes or cookies without a little experimentation. Baking recipes are much more malleable than you've been led to believe.

mix to make a smooth batter. With an electric mixer or whisk, beat the egg whites to stiff peaks. Gently fold the egg whites into the batter until incorporated. Divide the batter between the two pans.

Bake for about 25 minutes, until the cakes have risen, browned, pulled away from the sides, and they spring back to the touch. Remove from the oven, and cool on a wire rack for 15 minutes. Run a knife around the edges and invert on the rack to unmold and cool completely.

To prepare the icing, beat the butter in an electric mixer fitted with a paddle attachment until smooth. Add the cane syrup, vanilla, and salt, and beat until smooth. Beat in the confectioners' sugar to make a stiff paste, and slowly add just enough of the coconut milk to make a rich, spreadable frosting.

To assemble the cake, lay one of the layers upside down on a serving plate. Place strips of parchment or waxed paper under the edges of the cake to protect the dish. Brush some coconut milk on the surface of the cake to moisten it. Spread the lemon curd in an even layer on the cake. Brush the bottom of the second cake layer with coconut milk and place it on top of the lemon curd, right side up. Ice the cake with the frosting and cover with plenty of flaked coconut, pressing it in so it adheres. Chill until ready to serve.

PREP TIME: **40 minutes**

COOKING TIME: **25 minutes**

TOTAL TIME: 1½ hours (includes cooling time, plus chilling time)

ADVANCE PREP *Iced, covered, and uncut the cake will keep refrigerated for up to two days. You can* *freeze the layers for up to two months and, separately, the icing for up to six months.*

LEFTOVERS *The cake will keep for about a week in the fridge. Any leftover icing can be frozen for up to six months.*

Vanilla Cream Frosting

While French, Swiss, and Italian buttercreams are all delicious, this easy butter and sugar frosting is really versatile enough for most home-baking needs. I think of it as American buttercream. It's the kind of creamy, buttery frosting that's used on all those cupcakes for sale across the country. The corn syrup keeps the frosting from hardening. Use drops of food coloring to make pretty colors. Be sure the cake you are frosting has cooled completely; I like to chill my cakes for about 30 minutes so they are less crumbly and the icing goes on easily.

Makes about 2½ cups, enough for a 2-layer, 9-inch round cake

> 1 cup (2 sticks) unsalted butter, at room
>   temperature
> 1 tablespoon light corn syrup
> 1 tablespoon pure vanilla extract
> Pinch of kosher salt
> 4 cups confectioners' sugar (about 1 pound)
> ¼ cup heavy cream

Beat together the butter, corn syrup, vanilla, and salt until smooth. Blend in the sugar to form a stiff paste. Slowly beat in just enough of the heavy cream to make a spreadable frosting. If the frosting is too soft, add more sugar or chill it for a few minutes to firm up.

TOTAL TIME: 5 minutes

ADVANCE PREP *The frosting can be made several days in advance and refrigerated until needed. Bring back to room temperature and beat until smooth before using.*

LEFTOVERS *The frosting can be frozen for up to six months. Defrost at room temperature and beat until smooth before using.*

VARIATION
Lemon Frosting
Substitute 3 tablespoons fresh lemon juice for the heavy cream and proceed with the recipe as directed. A drop or two of yellow food coloring enhances the lemon effect.

Deep Dark Chocolate Frosting

This simple frosting has a creamy texture and deep chocolate flavor.

Makes about 2½ cups, enough for a 2-layer, 9-inch round cake

> 2 cups confectioners' sugar
> ¼ cup unsweetened cocoa powder (not Dutch-
>   processed)
> 8 ounces semisweet or bittersweet chocolate,
>   chopped
> ¼ cup heavy cream
> ¾ to 1 cup (1½ to 2 sticks) unsalted butter,
>   at room temperature
> Pinch of kosher salt
> 1 teaspoon pure vanilla extract

Sift together the sugar and cocoa and set aside. In a small saucepan over low heat or in the microwave, melt the chocolate with the cream, stirring until smooth. Be careful not to scorch

MAKING YOUR OWN VANILLA EXTRACT AND VANILLA SUGAR

Years ago I started to make my own vanilla extract and since then I've never bought commercially prepared vanilla. It's easy and it only gets better with time. Start with 6 fresh, plump vanilla beans. Cut them in half and then split each bean lengthwise. Scrape out the seeds with the point of a paring knife and place them into a glass bottle along with the pods. Fill the bottle with about 1½ cups whisky, bourbon, or brandy, or a combination. Shake and let stand for two or three weeks before using. As time passes and you use some of the extract, periodically top off the jar with more alcohol and throw in another bean or two. Shake it every once in a while, too. In ten years, I've never taken anything out of my vanilla bottle; I just keep adding to it.

To make vanilla sugar, you need one or two vanilla beans. Dry them before adding them to the sugar. Split the bean in half lengthwise. Combine the pod with 1½ cups sugar in an airtight container. Store for about two weeks. (You can also use vanilla bean pods that you've already used to infuse milk.) Use vanilla sugar on French Toast (page 105) and in anything that could stand a little extra boost of vanilla flavor.

the chocolate. Let this mixture cool completely to room temperature.

Beat ½ cup of the butter into the chocolate. Beat in the cocoa mixture along with the salt and vanilla to form a smooth, stiff paste. Continue beating, while adding in ¼ cup of the remaining butter. If the icing is still not quite smooth and shiny, but rather matte and a little grainy, beat in additional butter until it reaches the consistency and texture you desire.

TOTAL TIME: 40 minutes (includes cooling time)

ADVANCE PREP *The icing can be made in advance and kept at room temperature for several hours or refrigerated for three or four days until needed. Bring the icing back to room temperature and beat until smooth before using.*
LEFTOVERS *The icing can be frozen for up to six months. Bring back to room temperature and beat until smooth before using.*

Chocolate Ganache

This is a classic combination of chocolate and cream that can be used as an intense chocolate filling, icing, or glaze for cakes. The better the chocolate you use, the better your results. You can flavor the ganache with liquor or liqueur, such as bourbon, Grand Marnier, or Kahlua, to make simple truffles or an intense filling for tarts. Made with sour cream, ganache has a pleasant tang.
Makes about 1½ cups

   1 cup heavy or sour cream
   8 ounces semisweet chocolate, chopped

In a small saucepan, heat the cream over medium heat to a simmer. Add the chocolate and remove from the heat. Let sit for a minute or two, until the chocolate has melted. Stir until smooth. Cool until it reaches the desired consistency. For a glaze, it should be warm and pourable; for icing it should be at room temperature and spreadable; for truffles it should be chilled and firm.

ADVANCE PREP *Ganache can be made several days in advance and refrigerated until needed. To reheat, set in gently simmering water to melt to the desired consistency.*

LEFTOVERS *Ganache can be stored in the refrigerator for two or three weeks or frozen for up to two months.*

VARIATIONS

Flavored Ganache

Stir 1 tablespoon liquor or liqueur, such as bourbon, Grand Marnier, Kahlua, or Framboise, into the ganache and proceed as directed.

Chocolate Truffles

Reduce the cream to ³⁄₄ cup and chill the chocolate mixture completely. Using a melon baller, scoop little balls of chocolate and dump them into a bowl of unsweetened cocoa powder (not Dutch-processed). Roll the balls gently in your hands and roll again in the cocoa. Place the truffles on a parchment-lined cookie sheet and chill until serving.

Caramel Cream Cheese Frosting

This delicious frosting is good on all sorts of cakes, such as Applesauce Spice Cake (page 437), Banana Cake (page 444), or Devil's Food Cake (page 443).

Makes 2½ cups, enough to ice a 9-inch double layer cake, 2 loaf cakes, or one 9 by 13-inch cake.

³⁄₄ **cup sugar**
½ **cup heavy cream**
½ **teaspoon kosher salt**
1½ **cups (12 ounces) cream cheese, at room temperature**
6 **tablespoons (³⁄₄ stick) unsalted butter, at room temperature**

In a medium saucepan, combine the sugar with ¼ cup cold water. Set over medium-high heat and stir to dissolve the sugar. Bring to a boil and cook until the bubbles get slower, the syrup thickens, and the sugar starts to darken and caramelize, 8 to 10 minutes. The color change will begin in one or two sections of the pan. As soon as you see it, start swirling the pan so that you even out the caramelization process. Don't leave the pan, as the sugar can turn from caramelized to burnt very quickly. Keep swirling until the sugar has turned a dark, deep, mahogany caramel color. Remove from the heat and immediately but carefully pour in the heavy cream to stop the cooking. The caramel will bubble and froth at first, but if you keep swirling or stirring with a wooden spoon, it will settle down to a nice, thick, rich-looking sauce. Stir in the salt. Transfer to a small bowl and cool to room temperature, about 1 hour. The caramel will thicken considerably as it cools. You should have about ³⁄₄ cup.

In an electric mixer fitted with a paddle or in a heavy bowl with a wooden spoon, beat together the cream cheese and butter, scraping down the sides, until smooth and light. Beat in the cooled caramel until well blended, about 2 minutes. You can use the icing as is or chill it to stiffen somewhat before you put it on a cake.

PREP TIME: 10 minutes
COOKING TIME: 15 minutes
TOTAL TIME: 1½ hours (includes cooling time)

VARIATION
Caramel Sauce

Stop after you have added the cream to the caramel and you have a delicious sauce for ice cream, cakes, and other desserts.

Lemon Curd

This lemony custard can be used as a filling for cakes, tarts, or even crêpes. It's also delicious on its own.
Makes 1½ cups

> Finely grated zest of 1 lemon
> ¾ cup fresh lemon juice (from about 3 lemons)
> ¾ cup sugar
> ½ cup (1 stick) butter
> 6 large egg yolks

In a small saucepan, combine the lemon zest, juice, sugar, and butter. Set over medium-low heat and bring to a simmer, stirring to dissolve the sugar. Place the egg yolks in a medium bowl and whisk to blend. While continuing to whisk, pour about ½ cup of the hot lemon mixture into the yolks to temper them, then whisk in the rest. Return the mixture to the pot and set over low heat. Cook, whisking continuously, until the curd begins to thicken, 3 or 4 minutes.

The curd should not simmer or boil or it will curdle. Remove from the heat, strain into a bowl, and cover with plastic wrap pressed right onto the surface of the curd. Chill for several hours until firm.

TOTAL TIME: 10 minutes (plus chilling time)

VARIATIONS
Lime Curd

Substitute lime zest and juice for the lemon zest and juice.

Cranberry Curd

You can make a delicious crimson-colored curd by substituting ¾ cup unsweetened cranberry juice and 1 tablespoon lemon juice for the lemon juice and zest in the recipe. To make your own cranberry juice, in a saucepan combine 2 cups fresh cranberries and ½ cup orange juice or water and simmer, covered, for 20 minutes, or until soft. Mash the berries with a potato masher and pass through a fine-mesh sieve or a food mill fitted with a fine-holed disk. If necessary, add more orange or lemon juice to make ¾ cup.

Rhubarb Curd

Substitute 1½ pounds rhubarb cut into 1-inch chunks for the cranberries to make rhubarb juice (see Cranberry Curd) and then use this juice in place of the lemon juice and zest in the recipe.

Pomegranate Curd

Substitute ⅔ cup unsweetened pomegranate juice and 2 tablespoons fresh lemon juice for the lemon juice and zest in the recipe.

Chocolate Pudding

This childhood favorite pleases adults equally well. In this recipe, three types of chocolate produce a deep, dark chocolate flavor.

Makes about 2½ cups, enough for 6 servings

1¾ cups milk

½ cup sugar

2 ounces semisweet or bittersweet chocolate, chopped

2 ounces unsweetened chocolate, chopped

2 tablespoons cornstarch

1 tablespoon unsweetened cocoa powder (not Dutch-processed)

½ cup heavy cream or additional milk

1 teaspoon pure vanilla extract

Pinch of kosher salt

1 to 2 tablespoons unsalted butter (optional)

Combine the milk, sugar, and semisweet and unsweetened chocolates in a medium saucepan and scald over medium heat until almost boiling. Whisk once or twice to encourage the chocolate to melt evenly and prevent scorching.

Meanwhile, in a small bowl, combine the cornstarch and cocoa powder. Using a fork, beat in about half of the cream to form a paste without lumps. Add the rest of the cream and beat until smooth. Whisk this mixture into the scalded milk and keep heating until the mixture thickens and comes to a boil. Turn down the heat to low and simmer for about 7 minutes, whisking occasionally until the starchy consistency has cooked out.

Remove from the heat and stir in the vanilla, salt, and butter, if using, until melted. The pudding will seem loose, but it will thicken as it chills. Divide into serving cups and serve warm or chilled. To chill, place a piece of plastic wrap over each cup and press down so the plastic is pressing on the surface of the warm pudding (this will prevent a skin from forming).

PREP TIME: 7 minutes

COOKING TIME: 10 minutes

TOTAL TIME: 20 minutes

ADVANCE PREP *The chocolate pudding can be made two or three days in advance. Serve chilled.*
LEFTOVERS *The pudding will keep for about one week in the refrigerator.*

VARIATIONS

Mocha Pudding

Substitute ½ cup strong, cold coffee for the heavy cream.

Butterscotch Pudding

Omit both chocolates and the cocoa. Substitute ⅔ cup dark brown sugar for the ½ cup granulated sugar. Increase the cornstarch to 3 tablespoons and stir in the butter at the end.

Rice Pudding

This is a deliciously rich rice pudding made on top of the stove. Use medium- or long-grain white rice, not converted or instant. You can change the seasonings as you wish, adding cardamom pods, saffron threads, bay leaf, star anise, or any spices instead of or in addition to the cinnamon.

Makes 6 servings

> 2 tablespoons unsalted butter
> One 2-inch cinnamon stick
> 2 long strips orange or lemon zest (use a
>   vegetable peeler)
> Pinch of kosher salt
> ¾ cup medium- or long-grain white rice
> 1½ cups milk
> 2 cups heavy cream or half-and-half
> ½ cup sugar
> ½ cup raisins, dried cherries, or dried cranberries
>   (optional)
> 1 teaspoon pure vanilla extract

In a medium saucepan, combine 1¾ cups water with the butter, cinnamon stick, orange zest, and salt, and bring to a boil. Add the rice, stir, bring back to a boil, stir again, cover, lower the heat, and simmer over medium-low heat until all of the liquid has evaporated and the rice is tender, about 20 minutes.

Add the milk, 1½ cups cream, sugar, and raisins, if using, and cook over low heat, stirring frequently, until the mixture thickens and becomes creamy, about 25 minutes. Remove the cinnamon stick and zest. Stir in the vanilla and the remaining ½ cup cream and serve warm or chilled.

PREP TIME: 5 minutes
COOKING TIME: 55 minutes
TOTAL TIME: 1 hour

ADVANCE PREP *The rice pudding can be made a day or two in advance and refrigerated. It hardens* *somewhat when chilled. Remove from the fridge for about ½ hour and stir it up before serving.*
LEFTOVERS *The pudding will keep for about a week in the fridge.*

Bourbon Bread-and-Butter Pudding

Like an ordinary bread pudding, only richer and yummier. The brown sugar and bourbon combine to produce a delicate butterscotch flavor. Substitute stale panettone for the bread for a delicious variation.

Makes about 8 servings

> ¼ cup bourbon or dark rum
> ½ cup raisins
> ½ cup (1 stick) unsalted butter, at room
>   temperature
> 7 or 8 slices stale white bread, preferably from a
>   good bakery loaf
> About ⅓ cup light or dark brown sugar
> 4 large eggs
> ½ cup granulated sugar
> 4 cups milk, or 2 cups milk and 2 cups light or
>   heavy cream
> ¼ teaspoon kosher salt
> 1 teaspoon pure vanilla extract
> ¼ teaspoon ground cinnamon (optional)

Preheat the oven to 325°F. Pour the bourbon over the raisins and let soak. Butter a 2-quart baking dish. Generously butter one side of each of the pieces of bread. Sprinkle the buttered side evenly with the brown sugar and arrange the slices in an attractive pattern, sugared side up, on the bottom of the baking dish, overlapping them if necessary.

In a bowl, whisk together the eggs and the

granulated sugar. Beat in the milk. Add the raisins and bourbon, the salt, vanilla, and cinnamon, if using. Pour this mixture into the baking dish over the bread. Let sit at room temperature for about 30 minutes.

Bake for about 1 hour, or until the pudding has risen, set, and browned. Serve warm. The pudding will deflate as it cools.

PREP TIME: 15 minutes
COOKING TIME: 1 hour
TOTAL TIME: 1 hour 15 minutes

ADVANCE PREP *Before baking, the pudding can be assembled, covered, and refrigerated up to a day in advance.*

LEFTOVERS *The pudding will keep in the refrigerator for about a week. Serve it cold, room temperature, or reheated.*

VARIATION
Panettone Bread Pudding
Substitute ½ pound stale panettone, cubed, for the white bread. Omit the butter and brown sugar. Add the panettone to the egg mixture, pour into a buttered baking dish, let sit, and bake as directed above.

Chocolate Crème Brûlée
Somewhere between chocolate mousse and a molten chocolate cake, this crème brûlée is impossibly rich and delicious. If you don't want to bother brûléeing, simply serve it with a dollop of whipped cream.
Makes 12 to 16 servings

9 large egg yolks
1 cup granulated sugar

3¼ cups heavy cream
¾ cup milk
½ vanilla bean, split and scraped, or ½ teaspoon pure vanilla extract
8 ounces bittersweet chocolate, chopped
½ cup turbinado or light brown sugar

Preheat the oven to 325°F.

In the bowl of an electric mixer fitted with a whisk attachment, combine the egg yolks and ½ cup of the granulated sugar. Beat on high until the egg yolks are thick, golden yellow, and tripled in volume, about 10 minutes.

Meanwhile, in a medium saucepan, combine the cream, milk, the remaining ½ cup granulated sugar, and the vanilla bean, if using (add the extract later). Set over medium heat and cook just until the mixture is about to boil. Remove from the heat. Remove the vanilla bean pod and add the chocolate, stirring to melt. Beat about 1 cup of the chocolate mixture into the egg yolk mixture to temper the yolks, and then combine the two and mix well. Stir in the vanilla extract, if using. Divide the mixture among 12 to 16 ramekins or custard cups, 4 to 6 ounces each.

Place the ramekins in a baking dish and fill the dish with hot water to come halfway up the sides of the ramekins. Bake until set, 40 to 45 minutes. Carefully remove the pan from the oven and cool to room temperature. Remove the ramekins from the bath, wrap tightly with plastic wrap, and chill for several hours or overnight.

Set a rack 2 to 6 inches from the heating element and preheat the broiler for 10 minutes. Unwrap the ramekins and dab the top with paper towels to remove any moisture that may have accumulated. Coat the top of each custard with an even layer of turbinado sugar. Set the ramekins on a cookie sheet and broil until the sugar has melted evenly and caramelized, watching closely and moving the ramekins around to ensure even heating, a minute or two.

PREP TIME: 20 minutes

COOKING TIME: 1 hour

TOTAL TIME: 8 hours (includes chilling time)

ADVANCE PREP *The custards can be made up to a week in advance and stored in the refrigerator until needed. Brûlée the sugar on top just before serving.*

Halvah Pots de Crème

This rich pudding is flavored with halvah, a sweet Middle Eastern sesame paste confection that's like a sandy sesame fudge. The recipe was created by Todd Aarons, chef of Mosaica restaurant in New Jersey. Halvah is available fresh, by the pound, in specialty markets, or canned in the ethnic food section of most grocery stores.

Makes 8 servings

- 8 ounces plain or vanilla halvah
- 2 cups regular, plain soy, or almond milk
- 8 large egg yolks
- 1 large egg
- 1/3 cup sugar
- 1/2 vanilla bean, split and scraped, or 1/2 teaspoon pure vanilla extract

Preheat the oven to 350°F.

Break the halvah into chunks and place in the bowl of a food processor fitted with a metal chopping blade along with 1 cup of the milk and purée until smooth. Add the egg yolks and

egg and process for a minute to blend. Transfer to a large bowl.

In a saucepan, combine the remaining 1 cup milk, the sugar, and vanilla and bring to a boil, being careful not to let the milk boil over. Stir to dissolve the sugar.

Temper the halvah mixture with a third of the hot milk mixture, whisking to blend. Gradually add in the remaining hot milk. Mix the ingredients well. Pass the custard through a fine strainer, and divide among eight 4-ounce ramekins or custard cups. Place the cups in a baking or roasting dish and fill with water to come halfway up the side of the cups, in a bain-marie.

Bake until the center of the cream is thick and viscous, about 35 minutes; you'll have a semi-liquid circle in the middle of each pudding about the diameter of a nickel. Carefully remove from the oven, and let the ramekins cool in the bain-marie to finish cooking. Chill before serving.

PREP TIME: 10 minutes

COOKING TIME: 40 minutes

TOTAL TIME: 50 minutes (plus chilling time)

LEFTOVERS *The puddings will keep in the refrigerator, tightly wrapped, for up to a week.*

VARIATION

Chocolate Sesame Pots de Crème

Add 2 ounces chopped unsweetened chocolate to the saucepan with the milk.

Buttermilk Panna Cotta

Although panna cotta is a popular dessert in Italy—the Italian answer to crème brûlée—these days I think it might be more common in restaurants in the United States. The name means "cooked cream," but more often than not it is neither made with cream (it's often milk) nor cooked (it's usually thickened with gelatin and chilled). I like this variation because of the refreshing tang given to the sweetened cream by the addition of buttermilk or yogurt.

Makes 6 servings

2 teaspoons unflavored gelatin
1 cup heavy cream
$1/2$ cup sugar
$1/2$ vanilla bean, split lengthwise and scraped, or $3/4$ teaspoon pure vanilla extract
2 cups buttermilk or plain yogurt thinned with milk

Place 2 tablespoons of cold water in a small dish and sprinkle the gelatin on top of the water. Let the gelatin sit for 10 minutes or so to swell and soften.

Meanwhile, in a small saucepan, combine the cream and sugar. Add the vanilla bean, if using. Bring the mixture to a boil, stirring with a wooden spoon until the sugar dissolves. Remove from the heat. Add the softened gelatin and stir until it has dissolved into the cream. Allow this mixture to cool to room temperature, about 45 minutes.

When cool, stir in the buttermilk. If using vanilla extract, add it now. Strain this mixture through a sieve into a large measuring cup or pitcher. Divide evenly among six $3/4$-cup custard cups or other molds. Chill in the fridge for at least 6 hours or overnight. To unmold, run a warm knife around the edge of the mold and invert on a chilled plate.

PREP TIME: 10 minutes
COOKING TIME: 5 minutes
TOTAL TIME: 1 hour (includes cooling time; plus chilling time)

ADVANCE PREP The panna cotta can be made and chilled up to two days in advance.
LEFTOVERS Keep the cups in an airtight container or individually wrapped in the fridge for four or five days.

Lemon Pick-Me-Up

It's hard to escape tiramisù on restaurant menus, Italian or otherwise. It's not that I don't love it, but sometimes you just want something different. Here it is: a lemon variation created by my friend Bonnie. The bright, sunny flavor of this superb dessert is enough to make anyone joyful.

Makes 10 to 12 servings

$1 1/4$ cups sugar
3 large egg whites
$1 1/2$ cups Lemon Curd (page 451), chilled
About 1 pound (one 500 g tub) imported mascarpone, at room temperature
$1/2$ cup fresh lemon juice (from 3 lemons)
$1/2$ cup limoncello or other sweet, lemon-flavored liqueur
$1/4$ cup vodka
$3/4$ pound savoiardi (Italian ladyfingers)
10 ounces white chocolate, in a solid block

In a small saucepan, combine $3/4$ cup of the sugar with $3/4$ cup water. Set over medium-high heat and bring to a boil to dissolve the sugar. Boil for about 5 minutes, until the bubbles start to get bigger and lazier and the syrup thickens (234°F or the soft-ball stage).

Meanwhile, place the egg whites in the bowl of an electric mixer. Whip the whites on high until they hold firm peaks. With the mixer still on high, slowly pour in the hot sugar syrup and keep beating until all of it is incorporated. Keep running the mixer on high until the bowl feels cool to the touch and the egg whites are satiny, 8 to 10 minutes.

Whisk the lemon curd into the mascarpone in a large bowl. Using a large rubber spatula, fold about one fourth of the Italian meringue into the mascarpone mixture to lighten it. Dump the remaining meringue into the bowl and fold in until light and blended. Chill.

Prepare the dipping syrup by combining the lemon juice and the remaining ½ cup sugar in a saucepan. Heat for 5 minutes or so to dissolve the sugar. Remove from the heat and stir in the limoncello and vodka. Transfer to a wide soup bowl and chill.

To assemble the tiramisù, spoon about 1 cup of the lemon-mascarpone filling onto the bottom of a 3-quart serving dish and spread it out evenly. Dip two or three savoiardi into the limoncello syrup, turn them over quickly, and remove, shaking off any excess syrup. They shouldn't be soaked through. Arrange the cookies on the bottom of the baking dish and repeat to make an even layer. Spoon enough lemon filling on top of the cookies to cover them generously in an even layer. Dip more cookies and repeat layering with the filling to fill the dish, ending with a layer of lemon filling.

To finish, hold the white chocolate over the dish. Using a vegetable peeler, shave the chocolate onto the top of the tiramisù in shards and curls to cover the top generously. Wrap the tiramisù with plastic and refrigerate for several hours or overnight before serving.

TOTAL TIME: 1 hour (plus chilling time)

ADVANCE PREP *The tiramisù is best if made a day or even two in advance and refrigerated.*
LEFTOVERS *It will keep for a week or so in the fridge.*

Maxine's Peanut Butter Cookies

This is another recipe from my friend Adam's mother, Maxine, an excellent cook and baker. These are her chewy, crunchy peanut butter cookies. No matter your politics or health concerns, don't use fancy, organic, all-natural, unsweetened peanut butter; these cookies are much better with the cheap stuff—I've tried them both ways. And although a peanut lover might be tempted to use crunchy, the added texture from the rolled oats in this recipe means creamy is really all that's needed.

Makes 3 dozen large cookies

> ½ cup (1 stick) unsalted butter, at room temperature
> ½ cup vegetable shortening, at room temperature
> 1 cup light brown sugar
> ¾ cup plus 2 tablespoons granulated sugar
> 2 large eggs
> 1 large egg yolk
> 1 teaspoon pure vanilla extract
> 1 (12-ounce) jar creamy peanut butter (slightly more than 1 cup)
> 2 cups all-purpose flour, plus additional flour for shaping

2 teaspoons baking soda
$^{1}/_{2}$ teaspoon kosher salt
1 cup quick-cooking rolled oats

Preheat the oven to 350°F.

In an electric mixer fitted with a paddle attachment or in a bowl with a wooden spoon, beat together the butter and shortening until blended. Add the brown sugar and $^{3}/_{4}$ cup of the granulated sugar and beat until light and fluffy. Beat in the eggs and egg yolk and the vanilla. Beat in the peanut butter. In a separate bowl, combine the flour, baking soda, and salt, and mix well. Thoroughly mix this flour mixture into the peanut butter mixture. Stir in the oats.

With lightly moistened hands, roll heaping tablespoons of the cookie dough into balls about $1^{1}/_{2}$ inches in diameter. Place the balls on an ungreased cookie sheet, leaving a good $1^{1}/_{2}$ inches or so between the balls—the cookies will spread as they bake. Place some flour in a small bowl. Dip the tines of a dinner fork into the flour, tap off the excess, and use the fork to press down on the balls of cookie dough to flatten. Dip the fork in flour again and press down in the opposite direction, creating a cross-hatch pattern on the cookie. Don't press the cookies thinner than $^{3}/_{8}$ inch thick. Sprinkle each cookie with a pinch of the remaining 2 tablespoons granulated sugar.

Bake for about 12 minutes, turning the tray once to ensure even baking. When done, the cookies will have risen, spread, and lightly browned. Hairline cracks will be evident on the surface. Remove from the oven. Let cool on the cookie sheet for a minute or so, then transfer to a wire rack to finish cooling, being careful not to break the cookies, which are quite delicate until they cool completely.

PREP TIME: 10 minutes
COOKING TIME: 35 to 40 minutes
TOTAL TIME: 45 minutes

ADVANCE PREP *The cookie dough can be made and stored in the refrigerator for three or four days before baking. Soften to room temperature before shaping.*
LEFTOVERS *The cookies will keep in an airtight container at room temperature for about a week or in the freezer for two months.*

VARIATION
Chocolate Chip Peanut Butter Cookies
Stir 1 cup (6 ounces) or so semisweet chocolate chips into the cookie dough along with the rolled oats.

Chocolate Chunk Cookies
At a chocolate chip cookie tasting organized by my friend Jennifer, a recipe devised by pastry chef Chris Broberg at Café Gray in New York won hands down. Here's my adaptation, which produces cookies that are buttery, crisp, and chewy, all at once, with loads of chocolate.
Makes 3 dozen cookies

2$^{1}/_{3}$ cups all-purpose flour
$^{1}/_{2}$ teaspoon baking soda
Pinch of kosher salt
$^{3}/_{4}$ cup (1$^{1}/_{2}$ sticks) unsalted butter, at room
    temperature
1 cup light brown sugar
1$^{1}/_{2}$ tablespoons light corn syrup
2 large eggs
$^{1}/_{2}$ teaspoon pure vanilla extract
14 ounces semisweet or bittersweet chocolate,
    chopped, or chocolate chips

MAILING BAKED GOODS

I'm forever mailing baked goods to friends and relatives—at Christmastime, for birthdays, or just to remind my niece Helen that I'm thinking of her while she's at college. I have also been on the receiving end of many baked goods sent through the mail. As a result, I have some sound advice for anyone thinking of posting pastries.

First off, you have to pick something to mail that will be durable enough to withstand the journey and that won't go stale. Hard, dry cookies, such as biscotti, are ideal, as are whole cakes that improve with age. To hedge a little, I freeze everything I mail, believing that frozen things are more durable and the time it takes to defrost will add to the shelf life of whatever I'm sending. Of course, if you are really concerned, you can ship your baked goods overnight or via two-day express mail. Next you need the right container. Whether you are mailing cookies or cakes, you need to be able to pack them snugly in an airtight tin or plastic container. Finally, you need the shipping supplies, which include a box or carton that you can pack the container in and Styrofoam peanuts or bubble wrap, which will help absorb any undue shocks. Packing tape is also key.

To illustrate exactly what I'm describing, here's how I recently shipped a birthday cake to my brother: I made his favorite Streusel Coffee-Cake (page 116), wrapped it in plastic, and froze it. I placed the cake, still wrapped, in a metal tin and sealed the tin with packing tape. I tied a ribbon on the tin and cushioned it in a shipping box with plenty of Styrofoam peanuts. On the peanuts I strew some colored confetti just to make it more festive. Then I stuck the whole thing in my freezer until the next morning, when I took it to the post office to mail. Word has it the cake arrived in perfect condition.

Preheat the oven to 325°F.

Sift together the flour, baking soda, and salt. Set aside.

Beat together the butter, brown sugar, and corn syrup until smooth. Beat in the eggs, one at a time, beating well after each addition. Beat in the vanilla. Stir in the flour mixture and just when it is almost fully incorporated, add the chocolate. Mix until the chocolate is evenly distributed, but don't overmix or the cookies will be tough.

Drop tablespoonfuls of cookie dough on ungreased cookie sheets, leaving about $1\frac{1}{2}$ inches between cookies. Bake for about 8 minutes, until the edges begin to brown and the centers have puffed and set. Remove from the oven, transfer to wire racks, and let cool completely before serving.

PREP TIME: 10 minutes
COOKING TIME: 25 minutes
TOTAL TIME: 35 minutes

ADVANCE PREP The cookie dough can be made in advance and stored in the refrigerator for up to a week until ready to bake. It can also be frozen for up to a month.
LEFTOVERS The cookies will keep for about five days at room temperature. They can be frozen for up to two months.

VARIATIONS

Chocolate Chunk Cookies with Nuts
Stir in $\frac{3}{4}$ cup toasted and chopped walnuts or pecans along with the chocolate and proceed with the recipe as directed.

Oatmeal Chocolate Chunk Cookies
Stir in $\frac{1}{2}$ cup quick-cooking rolled oats along with the chocolate and proceed with the recipe

as directed. The oats give these cookies a pleasant, chewy texture.

Buckwheat Hazelnut Cookies

The recipe for these delicious cookies was based on an Italian recipe adapted by Melissa Clark for the *New York Times*. I was intrigued because I love buckwheat in just about any form and I had never seen a recipe for buckwheat cookies. These cookies are both chewy and crumbly, like a shortbread but with more resistance, or like an English oat cake but with more flavor. The faintly grassy taste of buckwheat is softened by the toasted hazelnuts, and crunchy bits of salt linger on the tongue. They are a grown-up cookie, perfect as a light dessert after a cheese course.

Makes 2 dozen cookies

$1/2$ cup buckwheat flour

$1/2$ cup unbleached all-purpose flour

$1/3$ cup sugar

$1/4$ teaspoon fleur de sel or other coarse salt

$1/4$ teaspoon baking powder

$1/4$ cup hazelnuts or $1/3$ cup walnuts, toasted (see page 10)

Finely grated zest of $1/2$ orange (optional)

$1/2$ cup (1 stick) unsalted butter, cut into $1/2$-inch chunks, chilled

1 large egg yolk

1 teaspoon pure vanilla extract

In the bowl of a food processor fitted with a metal chopping blade, combine the flours, sugar, salt, baking powder, and nuts. Pulse the machine on and off ten to fifteen times until the nuts are finely ground. Scrape down the sides of the work bowl. Add the orange zest, if using, and pulse once or twice. Add the butter and continue pulsing until the butter has also been finely ground, about ten times; the mixture will begin to clump. Scrape down the sides. Add the egg yolk and the vanilla and continue to pulse until the mixture forms a dough that starts to ball around the blade. Be sure the dough is evenly mixed.

Lay a piece of plastic wrap on the counter. Dump the cookie dough out of the food processor onto the plastic. Bunch up and roll the dough to form a log about $1\frac{1}{2}$ inches in diameter and wrap in the plastic. Chill for at least an hour or two.

Preheat the oven to 325°F. Line a cookie sheet with parchment paper or a silicone mat. Slice the dough in $1/2$-inch-thick rounds and place on the cookie sheet, leaving about $1\frac{1}{2}$ inches between cookies.

Bake the cookies for 18 to 20 minutes, turning the tray once to ensure even baking, until slightly puffed and browned around the edges. Remove from the oven and let cool on the pan for 5 minutes before transferring to a wire rack to cool completely.

PREP TIME: 15 minutes

COOKING TIME: 40 minutes

TOTAL TIME: 55 minutes (plus cooling time)

ADVANCE PREP *The cookie dough can be made up to three days in advance and refrigerated or frozen for up to a month before baking.*

LEFTOVERS *The cookies will keep for two or three days at room temperature in an airtight container or in the freezer for up to two months.*

Oatmeal Buttermilk Cookies

These cookies are both crisp and chewy. For mix-ins I alternate between raisins and chocolate chips, depending on my mood.

Makes 4 to 5 dozen cookies

- 1 1/2 cups all-purpose flour
- 1 teaspoon baking soda
- 3/4 teaspoon ground cinnamon
- 1/2 teaspoon kosher salt
- 1/2 cup (1 stick) unsalted butter, at room temperature
- 1/2 cup vegetable shortening or lard, at room temperature
- 3/4 cup granulated sugar
- 3/4 cup light brown sugar
- 2 large eggs
- 1 teaspoon pure vanilla extract
- 1/4 cup buttermilk
- Finely grated zest of 1 orange
- 3 cups old-fashioned or quick-cooking rolled oats (not instant)
- 1/2 cup chopped toasted walnuts (see page 10)
- 2/3 cup raisins or chocolate chips

Preheat the oven to 350°F. Line two cookie sheets with parchment paper or silicone mats, or grease them lightly with butter.

In a medium bowl, stir together the flour, baking soda, cinnamon, and salt. In a large bowl, by hand or with an electric mixer, beat together the butter and vegetable shortening. Beat in the sugars until the mixture is thoroughly blended. Add the eggs, beating after each one. Add the vanilla, buttermilk, and orange zest, and keep beating until the mixture is light and fluffy. Add the flour mixture to the butter mixture and mix until thoroughly com-

bined. Stir in the oats, walnuts, and raisins, and mix until evenly distributed.

Drop the cookie batter by heaping teaspoonfuls onto the prepared cookie sheets, leaving about 2 inches between them. Bake for 10 to 12 minutes, or until the cookies have spread and browned. Let cool for 1 minute on the pan and then transfer to a wire rack to cool completely.

PREP TIME: 20 minutes
COOKING TIME: 30 to 40 minutes
TOTAL TIME: 50 minutes (plus cooling time)

ADVANCE PREP *The cookie dough can be made in advance and refrigerated for up to two or three days or frozen for up to a month. Shape into a log and wrap in waxed paper and plastic wrap. Then slice the log just under 1/2 inch thick to bake.*
LEFTOVERS *The cookies will keep in an airtight container at room temperature for four days. Or they can be frozen for up to two months.*

Lavender Cookies

These delicate butter cookies are perfumed with lavender and dipped in dark or white chocolate. Even people who think they don't like lavender end up addicted.

Makes about 3 1/2 dozen cookies

- 1 cup (2 sticks) unsalted butter, at room temperature
- 2/3 cup sugar
- 1 large egg
- 1/2 teaspoon pure vanilla extract or the finely grated zest of 1/2 lemon
- 1 1/2 cups all-purpose flour

1 tablespoon fresh lavender buds, roughly chopped

8 ounces bittersweet chocolate or white chocolate, melted

Preheat the oven to 350°F. Line two cookie sheets with parchment paper or a silicone mat, or lightly grease with butter.

In a medium bowl, beat together the butter and sugar until smooth and creamy. Beat in the egg and vanilla. Stir in the flour and lavender just until blended.

Drop heaping teaspoonfuls of the dough onto the cookie sheets, leaving about $1\frac{1}{2}$ inches between them. Bake for 14 to 15 minutes, until the edges of the cookies have browned. Remove from the oven and transfer to wire racks to cool.

Turn over the parchment. Either dip the cookies into or drizzle with the melted chocolate, set them on the parchment, and chill for a few minutes to harden.

PREP TIME: 20 minutes

COOKING TIME: 30 minutes

TOTAL TIME: 50 minutes (plus chilling time)

LEFTOVERS *The cookies will keep for four or five days at room temperature or they can be frozen for up to one month.*

Salty Chocolate Sablés

Created by famous French pastry chef Pierre Hermé, adapted by famous American cookbook author Dorie Greenspan, and first prepared for me by my friend Hannah, these intensely flavored chocolate cookies with a sandy texture and salty aftertaste are simply amazing. Here is my version.

Makes 3 dozen cookies

$1\frac{1}{4}$ cups all-purpose flour

$\frac{1}{3}$ cup Dutch-processed unsweetened cocoa powder

$\frac{1}{2}$ teaspoon baking soda

$\frac{3}{4}$ cup ($1\frac{1}{2}$ sticks) unsalted butter, at room temperature

$\frac{2}{3}$ cup light brown sugar

$\frac{1}{4}$ cup granulated sugar

$\frac{1}{2}$ teaspoon fleur de sel or Maldon salt, or $\frac{1}{4}$ teaspoon fine sea salt

1 teaspoon pure vanilla extract

5 ounces bittersweet chocolate, finely chopped

Sift together the flour, cocoa, and baking soda.

Beat the butter with the sugars until smooth and creamy. Add the salt and vanilla. Stir in the dry ingredients to form a crumbly dough. Add the chocolate, and stir just to distribute. Don't overmix the dough. Turn the dough out onto a clean work surface and divide it in half. Work one half into a log about $1\frac{1}{2}$ inches in diameter; it may seem too dry at first but the heat of your hands will help make the dough cohere. Repeat with the remaining dough. Wrap in plastic and chill for at least 1 hour.

Preheat the oven to 325°F. Line two cookie sheets with parchment paper or silicone mats.

Slice the dough into $\frac{1}{2}$-inch-thick rounds and place the rounds on the parchment-lined pans. If they fall apart, press the pieces back together. Bake for 12 minutes, until set. They will look pretty much the same as when they went in the oven, but they will now hold their shape. Let cool on the pan to room temperature.

PREP TIME: 15 minutes

COOKING TIME: 25 minutes

TOTAL TIME: $1\frac{1}{2}$ hours (includes chilling time)

ADVANCE PREP *The cookie dough can be refrigerated for up to three days and frozen for up to a month. Slice and bake the dough from the freezer, increasing the baking time by a minute or two.*
LEFTOVERS *The cookies will keep at room temperature for about four days. They can be frozen for up to a month.*

Ginger Snaps

More chewy than snappy, these intensely flavored cookies are delicious with vanilla ice cream.
Makes 2½ dozen cookies

- ¾ cup (1½ sticks) unsalted butter, plus extra for greasing the pans, at room temperature
- 2 cups unbleached all-purpose flour
- 2 teaspoons baking soda
- 1 tablespoon ground ginger
- 1 teaspoon ground cinnamon
- Pinch of ground cloves
- ½ teaspoon kosher salt
- ¼ teaspoon freshly ground white pepper
- 1 cup dark brown sugar
- 1 large egg
- 1 tablespoon molasses
- 2 teaspoons grated fresh ginger
- 1 teaspoon finely grated lemon zest
- About ½ cup granulated sugar

Preheat the oven to 350°F and butter two cookie sheets or line with parchment paper.

Sift together the flour, baking soda, ground ginger, cinnamon, cloves, salt, and pepper. Set aside.

In an electric mixer fitted with a paddle attachment or by hand, beat the butter and brown sugar until smooth and creamy. Beat in the egg, and then add the molasses, fresh ginger, and lemon zest. Stir in the flour mixture to form a stiff dough.

Roll tablespoonfuls of the dough into balls in the palms of your hands and then roll the balls in the granulated sugar. Place the balls on the cookie sheets about 2 inches apart. Bake for 10 to 12 minutes, or until the cookies have spread and the tops have crackled. Remove from the cookie sheets to cool on wire racks.

PREP TIME: 10 minutes
COOKING TIME: 30 minutes
TOTAL TIME: 40 minutes (plus cooling time)

ADVANCE PREP *The cookie dough can be made a day or two in advance and refrigerated until ready to bake.*
LEFTOVERS *The cookies will keep four or five days at room temperature or up to a month in the freezer.*

Potato Chip Cookies

Before you write these delicious, crunchy, buttery, chewy, salty cookies off as some crazy whim, let me just say that I first made these with my stepgrandfather, Ken, when I was twelve years old. This was his recipe, sort of, and that makes them a classic. Don't make the mistake I once did of buying gourmet potato chips. They are too thick and taste too much like real potatoes for these cookies. The thinner and cheaper the chips, the better.
Makes about 3 dozen cookies

- 1 medium (2¾-ounce) package plain salted potato chips, about 3 cups

1 cup (2 sticks) unsalted butter, at room
    temperature
1 cup confectioners' sugar
1 large egg yolk
1 teaspoon pure vanilla extract
1 1/2 cups unbleached all-purpose flour
1/2 cup pecan halves, toasted (see page 10)

Preheat the oven to 350°F. Line two cookie sheets with parchment.

Using a rolling pin, crush the potato chips in the bag they came in (open it first to let out the air) or in a resealable plastic bag. You should have 1 cup of crushed chips. (Alternatively, you can crush them in a food processor with a metal chopping blade.)

In the bowl of a mixer or by hand, beat the butter and sugar until smooth. Add the egg yolk and vanilla and blend. Gradually stir in the flour; then add the potato chips and pecans. Drop tablespoonfuls of the dough onto the prepared sheets with enough room for the cookies to spread.

Bake for 12 minutes, or until the cookies have spread and browned nicely around the edges. Remove the pans from the oven and let cool for 5 minutes. Transfer the cookies to a wire rack to cool completely.

PREP TIME: 10 minutes
COOKING TIME: 30 minutes
TOTAL TIME: 40 minutes

ADVANCE PREP The cookie dough can be made in advance and refrigerated for two or three days before baking.
LEFTOVERS The cookies will keep in an airtight container at room temperature for about a week or in the freezer for up to two months.

Almond Biscotti

Biscotti means "twice cooked," and most recipes for biscotti are indeed cooked two times, once as a log and a second time as individual cookies. This is a recipe for Prato's famous almond biscotti. They can be quite hard, so they are traditionally dipped into sweet Vin Santo wine to soften them. They are pretty good dipped in cappuccino or tea, also.

Makes 3 dozen cookies

1 cup blanched almonds, toasted (see page 10)
    and coarsely chopped
1 3/4 cups all-purpose flour
1 cup sugar
1 teaspoon baking powder
Pinch of kosher salt
Finely grated zest of 1 lemon or orange
2 large eggs
1 teaspoon pure vanilla extract

Preheat the oven to 375°F. Line a cookie sheet with parchment.

In a medium bowl, combine the almonds, flour, sugar, baking powder, salt, and lemon zest. In a separate bowl, beat the eggs with the vanilla until frothy. Pour the eggs into the dry ingredients and mix to form a stiff dough. Turn out onto a clean work surface and knead until the mixture is smooth. Divide the dough into thirds and shape each third into a log about 1 1/2 inches thick. Place on the parchment-lined cookie sheet, leaving room for them to spread a little, and bake for about 30 minutes, or until they are firm.

Remove from the oven and let cool. Turn the oven temperature down to 325°F. Using a sharp serrated knife, slice the cookies on the diagonal about 1 inch thick. Lay the cookies on the cookie sheet cut side up and bake for 10 more minutes. Turn them over and bake for another 10 minutes. Remove from the oven and cool completely.

PREP TIME: 15 minutes

COOKING TIME: 1 hour 10 minutes

TOTAL TIME: 1 hour 25 minutes

LEFTOVERS *The cookies will keep at room temperature in an airtight container for up to three weeks. They can also be frozen for up to two months.*

Lemon Squares

My mother always kept lemon squares and brownies in her freezer, and that freezer was always our first stop when we visited. These bar cookies are best when freshly made, but they are pretty good eaten right out of the freezer, too.

Makes 16 squares

FOR THE CRUST

$1/2$ cup (1 stick) unsalted butter, at room temperature

$1/4$ cup confectioners' sugar, plus extra for dusting

Grated zest of $1/2$ lemon

Pinch of kosher salt

1 cup all-purpose flour

FOR THE FILLING

2 large eggs

1 cup granulated sugar

2 tablespoons all-purpose flour

$1/4$ cup fresh lemon juice (from 1 to $1 1/2$ lemons)

Grated zest of $1/2$ lemon

Preheat the oven to 350°F.

To prepare the crust, beat together the butter and confectioners' sugar until blended. Stir in the lemon zest and the salt. Beat in the flour to form a smooth dough. Dump the dough into the bottom of an 8-inch square baking pan and press it with your fingertips to form an even layer. Bake for 20 minutes, just until the crust has set and begun to brown. Remove from the oven and cool on a wire rack.

For the filling, whisk together the eggs, sugar, flour, lemon juice, and zest. Pour this mixture over the crust and bake for 20 to 25 minutes, or until just barely set. Remove from the oven and cool completely in the pan on a wire rack. Cut into squares and dust with additional confectioners' sugar before serving.

PREP TIME: 10 minutes

COOKING TIME: 40 minutes

TOTAL TIME: 50 minutes

LEFTOVERS *The lemon squares will keep at room temperature for up to five days. They can be frozen for up to two months.*

VARIATION
Cranberry Squares
Substitute $1/4$ cup pure, unsweetened cranberry juice (see page 451) for the lemon juice and proceed with the recipe as directed.

Brownies

Bakers are forever trying to find the richest, chocolatiest brownie recipe, but I think this old standby wins when you consider how easy the recipe is and how good the brownies are. You don't even have to dirty a mixing bowl. The secret, as with all brownies, is not to over-bake them so they remain fudgy.

Makes 16 brownies

½ cup (1 stick) unsalted butter
2 ounces unsweetened chocolate
1 cup sugar
2 large eggs
1 teaspoon pure vanilla extract
¾ cup all-purpose flour
½ cup chopped toasted walnuts or pecans (see page 10)

Preheat the oven to 350°F.

In a small saucepan, melt the butter and chocolate over medium-low heat. Be careful not to scorch the chocolate. Remove from the heat. Add the sugar and stir to dissolve. Add the eggs, one at a time, and stir in the vanilla. Stir in the flour and nuts. Pour the batter into an 8-inch square pan and set in the oven to bake for 20 to 25 minutes, just until the sides of the brownies begin to pull away from the pan and the middle has barely set. Remove from the oven, cool for 10 minutes or so, and cut into squares.

PREP TIME: 5 minutes
COOKING TIME: 20 minutes
TOTAL TIME: 25 minutes (plus cooling time)

LEFTOVERS *The brownies will keep for three or four days at room temperature or they can be frozen for up to two months.*

Rugelach

These flaky, rolled cookies are made with cream cheese pastry (see page 431) and filled with jam, raisins, and nuts. You can use any combination of jam and fillings. My favorite is apricot with walnuts, but raspberry jam and chocolate chips are also a delicious combination.

Makes 4 dozen rugelach

1 batch Cream Cheese Pastry (see page 431)
½ cup apricot or other jam
½ cup golden raisins or currants
½ cup chopped toasted walnuts or other nuts (see page 10)
1 egg beaten with 1 tablespoon cold water
Coarse sugar or turbinado sugar

Preheat the oven to 425°F. Line two cookie sheets with parchment paper.

Divide the dough into quarters and work with only one quarter at a time, keeping the rest chilled. On a lightly floured surface, roll out a quarter of the dough to a circle about 10 inches in diameter. Spread the dough evenly with about one fourth of the jam, right out to the edges. Sprinkle with raisins and nuts. Cut the circle of dough in half and then cut each half into five or six wedges or triangles. Don't worry too much if they aren't perfectly shaped—you'll be able to fix them when you roll them up. Use a thin spatula to loosen a triangle of dough off the counter. Starting from the wide end of the triangle, roll it up tightly like a miniature crescent roll. Tuck in the ends and turn them in to form a crescent and transfer to the prepared cookie sheets. Repeat, rolling up the remaining triangles. Leave about an inch of space between the rugelach so they can expand. Keep the tray of rugelach refrigerated while you work with the remaining dough.

When all of the dough is shaped, brush the rugelach lightly with the egg and sprinkle each

Candied Citrus Peel

A couple of times a year I make candied citrus peels to keep in the fridge so I have them to bake with. They last forever. I like to leave a little bit of the white pith on the zest to add a little bitterness to the sweet peel. The corn syrup helps keep the candied peel soft.

Makes as much zest as you have

> The peel of lemons, oranges, or grapefruits, cut into large sections or thin strips
> 1 cup sugar, plus extra for rolling
> 2 tablespoons corn syrup (optional)

Place the peels in a small saucepan and cover with cold water. Bring to a boil, turn down the heat, and simmer for 7 or 8 minutes. Drain. Place the peels back in the pot and cover with cold water again. Bring to a boil, simmer for 7 or 8 minutes more, and drain. Repeat twice more for a total of four blanchings. Set the peels aside.

In the same saucepan, combine the sugar and corn syrup, if using, with 1 cup water. You will need enough liquid to submerge the peel. If you need more, increase the sugar and water in the same proportions. Set over medium-high heat and bring to a boil, stirring to dissolve the sugar. Simmer for 5 minutes and then add the peel and simmer very gently for about 30 minutes, or until the peel is soft and almost translucent. Remove from the heat, cover, and let sit overnight.

The next day, gently heat again to melt the syrup. Lift the peel out of the pan, drain, and lay across a wire rack to dry for an hour or so. Roll the peel in sugar, and return to the rack to dry out completely for several hours. Roll in more sugar and store in an airtight container in the refrigerator.

PREP TIME: 30 minutes

COOKING TIME: 1 hour 10 minutes

TOTAL TIME: 9½ hours (includes resting time)

LEFTOVERS Candied peel will keep in the refrigerator for six months or more.

with a pinch of the sugar. Bake for 15 to 20 minutes, until the rugelach have risen and browned. Don't fret about any jam that has oozed out during baking. Remove from the oven and while still warm, carefully lift the rugelach off the paper and let cool on a wire rack.

PREP TIME: 30 minutes

COOKING TIME: 1 hour

TOTAL TIME: 1½ hours (plus cooling time)

ADVANCE PREP The rugelach are best freshly baked but they can be frozen for up to two months before baking.

Butterscotch Shortbread

Based on a recipe of my friend Karla's, this shortbread has a distinct butterscotch flavor because of the brown sugar. The rice flour produces a delicate texture.

Makes 16 to 24 cookies

> 1½ cups unbleached all-purpose flour
> ½ cup rice flour or cornstarch
> 1 cup (2 sticks) unsalted butter, at room temperature
> 1 cup light or dark brown sugar
> ½ teaspoon pure vanilla extract
> Pinch of salt

Preheat the oven to 325°F.

Blend the flours and set aside. With an electric mixer or by hand, beat the butter and brown sugar until light and creamy. Beat in the vanilla and the salt. Stir in the flour mixture. The shortbread will be crumbly, but that's okay. Dump into a 9-inch pie plate or spring-form pan or an 8-inch square pan. Press the mixture with your fingertips to form an even layer. Prick the shortbread all over with the tines of a fork. Bake for about 40 minutes, or until the edges have visibly browned and the middle has bubbled and set.

Remove from the oven and let cool for 15 minutes. While still warm, cut the shortbread into pieces, but don't remove them from the pan. Cool completely to room temperature before unmolding.

PREP TIME: 10 minutes

COOKING TIME: 40 minutes

TOTAL TIME: 50 minutes (plus cooling time)

ADVANCE PREP *The cookies are actually better the day after they are baked. Wrap tightly and keep at room temperature.*

LEFTOVERS *The shortbread will keep for about a week at room temperature in an airtight container, and up to four months frozen.*

Pumpkin Seed Brittle

This brittle comes out so beautifully translucent it looks like amber stained glass. The cumin is a tasty surprise. The recipe was adapted from Guy Reuge, chef/owner of Mirabelle on Long Island. He served it at his dinner at the James Beard House, and our staff loved it so much we wanted to know how to make it. Even better than how good it is to eat is how easy it is to make.

Makes about 2 pounds

$3/4$ teaspoon kosher salt

$3/8$ teaspoon baking soda

$1/2$ teaspoon ground cumin

$1 1/2$ cups sugar

$1/4$ cup light corn syrup

$2 1/2$ tablespoons unsalted butter, plus extra for greasing the pan

$1 3/4$ cups shelled raw pumpkin seeds (pepitas), toasted (see page 10)

Invert a cookie sheet and grease the bottom (now the top) with butter or place a silicone mat or piece of parchment on a clean work surface. In a small dish, combine the salt, baking soda, and cumin.

In a heavy saucepan, combine the sugar and corn syrup with $1/4$ cup water. Stir to combine and remove any lumps. Add the butter and set over medium heat. Bring to a simmer, stirring almost continuously. The mixture will become white and frothy. Keep simmering and stirring until the mixture turns to a medium-brown caramel, about 15 minutes. It will darken slowly at first and then go more quickly, becoming less frothy all the while. Remove from the heat and immediately whisk in the baking soda and cumin mixture. (Careful, the mixture will foam up, almost doubling in volume.) Quickly add the pumpkin seeds and stir until they are coated with the caramel. If the mixture hardens too much to stir or spread, set it over the heat for a minute or so to melt.

Pour the mixture onto the center of the prepared pan, and using a clean rolling pin, roll out to a $1/4$-inch thickness. The caramel may stick to the rolling pin at first, but as the mixture cools it will stop sticking; keep rolling. Cool completely. Break into bite-size pieces.

PREP TIME: 20 minutes

COOKING TIME: 15 minutes

TOTAL TIME: 35 minutes (plus cooling time)

LEFTOVERS *The brittle will keep at room temperature for about two weeks in an airtight container. It can be frozen for up to six months. Grind it up and use it as a topping for ice cream or in the center of a layer cake, anywhere you would use praline.*

VARIATION
Peanut Brittle

Follow the same directions, omitting the cumin and substituting 2 cups (10 ounces) of roasted peanuts, without their skin, for the pumpkin seeds. If the peanuts are salted, omit the salt in the recipe. Roll the finished brittle only ⅜ to ½ inch thick.

Almond Crack

Every year around holiday time I look forward to receiving a package of this bitter almond candy from my friend Karla. She calls it "crack" instead of brittle not only because it is hard and crunchy, meaning it cracks, but also because it is addictive like a drug. Luckily, she gave me the recipe so I can always get my fix. It's that rare candy recipe that doesn't require a special thermometer or any special technique.

Makes about 1 pound

   4 tablespoons (½ stick) unsalted butter

   2 cups slivered almonds

   1 cup light brown sugar

   Pinch of kosher salt

   1 teaspoon pure vanilla extract

Line a cookie sheet with aluminum foil and set aside.

In a heavy frying pan, melt the butter over medium heat. Add the almonds and stir so that they are totally coated with butter. Add the brown sugar and stir to distribute. Keep stirring until the sugar melts. The sugar goes through a few stages, first melting a little and then clumping and drying out as you stir. Don't despair, the nuts will toast while the mixture clumps. Keep stirring. After about 10 minutes the whole thing will suddenly loosen, start to ooze, and melt again. Stir for another minute or two until the mixture is really smooth and wet, the color of dark caramel, and it becomes a mass. If you smell the faintest burnt aroma, remove from the heat.

Remove the pan from the heat and quickly stir in the salt, and then the vanilla—be careful because it will splatter. Pour out onto the prepared cookie sheet and spread into a thin layer. Let cool to room temperature, about 20 minutes. Break apart into bite-size bits.

PREP TIME: 10 minutes

COOKING TIME: 15 minutes

TOTAL TIME: 25 minutes (plus cooling time)

LEFTOVERS *Keep the candy (hidden) at room temperature for up to a month or in the freezer for up to a year. For the first day or so, you may want to layer it between sheets of paper towels, as sometimes some of the butterfat sweats out of the crack. If you manage not to eat it all, you can grind leftover almond crack in a food processor and use it as a substitute for praline in dessert recipes or as a sprinkle for ice cream.*

Vanilla Cream Caramels

Though candy making is a craft that requires some time to master, these caramels are simple to make and the payoff—rich, buttery, chewy caramels with a deep flavor—is worth it. What makes them nearly foolproof is the substitution of condensed milk for the more traditional heavy cream. To assure success, you should have a candy thermometer, but that's about all you'll need. The most time-consuming part is wrapping them, but I do it in front of the television. I use cellophane bonbon wrappers that I mail-order online from Sweet Celebrations (www.sweetc.com), but you can also just use strips of waxed paper.

Makes 10 to 12 dozen

1 cup (2 sticks) unsalted butter, plus extra for greasing the pan

1 cup light corn syrup

2¼ cups sugar

½ teaspoon kosher salt

1 (14-ounce) can sweetened condensed milk

1 tablespoon pure vanilla extract

1 cup chopped toasted pecans, almonds, or hazelnuts (see page 10), optional

Very lightly butter a 9-inch square metal baking pan.

Melt the butter in a 3-quart saucepan over medium heat. Using a wooden spoon, add the corn syrup and stir to combine with the butter. Add the sugar and salt and stir until dissolved. Slowly add the condensed milk, stirring constantly. Bring the mixture to a boil, stirring all the while. Clip on a candy thermometer.

Cook over moderate heat, stirring constantly to prevent scorching, until the thermometer registers 248°F. The mixture will rise in temperature quickly at first, and then for the last 10 degrees it will rise much more slowly. The total cooking time should be 20 to 25 minutes. The mixture will not begin to color until around 238°F. At this point it is really important to keep stirring, and stirring pretty vigorously, making sure to cover the entire surface area of the bottom of the pot with the spoon to keep the mixture moving and prevent scorching. Resist the temptation to raise the heat.

As the mixture approaches 248°F, it will turn a deep caramel color. Right when it reaches 248°F, turn off the heat (or remove from the burner) and remove the thermometer. Stir it quickly for about 30 seconds, then let the mixture sit for 2 or 3 minutes. Stir in the vanilla extract and nuts, if using. It will sizzle as you stir the vanilla in. Once the mixture looks smooth again, pour it into the buttered pan. Make sure the pan is on a level surface and let it cool completely to room temperature, about 3 hours.

Unmold the caramel square onto a cutting board, and using a very sharp, heavy knife, cut it into ½-inch squares. Wrap each caramel in a strip of waxed paper or a little bonbon wrapper.

PREP TIME: 1 hour

COOKING TIME: 45 minutes

TOTAL TIME: 4 hours 45 minutes (includes cooling time and wrapping time)

LEFTOVERS *The caramels will keep at room temperature for four or five days before going stale. Wrapped in the freezer, they will keep more than six months. If you don't want to wrap all of the caramels or you don't need so many, you can store the leftovers in a block and melt them down to use in anything that calls for caramel.*

Chocolate Caramels

Add 2 ounces chopped unsweetened chocolate to the mixture at the beginning, after the butter is melted.

Hot Fudge Sauce

You'll never need another chocolate sauce recipe; this one is that good. I got the recipe years ago from pastry chef Dawn Rose, who was then at Olives in Boston. Because of all the other flavorings, you don't have to use the finest chocolate; even ordinary semisweet chocolate chips produce a delicious, chocolatey sauce.

Makes 1 quart

> 6 ounces semisweet or bittersweet chocolate, chopped, or semisweet chocolate chips
> ¾ cup (1½ sticks) unsalted butter
> ¼ cup strong coffee or espresso
> 1 cup heavy cream
> ¾ cup sugar
> ¾ cup unsweetened cocoa powder (not Dutch-processed)
> ½ cup light corn syrup
> Pinch of ground cinnamon
> Pinch of kosher salt

In a heavy-bottomed saucepan, combine the chocolate, butter, and coffee. Set over low heat and stir until the chocolate melts. Whisk in the cream, sugar, cocoa, corn syrup, cinnamon, and salt. Continue cooking, stirring frequently, until the sugar dissolves and the sauce has a smooth consistency, 5 to 7 minutes. Don't turn up the heat or you risk scorching the sauce. You can check if the sugar has dis-

solved by rubbing your finger on the back of the spoon: if you feel granules of sugar, it isn't ready.

TOTAL TIME: 10 minutes

LEFTOVERS The sauce will keep in an airtight container, such as a glass jar, in the refrigerator for months or in the freezer for at least one year. To reheat after chilling, spoon the amount of sauce you need in a small bowl and heat in a microwave for about a minute or in the top of a double boiler or a bowl set over simmering water.

Fruit Coulis

A coulis (pronounced coo-LEE) is a fresh fruit sauce. As with all fruit dishes, the riper the fruit, the better the flavor of the finished sauce. Berries are traditional, but you can use tropical fruits as well. Serve coulis with cakes or pies, or spooned over ice cream.

Makes about 1½ cups

> 1 pint fresh raspberries, strawberries, or blueberries or 1 (12-ounce) package frozen berries, defrosted
> 3 tablespoons sugar
> 1 tablespoon brandy, Cognac, or rum (optional)
> 1 tablespoon fresh lemon or lime juice
> Pinch of kosher salt

Place the fruit in the blender or a food processor fitted with a metal chopping blade. Add the sugar, brandy, if using, lemon juice, and salt. Purée until smooth. Pass through a fine-mesh strainer, using the back of a ladle or large spoon to force the sauce through. Adjust the seasoning with additional sugar or lemon juice, to taste.

TOTAL TIME: 10 minutes

ADVANCE PREP *A coulis will keep for four or five days in the refrigerator, after which it loses its characteristic fresh taste.*

LEFTOVERS *Use leftover coulis as part of the filling for pies or cobblers. You can also use it in drinks or to flavor ice cream.*

Vanilla Custard Sauce

This is a recipe for a traditional crème anglaise, English cream, or custard sauce. I could eat the whole thing with a spoon. Instead I restrain myself and spoon it over slices of cake or fresh fruits.

Makes 2½ cups

> 1 cup milk
> 1 cup heavy cream
> ½ vanilla bean, split and scraped, or 1 teaspoon pure vanilla extract
> 4 large egg yolks
> ⅓ cup sugar
> Pinch of kosher salt

Fill a large bowl halfway with ice, then fill it two thirds of the way to the top with cold water. Have a medium bowl and fine-mesh strainer at the ready.

In a medium saucepan, combine the milk, cream, and vanilla bean seeds and pod, if using. Bring to a simmer. Don't let it boil or it may boil over the top of the pot. Remove from the heat.

In a small bowl, whisk together the egg yolks, sugar, and salt. Whisk about ½ cup of

the hot milk mixture into the yolks, then pour the yolks back into the pot. Set over low heat and cook, stirring with a wooden spoon, until the mixture thickens enough to coat the back of a spoon. (An instant-read thermometer should register 170°F.) Don't let the sauce boil. Remove from the heat and strain into the medium bowl. Stir in the vanilla extract, if using. Set the bowl in the ice water bath (make sure the bath isn't too deep for the bowl), stirring to cool. Refrigerate until cold.

PREP TIME: 10 minutes
COOKING TIME: 10 minutes
TOTAL TIME: 20 minutes (plus cooling time)

LEFTOVERS *The custard sauce will keep for about a week in an airtight container in the refrigerator. You can incorporate leftover custard sauce into a trifle with some stale cake, sprinkled with some sort of alcohol and garnished with fresh fruit and/or nuts. You can use the custard sauce instead of some or all of the milk in a recipe for pancakes or waffles or bread pudding, or any sweet, eggy, vanilla-flavored dish.*

VARIATIONS

French Vanilla Ice Cream

Prepare the custard sauce as indicated, increasing the sugar to ½ cup. Freeze the custard in an ice-cream machine according to the manufacturer's instructions.

Chocolate Ice Cream

Follow the directions for French Vanilla Ice Cream, above. When the custard mixture has thickened, take it off the heat, add 6 ounces chopped bittersweet chocolate, and stir until melted. Churn the mixture in an ice-cream machine according to the manufacturer's directions.

Caramel Ice Cream

Prepare the French Vanilla Ice Cream as directed above. Add 1 cup of Caramel Sauce made with cream (page 451) to the hot custard mixture before churning in an ice-cream machine according to the manufacturer's directions.

The Easiest Vanilla Ice Cream Ever

This is an incredibly easy, delicious vanilla ice cream made without eggs. Although it is said to be typical of Philadelphia, I first tried it on Vancouver Island at my friends Clive and Suzanne's house. They served it with wild blackberry coulis (page 471) they made from blackberries they picked themselves. The delicate, sweet cream taste is delicious. Be sure to find a fresh heavy cream, without any additives, since that will determine the final flavor. It is a perfect base for mix-ins, such as minced crystallized ginger, broken candy bars, or toasted nuts. Be sure your ice-cream maker can handle a full quart of mix.

Makes about 1 quart

3 cups heavy cream, preferably without any gums or other additives and produced by a local, organic dairy

¾ cup plus 1 tablespoon sugar

1 vanilla bean, split and scraped, or 2 teaspoons pure vanilla extract

In a heavy saucepan, combine the cream, sugar, and vanilla bean (with scrapings), if using. Heat to dissolve the sugar without boiling. The cream should be scalded to the point that you see bubbles around the edges of the pan, but not on the surface. Turn off the heat and cool. If using vanilla extract, add it now. Chill the cream mixture in the refrigerator until very cold or overnight. Strain into an ice-cream machine and follow the manufacturer's directions. Firm up the ice cream in the freezer for 2 or 3 hours before serving.

PREP TIME: 10 minutes

COOKING TIME: 5 minutes

TOTAL TIME: 15 minutes (plus chilling, processing, and freezing times)

ADVANCE PREP *The base can be made two or three days before processing. Keep chilled.*

LEFTOVERS *The ice cream will keep for about one month in an airtight container in the freezer.*

VARIATIONS

Ginger Ice Cream

Add ½ cup minced crystallized ginger to the ice cream once it is processed. Freeze until hard. Don't worry that it is too much ginger— the flavor is mild once the ginger is frozen.

Candy Bar Ice Cream

Break 2 or 3 hard, brittle candy bars into little bits and stir into the ice cream after processing. Freeze until hard.

Cookies and Cream Ice Cream

Crush 8 to 10 chocolate wafers to crumbs and stir into the ice cream after processing. Freeze until hard.

Understanding the Recipes in this Book

IT BECAME CLEAR TO ME some years ago that, like all professions, cookbook writing has its jargon. Recipes are written in a certain way, with certain steps, and with certain words that home cooks and novice cooks alike don't always understand. I believe that these terms and techniques are part of the reason so many people are intimidated by cooking. As I wrote and tested the recipes for this book, I tried to think them through not as a professional food writer and experienced cook but as someone who didn't necessarily know his way around the kitchen.

In this section, and also in the recipes, you will find the answers to questions like, "What's a headnote?" "How big is a medium tomato?"

"A large pot?" "A pinch of salt?" "What exactly does it mean to sauté?" "To blanch?" "To make a roux?" Although this section will by no means be exhaustive—which would require a textbook, dictionary, and encyclopedia about food and cooking—it should help you learn how to read and use a recipe.

The Parts of a Recipe

ALTHOUGH I KNOW IT MAKES me sound like a schoolteacher, you should *always* read a recipe through before you begin it, to make sure you have everything you need and to understand what you are getting into. The following anatomy of a recipe should help you understand what you are looking at when you read a recipe in this book.

TITLE: Like items on a menu, recipes are named to entice. Recipe names are also similar to menu items in that they are subject to trends. Sometimes the trend veers toward homey, like Apple Pie. Other times it moves toward what I call chef-speak—that is, the names include all of the ingredients and techniques used to make a dish—for example, Cassia and Sugar Dusted Heirloom Apple Galette with Butter-Flake Pastry, which is just another way of saying Apple Pie. In this book you will find a combination of styles in the recipe names, not as an attempt to ride any particular trend but to reflect the nature of the dish. When I believe a foreign dish is common enough that most people know what it is, such as Chicken Paprikash (page 321), I use the foreign name. When I think that a dish is obscure and the foreign name might be confusing, such

as Crème Anglaise, I use an English equivalent, e.g., Vanilla Custard Sauce (page 472).

HEADNOTE: *Headnote* is publishing-speak for the introduction to a recipe—the few lines that precede the list of ingredients. Although many recipe headnotes in the world, including some of mine, are nothing more than clichés of the sort, "Served with a salad, this dish is perfect for a light lunch," often they contain important information that will help ensure success. Headnotes can convey details about ingredients, techniques, suitable substitutions, and other pertinent information.

YIELD: Deciding how many portions a recipe makes is a frustrating and somewhat arbitrary exercise. There are times when I could eat (and have eaten) half a cake from which you could technically cut 12 pieces. Does that mean the recipe serves 2 to 12? From experience with diets I have attempted to follow, I know I have a large appetite. In my indications about how many people a dish serves, I have tried to take this into account. The other complicating factor about determining yields is when in the order of courses you are serving the dish— appetizer or main course—and what you are serving with it. When appropriate, I have tried to give exact counts or volume measurements to help put things in perspective and make it easier for you to determine just how many of *your* friends or family members a recipe will serve.

INGREDIENTS: The list of ingredients is arranged in the order in which they are called for in the method. Don't fall into the trap of thinking that just because a recipe has a long list of ingredients it will be difficult to make. A recipe for Indian curry may have ten spices listed, but all you have to do is open the jars and mix them in. In magazines in particular, and cookbooks to some extent, there is pressure to keep the list of ingredients as short as possible. What I find is that this causes recipe writers to leave out some items that aren't essential but that can make the difference between something good and something great.

Whenever possible, I have given you the information you need to purchase and prepare your ingredients in the list of ingredients. Sometimes this includes directions for cleaning or cutting, toasting or tying. But when you have to treat an ingredient in a particular way, or I believe most people won't know how to handle the item, I have given the directions in the method of the recipe.

In many instances, I have recommended possible substitutions for listed ingredients, and when I have, they are given in my order of preference. Any of these substitutions, however, will produce delicious results. I have tested them all. In addition, these are not the only substitutions you can make. I really do think of recipes more as guidelines than as law. Just because you are missing a vegetable or a spice you should not necessarily give up and make something else. Even when baking, I think a good recipe offers leeway with ingredients (see page 447).

One of my pet peeves is recipes that call for all but a tablespoon of an ingredient that comes in a standard size container or when you must open an entire can of something only to use 1/4 cup. Wherever possible I have adjusted the amounts to make them consistent with the way ingredients are packaged and sold.

METHOD: As with shortened ingredients lists, publishers keep calling for shorter and shorter methods. I am wholeheartedly against this trend, especially in a basic cookbook such as this. While I don't think simple tasks should be belabored, I do think that if you take the time to explain what you expect people to do in a recipe, you can only help ensure more people will achieve success with it. Don't be put off by what looks like an extensive method until you read it and see what it's about. Although it might take up less space to say "bone a chicken" than it does to explain exactly how to do it, the former is not easier than the latter.

Similarly, one of the most common questions I get asked is how to know when something is done, so I have tried to include as much information about making that determination as possible—the reality is that as you cook more and more, this will become second nature.

Within the method are imbedded certain assumptions about what equipment and skill the average home cook might possess. If you've got a gadget that takes care of some technique I've described how to do by hand, use it. If you have your own trick to roasting a chicken or beating egg whites, don't let me stop you.

ESTIMATED TIMES: As with yields, determining the time it takes to do something is somewhat arbitrary. I am an experienced cook and I know exactly what I'm going to do, so timing myself following a recipe isn't necessarily useful. But I have taught many cooking classes and assisted many friends who don't have as much experience in the kitchen as I do, so I have assessed the time it takes a cook with average skills to complete the tasks at hand. If you know you are par-

ONE SIZE DOESN'T FIT ALL

Although recipes call for small and large ingredients and different kinds of pots and pans—onions, apples, carrots, mixing bowls, and frying pans, for example—the meanings of these words are relative, and therefore confusing. In a course on ingredients in the Food Studies Department of New York University where I teach, students are asked to bring in a medium potato. The variations in potato sizes are amazing. During the recipe testing for this book, which took place over three years, I weighed just about every piece of produce and measured every pan I cooked with. This has given me a clear sense of what I mean when I call for "a large onion" or "a small bowl." Here's a key.

Item	Adjective	Weight/Size
POTS, PANS, AND BOWLS		
Frying pan (measured across the bottom)	large	10 to 12 inches
	medium	8 inches
	small	6 inches
Saucepan	large	4 quarts
	medium	2½ quarts
	small	1½ quarts or less
Stock pot	large	10 to 12 quarts
	medium	8 quarts
Bowl	large	4½ to 5 quarts
	medium	2½ to 3 quarts
	small	1½ quarts or less

Item	Adjective	Weight/Size
PRODUCE		
Onion	very large	1 pound (16 ounces)
	large	8 ounces
	medium	6 ounces
	small	4 ounces
Carrot	large	5 to 6 ounces
	medium	4 ounces
Potato	large	8 ounces
	medium	6 ounces
Tomato	very large	1 pound (16 ounces)
	large	8 ounces
	medium	6 ounces
	small	4 ounces
Shallot	large	1 ounce
	small	½ ounce
Garlic clove	large	½ ounce
	small	¼ ounce
Apples, pears, peaches, and other fruit	large	8 to 9 ounces
	medium	6 ounces

ticularly slow or fast in the kitchen, you should adjust the time accordingly. Also note that for me the clock starts ticking after the ingredients are assembled. For example, if cooked beans or roasted peppers are in the ingredients list, I have not included the time it takes to make them as you may be substituting canned or jarred.

For the recipes in this book, *Prep time* corresponds more or less to active work time mixing, rolling out, shaping, and the like. *Cooking time* is self-evident, and although it can change if your oven runs hot or you adjust the temperature, these times are pretty accurate, to the best of my experience. *Total time* includes any soaking, chilling, resting, cooling, or other periods that don't require you do anything but wait. Don't be put off by big numbers; the time something takes to cook does not necessarily relate to how complicated it is to make. A beef stew may have to simmer for 2 hours, but you don't have to do anything during that time but stir it occasionally. The total time it takes to make beans may be 12 hours because the beans have to soak overnight before you cook them, but the active time is practically zero. With a little planning, most cooking—even things that take time— can seem effortless.

ADVANCE PREP: As part of the recipes, I've included information about what parts of them you can prepare in advance to speed things up or better use time before you serve the dish. Sometimes this means there are ingredients you can get ready, parts of dishes you can make ahead and chill or freeze, and other do-ahead tips. Other times my suggestion is to cook the whole dish and store it. Many dishes—soups and stews, for sure, but even some cakes and cookies—get better as they sit. If something needs to be eaten right away, you will not find an advance prep heading.

LEFTOVERS: I have also tried to advise what to do with leftovers—how long they will keep, how to reheat them, or when appropriate, what other dishes you can use them to make. Thinking up creative uses for leftovers is truly one of my favorite aspects of cooking. I'm not talking about turning everything into some big casserole and melting cheese on top, either. I stir leftover Chinese food into superb risotto and fold the remains of custard sauce into pancake or cake batter. I think frugality in the kitchen is a virtue. It isn't that I'm cheap— on the contrary, I spend an inordinate amount of money on food. And it's not that I think my eating a leftover boiled potato is going to help any of the hungry people in the world. It's just that I think you ought to treat good food—and all things, really—with respect, and throwing something away seems to me a last resort.

Note that there is a difference in my mind between making a dish in advance (see above) and leftovers. When something is cooked and left to rest before it is served for the first time, the advance preparation is intended to facilitate production or enhance the finished result. But once something has been served, the extra sitting around, chilling, and reheating can drastically alter a dish. That's not to say that I don't love cold pizza or leftover Thanksgiving dinner. It's just that they are drastically different from what they were when they were first served. And to make leftovers into something I would serve a guest again, I have to think of a creative way to reinvent what I've got.

VARIATIONS: When appropriate, I have listed variations after a recipe. These variations are usually further from the original recipe than the possible substitutions noted in the list of ingredients. There is a certain arbitrariness here, too, because sometimes recipe variations can go on forever. As I've already said, I rarely cook the same thing twice. But when I think a dish has the potential to produce some obvious and distinct alternatives, I've included the directions to make them.

Kitchen Words

ALTHOUGH MUCH CULINARY VOCABULARY and many techniques are universal, they don't always have the same meaning for every cook. When a French restaurant chef hears the word sauté, it means something quite different and more specific to him than it does to an American home cook. Below are some common kitchen words I use in my recipes and what I mean by them. The list is by no means comprehensive, and although some of the words seem obvious, I've included anything that my teaching experience has shown can be misinterpreted. For a good general kitchen dictionary that explains close to 6,000 words, pick up a copy of *The New Food Lover's Companion* by Sharon Tyler Herbst.

Food Terms

CHUNKS: When I say to cut something into chunks, I generally mean irregularly shaped pieces about $1\frac{1}{2}$ inches to 2 inches in size.

CUBES: In my mind, cubes are about 1-inch square pieces of food.

DICE: For me, *to dice* means to cut something up into small cubes, anywhere between $\frac{1}{4}$ inch and $\frac{1}{2}$ inch.

CHOP: In my recipes, unless otherwise specified, *chop* means to cut food into small pieces, finer than dice (above). It is less important that the items be in perfect cubes, though they should still be uniform in size. To *roughly* or *coarsely chop* means to cut pieces bigger and more irregularly shaped than if they were just chopped.

FINELY CHOP: Finer than chopped (above) but bigger than minced (below). The tiny pieces should be discernible and distinct.

MINCE: *To mince* something is to chop it as fine as possible, to the point of almost a purée.

SHRED: In my kitchen, shredding is coarser than grating. I shred cabbage for coleslaw but I grate cheese on pasta. Often the best way to shred certain ingredients, like that cabbage, is not with a shredding device at all, but simply by thinly slicing them with a knife or mandoline. Use the large holes of a box grater or the shredding disk of a food processor to shred a vegetable such as a carrot or a zucchini (and leave the stem end intact when you're using a grater so you can hold on to it while you work; discard it when you are done).

GRATE: Grating is finer than shredding in my mind, and unlike shredding, it requires a grater.

FINELY GRATE: When I say to finely grate something, I am almost always suggesting you use a Microplane grater, that is, a flat woodworker's plane with square-cut grooves instead of holes. It is ideal for finely grating citrus zest, cheese, even fresh ginger.

SLICE: Like other techniques in the kitchen, slicing is a skill; you get better with practice. The most important thing to have is a sharp knife. Whether you are slicing carrots, roast beef, or a loaf of bread, slices of even thickness are desirable. Wherever important, I've specified the thickness of slices in my recipes. When you are instructed to slice "on the bias," this means to angle your knife about 45 degrees, which elongates the slices.

THINLY SLICE: When I say to thinly slice something such as an onion or a lemon, I usually mean in the neighborhood of $\frac{1}{8}$-inch thickness. To slice something paper-thin, go down to $\frac{1}{16}$ inch. You can use a sharp knife or a mandoline, a metal or plastic device with a sharp blade designed to slice, for these tasks.

SEASON TO TASTE: Perhaps one of the most important directions in a recipe is to season to taste. I do not believe that guests should have to add salt and pepper at the table; that's the job of the cook. It is often remarkable how much difference a little salt can make in the flavor of something, even sweets. And salting as a dish cooks has a different effect than salting at the end. Seasoning to taste requires you, obviously, to taste what you are seasoning. In some cases, such as when cooking raw ground meat, you may want to fry a small piece to taste if it is properly seasoned.

Cooking Terms

HIGH, MEDIUM, AND LOW HEAT: Every burner throws off a different amount of heat, measured in British Thermal Units (BTUs). And since every pot conducts heat differently, it's difficult to explain what I mean by these relative terms. When I cook something on *high* heat, I turn the dial on as far as it will go, and then turn it back a notch. For *medium* heat, I pull it back about one third of the way. For *low*, it is two thirds back. And *very low* means just barely on.

SAUTÉ: *To sauté* usually means to cook quickly in fat over very high heat. When I use the term, I mean to cook quickly in fat over medium to medium-high heat, for a longer period of time than a classically trained French chef might believe. Unless otherwise stated, ingredients being sautéed shouldn't brown.

BOIL: When I say to bring a pot of water to a boil, I mean a good, strong, rapid, rolling boil. Boiling water only gets to 212°F (at sea level), not higher, so there's no need to worry it will get too hot. Soups, stews, and other items, on the other hand, should boil only gently. Rapid

boiling will destroy the integrity of the ingredients and may cause unnecessary cloudiness and scorching.

SIMMER: *To simmer* means to heat a liquid until it starts to bubble on the surface. Simmering is much less intense than boiling. To maintain a gentle simmer, you usually have to turn the burner down as low as it will go. Covering a pot, which traps the heat, causes something to simmer more vigorously. If your burners run hot or you find your long-cooked dishes burn on the bottom, you may want to consider buying a diffuser—a perforated metal or wire plate that you put over the burner, under the pot, to diffuse the heat and lower the temperature.

POACH: *Poaching* means to cook gently submerged in liquid. It is possible to cook fish or chicken in hot liquid that is just barely simmering or isn't even on the heat. To poach other items, such as pears, the liquid should simmer.

BRAISE: *To braise* means to cook slowly, covered, in moist heat, either in the oven or on top of the stove. It doesn't mean to submerge. Braising is an excellent technique for tough pieces of meat that break down after long, slow, moist cooking.

ROAST: *To roast* means to cook, uncovered, in hot, dry heat, as in an oven. It is important when roasting that the hot air be able to circulate freely around the oven. Roasting vegetables is one of my favorite ways to prepare them because the roasting process concentrates their flavor.

BROWN: Browning is an important step in many recipes because the process of browning, which involves the caramelization of sugars and other reactions, adds flavor. Degrees of browning are usually indicated by color, from very dark brown to light golden brown. Try not to cut the browning short or you'll cut the flavor short as well.

CARAMELIZE: Here's a term that's thrown around all the time because it sounds so sweet and appealing. It actually refers specifically to the browning of sugars, be they actual sugar or natural sugars found in fruits and vegetables. When you see something that says "cook until it has caramelized," what is usually meant is to cook until the food is the color of caramel.

SKIM: *To skim* means to lift off something that has floated to the surface of a liquid, usually fat or some sort of scum. Skimming is a skill that takes practice (my grandmother was amazing at it). To do it, you have to hold a large spoon or ladle almost parallel to the surface of the liquid and dip it down ever so slightly so that the fat runs into the spoon but the other liquid doesn't. Ideally, you will have time to chill whatever it is you need to skim so the fat will coagulate and you can just lift it off, which is much easier. There are a lot of nifty skimming gadgets available, but they don't always work as well as a large spoon.

Baking Terms

WHISK AND WHIP: *To whisk* and/or *whip* mean just that: to use a wire whisk to beat something quite vigorously, with the goal of incorporating plenty of air. Using a whisk, you can beat egg whites and heavy cream until stiff. You can also use a whisk to make sure your sauces are lump-free.

BEAT: To my mind, beating is less vigorous than whipping or whisking, and less air should be incorporated. You beat eggs with a fork to blend them before scrambling, but you whip egg whites to stiff peaks.

STIR: *Stirring* seems simple enough, but I've seen many people just move things around in a bowl when they were supposed to be stirring. The reasons for stirring are either to blend ingredients or to keep them moving so they don't burn. You've really got to move that spoon around to accomplish either of those goals.

MIX OR BLEND: Like *stirring*, these seem like obvious terms, but it's very important when making baked goods that ingredients are properly mixed. When you pour a cake batter into a pan and find a pocket of flour, you're in trouble, because although you can pour it all back into the bowl and mix it again, you run the risk of overmixing and making your cake tough. Pay attention and be sure ingredients are mixed and blended properly when they are supposed to be.

KNEAD: *Kneading* refers to the process of working dough by hand by folding it over itself on a work surface to develop the structure of the dough. The protein in the dough, called gluten, binds and stretches as you knead, making the dough smooth and elastic. Bread and pasta doughs are kneaded for a long time to develop their proper texture. Biscuits, scones, and pie doughs are kneaded for a very short time—just until the dough coheres—and overkneading would cause them to be tough. To knead a dough, turn it out onto a floured work surface. Bunch it together into a mound and flatten it out. Fold one side of the dough on top of the other and press it flat again. Turn the dough a quarter-turn and repeat. Each fold counts as one knead.

FOLD: Learning how to fold takes some practice. For years I was too timid and nothing ever came out right. You fold in things like beaten egg whites and whipped cream to incorporate them without deflating them. It helps to have a large rubber spatula. Always fold lighter mixtures into heavier mixtures. Add about one fourth of the lighter mixture to the heavier mixture and stir it gently to incorporate. Dump the remaining lighter mixture on top and using the spatula, scoop around under the batter and turn the heavier mixture on top of the lighter. Cut through the center of the bowl with the spatula and repeat, scraping under the other side and folding it on top. Repeat, turning the bowl as you work, until the two mixtures are well blended.

OVERMIXING: Because of the reaction of certain components of flour, namely protein, overmixing baked goods can make them tough. (The exception is bread, for which chewiness is desirable.) In general, you should stir in the dry ingredients in cakes and cookies just until they are fully incorporated, not more. And never beat anything after the flour has been added unless you are directed to do so.

Further Reading

There are more than 1,000 cookbooks published in America every year, many of them very good. It's impossible to keep up. But in my opinion an important aspect of a good cookbook is whether it can stand the test of time. I have hundreds of cookbooks in my small Manhattan apartment, but I turn to only a few of them again and again for recipes, information, and inspiration. Below is the list of those books. In most cases, any other books by the same authors are also worth owning. Though some of these books may be out of print, and a few of them are obscure, I have excellent luck finding just about everything I want on used book Web sites such as www.abebooks.com.

General (including American)

The Armchair James Beard edited by John Ferrone (Lyons Press, 1999)

The Cook's Bible: The Best of American Home Cooking by Christopher Kimball (Little, Brown, 1996)

Damon Lee Fowler's New Southern Kitchen by Damon Lee Fowler (Simon & Schuster, 2002)

The Fannie Farmer Cookbook by Marion Cunningham (Knopf, 1996)

Fish & Shellfish: The Cook's Indispensable Companion by James Peterson (William Morrow, 1996)

I Hear America Cooking by Betty Fussell (Viking, 1986)

How to Eat: The Pleasures and Principles of Good Food by Nigella Lawson (Wiley, 2002)

The Joy of Cooking by Irma S. Rombauer, Marion Rombauer Becker, and Ethan Becker (Scribner, 1997)

U.S.A. Cookbook by Sheila Lukins (Workman, 1997)

Baking

Austrian Pastries and Desserts by Maria Wiesmüller (Kompass, 2001)

Classic Home Desserts: A Treasury of Heirloom and Contemporary Recipes from Around the World by Richard Sax (Chapters, 1994)

The Fannie Farmer Baking Book by Marion Cunningham (Knopf, 1984)

How to Bake by Nick Malgieri (HarperCollins, 1995)

The Naturally Sweet Baker by Carrie Davis (Macmillan, 1997)—okay, she's my sister, but it's an excellent book

Reference

The New Food Lover's Companion, 3rd Edition, by Sharon Tyler Herbst (Barron's, 2001)

On Food and Cooking: The Science and Lore of the Kitchen by Harold McGee (Scribner, 2004 revised)

Asian

The Chinese Kitchen by Eileen Yin-Fei Lo (William Morrow, 1999)

Growing Up in a Korean Kitchen by Hi Soo Shin Hepinstall (Ten Speed, 2001)

Japanese Cooking: A Simple Art by Shizuo Tsuji (Kodansha, 1980)

Madhur Jaffrey Indian Cooking by Madhur Jaffrey (Barron's, 2003 revised)

Thai Food by David Thompson (Viking, 2002)

Vegetables, Grains, Legumes, and Vegetarian

Chez Panisse Vegetables by Alice Waters and the Cooks of Chez Panisse (HarperCollins, 1996)

Madhur Jaffrey's World Vegetarian by Madhur Jaffrey (Clarkson Potter, 1999)

The Versatile Grain and the Elegant Bean: A Celebration of the World's Most Healthful Foods by Sheryl and Mel London (Simon & Schuster, 1992)

French

Bistro Cooking by Patricia Wells (Workman, 1989)

Jacque Pépin's The Art of Cooking, Volumes I & II (Knopf, 1992)

La Varenne Pratique: The Complete Illustrated Cooking Course by Anne Willan (Crown, 1989)

Mastering the Art of French Cooking, Volumes I & II, by Julia Child, Louisette Bertholle, and Simone Beck (Knopf, 1961, 1970)

Simple French Food by Richard Olney (Wiley, 1992 reprint)

Italian

Celebrating Italy by Carol Field (William Morrow, 1990)

Essentials of Italian Cooking by Marcella Hazan (Knopf, 1992)

The Flavors of Tuscany: Traditional Recipes from the Tuscan Countryside by Nancy Harmon Jenkins (Broadway, 1998)

Rustico: Regional Italian Country Cooking by Micol Negrin (Clarkson Potter, 2002)

Sicilian Home Cooking: Family Recipes from Gangivecchio by Wanda and Giovanna Tornabene with Michele Evans (Knopf, 2001)

The Splendid Table: Recipes from Emilia-Romagna, the Heartland of Northern Italian Food by Lynne Rossetto Kasper (William Morrow, 1992)

Mediterranean

The Cooking of the Eastern Mediterranean by Paula Wolfert (HarperCollins, 1994)

Food and Wine of Greece by Diane Kochilas (St. Martin's Press, 1990)

The Foods & Wines of Spain by Penelope Casas (Knopf, 1988)

Honey from a Weed: Fasting and Feasting in Tuscany, Catalonia, The Cyclades, and Apulia by Patience Gray (Harper & Row, 1987)

The Legendary Cuisine of Persia by Margaret Shaida (Interlink, 2002)

German, Russian, Jewish, and Eastern European

The Cuisine of Hungary by George Lang (Bonanza, 1971)

From My Mother's Kitchen: Recipes & Reminiscences by Mimi Sheraton (HarperCollins, 1979 revised)

Jewish Cooking in America by Joan Nathan (Knopf, 1994)

Please to the Table: The Russian Cookbook by Anya von Bremzen and John Welchman (Workman, 1990)

Spoonfuls of Germany: Culinary Delights of the German Regions in 170 Recipes by Nadia Hassani (Hippocrene, 2004)

Traditional Ukrainian Cookery by Savella Stechishin (Trident, 1975)

Mexican and Latin American

Authentic Mexican: Regional Cooking from the Heart of Mexico by Rick Bayless with Deann Groen Bayless (William Morrow, 1987)

The Essential Cuisines of Mexico by Diana Kennedy (Clarkson Potter, 2000)

Restaurant Food

Alfred Portale's Gotham Bar and Grill Cookbook (Broadway, 1997)

The French Laundry Cookbook by Thomas Keller with Susie Heller and Michael Ruhlman (Artisan, 1999)

Think Like a Chef by Tom Colicchio (Clarkson Potter, 2000)

The Zuni Café Cookbook by Judy Rodgers (Norton, 2002)

Preserving

Preserving in Today's Kitchen: Easy, Modern Canning Methods—with 168 Recipes by Jeanne Lesem (Henry Holt, 1992)

Putting Food By by Janet Greene, Ruth Hertzber, and Beatrice Vaughan (Plume, 1991)

Acknowledgments

LIKE ALL BOOKS, this one wasn't easy. It began with an idea for a new way to think about American home cooking, and in the course of three years it morphed into several different projects, only to end up where it started. I am grateful for my former editor, Chris Pavone, and the folks at Clarkson Potter for having faith in my ability to pull off such a large project. And I am indebted to my new editor, Rica Allannic, and her assistants, Adrienne Jozwick and then Nikki Van Noy, without whose help I might have proved Chris's faith misplaced. Thanks to senior designer Maggie Hinders, production editor Trisha Howell, and publicity director Amy Corley. I am also thankful to my agent and friend, Lydia Wills, who is ever confident in my ability to finish the crazy ideas we cook up together—of course, that's what I pay her for.

Although we usually separate them into different categories, every cookbook is really a community cookbook because it involves so many people and because there are so few truly new recipes. I am fortunate to have a large community of close friends who are good cooks and/or food lovers. Perhaps two of my greatest sources of inspiration and ideas in the kitchen are Bonnie Stern and Dano Hutnik. If I didn't like to cook so much, I could easily live on their food. Other beloved friends whose inspiration to cook and think about food, whether by sharing ideas or breaking bread together, has had an impact on this book are: Clive Adamson, Mildred Amico, Ed Behr, Frank Bruni, Elizabeth Blau, Anya von Bremzen, Andrew Carmellini, Hannah Clark, Kerri Conan, Sebastiano Cossia-Castiglioni, Ian d'Agata, Michael Frank, Gabriella Ganugi, Karen Gilman, Michael and Laurie Ginor, Marko Gnann, Laurent Gras, Peggy Grodinsky, Dorita Hannah, Gwen Hyman, Phyllis Isaacson, Marcia and Jack Kelly, Tom Kelly, Judith Kim, Kate Krader, Jennifer Leuzzi, Oliver Ludwig, Michael and Sabine Maharam, Joe Meisel, Peter Meehan, Shelley Menaged, George Motz, Marcus Naubur, Marion Nestle, Fabio Parasecoli, Evelynne Patterson, Jane Patterson, Harold Rabinowitz, Felice Ramella, Suzanne Rannie, Adam Rapoport and his mother Maxine, Izabela and Howie Rumberg, Lisa and Eitan Sasson, Lonni Tanner, Karla Vermeulen, and Alexandra Zohn.

I am also honored to be part of a larger community of professional food writers and chefs on whose work I rely for inspiration and ideas. I am in awe of their knowledge, talent, and passion: Mark Bittman, Daniel Boulud, Giuliano Bugialli, Carla Capalbo, Melissa Clark, Dorie Greenspan, Monica Gullon, Madhur Jaffrey, Nancy Harmon Jenkins, Thomas Keller, Emily Luchetti, Nick Malgieri, Alice Medrich, Jacques Pépin, Jim Peterson, Fabio Picchi, Eric Ripert, Mimi Sheraton, Paula Wolfert, and Sherry Yard, just to name a few. Although they are no longer with us, I am also indebted to the work of Julia Child, Elizabeth David, Jean-Louis Palladin, Richard Olney, and Richard Sax; the joy of cooking for me begins by flipping through their books.

There would be no book without the understanding and generosity of, not to mention the covering of my you-know-what by, my staff—Anya Hoffman, Megan Krigbaum, Scott Meola, and Alison Tozzi-Liu—as well as my other colleagues at the James Beard Foundation. I am fortunate to be associated with an organization that takes food almost as seriously as I do. I can think of no group of people with whom I'd rather exchange recipes and share my testing successes (and failures).

Finally, I have to thank my family, the first good cooks and real food lovers I ever knew. My brother, Sheldon, and his family—Pauline, Helen, Aita, Sarah, and Nicole—prove that an enthusiasm for good food and cooking is both genetic and contagious. My sister Carrie can cry at the taste of an exquisite French pastry and make pastry that can make me cry, while her husband, John Morris, can politicize it. And my sister Leslie, whose love and support not only helps me get through giant, unwieldy projects like this one, but also helps keep me on the road to becoming the person I want to be.

Index

A

Aïoli, 406

Almond(s)
  Biscotti, 464–65
  Buttered, Apples, and Dried Cranberries, Wild
    Rice with, 232–33
  Crack, 469
  and Dates, Couscous with, 387
  Dukkah, 408–9
  Esther's Special Linzer Tart, 431–32
  and Orange Cake, Flourless, 440–41

Anchovies, White, with Garlic and Parsley, 30–31

Anchovy and Garlic Dressing, Wilted Arugula with,
    79–80

Appetizers. *See* Hors d'oeuvres

Apple(s)
  Baked, 417
  and Cheddar Tart, Savory, 25
  Chunky Applesauce, 416–17
  Cranberry Crisp, 433–34
  Dried Cranberries, and Buttered Almonds, Wild
    Rice with, 232–33
  Green, and Toasted Walnuts, Chicken Liver
    Mousse with, 18–19
  and Nutmeg, Butternut Squash Soup with, 38
  and Prunes, Pork Chops with, 374–75
  sizes, 478
  Tarte Tatin, 429–30

Applesauce, Chunky, 416–17

Applesauce Spice Cake, 437–38

Apricot Jam, Brandied, with Vanilla Bean, 134

Artichoke(s)
  and Chicken Lasagna, 261–62
  and Fava Bean Fricassée, 169–70
  Hearts, Marinated, 7
  preparing for cooking, 174
  Spread, 8–9

Arugula, Wilted, with Anchovy and Garlic Dress-
    ing, 79–80

Arugula and Walnut Pesto, 398

Asparagus, Roasted, 144

Asparagus Mignonette, 162–63

Asparagus Soup, Cream of, 37

Avocado(s)
  Guacamole, 14–15
  Salad, 58–59

B

Baba Ghanoush, 13–14

Bacon
  Frisée aux Lardons, 80–81
  and Red Onion, Wilted Spinach Salad with, 80
  roasting, 126
  Spaghetti alla Carbonara, 253
  and Tomato, Grilled Cheese with, 85

baked goods, shipping, 459

baking, technique, 447

Banana Cake, 444

Barbecue Sauce, Evelynne's, 406–7

Barley
  Mushroom Soup, 41–42
  with Orange and Dates, 236
  Salad, 72–73
  Salad, Warm, with Corn and Green Beans, 72

Basil
  Pesto, 398
  Pizza Margherita, 101
  and Roasted Garlic Mayonnaise, 406
  Sicilian Pesto with Almonds, Tomato, and Mint,
    399

Bean(s). *See also* Chickpea(s); Fava Bean(s); Green
    Beans
  Baked, Boston, with Country Bacon, 199–200
  Baked, Southwestern, with Chorizo, Poblanos,
    and Orange, 200–202
  Black, Soup, Cuban, 43–44
  Black, Soup in a Hurry, 44

Bean(s) (*cont.*)
  Black-Eyed Pea Fritters with Country Ham,
    196–97
  Buffalo Chili, 364–65
  Chili Dogs, 365
  cooking, 201
  dried, cooking, 201
  Edamame, 4–6
  Fraud Thai, 265–66
  Giant, in Tomato Sauce, 198–99
  Lentil and Root Vegetable Stew, 203
  Mushroom Barley Soup, 41–42
  and Mushroom Burrito, 94–95
  Peas and Rice, 206
  and Pickled Beets, Smoked Trout Salad with,
    77–78
  "Refried," 204–5
  Refried, with Cheese, 205
  Ribollita, 43
  soaking methods, 198
  Soup with Stinging Nettles, 42–43
  Split Pea Soup, 40–41
  Sprout Salad, Asian, 66
  Succotash, 170–71
  Vegetarian Chili, Baked, with Cheese, 204
  Vegetarian Chili with Bulgur and Cashews, 203–4
Beef. *See also* Meat
  Brisket, 354–57
  Buffalo Chili, 364–65
  Burgers, Gussied Up, 96
  Cheeseburgers, 96
  Chicken, or Shrimp, Curried Rice Noodles with,
    264
  Chicken, or Turkey Hash, 124–25
  Chili Dogs, 365
  Flank Steak, Marinated, 350
  Hamburger Heaven, 95–96
  Hanger Steaks, Soy-Marinated, 344
  Hash, 124–25
  Italian Meatballs, 365–66
  Meat and Vegetable Loaf, 364
  Meatloaf, 362–64
  Meatloaf with Roasted Potatoes, 364
  Mushroom Barley Soup, 41–42
  Pastitsio, 256–58
  Pot Roast, Beer-Braised, 359–60
  Pot Roast, Wine-Braised, 360

  Rib-Eye Roast, 343
  Rib-Eyes, Grilled, 344
  Rib Roast, Standing, with a Garlic and Herb
    Mustard Crust, 343
  Rib Roast, Standing or Prime, 342–43
  Rib Steaks, Grilled or Broiled, 343
  Salad, Vietnamese, with Watercress, 81–82
  Shepherd's Pie, 387–88
  Short Ribs, Barolo-Braised, 357–58
  Steak, Chicken-Fried, 346–48
  Steak, Pepper, 354
  Steak, Sliced, Smothered with Mushrooms and
    Onions, 349–50
  Stew, 358–59
  Tacos, Soft, 93
  T-Bone or Porterhouse Steaks, Grilled, 350–54
  Tenderloin, Mustard and Herb-Roasted, 349
  Tenderloin, Spiced Yogurt-Roasted, 349
  Tenderloin of, Roast, 348–49
  Tomato Sauce with Meat (Red Gravy), 251–52
Beet(s)
  and Goat Cheese Tart, Savory, 185–86
  greens, cooking, 150
  Pancakes, 188–89
  Pickled, and Beans, Smoked Trout Salad with,
    77–78
  Pickled, Spiced, 211
  Pickled, with Caraway, 210–11
  Roasted, 149
  Roasted, and Gorgonzola, Risotto with, 224
  Shredded, with Bacon and Sour Cream, 176
  Shredded, with Sour Cream and Dill, 176
  Steamed, 149
  Vinaigrette, 391–92
Belgian Endives
  Braised, 172
  Frisée aux Lardons, 80–81
  Oven-Braised, 172
Berry(ies). *See also* Blueberry; Cranberry(ies);
    Strawberry
  Fruit Coulis, 471–72
  Raspberry Vinaigrette, 394
  Summer, Galette, 428
Biscotti, Almond, 464–65
Biscuits
  Angel, 125–26
  Appenzeller and Peanut, 21

Buttermilk, 127
Cheese and Nut, 20–21
Cheese and Nut, Mini, 21
Scallion and Cheese, 127
Black-Eyed Pea Fritters with Country Ham, 196–97
Blanching, technique, 163
Blueberry
    Jam, Spiced, 136–37
    Lemon Sour Cream Muffins, 113–14
    Soup, 416
    Vinaigrette, 392–94
Blue cheese
    Cheese and Pepper Puffs, 26
    Cheese Spread, 17
    Gorgonzola Dressing, 394
    Risotto with Roasted Beets and Gorgonzola, 224
    Roasted Seckel Pear and Roquefort Salad with
        Walnuts, 60–61
    Savory Pear and Gorgonzola Tart, 24–25
Bok Choy, Baby, Chinese-Style, 158
Brandied Apricot Jam with Vanilla Bean, 134
Brandied Peach Jam with Vanilla, 135
Bread-based recipes
    Bourbon Bread-and-Butter Pudding, 453–54
    Bread Salad, 68–69
    Bruschetta, 23
    Crostini, 22–23
    French Toast, 105–7
    Grilled Pita Triangles with Za'atar, 24
    Lemon- or Orange-Infused French Toast, 107
    Oven-Toasted Croutons, 41
    Panettone Bread Pudding, 454
    Ribollita, 43
    Sausage and Bread Stuffing with Apples and Sage,
        228
    Savory Pumpkin Bread Pudding, 227–28
    Stove-Top Croutons, 41
    Wild Mushroom and Hazelnut Crostini, 23–24
Bread Crumbs, 370
Breadings, alternatives, 318
Breads. See also Focaccia; Pizza
    Angel Biscuits, 125–26
    bread crumbs, preparing, 370
    Buttermilk Biscuits, 127
    Chocolate Chip Scones, 115
    Cranberry Orange Scones, 115
    Honey-Buttermilk Cornbread, 224–25

Lemon Blueberry Sour Cream Muffins, 113–14
    Lemon Poppy Seed Scones, 115
    Scallion and Cheese Biscuits, 127
    Scones, 114–15
    Sesame Ginger Scones, 116
Broccoli
    Garlicky, 157
    Soup, Cream of, 37
Broccoli Rabe
    Baked, 177–78
    Pasta with, 248–49
    and Sausage, Pasta with, 249
Brownies, 465–66
Bruschetta, 23
Brussels Sprouts, Shredded, with Bacon, 156–57
Buckwheat, see also Kasha
    Buttermilk Bundt Cake with Orange Glaze, 118
    Buttermilk Bundt Cake with Walnuts, 117–18
    Hazelnut Cookies, 460
    Pancakes, Multigrain, 108–9
    Soba Salad, Chilled, 76
    Buffalo Chili, 364–65
Bulgur
    Baked Vegetarian Chili with Cheese, 204
    and Cashews, Vegetarian Chili with, 203–4
    Pilaf with Pine Nuts, 234
    Tabbouleh, 70–71
Burgers
    Cheeseburgers, 96
    Gussied Up, 96
    Hamburger Heaven, 95–96
Burrito, Mushroom and Bean, 94–95
Butter
    beurre manié, about, 45
    Chipotle, 407
    flavored, preparing, 116
    Sauce, 403–4
    Sauce, Orange, 404
    Sauce, Pink, 404
Buttermilk
    Biscuits, 127
    Buckwheat Bundt Cake with Orange Glaze,
        118
    Buckwheat Bundt Cake with Walnuts, 117–18
    -Honey Cornbread, 224–25
    Oatmeal Cookies, 461
    Pancakes, 107–8

Buttermilk (*cont.*)
    Panna Cotta, 455–56
    Polenta with Fresh Corn, 232
Butternut Squash Gratin, 184–85
Butternut Squash Soup with Apple and Nutmeg, 38
Butterscotch Pudding, 452
Butterscotch Shortbread, 467–68

C
Cabbage
    Herbed Coleslaw, 64
    Kimchee, 212–13
    Potstickers, 270–72
    Red, Braised, with Apples and Currants, 171
    Red, Slaw with Toasted Hazelnuts and Butter-
        milk Orange Dressing, 64–65
    shredding, 65
    and Snow Pea Slaw, Grilled Turkey Cutlets on,
        332–33
    Steamed Dumplings, 272
    Vegetarian Potstickers, 272
    Yakisoba, 266–67
Cakes. *See also* Coffee Cake
    Almond and Orange, Flourless, 440–41
    Applesauce Spice, 437–38
    Banana, 444
    Butter, 445
    Carrot, with Cream Cheese Frosting, 438–39
    Chocolate Cheesecake, 441–43
    Chocolate Cupcakes, 444
    Coconut Layer, 445–48
    Cranberry Upside Down, 436
    Date-Nut, 436–37
    Devil's Food, 443
    Devil's Food, Earl Grey's, 444
    Green Tomato, 440
    Jam, 438
    lining cake pans, 442
    Parsnip, 439–40
    Pineapple Upside-Down, 435–36
    Vanilla Cupcakes, 445
Calamari. *See* Squid
Candy
    Almond Crack, 469
    Candied Citrus Peel, 467
    Chocolate Caramels, 471
    Chocolate Truffles, 450

    Peanut Brittle, 469
    Pumpkin Seed Brittle, 468–69
    Vanilla Cream Caramels, 470–71
Candy Bar Ice Cream, 473
canning, technique, 136, 209
Cantaloupe Soup, 414
Caponata, Green Tomato, 168–69
Caramel
    Cream Cheese Frosting, 450–51
    Ice Cream, 473
    Sauce, 451
Caramels, Chocolate, 471
Caramels, Vanilla Cream, 470–71
Carrot(s)
    Cake with Cream Cheese Frosting, 438–39
    and Caraway Salad, 61–62
    and Ginger Soufflé, 131–34
    Glazed, 154–55
    and Raisin Raita, Madhur Jaffrey's, 402–3
    Roasted, with Spiced, 144
    Root Vegetable Purée Baked with Cheese, 180
    sizes, 478
    Slaw, Creamy, 64
    Soup, Cream of, 37
    Winter Mash, 179–80
Catfish, Cornmeal-Crusted, 302–3
Cauliflower
    Currants, and Pistachios, Spiced Millet with,
        233–34
    Curried, 165
    Garlicky, 157
    Gratin, 183
    Roasted, 147
    Roasted, and Pear Soup, 38–39
    Soup, Cream of, 37
    Soup, Curried, 39
Celery, Three, Soup, Cream of, 37–38
Celery Root
    cake, *see* Parsnip Cake
    Pancakes, 189
    Rémoulade, 62
    Rémoulade, Creamy, 62
    Root Vegetable Purée Baked with Cheese, 180
    Winter Mash, 179–80
Cereal
    Fruity Oatmeal Porridge, 112–13
    Oatmeal Made from Rolled Oats, 113

oatmeal mix-ins, 113
Savory Oatmeal, 113
Ceviche, 293–94
Ceviche, Shrimp or Calamari, 294
Charmoula, 400–401
Cheddar Cheese
    and Apple Tart, Savory, 25
    Baked Macaroni and Cheese with Tomatoes,
        258–59
    Butternut Squash Gratin, 184–85
    Cheese and Nut Biscuits, 20–21
    Cheese Grits, 129–30
    Cheese Grits "Soufflé," 130
    Cheese Spread, 17
    Root Vegetable Purée Baked with Cheese, 180
    Savory Cornbread with Ham, Cheese, and
        Jalapeño, 225
    Scallion and Cheese Biscuits, 127
    Soup, 44–46
    The Ultimate Macaroni and Cheese, 259–60
Cheese. *See also* Blue cheese; Cheddar Cheese;
        Cream Cheese; Mozzarella cheese; Parmesan
        cheese; Swiss cheese
    Appenzeller and Peanut Biscuits, 21
    Baked Vegetarian Chili with, 204
    Cheeseburgers, 96
    Cuban Sandwich, 88–89
    Goat, and Beet Tart, Savory, 185–86
    Goat, Tots, 21
    "Grilled," 85
    Grilled, with Bacon and Tomato, 85
    Grilled, with Ham and Onions, 85
    Grilled, with Smoked Salmon, 85–86
    Grits, 129–30
    Grits "Soufflé," 130
    Ham, and Jalapeño, Savory Cornbread with, 225
    Israeli Couscous Salad with Favas, Feta, Olives,
        Preserved Lemon, and Mint, 71–72
    Lace, 19–20
    Lace for a Crowd, 20
    Lasagna, 260–61
    Lemon Pick-Me-Up, 456–57
    Liptauer, 17–18
    Macaroni and, Baked, with Tomatoes, 258–59
    Macaroni and, The Ultimate, 259–60
    Muffuletta, 91
    Mushroom and Bean Burrito, 94–95

Naked Ravioli with Browned Butter, Sage, and
        Toasted Walnuts, 268–69
    Naked Ravioli with Tomato Sauce, 270
    and Nut Biscuits, 20–21
    and Nut Biscuits, Mini, 21
    and Pepper Puffs, 26
    Quesadilla, 22
    Refried Beans with, 205
    rinds, uses for, 43
    Roasted Figs with Mascarpone Mousse, 419–20
    and Scallion Biscuits, 127
    Sheep's Milk, and Black Pepper, Pasta with,
        253–54
    Sicilian Pesto with Almonds, Tomato, and Mint,
        399
    Soufflé, 130–31
    Spinach and Feta Rolls, 189–90
    Spread, 17
    "Thing," *see* Baked Macaroni and Cheese with
        Tomatoes
    Vegetable Lasagna, 261
Cheesecake, Chocolate, 441–43
Cheese "Thing," *see* Baked Macaroni and Cheese
        with Tomatoes
Cherry, Sour, Jam, 137
Cherry, Sour, Soup, 414–16
Chicken
    in Adobo, 382
    and Artichoke Lasagna, 261–62
    Barbecued, With or Without a Grill, 319–20
    Beef, or Shrimp, Curried Rice Noodles with, 264
    Beef, or Turkey Hash, 124–25
    breadings for, 318
    Breast, Cold Poached, 314–15
    Breasts, Sautéed, with Mushrooms, 316
    brining, 308
    Buttermilk Fried, with Cream Gravy, 325–26
    buying, 307–8
    Cacciatore, Summertime, 321
    carving, 313
    Casserole, 263
    cooked, cutting up, 313
    cooking, 308, 310
    Couscous with, 386
    and Dumplings, 324–25
    Fingers, Cracker-Crumb, 317–19
    Fraud Thai, 265–66

Chicken (*cont.*)
Greek Souvlaki, 384
Grilled Spice-Rubbed, 314
Hash, 124–25
Indian-Spiced, 326–27
Jerk, 316–17
Liver Mousse with Green Apple and Toasted
Walnuts, 18–19
Mock Tandoori, 328
or Turkey Gratin, 324
or Turkey Pot Pie, 322–24
Paprikash, 321–22
and Pepper Casserole, 320–21
raw, cutting up, 315
Roast, Crisp, with Herbs Under the Skin,
311–12
Roast, My Mother's, 310–11
Roast, Spice-Rubbed, 313–14
Roast, with Fresh Herbs, 311
Salad, 78
Soup, 50–51
testing for doneness, 310
trussing, 312
Yakisoba, 266–67
Chickpea(s)
The Best Hummus You've Ever Tasted,
11–12
Couscous with Chicken, 386
Couscous with Merguez, 387
Falafel, 197–98
Hummus in a Hurry, 12
Moroccan Couscous with Lamb, 384–86
Spicy, 202
Spicy, with Yogurt, 202–3
Spinach, and Cumin, Roasted Tomato Soup with,
36
and Spinach Salad, 68
Vegetarian Couscous, 386–87
Chile peppers
Chicken in Adobo, 382
Chipotle Butter, 407
Chipotle-Rubbed Turkey Breast, 330–32
Cilantro Chili Slather, 351
Grilled Tomato and Corn Salsa with Chipotle, 16
Jerk Chicken, 316–17
Mojo, 400
Peperonata, 167–68

Pork in Adobo, 381–82
Quinoa with Roasted Poblanos, Cilantro, and
Lime, 236–37
Savory Cornbread with Ham, Cheese, and
Jalapeño, 225
Soft Beef Tacos, 93
Soft Turkey Taco, 92–93
Southwestern Baked Beans with Chorizo,
Poblanos, and Orange, 200–202
Chili
Buffalo, 364–65
Vegetarian, Baked, with Cheese, 204
Vegetarian, with Bulgur and Cashews, 203–4
Chili Dogs, 365
Chili Sauce, Spicy Asian, 397
Chimichurri, 400
Chinese broccoli, *see* Bok Choy, Baby, Chinese-Style
Chocolate
Brownies, 465–66
Caramels, 471
Cheesecake, 441–43
Chip Peanut Butter Cookies, 458
Chip Scones, 115
Chunk, Cookies, Oatmeal, 459–60
Chunk Cookies, 458–59
Chunk Cookies with Nuts, 459
Cookie Crust, 427
Cookies and Cream Ice Cream, 473
Crème Brûlée, 454–55
Cupcakes, 444
Devil's Food Cake, 443
Earl Grey's Devil's Food Cake, 444
Flavored Ganache, 450
Frosting, Deep Dark, 448–49
Ganache, 449–50
Hot Fudge Sauce, 471
Ice Cream, 472–73
Lavender Cookies, 461–62
Mocha Pudding, 452
Pecan Pie, 425
Pudding, 452
Sablés, Salty, 462–63
Sesame Pots de Crème, 455
Truffles, 450
Chowder
Clam, Manhattan, 48–49
Clam, New England, 47–48

clams for, 47
Corn, Fresh, 49
Cilantro
    Charmoula, 400–401
    Chili Slather, 351
    Lime Mayonnaise, 406
    -Mint Sauce with Tomato, 399
Citrus, Candied Peel, 467
citrus, sectioning, 70
Clafoutis, 112
Clam(s)
    Buttermilk Fried, 282–84
    Buying, 278
    for chowder, 47
    Chowder, Manhattan, 48–49
    Chowder, New England, 47–48
    cleaning, 282
    Pasta with, 255
    shucking, 284
    Steamed, 283
cleaning, leafy greens, 60
cleaning, fava beans, fresh, 170
Cobbler, Summer Fruit, 432–33
Coconut Layer Cake, 445–48
Cod in the Basque Style, 304–5
Coffee Cake
    Buckwheat Buttermilk Bundt Cake with Orange
        Glaze, 118
    Buckwheat Buttermilk Bundt Cake with Walnuts,
        117–18
    Fig or Plum, 117
    Lemon Poppy Seed, 117
    Streusel, 116–17
Collard Greens, Southern-Style, 165–66
Condiments. *See also* Jams; Mayonnaise; Pesto;
    Salsa; Spices
    Bitter Orange Marmalade, 139–40
    Charmoula, 400–401
    Chimichurri, 400
    Evelynne's Barbecue Sauce, 406–7
    Fig Preserves, 140
    Fresh Corn and Tomato Relish, 207
    Gremolata, 361
    Kimchee, 212–13
    Madhur Jaffrey's Carrot and Raisin Raita, 402–3
    Marinated Eggplant Relish, 207
    Preserved Lemons, 409–10

Preserved Lemons with Spices, 410
    Preserved Limes, 410
    seasoned slathers, for meat, 351–52
    Spicy Asian Chili Sauce, 397
    Spicy Peanut Sauce, 397–98
Confit, Duck, 335–37
confit, lemons, *see* Lemons, Preserved
Cookies and bars
    Almond Biscotti, 464–65
    Brownies, 465–66
    Buckwheat Hazelnut Cookies, 460
    Butterscotch Shortbread, 467–68
    Chocolate Chunk Cookies, 458–59
    Chocolate Chunk Cookies Oatmeal, 459–60
    Chocolate Chunk Cookies with Nuts, 459
    Cranberry Squares, 465
    Ginger Snaps, 463
    Lavender Cookies, 461–62
    Lemon Squares, 465
    Peanut Butter Chocolate Chip Cookies, 458
    Peanut Butter Cookies, Maxine's, 457–58
    Potato Chip Cookies, 463–64
    Rugelach, 466
    Salty Chocolate Sablés, 462–63
Cookies and Cream Ice Cream, 473
Corn
    Chowder, Fresh, 49
    on the Cob, 151
    on the Cob, Grilled, 151–52
    on the Cob, Microwave, 151
    Cornbread Pudding, 226–27
    cutting kernels from, 50
    Fresh, and Rice Salad, Curried, with Golden
        Raisins, 74–75
    Fresh, Buttermilk Polenta with, 232
    Fresh, Cornbread with, 225
    Fritters, 194–95
    and Green Beans, Warm Barley Salad with, 72
    Grilled, and Tomato Salsa with Chipotle, 16
    Potato, and Mushroom Croquettes, 191
    Succotash, 170–71
    and Tomato Relish, Fresh, 207
Cornbread
    with Fresh Corn, 225
    Honey-Buttermilk, 224–25
    Pudding, 226–27
    Savory, with Ham, Cheese, and Jalapeño, 225

Cornbread (*cont.*)
  Skillet, Southern-Style, 225–26
  Stuffing with Fennel, Cranberries, and Toasted
    Pecans, 229
Cornmeal. *See also* Cornbread; Grits; Polenta
  Cranberry Johnnycakes, 109–10
  -Crusted Catfish, 302–3
Coulis, Fruit, 471–72
Couscous
  with Almonds and Dates, 387
  with Chicken, 386
  Israeli, Salad with Favas, Feta, Olives, Preserved
    Lemon, and Mint, 71–72
  with Lamb, Moroccan, 384–86
  with Merguez, 387
  Salad, Spiced Orange, with Currants and Carrots,
    69–70
  Vegetarian, 386–87
crab, buying, 278
Crab Cakes, 294–95
Crab Roll, 90
Cranberry(ies)
  Apple Crisp, 433–34
  Curd, 451
  Fennel, and Toasted Pecans, Cornbread Stuffing
    with, 229
  Johnnycakes, 109–10
  Orange Scones, 115
  Squares, 465
  Upside Down Cake, 436
Cream Cheese
  Caramel Frosting, 450–51
  Cheese Spread, 17
  Chocolate Cheesecake, 441–43
  flavored, preparing, 116
  Frosting, Carrot Cake with, 438–39
  Liptauer, 17–18
  Pastry, 431
  The Ultimate Macaroni and Cheese, 259–60
Creamsicle Pie, 425
Crème Brûlée, Chocolate, 454–55
Crisp, Apple Cranberry, 433–34
Croquettes
  breadings for, 318
  Goat Cheese Tots, 21
  Potato, Corn, and Mushroom, 191
  Potato and Ham, 191

Potato and Spinach, 190–91
Potato and Turnip, Beet, or Mustard Greens, 191
Crostini, 22–23
Crostini, Wild Mushroom and Hazelnut, 23–24
Croutons, Oven-Toasted, 41
Croutons, Stove-Top, 41
Cucumber(s)
  Bread and Butter Pickles, 207–9
  Chopped Middle Eastern Salad, 66–68
  Salad, Creamy, 63–64
  Sautéed, 160–61
  and Yogurt Salad, 64
Cupcakes, Chocolate, 444
Cupcakes, Vanilla, 445
Curd, Cranberry, 451
Curd, Lemon, 451
Curd, Lime, 451
Curd, Pomegranate, 452
Curd, Rhubarb, 451
Curry(ied)
  Cauliflower, 165
  Cauliflower Soup, 39
  Green Beans, 164–65
  Mayonnaise, 406
  Peas, 165
  Powder, 409
  Rice and Fresh Corn Salad with Golden Raisins,
    74–75
  Rice Noodles with Beef, Chicken, or Shrimp, 264
  Rice Noodles with Peanuts, 263–64
  Thai Slather, 352
  Turkey Salad with Dried Cranberries and Yogurt
    Dressing, 78–79

D
Dashi, 396
Date-Nut Cake, 436–37
Dates and Almonds, Couscous with, 387
Dates and Orange, Barley with, 236
Desserts. *See also* Cakes; Candy; Cookies and bars;
    Ice Cream; Pies; Tarts, dessert
  Apple Cranberry Crisp, 433–34
  Baked Apples, 417
  baked goods, ingredients for, 412
  baked goods, mailing, 459
  baked goods, preparing, 447
  Blueberry Soup, 416

Bourbon Bread-and-Butter Pudding, 453–54
Buttermilk Panna Cotta, 455–56
Butterscotch Pudding, 452
Cantaloupe Soup, 414
Caramel Sauce, 451
Chocolate Crème Brûlée, 454–55
Chocolate Pudding, 452
Chocolate Sesame Pots de Crème, 455
Chunky Applesauce, 416–17
Clafoutis, 112
Cranberry Curd, 451
Fruit Coulis, 471–72
Fruit Salad, 413
Fruit Salad with Lavender or Rosemary, 413
Halvah Pots de Crème, 455
Honeydew Soup, 413–14
Hot Fudge Sauce, 471
Lemon Curd, 451
Lemon Pick-Me-Up, 456–57
Lime Curd, 451
Mocha Pudding, 452
Panettone Bread Pudding, 454
Peach or Nectarine Soup, 414
Peach Shortcake, 435
Pear Sauce, 417
Pomegranate Curd, 452
Quince Paste, 418
Rhubarb Curd, 451
Rice Pudding, 452–53
Roasted Figs with Mascarpone Mousse,
    419–20
Sour Cherry Soup, 414–16
Strawberry Shortcake, 434–35
Summer Fruit Cobbler, 432–33
Vanilla Custard Sauce, 472
Watermelon Soup, 414
Wine-Poached Pears, 418–19
Dips. *See also* Salsa
Roasted Red Pepper and Garlic, 7–8
serving, 9
turning into spreads, 9
Duck
Breast, Grilled, 334–35
Confit, 335–37
cooking temperatures, 310
fat, rendering, 336
Prosciutto, 337

Stew, 335
testing for doneness, 310
Dukkah, 408–9
Dumplings
buying wrappers for, 271
Chicken and, 324–25
Chinese, about, 271
ethnic variations in, 240
making ahead, 271
Naked Ravioli with Browned Butter, Sage, and
    Toasted Walnuts, 268–69
Naked Ravioli with Tomato Sauce, 270
Potato Gnocchi, 267–68
Potato Gnocchi in Fresh Tomato Sauce,
    268
Potstickers, 270–72
Semolina, 270
Shu Mai, 272–73
Steamed, 272
Vegetarian Potstickers, 272

E
Earl Grey's Devil's Food Cake, 444
Edamame, 4–6
Fraud Thai, 265–66
Succotash, 170–71
Eggplant
Baba Ghanoush, 13–14
Focaccia, 101–2
Green Tomato Caponata, 168–69
Marinated, Relish, 207
Parmesan, Grilled, 152–54
Ratatouille, 166–67
Summertime Chicken Cacciatore, 321
Egg(s)
beating, for soufflés, 132
Beef, Chicken, or Turkey Hash, 124–25
Benedict, 123–24
Breakfast Strudel, 105
Carrot and Ginger Soufflé, 131–34
Cheese Soufflé, 130–31
Clafoutis, 112
Croque Madame, 86–87
Devilish, 28
Fried Rice, 222–23
and Fried Salami Sandwich, 121–23
Frisée aux Lardons, 80–81

Egg(s) (*cont.*)
  Frittata, 120–21
  hard-cooked, preparing, 29
  Poached, 122
  raw or undercooked, 125
  Scrambled, and Onions, Smoked Sturgeon with, 121
  soufflés, 132
  Spaghetti alla Carbonara, 253
  Spaghetti Frittata, 255–56
  Spanish Potato Omelet, 118–19
Endives. *See* Belgian Endives

F
Falafel, 197–98
Fats, trans, 422
Fava Bean(s)
  and Artichoke Fricassée, 169–70
  Feta, Olives, Preserved Lemon, and Mint, Israeli Couscous Salad with, 71–72
  fresh, cleaning and peeling, 170
  Hummus, 12–13
Fennel
  Cranberries, and Toasted Pecans, Cornbread Stuffing with, 229
  Roasted, 147–48
  Shaved, and Italian Tuna Sandwich with Black Olive Paste, 90–91
Fig and Shallot, Roasted, Dressing, 392
Fig or Plum Coffee Cake, 117
Fig Preserves, 140
Figs, Roasted, with Mascarpone Mousse, 419–20
Fish. *See also* Salmon; Tuna
  Anchovies, White, with Garlic and Parsley, 30–31
  Anchovy and Garlic Dressing, Wilted Arugula with, 79–80
  Beer Batter–Fried, 303–4
  breadings for, 318
  buying, 276, 278, 296
  Catfish, Cornmeal-Crusted, 302–3
  Ceviche, 293–94
  Cod in the Basque Style, 304–5
  endangered species, 276
  farmed, about, 275–76
  Fillets, Baked, with an Herbed Crust, 299
  Fillets, Baked, with Lemon and Olive Oil, 298–99

health benefits from, 275
poaching, in stock or oil, 301
raw, serving, 292
Salsa Verde, 401
Sardine Cream Sauce, Pasta with, 255
Seafood Pouches, 287–89
Simple Seafood Sausage, 289–90
Simple Seafood Terrine, 290
Skate, Crisp, with Brown Butter and Capers, 305–6
Skate, Mediterranean-Style, with Capers, 306
Sole, My Mother's Breaded, 303
Steaks, Spiced-Yogurt Grilled, 299–300
Steamed, Mediterranean Style, 296–97
Steamed, with Ginger, Scallion, and Soy, 295–96
Stock, 52–53
Sturgeon, Smoked, with Scrambled Eggs and Onions, 121
substituting, 296
Taco, 93–94
Trout, Smoked, Salad with Pickled Beets and Beans, 77–78
Whole, Baked in Salt, 297–98
whole, serving, 297
wild, about, 275–76
Flan, Jerusalem Artichoke, 175–76
Focaccia
  baking, 96–97
  Dough, 100
  Eggplant, 101–2
  Potato, 102
  toppings for, 97
French Fries, 191–93
French Fries with Garlic and Herbs, 193
French Toast, 105–7
French Toast, Lemon- or Orange-Infused, 107
Frisée aux Lardons, 80–81
Frittata, 120–21
Frittata, Spaghetti, 255–56
Fritters, Black-Eyed Pea, with Country Ham, 196–97
Fritters, Corn, 194–95
Frostings
  Caramel Cream Cheese, 450–51
  Chocolate, Deep Dark, 448–49
  Cream Cheese, Carrot Cake with, 438–39

Lemon, 448
Vanilla Cream, 448
Fruit. *See also specific fruits*
buying, 415
citrus, sectioning, 70
Citrus Peel, Candied, 467
Clafoutis, 112
Coulis, 471–72
Fruity Oatmeal Porridge, 112–13
ripening, 415
Salad, 413
Salad with Lavender or Rosemary, 413
sizes, 478
Summer, Cobbler, 432–33
Frying foods, 192

G
Garlic
Aïoli, 406
clove sizes, 478
Garlicky Broccoli, 157
Garlicky Cauliflower, 157
Garlicky Kohlrabi, 158
Garlicky Walnut and Potato Spread,
9–11
Gremolata, 361
and Herb Mustard Slather, 351
and Olive Oil, Pasta with, 247–48
or Shallot Vinaigrette, 391
Roasted, and Basil Mayonnaise, 406
Roasted, for Presentation, 152
and Roasted Red Pepper Dip, 7–8
Roasted Whole, 152
Gazpacho, Tomato, 34
Gazpacho, Watermelon, 35
Gazpacho, Yellow Tomato, 35
Ginger and Lemon Pie, 424
Ginger Ice Cream, 473
Ginger Sesame Scones, 116
Ginger Snaps, 463
Glossary of terms
baking terms, 483–84
cooking terms, 482–83
of food terms, 481–82
Gnocchi, Potato, 267–68
Gnocchi, Potato, in Fresh Tomato Sauce, 268
Goose, cooking, 310

Graham Cracker Crust, 427
Graham Cracker Crust, a 10–Inch, 427
Grains. *See also* Barley; Bulgur; Cornmeal; Cous-
cous; Oats; Rice
cooking, 215–17
Kasha Varnishkes, 236
Kasha with Wild Mushrooms and Walnuts,
235–36
Multigrain Pancakes, 108–9
Plain Kasha, 236
Plain Quinoa, 237
Quinoa with Roasted Poblanos, Cilantro, and
Lime, 236–37
Spiced Millet with Cauliflower, Currants, and
Pistachios, 233–34
storing, 215
Stuffed Peppers, 176–77
Wheat Berry Salad, 72
Gratins
Butternut Squash, 184–85
Cauliflower, 183
Chicken or Turkey, 324
Leek, 184
Potato, Beer-Baked, 182–83
Potato, Creamy, 181–82
Gravy
Cream, 325–26
Sausage, 127–28
Turkey, 328–30, 332
Green Beans
and Corn, Warm Barley Salad with, 72
Curried, 164–65
with Potato, Onion, and Bacon, 164
Smoked Trout Salad with Pickled Beets and
Beans, 77–78
Szechuan, 165
Greens. *See also* Broccoli Rabe; Cabbage;
Spinach
Bean Soup with Stinging Nettles, 42–43
beet or turnip, cooking, 150
cleaning and storing, 60
Collard, Southern-Style, 165–66
Frisée aux Lardons, 80–81
leafy, cleaning and storing, 60
mesclun, buying and storing, 61
Naked Ravioli with Browned Butter, Sage, and
Toasted Walnuts, 268–69

Greens (*cont.*)
  Naked Ravioli with Tomato Sauce, 270
  Radicchio Braised in Red Wine, 172–73
  Ribollita, 43
  Rice Noodle Bowl with Ginger and Watercress, 264–65
  Risotto with Radicchio and Barolo, 224
  Salad à la Française, 57
  Salad all'Italiana, 57
  Sausages with Kale, 372
  Turnip, Beet, or Mustard, and Potato Croquettes, 191
  Walnut and Arugula Pesto, 398
  Wilted Arugula with Anchovy and Garlic Dressing, 79–80
Gremolata, 361
grilling, pizza, 100
grilling, vegetables, 153
Grits, Basic, 130
Grits, Cheese, 129–30
Grits, Cheese, "Soufflé," 130
Guacamole, 14–15

H
Halvah Pots de Crème, 455
Ham
  Cheese, and Jalapeño, Savory Cornbread with, 225
  Croque Madame, 86–87
  Croque Monsieur, 86
  Cuban Sandwich, 88–89
  Eggs Benedict, 123–24
  Glazed, 377–78
  and Onions, Grilled Cheese with, 85
  and Potato Croquettes, 191
  prosciutto, about, 378
  Steaks with Red-Eye Gravy, 378–79
  types of, 378
Hash, Beef, Chicken, or Turkey, 124–25
Hazelnut(s)
  Buckwheat Cookies, 460
  Dukkah, 408–9
  Esther's Special Linzer Tart, 431–32
  and Wild Mushroom Crostini, 23–24
Herb(s). *See also* Basil; Cilantro
  and Garlic Mustard Slather, 351
  Gremolata, 361

  Herbed Syrups, 416
  Mint-Cilantro Sauce with Tomato, 399
  Minted Yogurt Sauce, 402
  Salsa Verde, 401
Hollandaise, *see* Egg(s), Benedict
Honeydew Soup, 413–14
Hors d'oeuvres. *See also* Spreads, savory
  Appenzeller and Peanut Biscuits, 21
  Baked Parsnip Chips, 27
  Bruschetta, 23
  Ceviche, 293–94
  Cheese and Nut Biscuits, 20–21
  Cheese and Pepper Puffs, 26
  Cheese Lace, 19–20
  Cheese Lace for a Crowd, 20
  Chorizo and Pepper Puffs, 25–26
  Crostini, 22–23
  Devilish Eggs, 28
  Edamame, 4–6
  Evelynne's Pickled Shrimp, 29–30
  Goat Cheese Tots, 21
  Grilled Pita Triangles with Za'atar, 24
  Herbed Olive Salad with Orange, 7
  Homemade Potato Chips, 26–27
  Marinated Artichoke Hearts, 7
  Mini Cheese and Nut Biscuits, 21
  number to serve, 5
  Party Nuts, 4
  Quesadilla, 22
  Roasted Red Pepper and Garlic Dip, 7–8
  Salmon Tartare with Preserved Lemon and Olives, 293
  Savory Apple and Cheddar Tart, 25
  Savory Pear and Gorgonzola Tart, 24–25
  serving, guidelines for, 5
  serving, in soup spoons, 30
  Shrimp Cocktail, 28–29
  Spicy Moroccan Olive Salad, 6–7
  Spicy Salmon Tartare, 293
  Tuna Tartare with Toasted Sesame, 292
  White Anchovies with Garlic and Parsley, 30–31
  Wild Mushroom and Hazelnut Crostini, 23–24
Hot dogs. *See* Chili Dogs
Hummus
  The Best You've Ever Tasted, 11–12
  Fava Bean, 12–13
  in a Hurry, 12

I

Ice Cream
  Candy Bar, 473
  Caramel, 473
  Chocolate, 472–73
  Cookies and Cream, 473
  Ginger, 473
  Vanilla, French, 472
  Vanilla, The Easiest Ever, 473
Ingredients, for recipes, 476–77
Ingredients, measuring, 446

J

Jam(s)
  Brandied Apricot, with Vanilla Bean, 134
  Brandied Peach, with Vanilla, 135
  Cake, 438
  canning techniques, 138
  Green Tomato Ginger, 139
  preparing, guidelines for, 135
  preparing, in microwave, 136
  Sour Cherry, 137
  Spiced Blueberry, 136–37
  Strawberry, 135–36
  Strawberry Rhubarb, 136
Jerk Chicken, 316–17
Jerusalem Artichoke Flan, 175–76
Jerusalem Artichokes, Roasted, 148–50
Jícama Slaw with Yogurt and Lime, 65–66

K

Kale, Sausages with, 372
Kasha
  Plain, 236
  Varnishkes, 236
  with Wild Mushrooms and Walnuts, 235–36
Kimchee, 212–13
Kohlrabi, Garlicky, 158
Kohlrabi, Shredded, with Caraway and Bacon,
  161–62

L

Lamb. *See also* Meat
  Chops, Grilled, with Salsa Verde, 383
  Greek Souvlaki, 384
  Irish Stew, 359
  Leg of, Grilled, 383–84

  Moroccan Couscous with, 384–86
  Moroccan-Spiced Meatballs with Preserved
    Lemon, Tomato, and Olive, 366–67
  Pastitsio, 256–58
  Roasted, Moroccan-Spiced, 383
  Roasted, Provençal, 382–83
  Shepherd's Pie, 387–88
  Sicilian Meatballs with Raisins and Pine Nuts,
    366
Lard, Homemade, 423
Lard, versus shortening, 422
Lasagna, 260–61
Lasagna, Chicken and Artichoke, 261–62
Lasagna, Vegetable, 261
Latkes (Potato Pancakes), 187
Lavender Cookies, 461–62
Leek(s)
  Braised, Chilled, with Vinaigrette, 175
  Braised, with Cream and Tarragon, 173–75
  Gratin, 184
Lemon(s)
  Candied Citrus Peel, 467
  Ceviche, 293–94
  Charmoula, 400–401
  Curd, 451
  Frosting, 448
  Mojo, 400
  Pick-Me-Up, 456–57
  Pie, 426
  Pie, Ginger and, 424
  Pie, Shaker, 422–24
  Poppy Seed Coffee Cake, 117
  Poppy Seed Scones, 115
  Preserved, 409–10
  Preserved, with Spices, 410
  sectioning, 70
  Squares, 465
  tiramisù, 456–57
Lentil(s)
  Mushroom Barley Soup, 41–42
  and Root Vegetable Stew, 203
Lime(s)
  Ceviche, 293–94
  Charmoula, 400–401
  Cilantro Mayonnaise, 406
  Curd, 451
  Key, Pie, 426

Lime(s) (*cont.*)
  Key, Pie, Mock, 426
  Preserved, 410
  sectioning, 70
Liptauer, 17–18
Liver, Chicken, Mousse with Green Apple and
    Toasted Walnuts, 18–19
Lobster
  buying, 278
  Cooked and Shelled, 288
  Roll, 89–90
  or Shrimp Stock, 53

M
Macaroni and Cheese, Baked, with Tomatoes,
    258–59
Macaroni and Cheese, Ultimate, 259–60
Mango, Green, or Green Papaya and Shrimp Salad,
    76–77
Marmalade, Bitter Orange, 139–40
Mayonnaise, 405
  Aïoli, 406
  Blender or Food Processor, 405–6
  broken, remedy for, 406
  Curried, 406
  Lime Cilantro, 406
  Roasted Garlic and Basil, 406
measuring ingredients, 446
Meat
  buying, 340, 347
  Chinese Stock, 52
  chops, about, 368
  cooking chart, 345
  Darker, Richer Stock, 52
  dry-aged, 350
  freezing, 340
  grades of, 347
  grinding at home, 363
  ground, storing, 340
  marinating, 353
  naturally raised, definition of, 347
  organic, definition of, 347
  or Poultry Stock, 51–52
  pan-frying, 355
  pan sauces for, 372
  sautéing, 355
  seasoned slathers for, 351–52
  stir-frying, 355
  storing, 340
  Stuffed Peppers with, 177
  testing for doneness, 345–46
  Tomato Sauce with (Red Gravy), 251–52
  wet-aged, 350
Meatballs
  Italian, 365–66
  Moroccan-Spiced, with Preserved Lemon,
    Tomato, and Olive, 366–67
  Sicilian, with Raisins and Pine Nuts, 366
Meatloaf, 362–64
  Meat and Vegetable Loaf, 364
  with Roasted Potatoes, 364
Melon
  Cantaloupe Soup, 414
  Honeydew Soup, 413–14
  Watermelon Gazpacho, 35
  Watermelon Soup, 414
Millet, Spiced, with Cauliflower, Currants, and Pis-
    tachios, 233–34
Mint-Cilantro Sauce with Tomato, 399
Minted Yogurt Sauce, 402
Mocha Pudding, 452
Mojo, 400
Mousse, Chicken Liver, with Green Apple and
    Toasted Walnuts, 18–19
Mousse, Mascarpone, Roasted Figs with, 419–20
Mozzarella cheese
  Grilled Eggplant Parmesan, 152–54
  Grilled Portobello Parmesan, 154
  Grilled Zucchini Parmesan, 154
  Lasagna, 260–61
  A New York Slice, 101
  Panini, 87–88
  Pasta with Uncooked Tomato Sauce, 249–50
  Pizza Margherita, 101
  Polenta Parmigiana, 231
  Veal Parmesan, 369–71
  Vegetable Lasagna, 261
  White Pizza, 100
Muffins, Lemon Blueberry Sour Cream,
    113–14
Muffuletta, 91
Mushroom(s)
  Barley Soup, 41–42
  and Bean Burrito, 94–95

Grilled Portobello and Sun-Dried Tomato Sandwich with Garlic Herbed Mayonnaise, 87
Grilled Portobello Parmesan, 154
Kasha Varnishkes, 236
and Onions, Sliced Steak Smothered with, 349–50
Porcini Risotto, 224
Potato, and Corn Croquettes, 191
Sautéed, 159–60
Sautéed Chicken Breasts with, 316
Shu Mai, 272–73
Wild, and Hazelnut Crostini, 23–24
Wild, and Marsala Sauce, Pork Cutlets with, 373–74
Wild, and Walnuts, Kasha with, 235–36
and Wild Rice Stuffing with Orange and Pine Nuts, 230
Mussels
  Belgian, 284–85
  buying, 278
  cleaning, 282
  Italian, 285–86
  Southeast Asian, 285
  Steamed, 284–86
Mustard Slather, Garlic and Herb, 351
Mustard Tarragon Sauce, 300–302

N
Nectarine or Peach Soup, 414
Nettles, Stinging, Bean Soup with, 42–43
Noodle(s)
  Chicken Casserole, 263
  Chilled Soba Salad, 76
  cooking, 239
  Fraud Thai, 265–66
  Fresh Tuna Casserole, 262–63
  Pad Thai, see Noodle(s), Fraud Thai
  Rice, Bowl with Ginger and Watercress, 264–65
  Rice, Curried, with Beef, Chicken, or Shrimp, 264
  Rice, Curried, with Peanuts, 263–64
  Spätzle, 246–47
  Yakisoba, 266–67
Nut(s). See also Almond(s); Pecan(s); Walnut(s)
  Appenzeller and Peanut Biscuits, 21
  Buckwheat Hazelnut Cookies, 460
  and Cheese Biscuits, 20–21
  and Cheese Biscuits, Mini, 21

Chocolate Chunk Cookies with, 459
Dukkah, 408–9
Esther's Special Linzer Tart, 431–32
grinding, 435
Party, 4
Peanut Brittle, 469
Peanut Pie, 425
Peanut Soup with Pickled Cherries and Crumbled Bacon, 46–47
Pesto, 398
Pine, and Raisins, Sicilian Meatballs with, 366
Rugelach, 466
Streusel Coffee Cake, 116–17
toasting, 10
Wild Mushroom and Hazelnut Crostini, 23–24

O
Oats
  Fruity Oatmeal Porridge, 112–13
  Oatmeal Buttermilk Cookies, 461
  Oatmeal Chocolate Chunk Cookies, 459–60
  Oatmeal Made from Rolled Oats, 113
  Savory Oatmeal, 113
Octopus, Stewed, 281–82
Oils, olive, about, 67
Okra, Pickled, 211
Okra, Roasted, 150
Olive oils, types of, 67
Olive(s)
  Black, Paste, Italian Tuna and Shaved Fennel Sandwich with Black Olive Paste, 90–91
  Duck Stew, 335
  Muffuletta, 91
  Preserved Lemon, and Tomato, Moroccan-Spiced Meatballs with, 366–67
  and Preserved Lemon, Salmon Tartare with, 293
  Salad, Herbed, with Orange, 7
  Salad, Spicy Moroccan, 6–7
  Tunisian Slather, 352
omelet, see also Fritatta
Omelet, Spanish Potato, 118–19
Omelet, Sweet Potato, see Spanish Potato Omelet
Onions
  Buttermilk Fried, 193–94
  Chimichurri, 400
  and Ham, Grilled Cheese with, 85

Onions (*cont.*)
  and Mushrooms, Sliced Steak Smothered with, 349–50
  Pearl, Glazed, 155–56
  Pickled, with Fresh Horseradish, 211–12
  sizes of, 478
Orange(s)
  and Almond Cake, Flourless, 440–41
  Bitter, Marmalade, 139–40
  Butter Sauce, 404
  Candied Citrus Peel, 467
  Ceviche, 293–94
  Charmoula, 400–401
  Cranberry Scones, 115
  Creamsicle Pie, 425
  Glaze, Buckwheat Buttermilk Bundt Cake with, 118
  Glazed Turkey, 330
  Mojo, 400
  sectioning, 70
  –Soy Sauce Salmon, 300
  –Soy Sauce Tuna, 300
Osso Buco, 360–62
oysters, buying, 278
Oysters, Buttermilk Fried, 284
Oysters, Scalloped, 286–87
oysters, shucking, 286

P
Pad Thai, *see* Noodle(s), Fraud Thai
Pancakes
  Beet, 188–89
  Buttermilk, 107–8
  Celery Root, 189
  Clafoutis, 112
  Cranberry Johnnycakes, 109–10
  Multigrain, 108–9
  Potato (Latkes), 187
Panettone, *see* Bread Pudding; French Toast
Panini, 87–88
Panna Cotta, Buttermilk, 455–56
Papaya, Green, or Green Mango and Shrimp Salad, 76–77
Parmesan cheese
  Chicken and Artichoke Lasagna, 261–62
  Creamy Cracked Pepper Dressing, 394–95
  Grilled Eggplant Parmesan, 152–54

Grilled Portobello Parmesan, 154
  Grilled Zucchini Parmesan, 154
  Lasagna, 260–61
  Pesto, 398
  Polenta Parmigiana, 231
  Sicilian Pesto with Almonds, Tomato, and Mint, 399
  Spaghetti alla Carbonara, 253
  The Ultimate Macaroni and Cheese, 259–60
  Veal Parmesan, 369–71
  Vegetable Lasagna, 261
  Walnut and Arugula Pesto, 398
Parsnip Cake, 439–40
Parsnip Chips, Baked, 27
Parsnips, Glazed, 155
party planning, 5
Pasta. *See also* Noodle(s)
  Baked Macaroni and Cheese with Tomatoes, 258–59
  with Broccoli Rabe, 248–49
  with Broccoli Rabe and Sausage, 249
  Chicken and Artichoke Lasagna, 261–62
  Chicken Casserole, 263
  with Clams, 255
  cooking *al dente*, 239
  cooking water, adding to sauce, 248
  Dough, Flavored, 246
  Dough, Fresh (Egg Noodles), 242–46
  dried, buying, 243
  Dried, Cooking, 241
  fresh, buying, 243
  Fresh, Cooking, 244
  Fresh Tuna Casserole, 262–63
  with Garlic and Olive Oil, 247–48
  Kasha Varnishkes, 236
  Lasagna, 260–61
  Macaroni Salad, 75–76
  Pastitsio, 256–58
  with Sardine Cream Sauce, 255
  sauce, finishing, 248
  Seafood, 254–55
  with Sheep's Milk Cheese and Black Pepper, 253–54
  Spaghetti alla Carbonara, 253
  Spaghetti Frittata, 255–56
  Spaghetti with Tomato Sauce, 249

The Ultimate Macaroni and Cheese, 259–60
  with Uncooked Tomato Sauce, 249–50
  Vegetable Lasagna, 261
  Yakisoba, 266–67
Pastitsio, 256–58
Pastry dough
  Cream Cheese, 431
  Pie Dough, 421
  pre-baking, 426
Peach(es)
  Galette, 427–28
  Jam, Brandied, with Vanilla, 135
  or Nectarine Soup, 414
  peeling, 429
  Shortcake, 435
  sizes, 478
Peanut
  and Appenzeller Biscuits, 21
  Brittle, 469
  Pie, 425
Peanut Butter
  Cookies, Chocolate Chip, 458
  Cookies, Maxine's, 457–58
  Peanut Pie, 425
  Peanut Soup with Pickled Cherries and Crumbled Bacon, 46–47
  Spicy Peanut Sauce, 397–98
Pear(s)
  Curried Cauliflower Soup, 39
  and Gorgonzola Tart, Savory, 24–25
  and Roasted Cauliflower Soup, 38–39
  Roasted Seckel, and Roquefort Salad with Walnuts, 60–61
  Sauce, 417
  sizes, 478
  Wine-Poached, 418–19
Pea(s)
  Curried, 165
  Snow, and Cabbage Slaw, Grilled Turkey Cutlets on, 332–33
Pecan(s)
  Cheese and Nut Biscuits, 20–21
  Ground, Pie, Anya's, 424–25
  Pie, Chocolate, 425
  Pie, Traditional, 425
  Toasted, Fennel, and Cranberries, Cornbread Stuffing with, 229

Pepper(s). *See also* Chile peppers
  and Chicken Casserole, 320–21
  Cod in the Basque Style, 304–5
  Peperonata, 167–68
  Roasted, 146
  Roasted Red, and Garlic Dip, 7–8
  Spanish Romesco Sauce, 401
  Steak, 354
  Stuffed, 176–77
  Stuffed, with Meat, 177
Pesto, 398
Pesto, Sicilian, with Almonds, Tomato, and Mint, 399
Pesto, Walnut and Arugula, 398
Phyllo
  Breakfast Strudel, 105
  Spinach and Feta Rolls, 189–90
  working with, 106
Pickles
  Bread and Butter, 207–9
  Bread and Butter, Summer Squash, 210
  Kimchee, 212–13
  Pickled Beets, Spiced, 211
  Pickled Beets with Caraway, 210–11
  Pickled Okra, 211
  Pickled Onions with Fresh Horseradish, 211–12
  Polish, Soup, Izabela's, 39–40
  preserving, 209
  quick, preparing, 212
Pie crusts
  Chocolate Cookie, 427
  Graham Cracker, 427
  Graham Cracker, a 10-Inch, 427
  Pie Dough, 421
  pre-baking, 426
Pies
  Apple, 420–22
  Creamsicle, 425
  Key Lime, 426
  Key Lime, Mock, 426
  Lemon, 426
  Lemon, Shaker, 422–24
  Lemon and Ginger, 424
  Peanut, 425
  Pecan, Ground, Anya's, 424–25
  Pecan, Traditional, 425

Pies (*cont.*)
 Pecan Chocolate, 425
 Pumpkin Chiffon, 426–27
Pilaf, Bulgur, with Pine Nuts, 234
Pilaf, Rice, 220–21
Pilaf in the Oven, 221
Pineapple, Grilled, Salsa, 16–17
Pineapple Upside-Down Cake, 435–36
Pine Nut(s)
 Pesto, 398
 and Raisins, Sicilian Meatballs with, 366
Pizza, 97
 baking, 96–97
 Dough, Neapolitan-Style, 99
 Dough, Quick, 98
 grilling, 100
 Margherita, 101
 A New York Slice, 101
 toppings for, 97
 White, 100
Plum or Fig Coffee Cake, 117
Plum Tart, 428–29
Polenta
 Buttermilk, with Fresh Corn, 232
 Fried, 231
 Grilled, 231
 with Herbs, 230–31
 Parmigiana, 231
Pomegranate Curd, 452
Pomegranate Slather, 352
Pomegranate Vinaigrette, Warm, Seared Scallops
  with, 290–91
Pork. *See also* Bacon; Ham; Meat; Pork sausages
 in Adobo, 381–82
 Barbecued, Chinese, 380–81
 Barbecued Ribs, Braised, 380
 Barbecued Spareribs, 379–80
 Chops, Smoked, with Mustard and Bread
   Crumbs, 375–76
 Chops with Apples and Prunes, 374–75
 Cuban Sandwich, 88–89
 Cutlets with Marsala and Wild Mushroom Sauce,
   373–74
 Greek Souvlaki, 384
 Oven-Roasted, 373
 Potstickers, 270–72
 Pulled, 376–77

 Pulled, Less, 377
 Roast, Tuscan-Style, 372–73
 Shu Mai, 272–73
 Steamed Dumplings, 272
 Tomato Sauce with Meat (Red Gravy), 251–52
Pork sausages
 Chorizo and Pepper Puffs, 25–26
 Fried Salami and Egg Sandwich, 121–23
 Muffuletta, 91
 Panini, 87–88
 Pasta with Broccoli Rabe and Sausage, 249
 Sausage and Bread Stuffing with Apples and Sage,
   228
 Sausage Gravy, 127–28
 Sausages with Kale, 372
 Southwestern Baked Beans with Chorizo,
   Poblanos, and Orange, 200–202
 Spaghetti Frittata, 255–56
 Tomato Sauce with Meat (Red Gravy), 251–52
Potato(es). *See also* Sweet Potato(es)
 Beef, Chicken, or Turkey Hash, 124–25
 Beef Stew, 358–59
 Chip Cookies, 463–64
 Chips, Homemade, 26–27
 Corn, and Mushroom Croquettes, 191
 Focaccia, 102
 French Fries, 191–93
 French Fries with Garlic and Herbs, 193
 Gnocchi, 267–68
 Gnocchi in Fresh Tomato Sauce, 268
 Gratin, Beer-Baked, 182–83
 Gratin, Creamy, 181–82
 and Ham Croquettes, 191
 Home Fries, 128
 Irish Stew, 359
 Izabela's Polish Pickle Soup, 39–40
 Mashed, 178–79
 Mashed, Make-Ahead, 179
 Mashed, Mediterranean, 179
 Omelet, Spanish, 118–19
 Onion, and Bacon, Green Beans with, 164
 Pancakes (Latkes), 187
 Roasted, Meatloaf with, 364
 Root Vegetable Purée Baked with Cheese, 180
 Salad, 72–73
 Seedy, 180–81
 Shepherd's Pie, 387–88

sizes, 478
and Spinach Croquettes, 190–91
and Turnip, Beet, or Mustard Greens Croquettes, 191
and Turnip Galette, 185
and Turnips, Sautéed, 181
and Walnut Spread, Garlicky, 9–11
Winter Mash, 179–80
Pot Pie, Chicken or Turkey, 322–24
Pots and pans, 478
Pots de Crème, Chocolate Sesame, 455
Pots de Crème, Halvah, 455
Potstickers, 270–72
Potstickers, Vegetarian, 272
Poultry. *See also* Chicken; Duck; Goose; Turkey
brining, 308
buying, 307–8
Chinese Stock, 52
cooking, 308
cooking temperatures, 310
Darker, Richer Stock, 52
deep-fried, 330
Duck Confit, 335–37
duck fat, rendering, 336
Duck Prosciutto, 337
Duck Stew, 335
Grilled Duck Breast, 334–35
or Meat Stock, 51–52
pan sauces for, 372
popular cooking fads, 330
testing for doneness, 310
trussing, 312
turducken, 330
Prosciutto ham, about, 378
Prunes and Apples, Pork Chops with, 374–75
Pudding(s)
Bread, Panettone, 454
Bread, Savory Pumpkin, 227–28
Bread-and-Butter, Bourbon, 453–54
Buttermilk Panna Cotta, 455–56
Butterscotch, 452
Chocolate, 452
Chocolate Sesame Pots de Crème, 455
Cornbread, 226–27
Halvah Pots de Crème, 455
Mocha, 452
Rice, 452–53

Pumpkin
Bread Pudding, Savory, 227–28
Chiffon Pie, 426–27
Seed Brittle, 468–69

Q
Quesadilla, 22
Quince Paste, 418
Quinoa, Plain, 237
Quinoa with Roasted Poblanos, Cilantro, and Lime, 236–37

R
Radicchio and Barolo, Risotto with, 224
Radicchio Braised in Red Wine, 172–73
Radishes, Glazed, 155
Raisin and Carrot Raita, Madhur Jaffrey's, 402–3
Raita, Carrot and Raisin, Madhur Jaffrey's, 402–3
Raspberry Vinaigrette, 394
Ratatouille, 166–67
Recipes
advance prep time, 479
baking terms, 483–84
cooking terms, 482–83
estimated times, 477–79
food terms, 481–82
headnotes to, 476
ingredients, 476–77
leftovers, notes about, 479
measuring Ingredients for, 446
pots and pans for, 478
titles to, 476
variations, about, 479
Relish, Fresh Corn and Tomato, 207
Relish, Marinated Eggplant, 207
Rhubarb Curd, 451
Rhubarb Galette, 428
Rhubarb Strawberry Jam, 136
Ribollita, 43
Rice. *See also* Risotto
Basmati, 218–19
Brown, 220
and Fresh Corn Salad, Curried, with Golden Raisins, 74–75
Fried, 222–23
Jasmine, 219–20
Mushroom and Bean Burrito, 94–95

Rice (*cont.*)
Peas and, 206
Pilaf, 220–21
Pilaf in the Oven, 221
Pudding, 452–53
reheating, 219
Stuffed Peppers, 176–77
Tomato, 221–22
White, Basic, 218
White, Converted, 218
Wild, and Mushroom Stuffing with Orange and Pine Nuts, 230
Wild, with Apples, Dried Cranberries, and Buttered Almonds, 232–33
Yellow, 218
Yellow, Cuban-Style, 221
Risotto, 223–24
Porcini, 224
with Radicchio and Barolo, 224
with Roasted Beets and Gorgonzola, 224
Saffron, 224
Roasted
Beets, 149
Garlic, Whole, 152
Peppers, 146
vegetables, 148
Rugelach, 466
Rutabagas
Glazed, 155
Root Vegetable Purée Baked with Cheese, 180
Winter Mash, 179–80

S
Saffron Risotto, 224
Salad dressings. *See also* Vinaigrettes
Creamy Cracked Pepper, 394–95
Gorgonzola, 394
Roasted Shallot and Fig, 392
Sesame, 396
Salads
à la Française, 57
all'Italiana, 57
Arugula, Wilted, with Anchovy and Garlic Dressing, 79–80
Avocado, 58–59
Barley, 72–73
Barley, Warm, with Corn and Green Beans, 72

Bean Sprout, Asian, 66
Beef, Vietnamese, with Watercress, 81–82
Bread, 68–69
Carrot and Caraway, 61–62
Carrot Slaw, Creamy, 64
Celery Root Rémoulade, 62
Celery Root Rémoulade, Creamy, 62
Chicken, 78
Chickpea and Spinach, 68
Coleslaw, Herbed, 64
Couscous, Spiced Orange, with Currants and Carrots, 69–70
Cucumber, Creamy, 63–64
Cucumber and Yogurt, 64
Frisée aux Lardons, 80–81
Fruit, 413
Fruit, with Lavender or Rosemary, 413
Israeli Couscous, with Favas, Feta, Olives, Preserved Lemon, and Mint, 71–72
Jícama Slaw with Yogurt and Lime, 65–66
Macaroni, 75–76
Middle Eastern, Chopped, 66–68
Potato, 72–73
Red Cabbage Slaw with Toasted Hazelnuts and Buttermilk Orange Dressing, 64–65
Rice and Fresh Corn, Curried, with Golden Raisins, 74–75
Seckel Pear, Roasted, and Roquefort, with Walnuts, 60–61
serving, 55–56
Shrimp and Green Mango or Green Papaya, 76–77
Smoked Trout, with Pickled Beets and Beans, 77–78
Soba, Chilled, 76
Spinach, Wilted, with Red Onion and Bacon, 80
Tabbouleh, 70–71
Tomato, with Browned Butter and Caper Dressing, 59
Turkey, Curried, with Dried Cranberries and Yogurt Dressing, 78–79
varieties of, 55–56
Wheat Berry, 72
Salmon
Baked, 298
Chardonnay-Poached, with Mustard Tarragon Sauce, 300–302

farmed, versus wild, 275–76
Orange–Soy Sauce, 300
Smoked, Grilled Cheese with, 85–86
Tartare, Spicy, 293
Tartare with Preserved Lemon and Olives, 293
Salsa
Fresh Red and Yellow Tomato, 15–16
Grilled Pineapple, 16–17
Grilled Tomato and Corn, with Chipotle, 16
Verde, 401
Sandwiches
Cheeseburgers, 96
Chili Dogs, 365
Crab Roll, 90
Croque Madame, 86–87
Croque Monsieur, 86
Cuban, 88–89
Fish Taco, 93–94
Fried Salami and Egg, 121–23
"Grilled"Cheese, 85
Grilled Cheese with Bacon and Tomato, 85
Grilled Cheese with Ham and Onions, 85
Grilled Cheese with Smoked Salmon, 85–86
Grilled Portobello and Sun-Dried Tomato, with
    Garlic Herbed Mayonnaise, 87
Gussied Up Burgers, 96
Hamburger Heaven, 95–96
Lobster Roll, 89–90
Muffuletta, 91
Mushroom and Bean Burrito, 94–95
Panini, 87–88
Shrimp Roll, 90
Smoked Turkey, with Green Apple, Curried
    Mayonnaise, and Pickled Red Onions, 91–92
Soft Beef Tacos, 93
Soft Turkey Taco, 92–93
Tuna, Italian, and Shaved Fennel, with Black
    Olive Paste, 90–91
Sardine Cream Sauce, Pasta with, 255
Sauces. See also Mayonnaise; Pesto; Salsa
Barbecue, Evelynne's, 406–7
Butter, 403–4
Butter, Orange, 404
Butter, Pink, 404
Caramel, 451
Charmoula, 400–401
Chili, Spicy Asian, 397

Chimichurri, 400
Chunky Applesauce, 416–17
Cilantro-Mint, with Tomato, 399
Cocktail, for shrimp, 28–29
Cream, 404–5
finishing, with pasta water, 248
Fruit Coulis, 471–72
Hot Fudge, 471
Madhur Jaffrey's Carrot and Raisin Raita, 402–3
Mojo, 400
Mustard Tarragon, 300–302
pan, for meat and poultry, 372
Peanut, Spicy, 397–98
Pear, 417
Romesco, Spanish, 401
Spaghetti, 251
Tomato, Quick, 250–51
Tomato, with Meat (Red Gravy), 251–52
Vanilla Custard, 472
Vegetarian Red Gravy, 253
Yogurt, Minted, 402
Sausage(s). See also Pork sausages
Couscous with Merguez, 387
Seafood, Simple, 289–90
Scallops
buying, 278
preparing for cooking, 291
Seafood Pasta, 254–55
Seafood Pouches, 287–89
Seared, with Warm Pomegranate Vinaigrette,
    290–91
Simple Seafood Sausage, 289–90
Simple Seafood Terrine, 290
Scones, 114–15
Chocolate Chip, 115
Cranberry Orange, 115
Lemon Poppy Seed, 115
Sesame Ginger, 116
Seafood, see Shellfish; specific types
Seeds, toasting, 10
Sesame
Chocolate Pots de Crème, 455
Halvah Pots de Crème, 455
seeds, toasting, 10
tahini sauce, see Falafel
Za'atar, 407–8
Shallot and Fig, Roasted, Dressing, 392

Shallot or Garlic Vinaigrette, 391
Shallot sizes, 478
Shellfish. *See also* Clam(s); Mussels; Shrimp;
    Squid
  Buttermilk Fried Oysters, 284
  buying, 278
  Cooked and Shelled Lobster, 288
  Crab Cakes, 294–95
  Crab Roll, 90
  health benefits from, 275
  Lobster or Shrimp Stock, 53
  Lobster Roll, 89–90
  oysters, shucking, 286
  raw, serving, 292
  Scalloped Oysters, 286–87
  Seafood Pasta, 254–55
  Seafood Pouches, 287–89
  Seared Scallops with Warm Pomegranate Vinai-
    grette, 290–91
  Simple Seafood Sausage, 289–90
  Simple Seafood Terrine, 290
  Stewed Octopus, 281–82
Shepherd's Pie, 387–88
shipping, baked goods, 459
Shortbread, Butterscotch, 467–68
Shortcake
  Peach, 435
  Strawberry, 434–35
  Strawberry, Herbed, 435
Shortening, versus lard, 422
Shrimp
  Beef, or Chicken, Curried Rice Noodles with, 264
  brining, 280
  Buttermilk Fried, 284
  buying, 278
  Cocktail, 28–29
  Cooked, Simple, 279
  Fraud Thai, 265–66
  and Green Mango or Green Papaya Salad, 76–77
  Grilled, 278–80
  or Calamari Ceviche, 294
  or Lobster Stock, 53
  Pickled, Evelynne's, 29–30
  Roll, 90
  Seafood Pasta, 254–55
  Seafood Pouches, 287–89
  Shu Mai, 272–73

  Simple Seafood Sausage, 289–90
  Simple Seafood Terrine, 290
  size counts, 279
  Yakisoba, 266–67
Shu Mai, 272–73
Skate, Crisp, with Brown Butter and Capers, 305–6
Skate, Mediterranean-Style, with Capers, 306
Slathers, seasoned, for meat, 351–52
Smoked Sturgeon with Scrambled Eggs and
    Onions, 121
Smoked Trout Salad with Pickled Beets and Beans,
    77–78
Soba Salad, Chilled, 76
Sole, My Mother's Breaded, 303
Soufflé
  Carrot and Ginger, 131–34
  Cheese, 130–31
  preparing, 132
"Soufflé," Cheese Grits, 130
Soups. *See also* Chowder; Stews; Stocks
  Asparagus, Cream of, 37
  Bean, with Stinging Nettles, 42–43
  Black Bean, Cuban, 43–44
  Black Bean, in a Hurry, 44
  Blueberry, 416
  Broccoli, Cream of, 37
  Butternut Squash, with Apple and Nutmeg, 38
  Cantaloupe, 414
  Carrot, Cream of, 37
  Cauliflower, Cream of, 37
  Cauliflower, Curried, 39
  Cauliflower, Roasted, and Pear, 38–39
  Celery, Three, Cream of, 37–38
  Cheddar Cheese, 44–46
  Chicken, 50–51
  cook-ins, suggested, 51
  garnishes for, 51
  Honeydew, 413–14
  Mushroom Barley, 41–42
  Peach or Nectarine, 414
  Peanut, with Pickled Cherries and Crumbled
    Bacon, 46–47
  Polish Pickle, Izabela's, 39–40
  preparing, technique for, 33
  Ribollita, 43
  Rice Noodle Bowl with Ginger and Watercress,
    264–65

Sour Cherry, 414–16
Split Pea, 40–41
thickening, methods for, 45
Tomato, Roasted, with Chickpeas, Spinach, and Cumin, 36
Tomato Gazpacho, 34
Watermelon, 414
Watermelon Gazpacho, 35
Yellow Tomato Gazpacho, 35
Souvlaki, Greek, 384
Soybeans. *See* Edamame
Soy Sauce Slather, 351
Spätzle, 246–47
Spices
    Curry Powder, 409
    Dukkah, 408–9
    toasting, 10
    Za'atar, 407–8
Spinach
    Chickpeas, and Cumin, Roasted Tomato Soup with, 36
    and Chickpea Salad, 68
    Creamed, 159
    and Feta Rolls, 189–90
    Naked Ravioli with Browned Butter, Sage, and Toasted Walnuts, 268–69
    Naked Ravioli with Tomato Sauce, 270
    and Potato Croquettes, 190–91
    Sautéed, American Style, 159
    Sautéed, Italian Style, 158–59
    Spaghetti Frittata, 255–56
    Wilted, Salad with Red Onion and Bacon, 80
Split Pea Soup, 40–41
Spreads, savory
    Artichoke, 8–9
    Baba Ghanoush, 13–14
    The Best Hummus You've Ever Tasted, 11–12
    Cheese, 17
    Chicken Liver Mousse with Green Apple and Toasted Walnuts, 18–19
    Fava Bean Hummus, 12–13
    Garlicky Walnut and Potato, 9–11
    Green Tomato Ginger Jam, 139
    Guacamole, 14–15
    Hummus in a Hurry, 12
    Liptauer, 17–18

serving, 9
    Strained Yogurt, 63
    turning into dips, 9
Spreads, sweet. *See also* Jams
    Bitter Orange Marmalade, 139–40
    Fig Preserves, 140
Squash. *See also* Pumpkin; Zucchini
    Butternut, Gratin, 184–85
    Butternut, Soup with Apple and Nutmeg, 38
    Summer, Bread and Butter Pickles, 210
    Winter, Roasted, 145
Squid
    Buttermilk Fried Calamari, 284
    cleaning, 280
    Fried Calamari, 280–81
    Seafood Pasta, 254–55
    Shrimp or Calamari Ceviche, 294
Stews
    Beef, 358–59
    Chicken in Adobo, 382
    Couscous with Chicken, 386
    Couscous with Merguez, 387
    Duck, 335
    Irish, 359
    Lentil and Root Vegetable, 203
    Moroccan Couscous with Lamb, 384–86
    Pork in Adobo, 381–82
    Vegetarian Couscous, 386–87
Stinging Nettles, Bean Soup with, 42–43
Stocks
    Chinese, 52
    Darker, Richer, 52
    Dashi, 396
    Fish, 52–53
    Lobster or Shrimp, 53
    Poultry or Meat, 51–52
    Vegetable, 53
    vegetable, quick, preparing, 151
storing leafy greens, 60
storing olive oil, 67
Strawberry
    Jam, 135–36
    Rhubarb Jam, 136
    Shortcake, 434–35
    Shortcake, Herbed, 435
Strudel, Breakfast, 105

Stuffings
  Cornbread, with Fennel, Cranberries, and
    Toasted Pecans, 229
  Mushroom and Wild Rice, with Orange and Pine
    Nuts, 230
  Sausage and Bread, with Apples and Sage, 228
Sturgeon, Smoked, with Scrambled Eggs and
    Onions, 121
Succotash, 170–71
Sweet Potato(es)
  Home Fries, 128–29
  Root Vegetable Purée Baked with Cheese, 180
  Wedges, Roasted, 145–47
  Wedges, Roasted, with Herbs, 147
  Winter Mash, 179–80
Swiss cheese
  Cauliflower Gratin, 183
  Chicken and Artichoke Lasagna, 261–62
  Chicken Casserole, 263
  Chicken or Turkey Gratin, 324
  Creamy Potato Gratin, 181–82
  Croque Madame, 86–87
  Croque Monsieur, 86
  Fresh Tuna Casserole, 262–63
  Leek Gratin, 184
  Root Vegetable Purée Baked with Cheese, 180
  Turnip and Potato Galette, 185
Syrups, Herbed, 416

T
Tabbouleh, 70–71
Taco, Fish, 93–94
Taco, Soft Turkey, 92–93
Tacos, Soft Beef, 93
tahini sauce, see Falafel
Tarts, Savory
  Apple and Cheddar, 25
  Beet and Goat Cheese, 185–86
  Pear and Gorgonzola, 24–25
  Turnip and Potato Galette, 185
Tarts, sweet
  Linzer, Esther's Special, 431–32
  Peach Galette, 427–28
  Plum, 428–29
  Rhubarb Galette, 428
  Summer Berry Galette, 428
  Tarte Tatin, 429–30

Tea
  Earl Grey's Devil's Food Cake, 444
  Slather, 352
Tiramisù, see Lemon, Pick-Me-Up
Tofu, Baked, 206–7
Tomato(es)
  Almonds, and Mint, Sicilian Pesto with, 399
  and Bacon, Grilled Cheese with, 85
  Baked Macaroni and Cheese with, 258–59
  Bread Salad, 68–69
  Cherry, Burst, 162
  Chopped Middle Eastern Salad, 66–68
  and Corn Relish, Fresh, 207
  Fresh Red and Yellow, Salsa, 15–16
  Gazpacho, 34
  Green, Cake, 440
  Green, Caponata, 168–69
  Green, Fried, 194
  Green, Ginger Jam, 139
  Grilled, and Corn Salsa with Chipotle, 16
  Manhattan Clam Chowder, 48–49
  peeling, 429
  Peperonata, 167–68
  Pizza Margherita, 101
  Ratatouille, 166–67
  Rice, 221–22
  Roasted, Soup with Chickpeas, Spinach, and
    Cumin, 36
  Salad with Browned Butter and Caper Dressing,
    59
  Sauce, Fresh, Potato Gnocchi in, 268
  Sauce, Giant Beans in, 198–99
  Sauce, Naked Ravioli with, 270
  Sauce, Quick, 250–51
  Sauce, Spaghetti with, 249
  Sauce, Uncooked, Pasta with, 249–50
  Sauce with Meat (Red Gravy), 251–52
  sizes, 478
  Spaghetti Sauce, 251
  Summertime Chicken Cacciatore, 321
  Sun-Dried, and Grilled Portobello Sandwich with
    Garlic Herbed Mayonnaise, 87
  Vegetarian Red Gravy, 253
  Yellow, Gazpacho, 35
Tortillas
  Fish Taco, 93–94
  Mushroom and Bean Burrito, 94–95

Quesadilla, 22
Soft Beef Tacos, 93
Soft Turkey Taco, 92–93
Trans fats, 422
Trout, Smoked, Salad with Pickled Beets and Beans, 77–78
Truffles, Chocolate, 450
trussing poultry, 312
Tuna
    Fresh, Casserole, 262–63
    Italian, and Shaved Fennel Sandwich with Black Olive Paste, 90–91
    Orange–Soy Sauce, 300
    Tartare with Toasted Sesame, 292
turducken, 330
Turkey
    Beef, or Chicken Hash, 124–25
    Breast, Chipotle-Rubbed, 330–32
    brining, 308, 331
    buying, 307–8
    carving, 331
    cooking, 308, 310
    Cutlets, Grilled, on Cabbage and Snow Pea Slaw, 332–33
    deep-fried, about, 330
    defrosting, 331
    gravy for, 332
    Ground, with Scallion and Chili, 333–34
    Hash, 124–25
    Orange Glazed, 330
    or Chicken Gratin, 324
    or Chicken Pot Pie, 322–24
    roast, slathers for, 330
    Roast, with Gravy, 328–30
    Salad, Curried, with Dried Cranberries and Yogurt Dressing, 78–79
    Smoked, Sandwich with Green Apple, Curried Mayonnaise, and Pickled Red Onions, 91–92
    stuffing, 331
    Taco, Soft, 92–93
    testing for doneness, 310
    trussing, 312
Turnip(s)
    Glazed, 155
    greens, cooking, 150
    Lentil and Root Vegetable Stew, 203

    and Potatoes, Sautéed, 181
    and Potato Galette, 185

V
Vanilla Cream Caramels, 470–71
Vanilla Cream Frosting, 448
Vanilla Cupcakes, 445
Vanilla Custard Sauce, 472
Vanilla extract, homemade, 449
Vanilla Ice Cream, French, 472
Vanilla Ice Cream, The Easiest Ever, 473
Vanilla sugar, homemade, 449
Veal. *See also* Meat
    alla Milanese or Wiener Schnitzel, 371
    Chops, Grilled, with Charmoula, 368–69
    Osso Buco, 360–62
    Parmesan, 369–71
    Scaloppine, Sautéed, with Capers and Lemon, 371
Vegetable(s). *See also specific vegetables*
    blanching, 163
    breadings for, 318
    Couscous with Chicken, 386
    Couscous with Merguez, 387
    Frittata, 120–21
    grilling, 153
    Lasagna, 261
    and Meat Loaf, 364
    Moroccan Couscous with Lamb, 384–86
    organic, buying, 142–43
    Panini, 87–88
    roasting, 148
    seasonal, buying, 142
    Stock, 53
    stocks, quick, preparing, 151
    Vegetarian Couscous, 386–87
Vinaigrettes
    Basic, 391
    Beet, 391–92
    Blueberry, 392–94
    emusifying agents, 395
    Garlic or Shallot, 391
    Herbed, 391
    preparing, 58
    Raspberry, 394
    variations, 393

W
Waffles, Sour Cream, 111
Waffles, Yeast-Raised, 110–11
Walnut(s)
    and Arugula Pesto, 398
    Buckwheat Buttermilk Bundt Cake with, 117–18
    Chocolate Chunk Cookies with Nuts, 459
    Date-Nut Cake, 436–37
    Esther's Special Linzer Tart, 431–32
    and Potato Spread, Garlicky, 9–11
    and Wild Mushrooms, Kasha with, 235–36
Watercress
    Baby Bok Choy, Chinese-Style, 158
    and Ginger, Rice Noodle Bowl with, 264–65
Watermelon Gazpacho, 35
Watermelon Soup, 414
Wheat Berry Salad, 72
Wild Rice and Mushroom Stuffing with Orange and
    Pine Nuts, 230
Wild Rice with Apples, Dried Cranberries, and But-
    tered Almonds, 232–33
Wine
    Barolo-Braised Short Ribs, 357–58
    -Braised Pot Roast, 360
    -Poached Pears, 418–19
    Red, Slather, 351
    White, Slather, 352

Y
Yakisoba, 266–67
yellow cake, see Cake, Butter
Yogurt
    and Cucumber Salad, 64
    Dressing, Curried Turkey Salad with Dried
        Cranberries and, 78–79
    Homemade, 133
    and Lime, Jícama Slaw with, 65–66
    Madhur Jaffrey's Carrot and Raisin Raita,
        402–3
    Mock Tandoori Chicken, 328
    Sauce, Minted, 402
    Slather, Spiced, 351
    Spiced-, Grilled Fish Steaks, 299–300
    Spicy Chickpeas with, 202–3
    Strained, 63

Z
Za'atar, 407–8
Za'atar, Grilled Pita Triangles with, 24
Zucchini
    Flowers, Fried, with Fried Sage Leaves, 195–96
    Parmesan, Grilled, 154
    Ratatouille, 166–67
    Sautéed, with Toasted Almonds and Mint, 160
    Summer Squash Bread and Butter Pickles, 210